Family Maps
of
Newaygo County, Michigan
Deluxe Edition

With Homesteads, Roads, Waterways, Towns, Cemeteries, Railroads, and More

Family Maps
of
Newaygo County, Michigan
Deluxe Edition

With Homesteads, Roads, Waterways, Towns, Cemeteries, Railroads, and More

by Gregory A. Boyd, J.D.

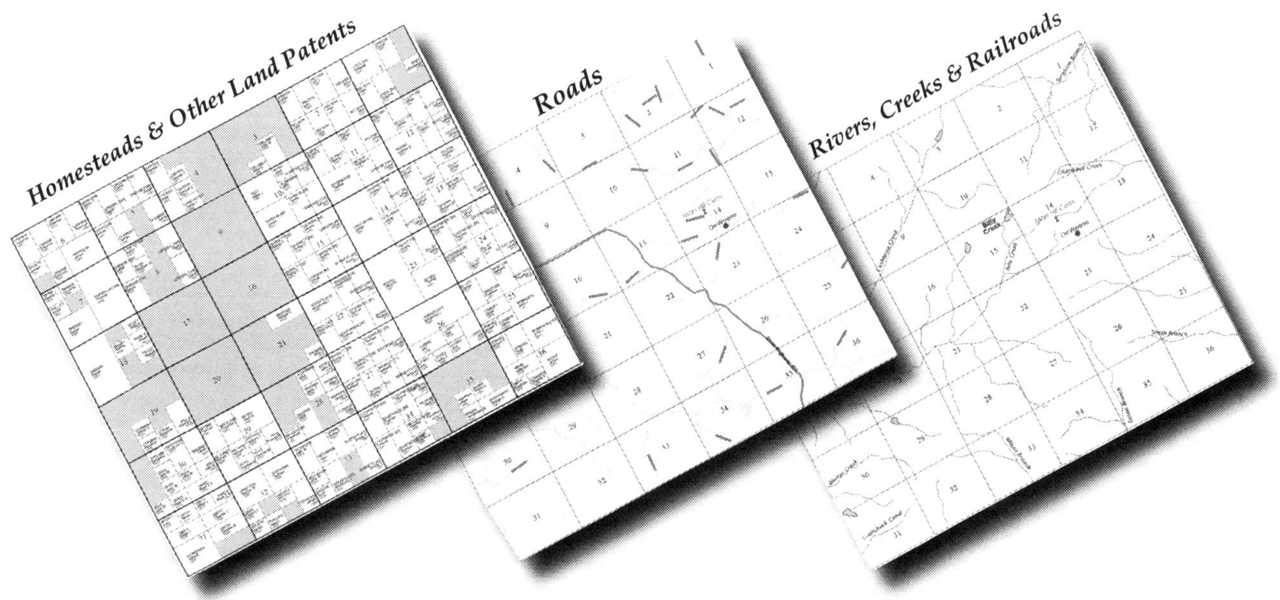

Featuring 3 Maps Per Township ...

Arphax Publishing Co.
www.arphax.com

Family Maps of Newaygo County, Michigan, Deluxe Edition: With Homesteads, Roads, Waterways, Towns, Cemeteries, Railroads, and More.
by Gregory A. Boyd, J.D.

ISBN 1-4203-1496-3

Printed in the United States of America

Published by Arphax Publishing Co., 2210 Research Park Blvd., Norman, Oklahoma, USA 73069
www.arphax.com

First Edition

—LEGAL—

The contents of this book rely on data published by the United States Government and its various agencies and departments, including but not limited to the General Land Office–Bureau of Land Management, the Department of the Interior, and the U.S. Census Bureau. The author has relied on said government agencies or re-sellers of its data, but makes no guarantee of the data's accuracy or of its representation herein, neither in its text nor maps. Said maps have been proportioned and scaled in a manner reflecting the author's primary goal—to make patentee names readable. This book will assist in the discovery of possible relationships between people, places, locales, rivers, streams, cemeteries, etc., but "proving" those relationships or exact geographic locations of any of the elements contained in the maps will require the use of other source material, which could include, but not be limited to: land patents, surveys, the patentees' applications, professionally drawn road-maps, etc.

Neither the author nor publisher makes any claim that the contents herein represent a complete or accurate record of the data it presents and disclaims any liability for reader's use of the book's contents. Many circumstances exist where human, computer, or data delivery errors could cause records to have been missed or to be inaccurately represented herein. Neither the author nor publisher shall assume any liability whatsoever for errors, inaccuracies, omissions or other inconsistencies herein.

This book is dedicated to my wonderful family:

Vicki, Jordan, & Amy Boyd

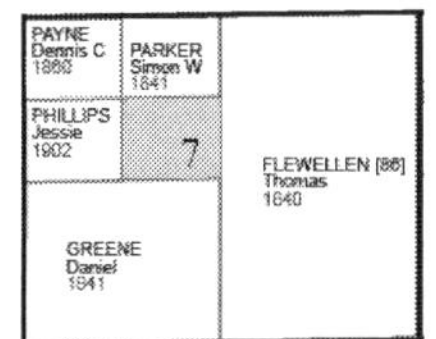

Contents

Preface....1
How to Use this Book - A Graphical Summary....2
How to Use This Book....3

- Part I -

The Big Picture

Map **A** - Where Newaygo County, Michigan Lies Within the State....11
Map **B** - Newaygo County, Michigan and Surrounding Counties....12
Map **C** - Congressional Townships of Newaygo County, Michigan....13
Map **D** - Cities & Towns of Newaygo County, Michigan....14
Map **E** - Cemeteries of Newaygo County, Michigan....16
Surnames in Newaygo County, Michigan Patents....18
Surname/Township Index....23

- Part II -

Township Map Groups

(each Map Group contains a Patent Index, Patent Map, Road Map, & Historical Map)

Map Group **1** - Township 16-North Range 14-West....56
Map Group **2** - Township 16-North Range 13-West....66
Map Group **3** - Township 16-North Range 12-West....76
Map Group **4** - Township 16-North Range 11-West....86
Map Group **5** - Township 15-North Range 14-West....98
Map Group **6** - Township 15-North Range 13-West....106
Map Group **7** - Township 15-North Range 12-West.....114
Map Group **8** - Township 15-North Range 11-West....122
Map Group **9** - Township 14-North Range 14-West....134
Map Group **10** - Township 14-North Range 13-West....144
Map Group **11** - Township 14-North Range 12-West....154
Map Group **12** - Township 14-North Range 11-West....164
Map Group **13** - Township 13-North Range 14-West....176
Map Group **14** - Township 13-North Range 13-West....188
Map Group **15** - Township 13-North Range 12-West....200
Map Group **16** - Township 13-North Range 11-West....210
Map Group **17** - Township 12-North Range 14-West....222
Map Group **18** - Township 12-North Range 13-West....234
Map Group **19** - Township 12-North Range 12-West....244

Map Group **20** - Township 12-North Range 11-West 254
Map Group **21** - Township 11-North Range 14-West 264
Map Group **22** - Township 11-North Range 13-West 276
Map Group **23** - Township 11-North Range 12-West 286
Map Group **24** - Township 11-North Range 11-West 294

Appendices

Appendix A - Congressional Authority for Land Patents 308
Appendix B - Section Parts (Aliquot Parts) 309
Appendix C - Multi-Patentee Groups in Newaygo County 313

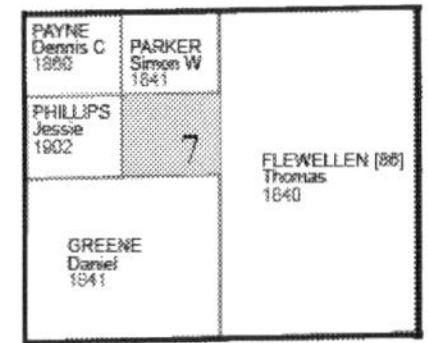

Preface

The quest for the discovery of my ancestors' origins, migrations, beliefs, and life-ways has brought me rewards that I could never have imagined. The *Family Maps* series of books is my first effort to share with historical and genealogical researchers, some of the tools that I have developed to achieve my research goals. I firmly believe that this effort will allow many people to reap the same sorts of treasures that I have.

Our Federal government's General Land Office of the Bureau of Land Management (the "GLO") has given genealogists and historians an incredible gift by virtue of its enormous database housed on its web-site at glorecords.blm.gov. Here, you can search for and find millions of parcels of land purchased by our ancestors in about thirty states.

This GLO web-site is one of the best FREE on-line tools available to family researchers. But, it is not for the faint of heart, nor is it for those unwilling or unable to to sift through and analyze the thousands of records that exist for most counties.

My immediate goal with this series is to spare you the hundreds of hours of work that it would take you to map the Land Patents for this county. Every Newaygo County homestead or land patent that I have gleaned from public GLO databases is mapped here. Consequently, I can usually show you in an instant, where your ancestor's land is located, as well as the names of nearby land-owners.

Originally, that was my primary goal. But after speaking to other genealogists, it became clear that there was much more that they wanted. Taking their advice set me back almost a full year, but I think you will agree it was worth the wait. Because now, you can learn so much more.

Now, this book answers these sorts of questions:

- Are there any variant spellings for surnames that I have missed in searching GLO records?
- Where is my family's traditional home-place?
- What cemeteries are near Grandma's house?
- My Granddad used to swim in such-and-such-Creek—where is that?
- How close is this little community to that one?
- Are there any other people with the same surname who bought land in the county?
- How about cousins and in-laws—did they buy land in the area?

And these are just for starters!

The rules for using the *Family Maps* books are simple, but the strategies for success are many. Some techniques are apparent on first use, but many are gained with time and experience. Please take the time to notice the roads, cemeteries, creek-names, family names, and unique first-names throughout the whole county. You cannot imagine what YOU might be the first to discover.

I hope to learn that many of you have answered age-old research questions within these pages or that you have discovered relationships previously not even considered. When these sorts of things happen to you, will you please let me hear about it? I would like nothing better. My contact information can always be found at www.arphax.com.

One more thing: please read the "How To Use This Book" chapter; it starts on the next page. This will give you the very best chance to find the treasures that lie within these pages.

My family and I wish you the very best of luck, both in life, and in your research. Greg Boyd

How to Use This Book - A Graphical Summary

Part I

"The Big Picture"

Map A ▸ *Counties in the State*
Map B ▸ *Surrounding Counties*
Map C ▸ *Congressional Townships (Map Groups) in the County*
Map D ▸ *Cities & Towns in the County*
Map E ▸ *Cemeteries in the County*
Surnames in the County ▸ *Number of Land-Parcels for Each Surname*
Surname/Township Index ▸ Directs you to Township Map Groups in Part II

The Surname/Township Index can direct you to any number of **Township Map Groups**

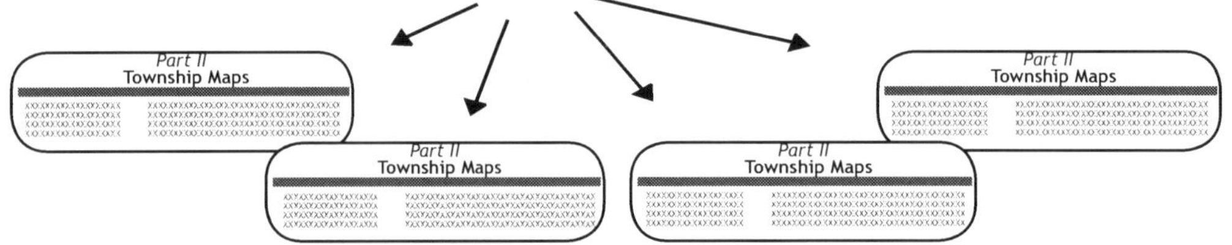

Part II

Township Map Groups

(1 for each Township in the County)

Each Township Map Group contains all four of of the following tools . . .

Land Patent Index ▸ *Every-name Index of Patents Mapped in this Township*
Land Patent Map ▸ *Map of Patents as listed in above Index*
Road Map ▸ *Map of Roads, City-centers, and Cemeteries in the Township*
Historical Map ▸ *Map of Railroads, Lakes, Rivers, Creeks, City-Centers, and Cemeteries*

Appendices

Appendix A ▸ *Congressional Authority enabling Patents within our Maps*
Appendix B ▸ *Section-Parts / Aliquot Parts (a comprehensive list)*
Appendix C ▸ *Multi-patentee Groups (Individuals within Buying Groups)*

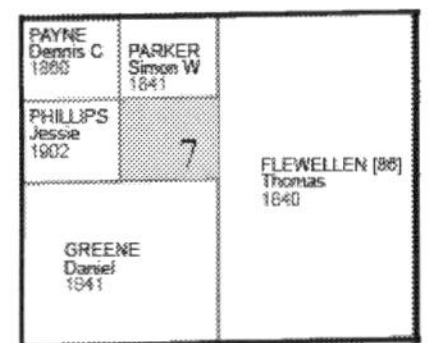

How to Use This Book

The two "Parts" of this *Family Maps* volume seek to answer two different types of questions. Part I deals with broad questions like: what counties surround Newaygo County, are there any ASHCRAFTs in Newaygo County, and if so, in which Townships or Maps can I find them? Ultimately, though, Part I should point you to a particular Township Map Group in Part II.

Part II concerns itself with details like: where exactly is this family's land, who else bought land in the area, and what roads and streams run through the land, or are located nearby. The Chart on the opposite page, and the remainder of this chapter attempt to convey to you the particulars of these two "parts", as well as how best to use them to achieve your research goals.

Part I
"The Big Picture"

Within Part I, you will find five "Big Picture" maps and two county-wide surname tools.

These include:

- Map A - Where Newaygo County lies within the state
- Map B - Counties that surround Newaygo County
- Map C - Congressional Townships of Newaygo County (+ Map Group Numbers)
- Map D - Cities & Towns of Newaygo County (with Index)
- Map E - Cemeteries of Newaygo County (with Index)
- Surnames in Newaygo County Patents (with Parcel-counts for each surname)
- Surname/Township Index (with Parcel-counts for each surname by Township)

The five "Big-Picture" Maps are fairly self-explanatory, yet should not be overlooked. This is particularly true of Maps "C", "D", and "E", all of which show Newaygo County and its Congressional Townships (and their assigned Map Group Numbers).

Let me briefly explain this concept of Map Group Numbers. These are a device completely of our own invention. They were created to help you quickly locate maps without having to remember the full legal name of the various Congressional Townships. It is simply easier to remember "Map Group 1" than a legal name like: "Township 9-North Range 6-West, 5th Principal Meridian." But the fact is that the TRUE legal name for these Townships IS terribly important. These are the designations that others will be familiar with and you will need to accurately record them in your notes. This is why both Map Group numbers AND legal descriptions of Townships are almost always displayed together.

Map "C" will be your first intoduction to "Map Group Numbers", and that is all it contains: legal Township descriptions and their assigned Map Group Numbers. Once you get further into your research, and more immersed in the details, you will likely want to refer back to Map "C" from time to time, in order to regain your bearings on just where in the county you are researching.

Remember, township boundaries are a completely artificial device, created to standardize land descriptions. But do not let them become a boundary in your mind when choosing which townships to research. Your relative's in-laws, children, cousins, siblings, and mamas and papas, might just as easily have lived in the township next to the one your grandfather lived in—rather than in the one where he actually lived. So Map "C" can be your guide to which other Townships/Map Groups you likewise ought to analyze.

Of course, the same holds true for County lines; this is the purpose behind Map "B". It shows you surrounding counties that you may want to consider for further reserarch.

Map "D", the Cities and Towns map, is the first map with an index. Map "E" is the second (Cemeteries). Both, Maps "D" and "E" give you broad views of City (or Cemetery) locations in the County. But they go much further by pointing you toward pertinent Township Map Groups so you can locate the patents, roads, and waterways located near a particular city or cemetery.

Once you are familiar with these *Family Maps* volumes and the county you are researching, the "Surnames In Newaygo County" chapter (or its sister chapter in other volumes) is where you'll likely start your future research sessions. Here, you can quickly scan its few pages and see if anyone in the county possesses the surnames you are researching. The "Surnames in Newaygo County" list shows only two things: surnames and the number of parcels of land we have located for that surname in Newaygo County. But whether or not you immediately locate the surnames you are researching, please do not go any further without taking a few moments to scan ALL the surnames in these very few pages.

You cannot imagine how many lost ancestors are waiting to be found by someone willing to take just a little longer to scan the "Surnames In Newaygo County" list. Misspellings and typographical errors abound in most any index of this sort. Don't miss out on finding your Kinard that was written Rynard or Cox that was written Lox. If it looks funny or wrong, it very often is. And one of those little errors may well be your relative.

Now, armed with a surname and the knowledge that it has one or more entries in this book, you are ready for the "Surname/Township Index." Unlike the "Surnames In Newaygo County", which has only one line per Surname, the "Surname/Township Index" contains one line-item for each Township Map Group in which each surname is found. In other words, each line represents a different Township Map Group that you will need to review.

Specifically, each line of the Surname/Township Index contains the following four columns of information:

1. Surname
2. Township Map Group Number (these Map Groups are found in Part II)
3. Parcels of Land (number of them with the given Surname within the Township)
4. Meridian/Township/Range (the legal description for this Township Map Group)

The key column here is that of the Township Map Group Number. While you should definitely record the Meridian, Township, and Range, you can do that later. Right now, you need to dig a little deeper. That Map Group Number tells you where in Part II that you need to start digging.

But before you leave the "Surname/Township Index", do the same thing that you did with the "Surnames in Newaygo County" list: take a moment to scan the pages of the Index and see if there are similarly spelled or misspelled surnames that deserve your attention. Here again, is an easy opportunity to discover grossly misspelled family names with very little effort. Now you are ready to turn to . . .

Part II
"Township Map Groups"

You will normally arrive here in Part II after being directed to do so by one or more "Map Group Numbers" in the Surname/Township Index of Part I.

Each Map Group represents a set of four tools dedicated to a single Congressional Township that is either wholly or partially within the county. If you are trying to learn all that you can about a particular family or their land, then these tools should usually be viewed in the order they are presented.

These four tools include:

1. a Land Patent Index
2. a Land Patent Map
3. a Road Map, and
4. an Historical Map

As I mentioned earlier, each grouping of this sort is assigned a Map Group Number. So, let's now move on to a discussion of the four tools that make up one of these Township Map Groups.

Land Patent Index

Each Township Map Group's Index begins with a title, something along these lines:

MAP GROUP 1: Index to Land Patents
Township 16-North Range 5-West (2nd PM)

The Index contains seven (7) columns. They are:

1. ID (a unique ID number for this Individual and a corresponding Parcel of land in this Township)
2. Individual in Patent (name)
3. Sec. (Section), and
4. Sec. Part (Section Part, or Aliquot Part)
5. Date Issued (Patent)
6. Other Counties (often means multiple counties were mentioned in GLO records, or the section lies within multiple counties).
7. For More Info . . . (points to other places within this index or elsewhere in the book where you can find more information)

While most of the seven columns are self-explanatory, I will take a few moments to explain the "Sec. Part." and "For More Info" columns.

The "Sec. Part" column refers to what surveryors and other land professionals refer to as an Aliquot Part. The origins and use of such a term mean little to a non-surveyor, and I have chosen to simply call these sub-sections of land what they are: a "Section Part". No matter what we call them, what we are referring to are things like a quarter-section or half-section or quarter-quarter-section. See Appendix "B" for most of the "Section Parts" you will come across (and many you will not) and what size land-parcel they represent.

The "For More Info" column of the Index may seem like a small appendage to each line, but please recognize quickly that this is not so. And to understand the various items you might find here, you need to become familiar with the Legend that appears at the top of each Land Patent Index.

Here is a sample of the Legend . . .

LEGEND

"For More Info . . . " column

A = Authority (Legislative Act, See Appendix "A")
B = Block or Lot (location in Section unknown)
C = Cancelled Patent
F = Fractional Section
G = Group (Multi-Patentee Patent, see Appendix "C")
V = Overlaps another Parcel
R = Re-Issued (Parcel patented more than once)

Most parcels of land will have only one or two of these items in their "For More Info" columns, but when that is not the case, there is often some valuable information to be gained from further investigation. Below, I will explain what each of these items means to you you as a researcher.

A = Authority
(Legislative Act, See Appendix "A")

All Federal Land Patents were issued because some branch of our government (usually the U.S. Congress) passed a law making such a transfer of title possible. And therefore every patent within these pages will have an "A" item next to it in the index. The number after the "A" indicates which item in Appendix "A" holds the citation to the particular law which authorized the transfer of land to the public. As it stands, most of the Public Land data compiled and released by our government, and which serves as the basis for the patents mapped here, concerns itself with "Cash Sale" homesteads. So in some Counties, the law which authorized cash sales will be the primary, if not the only, entry in the Appendix.

B = Block or Lot (location in Section unknown)

A "B" designation in the Index is a tip-off that the EXACT location of the patent within the map is not apparent from the legal description. This Patent will nonetheless be noted within the proper

Section along with any other Lots purchased in the Section. Given the scope of this project (many states and many Counties are being mapped), trying to locate all relevant plats for Lots (if they even exist) and accurately mapping them would have taken one person several lifetimes. But since our primary goal from the onset has been to establish relationships between neighbors and families, very little is lost to this goal since we can still observe who all lived in which Section.

C = Cancelled Patent

A Cancelled Patent is just that: cancelled. Whether the original Patentee forfeited his or her patent due to fraud, a technicality, non-payment, or whatever, the fact remains that it is significant to know who received patents for what parcels and when. A cancellation may be evidence that the Patentee never physically re-located to the land, but does not in itself prove that point. Further evidence would be required to prove that. *See also*, Re-issued Patents, *below*.

F = Fractional Section

A Fractional Section is one that contains less than 640 acres, almost always because of a body of water. The exact size and shape of land-parcels contained in such sections may not be ascertainable, but we map them nonetheless. Just keep in mind that we are not mapping an actual parcel to scale in such instances. Another point to consider is that we have located some fractional sections that are not so designated by the Bureau of Land Management in their data. This means that not all fractional sections have been so identified in our indexes.

G = Group
(Multi-Patentee Patent, see Appendix "C")

A "G" designation means that the Patent was issued to a GROUP of people (Multi-patentees). The "G" will always be followed by a number. Some such groups were quite large and it was impractical if not impossible to display each individual in our maps without unduly affecting readability. EACH person in the group is named in the Index, but they won't all be found on the Map. You will find the name of the first person in such a Group on the map with the Group number next to it, enclosed in [square brackets].

To find all the members of the Group you can either scan the Index for all people with the same Group Number or you can simply refer to Appendix "C" where all members of the Group are listed next to their number.

O = Overlaps another Parcel

An Overlap is one where PART of a parcel of land gets issued on more than one patent. For genealogical purposes, both transfers of title are important and both Patentees are mapped. If the ENTIRE parcel of land is re-issued, that is what we call it, a Re-Issued Patent (*see below*). The number after the "O" indicates the ID for the overlapping Patent(s) contained within the same Index. Like Re-Issued and Cancelled Patents, Overlaps may cause a map-reader to be confused at first, but for genealogical purposes, all of these parties' relationships to the underlying land is important, and therefore, we map them.

R = Re-Issued (Parcel patented more than once)

The label, "Re-issued Patent" describes Patents which were issued more than once for land with the EXACT SAME LEGAL DESCRIPTION. Whether the original patent was cancelled or not, there were a good many parcels which were patented more than once. The number after the "R" indicates the ID for the other Patent contained within the same Index that was for the same land. A quick glance at the map itself within the relevant Section will be the quickest way to find the other Patentee to whom the Parcel was transferred. They should both be mapped in the same general area.

I have gone to some length describing all sorts of anomalies either in the underlying data or in their representation on the maps and indexes in this book. Most of this will bore the most ardent reseracher, but I do this with all due respect to those researchers who will inevitably (and rightfully) ask: *"Why isn't so-and-so's name on the exact spot that the index says it should be?"*

In most cases it will be due to the existence of a Multi-Patentee Patent, a Re-issued Patent, a Cancelled Patent, or Overlapping Parcels named in separate Patents. I don't pretend that this discussion will answer every question along these lines, but I hope it will at least convince you of the complexity of the subject.

Not to despair, this book's companion web-site will offer a way to further explain "odd-ball" or errant data. Each book (County) will have its own web-page or pages to discuss such situations. You can go to www.arphax.com to find the relevant web-page for Newaygo County.

Land Patent Map

On the first two-page spread following each Township's Index to Land Patents, you'll find the corresponding Land Patent Map. And here lies the real heart of our work. For the first time anywhere, researchers will be able to observe and analyze, on a grand scale, most of the original land-owners for an area AND see them mapped in proximity to each one another.

We encourage you to make vigorous use of the accompanying Index described above, but then later, to abandon it, and just stare at these maps for a while. This is a great way to catch misspellings or to find collateral kin you'd not known were in the area.

Each Land Patent Map represents one Congressional Township containing approximately 36-square miles. Each of these square miles is labeled by an accompanying Section Number (1 through 36, in most cases). Keep in mind, that this book concerns itself solely with Newaygo County's patents. Townships which creep into one or more other counties will not be shown in their entirety in any one book. You will need to consult other books, as they become available, in order to view other countys' patents, cities, cemeteries, etc.

But getting back to Newaygo County: each Land Patent Map contains a Statistical Chart that looks like the following:

Township Statistics

Parcels Mapped	:	173
Number of Patents	:	163
Number of Individuals	:	152
Patentees Identified	:	151
Number of Surnames	:	137
Multi-Patentee Parcels	:	4
Oldest Patent Date	:	11/27/1820
Most Recent Patent	:	9/28/1917
Block/Lot Parcels	:	0
Parcels Re-Issued	:	3
Parcels that Overlap	:	8
Cities and Towns	:	6
Cemeteries	:	6

This information may be of more use to a social statistician or historian than a genealogist, but I think all three will find it interesting.

Most of the statistics are self-explanatory, and what is not, was described in the above discussion of the Index's Legend, but I do want to mention a few of them that may affect your understanding of the Land Patent Maps.

First of all, Patents often contain more than one Parcel of land, so it is common for there to be more Parcels than Patents. Also, the Number of Individuals will more often than not, not match the number of Patentees. A Patentee is literally the person or PERSONS named in a patent. So, a Patent may have a multi-person Patentee or a single-person patentee. Nonetheless, we account for all these individuals in our indexes.

On the lower-righthand side of the Patent Map is a Legend which describes various features in the map, including Section Boundaries, Patent (land) Boundaries, Lots (numbered), and Multi-Patentee Group Numbers. You'll also find a "Helpful Hints" Box that will assist you.

One important note: though the vast majority of Patents mapped in this series will prove to be reasonably accurate representations of their actual locations, we cannot claim this for patents lying along state and county lines, or waterways, or that have been platted (lots).

Shifting boundaries and sparse legal descriptions in the GLO data make this a reality that we have nonetheless tried to overcome by estimating these patents' locations the best that we can.

Road Map

On the two-page spread following each Patent Map you will find a Road Map covering the exact same area (the same Congressional Township).

For me, fully exploring the past means that every once in a while I must leave the library and travel to the actual locations where my ancestors once walked and worked the land. Our Township Road Maps are a great place to begin such a quest.

Keep in mind that the scaling and proportion of these maps was chosen in order to squeeze hundreds of people-names, road-names, and place-names into tinier spaces than you would traditionally see. These are not professional road-maps, and like any secondary genealogical source, should be looked upon as an entry-way to original sources—in this case, original patents and applications, professionally produced maps and surveys, etc.

Both our Road Maps and Historical Maps contain cemeteries and city-centers, along with a listing of these on the left-hand side of the map. I should note that I am showing you city center-points, rather than city-limit boundaries, because in many instances, this will represent a place where settlement began. This may be a good time to mention that many cemeteries are located on private property, Always check with a local historical or genealogical society to see if a particular cemetery is publicly accessible (if it is not obviously so). As a final point, look for your surnames among the road-names. You will often be surprised by what you find.

Historical Map

The third and final map in each Map Group is our attempt to display what each Township might have looked like before the advent of modern roads. In frontier times, people were usually more determined to settle near rivers and creeks than they were near roads, which were often few and far between. As was the case with the Road Map, we've included the same cemeteries and city-centers. We've also included railroads, many of which came along before most roads.

While some may claim "Historical Map" to be a bit of a misnomer for this tool, we settled for this label simply because it was almost as accurate as saying "Railroads, Lakes, Rivers, Cities, and Cemeteries," and it is much easier to remember.

In Closing . . .

By way of example, here is *A Really Good Way to Use a Township Map Group.* First, find the person you are researching in the Township's Index to Land Patents, which will direct you to the proper Section and parcel on the Patent Map. But before leaving the Index, scan all the patents within it, looking for other names of interest. Now, turn to the Patent Map and locate your parcels of land. Pay special attention to the names of patent-holders who own land surrounding your person of interest. Next, turn the page and look at the same Section(s) on the Road Map. Note which roads are closest to your parcels and also the names of nearby towns and cemeteries. Using other resources, you may be able to learn of kin who have been buried here, plus, you may choose to visit these cemeteries the next time you are in the area.

Finally, turn to the Historical Map. Look once more at the same Sections where you found your research subject's land. Note the nearby streams, creeks, and other geographical features. You may be surprised to find family names were used to name them, or you may see a name you haven't heard mentioned in years and years—and a new research possibility is born.

Many more techniques for using these *Family Maps* volumes will no doubt be discovered. If from time to time, you will navigate to Newaygo County's web-page at www.arphax.com (use the "Research" link), you can learn new tricks as they become known (or you can share ones you have employed). But for now, you are ready to get started. So, go, and good luck.

– Part I –

The Big Picture

Map A - Where Newaygo County, Michigan Lies Within the State

Legend

State Boundary

County Boundaries

Newaygo County, Michigan

Helpful Hints

1 We start with Map "A" which simply shows us where within the State this county lies.

2 Map "B" zooms in further to help us more easily identify surrounding Counties.

3 Map "C" zooms in even further to reveal the Congressional Townships that either lie within or intersect Newaygo County.

Map B - Newaygo County, Michigan and Surrounding Counties

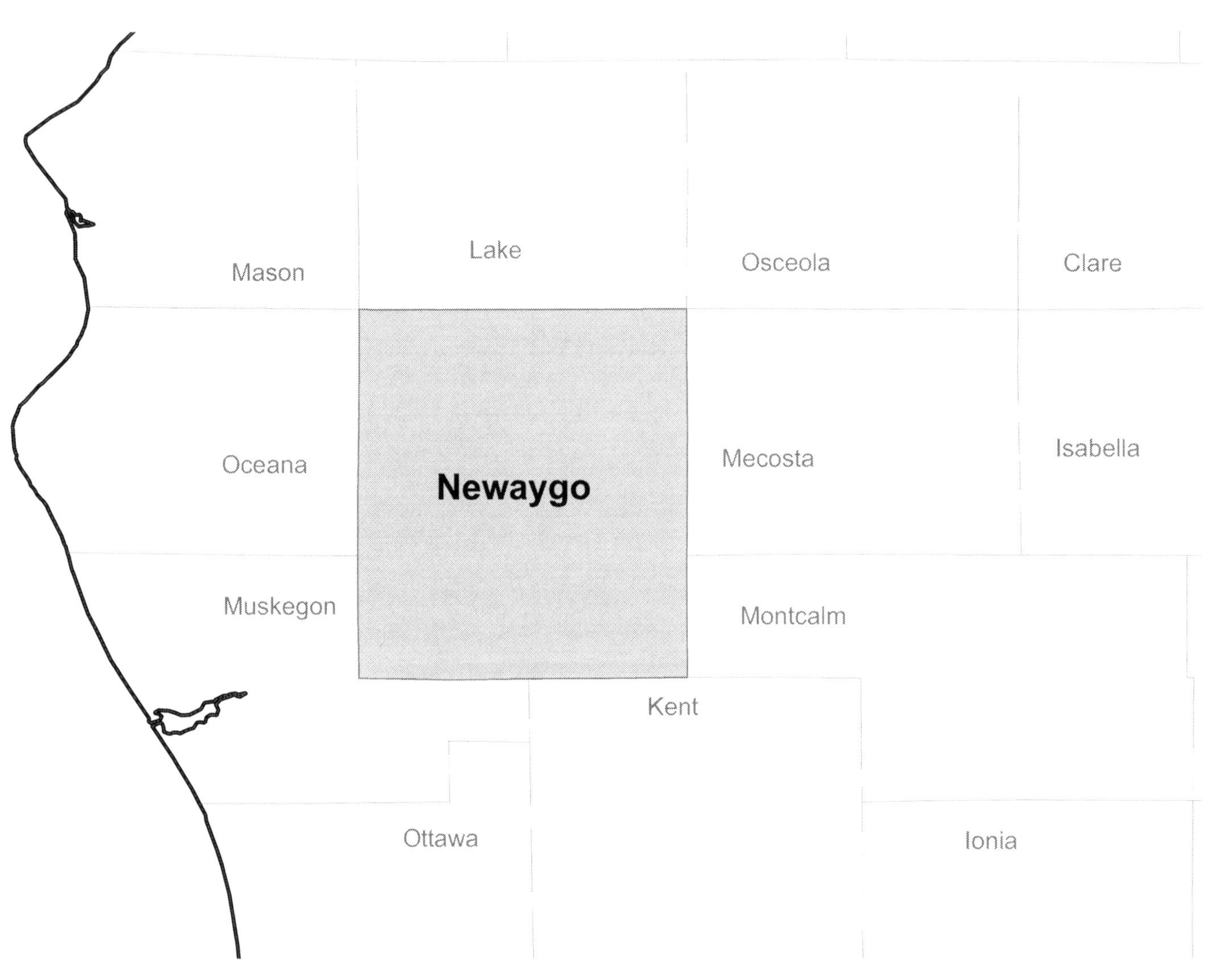

Legend

State Boundaries (when applicable)

County Boundary

Helpful Hints

1 Many Patent-holders and their families settled across county lines. It is always a good idea to check nearby counties for your families.

2 Refer to Map "A" to see a broader view of where this County lies within the State, and Map "C" to see which Congressional Townships lie within Newaygo County.

Map C - Congressional Townships of Newaygo County, Michigan

Map Group 1 Township 16-N Range 14-W	Map Group 2 Township 16-N Range 13-W	Map Group 3 Township 16-N Range 12-W	Map Group 4 Township 16-N Range 11-W
Map Group 5 Township 15-N Range 14-W	Map Group 6 Township 15-N Range 13-W	Map Group 7 Township 15-N Range 12-W	Map Group 8 Township 15-N Range 11-W
Map Group 9 Township 14-N Range 14-W	Map Group 10 Township 14-N Range 13-W	Map Group 11 Township 14-N Range 12-W	Map Group 12 Township 14-N Range 11-W
Map Group 13 Township 13-N Range 14-W	Map Group 14 Township 13-N Range 13-W	Map Group 15 Township 13-N Range 12-W	Map Group 16 Township 13-N Range 11-W
Map Group 17 Township 12-N Range 14-W	Map Group 18 Township 12-N Range 13-W	Map Group 19 Township 12-N Range 12-W	Map Group 20 Township 12-N Range 11-W
Map Group 21 Township 11-N Range 14-W	Map Group 22 Township 11-N Range 13-W	Map Group 23 Township 11-N Range 12-W	Map Group 24 Township 11-N Range 11-W

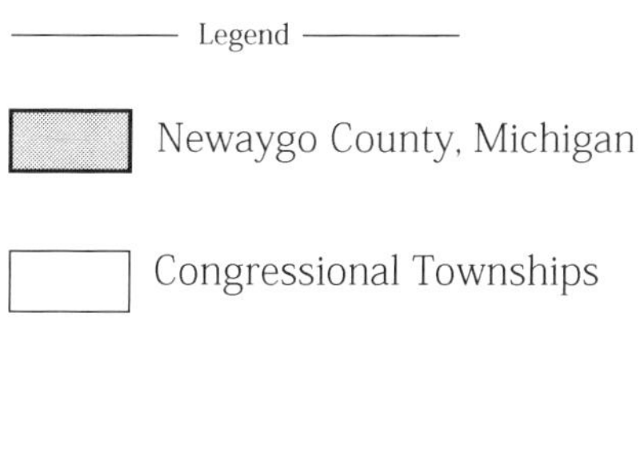

Helpful Hints

1 Many Patent-holders and their families settled across county lines. It is always a good idea to check nearby counties for your families (See Map "B").

2 Refer to Map "A" to see a broader view of where this county lies within the State, and Map "B" for a view of the counties surrounding Newaygo County.

Map D Index: Cities & Towns of Newaygo County, Michigan

The following represents the Cities and Towns of Newaygo County, along with the corresponding Map Group in which each is found. Cities and Towns are displayed in both the Road and Historical maps in the Group.

City/Town	Map Group No.
Aetna	9
Ashland	22
Ashland Center	22
Big Bend	16
Big Prairie	16
Bishop	18
Bitely	2
Bridgeton	21
Brohman	6
Croton	20
Croton Heights	20
Dayton Center	13
Ensley Center	24
Fremont	13
Grant	22
Hawkins	4
Huber	9
Jugville	14
Lilley	2
Newaygo	19
Oxbow	16
Oxbow Park	16
Ramona	10
Reeman	17
Riverview	20
Sitka	17
Sun	23
Tift Corner	20
Troy	1
Volney	5
Walgamor Corners	1
White Cloud	15
Woodland Park	6
Woodville	7
Wooster	14

Map D - Cities & Towns of Newaygo County, Michigan

Map Group 1 Township 16-N Range 14-W Troy Walgamor Corners	Map Group 2 Township 16-N Range 13-W Lilley Bitely	Map Group 3 Township 16-N Range 12-W	Hawkins Map Group 4 Township 16-N Range 11-W
Volney Map Group 5 Township 15-N Range 14-W	Woodland Park Brohman Map Group 6 Township 15-N Range 13-W	Map Group 7 Township 15-N Range 12-W	Map Group 8 Township 15-N Range 11-W Woodville
Huber Map Group 9 Township 14-N Range 14-W Aetna	Ramona Map Group 10 Township 14-N Range 13-W	Map Group 11 Township 14-N Range 12-W	Map Group 12 Township 14-N Range 11-W
Map Group 13 Township 13-N Range 14-W Dayton Center Fremont	Jugville Wooster Map Group 14 Township 13-N Range 13-W	White Cloud Map Group 15 Township 13-N Range 12-W	Map Group 16 Township 13-N Range 11-W Big Bend Big Prairie Oxbow Park Oxbow
Reeman Map Group 17 Township 12-N Range 14-W Sitka	Map Group 18 Township 12-N Range 13-W Bishop	Map Group 19 Township 12-N Range 12-W Newaygo	Croton Heights Riverview Croton Map Group 20 Township 12-N Range 11-W Tift Corner
Bridgeton Map Group 21 Township 11-N Range 14-W	Map Group 22 Township 11-N Range 13-W Ashland Center Grant Ashland	Map Group 23 Township 11-N Range 12-W Sun	Map Group 24 Township 11-N Range 11-W Ensley Center

Legend

Newaygo County, Michigan

Congressional Townships

Helpful Hints

1 Cities and towns are marked only at their center-points as published by the USGS and/or NationalAtlas.gov. This often enables us to more closely approximate where these might have existed when first settled.

2 To see more specifically where these Cities & Towns are located within the county, refer to both the Road and Historical maps in the Map-Group referred to above. See also, the Map "D" Index on the opposite page.

Map E Index: Cemeteries of Newaygo County, Michigan

The following represents many of the Cemeteries of Newaygo County, along with the corresponding Township Map Group in which each is found. Cemeteries are displayed in both the Road and Historical maps in the Map Groups referred to below.

Cemetery	Map Group No.
Amish Cem.	11
Big Prairie-Everett Cem.	15
Bull Cem.	9
Christian Plains Cem.	20
Clark Cem.	13
Crandall Cem.	24
Croton Cem.	20
Curtice Cem.	3
Dayton Center Cem.	13
Evans Cem.	13
Goodwell Cem.	12
Gulp Cem.	20
Hillers Cem.	6
Hillside Cem.	23
Hungerford Cem.	8
Lincoln Cem.	10
North Ensley Cem.	24
Oak Grove Cem.	20
Prairie Cem.	20
Prospect Hill Cem.	15
Reeman Cem.	17
Saint John Cem.	24
Saint Marks Cem.	18
Saint Michaels Cem.	17
Shippy Cem.	22
Whipple Cem.	3

Map E - Cemeteries of Newaygo County, Michigan

Map Group 1 Township 16-N Range 14-W	Map Group 2 Township 16-N Range 13-W	Curtice Whipple Map Group 3 Township 16-N Range 12-W	Map Group 4 Township 16-N Range 11-W
Map Group 5 Township 15-N Range 14-W	Map Group 6 Township 15-N Range 13-W Hillers	Map Group 7 Township 15-N Range 12-W	Hungerford Map Group 8 Township 15-N Range 11-W
Map Group 9 Township 14-N Range 14-W Bull	Lincoln Map Group 10 Township 14-N Range 13-W	Map Group 11 Township 14-N Range 12-W Amish	Map Group 12 Township 14-N Range 11-W Goodwell
Map Group 13 Township 13-N Range 14-W Dayton Center Evans Clark	Map Group 14 Township 13-N Range 13-W	Prospect Hill Big Prairie-Everett Map Group 15 Township 13-N Range 12-W	Map Group 16 Township 13-N Range 11-W
Saint Michaels Reeman Map Group 17 Township 12-N Range 14-W	Map Group 18 Township 12-N Range 13-W Saint Marks	Map Group 19 Township 12-N Range 12-W	Gulp Prairie Croton Map Group 20 Township 12-N Range 11-W Oak Grove Christian Plains
Map Group 21 Township 11-N Range 14-W	Map Group 22 Township 11-N Range 13-W Shippy	Map Group 23 Township 11-N Range 12-W Hillside	North Ensley Saint John Map Group 24 Township 11-N Range 11-W Crandall

Legend

Newaygo County, Michigan

Congressional Townships

Helpful Hints

1 Cemeteries are marked at locations as published by the USGS and/or NationalAtlas.gov.

2 To see more specifically where these Cemeteries are located, refer to the Road & Historical maps in the Map-Group referred to above. See also, the Map "E" Index on the opposite page to make sure you don't miss any of the Cemeteries located within this Congressional township.

Surnames in Newaygo County, Michigan Patents

The following list represents the surnames that we have located in Newaygo County, Michigan Patents and the number of parcels that we have mapped for each one. Here is a quick way to determine the existence (or not) of Patents to be found in the subsequent indexes and maps of this volume.

Surname	# of Land Parcels	Surname	# of Land Parcels	Surname	# of Land Parcels	Surname	# of Land Parcels
ACHENBACH	3	BELL	8	BUTLER	3	CRANDALL	3
ACKLEY	2	BELMEAR	2	BUTTON	1	CRANDELL	1
ADAMS	5	BEMENT	2	BUZZLE	1	CRARY	2
ADSIT	2	BENDER	2	CADY	5	CRAWFORD	4
AGARD	1	BENJAMIN	29	CAIRNS	2	CREPIN	2
AITKEN	1	BENNETT	14	CALHOUN	1	CRESSMAN	2
ALBERTSON	2	BENNITT	1	CALLAR	3	CRITCHLOW	2
ALEXANDER	2	BENTON	6	CALLENDER	1	CRITTENDON	6
ALLEN	6	BERRY	2	CARLISLE	1	CROFF	1
ALLERS	1	BESHER	4	CARLSON	1	CROFOOT	8
ALLEY	9	BEVIER	1	CARPENTER	13	CROMAN	2
AMES	1	BIGELOW	9	CARR	3	CROSS	2
AMOS	1	BIGGS	1	CARTER	2	CROSSMAN	3
ANDERSON	2	BILLS	6	CASE	2	CROY	1
ANDREWS	3	BINGHAM	1	CASS	1	CRUM	1
ANDRIE	1	BIRCHARD	2	CASTLE	1	CUDABACK	5
ANGEL	1	BIRDSELL	3	CAVENDAR	1	CULP	2
ARMS	10	BISBEE	2	CAVENDER	2	CULVER	1
ARMSTRONG	2	BISSETT	1	CAYWOOD	1	CUMINGS	1
ARNOLD	3	BLACK	4	CHADWICK	2	CUMMINGS	2
ASHCRAFT	1	BLACKWELL	3	CHAFFEE	1	CURDY	1
ASHLEY	1	BLAIR	1	CHAPIN	1	CURTICE	3
ATWATER	1	BLANCHARD	5	CHAPMAN	4	CURTIS	1
ATWOOD	1	BLAZO	1	CHARLES	2	DAGAN	2
AUGERINE	1	BLINDBERRY	2	CHARLOE	1	DAGGETT	1
AVERY	12	BLISS	1	CHASE	1	DAKE	6
AYER	2	BLOOD	3	CHEENEY	7	DANA	7
BABCOCK	2	BOHNE	4	CHENEY	10	DANIEL	2
BACKARD	2	BOLDMAN	1	CHICK	4	DANIELS	2
BACKART	7	BONNEY	3	CHILD	1	DARLING	35
BACKHART	1	BORDEN	3	CHILDS	1	DAVENPORT	3
BADGEROW	3	BOTSFORD	1	CHIPMAN	1	DAVIDSON	1
BAILEY	1	BOWEN	5	CHRISTIAN	2	DAVIS	13
BAKER	1	BOWER	1	CHURCH	1	DE BOIS	5
BALDWIN	8	BOWLEY	3	CILLEY	2	DE MOO	1
BALEY	1	BOWMAN	4	CLARK	18	DE PUNG	1
BALFOUR	2	BOYD	2	CLAY	4	DEAN	1
BALL	91	BRACE	1	CLENLEY	2	DEANE	2
BALLINGER	1	BRENNAN	2	COCHRAN	3	DEARTH	2
BALLOU	5	BRIGGS	8	COGSWELL	3	DECKER	4
BAMBER	2	BRIGHAM	9	COLBURN	1	DELAHOUSSAYE	2
BANCROFT	2	BRITTAIN	1	COLE	7	DELANO	3
BANKER	1	BRITTON	2	COLLINS	3	DENIS	1
BARB	2	BROMLEY	1	COLVER	1	DENSLOW	1
BARBER	2	BROOKS	20	COMSTOCK	12	DEVER	2
BARKER	2	BROTHERTON	2	CONKLIN	4	DEWOLF	1
BARNES	2	BROWN	9	CONKWRIGHT	3	DICKERSON	1
BARNHARD	6	BRUBAKER	3	CONLEY	1	DICKINSON	6
BARNUM	1	BRUCE	3	CONOVER	1	DICKISON	3
BARRON	2	BRUNSON	1	COOK	61	DINGMAN	2
BARSTOW	2	BUCK	5	COOLBAUGH	1	DIRSTEIN	2
BARTON	24	BUGGS	3	COOLEY	1	DIXON	1
BATES	1	BUHL	1	COON	2	DOANE	1
BEAN	5	BUICK	2	COOPER	6	DOBE	2
BEATON	1	BULL	3	COULTER	2	DOBSON	1
BEAUCHAMP	2	BULSON	1	COUNTRIMAN	1	DOCHERTY	1
BEAZLEY	2	BUMSTED	2	COWLES	3	DOTY	1
BEDIENT	2	BURKE	1	COWN	1	DOUD	1
BEEG	1	BURRIL	2	COX	1	DOUGLAS	1
BEERS	1	BURT	1	CRABTREE	2	DOUGLASS	9
BEIDLER	2	BUSH	7	CRADIT	1	DOVE	2
BELDEN	4	BUSHNELL	4	CRAM	1	DOWLING	2

Surname	# of Land Parcels
DOWNING	1
DOYLE	1
DRAGOO	1
DRAPER	2
DRESSER	1
DRUHER	1
DUBOIS	2
DUDLEY	2
DUELL	1
DUFFY	1
DUNFEE	1
DUNGAN	1
DUNLAP	1
DUNN	6
DUNNING	1
DUTCHER	1
EAEGLE	1
EANES	2
EARLY	2
EASTMAN	79
ECHTINAW	3
ECKELS	1
EDDY	11
EDGCOMB	2
EDMESTON	1
EDMONSON	1
EDMUNDS	1
EDWARDS	2
EHLE	1
EICHENLAUB	1
ELDRED	2
ELDREDGE	2
ELDRIDGE	10
ELLIOTT	2
ELMS	2
ELPHICK	1
ELTING	2
ELWELL	2
ELY	13
EMBREE	2
ENSLEY	1
ERRICKSON	1
EUT	1
EVANS	4
EWERS	2
EWING	3
EYCK	2
FAIRCHILDES	2
FALES	1
FARINHOLT	2
FARNHAM	3
FELLOWS	2
FENNER	1
FERRAN	1
FERRISS	2
FERRY	5
FIFIELD	1
FILER	4
FINCH	4
FISCHER	2
FLAGG	2
FLANDERS	2
FOGG	2
FOLJAMBE	2
FORBES	3
FORD	7
FORSHAY	1
FOSTER	5
FOWLER	3
FOWTER	1
FOX	1
FRANKLIN	2
FREEMAN	2
FRENCH	10
FRISBY	1
FROST	1
FRY	4
FULLER	10
FULLMER	1
FURGERSON	3
FURMAN	9
FURRY	3
GALLUP	1
GAMBLE	2
GARD	1
GARDNER	4
GARNER	1
GASTON	1
GATES	3
GATEWOOD	2
GAUWEILER	2
GAY	2
GAYLORD	4
GERRY	3
GETTY	4
GEYASHE	1
GIBB	5
GIBBS	2
GIDDINGS	3
GILBERT	4
GILL	2
GILLILAND	2
GLASS	2
GLAZE	2
GLAZIER	2
GLOVER	2
GO	1
GODFREY	7
GOLLADAY	2
GOOCH	7
GOODALE	2
GOODALL	2
GOODRICH	5
GOODRIDGE	1
GOODWILL	1
GORDON	2
GORING	1
GOULD	2
GRACEY	1
GRAHAM	3
GRANADE	1
GRANGER	1
GRAVES	4
GRAY	10
GREEN	3
GREENFIELD	2
GREGORY	1
GREY	2
GRIFFES	1
GRIFFIN	7
GRIFFITTS	5
GROVE	2
GROVENBERRY	3
GROVESTEEN	6
GROW	4
GUDGELL	1
GUOM	1
GUSTROUS	4
HAGERMANN	1
HAIG	2
HAIGHT	1
HAINES	4
HAIST	2
HALCOMB	2
HALL	23
HALLOCK	1
HAMENT	1
HAMILTON	7
HAMMOND	2
HANCOCK	2
HARDEN	2
HARNESS	2
HARPER	4
HARRIES	3
HARRINGTON	7
HARRIS	5
HARRISON	3
HART	6
HARTZER	2
HASCALL	6
HASKELL	4
HATFIELD	2
HATHERLEY	1
HAWKINS	1
HAYWARD	2
HAYWOOD	1
HEADLEY	2
HEALD	26
HEATH	4
HEATON	6
HEBEL	2
HEFFERAN	2
HEMSWORTH	1
HENNESSY	1
HENRY	3
HERENDEEN	2
HERINGTON	1
HERRICK	4
HERRINGTON	1
HERSHBERGER	2
HERTZER	3
HESS	2
HETSLER	3
HEWES	3
HEWIT	1
HICKS	2
HIGBE	3
HIGBEE	3
HIGGS	2
HILDRETH	6
HILES	1
HILL	5
HILLMAN	6
HILLS	8
HINDES	1
HINDS	1
HINE	4
HINMAN	10
HOBLER	1
HODGES	1
HOLE	1
HOLLOWAY	2
HOLMES	7
HOOD	3
HOOKER	2
HOOPER	2
HOPKINS	6
HOSKIN	1
HOUGHTALING	2
HOUGHTON	3
HOULDING	5
HOUSE	4
HOUSTON	2
HOVEY	9
HOW	1
HOWE	28
HOWELL	1
HOWLETT	16
HOWSE	1
HOYT	2
HUBBARD	10
HUCKLEBERRY	1
HUDLER	2
HUGHES	4
HULL	4
HUNSINGER	1
HUNT	4
HUNTER	3
HUSTON	2
HUTCHERSON	2
HUZZEY	3
HYDE	1
INGALLS	1
INMAN	3
IRONS	2
ISBELL	1
ISH	3
ISHAM	1
IVES	201
JACKLIN	3
JACKSON	1
JACOBS	1
JARVIS	1
JAY	1
JENKINS	1
JENNE	1
JEWELL	3
JIBSON	3
JOACHIM	1
JOBBITT	1
JOHNSON	54
JONES	8
JOSLIN	3
JOY	1
JUDSON	3
KAKE	1
KAUFMAN	2
KEATING	1
KEELEAN	1
KEENEY	2
KEINER	2
KELLEY	1
KELLOGG	6
KEMP	2
KENDALL	42
KENDULL	16
KENNE	7
KENNEDY	1
KENNEY	2
KETCHUM	1
KIDD	1
KIEFER	12
KIEFFER	1
KILBY	1
KIMBALL	5
KIMBELL	4
KING	3
KINGSLEY	2
KINNEY	1
KITCHEN	3

Surname	# of Land Parcels	Surname	# of Land Parcels	Surname	# of Land Parcels	Surname	# of Land Parcels
KLETT	1	LYONS	20	MONROE	5	PENNOYER	4
KLINE	1	MABIE	2	MOODY	1	PERKINS	1
KNAPP	3	MACK	2	MOORE	8	PERRIGO	2
KNICKERBOCKER	1	MACOMBER	2	MOOTE	1	PETER	1
KNISS	1	MAHAN	2	MORELL	1	PETERS	1
KNOWLES	1	MALLERY	3	MORGAN	4	PETERSON	28
KNOX	1	MALLET	2	MORLEY	1	PETTIBONE	3
KONKEL	2	MANLEY	2	MORRIS	32	PHELPS	1
KOON	3	MANNING	5	MORRISON	18	PHILLIPS	3
KRICK	1	MANROW	1	MORTON	1	PICHETTE	1
KRIGER	2	MANSFIELD	6	MOSES	5	PIGEON	1
KUPRECHT	1	MAPES	1	MOSHER	8	PIKE	1
LACEY	2	MARKLE	3	MOSS	2	PILLSBURY	7
LACKEY	2	MARSH	3	MOST	1	PITTS	3
LAFFERTY	1	MARSHALL	7	MOYE	1	PIXLEY	1
LAHR	2	MARTIN	12	MUDGE	1	PLACKARD	1
LAKE	5	MARVIN	2	MULDER	1	PLATT	6
LALOTTE	1	MATHERS	1	MUNDY	1	PODOSZKIE	1
LANBAUGH	1	MATHEW	5	MURPHY	9	POLLARD	2
LANCASTER	3	MATTESON	3	MURRAY	1	POMROY	2
LANE	1	MATTHEW	3	MURRY	4	PORTER	3
LANGFORD	2	MAXIM	9	NASON	2	POST	1
LANNING	2	MAYBEE	2	NEAL	2	POTTER	11
LASHER	2	MAYNARD	1	NELLIS	4	POWERS	2
LASLEY	6	MAZE	1	NELSON	2	PRATT	3
LATHROP	5	MCBRIDE	5	NEVILLE	2	PRENTICE	1
LAVANCE	1	MCCAB	1	NEWELL	1	PRESTON	14
LAVERGNE	2	MCCALL	4	NEWTON	1	PRICE	2
LAVERTY	1	MCCLAIN	2	NICHOLS	10	PRINGLE	1
LAWRENCE	12	MCCLUNG	2	NIEGLESON	1	PROBASCO	8
LAWSON	2	MCCLURE	4	NININGER	1	PROVIN	2
LE BARON	2	MCCOY	1	NO	1	PRUDDEN	2
LE BARRON	1	MCCRACKEN	1	NORTH	2	PRUYN	3
LEACH	2	MCCUNE	2	NORTHROP	122	PULLER	2
LEE	1	MCDUFFIE	1	NORTON	33	PUNK-E-NOB-BI-NO	2
LEHMANN	1	MCFARLAN	2	OBRIEN	2	PUTNAM	8
LEMAIRE	1	MCGHAN	2	OCONNOR	1	QUICK	1
LEMONS	1	MCGUIRE	1	ODELL	3	QUIGLEY	2
LENNEN	2	MCINTOSH	4	OLDS	2	QUOT	1
LEONARD	207	MCKEE	11	ONDERDONK	2	RAIDER	1
LESTER	2	MCKENZIE	4	ONEIL	4	RAMSEY	1
LESUEUR	2	MCKIE	3	ORCUTT	1	RANDALL	2
LETCH	1	MCNIEL	1	ORN	1	RANDLE	1
LEVI	2	MCNITT	3	ORTON	12	RANDOLPH	3
LEWIS	11	MCQUEEN	3	OSBURN	1	RANK	1
LICHTENBERG	12	MEAD	2	OSTRANDER	2	RASSEDIR	1
LIFER	1	MEE	2	PADDOCK	13	RAY	3
LINCOLN	1	MEIER	2	PAGE	17	RAYBORNE	2
LINDEN	1	MELANCON	3	PAINTER	5	RAYNSFORD	12
LINDON	2	MELENDY	24	PALMER	4	REARDON	1
LINGLE	1	MERCHANT	2	PARDEE	1	REASMON	2
LINGO	1	MERRICK	5	PARK	2	REDDIN	2
LOGAN	1	MERRILL	8	PARKER	4	REED	17
LONG	1	MERRITT	3	PARKS	1	REEVES	2
LOOMIS	1	MERWIN	44	PARMETER	1	RESSEGINE	9
LORDAN	2	METEVY	1	PARSHALL	2	RETERSTOFF	1
LORDON	1	MICHIGAN	1	PATEN	2	REWALT	2
LOREE	4	MIDDAUGH	2	PATTERSON	2	REYNOLDS	5
LOSINGER	1	MILES	20	PATTESON	1	RHOADES	2
LOVELL	16	MILLARD	1	PATTISON	1	RHYAN	1
LUCE	1	MILLER	22	PAYNE	3	RIBLET	2
LUDINGTON	31	MILLIMAN	3	PAYSON	1	RICE	12
LULL	50	MILLIS	8	PEACOCK	1	RICHARDSON	5
LUNDY	3	MILLS	2	PEAK	1	RIGGS	1
LUTES	3	MINK	3	PEARSON	5	RIPLEY	1
LUTZ	1	MISNER	1	PEAT	1	RISSEGUIE	2
LYKINE	1	MITCHELL	19	PECK	4	RIVERS	1
LYMAN	5	MIX	2	PEIRCE	1	ROACH	1
LYNN	2	MIZNER	1	PELTON	2	ROBBINS	2
LYON	10	MOE	3	PENCE	1	ROBERTS	19

Surname	# of Land Parcels	Surname	# of Land Parcels	Surname	# of Land Parcels	Surname	# of Land Parcels
ROBERTSON	1	SHERMAN	8	SWAIN	22	WALTON	1
ROBINSON	3	SHORTER	1	SWARTWOUT	3	WARANGASOE	1
ROBISON	1	SHOWARD	2	SWAYER	1	WARD	20
ROCHESTER	5	SHUTTS	1	SWEAT	2	WARDWELL	7
RODES	1	SIBLEY	4	SWITZER	1	WARREN	20
ROGERS	7	SIDERS	2	TAGUASON	1	WART	3
ROLSTONE	1	SIMMONS	1	TANNER	1	WARTROUS	1
RONAN	2	SIMMS	1	TARR	1	WASHBURN	4
ROOKE	2	SIMONDS	1	TAYLOR	4	WATERHOUSE	1
ROOT	5	SIMONS	2	TENANT	1	WATERMAN	2
ROSE	15	SIMPSON	1	TENNY	3	WATERS	14
ROSENBERGER	3	SINE	1	TERRY	1	WATSON	22
ROSS	5	SKEELS	5	TERWILLIGER	10	WAU-BA-TO	1
ROSSEDIR	1	SKELTON	2	THAYER	1	WEAVER	11
ROUNDS	3	SKINNER	5	THOMAS	4	WEBB	2
ROWAN	3	SLADE	5	THOMPSON	11	WEBBER	12
ROWE	2	SLAGHT	1	THORP	2	WEBSTER	12
ROWLAND	2	SLAIGHT	1	THURSTON	1	WEDD	1
RUDES	1	SLATER	5	TIBBITS	1	WEIDMAN	2
RUFRECHT	1	SLAUGHTER	2	TIBBITTS	7	WELCH	5
RUMSEY	1	SLOCUM	5	TICHENOR	1	WELLES	7
RUPRECHT	6	SLOSSON	6	TIFT	13	WELLING	2
RUSH	2	SMITH	51	TINDALL	8	WELLS	3
RUSHMORE	5	SNYDER	1	TINDOLL	1	WERT	1
RUSSEL	1	SOEVYN	2	TINKHAM	5	WESTCOTT	1
RUSSELL	13	SOPER	1	TITUS	1	WESTERBERG	1
RYAN	5	SOULE	2	TOBY	2	WESTGATE	1
RYDER	2	SOUTHWORTH	2	TONER	1	WESTON	27
RYERSON	43	SPAIDS	2	TOWER	9	WHALEN	1
SACKS	1	SPALDING	2	TOWNE	1	WHEAT	1
SAGE	3	SPARKS	1	TOWNSEND	9	WHEELER	10
SAIEN	4	SPAULDING	3	TRACY	6	WHEELOCK	10
SAMMIS	2	SPEIRS	1	TRAHAN	2	WHIPPLE	6
SAMPSON	1	SPENCER	6	TRAIN	2	WHITE	17
SAMUEL	2	SPES	4	TRASK	1	WHITEHEAD	3
SANBORN	9	SQUIER	13	TRENBLER	1	WHITEHURST	2
SANDS	1	ST PETER	4	TREXELL	2	WHITEMAN	1
SANFORD	117	STAAB	1	TRIPP	4	WHITMAN	5
SANGER	1	STAILER	1	TROMBLY	3	WHITNEY	8
SAPP	2	STAKER	3	TROTT	5	WIGGINS	4
SAUNDERS	11	STANDISH	1	TROUNBLEY	1	WILCOX	24
SAVAGE	6	STANLEY	14	TROUTIER	1	WILDER	5
SAVERCOOL	1	STARR	2	TROWBRIDGE	2	WILKIN	2
SAWYER	1	STAUDT	2	TRUDE	2	WILLARD	4
SAXTON	1	STEBBINS	2	TRUFONT	2	WILLETS	1
SCHANK	1	STEINER	4	TUBBS	1	WILLIAMS	7
SCHOONOVER	2	STEVENS	19	TUCK	2	WILLINS	1
SCHURCK	4	STEVENSON	11	TUCKER	4	WILLIUS	2
SCHWEITZER	2	STEWART	2	TURNER	5	WILLMER	3
SCOFIELD	1	STICKNEY	2	TUSK	1	WILSON	28
SCOTT	1	STILES	3	TUTHILL	2	WINN	2
SCOUGHTON	1	STILWELL	3	TUTTLE	1	WINSTON	1
SCOVILLE	2	STIMPSON	1	UPTON	6	WISENFIELD	1
SE	1	STIMSON	3	UTLEY	12	WISWELL	1
SEAFORD	1	STINGEL	1	VALLANCE	1	WITHEROW	2
SEAMAN	5	STOCKING	2	VAN ALSTINE	1	WONCH	1
SEARLES	1	STODDARD	3	VAN BRUNT	1	WOOD	177
SECORD	1	STONE	4	VAN BUREN	1	WOODARD	1
SEELEY	2	STORMS	2	VAN LIEW	1	WOODBURY	4
SEEVERS	1	STROH	12	VAN NARTEVICK	1	WOODFORD	1
SELFRIDGE	2	STRONACH	1	VAN WILTENBURG	9	WOODHOUSE	2
SELLEARS	2	STRONG	7	VANDAWATERS	1	WOODMAN	6
SHALAH	1	STUART	9	VANDUSEN	1	WOODRUFF	1
SHARAR	1	STUDLEY	1	VANO	6	WOODS	6
SHAW	5	SUMNER	1	VARNUM	1	WRENN	2
SHE	1	SURRARRER	1	WAH	1	WRIGHT	12
SHEAR	1	SUTFIN	1	WAKE	1	WUTCH	1
SHEARMAN	1	SUTHERLAND	3	WALKER	5	YATES	3
SHELDON	2	SUTLIFF	9	WALLACE	1	YERKES	4
SHERK	1	SVANO	2	WALTERHOUSE	2	YOUNG	7

Surname	# of Land Parcels
YOUNGS	1
YUNG	1
ZERLANT	3

Surname/Township Index

This Index allows you to determine which *Township Map Group(s)* contain individuals with the following surnames. Each *Map Group* has a corresponding full-name index of all individuals who obtained patents for land within its Congressional township's borders. After each index you will find the Patent Map to which it refers, and just thereafter, you can view the township's Road Map and Historical Map, with the latter map displaying streams, railroads, and more.

So, once you find your Surname here, proceed to the Index at the beginning of the **Map Group** indicated below.

Surname	Map Group	Parcels of Land	Meridian/Township/Range		
ACHENBACH	**21**	3	Michigan-Toledo Strip	11-N	14-W
ACKLEY	**21**	2	Michigan-Toledo Strip	11-N	14-W
ADAMS	**10**	3	Michigan-Toledo Strip	14-N	13-W
" "	**18**	2	Michigan-Toledo Strip	12-N	13-W
ADSIT	**24**	2	Michigan-Toledo Strip	11-N	11-W
AGARD	**3**	1	Michigan-Toledo Strip	16-N	12-W
AITKEN	**4**	1	Michigan-Toledo Strip	16-N	11-W
ALBERTSON	**13**	2	Michigan-Toledo Strip	13-N	14-W
ALEXANDER	**17**	1	Michigan-Toledo Strip	12-N	14-W
" "	**3**	1	Michigan-Toledo Strip	16-N	12-W
ALLEN	**16**	3	Michigan-Toledo Strip	13-N	11-W
" "	**13**	2	Michigan-Toledo Strip	13-N	14-W
" "	**23**	1	Michigan-Toledo Strip	11-N	12-W
ALLERS	**16**	1	Michigan-Toledo Strip	13-N	11-W
ALLEY	**15**	4	Michigan-Toledo Strip	13-N	12-W
" "	**11**	2	Michigan-Toledo Strip	14-N	12-W
" "	**10**	2	Michigan-Toledo Strip	14-N	13-W
" "	**12**	1	Michigan-Toledo Strip	14-N	11-W
AMES	**21**	1	Michigan-Toledo Strip	11-N	14-W
AMOS	**13**	1	Michigan-Toledo Strip	13-N	14-W
ANDERSON	**14**	1	Michigan-Toledo Strip	13-N	13-W
" "	**10**	1	Michigan-Toledo Strip	14-N	13-W
ANDREWS	**20**	2	Michigan-Toledo Strip	12-N	11-W
" "	**18**	1	Michigan-Toledo Strip	12-N	13-W
ANDRIE	**21**	1	Michigan-Toledo Strip	11-N	14-W
ANGEL	**21**	1	Michigan-Toledo Strip	11-N	14-W
ARMS	**19**	4	Michigan-Toledo Strip	12-N	12-W
" "	**14**	4	Michigan-Toledo Strip	13-N	13-W
" "	**24**	1	Michigan-Toledo Strip	11-N	11-W
" "	**20**	1	Michigan-Toledo Strip	12-N	11-W
ARMSTRONG	**22**	2	Michigan-Toledo Strip	11-N	13-W
ARNOLD	**10**	2	Michigan-Toledo Strip	14-N	13-W
" "	**3**	1	Michigan-Toledo Strip	16-N	12-W
ASHCRAFT	**17**	1	Michigan-Toledo Strip	12-N	14-W
ASHLEY	**12**	1	Michigan-Toledo Strip	14-N	11-W
ATWATER	**21**	1	Michigan-Toledo Strip	11-N	14-W
ATWOOD	**1**	1	Michigan-Toledo Strip	16-N	14-W
AUGERINE	**19**	1	Michigan-Toledo Strip	12-N	12-W
AVERY	**11**	5	Michigan-Toledo Strip	14-N	12-W
" "	**14**	3	Michigan-Toledo Strip	13-N	13-W
" "	**9**	3	Michigan-Toledo Strip	14-N	14-W
" "	**15**	1	Michigan-Toledo Strip	13-N	12-W
AYER	**11**	2	Michigan-Toledo Strip	14-N	12-W
BABCOCK	**21**	2	Michigan-Toledo Strip	11-N	14-W

Surname	Map Group	Parcels of Land	Meridian/Township/Range		
BACKARD	**20**	2	Michigan-Toledo Strip	12-N	11-W
BACKART	**20**	7	Michigan-Toledo Strip	12-N	11-W
BACKHART	**20**	1	Michigan-Toledo Strip	12-N	11-W
BADGEROW	**15**	2	Michigan-Toledo Strip	13-N	12-W
" "	**4**	1	Michigan-Toledo Strip	16-N	11-W
BAILEY	**3**	1	Michigan-Toledo Strip	16-N	12-W
BAKER	**24**	1	Michigan-Toledo Strip	11-N	11-W
BALDWIN	**1**	4	Michigan-Toledo Strip	16-N	14-W
" "	**15**	3	Michigan-Toledo Strip	13-N	12-W
" "	**17**	1	Michigan-Toledo Strip	12-N	14-W
BALEY	**3**	1	Michigan-Toledo Strip	16-N	12-W
BALFOUR	**18**	2	Michigan-Toledo Strip	12-N	13-W
BALL	**21**	27	Michigan-Toledo Strip	11-N	14-W
" "	**22**	16	Michigan-Toledo Strip	11-N	13-W
" "	**15**	13	Michigan-Toledo Strip	13-N	12-W
" "	**18**	7	Michigan-Toledo Strip	12-N	13-W
" "	**14**	7	Michigan-Toledo Strip	13-N	13-W
" "	**24**	4	Michigan-Toledo Strip	11-N	11-W
" "	**16**	4	Michigan-Toledo Strip	13-N	11-W
" "	**8**	4	Michigan-Toledo Strip	15-N	11-W
" "	**23**	3	Michigan-Toledo Strip	11-N	12-W
" "	**12**	3	Michigan-Toledo Strip	14-N	11-W
" "	**17**	2	Michigan-Toledo Strip	12-N	14-W
" "	**19**	1	Michigan-Toledo Strip	12-N	12-W
BALLINGER	**9**	1	Michigan-Toledo Strip	14-N	14-W
BALLOU	**13**	4	Michigan-Toledo Strip	13-N	14-W
" "	**14**	1	Michigan-Toledo Strip	13-N	13-W
BAMBER	**14**	2	Michigan-Toledo Strip	13-N	13-W
BANCROFT	**24**	2	Michigan-Toledo Strip	11-N	11-W
BANKER	**22**	1	Michigan-Toledo Strip	11-N	13-W
BARB	**4**	2	Michigan-Toledo Strip	16-N	11-W
BARBER	**2**	2	Michigan-Toledo Strip	16-N	13-W
BARKER	**23**	2	Michigan-Toledo Strip	11-N	12-W
BARNES	**24**	2	Michigan-Toledo Strip	11-N	11-W
BARNHARD	**19**	2	Michigan-Toledo Strip	12-N	12-W
" "	**13**	2	Michigan-Toledo Strip	13-N	14-W
" "	**9**	2	Michigan-Toledo Strip	14-N	14-W
BARNUM	**19**	1	Michigan-Toledo Strip	12-N	12-W
BARRON	**15**	2	Michigan-Toledo Strip	13-N	12-W
BARSTOW	**4**	2	Michigan-Toledo Strip	16-N	11-W
BARTON	**16**	13	Michigan-Toledo Strip	13-N	11-W
" "	**15**	6	Michigan-Toledo Strip	13-N	12-W
" "	**8**	3	Michigan-Toledo Strip	15-N	11-W
" "	**20**	1	Michigan-Toledo Strip	12-N	11-W
" "	**4**	1	Michigan-Toledo Strip	16-N	11-W
BATES	**16**	1	Michigan-Toledo Strip	13-N	11-W
BEAN	**20**	3	Michigan-Toledo Strip	12-N	11-W
" "	**9**	2	Michigan-Toledo Strip	14-N	14-W
BEATON	**3**	1	Michigan-Toledo Strip	16-N	12-W
BEAUCHAMP	**24**	2	Michigan-Toledo Strip	11-N	11-W
BEAZLEY	**8**	2	Michigan-Toledo Strip	15-N	11-W
BEDIENT	**8**	2	Michigan-Toledo Strip	15-N	11-W
BEEG	**17**	1	Michigan-Toledo Strip	12-N	14-W
BEERS	**9**	1	Michigan-Toledo Strip	14-N	14-W
BEIDLER	**24**	2	Michigan-Toledo Strip	11-N	11-W
BELDEN	**21**	2	Michigan-Toledo Strip	11-N	14-W
" "	**18**	1	Michigan-Toledo Strip	12-N	13-W
" "	**17**	1	Michigan-Toledo Strip	12-N	14-W
BELL	**6**	3	Michigan-Toledo Strip	15-N	13-W
" "	**17**	2	Michigan-Toledo Strip	12-N	14-W

Surname	Map Group	Parcels of Land	Meridian/Township/Range		
BELL (Cont'd)	**14**	1	Michigan-Toledo Strip	13-N	13-W
" "	**7**	1	Michigan-Toledo Strip	15-N	12-W
" "	**2**	1	Michigan-Toledo Strip	16-N	13-W
BELMEAR	**2**	2	Michigan-Toledo Strip	16-N	13-W
BEMENT	**19**	2	Michigan-Toledo Strip	12-N	12-W
BENDER	**12**	1	Michigan-Toledo Strip	14-N	11-W
" "	**10**	1	Michigan-Toledo Strip	14-N	13-W
BENJAMIN	**8**	10	Michigan-Toledo Strip	15-N	11-W
" "	**3**	9	Michigan-Toledo Strip	16-N	12-W
" "	**2**	9	Michigan-Toledo Strip	16-N	13-W
" "	**4**	1	Michigan-Toledo Strip	16-N	11-W
BENNETT	**15**	4	Michigan-Toledo Strip	13-N	12-W
" "	**19**	3	Michigan-Toledo Strip	12-N	12-W
" "	**8**	3	Michigan-Toledo Strip	15-N	11-W
" "	**18**	2	Michigan-Toledo Strip	12-N	13-W
" "	**20**	1	Michigan-Toledo Strip	12-N	11-W
" "	**12**	1	Michigan-Toledo Strip	14-N	11-W
BENNITT	**20**	1	Michigan-Toledo Strip	12-N	11-W
BENTON	**24**	6	Michigan-Toledo Strip	11-N	11-W
BERRY	**19**	2	Michigan-Toledo Strip	12-N	12-W
BESHER	**15**	4	Michigan-Toledo Strip	13-N	12-W
BEVIER	**4**	1	Michigan-Toledo Strip	16-N	11-W
BIGELOW	**19**	5	Michigan-Toledo Strip	12-N	12-W
" "	**15**	4	Michigan-Toledo Strip	13-N	12-W
BIGGS	**24**	1	Michigan-Toledo Strip	11-N	11-W
BILLS	**20**	4	Michigan-Toledo Strip	12-N	11-W
" "	**24**	2	Michigan-Toledo Strip	11-N	11-W
BINGHAM	**9**	1	Michigan-Toledo Strip	14-N	14-W
BIRCHARD	**17**	2	Michigan-Toledo Strip	12-N	14-W
BIRDSELL	**17**	3	Michigan-Toledo Strip	12-N	14-W
BISBEE	**19**	2	Michigan-Toledo Strip	12-N	12-W
BISSETT	**1**	1	Michigan-Toledo Strip	16-N	14-W
BLACK	**4**	4	Michigan-Toledo Strip	16-N	11-W
BLACKWELL	**20**	3	Michigan-Toledo Strip	12-N	11-W
BLAIR	**17**	1	Michigan-Toledo Strip	12-N	14-W
BLANCHARD	**20**	2	Michigan-Toledo Strip	12-N	11-W
" "	**17**	2	Michigan-Toledo Strip	12-N	14-W
" "	**3**	1	Michigan-Toledo Strip	16-N	12-W
BLAZO	**10**	1	Michigan-Toledo Strip	14-N	13-W
BLINDBERRY	**24**	2	Michigan-Toledo Strip	11-N	11-W
BLISS	**4**	1	Michigan-Toledo Strip	16-N	11-W
BLOOD	**22**	3	Michigan-Toledo Strip	11-N	13-W
BOHNE	**20**	4	Michigan-Toledo Strip	12-N	11-W
BOLDMAN	**6**	1	Michigan-Toledo Strip	15-N	13-W
BONNEY	**16**	3	Michigan-Toledo Strip	13-N	11-W
BORDEN	**20**	2	Michigan-Toledo Strip	12-N	11-W
" "	**24**	1	Michigan-Toledo Strip	11-N	11-W
BOTSFORD	**20**	1	Michigan-Toledo Strip	12-N	11-W
BOWEN	**15**	5	Michigan-Toledo Strip	13-N	12-W
BOWER	**4**	1	Michigan-Toledo Strip	16-N	11-W
BOWLEY	**13**	3	Michigan-Toledo Strip	13-N	14-W
BOWMAN	**12**	2	Michigan-Toledo Strip	14-N	11-W
" "	**13**	1	Michigan-Toledo Strip	13-N	14-W
" "	**4**	1	Michigan-Toledo Strip	16-N	11-W
BOYD	**24**	1	Michigan-Toledo Strip	11-N	11-W
" "	**12**	1	Michigan-Toledo Strip	14-N	11-W
BRACE	**23**	1	Michigan-Toledo Strip	11-N	12-W
BRENNAN	**16**	2	Michigan-Toledo Strip	13-N	11-W
BRIGGS	**13**	5	Michigan-Toledo Strip	13-N	14-W
" "	**24**	1	Michigan-Toledo Strip	11-N	11-W

Surname	Map Group	Parcels of Land	Meridian/Township/Range		
BRIGGS (Cont'd)	**17**	1	Michigan-Toledo Strip	12-N	14-W
" "	**9**	1	Michigan-Toledo Strip	14-N	14-W
BRIGHAM	**10**	5	Michigan-Toledo Strip	14-N	13-W
" "	**14**	4	Michigan-Toledo Strip	13-N	13-W
BRITTAIN	**23**	1	Michigan-Toledo Strip	11-N	12-W
BRITTON	**18**	1	Michigan-Toledo Strip	12-N	13-W
" "	**3**	1	Michigan-Toledo Strip	16-N	12-W
BROMLEY	**1**	1	Michigan-Toledo Strip	16-N	14-W
BROOKS	**19**	7	Michigan-Toledo Strip	12-N	12-W
" "	**18**	4	Michigan-Toledo Strip	12-N	13-W
" "	**14**	3	Michigan-Toledo Strip	13-N	13-W
" "	**21**	2	Michigan-Toledo Strip	11-N	14-W
" "	**13**	2	Michigan-Toledo Strip	13-N	14-W
" "	**22**	1	Michigan-Toledo Strip	11-N	13-W
" "	**16**	1	Michigan-Toledo Strip	13-N	11-W
BROTHERTON	**13**	2	Michigan-Toledo Strip	13-N	14-W
BROWN	**22**	2	Michigan-Toledo Strip	11-N	13-W
" "	**18**	2	Michigan-Toledo Strip	12-N	13-W
" "	**23**	1	Michigan-Toledo Strip	11-N	12-W
" "	**11**	1	Michigan-Toledo Strip	14-N	12-W
" "	**9**	1	Michigan-Toledo Strip	14-N	14-W
" "	**8**	1	Michigan-Toledo Strip	15-N	11-W
" "	**6**	1	Michigan-Toledo Strip	15-N	13-W
BRUBAKER	**14**	3	Michigan-Toledo Strip	13-N	13-W
BRUCE	**20**	1	Michigan-Toledo Strip	12-N	11-W
" "	**16**	1	Michigan-Toledo Strip	13-N	11-W
" "	**9**	1	Michigan-Toledo Strip	14-N	14-W
BRUNSON	**8**	1	Michigan-Toledo Strip	15-N	11-W
BUCK	**13**	3	Michigan-Toledo Strip	13-N	14-W
" "	**16**	1	Michigan-Toledo Strip	13-N	11-W
" "	**12**	1	Michigan-Toledo Strip	14-N	11-W
BUGGS	**13**	3	Michigan-Toledo Strip	13-N	14-W
BUHL	**22**	1	Michigan-Toledo Strip	11-N	13-W
BUICK	**9**	2	Michigan-Toledo Strip	14-N	14-W
BULL	**9**	3	Michigan-Toledo Strip	14-N	14-W
BULSON	**1**	1	Michigan-Toledo Strip	16-N	14-W
BUMSTED	**21**	2	Michigan-Toledo Strip	11-N	14-W
BURKE	**20**	1	Michigan-Toledo Strip	12-N	11-W
BURRIL	**22**	2	Michigan-Toledo Strip	11-N	13-W
BURT	**24**	1	Michigan-Toledo Strip	11-N	11-W
BUSH	**8**	4	Michigan-Toledo Strip	15-N	11-W
" "	**20**	2	Michigan-Toledo Strip	12-N	11-W
" "	**15**	1	Michigan-Toledo Strip	13-N	12-W
BUSHNELL	**3**	4	Michigan-Toledo Strip	16-N	12-W
BUTLER	**18**	3	Michigan-Toledo Strip	12-N	13-W
BUTTON	**8**	1	Michigan-Toledo Strip	15-N	11-W
BUZZLE	**4**	1	Michigan-Toledo Strip	16-N	11-W
CADY	**20**	2	Michigan-Toledo Strip	12-N	11-W
" "	**14**	2	Michigan-Toledo Strip	13-N	13-W
" "	**1**	1	Michigan-Toledo Strip	16-N	14-W
CAIRNS	**13**	2	Michigan-Toledo Strip	13-N	14-W
CALHOUN	**15**	1	Michigan-Toledo Strip	13-N	12-W
CALLAR	**20**	2	Michigan-Toledo Strip	12-N	11-W
" "	**24**	1	Michigan-Toledo Strip	11-N	11-W
CALLENDER	**2**	1	Michigan-Toledo Strip	16-N	13-W
CARLISLE	**16**	1	Michigan-Toledo Strip	13-N	11-W
CARLSON	**7**	1	Michigan-Toledo Strip	15-N	12-W
CARPENTER	**16**	6	Michigan-Toledo Strip	13-N	11-W
" "	**24**	3	Michigan-Toledo Strip	11-N	11-W
" "	**13**	3	Michigan-Toledo Strip	13-N	14-W

Surname	Map Group	Parcels of Land	Meridian/Township/Range		
CARPENTER (Cont'd)	**20**	1	Michigan-Toledo Strip	12-N	11-W
CARR	**21**	3	Michigan-Toledo Strip	11-N	14-W
CARTER	**22**	1	Michigan-Toledo Strip	11-N	13-W
" "	**12**	1	Michigan-Toledo Strip	14-N	11-W
CASE	**4**	2	Michigan-Toledo Strip	16-N	11-W
CASS	**19**	1	Michigan-Toledo Strip	12-N	12-W
CASTLE	**17**	1	Michigan-Toledo Strip	12-N	14-W
CAVENDAR	**15**	1	Michigan-Toledo Strip	13-N	12-W
CAVENDER	**20**	2	Michigan-Toledo Strip	12-N	11-W
CAYWOOD	**24**	1	Michigan-Toledo Strip	11-N	11-W
CHADWICK	**3**	2	Michigan-Toledo Strip	16-N	12-W
CHAFFEE	**14**	1	Michigan-Toledo Strip	13-N	13-W
CHAPIN	**4**	1	Michigan-Toledo Strip	16-N	11-W
CHAPMAN	**21**	2	Michigan-Toledo Strip	11-N	14-W
" "	**22**	1	Michigan-Toledo Strip	11-N	13-W
" "	**3**	1	Michigan-Toledo Strip	16-N	12-W
CHARLES	**3**	2	Michigan-Toledo Strip	16-N	12-W
CHARLOE	**19**	1	Michigan-Toledo Strip	12-N	12-W
CHASE	**4**	1	Michigan-Toledo Strip	16-N	11-W
CHEENEY	**14**	7	Michigan-Toledo Strip	13-N	13-W
CHENEY	**19**	4	Michigan-Toledo Strip	12-N	12-W
" "	**14**	4	Michigan-Toledo Strip	13-N	13-W
" "	**24**	1	Michigan-Toledo Strip	11-N	11-W
" "	**20**	1	Michigan-Toledo Strip	12-N	11-W
CHICK	**1**	2	Michigan-Toledo Strip	16-N	14-W
" "	**10**	1	Michigan-Toledo Strip	14-N	13-W
" "	**7**	1	Michigan-Toledo Strip	15-N	12-W
CHILD	**4**	1	Michigan-Toledo Strip	16-N	11-W
CHILDS	**3**	1	Michigan-Toledo Strip	16-N	12-W
CHIPMAN	**15**	1	Michigan-Toledo Strip	13-N	12-W
CHRISTIAN	**6**	2	Michigan-Toledo Strip	15-N	13-W
CHURCH	**19**	1	Michigan-Toledo Strip	12-N	12-W
CILLEY	**9**	2	Michigan-Toledo Strip	14-N	14-W
CLARK	**8**	12	Michigan-Toledo Strip	15-N	11-W
" "	**13**	2	Michigan-Toledo Strip	13-N	14-W
" "	**2**	2	Michigan-Toledo Strip	16-N	13-W
" "	**17**	1	Michigan-Toledo Strip	12-N	14-W
" "	**10**	1	Michigan-Toledo Strip	14-N	13-W
CLAY	**11**	3	Michigan-Toledo Strip	14-N	12-W
" "	**19**	1	Michigan-Toledo Strip	12-N	12-W
CLENLEY	**10**	2	Michigan-Toledo Strip	14-N	13-W
COCHRAN	**10**	3	Michigan-Toledo Strip	14-N	13-W
COGSWELL	**13**	3	Michigan-Toledo Strip	13-N	14-W
COLBURN	**13**	1	Michigan-Toledo Strip	13-N	14-W
COLE	**19**	3	Michigan-Toledo Strip	12-N	12-W
" "	**18**	1	Michigan-Toledo Strip	12-N	13-W
" "	**16**	1	Michigan-Toledo Strip	13-N	11-W
" "	**15**	1	Michigan-Toledo Strip	13-N	12-W
" "	**4**	1	Michigan-Toledo Strip	16-N	11-W
COLLINS	**13**	2	Michigan-Toledo Strip	13-N	14-W
" "	**7**	1	Michigan-Toledo Strip	15-N	12-W
COLVER	**20**	1	Michigan-Toledo Strip	12-N	11-W
COMSTOCK	**11**	12	Michigan-Toledo Strip	14-N	12-W
CONKLIN	**3**	3	Michigan-Toledo Strip	16-N	12-W
" "	**8**	1	Michigan-Toledo Strip	15-N	11-W
CONKWRIGHT	**15**	2	Michigan-Toledo Strip	13-N	12-W
" "	**16**	1	Michigan-Toledo Strip	13-N	11-W
CONLEY	**4**	1	Michigan-Toledo Strip	16-N	11-W
CONOVER	**24**	1	Michigan-Toledo Strip	11-N	11-W
COOK	**10**	26	Michigan-Toledo Strip	14-N	13-W

Surname	Map Group	Parcels of Land	Meridian/Township/Range		
COOK (Cont'd)	**13**	8	Michigan-Toledo Strip	13-N	14-W
" "	**9**	6	Michigan-Toledo Strip	14-N	14-W
" "	**24**	4	Michigan-Toledo Strip	11-N	11-W
" "	**16**	4	Michigan-Toledo Strip	13-N	11-W
" "	**4**	3	Michigan-Toledo Strip	16-N	11-W
" "	**3**	3	Michigan-Toledo Strip	16-N	12-W
" "	**19**	2	Michigan-Toledo Strip	12-N	12-W
" "	**15**	2	Michigan-Toledo Strip	13-N	12-W
" "	**23**	1	Michigan-Toledo Strip	11-N	12-W
" "	**12**	1	Michigan-Toledo Strip	14-N	11-W
" "	**11**	1	Michigan-Toledo Strip	14-N	12-W
COOLBAUGH	**15**	1	Michigan-Toledo Strip	13-N	12-W
COOLEY	**16**	1	Michigan-Toledo Strip	13-N	11-W
COON	**21**	2	Michigan-Toledo Strip	11-N	14-W
COOPER	**24**	2	Michigan-Toledo Strip	11-N	11-W
" "	**9**	2	Michigan-Toledo Strip	14-N	14-W
" "	**5**	2	Michigan-Toledo Strip	15-N	14-W
COULTER	**16**	2	Michigan-Toledo Strip	13-N	11-W
COUNTRIMAN	**4**	1	Michigan-Toledo Strip	16-N	11-W
COWLES	**14**	3	Michigan-Toledo Strip	13-N	13-W
COWN	**21**	1	Michigan-Toledo Strip	11-N	14-W
COX	**22**	1	Michigan-Toledo Strip	11-N	13-W
CRABTREE	**16**	2	Michigan-Toledo Strip	13-N	11-W
CRADIT	**17**	1	Michigan-Toledo Strip	12-N	14-W
CRAM	**20**	1	Michigan-Toledo Strip	12-N	11-W
CRANDALL	**24**	3	Michigan-Toledo Strip	11-N	11-W
CRANDELL	**18**	1	Michigan-Toledo Strip	12-N	13-W
CRARY	**12**	2	Michigan-Toledo Strip	14-N	11-W
CRAWFORD	**17**	2	Michigan-Toledo Strip	12-N	14-W
" "	**5**	2	Michigan-Toledo Strip	15-N	14-W
CREPIN	**9**	1	Michigan-Toledo Strip	14-N	14-W
" "	**5**	1	Michigan-Toledo Strip	15-N	14-W
CRESSMAN	**13**	2	Michigan-Toledo Strip	13-N	14-W
CRITCHLOW	**11**	2	Michigan-Toledo Strip	14-N	12-W
CRITTENDON	**3**	6	Michigan-Toledo Strip	16-N	12-W
CROFF	**24**	1	Michigan-Toledo Strip	11-N	11-W
CROFOOT	**9**	4	Michigan-Toledo Strip	14-N	14-W
" "	**15**	3	Michigan-Toledo Strip	13-N	12-W
" "	**19**	1	Michigan-Toledo Strip	12-N	12-W
CROMAN	**15**	2	Michigan-Toledo Strip	13-N	12-W
CROSS	**5**	2	Michigan-Toledo Strip	15-N	14-W
CROSSMAN	**18**	3	Michigan-Toledo Strip	12-N	13-W
CROY	**13**	1	Michigan-Toledo Strip	13-N	14-W
CRUM	**4**	1	Michigan-Toledo Strip	16-N	11-W
CUDABACK	**8**	5	Michigan-Toledo Strip	15-N	11-W
CULP	**20**	1	Michigan-Toledo Strip	12-N	11-W
" "	**16**	1	Michigan-Toledo Strip	13-N	11-W
CULVER	**19**	1	Michigan-Toledo Strip	12-N	12-W
CUMINGS	**4**	1	Michigan-Toledo Strip	16-N	11-W
CUMMINGS	**3**	2	Michigan-Toledo Strip	16-N	12-W
CURDY	**17**	1	Michigan-Toledo Strip	12-N	14-W
CURTICE	**13**	3	Michigan-Toledo Strip	13-N	14-W
CURTIS	**19**	1	Michigan-Toledo Strip	12-N	12-W
DAGAN	**21**	2	Michigan-Toledo Strip	11-N	14-W
DAGGETT	**20**	1	Michigan-Toledo Strip	12-N	11-W
DAKE	**9**	6	Michigan-Toledo Strip	14-N	14-W
DANA	**21**	3	Michigan-Toledo Strip	11-N	14-W
" "	**18**	3	Michigan-Toledo Strip	12-N	13-W
" "	**22**	1	Michigan-Toledo Strip	11-N	13-W
DANIEL	**12**	2	Michigan-Toledo Strip	14-N	11-W

Surname	Map Group	Parcels of Land	Meridian/Township/Range		
DANIELS	**23**	2	Michigan-Toledo Strip	11-N	12-W
DARLING	**24**	17	Michigan-Toledo Strip	11-N	11-W
" "	**13**	13	Michigan-Toledo Strip	13-N	14-W
" "	**11**	5	Michigan-Toledo Strip	14-N	12-W
DAVENPORT	**4**	3	Michigan-Toledo Strip	16-N	11-W
DAVIDSON	**20**	1	Michigan-Toledo Strip	12-N	11-W
DAVIS	**4**	4	Michigan-Toledo Strip	16-N	11-W
" "	**19**	3	Michigan-Toledo Strip	12-N	12-W
" "	**18**	3	Michigan-Toledo Strip	12-N	13-W
" "	**14**	2	Michigan-Toledo Strip	13-N	13-W
" "	**7**	1	Michigan-Toledo Strip	15-N	12-W
DE BOIS	**21**	5	Michigan-Toledo Strip	11-N	14-W
DE MOO	**17**	1	Michigan-Toledo Strip	12-N	14-W
DE PUNG	**24**	1	Michigan-Toledo Strip	11-N	11-W
DEAN	**16**	1	Michigan-Toledo Strip	13-N	11-W
DEANE	**18**	2	Michigan-Toledo Strip	12-N	13-W
DEARTH	**3**	2	Michigan-Toledo Strip	16-N	12-W
DECKER	**19**	3	Michigan-Toledo Strip	12-N	12-W
" "	**4**	1	Michigan-Toledo Strip	16-N	11-W
DELAHOUSSAYE	**4**	2	Michigan-Toledo Strip	16-N	11-W
DELANO	**20**	3	Michigan-Toledo Strip	12-N	11-W
DENIS	**24**	1	Michigan-Toledo Strip	11-N	11-W
DENSLOW	**18**	1	Michigan-Toledo Strip	12-N	13-W
DEVER	**3**	2	Michigan-Toledo Strip	16-N	12-W
DEWOLF	**14**	1	Michigan-Toledo Strip	13-N	13-W
DICKERSON	**19**	1	Michigan-Toledo Strip	12-N	12-W
DICKINSON	**15**	4	Michigan-Toledo Strip	13-N	12-W
" "	**13**	2	Michigan-Toledo Strip	13-N	14-W
DICKISON	**9**	3	Michigan-Toledo Strip	14-N	14-W
DINGMAN	**6**	1	Michigan-Toledo Strip	15-N	13-W
" "	**2**	1	Michigan-Toledo Strip	16-N	13-W
DIRSTEIN	**4**	2	Michigan-Toledo Strip	16-N	11-W
DIXON	**24**	1	Michigan-Toledo Strip	11-N	11-W
DOANE	**3**	1	Michigan-Toledo Strip	16-N	12-W
DOBE	**17**	2	Michigan-Toledo Strip	12-N	14-W
DOBSON	**13**	1	Michigan-Toledo Strip	13-N	14-W
DOCHERTY	**4**	1	Michigan-Toledo Strip	16-N	11-W
DOTY	**20**	1	Michigan-Toledo Strip	12-N	11-W
DOUD	**13**	1	Michigan-Toledo Strip	13-N	14-W
DOUGLAS	**11**	1	Michigan-Toledo Strip	14-N	12-W
DOUGLASS	**15**	7	Michigan-Toledo Strip	13-N	12-W
" "	**12**	2	Michigan-Toledo Strip	14-N	11-W
DOVE	**3**	2	Michigan-Toledo Strip	16-N	12-W
DOWLING	**9**	2	Michigan-Toledo Strip	14-N	14-W
DOWNING	**24**	1	Michigan-Toledo Strip	11-N	11-W
DOYLE	**13**	1	Michigan-Toledo Strip	13-N	14-W
DRAGOO	**13**	1	Michigan-Toledo Strip	13-N	14-W
DRAPER	**21**	2	Michigan-Toledo Strip	11-N	14-W
DRESSER	**21**	1	Michigan-Toledo Strip	11-N	14-W
DRUHER	**21**	1	Michigan-Toledo Strip	11-N	14-W
DUBOIS	**17**	1	Michigan-Toledo Strip	12-N	14-W
" "	**4**	1	Michigan-Toledo Strip	16-N	11-W
DUDLEY	**24**	2	Michigan-Toledo Strip	11-N	11-W
DUELL	**18**	1	Michigan-Toledo Strip	12-N	13-W
DUFFY	**4**	1	Michigan-Toledo Strip	16-N	11-W
DUNFEE	**13**	1	Michigan-Toledo Strip	13-N	14-W
DUNGAN	**6**	1	Michigan-Toledo Strip	15-N	13-W
DUNLAP	**9**	1	Michigan-Toledo Strip	14-N	14-W
DUNN	**21**	3	Michigan-Toledo Strip	11-N	14-W
" "	**15**	2	Michigan-Toledo Strip	13-N	12-W

Surname	Map Group	Parcels of Land	Meridian/Township/Range		
DUNN (Cont'd)	**6**	1	Michigan-Toledo Strip	15-N	13-W
DUNNING	**9**	1	Michigan-Toledo Strip	14-N	14-W
DUTCHER	**4**	1	Michigan-Toledo Strip	16-N	11-W
EAEGLE	**5**	1	Michigan-Toledo Strip	15-N	14-W
EANES	**12**	2	Michigan-Toledo Strip	14-N	11-W
EARLY	**10**	2	Michigan-Toledo Strip	14-N	13-W
EASTMAN	**16**	49	Michigan-Toledo Strip	13-N	11-W
" "	**11**	13	Michigan-Toledo Strip	14-N	12-W
" "	**20**	10	Michigan-Toledo Strip	12-N	11-W
" "	**17**	3	Michigan-Toledo Strip	12-N	14-W
" "	**15**	3	Michigan-Toledo Strip	13-N	12-W
" "	**7**	1	Michigan-Toledo Strip	15-N	12-W
ECHTINAW	**21**	3	Michigan-Toledo Strip	11-N	14-W
ECKELS	**24**	1	Michigan-Toledo Strip	11-N	11-W
EDDY	**9**	5	Michigan-Toledo Strip	14-N	14-W
" "	**13**	4	Michigan-Toledo Strip	13-N	14-W
" "	**17**	2	Michigan-Toledo Strip	12-N	14-W
EDGCOMB	**16**	2	Michigan-Toledo Strip	13-N	11-W
EDMESTON	**23**	1	Michigan-Toledo Strip	11-N	12-W
EDMONSON	**19**	1	Michigan-Toledo Strip	12-N	12-W
EDMUNDS	**18**	1	Michigan-Toledo Strip	12-N	13-W
EDWARDS	**12**	1	Michigan-Toledo Strip	14-N	11-W
" "	**1**	1	Michigan-Toledo Strip	16-N	14-W
EHLE	**16**	1	Michigan-Toledo Strip	13-N	11-W
EICHENLAUB	**21**	1	Michigan-Toledo Strip	11-N	14-W
ELDRED	**24**	2	Michigan-Toledo Strip	11-N	11-W
ELDREDGE	**11**	2	Michigan-Toledo Strip	14-N	12-W
ELDRIDGE	**11**	9	Michigan-Toledo Strip	14-N	12-W
" "	**10**	1	Michigan-Toledo Strip	14-N	13-W
ELLIOTT	**13**	1	Michigan-Toledo Strip	13-N	14-W
" "	**9**	1	Michigan-Toledo Strip	14-N	14-W
ELMS	**4**	2	Michigan-Toledo Strip	16-N	11-W
ELPHICK	**22**	1	Michigan-Toledo Strip	11-N	13-W
ELTING	**17**	2	Michigan-Toledo Strip	12-N	14-W
ELWELL	**3**	2	Michigan-Toledo Strip	16-N	12-W
ELY	**8**	12	Michigan-Toledo Strip	15-N	11-W
" "	**17**	1	Michigan-Toledo Strip	12-N	14-W
EMBREE	**13**	2	Michigan-Toledo Strip	13-N	14-W
ENSLEY	**24**	1	Michigan-Toledo Strip	11-N	11-W
ERRICKSON	**21**	1	Michigan-Toledo Strip	11-N	14-W
EUT	**10**	1	Michigan-Toledo Strip	14-N	13-W
EVANS	**23**	3	Michigan-Toledo Strip	11-N	12-W
" "	**16**	1	Michigan-Toledo Strip	13-N	11-W
EWERS	**14**	2	Michigan-Toledo Strip	13-N	13-W
EWING	**8**	2	Michigan-Toledo Strip	15-N	11-W
" "	**23**	1	Michigan-Toledo Strip	11-N	12-W
EYCK	**8**	2	Michigan-Toledo Strip	15-N	11-W
FAIRCHILDES	**18**	2	Michigan-Toledo Strip	12-N	13-W
FALES	**7**	1	Michigan-Toledo Strip	15-N	12-W
FARINHOLT	**8**	2	Michigan-Toledo Strip	15-N	11-W
FARNHAM	**13**	2	Michigan-Toledo Strip	13-N	14-W
" "	**17**	1	Michigan-Toledo Strip	12-N	14-W
FELLOWS	**22**	2	Michigan-Toledo Strip	11-N	13-W
FENNER	**21**	1	Michigan-Toledo Strip	11-N	14-W
FERRAN	**10**	1	Michigan-Toledo Strip	14-N	13-W
FERRISS	**8**	2	Michigan-Toledo Strip	15-N	11-W
FERRY	**11**	4	Michigan-Toledo Strip	14-N	12-W
" "	**16**	1	Michigan-Toledo Strip	13-N	11-W
FIFIELD	**2**	1	Michigan-Toledo Strip	16-N	13-W
FILER	**2**	3	Michigan-Toledo Strip	16-N	13-W

Surname	Map Group	Parcels of Land	Meridian/Township/Range		
FILER (Cont'd)	**1**	1	Michigan-Toledo Strip	16-N	14-W
FINCH	**20**	3	Michigan-Toledo Strip	12-N	11-W
" "	**3**	1	Michigan-Toledo Strip	16-N	12-W
FISCHER	**8**	2	Michigan-Toledo Strip	15-N	11-W
FLAGG	**1**	2	Michigan-Toledo Strip	16-N	14-W
FLANDERS	**9**	2	Michigan-Toledo Strip	14-N	14-W
FOGG	**8**	2	Michigan-Toledo Strip	15-N	11-W
FOLJAMBE	**1**	2	Michigan-Toledo Strip	16-N	14-W
FORBES	**13**	1	Michigan-Toledo Strip	13-N	14-W
" "	**10**	1	Michigan-Toledo Strip	14-N	13-W
" "	**9**	1	Michigan-Toledo Strip	14-N	14-W
FORD	**8**	6	Michigan-Toledo Strip	15-N	11-W
" "	**14**	1	Michigan-Toledo Strip	13-N	13-W
FORSHAY	**6**	1	Michigan-Toledo Strip	15-N	13-W
FOSTER	**16**	4	Michigan-Toledo Strip	13-N	11-W
" "	**1**	1	Michigan-Toledo Strip	16-N	14-W
FOWLER	**13**	3	Michigan-Toledo Strip	13-N	14-W
FOWTER	**12**	1	Michigan-Toledo Strip	14-N	11-W
FOX	**13**	1	Michigan-Toledo Strip	13-N	14-W
FRANKLIN	**16**	1	Michigan-Toledo Strip	13-N	11-W
" "	**10**	1	Michigan-Toledo Strip	14-N	13-W
FREEMAN	**1**	2	Michigan-Toledo Strip	16-N	14-W
FRENCH	**24**	5	Michigan-Toledo Strip	11-N	11-W
" "	**14**	3	Michigan-Toledo Strip	13-N	13-W
" "	**16**	2	Michigan-Toledo Strip	13-N	11-W
FRISBY	**19**	1	Michigan-Toledo Strip	12-N	12-W
FROST	**20**	1	Michigan-Toledo Strip	12-N	11-W
FRY	**12**	2	Michigan-Toledo Strip	14-N	11-W
" "	**3**	2	Michigan-Toledo Strip	16-N	12-W
FULLER	**24**	8	Michigan-Toledo Strip	11-N	11-W
" "	**22**	2	Michigan-Toledo Strip	11-N	13-W
FULLMER	**19**	1	Michigan-Toledo Strip	12-N	12-W
FURGERSON	**15**	3	Michigan-Toledo Strip	13-N	12-W
FURMAN	**18**	5	Michigan-Toledo Strip	12-N	13-W
" "	**19**	3	Michigan-Toledo Strip	12-N	12-W
" "	**22**	1	Michigan-Toledo Strip	11-N	13-W
FURRY	**4**	3	Michigan-Toledo Strip	16-N	11-W
GALLUP	**24**	1	Michigan-Toledo Strip	11-N	11-W
GAMBLE	**10**	2	Michigan-Toledo Strip	14-N	13-W
GARD	**4**	1	Michigan-Toledo Strip	16-N	11-W
GARDNER	**24**	2	Michigan-Toledo Strip	11-N	11-W
" "	**20**	2	Michigan-Toledo Strip	12-N	11-W
GARNER	**10**	1	Michigan-Toledo Strip	14-N	13-W
GASTON	**8**	1	Michigan-Toledo Strip	15-N	11-W
GATES	**1**	2	Michigan-Toledo Strip	16-N	14-W
" "	**14**	1	Michigan-Toledo Strip	13-N	13-W
GATEWOOD	**8**	2	Michigan-Toledo Strip	15-N	11-W
GAUWEILER	**20**	1	Michigan-Toledo Strip	12-N	11-W
" "	**16**	1	Michigan-Toledo Strip	13-N	11-W
GAY	**21**	2	Michigan-Toledo Strip	11-N	14-W
GAYLORD	**17**	3	Michigan-Toledo Strip	12-N	14-W
" "	**2**	1	Michigan-Toledo Strip	16-N	13-W
GERRY	**2**	3	Michigan-Toledo Strip	16-N	13-W
GETTY	**17**	3	Michigan-Toledo Strip	12-N	14-W
" "	**14**	1	Michigan-Toledo Strip	13-N	13-W
GEYASHE	**21**	1	Michigan-Toledo Strip	11-N	14-W
GIBB	**18**	3	Michigan-Toledo Strip	12-N	13-W
" "	**17**	2	Michigan-Toledo Strip	12-N	14-W
GIBBS	**16**	1	Michigan-Toledo Strip	13-N	11-W
" "	**12**	1	Michigan-Toledo Strip	14-N	11-W

Surname	Map Group	Parcels of Land	Meridian/Township/Range		
GIDDINGS	**5**	3	Michigan-Toledo Strip	15-N	14-W
GILBERT	**19**	2	Michigan-Toledo Strip	12-N	12-W
" "	**18**	2	Michigan-Toledo Strip	12-N	13-W
GILL	**4**	2	Michigan-Toledo Strip	16-N	11-W
GILLILAND	**4**	2	Michigan-Toledo Strip	16-N	11-W
GLASS	**17**	2	Michigan-Toledo Strip	12-N	14-W
GLAZE	**3**	2	Michigan-Toledo Strip	16-N	12-W
GLAZIER	**16**	2	Michigan-Toledo Strip	13-N	11-W
GLOVER	**23**	2	Michigan-Toledo Strip	11-N	12-W
GO	**17**	1	Michigan-Toledo Strip	12-N	14-W
GODFREY	**15**	5	Michigan-Toledo Strip	13-N	12-W
" "	**16**	2	Michigan-Toledo Strip	13-N	11-W
GOLLADAY	**12**	2	Michigan-Toledo Strip	14-N	11-W
GOOCH	**12**	4	Michigan-Toledo Strip	14-N	11-W
" "	**13**	2	Michigan-Toledo Strip	13-N	14-W
" "	**11**	1	Michigan-Toledo Strip	14-N	12-W
GOODALE	**23**	2	Michigan-Toledo Strip	11-N	12-W
GOODALL	**6**	2	Michigan-Toledo Strip	15-N	13-W
GOODRICH	**13**	3	Michigan-Toledo Strip	13-N	14-W
" "	**16**	2	Michigan-Toledo Strip	13-N	11-W
GOODRIDGE	**19**	1	Michigan-Toledo Strip	12-N	12-W
GOODWILL	**20**	1	Michigan-Toledo Strip	12-N	11-W
GORDON	**5**	2	Michigan-Toledo Strip	15-N	14-W
GORING	**10**	1	Michigan-Toledo Strip	14-N	13-W
GOULD	**11**	2	Michigan-Toledo Strip	14-N	12-W
GRACEY	**13**	1	Michigan-Toledo Strip	13-N	14-W
GRAHAM	**12**	2	Michigan-Toledo Strip	14-N	11-W
" "	**21**	1	Michigan-Toledo Strip	11-N	14-W
GRANADE	**3**	1	Michigan-Toledo Strip	16-N	12-W
GRANGER	**9**	1	Michigan-Toledo Strip	14-N	14-W
GRAVES	**15**	4	Michigan-Toledo Strip	13-N	12-W
GRAY	**1**	4	Michigan-Toledo Strip	16-N	14-W
" "	**18**	2	Michigan-Toledo Strip	12-N	13-W
" "	**23**	1	Michigan-Toledo Strip	11-N	12-W
" "	**17**	1	Michigan-Toledo Strip	12-N	14-W
" "	**13**	1	Michigan-Toledo Strip	13-N	14-W
" "	**5**	1	Michigan-Toledo Strip	15-N	14-W
GREEN	**12**	2	Michigan-Toledo Strip	14-N	11-W
" "	**23**	1	Michigan-Toledo Strip	11-N	12-W
GREENFIELD	**4**	2	Michigan-Toledo Strip	16-N	11-W
GREGORY	**14**	1	Michigan-Toledo Strip	13-N	13-W
GREY	**21**	1	Michigan-Toledo Strip	11-N	14-W
" "	**1**	1	Michigan-Toledo Strip	16-N	14-W
GRIFFES	**20**	1	Michigan-Toledo Strip	12-N	11-W
GRIFFIN	**20**	6	Michigan-Toledo Strip	12-N	11-W
" "	**22**	1	Michigan-Toledo Strip	11-N	13-W
GRIFFITTS	**24**	5	Michigan-Toledo Strip	11-N	11-W
GROVE	**24**	2	Michigan-Toledo Strip	11-N	11-W
GROVENBERRY	**9**	3	Michigan-Toledo Strip	14-N	14-W
GROVESTEEN	**14**	4	Michigan-Toledo Strip	13-N	13-W
" "	**15**	1	Michigan-Toledo Strip	13-N	12-W
" "	**11**	1	Michigan-Toledo Strip	14-N	12-W
GROW	**20**	4	Michigan-Toledo Strip	12-N	11-W
GUDGELL	**5**	1	Michigan-Toledo Strip	15-N	14-W
GUOM	**17**	1	Michigan-Toledo Strip	12-N	14-W
GUSTROUS	**14**	2	Michigan-Toledo Strip	13-N	13-W
" "	**11**	2	Michigan-Toledo Strip	14-N	12-W
HAGERMANN	**11**	1	Michigan-Toledo Strip	14-N	12-W
HAIG	**20**	2	Michigan-Toledo Strip	12-N	11-W
HAIGHT	**16**	1	Michigan-Toledo Strip	13-N	11-W

Surname	Map Group	Parcels of Land	Meridian/Township/Range		
HAINES	**16**	3	Michigan-Toledo Strip	13-N	11-W
" "	**2**	1	Michigan-Toledo Strip	16-N	13-W
HAIST	**20**	2	Michigan-Toledo Strip	12-N	11-W
HALCOMB	**16**	2	Michigan-Toledo Strip	13-N	11-W
HALL	**9**	8	Michigan-Toledo Strip	14-N	14-W
" "	**16**	3	Michigan-Toledo Strip	13-N	11-W
" "	**8**	3	Michigan-Toledo Strip	15-N	11-W
" "	**3**	3	Michigan-Toledo Strip	16-N	12-W
" "	**22**	2	Michigan-Toledo Strip	11-N	13-W
" "	**10**	2	Michigan-Toledo Strip	14-N	13-W
" "	**15**	1	Michigan-Toledo Strip	13-N	12-W
" "	**4**	1	Michigan-Toledo Strip	16-N	11-W
HALLOCK	**20**	1	Michigan-Toledo Strip	12-N	11-W
HAMENT	**18**	1	Michigan-Toledo Strip	12-N	13-W
HAMILTON	**4**	7	Michigan-Toledo Strip	16-N	11-W
HAMMOND	**2**	2	Michigan-Toledo Strip	16-N	13-W
HANCOCK	**6**	1	Michigan-Toledo Strip	15-N	13-W
" "	**4**	1	Michigan-Toledo Strip	16-N	11-W
HARDEN	**10**	2	Michigan-Toledo Strip	14-N	13-W
HARNESS	**3**	2	Michigan-Toledo Strip	16-N	12-W
HARPER	**11**	2	Michigan-Toledo Strip	14-N	12-W
" "	**1**	2	Michigan-Toledo Strip	16-N	14-W
HARRIES	**20**	3	Michigan-Toledo Strip	12-N	11-W
HARRINGTON	**9**	5	Michigan-Toledo Strip	14-N	14-W
" "	**22**	1	Michigan-Toledo Strip	11-N	13-W
" "	**2**	1	Michigan-Toledo Strip	16-N	13-W
HARRIS	**15**	2	Michigan-Toledo Strip	13-N	12-W
" "	**6**	2	Michigan-Toledo Strip	15-N	13-W
" "	**14**	1	Michigan-Toledo Strip	13-N	13-W
HARRISON	**6**	2	Michigan-Toledo Strip	15-N	13-W
" "	**20**	1	Michigan-Toledo Strip	12-N	11-W
HART	**19**	3	Michigan-Toledo Strip	12-N	12-W
" "	**20**	2	Michigan-Toledo Strip	12-N	11-W
" "	**23**	1	Michigan-Toledo Strip	11-N	12-W
HARTZER	**12**	2	Michigan-Toledo Strip	14-N	11-W
HASCALL	**17**	4	Michigan-Toledo Strip	12-N	14-W
" "	**19**	2	Michigan-Toledo Strip	12-N	12-W
HASKELL	**15**	4	Michigan-Toledo Strip	13-N	12-W
HATFIELD	**8**	2	Michigan-Toledo Strip	15-N	11-W
HATHERLEY	**13**	1	Michigan-Toledo Strip	13-N	14-W
HAWKINS	**4**	1	Michigan-Toledo Strip	16-N	11-W
HAYWARD	**17**	2	Michigan-Toledo Strip	12-N	14-W
HAYWOOD	**4**	1	Michigan-Toledo Strip	16-N	11-W
HEADLEY	**22**	2	Michigan-Toledo Strip	11-N	13-W
HEALD	**18**	6	Michigan-Toledo Strip	12-N	13-W
" "	**4**	5	Michigan-Toledo Strip	16-N	11-W
" "	**11**	4	Michigan-Toledo Strip	14-N	12-W
" "	**9**	4	Michigan-Toledo Strip	14-N	14-W
" "	**12**	3	Michigan-Toledo Strip	14-N	11-W
" "	**14**	2	Michigan-Toledo Strip	13-N	13-W
" "	**15**	1	Michigan-Toledo Strip	13-N	12-W
" "	**5**	1	Michigan-Toledo Strip	15-N	14-W
HEATH	**15**	2	Michigan-Toledo Strip	13-N	12-W
" "	**24**	1	Michigan-Toledo Strip	11-N	11-W
" "	**4**	1	Michigan-Toledo Strip	16-N	11-W
HEATON	**15**	6	Michigan-Toledo Strip	13-N	12-W
HEBEL	**23**	2	Michigan-Toledo Strip	11-N	12-W
HEFFERAN	**11**	1	Michigan-Toledo Strip	14-N	12-W
" "	**7**	1	Michigan-Toledo Strip	15-N	12-W
HEMSWORTH	**3**	1	Michigan-Toledo Strip	16-N	12-W

Surname	Map Group	Parcels of Land	Meridian/Township/Range		
HENNESSY	**18**	1	Michigan-Toledo Strip	12-N	13-W
HENRY	**2**	3	Michigan-Toledo Strip	16-N	13-W
HERENDEEN	**13**	2	Michigan-Toledo Strip	13-N	14-W
HERINGTON	**14**	1	Michigan-Toledo Strip	13-N	13-W
HERRICK	**9**	4	Michigan-Toledo Strip	14-N	14-W
HERRINGTON	**18**	1	Michigan-Toledo Strip	12-N	13-W
HERSHBERGER	**14**	2	Michigan-Toledo Strip	13-N	13-W
HERTZER	**16**	3	Michigan-Toledo Strip	13-N	11-W
HESS	**18**	1	Michigan-Toledo Strip	12-N	13-W
" "	**17**	1	Michigan-Toledo Strip	12-N	14-W
HETSLER	**13**	3	Michigan-Toledo Strip	13-N	14-W
HEWES	**13**	3	Michigan-Toledo Strip	13-N	14-W
HEWIT	**2**	1	Michigan-Toledo Strip	16-N	13-W
HICKS	**21**	1	Michigan-Toledo Strip	11-N	14-W
" "	**17**	1	Michigan-Toledo Strip	12-N	14-W
HIGBE	**4**	3	Michigan-Toledo Strip	16-N	11-W
HIGBEE	**20**	2	Michigan-Toledo Strip	12-N	11-W
" "	**19**	1	Michigan-Toledo Strip	12-N	12-W
HIGGS	**9**	2	Michigan-Toledo Strip	14-N	14-W
HILDRETH	**8**	6	Michigan-Toledo Strip	15-N	11-W
HILES	**9**	1	Michigan-Toledo Strip	14-N	14-W
HILL	**22**	2	Michigan-Toledo Strip	11-N	13-W
" "	**10**	2	Michigan-Toledo Strip	14-N	13-W
" "	**13**	1	Michigan-Toledo Strip	13-N	14-W
HILLMAN	**24**	6	Michigan-Toledo Strip	11-N	11-W
HILLS	**17**	3	Michigan-Toledo Strip	12-N	14-W
" "	**19**	2	Michigan-Toledo Strip	12-N	12-W
" "	**3**	2	Michigan-Toledo Strip	16-N	12-W
" "	**14**	1	Michigan-Toledo Strip	13-N	13-W
HINDES	**14**	1	Michigan-Toledo Strip	13-N	13-W
HINDS	**16**	1	Michigan-Toledo Strip	13-N	11-W
HINE	**17**	3	Michigan-Toledo Strip	12-N	14-W
" "	**18**	1	Michigan-Toledo Strip	12-N	13-W
HINMAN	**2**	8	Michigan-Toledo Strip	16-N	13-W
" "	**7**	1	Michigan-Toledo Strip	15-N	12-W
" "	**3**	1	Michigan-Toledo Strip	16-N	12-W
HOBLER	**11**	1	Michigan-Toledo Strip	14-N	12-W
HODGES	**20**	1	Michigan-Toledo Strip	12-N	11-W
HOLE	**4**	1	Michigan-Toledo Strip	16-N	11-W
HOLLOWAY	**8**	2	Michigan-Toledo Strip	15-N	11-W
HOLMES	**24**	4	Michigan-Toledo Strip	11-N	11-W
" "	**14**	1	Michigan-Toledo Strip	13-N	13-W
" "	**13**	1	Michigan-Toledo Strip	13-N	14-W
" "	**9**	1	Michigan-Toledo Strip	14-N	14-W
HOOD	**23**	3	Michigan-Toledo Strip	11-N	12-W
HOOKER	**16**	2	Michigan-Toledo Strip	13-N	11-W
HOOPER	**16**	2	Michigan-Toledo Strip	13-N	11-W
HOPKINS	**21**	2	Michigan-Toledo Strip	11-N	14-W
" "	**14**	2	Michigan-Toledo Strip	13-N	13-W
" "	**13**	2	Michigan-Toledo Strip	13-N	14-W
HOSKIN	**9**	1	Michigan-Toledo Strip	14-N	14-W
HOUGHTALING	**2**	2	Michigan-Toledo Strip	16-N	13-W
HOUGHTON	**16**	2	Michigan-Toledo Strip	13-N	11-W
" "	**24**	1	Michigan-Toledo Strip	11-N	11-W
HOULDING	**22**	5	Michigan-Toledo Strip	11-N	13-W
HOUSE	**20**	3	Michigan-Toledo Strip	12-N	11-W
" "	**24**	1	Michigan-Toledo Strip	11-N	11-W
HOUSTON	**8**	2	Michigan-Toledo Strip	15-N	11-W
HOVEY	**9**	3	Michigan-Toledo Strip	14-N	14-W
" "	**3**	2	Michigan-Toledo Strip	16-N	12-W

Surname	Map Group	Parcels of Land	Meridian/Township/Range		
HOVEY (Cont'd)	**2**	2	Michigan-Toledo Strip	16-N	13-W
" "	**1**	2	Michigan-Toledo Strip	16-N	14-W
HOW	**13**	1	Michigan-Toledo Strip	13-N	14-W
HOWE	**15**	19	Michigan-Toledo Strip	13-N	12-W
" "	**19**	4	Michigan-Toledo Strip	12-N	12-W
" "	**14**	4	Michigan-Toledo Strip	13-N	13-W
" "	**9**	1	Michigan-Toledo Strip	14-N	14-W
HOWELL	**17**	1	Michigan-Toledo Strip	12-N	14-W
HOWLETT	**22**	7	Michigan-Toledo Strip	11-N	13-W
" "	**21**	7	Michigan-Toledo Strip	11-N	14-W
" "	**18**	2	Michigan-Toledo Strip	12-N	13-W
HOWSE	**20**	1	Michigan-Toledo Strip	12-N	11-W
HOYT	**12**	2	Michigan-Toledo Strip	14-N	11-W
HUBBARD	**15**	10	Michigan-Toledo Strip	13-N	12-W
HUCKLEBERRY	**24**	1	Michigan-Toledo Strip	11-N	11-W
HUDLER	**20**	2	Michigan-Toledo Strip	12-N	11-W
HUGHES	**3**	3	Michigan-Toledo Strip	16-N	12-W
" "	**20**	1	Michigan-Toledo Strip	12-N	11-W
HULL	**17**	2	Michigan-Toledo Strip	12-N	14-W
" "	**12**	2	Michigan-Toledo Strip	14-N	11-W
HUNSINGER	**23**	1	Michigan-Toledo Strip	11-N	12-W
HUNT	**17**	2	Michigan-Toledo Strip	12-N	14-W
" "	**13**	2	Michigan-Toledo Strip	13-N	14-W
HUNTER	**24**	1	Michigan-Toledo Strip	11-N	11-W
" "	**23**	1	Michigan-Toledo Strip	11-N	12-W
" "	**8**	1	Michigan-Toledo Strip	15-N	11-W
HUSTON	**8**	2	Michigan-Toledo Strip	15-N	11-W
HUTCHERSON	**8**	2	Michigan-Toledo Strip	15-N	11-W
HUZZEY	**12**	3	Michigan-Toledo Strip	14-N	11-W
HYDE	**19**	1	Michigan-Toledo Strip	12-N	12-W
INGALLS	**2**	1	Michigan-Toledo Strip	16-N	13-W
INMAN	**3**	3	Michigan-Toledo Strip	16-N	12-W
IRONS	**19**	2	Michigan-Toledo Strip	12-N	12-W
ISBELL	**2**	1	Michigan-Toledo Strip	16-N	13-W
ISH	**13**	3	Michigan-Toledo Strip	13-N	14-W
ISHAM	**24**	1	Michigan-Toledo Strip	11-N	11-W
IVES	**8**	103	Michigan-Toledo Strip	15-N	11-W
" "	**12**	50	Michigan-Toledo Strip	14-N	11-W
" "	**4**	44	Michigan-Toledo Strip	16-N	11-W
" "	**7**	4	Michigan-Toledo Strip	15-N	12-W
JACKLIN	**13**	2	Michigan-Toledo Strip	13-N	14-W
" "	**14**	1	Michigan-Toledo Strip	13-N	13-W
JACKSON	**3**	1	Michigan-Toledo Strip	16-N	12-W
JACOBS	**8**	1	Michigan-Toledo Strip	15-N	11-W
JARVIS	**4**	1	Michigan-Toledo Strip	16-N	11-W
JAY	**12**	1	Michigan-Toledo Strip	14-N	11-W
JENKINS	**7**	1	Michigan-Toledo Strip	15-N	12-W
JENNE	**13**	1	Michigan-Toledo Strip	13-N	14-W
JEWELL	**13**	2	Michigan-Toledo Strip	13-N	14-W
" "	**14**	1	Michigan-Toledo Strip	13-N	13-W
JIBSON	**21**	3	Michigan-Toledo Strip	11-N	14-W
JOACHIM	**20**	1	Michigan-Toledo Strip	12-N	11-W
JOBBITT	**1**	1	Michigan-Toledo Strip	16-N	14-W
JOHNSON	**10**	10	Michigan-Toledo Strip	14-N	13-W
" "	**9**	10	Michigan-Toledo Strip	14-N	14-W
" "	**14**	7	Michigan-Toledo Strip	13-N	13-W
" "	**3**	7	Michigan-Toledo Strip	16-N	12-W
" "	**21**	6	Michigan-Toledo Strip	11-N	14-W
" "	**11**	4	Michigan-Toledo Strip	14-N	12-W
" "	**17**	2	Michigan-Toledo Strip	12-N	14-W

Surname	Map Group	Parcels of Land	Meridian/Township/Range		
JOHNSON (Cont'd)	**8**	2	Michigan-Toledo Strip	15-N	11-W
" "	**23**	1	Michigan-Toledo Strip	11-N	12-W
" "	**20**	1	Michigan-Toledo Strip	12-N	11-W
" "	**18**	1	Michigan-Toledo Strip	12-N	13-W
" "	**12**	1	Michigan-Toledo Strip	14-N	11-W
" "	**6**	1	Michigan-Toledo Strip	15-N	13-W
" "	**1**	1	Michigan-Toledo Strip	16-N	14-W
JONES	**21**	2	Michigan-Toledo Strip	11-N	14-W
" "	**13**	2	Michigan-Toledo Strip	13-N	14-W
" "	**8**	2	Michigan-Toledo Strip	15-N	11-W
" "	**20**	1	Michigan-Toledo Strip	12-N	11-W
" "	**12**	1	Michigan-Toledo Strip	14-N	11-W
JOSLIN	**13**	3	Michigan-Toledo Strip	13-N	14-W
JOY	**1**	1	Michigan-Toledo Strip	16-N	14-W
JUDSON	**12**	3	Michigan-Toledo Strip	14-N	11-W
KAKE	**17**	1	Michigan-Toledo Strip	12-N	14-W
KAUFMAN	**20**	1	Michigan-Toledo Strip	12-N	11-W
" "	**16**	1	Michigan-Toledo Strip	13-N	11-W
KEATING	**22**	1	Michigan-Toledo Strip	11-N	13-W
KEELEAN	**4**	1	Michigan-Toledo Strip	16-N	11-W
KEENEY	**24**	1	Michigan-Toledo Strip	11-N	11-W
" "	**16**	1	Michigan-Toledo Strip	13-N	11-W
KEINER	**2**	2	Michigan-Toledo Strip	16-N	13-W
KELLEY	**13**	1	Michigan-Toledo Strip	13-N	14-W
KELLOGG	**24**	4	Michigan-Toledo Strip	11-N	11-W
" "	**20**	2	Michigan-Toledo Strip	12-N	11-W
KEMP	**17**	2	Michigan-Toledo Strip	12-N	14-W
KENDALL	**12**	21	Michigan-Toledo Strip	14-N	11-W
" "	**22**	5	Michigan-Toledo Strip	11-N	13-W
" "	**19**	5	Michigan-Toledo Strip	12-N	12-W
" "	**18**	4	Michigan-Toledo Strip	12-N	13-W
" "	**13**	2	Michigan-Toledo Strip	13-N	14-W
" "	**24**	1	Michigan-Toledo Strip	11-N	11-W
" "	**23**	1	Michigan-Toledo Strip	11-N	12-W
" "	**17**	1	Michigan-Toledo Strip	12-N	14-W
" "	**16**	1	Michigan-Toledo Strip	13-N	11-W
" "	**4**	1	Michigan-Toledo Strip	16-N	11-W
KENDULL	**19**	11	Michigan-Toledo Strip	12-N	12-W
" "	**18**	3	Michigan-Toledo Strip	12-N	13-W
" "	**22**	2	Michigan-Toledo Strip	11-N	13-W
KENNE	**17**	7	Michigan-Toledo Strip	12-N	14-W
KENNEDY	**3**	1	Michigan-Toledo Strip	16-N	12-W
KENNEY	**24**	2	Michigan-Toledo Strip	11-N	11-W
KETCHUM	**19**	1	Michigan-Toledo Strip	12-N	12-W
KIDD	**16**	1	Michigan-Toledo Strip	13-N	11-W
KIEFER	**7**	8	Michigan-Toledo Strip	15-N	12-W
" "	**5**	2	Michigan-Toledo Strip	15-N	14-W
" "	**1**	2	Michigan-Toledo Strip	16-N	14-W
KIEFFER	**16**	1	Michigan-Toledo Strip	13-N	11-W
KILBY	**2**	1	Michigan-Toledo Strip	16-N	13-W
KIMBALL	**17**	3	Michigan-Toledo Strip	12-N	14-W
" "	**16**	2	Michigan-Toledo Strip	13-N	11-W
KIMBELL	**18**	4	Michigan-Toledo Strip	12-N	13-W
KING	**12**	2	Michigan-Toledo Strip	14-N	11-W
" "	**3**	1	Michigan-Toledo Strip	16-N	12-W
KINGSLEY	**21**	2	Michigan-Toledo Strip	11-N	14-W
KINNEY	**24**	1	Michigan-Toledo Strip	11-N	11-W
KITCHEN	**3**	2	Michigan-Toledo Strip	16-N	12-W
" "	**4**	1	Michigan-Toledo Strip	16-N	11-W
KLETT	**13**	1	Michigan-Toledo Strip	13-N	14-W

Surname	Map Group	Parcels of Land	Meridian/Township/Range		
KLINE	**20**	1	Michigan-Toledo Strip	12-N	11-W
KNAPP	**5**	3	Michigan-Toledo Strip	15-N	14-W
KNICKERBOCKER	**18**	1	Michigan-Toledo Strip	12-N	13-W
KNISS	**20**	1	Michigan-Toledo Strip	12-N	11-W
KNOWLES	**5**	1	Michigan-Toledo Strip	15-N	14-W
KNOX	**15**	1	Michigan-Toledo Strip	13-N	12-W
KONKEL	**15**	2	Michigan-Toledo Strip	13-N	12-W
KOON	**21**	3	Michigan-Toledo Strip	11-N	14-W
KRICK	**20**	1	Michigan-Toledo Strip	12-N	11-W
KRIGER	**22**	2	Michigan-Toledo Strip	11-N	13-W
KUPRECHT	**21**	1	Michigan-Toledo Strip	11-N	14-W
LACEY	**21**	2	Michigan-Toledo Strip	11-N	14-W
LACKEY	**4**	2	Michigan-Toledo Strip	16-N	11-W
LAFFERTY	**16**	1	Michigan-Toledo Strip	13-N	11-W
LAHR	**24**	2	Michigan-Toledo Strip	11-N	11-W
LAKE	**13**	5	Michigan-Toledo Strip	13-N	14-W
LALOTTE	**20**	1	Michigan-Toledo Strip	12-N	11-W
LANBAUGH	**18**	1	Michigan-Toledo Strip	12-N	13-W
LANCASTER	**17**	2	Michigan-Toledo Strip	12-N	14-W
" "	**23**	1	Michigan-Toledo Strip	11-N	12-W
LANE	**3**	1	Michigan-Toledo Strip	16-N	12-W
LANGFORD	**8**	2	Michigan-Toledo Strip	15-N	11-W
LANNING	**4**	2	Michigan-Toledo Strip	16-N	11-W
LASHER	**12**	2	Michigan-Toledo Strip	14-N	11-W
LASLEY	**19**	3	Michigan-Toledo Strip	12-N	12-W
" "	**21**	2	Michigan-Toledo Strip	11-N	14-W
" "	**16**	1	Michigan-Toledo Strip	13-N	11-W
LATHROP	**24**	5	Michigan-Toledo Strip	11-N	11-W
LAVANCE	**20**	1	Michigan-Toledo Strip	12-N	11-W
LAVERGNE	**4**	2	Michigan-Toledo Strip	16-N	11-W
LAVERTY	**16**	1	Michigan-Toledo Strip	13-N	11-W
LAWRENCE	**19**	3	Michigan-Toledo Strip	12-N	12-W
" "	**18**	3	Michigan-Toledo Strip	12-N	13-W
" "	**15**	3	Michigan-Toledo Strip	13-N	12-W
" "	**8**	2	Michigan-Toledo Strip	15-N	11-W
" "	**12**	1	Michigan-Toledo Strip	14-N	11-W
LAWSON	**24**	2	Michigan-Toledo Strip	11-N	11-W
LE BARON	**16**	2	Michigan-Toledo Strip	13-N	11-W
LE BARRON	**16**	1	Michigan-Toledo Strip	13-N	11-W
LEACH	**8**	2	Michigan-Toledo Strip	15-N	11-W
LEE	**24**	1	Michigan-Toledo Strip	11-N	11-W
LEHMANN	**21**	1	Michigan-Toledo Strip	11-N	14-W
LEMAIRE	**20**	1	Michigan-Toledo Strip	12-N	11-W
LEMONS	**2**	1	Michigan-Toledo Strip	16-N	13-W
LENNEN	**8**	2	Michigan-Toledo Strip	15-N	11-W
LEONARD	**8**	102	Michigan-Toledo Strip	15-N	11-W
" "	**12**	50	Michigan-Toledo Strip	14-N	11-W
" "	**4**	44	Michigan-Toledo Strip	16-N	11-W
" "	**7**	4	Michigan-Toledo Strip	15-N	12-W
" "	**1**	4	Michigan-Toledo Strip	16-N	14-W
" "	**24**	2	Michigan-Toledo Strip	11-N	11-W
" "	**2**	1	Michigan-Toledo Strip	16-N	13-W
LESTER	**19**	2	Michigan-Toledo Strip	12-N	12-W
LESUEUR	**6**	2	Michigan-Toledo Strip	15-N	13-W
LETCH	**21**	1	Michigan-Toledo Strip	11-N	14-W
LEVI	**13**	2	Michigan-Toledo Strip	13-N	14-W
LEWIS	**19**	2	Michigan-Toledo Strip	12-N	12-W
" "	**16**	2	Michigan-Toledo Strip	13-N	11-W
" "	**13**	2	Michigan-Toledo Strip	13-N	14-W
" "	**9**	2	Michigan-Toledo Strip	14-N	14-W

Surname	Map Group	Parcels of Land	Meridian/Township/Range		
LEWIS (Cont'd)	**24**	1	Michigan-Toledo Strip	11-N	11-W
" "	**14**	1	Michigan-Toledo Strip	13-N	13-W
" "	**10**	1	Michigan-Toledo Strip	14-N	13-W
LICHTENBERG	**7**	8	Michigan-Toledo Strip	15-N	12-W
" "	**5**	2	Michigan-Toledo Strip	15-N	14-W
" "	**1**	2	Michigan-Toledo Strip	16-N	14-W
LIFER	**17**	1	Michigan-Toledo Strip	12-N	14-W
LINCOLN	**4**	1	Michigan-Toledo Strip	16-N	11-W
LINDEN	**17**	1	Michigan-Toledo Strip	12-N	14-W
LINDON	**17**	2	Michigan-Toledo Strip	12-N	14-W
LINGLE	**2**	1	Michigan-Toledo Strip	16-N	13-W
LINGO	**24**	1	Michigan-Toledo Strip	11-N	11-W
LOGAN	**15**	1	Michigan-Toledo Strip	13-N	12-W
LONG	**2**	1	Michigan-Toledo Strip	16-N	13-W
LOOMIS	**22**	1	Michigan-Toledo Strip	11-N	13-W
LORDAN	**17**	2	Michigan-Toledo Strip	12-N	14-W
LORDON	**17**	1	Michigan-Toledo Strip	12-N	14-W
LOREE	**20**	4	Michigan-Toledo Strip	12-N	11-W
LOSINGER	**20**	1	Michigan-Toledo Strip	12-N	11-W
LOVELL	**17**	5	Michigan-Toledo Strip	12-N	14-W
" "	**18**	4	Michigan-Toledo Strip	12-N	13-W
" "	**12**	3	Michigan-Toledo Strip	14-N	11-W
" "	**22**	1	Michigan-Toledo Strip	11-N	13-W
" "	**19**	1	Michigan-Toledo Strip	12-N	12-W
" "	**16**	1	Michigan-Toledo Strip	13-N	11-W
" "	**15**	1	Michigan-Toledo Strip	13-N	12-W
LUCE	**4**	1	Michigan-Toledo Strip	16-N	11-W
LUDINGTON	**3**	12	Michigan-Toledo Strip	16-N	12-W
" "	**1**	7	Michigan-Toledo Strip	16-N	14-W
" "	**2**	5	Michigan-Toledo Strip	16-N	13-W
" "	**4**	4	Michigan-Toledo Strip	16-N	11-W
" "	**6**	3	Michigan-Toledo Strip	15-N	13-W
LULL	**16**	22	Michigan-Toledo Strip	13-N	11-W
" "	**20**	12	Michigan-Toledo Strip	12-N	11-W
" "	**11**	9	Michigan-Toledo Strip	14-N	12-W
" "	**12**	4	Michigan-Toledo Strip	14-N	11-W
" "	**15**	2	Michigan-Toledo Strip	13-N	12-W
" "	**7**	1	Michigan-Toledo Strip	15-N	12-W
LUNDY	**20**	3	Michigan-Toledo Strip	12-N	11-W
LUTES	**24**	3	Michigan-Toledo Strip	11-N	11-W
LUTZ	**12**	1	Michigan-Toledo Strip	14-N	11-W
LYKINE	**12**	1	Michigan-Toledo Strip	14-N	11-W
LYMAN	**1**	5	Michigan-Toledo Strip	16-N	14-W
LYNN	**14**	1	Michigan-Toledo Strip	13-N	13-W
" "	**10**	1	Michigan-Toledo Strip	14-N	13-W
LYON	**4**	4	Michigan-Toledo Strip	16-N	11-W
" "	**20**	3	Michigan-Toledo Strip	12-N	11-W
" "	**18**	3	Michigan-Toledo Strip	12-N	13-W
LYONS	**12**	10	Michigan-Toledo Strip	14-N	11-W
" "	**18**	6	Michigan-Toledo Strip	12-N	13-W
" "	**16**	3	Michigan-Toledo Strip	13-N	11-W
" "	**4**	1	Michigan-Toledo Strip	16-N	11-W
MABIE	**10**	2	Michigan-Toledo Strip	14-N	13-W
MACK	**13**	2	Michigan-Toledo Strip	13-N	14-W
MACOMBER	**9**	2	Michigan-Toledo Strip	14-N	14-W
MAHAN	**14**	2	Michigan-Toledo Strip	13-N	13-W
MALLERY	**22**	1	Michigan-Toledo Strip	11-N	13-W
" "	**18**	1	Michigan-Toledo Strip	12-N	13-W
" "	**14**	1	Michigan-Toledo Strip	13-N	13-W
MALLET	**3**	1	Michigan-Toledo Strip	16-N	12-W

Surname	Map Group	Parcels of Land	Meridian/Township/Range		
MALLET (Cont'd)	**2**	1	Michigan-Toledo Strip	16-N	13-W
MANLEY	**8**	2	Michigan-Toledo Strip	15-N	11-W
MANNING	**9**	3	Michigan-Toledo Strip	14-N	14-W
" "	**13**	2	Michigan-Toledo Strip	13-N	14-W
MANROW	**15**	1	Michigan-Toledo Strip	13-N	12-W
MANSFIELD	**9**	6	Michigan-Toledo Strip	14-N	14-W
MAPES	**23**	1	Michigan-Toledo Strip	11-N	12-W
MARKLE	**17**	3	Michigan-Toledo Strip	12-N	14-W
MARSH	**4**	2	Michigan-Toledo Strip	16-N	11-W
" "	**20**	1	Michigan-Toledo Strip	12-N	11-W
MARSHALL	**21**	5	Michigan-Toledo Strip	11-N	14-W
" "	**1**	2	Michigan-Toledo Strip	16-N	14-W
MARTIN	**17**	6	Michigan-Toledo Strip	12-N	14-W
" "	**18**	2	Michigan-Toledo Strip	12-N	13-W
" "	**13**	2	Michigan-Toledo Strip	13-N	14-W
" "	**8**	2	Michigan-Toledo Strip	15-N	11-W
MARVIN	**23**	1	Michigan-Toledo Strip	11-N	12-W
" "	**21**	1	Michigan-Toledo Strip	11-N	14-W
MATHERS	**7**	1	Michigan-Toledo Strip	15-N	12-W
MATHEW	**21**	3	Michigan-Toledo Strip	11-N	14-W
" "	**17**	2	Michigan-Toledo Strip	12-N	14-W
MATTESON	**4**	2	Michigan-Toledo Strip	16-N	11-W
" "	**9**	1	Michigan-Toledo Strip	14-N	14-W
MATTHEW	**21**	3	Michigan-Toledo Strip	11-N	14-W
MAXIM	**22**	6	Michigan-Toledo Strip	11-N	13-W
" "	**21**	3	Michigan-Toledo Strip	11-N	14-W
MAYBEE	**18**	2	Michigan-Toledo Strip	12-N	13-W
MAYNARD	**9**	1	Michigan-Toledo Strip	14-N	14-W
MAZE	**17**	1	Michigan-Toledo Strip	12-N	14-W
MCBRIDE	**15**	3	Michigan-Toledo Strip	13-N	12-W
" "	**19**	1	Michigan-Toledo Strip	12-N	12-W
" "	**16**	1	Michigan-Toledo Strip	13-N	11-W
MCCAB	**16**	1	Michigan-Toledo Strip	13-N	11-W
MCCALL	**20**	2	Michigan-Toledo Strip	12-N	11-W
" "	**16**	2	Michigan-Toledo Strip	13-N	11-W
MCCLAIN	**6**	2	Michigan-Toledo Strip	15-N	13-W
MCCLUNG	**4**	2	Michigan-Toledo Strip	16-N	11-W
MCCLURE	**13**	2	Michigan-Toledo Strip	13-N	14-W
" "	**2**	2	Michigan-Toledo Strip	16-N	13-W
MCCOY	**12**	1	Michigan-Toledo Strip	14-N	11-W
MCCRACKEN	**9**	1	Michigan-Toledo Strip	14-N	14-W
MCCUNE	**18**	2	Michigan-Toledo Strip	12-N	13-W
MCDUFFIE	**8**	1	Michigan-Toledo Strip	15-N	11-W
MCFARLAN	**6**	2	Michigan-Toledo Strip	15-N	13-W
MCGHAN	**9**	2	Michigan-Toledo Strip	14-N	14-W
MCGUIRE	**17**	1	Michigan-Toledo Strip	12-N	14-W
MCINTOSH	**21**	4	Michigan-Toledo Strip	11-N	14-W
MCKEE	**21**	11	Michigan-Toledo Strip	11-N	14-W
MCKENZIE	**2**	2	Michigan-Toledo Strip	16-N	13-W
" "	**13**	1	Michigan-Toledo Strip	13-N	14-W
" "	**3**	1	Michigan-Toledo Strip	16-N	12-W
MCKIE	**21**	3	Michigan-Toledo Strip	11-N	14-W
MCNIEL	**16**	1	Michigan-Toledo Strip	13-N	11-W
MCNITT	**8**	3	Michigan-Toledo Strip	15-N	11-W
MCQUEEN	**17**	3	Michigan-Toledo Strip	12-N	14-W
MEAD	**23**	1	Michigan-Toledo Strip	11-N	12-W
" "	**22**	1	Michigan-Toledo Strip	11-N	13-W
MEE	**17**	2	Michigan-Toledo Strip	12-N	14-W
MEIER	**16**	2	Michigan-Toledo Strip	13-N	11-W
MELANCON	**19**	2	Michigan-Toledo Strip	12-N	12-W

Surname	Map Group	Parcels of Land	Meridian/Township/Range		
MELANCON (Cont'd)	**15**	1	Michigan-Toledo Strip	13-N	12-W
MELENDY	**2**	17	Michigan-Toledo Strip	16-N	13-W
" "	**3**	4	Michigan-Toledo Strip	16-N	12-W
" "	**1**	2	Michigan-Toledo Strip	16-N	14-W
" "	**5**	1	Michigan-Toledo Strip	15-N	14-W
MERCHANT	**17**	2	Michigan-Toledo Strip	12-N	14-W
MERRICK	**10**	2	Michigan-Toledo Strip	14-N	13-W
" "	**3**	2	Michigan-Toledo Strip	16-N	12-W
" "	**2**	1	Michigan-Toledo Strip	16-N	13-W
MERRILL	**21**	6	Michigan-Toledo Strip	11-N	14-W
" "	**22**	1	Michigan-Toledo Strip	11-N	13-W
" "	**19**	1	Michigan-Toledo Strip	12-N	12-W
MERRITT	**9**	2	Michigan-Toledo Strip	14-N	14-W
" "	**4**	1	Michigan-Toledo Strip	16-N	11-W
MERWIN	**17**	24	Michigan-Toledo Strip	12-N	14-W
" "	**14**	20	Michigan-Toledo Strip	13-N	13-W
METEVY	**19**	1	Michigan-Toledo Strip	12-N	12-W
MICHIGAN	**16**	1	Michigan-Toledo Strip	13-N	11-W
MIDDAUGH	**24**	2	Michigan-Toledo Strip	11-N	11-W
MILES	**11**	10	Michigan-Toledo Strip	14-N	12-W
" "	**10**	7	Michigan-Toledo Strip	14-N	13-W
" "	**16**	2	Michigan-Toledo Strip	13-N	11-W
" "	**12**	1	Michigan-Toledo Strip	14-N	11-W
MILLARD	**4**	1	Michigan-Toledo Strip	16-N	11-W
MILLER	**13**	9	Michigan-Toledo Strip	13-N	14-W
" "	**4**	4	Michigan-Toledo Strip	16-N	11-W
" "	**20**	2	Michigan-Toledo Strip	12-N	11-W
" "	**18**	2	Michigan-Toledo Strip	12-N	13-W
" "	**17**	1	Michigan-Toledo Strip	12-N	14-W
" "	**11**	1	Michigan-Toledo Strip	14-N	12-W
" "	**9**	1	Michigan-Toledo Strip	14-N	14-W
" "	**8**	1	Michigan-Toledo Strip	15-N	11-W
" "	**7**	1	Michigan-Toledo Strip	15-N	12-W
MILLIMAN	**12**	3	Michigan-Toledo Strip	14-N	11-W
MILLIS	**9**	7	Michigan-Toledo Strip	14-N	14-W
" "	**1**	1	Michigan-Toledo Strip	16-N	14-W
MILLS	**15**	2	Michigan-Toledo Strip	13-N	12-W
MINK	**10**	2	Michigan-Toledo Strip	14-N	13-W
" "	**11**	1	Michigan-Toledo Strip	14-N	12-W
MISNER	**4**	1	Michigan-Toledo Strip	16-N	11-W
MITCHELL	**11**	7	Michigan-Toledo Strip	14-N	12-W
" "	**16**	6	Michigan-Toledo Strip	13-N	11-W
" "	**10**	3	Michigan-Toledo Strip	14-N	13-W
" "	**22**	1	Michigan-Toledo Strip	11-N	13-W
" "	**5**	1	Michigan-Toledo Strip	15-N	14-W
" "	**3**	1	Michigan-Toledo Strip	16-N	12-W
MIX	**1**	2	Michigan-Toledo Strip	16-N	14-W
MIZNER	**21**	1	Michigan-Toledo Strip	11-N	14-W
MOE	**16**	2	Michigan-Toledo Strip	13-N	11-W
" "	**13**	1	Michigan-Toledo Strip	13-N	14-W
MONROE	**15**	3	Michigan-Toledo Strip	13-N	12-W
" "	**3**	2	Michigan-Toledo Strip	16-N	12-W
MOODY	**4**	1	Michigan-Toledo Strip	16-N	11-W
MOORE	**1**	2	Michigan-Toledo Strip	16-N	14-W
" "	**24**	1	Michigan-Toledo Strip	11-N	11-W
" "	**23**	1	Michigan-Toledo Strip	11-N	12-W
" "	**18**	1	Michigan-Toledo Strip	12-N	13-W
" "	**17**	1	Michigan-Toledo Strip	12-N	14-W
" "	**15**	1	Michigan-Toledo Strip	13-N	12-W
" "	**4**	1	Michigan-Toledo Strip	16-N	11-W

Surname	Map Group	Parcels of Land	Meridian/Township/Range		
MOOTE	**4**	1	Michigan-Toledo Strip	16-N	11-W
MORELL	**13**	1	Michigan-Toledo Strip	13-N	14-W
MORGAN	**23**	1	Michigan-Toledo Strip	11-N	12-W
" "	**19**	1	Michigan-Toledo Strip	12-N	12-W
" "	**11**	1	Michigan-Toledo Strip	14-N	12-W
" "	**1**	1	Michigan-Toledo Strip	16-N	14-W
MORLEY	**24**	1	Michigan-Toledo Strip	11-N	11-W
MORRIS	**18**	14	Michigan-Toledo Strip	12-N	13-W
" "	**14**	9	Michigan-Toledo Strip	13-N	13-W
" "	**22**	3	Michigan-Toledo Strip	11-N	13-W
" "	**21**	3	Michigan-Toledo Strip	11-N	14-W
" "	**12**	3	Michigan-Toledo Strip	14-N	11-W
MORRISON	**20**	12	Michigan-Toledo Strip	12-N	11-W
" "	**16**	6	Michigan-Toledo Strip	13-N	11-W
MORTON	**13**	1	Michigan-Toledo Strip	13-N	14-W
MOSES	**14**	3	Michigan-Toledo Strip	13-N	13-W
" "	**11**	2	Michigan-Toledo Strip	14-N	12-W
MOSHER	**18**	5	Michigan-Toledo Strip	12-N	13-W
" "	**13**	2	Michigan-Toledo Strip	13-N	14-W
" "	**20**	1	Michigan-Toledo Strip	12-N	11-W
MOSS	**14**	2	Michigan-Toledo Strip	13-N	13-W
MOST	**20**	1	Michigan-Toledo Strip	12-N	11-W
MOYE	**19**	1	Michigan-Toledo Strip	12-N	12-W
MUDGE	**5**	1	Michigan-Toledo Strip	15-N	14-W
MULDER	**14**	1	Michigan-Toledo Strip	13-N	13-W
MUNDY	**19**	1	Michigan-Toledo Strip	12-N	12-W
MURPHY	**11**	5	Michigan-Toledo Strip	14-N	12-W
" "	**15**	1	Michigan-Toledo Strip	13-N	12-W
" "	**14**	1	Michigan-Toledo Strip	13-N	13-W
" "	**9**	1	Michigan-Toledo Strip	14-N	14-W
" "	**5**	1	Michigan-Toledo Strip	15-N	14-W
MURRAY	**24**	1	Michigan-Toledo Strip	11-N	11-W
MURRY	**16**	4	Michigan-Toledo Strip	13-N	11-W
NASON	**20**	1	Michigan-Toledo Strip	12-N	11-W
" "	**4**	1	Michigan-Toledo Strip	16-N	11-W
NEAL	**14**	2	Michigan-Toledo Strip	13-N	13-W
NELLIS	**20**	4	Michigan-Toledo Strip	12-N	11-W
NELSON	**9**	1	Michigan-Toledo Strip	14-N	14-W
" "	**5**	1	Michigan-Toledo Strip	15-N	14-W
NEVILLE	**16**	2	Michigan-Toledo Strip	13-N	11-W
NEWELL	**18**	1	Michigan-Toledo Strip	12-N	13-W
NEWTON	**12**	1	Michigan-Toledo Strip	14-N	11-W
NICHOLS	**11**	7	Michigan-Toledo Strip	14-N	12-W
" "	**19**	3	Michigan-Toledo Strip	12-N	12-W
NIEGLESON	**19**	1	Michigan-Toledo Strip	12-N	12-W
NININGER	**14**	1	Michigan-Toledo Strip	13-N	13-W
NO	**17**	1	Michigan-Toledo Strip	12-N	14-W
NORTH	**9**	2	Michigan-Toledo Strip	14-N	14-W
NORTHROP	**17**	61	Michigan-Toledo Strip	12-N	14-W
" "	**14**	27	Michigan-Toledo Strip	13-N	13-W
" "	**12**	16	Michigan-Toledo Strip	14-N	11-W
" "	**24**	8	Michigan-Toledo Strip	11-N	11-W
" "	**18**	7	Michigan-Toledo Strip	12-N	13-W
" "	**8**	2	Michigan-Toledo Strip	15-N	11-W
" "	**19**	1	Michigan-Toledo Strip	12-N	12-W
NORTON	**21**	20	Michigan-Toledo Strip	11-N	14-W
" "	**22**	13	Michigan-Toledo Strip	11-N	13-W
OBRIEN	**13**	2	Michigan-Toledo Strip	13-N	14-W
OCONNOR	**23**	1	Michigan-Toledo Strip	11-N	12-W
ODELL	**14**	3	Michigan-Toledo Strip	13-N	13-W

Surname	Map Group	Parcels of Land	Meridian/Township/Range		
OLDS	**13**	2	Michigan-Toledo Strip	13-N	14-W
ONDERDONK	**24**	2	Michigan-Toledo Strip	11-N	11-W
ONEIL	**16**	4	Michigan-Toledo Strip	13-N	11-W
ORCUTT	**21**	1	Michigan-Toledo Strip	11-N	14-W
ORN	**4**	1	Michigan-Toledo Strip	16-N	11-W
ORTON	**19**	5	Michigan-Toledo Strip	12-N	12-W
" "	**17**	5	Michigan-Toledo Strip	12-N	14-W
" "	**21**	2	Michigan-Toledo Strip	11-N	14-W
OSBURN	**24**	1	Michigan-Toledo Strip	11-N	11-W
OSTRANDER	**21**	2	Michigan-Toledo Strip	11-N	14-W
PADDOCK	**12**	8	Michigan-Toledo Strip	14-N	11-W
" "	**19**	4	Michigan-Toledo Strip	12-N	12-W
" "	**15**	1	Michigan-Toledo Strip	13-N	12-W
PAGE	**6**	9	Michigan-Toledo Strip	15-N	13-W
" "	**16**	2	Michigan-Toledo Strip	13-N	11-W
" "	**12**	2	Michigan-Toledo Strip	14-N	11-W
" "	**10**	2	Michigan-Toledo Strip	14-N	13-W
" "	**20**	1	Michigan-Toledo Strip	12-N	11-W
" "	**8**	1	Michigan-Toledo Strip	15-N	11-W
PAINTER	**1**	3	Michigan-Toledo Strip	16-N	14-W
" "	**5**	2	Michigan-Toledo Strip	15-N	14-W
PALMER	**19**	1	Michigan-Toledo Strip	12-N	12-W
" "	**15**	1	Michigan-Toledo Strip	13-N	12-W
" "	**5**	1	Michigan-Toledo Strip	15-N	14-W
" "	**1**	1	Michigan-Toledo Strip	16-N	14-W
PARDEE	**20**	1	Michigan-Toledo Strip	12-N	11-W
PARK	**21**	2	Michigan-Toledo Strip	11-N	14-W
PARKER	**13**	2	Michigan-Toledo Strip	13-N	14-W
" "	**7**	1	Michigan-Toledo Strip	15-N	12-W
" "	**2**	1	Michigan-Toledo Strip	16-N	13-W
PARKS	**4**	1	Michigan-Toledo Strip	16-N	11-W
PARMETER	**4**	1	Michigan-Toledo Strip	16-N	11-W
PARSHALL	**13**	2	Michigan-Toledo Strip	13-N	14-W
PATEN	**3**	2	Michigan-Toledo Strip	16-N	12-W
PATTERSON	**22**	1	Michigan-Toledo Strip	11-N	13-W
" "	**11**	1	Michigan-Toledo Strip	14-N	12-W
PATTESON	**24**	1	Michigan-Toledo Strip	11-N	11-W
PATTISON	**21**	1	Michigan-Toledo Strip	11-N	14-W
PAYNE	**9**	2	Michigan-Toledo Strip	14-N	14-W
" "	**12**	1	Michigan-Toledo Strip	14-N	11-W
PAYSON	**21**	1	Michigan-Toledo Strip	11-N	14-W
PEACOCK	**18**	1	Michigan-Toledo Strip	12-N	13-W
PEAK	**15**	1	Michigan-Toledo Strip	13-N	12-W
PEARSON	**11**	2	Michigan-Toledo Strip	14-N	12-W
" "	**15**	1	Michigan-Toledo Strip	13-N	12-W
" "	**4**	1	Michigan-Toledo Strip	16-N	11-W
" "	**1**	1	Michigan-Toledo Strip	16-N	14-W
PEAT	**7**	1	Michigan-Toledo Strip	15-N	12-W
PECK	**14**	4	Michigan-Toledo Strip	13-N	13-W
PEIRCE	**19**	1	Michigan-Toledo Strip	12-N	12-W
PELTON	**14**	2	Michigan-Toledo Strip	13-N	13-W
PENCE	**1**	1	Michigan-Toledo Strip	16-N	14-W
PENNOYER	**19**	4	Michigan-Toledo Strip	12-N	12-W
PERKINS	**4**	1	Michigan-Toledo Strip	16-N	11-W
PERRIGO	**24**	2	Michigan-Toledo Strip	11-N	11-W
PETER	**17**	1	Michigan-Toledo Strip	12-N	14-W
PETERS	**15**	1	Michigan-Toledo Strip	13-N	12-W
PETERSON	**14**	12	Michigan-Toledo Strip	13-N	13-W
" "	**10**	9	Michigan-Toledo Strip	14-N	13-W
" "	**3**	4	Michigan-Toledo Strip	16-N	12-W

Surname	Map Group	Parcels of Land	Meridian/Township/Range		
PETERSON (Cont'd)	**2**	2	Michigan-Toledo Strip	16-N	13-W
" "	**21**	1	Michigan-Toledo Strip	11-N	14-W
PETTIBONE	**2**	2	Michigan-Toledo Strip	16-N	13-W
" "	**3**	1	Michigan-Toledo Strip	16-N	12-W
PHELPS	**8**	1	Michigan-Toledo Strip	15-N	11-W
PHILLIPS	**9**	2	Michigan-Toledo Strip	14-N	14-W
" "	**24**	1	Michigan-Toledo Strip	11-N	11-W
PICHETTE	**21**	1	Michigan-Toledo Strip	11-N	14-W
PIGEON	**17**	1	Michigan-Toledo Strip	12-N	14-W
PIKE	**2**	1	Michigan-Toledo Strip	16-N	13-W
PILLSBURY	**3**	7	Michigan-Toledo Strip	16-N	12-W
PITTS	**8**	2	Michigan-Toledo Strip	15-N	11-W
" "	**20**	1	Michigan-Toledo Strip	12-N	11-W
PIXLEY	**15**	1	Michigan-Toledo Strip	13-N	12-W
PLACKARD	**4**	1	Michigan-Toledo Strip	16-N	11-W
PLATT	**19**	2	Michigan-Toledo Strip	12-N	12-W
" "	**18**	2	Michigan-Toledo Strip	12-N	13-W
" "	**23**	1	Michigan-Toledo Strip	11-N	12-W
" "	**15**	1	Michigan-Toledo Strip	13-N	12-W
PODOSZKIE	**20**	1	Michigan-Toledo Strip	12-N	11-W
POLLARD	**22**	2	Michigan-Toledo Strip	11-N	13-W
POMROY	**20**	2	Michigan-Toledo Strip	12-N	11-W
PORTER	**21**	2	Michigan-Toledo Strip	11-N	14-W
" "	**19**	1	Michigan-Toledo Strip	12-N	12-W
POST	**23**	1	Michigan-Toledo Strip	11-N	12-W
POTTER	**1**	5	Michigan-Toledo Strip	16-N	14-W
" "	**2**	3	Michigan-Toledo Strip	16-N	13-W
" "	**3**	2	Michigan-Toledo Strip	16-N	12-W
" "	**4**	1	Michigan-Toledo Strip	16-N	11-W
POWERS	**20**	2	Michigan-Toledo Strip	12-N	11-W
PRATT	**19**	2	Michigan-Toledo Strip	12-N	12-W
" "	**15**	1	Michigan-Toledo Strip	13-N	12-W
PRENTICE	**21**	1	Michigan-Toledo Strip	11-N	14-W
PRESTON	**13**	4	Michigan-Toledo Strip	13-N	14-W
" "	**19**	2	Michigan-Toledo Strip	12-N	12-W
" "	**16**	2	Michigan-Toledo Strip	13-N	11-W
" "	**3**	2	Michigan-Toledo Strip	16-N	12-W
" "	**1**	2	Michigan-Toledo Strip	16-N	14-W
" "	**8**	1	Michigan-Toledo Strip	15-N	11-W
" "	**7**	1	Michigan-Toledo Strip	15-N	12-W
PRICE	**13**	1	Michigan-Toledo Strip	13-N	14-W
" "	**9**	1	Michigan-Toledo Strip	14-N	14-W
PRINGLE	**13**	1	Michigan-Toledo Strip	13-N	14-W
PROBASCO	**20**	6	Michigan-Toledo Strip	12-N	11-W
" "	**7**	2	Michigan-Toledo Strip	15-N	12-W
PROVIN	**24**	2	Michigan-Toledo Strip	11-N	11-W
PRUDDEN	**19**	2	Michigan-Toledo Strip	12-N	12-W
PRUYN	**9**	2	Michigan-Toledo Strip	14-N	14-W
" "	**16**	1	Michigan-Toledo Strip	13-N	11-W
PULLER	**8**	2	Michigan-Toledo Strip	15-N	11-W
PUNK-E-NOB-BI-NO	**17**	2	Michigan-Toledo Strip	12-N	14-W
PUTNAM	**17**	3	Michigan-Toledo Strip	12-N	14-W
" "	**13**	3	Michigan-Toledo Strip	13-N	14-W
" "	**21**	2	Michigan-Toledo Strip	11-N	14-W
QUICK	**21**	1	Michigan-Toledo Strip	11-N	14-W
QUIGLEY	**20**	2	Michigan-Toledo Strip	12-N	11-W
QUOT	**17**	1	Michigan-Toledo Strip	12-N	14-W
RAIDER	**24**	1	Michigan-Toledo Strip	11-N	11-W
RAMSEY	**8**	1	Michigan-Toledo Strip	15-N	11-W
RANDALL	**4**	2	Michigan-Toledo Strip	16-N	11-W

Surname	Map Group	Parcels of Land	Meridian/Township/Range		
RANDLE	22	1	Michigan-Toledo Strip	11-N	13-W
RANDOLPH	15	2	Michigan-Toledo Strip	13-N	12-W
" "	9	1	Michigan-Toledo Strip	14-N	14-W
RANK	20	1	Michigan-Toledo Strip	12-N	11-W
RASSEDIR	9	1	Michigan-Toledo Strip	14-N	14-W
RAY	15	3	Michigan-Toledo Strip	13-N	12-W
RAYBORNE	12	2	Michigan-Toledo Strip	14-N	11-W
RAYNSFORD	8	12	Michigan-Toledo Strip	15-N	11-W
REARDON	12	1	Michigan-Toledo Strip	14-N	11-W
REASMON	11	2	Michigan-Toledo Strip	14-N	12-W
REDDIN	9	2	Michigan-Toledo Strip	14-N	14-W
REED	13	6	Michigan-Toledo Strip	13-N	14-W
" "	14	4	Michigan-Toledo Strip	13-N	13-W
" "	23	2	Michigan-Toledo Strip	11-N	12-W
" "	19	2	Michigan-Toledo Strip	12-N	12-W
" "	15	2	Michigan-Toledo Strip	13-N	12-W
" "	17	1	Michigan-Toledo Strip	12-N	14-W
REEVES	19	2	Michigan-Toledo Strip	12-N	12-W
RESSEGINE	6	9	Michigan-Toledo Strip	15-N	13-W
RETERSTOFF	1	1	Michigan-Toledo Strip	16-N	14-W
REWALT	5	2	Michigan-Toledo Strip	15-N	14-W
REYNOLDS	4	2	Michigan-Toledo Strip	16-N	11-W
" "	2	2	Michigan-Toledo Strip	16-N	13-W
" "	12	1	Michigan-Toledo Strip	14-N	11-W
RHOADES	24	2	Michigan-Toledo Strip	11-N	11-W
RHYAN	16	1	Michigan-Toledo Strip	13-N	11-W
RIBLET	19	1	Michigan-Toledo Strip	12-N	12-W
" "	17	1	Michigan-Toledo Strip	12-N	14-W
RICE	1	4	Michigan-Toledo Strip	16-N	14-W
" "	20	3	Michigan-Toledo Strip	12-N	11-W
" "	3	3	Michigan-Toledo Strip	16-N	12-W
" "	16	2	Michigan-Toledo Strip	13-N	11-W
RICHARDSON	13	2	Michigan-Toledo Strip	13-N	14-W
" "	4	2	Michigan-Toledo Strip	16-N	11-W
" "	3	1	Michigan-Toledo Strip	16-N	12-W
RIGGS	2	1	Michigan-Toledo Strip	16-N	13-W
RIPLEY	2	1	Michigan-Toledo Strip	16-N	13-W
RISSEGUIE	10	2	Michigan-Toledo Strip	14-N	13-W
RIVERS	15	1	Michigan-Toledo Strip	13-N	12-W
ROACH	24	1	Michigan-Toledo Strip	11-N	11-W
ROBBINS	13	2	Michigan-Toledo Strip	13-N	14-W
ROBERTS	17	17	Michigan-Toledo Strip	12-N	14-W
" "	9	2	Michigan-Toledo Strip	14-N	14-W
ROBERTSON	24	1	Michigan-Toledo Strip	11-N	11-W
ROBINSON	13	2	Michigan-Toledo Strip	13-N	14-W
" "	3	1	Michigan-Toledo Strip	16-N	12-W
ROBISON	3	1	Michigan-Toledo Strip	16-N	12-W
ROCHESTER	1	4	Michigan-Toledo Strip	16-N	14-W
" "	19	1	Michigan-Toledo Strip	12-N	12-W
RODES	13	1	Michigan-Toledo Strip	13-N	14-W
ROGERS	19	2	Michigan-Toledo Strip	12-N	12-W
" "	16	2	Michigan-Toledo Strip	13-N	11-W
" "	12	2	Michigan-Toledo Strip	14-N	11-W
" "	4	1	Michigan-Toledo Strip	16-N	11-W
ROLSTONE	4	1	Michigan-Toledo Strip	16-N	11-W
RONAN	16	2	Michigan-Toledo Strip	13-N	11-W
ROOKE	13	2	Michigan-Toledo Strip	13-N	14-W
ROOT	18	4	Michigan-Toledo Strip	12-N	13-W
" "	3	1	Michigan-Toledo Strip	16-N	12-W
ROSE	18	15	Michigan-Toledo Strip	12-N	13-W

Surname	Map Group	Parcels of Land	Meridian/Township/Range		
ROSENBERGER	**17**	3	Michigan-Toledo Strip	12-N	14-W
ROSS	**15**	4	Michigan-Toledo Strip	13-N	12-W
" "	**16**	1	Michigan-Toledo Strip	13-N	11-W
ROSSEDIR	**9**	1	Michigan-Toledo Strip	14-N	14-W
ROUNDS	**2**	3	Michigan-Toledo Strip	16-N	13-W
ROWAN	**16**	3	Michigan-Toledo Strip	13-N	11-W
ROWE	**5**	2	Michigan-Toledo Strip	15-N	14-W
ROWLAND	**2**	2	Michigan-Toledo Strip	16-N	13-W
RUDES	**24**	1	Michigan-Toledo Strip	11-N	11-W
RUFRECHT	**17**	1	Michigan-Toledo Strip	12-N	14-W
RUMSEY	**10**	1	Michigan-Toledo Strip	14-N	13-W
RUPRECHT	**21**	5	Michigan-Toledo Strip	11-N	14-W
" "	**17**	1	Michigan-Toledo Strip	12-N	14-W
RUSH	**8**	2	Michigan-Toledo Strip	15-N	11-W
RUSHMORE	**13**	5	Michigan-Toledo Strip	13-N	14-W
RUSSEL	**24**	1	Michigan-Toledo Strip	11-N	11-W
RUSSELL	**20**	6	Michigan-Toledo Strip	12-N	11-W
" "	**9**	5	Michigan-Toledo Strip	14-N	14-W
" "	**23**	2	Michigan-Toledo Strip	11-N	12-W
RYAN	**20**	4	Michigan-Toledo Strip	12-N	11-W
" "	**16**	1	Michigan-Toledo Strip	13-N	11-W
RYDER	**2**	1	Michigan-Toledo Strip	16-N	13-W
" "	**1**	1	Michigan-Toledo Strip	16-N	14-W
RYERSON	**18**	14	Michigan-Toledo Strip	12-N	13-W
" "	**14**	10	Michigan-Toledo Strip	13-N	13-W
" "	**21**	9	Michigan-Toledo Strip	11-N	14-W
" "	**12**	4	Michigan-Toledo Strip	14-N	11-W
" "	**22**	3	Michigan-Toledo Strip	11-N	13-W
" "	**17**	3	Michigan-Toledo Strip	12-N	14-W
SACKS	**21**	1	Michigan-Toledo Strip	11-N	14-W
SAGE	**17**	3	Michigan-Toledo Strip	12-N	14-W
SAIEN	**16**	4	Michigan-Toledo Strip	13-N	11-W
SAMMIS	**4**	2	Michigan-Toledo Strip	16-N	11-W
SAMPSON	**20**	1	Michigan-Toledo Strip	12-N	11-W
SAMUEL	**4**	2	Michigan-Toledo Strip	16-N	11-W
SANBORN	**21**	3	Michigan-Toledo Strip	11-N	14-W
" "	**13**	3	Michigan-Toledo Strip	13-N	14-W
" "	**23**	2	Michigan-Toledo Strip	11-N	12-W
" "	**24**	1	Michigan-Toledo Strip	11-N	11-W
SANDS	**18**	1	Michigan-Toledo Strip	12-N	13-W
SANFORD	**17**	60	Michigan-Toledo Strip	12-N	14-W
" "	**14**	27	Michigan-Toledo Strip	13-N	13-W
" "	**24**	10	Michigan-Toledo Strip	11-N	11-W
" "	**18**	9	Michigan-Toledo Strip	12-N	13-W
" "	**12**	9	Michigan-Toledo Strip	14-N	11-W
" "	**22**	2	Michigan-Toledo Strip	11-N	13-W
SANGER	**24**	1	Michigan-Toledo Strip	11-N	11-W
SAPP	**16**	2	Michigan-Toledo Strip	13-N	11-W
SAUNDERS	**11**	6	Michigan-Toledo Strip	14-N	12-W
" "	**20**	2	Michigan-Toledo Strip	12-N	11-W
" "	**16**	2	Michigan-Toledo Strip	13-N	11-W
" "	**12**	1	Michigan-Toledo Strip	14-N	11-W
SAVAGE	**17**	3	Michigan-Toledo Strip	12-N	14-W
" "	**13**	3	Michigan-Toledo Strip	13-N	14-W
SAVERCOOL	**16**	1	Michigan-Toledo Strip	13-N	11-W
SAWYER	**3**	1	Michigan-Toledo Strip	16-N	12-W
SAXTON	**16**	1	Michigan-Toledo Strip	13-N	11-W
SCHANK	**21**	1	Michigan-Toledo Strip	11-N	14-W
SCHOONOVER	**18**	2	Michigan-Toledo Strip	12-N	13-W
SCHURCK	**15**	4	Michigan-Toledo Strip	13-N	12-W

Surname	Map Group	Parcels of Land	Meridian/Township/Range		
SCHWEITZER	**18**	2	Michigan-Toledo Strip	12-N	13-W
SCOFIELD	**18**	1	Michigan-Toledo Strip	12-N	13-W
SCOTT	**13**	1	Michigan-Toledo Strip	13-N	14-W
SCOUGHTON	**21**	1	Michigan-Toledo Strip	11-N	14-W
SCOVILLE	**9**	2	Michigan-Toledo Strip	14-N	14-W
SE	**17**	1	Michigan-Toledo Strip	12-N	14-W
SEAFORD	**4**	1	Michigan-Toledo Strip	16-N	11-W
SEAMAN	**19**	3	Michigan-Toledo Strip	12-N	12-W
" "	**6**	2	Michigan-Toledo Strip	15-N	13-W
SEARLES	**21**	1	Michigan-Toledo Strip	11-N	14-W
SECORD	**4**	1	Michigan-Toledo Strip	16-N	11-W
SEELEY	**16**	2	Michigan-Toledo Strip	13-N	11-W
SEEVERS	**20**	1	Michigan-Toledo Strip	12-N	11-W
SELFRIDGE	**13**	2	Michigan-Toledo Strip	13-N	14-W
SELLEARS	**8**	2	Michigan-Toledo Strip	15-N	11-W
SHALAH	**20**	1	Michigan-Toledo Strip	12-N	11-W
SHARAR	**17**	1	Michigan-Toledo Strip	12-N	14-W
SHAW	**23**	2	Michigan-Toledo Strip	11-N	12-W
" "	**13**	2	Michigan-Toledo Strip	13-N	14-W
" "	**18**	1	Michigan-Toledo Strip	12-N	13-W
SHE	**17**	1	Michigan-Toledo Strip	12-N	14-W
SHEAR	**15**	1	Michigan-Toledo Strip	13-N	12-W
SHEARMAN	**17**	1	Michigan-Toledo Strip	12-N	14-W
SHELDON	**22**	2	Michigan-Toledo Strip	11-N	13-W
SHERK	**22**	1	Michigan-Toledo Strip	11-N	13-W
SHERMAN	**17**	7	Michigan-Toledo Strip	12-N	14-W
" "	**16**	1	Michigan-Toledo Strip	13-N	11-W
SHORTER	**16**	1	Michigan-Toledo Strip	13-N	11-W
SHOWARD	**8**	2	Michigan-Toledo Strip	15-N	11-W
SHUTTS	**20**	1	Michigan-Toledo Strip	12-N	11-W
SIBLEY	**11**	2	Michigan-Toledo Strip	14-N	12-W
" "	**15**	1	Michigan-Toledo Strip	13-N	12-W
" "	**10**	1	Michigan-Toledo Strip	14-N	13-W
SIDERS	**4**	2	Michigan-Toledo Strip	16-N	11-W
SIMMONS	**20**	1	Michigan-Toledo Strip	12-N	11-W
SIMMS	**7**	1	Michigan-Toledo Strip	15-N	12-W
SIMONDS	**22**	1	Michigan-Toledo Strip	11-N	13-W
SIMONS	**18**	2	Michigan-Toledo Strip	12-N	13-W
SIMPSON	**24**	1	Michigan-Toledo Strip	11-N	11-W
SINE	**13**	1	Michigan-Toledo Strip	13-N	14-W
SKEELS	**14**	4	Michigan-Toledo Strip	13-N	13-W
" "	**17**	1	Michigan-Toledo Strip	12-N	14-W
SKELTON	**8**	2	Michigan-Toledo Strip	15-N	11-W
SKINNER	**6**	3	Michigan-Toledo Strip	15-N	13-W
" "	**9**	1	Michigan-Toledo Strip	14-N	14-W
" "	**5**	1	Michigan-Toledo Strip	15-N	14-W
SLADE	**16**	3	Michigan-Toledo Strip	13-N	11-W
" "	**19**	2	Michigan-Toledo Strip	12-N	12-W
SLAGHT	**13**	1	Michigan-Toledo Strip	13-N	14-W
SLAIGHT	**24**	1	Michigan-Toledo Strip	11-N	11-W
SLATER	**21**	2	Michigan-Toledo Strip	11-N	14-W
" "	**2**	2	Michigan-Toledo Strip	16-N	13-W
" "	**12**	1	Michigan-Toledo Strip	14-N	11-W
SLAUGHTER	**24**	2	Michigan-Toledo Strip	11-N	11-W
SLOCUM	**9**	4	Michigan-Toledo Strip	14-N	14-W
" "	**1**	1	Michigan-Toledo Strip	16-N	14-W
SLOSSON	**4**	6	Michigan-Toledo Strip	16-N	11-W
SMITH	**16**	8	Michigan-Toledo Strip	13-N	11-W
" "	**24**	5	Michigan-Toledo Strip	11-N	11-W
" "	**18**	5	Michigan-Toledo Strip	12-N	13-W

Surname	Map Group	Parcels of Land	Meridian/Township/Range		
SMITH (Cont'd)	**20**	4	Michigan-Toledo Strip	12-N	11-W
" "	**12**	4	Michigan-Toledo Strip	14-N	11-W
" "	**4**	4	Michigan-Toledo Strip	16-N	11-W
" "	**19**	3	Michigan-Toledo Strip	12-N	12-W
" "	**13**	3	Michigan-Toledo Strip	13-N	14-W
" "	**10**	3	Michigan-Toledo Strip	14-N	13-W
" "	**21**	2	Michigan-Toledo Strip	11-N	14-W
" "	**17**	2	Michigan-Toledo Strip	12-N	14-W
" "	**9**	2	Michigan-Toledo Strip	14-N	14-W
" "	**2**	2	Michigan-Toledo Strip	16-N	13-W
" "	**22**	1	Michigan-Toledo Strip	11-N	13-W
" "	**15**	1	Michigan-Toledo Strip	13-N	12-W
" "	**7**	1	Michigan-Toledo Strip	15-N	12-W
" "	**3**	1	Michigan-Toledo Strip	16-N	12-W
SNYDER	**17**	1	Michigan-Toledo Strip	12-N	14-W
SOEVYN	**3**	2	Michigan-Toledo Strip	16-N	12-W
SOPER	**3**	1	Michigan-Toledo Strip	16-N	12-W
SOULE	**13**	2	Michigan-Toledo Strip	13-N	14-W
SOUTHWORTH	**8**	2	Michigan-Toledo Strip	15-N	11-W
SPAIDS	**12**	2	Michigan-Toledo Strip	14-N	11-W
SPALDING	**24**	2	Michigan-Toledo Strip	11-N	11-W
SPARKS	**8**	1	Michigan-Toledo Strip	15-N	11-W
SPAULDING	**24**	1	Michigan-Toledo Strip	11-N	11-W
" "	**8**	1	Michigan-Toledo Strip	15-N	11-W
" "	**3**	1	Michigan-Toledo Strip	16-N	12-W
SPEIRS	**20**	1	Michigan-Toledo Strip	12-N	11-W
SPENCER	**9**	2	Michigan-Toledo Strip	14-N	14-W
" "	**20**	1	Michigan-Toledo Strip	12-N	11-W
" "	**19**	1	Michigan-Toledo Strip	12-N	12-W
" "	**16**	1	Michigan-Toledo Strip	13-N	11-W
" "	**12**	1	Michigan-Toledo Strip	14-N	11-W
SPES	**16**	4	Michigan-Toledo Strip	13-N	11-W
SQUIER	**21**	5	Michigan-Toledo Strip	11-N	14-W
" "	**6**	4	Michigan-Toledo Strip	15-N	13-W
" "	**17**	2	Michigan-Toledo Strip	12-N	14-W
" "	**2**	2	Michigan-Toledo Strip	16-N	13-W
ST PETER	**21**	4	Michigan-Toledo Strip	11-N	14-W
STAAB	**4**	1	Michigan-Toledo Strip	16-N	11-W
STAILER	**19**	1	Michigan-Toledo Strip	12-N	12-W
STAKER	**21**	3	Michigan-Toledo Strip	11-N	14-W
STANDISH	**22**	1	Michigan-Toledo Strip	11-N	13-W
STANLEY	**10**	7	Michigan-Toledo Strip	14-N	13-W
" "	**9**	4	Michigan-Toledo Strip	14-N	14-W
" "	**17**	2	Michigan-Toledo Strip	12-N	14-W
" "	**16**	1	Michigan-Toledo Strip	13-N	11-W
STARR	**22**	2	Michigan-Toledo Strip	11-N	13-W
STAUDT	**17**	2	Michigan-Toledo Strip	12-N	14-W
STEBBINS	**10**	1	Michigan-Toledo Strip	14-N	13-W
" "	**4**	1	Michigan-Toledo Strip	16-N	11-W
STEINER	**21**	3	Michigan-Toledo Strip	11-N	14-W
" "	**17**	1	Michigan-Toledo Strip	12-N	14-W
STEVENS	**17**	10	Michigan-Toledo Strip	12-N	14-W
" "	**20**	4	Michigan-Toledo Strip	12-N	11-W
" "	**12**	3	Michigan-Toledo Strip	14-N	11-W
" "	**10**	1	Michigan-Toledo Strip	14-N	13-W
" "	**1**	1	Michigan-Toledo Strip	16-N	14-W
STEVENSON	**1**	6	Michigan-Toledo Strip	16-N	14-W
" "	**5**	4	Michigan-Toledo Strip	15-N	14-W
" "	**13**	1	Michigan-Toledo Strip	13-N	14-W
STEWART	**17**	2	Michigan-Toledo Strip	12-N	14-W

Surname	Map Group	Parcels of Land	Meridian/Township/Range		
STICKNEY	22	1	Michigan-Toledo Strip	11-N	13-W
" "	21	1	Michigan-Toledo Strip	11-N	14-W
STILES	20	3	Michigan-Toledo Strip	12-N	11-W
STILWELL	18	2	Michigan-Toledo Strip	12-N	13-W
" "	22	1	Michigan-Toledo Strip	11-N	13-W
STIMPSON	20	1	Michigan-Toledo Strip	12-N	11-W
STIMSON	20	1	Michigan-Toledo Strip	12-N	11-W
" "	19	1	Michigan-Toledo Strip	12-N	12-W
" "	4	1	Michigan-Toledo Strip	16-N	11-W
STINGEL	16	1	Michigan-Toledo Strip	13-N	11-W
STOCKING	24	1	Michigan-Toledo Strip	11-N	11-W
" "	13	1	Michigan-Toledo Strip	13-N	14-W
STODDARD	19	3	Michigan-Toledo Strip	12-N	12-W
STONE	13	2	Michigan-Toledo Strip	13-N	14-W
" "	18	1	Michigan-Toledo Strip	12-N	13-W
" "	4	1	Michigan-Toledo Strip	16-N	11-W
STORMS	9	2	Michigan-Toledo Strip	14-N	14-W
STROH	7	8	Michigan-Toledo Strip	15-N	12-W
" "	5	2	Michigan-Toledo Strip	15-N	14-W
" "	1	2	Michigan-Toledo Strip	16-N	14-W
STRONACH	21	1	Michigan-Toledo Strip	11-N	14-W
STRONG	18	4	Michigan-Toledo Strip	12-N	13-W
" "	22	3	Michigan-Toledo Strip	11-N	13-W
STUART	13	6	Michigan-Toledo Strip	13-N	14-W
" "	17	1	Michigan-Toledo Strip	12-N	14-W
" "	14	1	Michigan-Toledo Strip	13-N	13-W
" "	5	1	Michigan-Toledo Strip	15-N	14-W
STUDLEY	9	1	Michigan-Toledo Strip	14-N	14-W
SUMNER	24	1	Michigan-Toledo Strip	11-N	11-W
SURRARRER	19	1	Michigan-Toledo Strip	12-N	12-W
SUTFIN	24	1	Michigan-Toledo Strip	11-N	11-W
SUTHERLAND	16	3	Michigan-Toledo Strip	13-N	11-W
SUTLIFF	21	7	Michigan-Toledo Strip	11-N	14-W
" "	22	2	Michigan-Toledo Strip	11-N	13-W
SVANO	11	1	Michigan-Toledo Strip	14-N	12-W
" "	10	1	Michigan-Toledo Strip	14-N	13-W
SWAIN	16	7	Michigan-Toledo Strip	13-N	11-W
" "	10	7	Michigan-Toledo Strip	14-N	13-W
" "	19	4	Michigan-Toledo Strip	12-N	12-W
" "	21	2	Michigan-Toledo Strip	11-N	14-W
" "	15	1	Michigan-Toledo Strip	13-N	12-W
" "	8	1	Michigan-Toledo Strip	15-N	11-W
SWARTWOUT	16	3	Michigan-Toledo Strip	13-N	11-W
SWAYER	20	1	Michigan-Toledo Strip	12-N	11-W
SWEAT	5	2	Michigan-Toledo Strip	15-N	14-W
SWITZER	16	1	Michigan-Toledo Strip	13-N	11-W
TAGUASON	18	1	Michigan-Toledo Strip	12-N	13-W
TANNER	13	1	Michigan-Toledo Strip	13-N	14-W
TARR	3	1	Michigan-Toledo Strip	16-N	12-W
TAYLOR	11	2	Michigan-Toledo Strip	14-N	12-W
" "	17	1	Michigan-Toledo Strip	12-N	14-W
" "	10	1	Michigan-Toledo Strip	14-N	13-W
TENANT	17	1	Michigan-Toledo Strip	12-N	14-W
TENNY	4	3	Michigan-Toledo Strip	16-N	11-W
TERRY	16	1	Michigan-Toledo Strip	13-N	11-W
TERWILLIGER	24	6	Michigan-Toledo Strip	11-N	11-W
" "	15	3	Michigan-Toledo Strip	13-N	12-W
" "	20	1	Michigan-Toledo Strip	12-N	11-W
THAYER	15	1	Michigan-Toledo Strip	13-N	12-W
THOMAS	20	3	Michigan-Toledo Strip	12-N	11-W

Surname	Map Group	Parcels of Land	Meridian/Township/Range		
THOMAS (Cont'd)	**22**	1	Michigan-Toledo Strip	11-N	13-W
THOMPSON	**22**	2	Michigan-Toledo Strip	11-N	13-W
" "	**21**	2	Michigan-Toledo Strip	11-N	14-W
" "	**10**	2	Michigan-Toledo Strip	14-N	13-W
" "	**9**	2	Michigan-Toledo Strip	14-N	14-W
" "	**3**	2	Michigan-Toledo Strip	16-N	12-W
" "	**19**	1	Michigan-Toledo Strip	12-N	12-W
THORP	**9**	2	Michigan-Toledo Strip	14-N	14-W
THURSTON	**21**	1	Michigan-Toledo Strip	11-N	14-W
TIBBITS	**17**	1	Michigan-Toledo Strip	12-N	14-W
TIBBITTS	**17**	6	Michigan-Toledo Strip	12-N	14-W
" "	**13**	1	Michigan-Toledo Strip	13-N	14-W
TICHENOR	**3**	1	Michigan-Toledo Strip	16-N	12-W
TIFT	**20**	7	Michigan-Toledo Strip	12-N	11-W
" "	**16**	6	Michigan-Toledo Strip	13-N	11-W
TINDALL	**9**	4	Michigan-Toledo Strip	14-N	14-W
" "	**13**	3	Michigan-Toledo Strip	13-N	14-W
" "	**17**	1	Michigan-Toledo Strip	12-N	14-W
TINDOLL	**13**	1	Michigan-Toledo Strip	13-N	14-W
TINKHAM	**11**	4	Michigan-Toledo Strip	14-N	12-W
" "	**15**	1	Michigan-Toledo Strip	13-N	12-W
TITUS	**17**	1	Michigan-Toledo Strip	12-N	14-W
TOBY	**13**	2	Michigan-Toledo Strip	13-N	14-W
TONER	**4**	1	Michigan-Toledo Strip	16-N	11-W
TOWER	**16**	2	Michigan-Toledo Strip	13-N	11-W
" "	**6**	2	Michigan-Toledo Strip	15-N	13-W
" "	**5**	2	Michigan-Toledo Strip	15-N	14-W
" "	**1**	2	Michigan-Toledo Strip	16-N	14-W
" "	**2**	1	Michigan-Toledo Strip	16-N	13-W
TOWNE	**16**	1	Michigan-Toledo Strip	13-N	11-W
TOWNSEND	**10**	8	Michigan-Toledo Strip	14-N	13-W
" "	**11**	1	Michigan-Toledo Strip	14-N	12-W
TRACY	**12**	4	Michigan-Toledo Strip	14-N	11-W
" "	**16**	2	Michigan-Toledo Strip	13-N	11-W
TRAHAN	**4**	2	Michigan-Toledo Strip	16-N	11-W
TRAIN	**23**	2	Michigan-Toledo Strip	11-N	12-W
TRASK	**16**	1	Michigan-Toledo Strip	13-N	11-W
TRENBLER	**21**	1	Michigan-Toledo Strip	11-N	14-W
TREXELL	**23**	2	Michigan-Toledo Strip	11-N	12-W
TRIPP	**19**	3	Michigan-Toledo Strip	12-N	12-W
" "	**16**	1	Michigan-Toledo Strip	13-N	11-W
TROMBLY	**21**	3	Michigan-Toledo Strip	11-N	14-W
TROTT	**1**	4	Michigan-Toledo Strip	16-N	14-W
" "	**10**	1	Michigan-Toledo Strip	14-N	13-W
TROUNBLEY	**21**	1	Michigan-Toledo Strip	11-N	14-W
TROUTIER	**21**	1	Michigan-Toledo Strip	11-N	14-W
TROWBRIDGE	**19**	1	Michigan-Toledo Strip	12-N	12-W
" "	**18**	1	Michigan-Toledo Strip	12-N	13-W
TRUDE	**19**	2	Michigan-Toledo Strip	12-N	12-W
TRUFONT	**16**	2	Michigan-Toledo Strip	13-N	11-W
TUBBS	**16**	1	Michigan-Toledo Strip	13-N	11-W
TUCK	**3**	2	Michigan-Toledo Strip	16-N	12-W
TUCKER	**16**	4	Michigan-Toledo Strip	13-N	11-W
TURNER	**24**	2	Michigan-Toledo Strip	11-N	11-W
" "	**15**	1	Michigan-Toledo Strip	13-N	12-W
" "	**14**	1	Michigan-Toledo Strip	13-N	13-W
" "	**5**	1	Michigan-Toledo Strip	15-N	14-W
TUSK	**17**	1	Michigan-Toledo Strip	12-N	14-W
TUTHILL	**10**	2	Michigan-Toledo Strip	14-N	13-W
TUTTLE	**7**	1	Michigan-Toledo Strip	15-N	12-W

Surname	Map Group	Parcels of Land	Meridian/Township/Range		
UPTON	**22**	1	Michigan-Toledo Strip	11-N	13-W
" "	**19**	1	Michigan-Toledo Strip	12-N	12-W
" "	**18**	1	Michigan-Toledo Strip	12-N	13-W
" "	**17**	1	Michigan-Toledo Strip	12-N	14-W
" "	**14**	1	Michigan-Toledo Strip	13-N	13-W
" "	**13**	1	Michigan-Toledo Strip	13-N	14-W
UTLEY	**16**	6	Michigan-Toledo Strip	13-N	11-W
" "	**15**	6	Michigan-Toledo Strip	13-N	12-W
VALLANCE	**4**	1	Michigan-Toledo Strip	16-N	11-W
VAN ALSTINE	**4**	1	Michigan-Toledo Strip	16-N	11-W
VAN BRUNT	**15**	1	Michigan-Toledo Strip	13-N	12-W
VAN BUREN	**1**	1	Michigan-Toledo Strip	16-N	14-W
VAN LIEW	**24**	1	Michigan-Toledo Strip	11-N	11-W
VAN NARTEVICK	**1**	1	Michigan-Toledo Strip	16-N	14-W
VAN WILTENBURG	**2**	6	Michigan-Toledo Strip	16-N	13-W
" "	**3**	3	Michigan-Toledo Strip	16-N	12-W
VANDAWATERS	**4**	1	Michigan-Toledo Strip	16-N	11-W
VANDUSEN	**4**	1	Michigan-Toledo Strip	16-N	11-W
VANO	**11**	4	Michigan-Toledo Strip	14-N	12-W
" "	**10**	2	Michigan-Toledo Strip	14-N	13-W
VARNUM	**12**	1	Michigan-Toledo Strip	14-N	11-W
WAH	**17**	1	Michigan-Toledo Strip	12-N	14-W
WAKE	**3**	1	Michigan-Toledo Strip	16-N	12-W
WALKER	**13**	4	Michigan-Toledo Strip	13-N	14-W
" "	**1**	1	Michigan-Toledo Strip	16-N	14-W
WALLACE	**13**	1	Michigan-Toledo Strip	13-N	14-W
WALTERHOUSE	**17**	2	Michigan-Toledo Strip	12-N	14-W
WALTON	**21**	1	Michigan-Toledo Strip	11-N	14-W
WARANGASOE	**19**	1	Michigan-Toledo Strip	12-N	12-W
WARD	**24**	14	Michigan-Toledo Strip	11-N	11-W
" "	**9**	5	Michigan-Toledo Strip	14-N	14-W
" "	**2**	1	Michigan-Toledo Strip	16-N	13-W
WARDWELL	**4**	7	Michigan-Toledo Strip	16-N	11-W
WARREN	**12**	10	Michigan-Toledo Strip	14-N	11-W
" "	**10**	3	Michigan-Toledo Strip	14-N	13-W
" "	**14**	2	Michigan-Toledo Strip	13-N	13-W
" "	**8**	2	Michigan-Toledo Strip	15-N	11-W
" "	**6**	2	Michigan-Toledo Strip	15-N	13-W
" "	**24**	1	Michigan-Toledo Strip	11-N	11-W
WART	**22**	2	Michigan-Toledo Strip	11-N	13-W
" "	**16**	1	Michigan-Toledo Strip	13-N	11-W
WARTROUS	**19**	1	Michigan-Toledo Strip	12-N	12-W
WASHBURN	**9**	3	Michigan-Toledo Strip	14-N	14-W
" "	**8**	1	Michigan-Toledo Strip	15-N	11-W
WATERHOUSE	**18**	1	Michigan-Toledo Strip	12-N	13-W
WATERMAN	**4**	2	Michigan-Toledo Strip	16-N	11-W
WATERS	**16**	7	Michigan-Toledo Strip	13-N	11-W
" "	**13**	4	Michigan-Toledo Strip	13-N	14-W
" "	**14**	3	Michigan-Toledo Strip	13-N	13-W
WATSON	**19**	8	Michigan-Toledo Strip	12-N	12-W
" "	**18**	8	Michigan-Toledo Strip	12-N	13-W
" "	**17**	2	Michigan-Toledo Strip	12-N	14-W
" "	**14**	2	Michigan-Toledo Strip	13-N	13-W
" "	**22**	1	Michigan-Toledo Strip	11-N	13-W
" "	**13**	1	Michigan-Toledo Strip	13-N	14-W
WAU-BA-TO	**17**	1	Michigan-Toledo Strip	12-N	14-W
WEAVER	**13**	8	Michigan-Toledo Strip	13-N	14-W
" "	**18**	2	Michigan-Toledo Strip	12-N	13-W
" "	**17**	1	Michigan-Toledo Strip	12-N	14-W
WEBB	**17**	2	Michigan-Toledo Strip	12-N	14-W

Surname	Map Group	Parcels of Land	Meridian/Township/Range		
WEBBER	**1**	5	Michigan-Toledo Strip	16-N	14-W
" "	**2**	3	Michigan-Toledo Strip	16-N	13-W
" "	**4**	2	Michigan-Toledo Strip	16-N	11-W
" "	**3**	2	Michigan-Toledo Strip	16-N	12-W
WEBSTER	**16**	9	Michigan-Toledo Strip	13-N	11-W
" "	**4**	2	Michigan-Toledo Strip	16-N	11-W
" "	**5**	1	Michigan-Toledo Strip	15-N	14-W
WEDD	**3**	1	Michigan-Toledo Strip	16-N	12-W
WEIDMAN	**16**	2	Michigan-Toledo Strip	13-N	11-W
WELCH	**11**	4	Michigan-Toledo Strip	14-N	12-W
" "	**14**	1	Michigan-Toledo Strip	13-N	13-W
WELLES	**18**	2	Michigan-Toledo Strip	12-N	13-W
" "	**9**	2	Michigan-Toledo Strip	14-N	14-W
" "	**24**	1	Michigan-Toledo Strip	11-N	11-W
" "	**20**	1	Michigan-Toledo Strip	12-N	11-W
" "	**19**	1	Michigan-Toledo Strip	12-N	12-W
WELLING	**1**	2	Michigan-Toledo Strip	16-N	14-W
WELLS	**5**	3	Michigan-Toledo Strip	15-N	14-W
WERT	**4**	1	Michigan-Toledo Strip	16-N	11-W
WESTCOTT	**20**	1	Michigan-Toledo Strip	12-N	11-W
WESTERBERG	**4**	1	Michigan-Toledo Strip	16-N	11-W
WESTGATE	**16**	1	Michigan-Toledo Strip	13-N	11-W
WESTON	**10**	17	Michigan-Toledo Strip	14-N	13-W
" "	**14**	6	Michigan-Toledo Strip	13-N	13-W
" "	**11**	2	Michigan-Toledo Strip	14-N	12-W
" "	**9**	2	Michigan-Toledo Strip	14-N	14-W
WHALEN	**14**	1	Michigan-Toledo Strip	13-N	13-W
WHEAT	**22**	1	Michigan-Toledo Strip	11-N	13-W
WHEELER	**10**	5	Michigan-Toledo Strip	14-N	13-W
" "	**14**	4	Michigan-Toledo Strip	13-N	13-W
" "	**9**	1	Michigan-Toledo Strip	14-N	14-W
WHEELOCK	**14**	7	Michigan-Toledo Strip	13-N	13-W
" "	**15**	3	Michigan-Toledo Strip	13-N	12-W
WHIPPLE	**3**	5	Michigan-Toledo Strip	16-N	12-W
" "	**4**	1	Michigan-Toledo Strip	16-N	11-W
WHITE	**20**	5	Michigan-Toledo Strip	12-N	11-W
" "	**16**	4	Michigan-Toledo Strip	13-N	11-W
" "	**15**	2	Michigan-Toledo Strip	13-N	12-W
" "	**5**	2	Michigan-Toledo Strip	15-N	14-W
" "	**4**	2	Michigan-Toledo Strip	16-N	11-W
" "	**24**	1	Michigan-Toledo Strip	11-N	11-W
" "	**13**	1	Michigan-Toledo Strip	13-N	14-W
WHITEHEAD	**21**	2	Michigan-Toledo Strip	11-N	14-W
" "	**13**	1	Michigan-Toledo Strip	13-N	14-W
WHITEHURST	**24**	2	Michigan-Toledo Strip	11-N	11-W
WHITEMAN	**21**	1	Michigan-Toledo Strip	11-N	14-W
WHITMAN	**18**	3	Michigan-Toledo Strip	12-N	13-W
" "	**21**	2	Michigan-Toledo Strip	11-N	14-W
WHITNEY	**20**	4	Michigan-Toledo Strip	12-N	11-W
" "	**19**	3	Michigan-Toledo Strip	12-N	12-W
" "	**16**	1	Michigan-Toledo Strip	13-N	11-W
WIGGINS	**23**	2	Michigan-Toledo Strip	11-N	12-W
" "	**19**	2	Michigan-Toledo Strip	12-N	12-W
WILCOX	**18**	6	Michigan-Toledo Strip	12-N	13-W
" "	**4**	5	Michigan-Toledo Strip	16-N	11-W
" "	**12**	3	Michigan-Toledo Strip	14-N	11-W
" "	**22**	2	Michigan-Toledo Strip	11-N	13-W
" "	**14**	2	Michigan-Toledo Strip	13-N	13-W
" "	**13**	2	Michigan-Toledo Strip	13-N	14-W
" "	**11**	2	Michigan-Toledo Strip	14-N	12-W

Surname	Map Group	Parcels of Land	Meridian/Township/Range		
WILCOX (Cont'd)	**15**	1	Michigan-Toledo Strip	13-N	12-W
" "	**1**	1	Michigan-Toledo Strip	16-N	14-W
WILDER	**13**	3	Michigan-Toledo Strip	13-N	14-W
" "	**9**	2	Michigan-Toledo Strip	14-N	14-W
WILKIN	**24**	1	Michigan-Toledo Strip	11-N	11-W
" "	**20**	1	Michigan-Toledo Strip	12-N	11-W
WILLARD	**11**	2	Michigan-Toledo Strip	14-N	12-W
" "	**8**	2	Michigan-Toledo Strip	15-N	11-W
WILLETS	**9**	1	Michigan-Toledo Strip	14-N	14-W
WILLIAMS	**19**	2	Michigan-Toledo Strip	12-N	12-W
" "	**2**	2	Michigan-Toledo Strip	16-N	13-W
" "	**18**	1	Michigan-Toledo Strip	12-N	13-W
" "	**17**	1	Michigan-Toledo Strip	12-N	14-W
" "	**3**	1	Michigan-Toledo Strip	16-N	12-W
WILLINS	**21**	1	Michigan-Toledo Strip	11-N	14-W
WILLIUS	**21**	2	Michigan-Toledo Strip	11-N	14-W
WILLMER	**20**	3	Michigan-Toledo Strip	12-N	11-W
WILSON	**2**	8	Michigan-Toledo Strip	16-N	13-W
" "	**6**	6	Michigan-Toledo Strip	15-N	13-W
" "	**20**	3	Michigan-Toledo Strip	12-N	11-W
" "	**12**	2	Michigan-Toledo Strip	14-N	11-W
" "	**5**	2	Michigan-Toledo Strip	15-N	14-W
" "	**22**	1	Michigan-Toledo Strip	11-N	13-W
" "	**19**	1	Michigan-Toledo Strip	12-N	12-W
" "	**16**	1	Michigan-Toledo Strip	13-N	11-W
" "	**15**	1	Michigan-Toledo Strip	13-N	12-W
" "	**11**	1	Michigan-Toledo Strip	14-N	12-W
" "	**9**	1	Michigan-Toledo Strip	14-N	14-W
" "	**1**	1	Michigan-Toledo Strip	16-N	14-W
WINN	**6**	2	Michigan-Toledo Strip	15-N	13-W
WINSTON	**9**	1	Michigan-Toledo Strip	14-N	14-W
WISENFIELD	**21**	1	Michigan-Toledo Strip	11-N	14-W
WISWELL	**13**	1	Michigan-Toledo Strip	13-N	14-W
WITHEROW	**6**	2	Michigan-Toledo Strip	15-N	13-W
WONCH	**20**	1	Michigan-Toledo Strip	12-N	11-W
WOOD	**24**	39	Michigan-Toledo Strip	11-N	11-W
" "	**14**	26	Michigan-Toledo Strip	13-N	13-W
" "	**2**	26	Michigan-Toledo Strip	16-N	13-W
" "	**23**	15	Michigan-Toledo Strip	11-N	12-W
" "	**17**	11	Michigan-Toledo Strip	12-N	14-W
" "	**3**	11	Michigan-Toledo Strip	16-N	12-W
" "	**18**	9	Michigan-Toledo Strip	12-N	13-W
" "	**7**	9	Michigan-Toledo Strip	15-N	12-W
" "	**6**	9	Michigan-Toledo Strip	15-N	13-W
" "	**15**	7	Michigan-Toledo Strip	13-N	12-W
" "	**8**	4	Michigan-Toledo Strip	15-N	11-W
" "	**19**	3	Michigan-Toledo Strip	12-N	12-W
" "	**22**	2	Michigan-Toledo Strip	11-N	13-W
" "	**16**	2	Michigan-Toledo Strip	13-N	11-W
" "	**21**	1	Michigan-Toledo Strip	11-N	14-W
" "	**20**	1	Michigan-Toledo Strip	12-N	11-W
" "	**12**	1	Michigan-Toledo Strip	14-N	11-W
" "	**9**	1	Michigan-Toledo Strip	14-N	14-W
WOODARD	**4**	1	Michigan-Toledo Strip	16-N	11-W
WOODBURY	**2**	4	Michigan-Toledo Strip	16-N	13-W
WOODFORD	**20**	1	Michigan-Toledo Strip	12-N	11-W
WOODHOUSE	**24**	2	Michigan-Toledo Strip	11-N	11-W
WOODMAN	**20**	3	Michigan-Toledo Strip	12-N	11-W
" "	**14**	2	Michigan-Toledo Strip	13-N	13-W
" "	**10**	1	Michigan-Toledo Strip	14-N	13-W

Surname	Map Group	Parcels of Land	Meridian/Township/Range		
WOODRUFF	**19**	1	Michigan-Toledo Strip	12-N	12-W
WOODS	**24**	3	Michigan-Toledo Strip	11-N	11-W
" "	**2**	3	Michigan-Toledo Strip	16-N	13-W
WRENN	**8**	2	Michigan-Toledo Strip	15-N	11-W
WRIGHT	**20**	6	Michigan-Toledo Strip	12-N	11-W
" "	**13**	2	Michigan-Toledo Strip	13-N	14-W
" "	**8**	2	Michigan-Toledo Strip	15-N	11-W
" "	**7**	2	Michigan-Toledo Strip	15-N	12-W
WUTCH	**18**	1	Michigan-Toledo Strip	12-N	13-W
YATES	**1**	3	Michigan-Toledo Strip	16-N	14-W
YERKES	**16**	4	Michigan-Toledo Strip	13-N	11-W
YOUNG	**10**	6	Michigan-Toledo Strip	14-N	13-W
" "	**16**	1	Michigan-Toledo Strip	13-N	11-W
YOUNGS	**4**	1	Michigan-Toledo Strip	16-N	11-W
YUNG	**17**	1	Michigan-Toledo Strip	12-N	14-W
ZERLANT	**17**	3	Michigan-Toledo Strip	12-N	14-W

– Part II –

Township Map Groups

Map Group 1: Index to Land Patents

Township 16-North Range 14-West (Michigan-Toledo Strip)

After you locate an individual in this Index, take note of the Section and Section Part then proceed to the Land Patent map on the pages immediately following. You should have no difficulty locating the corresponding parcel of land.

The "For More Info" Column will lead you to more information about the underlying Patents. See the *Legend* at right, and the "How to Use this Book" chapter, for more information.

LEGEND

"For More Info . . . " column

A = Authority (Legislative Act, See Appendix "A")
B = Block or Lot (location in Section unknown)
C = Cancelled Patent
F = Fractional Section
G = Group (Multi-Patentee Patent, see Appendix "C")
V = Overlaps another Parcel
R = Re-Issued (Parcel patented more than once)

(A & G items require you to look in the Appendixes referred to above. All other Letter-designations followed by a number require you to locate line-items in this index that possess the ID number found after the letter).

ID	Individual in Patent	Sec.	Sec. Part	Date Issued	Other Counties	For More Info . . .
63	ATWOOD, Mary	6	S½NE	1869-07-01		A3 G149
36	BALDWIN, Edwin	2	S½NW	1884-05-15		A4
37	" "	2	W½SW	1884-05-15		A4
34	" "	2	NENE	1885-01-07		A1 F
35	" "	2	NWNE	1885-01-07		A1 F
19	BISSETT, Bethiah	18	SW	1864-02-10		A3 G118 F
83	BROMLEY, William H	30	NE	1872-01-01		A4
82	BULSON, Washington J	2	NENW	1905-09-11		A4
62	CADY, Levinia	6	SE	1866-01-10		A3 G151
16	CHICK, Charles H	4	SENW	1884-04-15		A1
15	" "	14	SWNE	1885-01-07		A1
66	EDWARDS, Louis	6	N½NE	1912-08-19		A4
27	FILER, Delos L	14	NESW	1873-05-15		A1
60	FLAGG, Betsey	8	N½NE	1867-02-01		A3 G152 F
61	" "	8	N½NW	1867-02-01		A3 G152 F
78	FOLJAMBE, Charles	32	E½SE	1869-09-01		A3 G266
79	" "	32	NWSE	1869-09-01		A3 G266
19	FOSTER, James	18	SW	1864-02-10		A3 G118 F
1	FREEMAN, Addison	30	SW	1869-11-01		A4
14	FREEMAN, Charles	30	SE	1873-06-10		A4
39	GATES, George	4	N½NE	1903-06-12		A4
40	" "	4	NENW	1903-06-12		A4
64	GRAY, Edgar L	8	NESE	1866-06-05		A1 G229 F
28	" "	8	NWSE	1867-05-10		A3 G72 R29
28	" "	8	NWSE	1867-05-10		A3 G72 C R29
29	" "	8	NWSE	1867-05-10		A3 G72 R28
29	" "	8	NWSE	1867-05-10		A3 G72 C R28
30	" "	8	SENW	1867-05-10		A3 G72 R31
30	" "	8	SENW	1867-05-10		A3 G72 C R31
31	" "	8	SENW	1867-05-10		A3 G72 R30
31	" "	8	SENW	1867-05-10		A3 G72 C R30
32	" "	8	SWNE	1867-05-10		A3 G72 R33
32	" "	8	SWNE	1867-05-10		A3 G72 C R33
33	" "	8	SWNE	1867-05-10		A3 G72 R32
33	" "	8	SWNE	1867-05-10		A3 G72 C R32
13	GREY, Charles	28	W½SE	1868-12-01		A3 G213
25	HARPER, John L	2	E½SW	1872-07-01		A1 G222
26	" "	2	S½NE	1872-07-01		A1 G222
72	HOVEY, Silas P	4	N½SW	1881-10-19		A1
73	" "	4	SWNW	1881-10-19		A1
56	JOBBITT, James	10	W½SE	1883-10-01		A4
80	JOHNSON, Davis	32	NW	1869-09-01		A3 G267
59	JOY, Abigail	6	SW	1866-12-15		A3 G153 F
7	KIEFER, Herman	36	NESE	1869-09-10		A1 G273
8	" "	36	SWNE	1869-09-10		A1 G273
17	LEONARD, Charles W	18	S½NE	1864-02-10		A3 G117

ID	Individual in Patent	Sec.	Sec. Part	Date Issued	Other Counties	For More Info . . .
18	LEONARD, Charles W (Cont'd)	18	S½NW	1864-02-10		A3 G117 F
20	" "	18	SE	1864-02-10		A3 G119
19	" "	18	SW	1864-02-10		A3 G118 F
7	LICHTENBERG, Gustav B	36	NESE	1869-09-10		A1 G273
8	" "	36	SWNE	1869-09-10		A1 G273
62	LUDINGTON, James	6	SE	1866-01-10		A3 G151
59	" "	6	SW	1866-12-15		A3 G153 F
57	" "	6	SWNW	1867-01-10		A1 F
60	" "	8	N½NE	1867-02-01		A3 G152 F
61	" "	8	N½NW	1867-02-01		A3 G152 F
63	" "	6	S½NE	1869-07-01		A3 G149
58	" "	8	SENE	1869-09-10		A1 F
41	LYMAN, George N	22	E½SW	1870-05-02		A1
42	" "	22	S½NE	1870-05-02		A1
43	" "	22	SENW	1870-05-02		A1
44	" "	26	W½NW	1870-05-02		A1
45	" "	4	S½SE	1870-05-02		A1
21	MARSHALL, William R	22	NWSW	1870-06-01		A3 G175
22	" "	22	SWNW	1870-06-01		A3 G175
21	MELENDY, David A	22	NWSW	1870-06-01		A3 G175
22	" "	22	SWNW	1870-06-01		A3 G175
53	MILLIS, Hiram S	14	W½SW	1884-05-10		A4
74	MIX, Sylvenus S	22	N½NE	1865-10-20		A3 G193
75	" "	22	N½NW	1865-10-20		A3 G193
74	MIX, Sylvester	22	N½NE	1865-10-20		A3 G193
75	" "	22	N½NW	1865-10-20		A3 G193
24	MOORE, David	14	W½NW	1883-09-15		A4
23	" "	14	E½NW	1884-12-20		A4
67	MORGAN, Moses	10	NW	1877-07-20		A4
4	PAINTER, Andrew J	28	NESW	1881-02-10		A4
5	" "	28	SENW	1881-02-10		A4
6	" "	28	SWNE	1881-02-10		A4
13	PALMER, Chandler	28	W½SE	1868-12-01		A3 G213
71	PEARSON, Daniel K	10	E½SE	1872-03-20		A1 G315 F
54	PENCE, Isaac	2	NWNW	1889-04-05		A1 F
48	POTTER, Henry C	14	SESW	1872-07-01		A1 G221
50	" "	4	NWNW	1872-07-01		A1 G221
49	" "	24	SWSW	1872-08-30		A1 G221
51	" "	4	S½SW	1872-08-30		A1 G221
52	" "	6	SENW	1872-08-30		A1 G221 C R12
25	PRESTON, David	2	E½SW	1872-07-01		A1 G222
26	" "	2	S½NE	1872-07-01		A1 G222
65	RETERSTOFF, Lewis	10	SW	1903-06-12		A4
9	RICE, Catherine	36	S½SE	1868-02-15		A1
10	" "	36	SENE	1868-02-15		A1
11	" "	36	SWNW	1868-02-15		A1
12	" "	6	SENW	1875-01-05		A1 F R52
64	ROCHESTER, John W	8	NESE	1866-06-05		A1 G229 F
28	" "	8	NWSE	1867-05-10		A3 G72 R29
28	" "	8	NWSE	1867-05-10		A3 G72 C R29
29	" "	8	NWSE	1867-05-10		A3 G72 R28
29	" "	8	NWSE	1867-05-10		A3 G72 C R28
30	" "	8	SENW	1867-05-10		A3 G72 R31
30	" "	8	SENW	1867-05-10		A3 G72 C R31
31	" "	8	SENW	1867-05-10		A3 G72 R30
31	" "	8	SENW	1867-05-10		A3 G72 C R30
32	" "	8	SWNE	1867-05-10		A3 G72 R33
32	" "	8	SWNE	1867-05-10		A3 G72 C R33
33	" "	8	SWNE	1867-05-10		A3 G72 R32
33	" "	8	SWNE	1867-05-10		A3 G72 C R32
46	RYDER, Dinah	36	SW	1869-09-01		A3 G318
70	SLOCUM, Richard C	26	E½NW	1877-05-15		A4
20	STEVENS, Jane	18	SE	1864-02-10		A3 G119
78	STEVENSON, Thomas G	32	E½SE	1869-09-01		A3 G266
76	" "	32	NE	1869-09-01		A3
80	" "	32	NW	1869-09-01		A3 G267
79	" "	32	NWSE	1869-09-01		A3 G266
81	" "	32	SW	1869-09-01		A3 G269
77	" "	32	SWSE	1871-11-15		A1
7	STROH, Bernhard	36	NESE	1869-09-10		A1 G273
8	" "	36	SWNE	1869-09-10		A1 G273
68	TOWER, Osmond S	36	NWSE	1872-07-01		A1
69	" "	36	SENW	1872-07-01		A1

ID	Individual in Patent	Sec.	Sec. Part	Date Issued	Other Counties	For More Info . . .
17	TROTT, Levi L	18	S½NE	1864-02-10		A3 G117
18	" "	18	S½NW	1864-02-10		A3 G117 F
20	" "	18	SE	1864-02-10		A3 G119
19	" "	18	SW	1864-02-10		A3 G118 F
81	VAN BUREN, MARIA	32	SW	1869-09-01		A3 G269
55	VAN NARTEVICK, JAMES H	6	N½NW	1870-05-02		A1 F
38	WALKER, Ezekiel	14	N½NE	1891-11-23		A4
48	WEBBER, William L	14	SESW	1872-07-01		A1 G221
50	" "	4	NWNW	1872-07-01		A1 G221
49	" "	24	SWSW	1872-08-30		A1 G221
51	" "	4	S½SW	1872-08-30		A1 G221
52	" "	6	SENW	1872-08-30		A1 G221 C R12
74	WELLING, Cornelia	22	N½NE	1865-10-20		A3 G193
75	" "	22	N½NW	1865-10-20		A3 G193
71	WILCOX, Sextus N	10	E½SE	1872-03-20		A1 G315 F
46	WILSON, Gilbert F D	36	SW	1869-09-01		A3 G318
2	YATES, Alonzo	18	N½NW	1870-06-20		A4 F
3	" "	18	NWNE	1870-06-20		A4 F
47	YATES, Gilbert	30	NW	1877-06-04		A4 F

Patent Map

T16-N R14-W
Michigan-Toledo Strip Meridian

Map Group 1

Township Statistics

Parcels Mapped	:	83
Number of Patents	:	61
Number of Individuals	:	59
Patentees Identified	:	47
Number of Surnames	:	56
Multi-Patentee Parcels	:	36
Oldest Patent Date	:	2/10/1864
Most Recent Patent	:	8/19/1912
Block/Lot Parcels	:	0
Parcels Re - Issued	:	4
Parcels that Overlap	:	0
Cities and Towns	:	2
Cemeteries	:	0

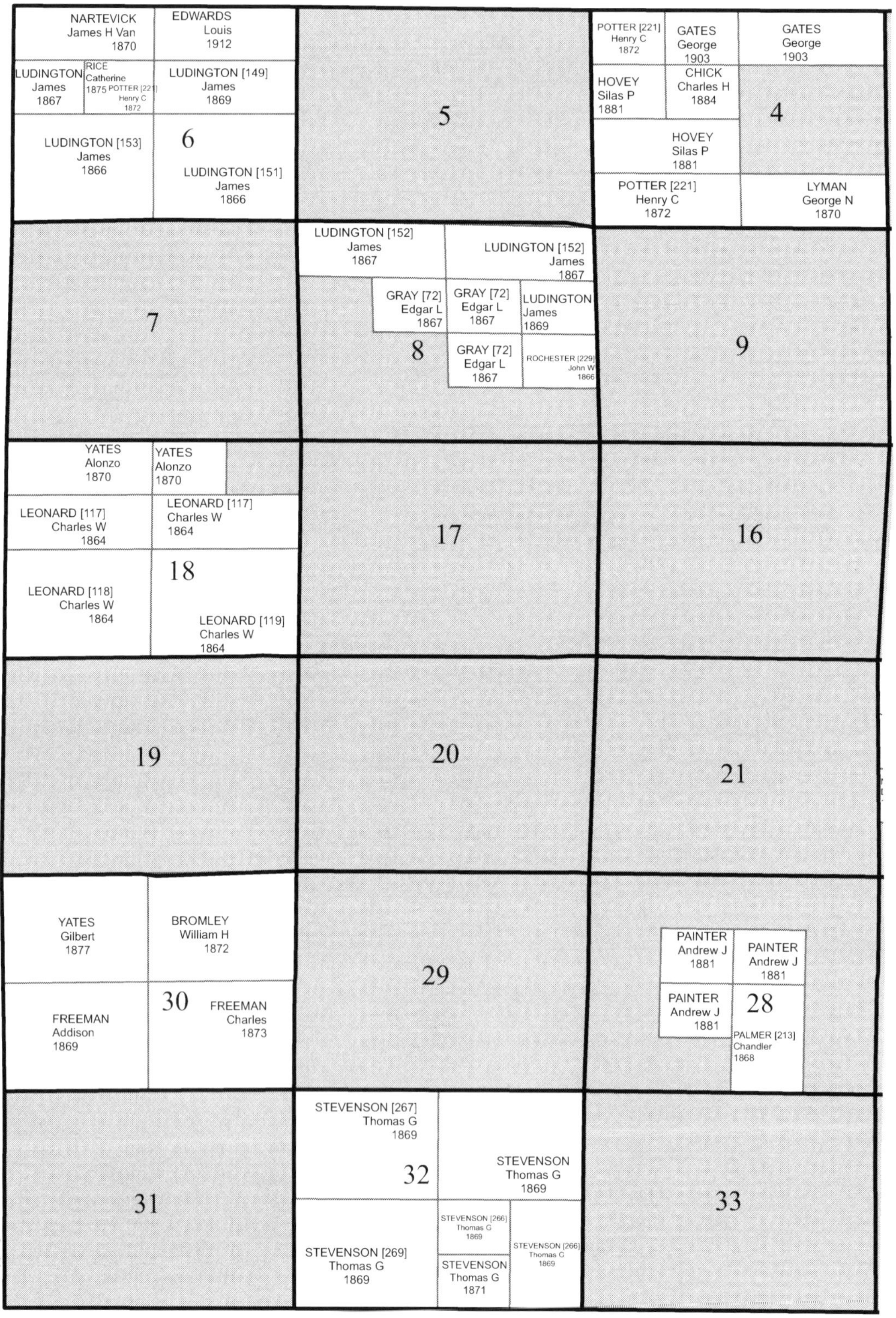

NARTEVICK James H Van 1870
EDWARDS Louis 1912
LUDINGTON James 1867
RICE Catherine 1875
POTTER [221] Henry C 1872
LUDINGTON [149] James 1869
LUDINGTON [153] James 1866
6
LUDINGTON [151] James 1866

5

POTTER [221] Henry C 1872
GATES George 1903
GATES George 1903
HOVEY Silas P 1881
CHICK Charles H 1884
4
HOVEY Silas P 1881
POTTER [221] Henry C 1872
LYMAN George N 1870

7

LUDINGTON [152] James 1867
LUDINGTON [152] James 1867
GRAY [72] Edgar L 1867
GRAY [72] Edgar L 1867
LUDINGTON James 1869
8
GRAY [72] Edgar L 1867
ROCHESTER [229] John W 1866

9

YATES Alonzo 1870
YATES Alonzo 1870
LEONARD [117] Charles W 1864
LEONARD [117] Charles W 1864
18
LEONARD [118] Charles W 1864
LEONARD [119] Charles W 1864

17

16

19

20

21

YATES Gilbert 1877
BROMLEY William H 1872
30
FREEMAN Addison 1869
FREEMAN Charles 1873

29

PAINTER Andrew J 1881
PAINTER Andrew J 1881
PAINTER Andrew J 1881
28
PALMER [213] Chandler 1868

31

STEVENSON [267] Thomas G 1869
32
STEVENSON Thomas G 1869
STEVENSON [266] Thomas G 1869
STEVENSON [266] Thomas G 1869
STEVENSON [269] Thomas G 1869
STEVENSON Thomas G 1871

33

Helpful Hints

1. This Map's INDEX can be found on the preceding pages.
2. Refer to Map "C" to see where this Township lies within Newaygo County, Michigan.
3. Numbers within square brackets [ ] denote a multi-patentee land parcel (multi-owner). Refer to Appendix "C" for a full list of members in this group.
4. Areas that look to be crowded with Patentees usually indicate multiple sales of the same parcel (Re-issues) or Overlapping parcels. See this Township's Index for an explanation of these and other circumstances that might explain "odd" groupings of Patentees on this map.

Legend

Patent Boundary

Section Boundary

No Patents Found (or Outside County)

1., 2., 3., ... Lot Numbers (when beside a name)

[ ] Group Number (see Appendix "C")

Scale: Section = 1 mile X 1 mile (generally, with some exceptions)

Road Map

T16-N R14-W
Michigan-Toledo Strip Meridian

Map Group 1

Cities & Towns

Troy
Walgamor Corners

Cemeteries

None

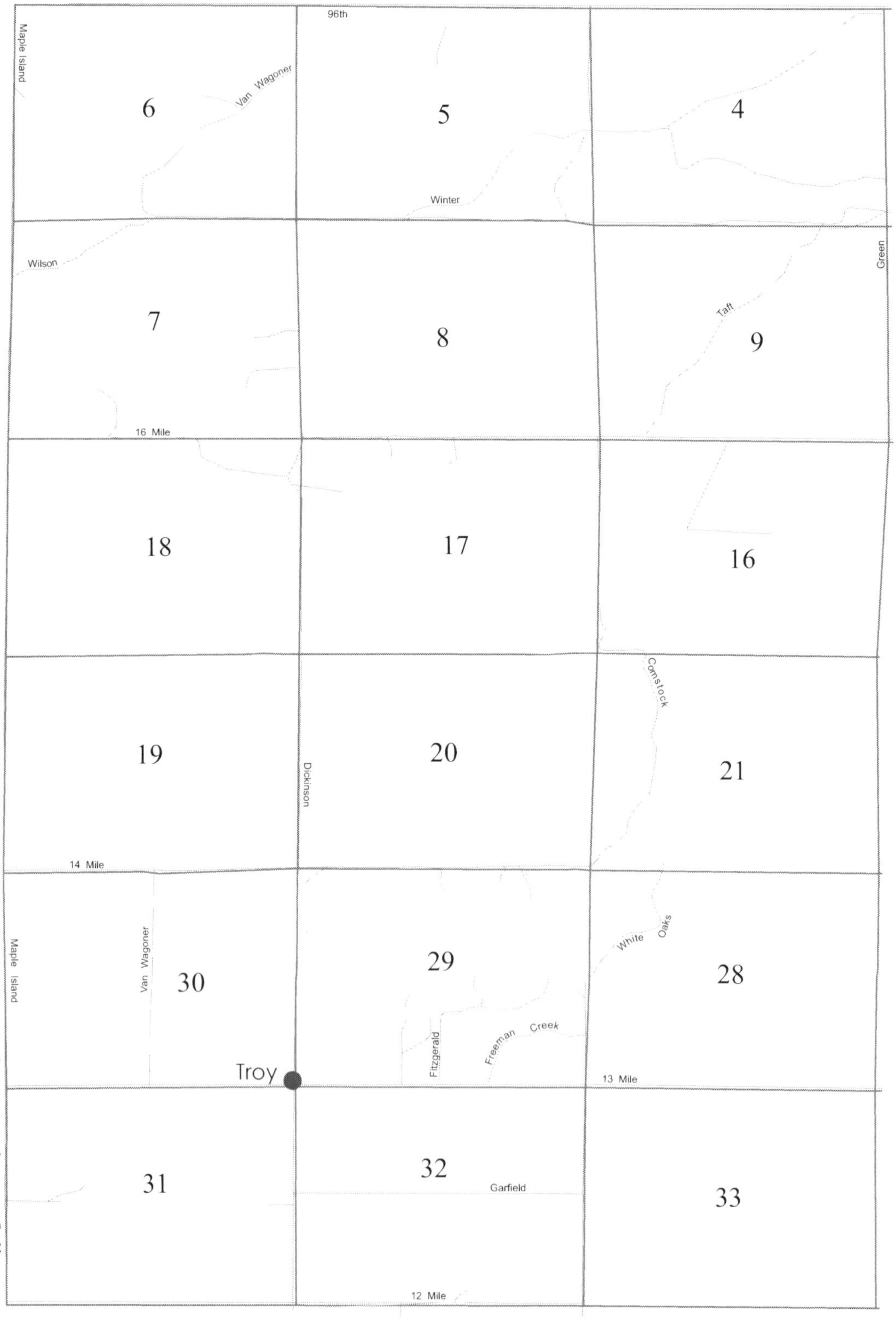

Osborn
Tower
Coolidge
3
2
1
17 Mile
Harding
10
11
12
Badger
16 Mile
15
14
13
22
23
24
Osborn
27
26
25
Walgamor Corners
Hill
Cleveland
34
35
36
Filbert
Warner

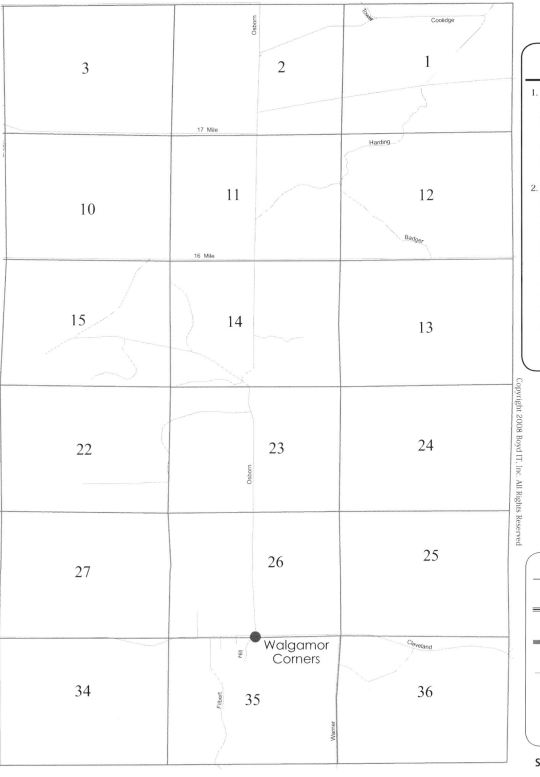

Helpful Hints

1. This road map has a number of uses, but primarily it is to help you: a) find the present location of land owned by your ancestors (at least the general area), b) find cemeteries and city-centers, and c) estimate the route/roads used by Census-takers & tax-assessors.

2. If you plan to travel to Newaygo County to locate cemeteries or land parcels, please pick up a modern travel map for the area before you do. Mapping old land parcels on modern maps is not as exact a science as you might think. Just the slightest variations in public land survey coordinates, estimates of parcel boundaries, or road-map deviations can greatly alter a map's representation of how a road either does or doesn't cross a particular parcel of land.

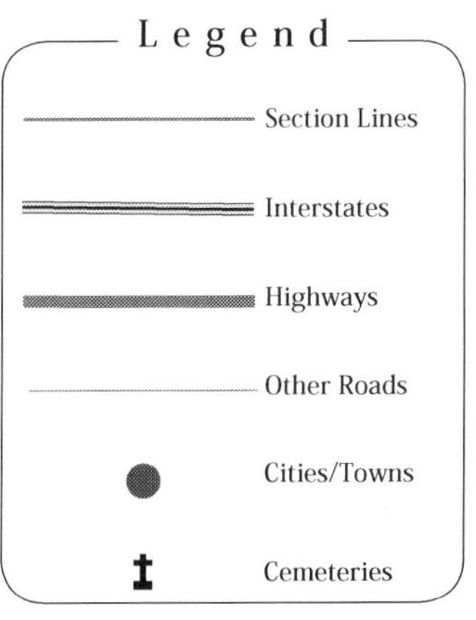

Scale: Section = 1 mile X 1 mile
(generally, with some exceptions)

Historical Map

T16-N R14-W
Michigan-Toledo Strip Meridian

Map Group 1

Cities & Towns

Troy
Walgamor Corners

Cemeteries

None

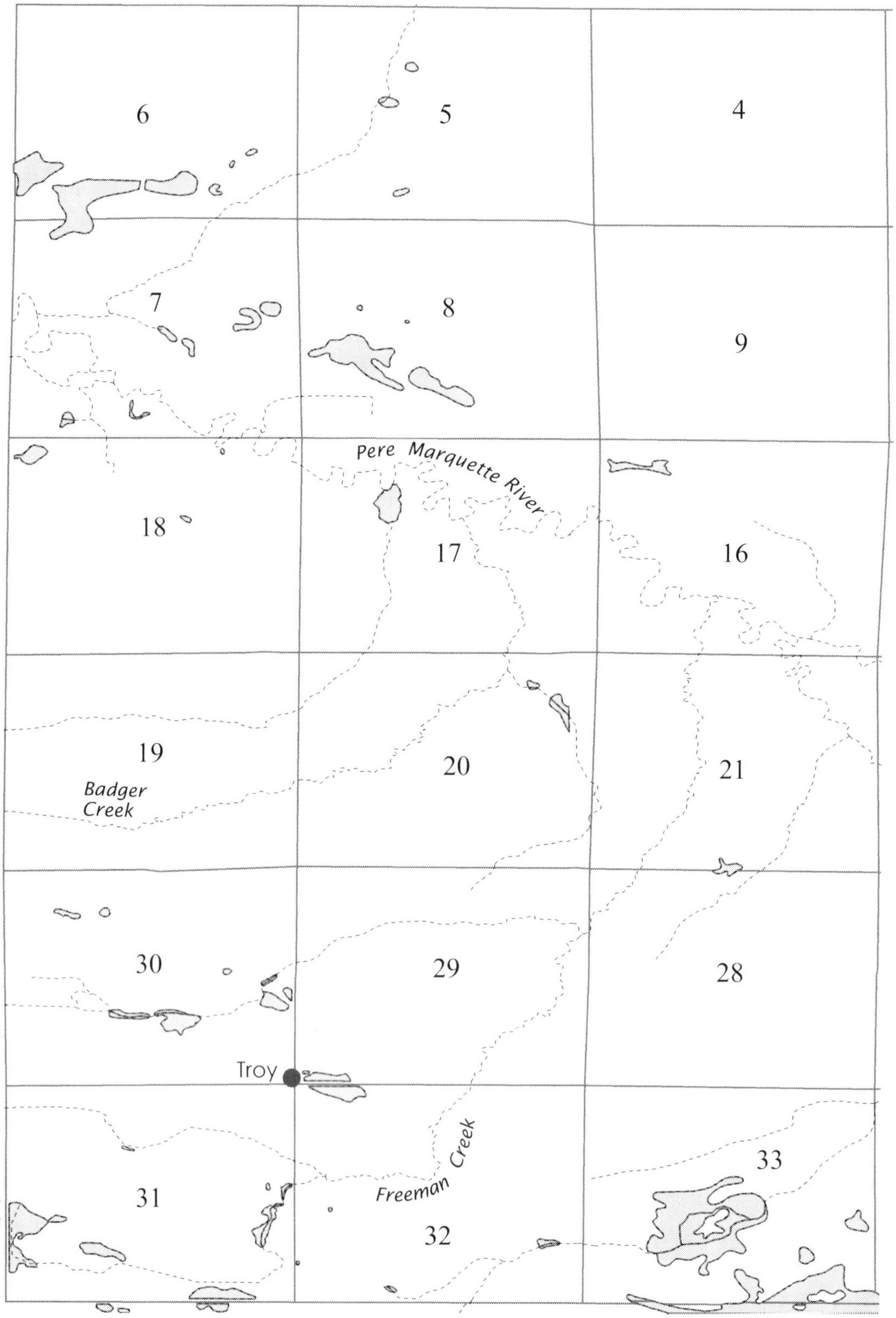

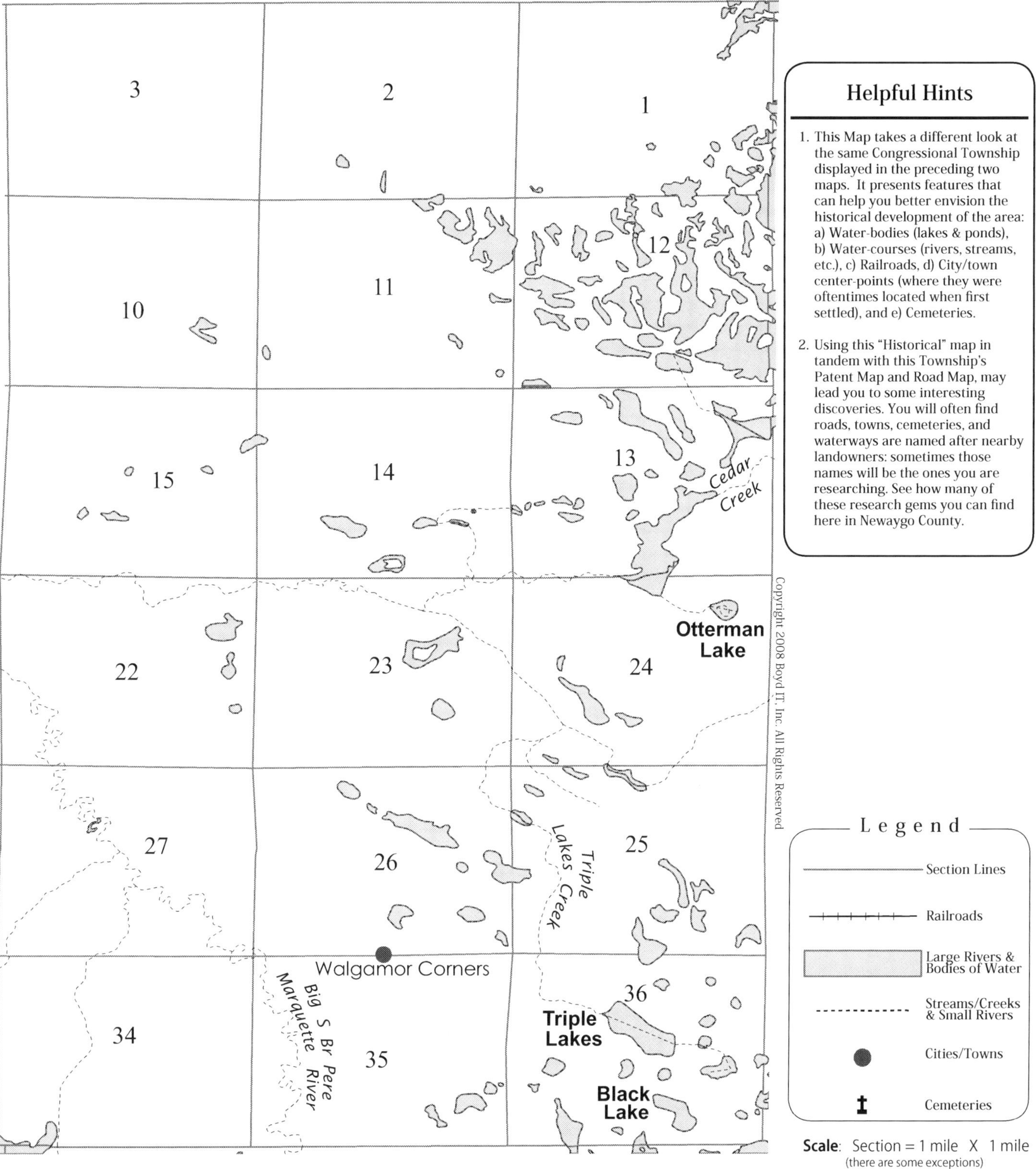

Helpful Hints

1. This Map takes a different look at the same Congressional Township displayed in the preceding two maps. It presents features that can help you better envision the historical development of the area: a) Water-bodies (lakes & ponds), b) Water-courses (rivers, streams, etc.), c) Railroads, d) City/town center-points (where they were oftentimes located when first settled), and e) Cemeteries.

2. Using this "Historical" map in tandem with this Township's Patent Map and Road Map, may lead you to some interesting discoveries. You will often find roads, towns, cemeteries, and waterways are named after nearby landowners: sometimes those names will be the ones you are researching. See how many of these research gems you can find here in Newaygo County.

Legend

- Section Lines
- Railroads
- Large Rivers & Bodies of Water
- Streams/Creeks & Small Rivers
- Cities/Towns
- Cemeteries

Scale: Section = 1 mile X 1 mile
(there are some exceptions)

Map Group 2: Index to Land Patents

Township 16-North Range 13-West (Michigan-Toledo Strip)

After you locate an individual in this Index, take note of the Section and Section Part then proceed to the Land Patent map on the pages immediately following. You should have no difficulty locating the corresponding parcel of land.

The "For More Info" Column will lead you to more information about the underlying Patents. See the *Legend* at right, and the "How to Use this Book" chapter, for more information.

LEGEND

"For More Info . . . " column

- **A** = Authority (Legislative Act, See Appendix "A")
- **B** = Block or Lot (location in Section unknown)
- **C** = Cancelled Patent
- **F** = Fractional Section
- **G** = Group (Multi-Patentee Patent, see Appendix "C")
- **V** = Overlaps another Parcel
- **R** = Re-Issued (Parcel patented more than once)

(A & G items require you to look in the Appendixes referred to above. All other Letter-designations followed by a number require you to locate line-items in this index that possess the ID number found after the letter).

ID	Individual in Patent	Sec.	Sec. Part	Date Issued	Other Counties	For More Info . . .
163	BARBER, Clara	24	E½NE	1869-09-01		A3 G322
164	" "	24	SWNE	1869-09-01		A3 G322
98	BELL, Darwin G	34	SENE	1885-01-07		A1
159	BELMEAR, Catharine	26	N½NE	1869-09-01		A3 G323
160	" "	26	NENW	1869-09-01		A3 G323
87	BENJAMIN, D M	10	SESE	1869-09-10		A1 F
88	BENJAMIN, D Marcellus	10	E½NW	1869-06-15		A3
95	" "	10	NE	1869-06-15		A3 G19
89	" "	12	NENW	1869-06-15		A3
90	" "	12	S½NW	1869-06-15		A3
91	" "	12	SWNE	1869-06-15		A3
92	" "	10	SW	1869-07-01		A3 G12
93	" "	10	NESE	1869-09-01		A3 G20
94	" "	10	W½SE	1869-09-01		A3 G20
135	CALLENDER, James E	18	W½SW	1894-08-17		A4
166	CLARK, John	22	N½SW	1869-09-01		A3 G324
167	" "	22	S½NW	1869-09-01		A3 G324
189	DINGMAN, Thomas	36	S½SE	1880-11-20		A1
97	FIFIELD, Daniel	2	NE	1906-06-30		A4
119	FILER, Delos L	2	N½SW	1873-05-15		A1
120	" "	2	NWSE	1873-05-15		A1
121	" "	2	SESW	1873-05-15		A1
127	GAYLORD, Josiah A	32	SW	1869-09-01		A3 G317 F
105	GERRY, Elizabeth	20	N½SE	1870-06-01		A3 G172
106	" "	20	SESW	1870-06-01		A3 G172
107	" "	20	SWSE	1870-06-01		A3 G172
92	HAINES, James	10	SW	1869-07-01		A3 G12
128	HAMMOND, Mercy	30	SW	1869-09-01		A3 G316 F
129	" "	30	SWNW	1869-09-01		A3 G316 F
183	HARRINGTON, Owen D	2	E½SE	1907-09-27		A4
136	HENRY, James	8	NESW	1872-07-01		A1
137	" "	8	SENW	1872-07-01		A1
138	" "	8	SWSW	1872-07-01		A1
96	HEWIT, Daniel B	18	N½SE	1875-07-01		A4
192	HINMAN, William G	10	W½NW	1870-08-10		A1
193	" "	12	NESE	1870-08-10		A1
194	" "	12	SWSE	1870-08-10		A1
195	" "	14	NWNE	1870-08-10		A1
196	" "	18	SENE	1870-08-10		A1
197	" "	18	W½NE	1870-08-10		A1
198	" "	4	SENE	1870-08-10		A1
199	" "	4	W½SW	1870-08-10		A1
200	HOUGHTALING, William	18	E½NW	1875-09-01		A4
201	" "	18	NESW	1875-09-01		A4
187	HOVEY, Silas P	18	SESW	1880-03-05		A1
188	" "	8	NWSW	1880-03-05		A1

ID	Individual in Patent	Sec.	Sec. Part	Date Issued	Other Counties	For More Info . . .
169	INGALLS, Mercy	24	SE	1869-09-01		A3 G328
114	ISBELL, Yearby H	30	W½NE	1870-06-01		A3 G173
161	KEINER, Catharine	24	E½SW	1869-09-01		A3 G329
162	" "	24	SENW	1869-09-01		A3 G329
165	KILBY, Hannah	4	SE	1869-09-01		A3 G330
140	LEMONS, Aley	24	W½NW	1869-06-15		A3 G156 R141
140	" "	24	W½NW	1869-06-15		A3 G156 C R141
141	" "	24	W½NW	1869-06-15		A3 G156 R140
141	" "	24	W½NW	1869-06-15		A3 G156 C R140
114	LEONARD, Mary	30	W½NE	1870-06-01		A3 G173
114	LEONARD, Samuel L	30	W½NE	1870-06-01		A3 G173
114	LINGLE, John S	30	W½NE	1870-06-01		A3 G173
115	LONG, Priscilla	18	S½SE	1870-06-01		A3 G174
140	LUDINGTON, James	24	W½NW	1869-06-15		A3 G156 R141
140	" "	24	W½NW	1869-06-15		A3 G156 C R141
141	" "	24	W½NW	1869-06-15		A3 G156 R140
141	" "	24	W½NW	1869-06-15		A3 G156 C R140
142	" "	34	N½NE	1869-06-15		A3 G159
143	" "	34	SENW	1869-06-15		A3 G159
144	" "	34	SWNE	1869-06-15		A3 G159
139	" "	34	N½NW	1869-09-10		A1 F
184	MALLET, Richmond D	22	SWNE	1881-10-19		A1
190	MCCLURE, William C	2	SWSW	1872-11-06		A1
191	" "	22	SWSW	1872-11-06		A1
174	MCKENZIE, Kenneth	36	NWSE	1875-02-10		A4
175	" "	36	SWNE	1875-02-10		A4
102	MELENDY, David A	30	SENE	1870-05-10		A1
103	" "	34	NESE	1870-05-10		A1
104	" "	34	SWNW	1870-05-10		A1
115	" "	18	S½SE	1870-06-01		A3 G174
105	" "	20	N½SE	1870-06-01		A3 G172
106	" "	20	SESW	1870-06-01		A3 G172
107	" "	20	SWSE	1870-06-01		A3 G172
108	" "	22	N½NE	1870-06-01		A3 G176
109	" "	22	N½NW	1870-06-01		A3 G176
100	" "	26	S½SE	1870-06-01		A3
101	" "	26	S½SW	1870-06-01		A3
110	" "	28	2	1870-06-01		A3 G177
111	" "	28	3	1870-06-01		A3 G177
112	" "	28	SESW	1870-06-01		A3 G177
113	" "	28	SWSE	1870-06-01		A3 G177 F
114	" "	30	W½NE	1870-06-01		A3 G173
99	" "	12	NWNW	1872-03-20		A1
95	MERRICK, E T	10	NE	1869-06-15		A3 G19
168	PARKER, Jonas	8	NE	1869-09-01		A3 G331
84	PETERSON, Charles	8	S½SE	1872-03-20		A1
85	" "	8	SESW	1872-03-20		A1
185	PETTIBONE, Roger	36	NESE	1876-01-20		A4
186	" "	36	SENE	1876-01-20		A4
116	PIKE, David	36	N½NE	1875-02-10		A4
133	POTTER, Henry C	12	SWSW	1872-08-30		A1 G221 C
134	" "	24	NENW	1872-08-30		A1 G221 F
132	" "	12	SESW	1883-08-13		A1 G221
122	REYNOLDS, Ezra B	36	E½NW	1875-08-20		A4
123	" "	36	E½SW	1875-08-20		A4
127	RIGGS, Clinton D	32	SW	1869-09-01		A3 G317 F
127	RIGGS, Mary Jane	32	SW	1869-09-01		A3 G317 F
95	RIPLEY, Joseph O	10	NE	1869-06-15		A3 G19
95	RIPLEY, Mercy J	10	NE	1869-06-15		A3 G19
142	ROUNDS, Mina	34	N½NE	1869-06-15		A3 G159
143	" "	34	SENW	1869-06-15		A3 G159
144	" "	34	SWNE	1869-06-15		A3 G159
108	ROWLAND, James A	22	N½NE	1870-06-01		A3 G176
109	" "	22	N½NW	1870-06-01		A3 G176
126	RYDER, Lurana	32	SE	1869-09-01		A3 G319 F
93	SLATER, John M	10	NESE	1869-09-01		A3 G20
94	" "	10	W½SE	1869-09-01		A3 G20
93	SMITH, Joseph B	10	NESE	1869-09-01		A3 G20
94	" "	10	W½SE	1869-09-01		A3 G20
117	SQUIER, David W	6	NENW	1867-01-10		A1 F
118	" "	6	W½NW	1867-01-10		A1 F
182	TOWER, Osmond S	22	SWSE	1871-02-01		A1
176	VAN WILTENBURG, MICHAEL	12	E½NE	1872-07-01		A1

ID	Individual in Patent	Sec.	Sec. Part	Date Issued	Other Counties	For More Info . . .
177	VAN WILTENBURG, MICHAEL (Cont'd)	12	NWNE	1872-07-01		A1
178	" "	18	NENE	1872-07-01		A1
179	" "	2	SWSE	1872-07-01		A1
180	" "	20	SENE	1872-07-01		A1 F
181	" "	28	SWNE	1872-07-01		A1
86	WARD, Charles T	2	NW	1875-05-10		A4 F
133	WEBBER, William L	12	SWSW	1872-08-30		A1 G221 C
134	" "	24	NENW	1872-08-30		A1 G221 F
132	" "	12	SESW	1883-08-13		A1 G221
166	WILLIAMS, Simeon	22	N½SW	1869-09-01		A3 G324
167	" "	22	S½NW	1869-09-01		A3 G324
131	WILSON, Gilbert F	34	S½SE	1871-11-15		A1
130	" "	32	N½NE	1872-08-30		A1
124	WILSON, Gilbert F D	30	SE	1869-09-01		A3
128	" "	30	SW	1869-09-01		A3 G316 F
129	" "	30	SWNW	1869-09-01		A3 G316 F
125	" "	32	NW	1869-09-01		A3 F
126	" "	32	SE	1869-09-01		A3 G319 F
127	" "	32	SW	1869-09-01		A3 G317 F
173	WOOD, John	8	N½SE	1869-11-30		A1
166	WOOD, John L	22	N½SW	1869-09-01		A3 G324
167	" "	22	S½NW	1869-09-01		A3 G324
163	" "	24	E½NE	1869-09-01		A3 G322
161	" "	24	E½SW	1869-09-01		A3 G329
169	" "	24	SE	1869-09-01		A3 G328
162	" "	24	SENW	1869-09-01		A3 G329
164	" "	24	SWNE	1869-09-01		A3 G322
159	" "	26	N½NE	1869-09-01		A3 G323
155	" "	26	N½SE	1869-09-01		A3
160	" "	26	NENW	1869-09-01		A3 G323
156	" "	26	S½NE	1869-09-01		A3
165	" "	4	SE	1869-09-01		A3 G330
168	" "	8	NE	1869-09-01		A3 G331
145	" "	20	1	1869-11-30		A1 F
146	" "	20	2	1869-11-30		A1 F
147	" "	20	3	1869-11-30		A1 F
148	" "	20	4	1869-11-30		A1 F
149	" "	20	6	1869-11-30		A1 F
150	" "	20	N½SW	1869-11-30		A1 F
151	" "	20	NWNW	1869-11-30		A1 F
152	" "	20	SENW	1869-11-30		A1 F
153	" "	20	W½SW	1869-11-30		A1 F
154	" "	24	NWNE	1869-11-30		A1 F
157	" "	28	1	1869-11-30		A1
158	" "	30	NENE	1869-11-30		A1
110	WOODBURY, Joseph B	28	2	1870-06-01		A3 G177
111	" "	28	3	1870-06-01		A3 G177
112	" "	28	SESW	1870-06-01		A3 G177
113	" "	28	SWSE	1870-06-01		A3 G177 F
170	WOODS, John L	28	E½NE	1869-09-01		A3
171	" "	28	NW	1869-09-01		A3
172	" "	28	NWNE	1869-09-01		A3

Patent Map

T16-N R13-W
Michigan-Toledo Strip Meridian

Map Group 2

Township Statistics

Parcels Mapped	:	118
Number of Patents	:	77
Number of Individuals	:	62
Patentees Identified	:	52
Number of Surnames	:	56
Multi-Patentee Parcels	:	38
Oldest Patent Date	:	1/10/1867
Most Recent Patent	:	9/27/1907
Block/Lot Parcels	:	8
Parcels Re - Issued	:	1
Parcels that Overlap	:	0
Cities and Towns	:	2
Cemeteries	:	0

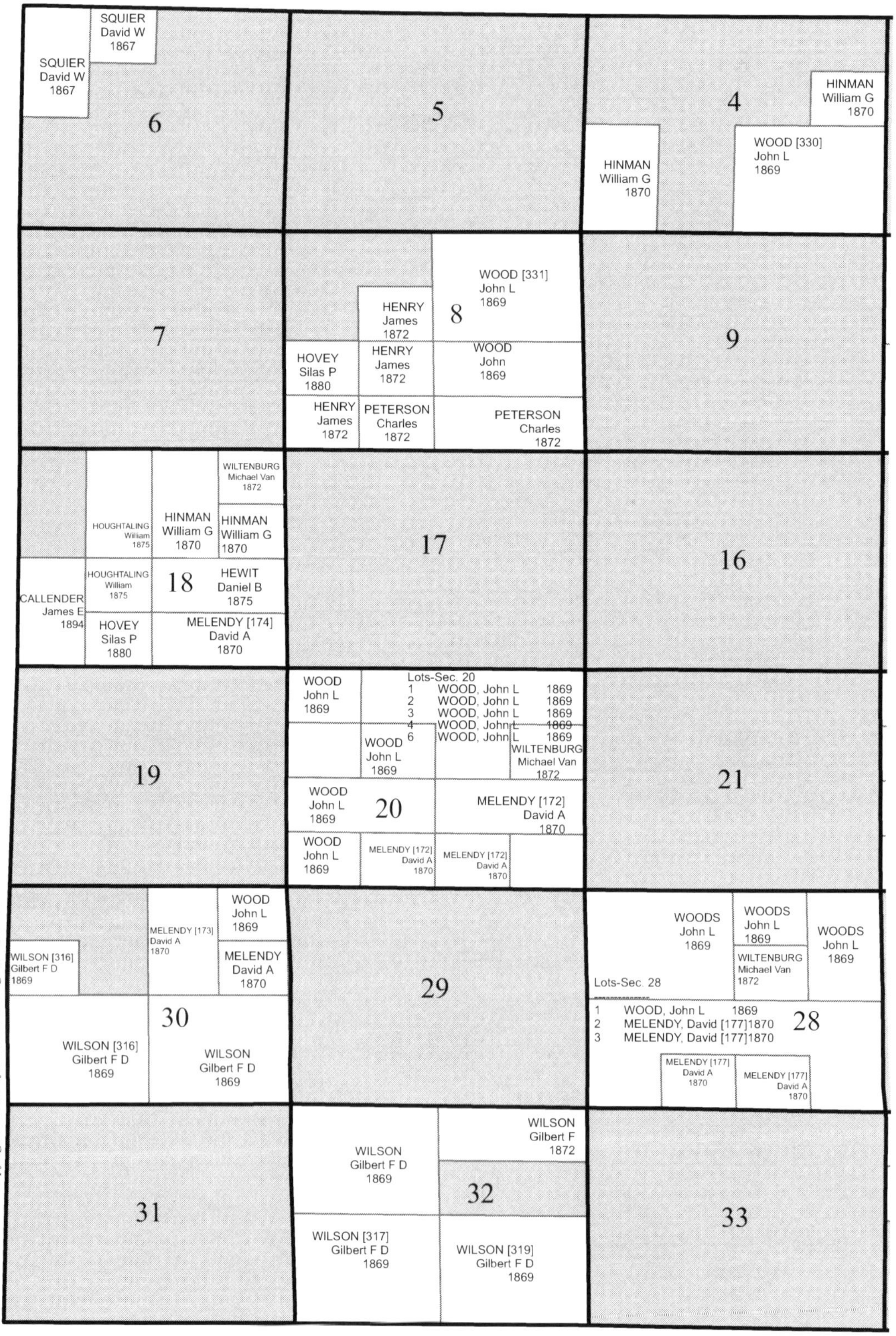

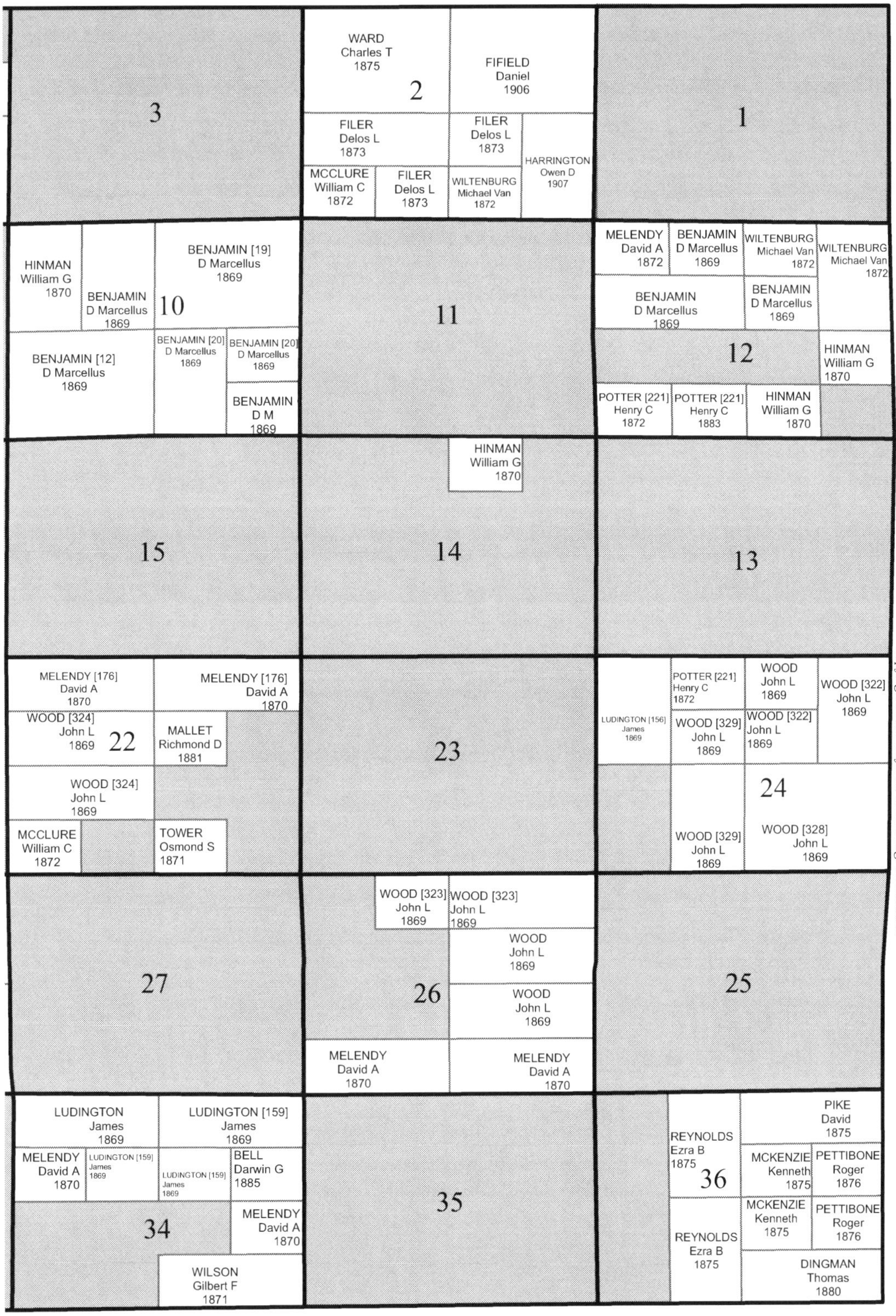

Helpful Hints

1. This Map's INDEX can be found on the preceding pages.
2. Refer to Map "C" to see where this Township lies within Newaygo County, Michigan.
3. Numbers within square brackets [ ] denote a multi-patentee land parcel (multi-owner). Refer to Appendix "C" for a full list of members in this group.
4. Areas that look to be crowded with Patentees usually indicate multiple sales of the same parcel (Re-issues) or Overlapping parcels. See this Township's Index for an explanation of these and other circumstances that might explain "odd" groupings of Patentees on this map.

Legend

Patent Boundary

Section Boundary

No Patents Found (or Outside County)

1., 2., 3., ... Lot Numbers (when beside a name)

[ ] Group Number (see Appendix "C")

Scale: Section = 1 mile X 1 mile (generally, with some exceptions)

Road Map

T16-N R13-W
Michigan-Toledo Strip Meridian

Map Group 2

Cities & Towns

Bitely
Lilley

Cemeteries

None

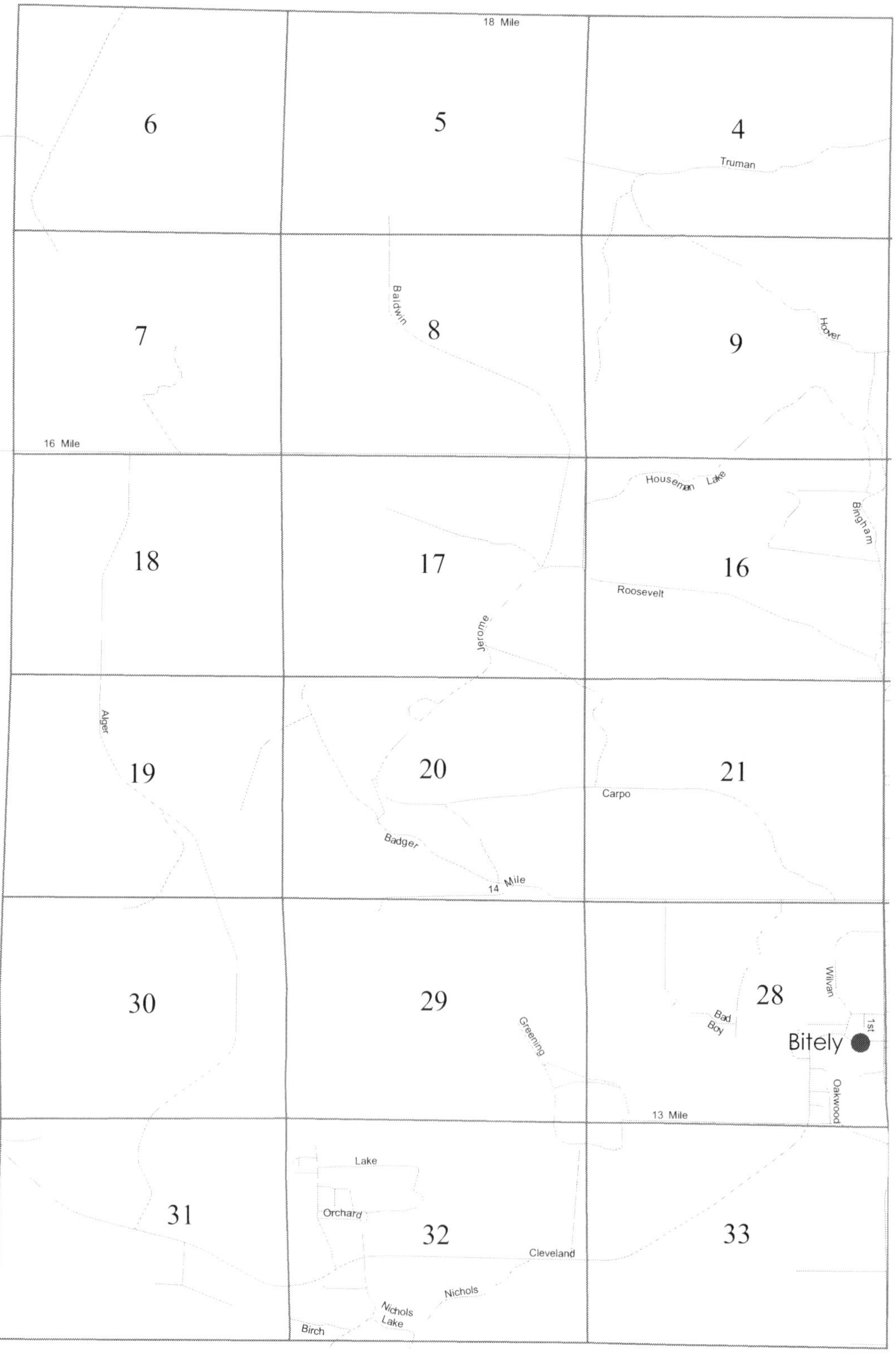

18 Mile
6
5
4
Truman
Baldwin
7
8
9
Hover
16 Mile
Houseman Lake
Bingham
18
17
16
Roosevelt
Jerome
Alger
19
20
21
Carpo
Badger
14 Mile
30
29
28
Wilvan
Greening
Bad Boy
1st
Bitely
Oakwood
13 Mile
Lake
Orchard
31
32
33
Cleveland
Nichols
Nichols Lake
Birch

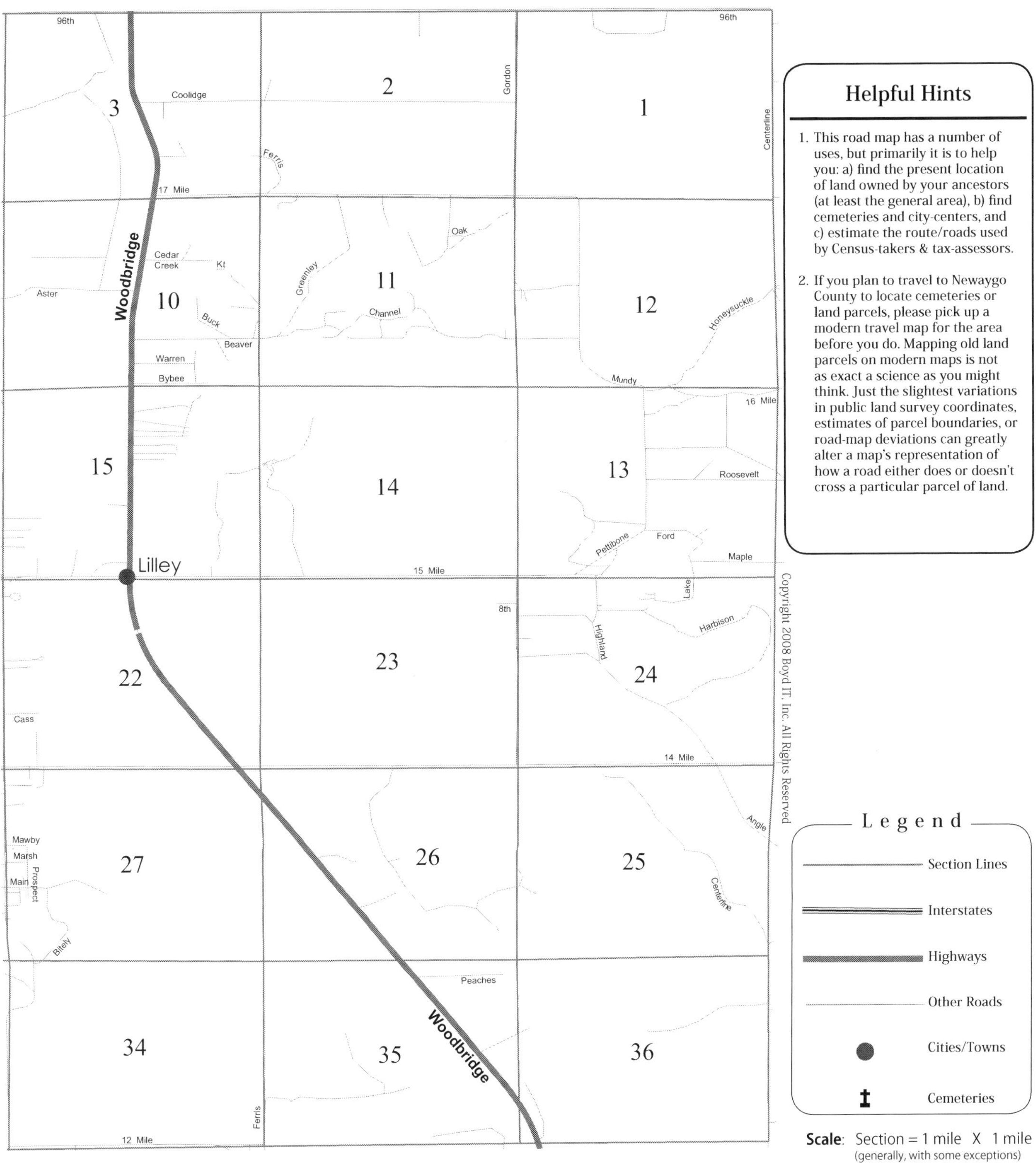
96th
Coolidge
3
2
Gordon
1
Centerline
Ferris
17 Mile
Oak
Woodbridge
Cedar Creek
Kt
Greenley
11
Aster
10
Channel
12
Honeysuckle
Buck
Beaver
Warren
Bybee
Mundy
16 Mile
15
14
13
Roosevelt
Ford
Pettibone
Maple
Lilley
15 Mile
Lake
8th
Harbison
Highland
23
22
24
Cass
14 Mile
Angle
Mawby
Marsh
Main
Prospect
27
26
25
Centerline
Bitely
Peaches
Woodbridge
34
35
36
Ferris
12 Mile
Copyright 2008 Boyd IT, Inc. All Rights Reserved
Helpful Hints
1. This road map has a number of uses, but primarily it is to help you: a) find the present location of land owned by your ancestors (at least the general area), b) find cemeteries and city-centers, and c) estimate the route/roads used by Census-takers & tax-assessors.
2. If you plan to travel to Newaygo County to locate cemeteries or land parcels, please pick up a modern travel map for the area before you do. Mapping old land parcels on modern maps is not as exact a science as you might think. Just the slightest variations in public land survey coordinates, estimates of parcel boundaries, or road-map deviations can greatly alter a map's representation of how a road either does or doesn't cross a particular parcel of land.
Legend
Section Lines
Interstates
Highways
Other Roads
Cities/Towns
Cemeteries
Scale: Section = 1 mile X 1 mile
(generally, with some exceptions)

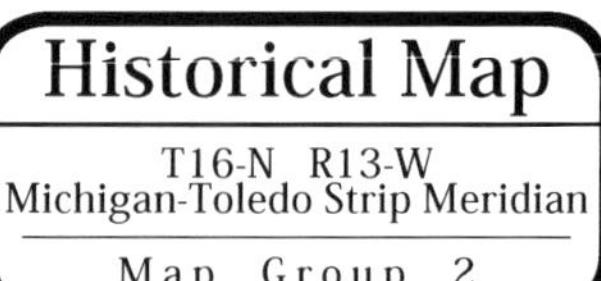

Cities & Towns

Bitely
Lilley

Cemeteries

None

6
5
4
7
8
9
Houseman Lake
Cedar Creek
18
17
16
Kenosha Lake
19
Pickeral Lake
20
Amoung Lake
21
Halfmoon Lake
Mawby Lake
30
29
28
Bitely
Walk Up Lake
Greening Lake
Musketeer Lake
31
Todd Lake
Bitely Lake
33
Walkup Lake
Nichols Lake
32
Jars Lake
Tank Creek

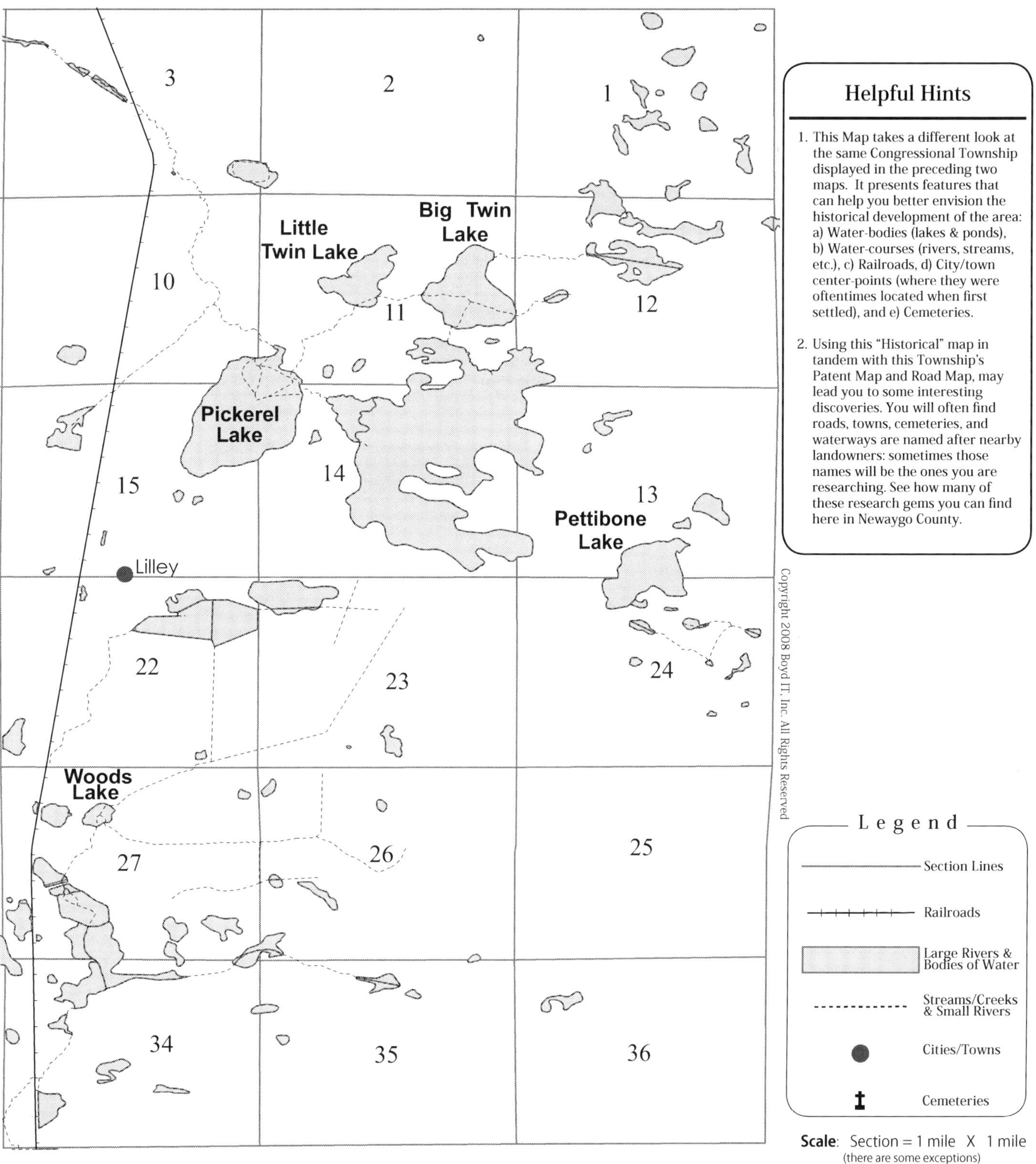

Helpful Hints

1. This Map takes a different look at the same Congressional Township displayed in the preceding two maps. It presents features that can help you better envision the historical development of the area: a) Water-bodies (lakes & ponds), b) Water-courses (rivers, streams, etc.), c) Railroads, d) City/town center-points (where they were oftentimes located when first settled), and e) Cemeteries.

2. Using this "Historical" map in tandem with this Township's Patent Map and Road Map, may lead you to some interesting discoveries. You will often find roads, towns, cemeteries, and waterways are named after nearby landowners: sometimes those names will be the ones you are researching. See how many of these research gems you can find here in Newaygo County.

Scale: Section = 1 mile X 1 mile
(there are some exceptions)

Map Group 3: Index to Land Patents

Township 16-North Range 12-West (Michigan-Toledo Strip)

After you locate an individual in this Index, take note of the Section and Section Part then proceed to the Land Patent map on the pages immediately following. You should have no difficulty locating the corresponding parcel of land.

The "For More Info" Column will lead you to more information about the underlying Patents. See the *Legend* at right, and the "How to Use this Book" chapter, for more information.

LEGEND

"For More Info . . . " column

A = Authority (Legislative Act, See Appendix "A")
B = Block or Lot (location in Section unknown)
C = Cancelled Patent
F = Fractional Section
G = Group (Multi-Patentee Patent, see Appendix "C")
V = Overlaps another Parcel
R = Re-Issued (Parcel patented more than once)

(A & G items require you to look in the Appendixes referred to above. All other Letter-designations followed by a number require you to locate line-items in this index that possess the ID number found after the letter).

ID	Individual in Patent	Sec.	Sec. Part	Date Issued	Other Counties	For More Info . . .
261	AGARD, Alexaniller	8	SW	1866-02-20		A3 G148 F
261	AGARD, Noah	8	SW	1866-02-20		A3 G148 F
296	ALEXANDER, Elizabeth	14	SE	1869-06-15		A3 G217
296	ALEXANDER, Robert C	14	SE	1869-06-15		A3 G217
221	ARNOLD, Nancy	8	E½SE	1869-07-01		A3 G8 C F R257
261	BAILEY, Gilbert D	8	SW	1866-02-20		A3 G148 F
261	BALEY, Arma M	8	SW	1866-02-20		A3 G148 F
230	BEATON, Duncan	36	S½SW	1875-02-10		A4
215	BENJAMIN, D M	20	NENW	1970-10-29		A3
217	BENJAMIN, D Marcellus	20	N½NW	1869-07-01		A3 G17 C
218	" "	20	S½NE	1869-07-01		A3 G17
221	" "	8	E½SE	1869-07-01		A3 G8 C F R257
219	" "	8	NWNE	1869-07-01		A3 G9 F
220	" "	8	S½NE	1869-07-01		A3 G9 F
222	" "	14	N½NW	1870-06-01		A3 G18
216	" "	14	NE	1870-06-01		A3 G11
223	" "	14	SENW	1870-06-01		A3 G18
258	BLANCHARD, Irena	18	NW	1867-02-01		A3 G150 F
214	BRITTON, Christopher H	24	E½SW	1873-06-10		A4
298	BUSHNELL, William	10	SESW	1869-06-15		A3 G218 F
299	" "	10	W½SE	1869-06-15		A3 G218 F
300	" "	4	N½SE	1869-06-15		A3 G218 F
301	" "	4	SWSE	1869-06-15		A3 G218 F
243	CHADWICK, Rachel	2	S½SE	1870-02-18		A3 G108
244	" "	2	S½SW	1870-02-18		A3 G108
282	CHAPMAN, Justus	36	N½SE	1873-06-10		A4
219	CHARLES, James	8	NWNE	1869-07-01		A3 G9 F
220	" "	8	S½NE	1869-07-01		A3 G9 F
278	CHILDS, Joshua G	26	W½SE	1877-04-05		A4 F
204	CONKLIN, Catharine	24	W½SW	1884-05-10		A4 G37
235	CONKLIN, Frank	26	W½NW	1884-05-10		A4 G38 F
204	CONKLIN, George	24	W½SW	1884-05-10		A4 G37
235	CONKLIN, Thomas	26	W½NW	1884-05-10		A4 G38 F
235	CONKLIN, Walter	26	W½NW	1884-05-10		A4 G38 F
312	CONKLIN, William H	26	S½NE	1877-04-05		A4
279	COOK, Josiah M	12	NENE	1868-02-15		A1 F
281	" "	12	NWNE	1869-09-10		A1 G45 F
280	" "	12	SENE	1870-05-02		A1 G46 F
241	CRITTENDON, Israel L	2	N½NE	1870-02-18		A3 G110 F
239	" "	2	N½SE	1870-02-18		A3 G109
242	" "	2	NENW	1870-02-18		A3 G110 F
240	" "	2	S½NE	1870-02-18		A3 G109
243	" "	2	S½SE	1870-02-18		A3 G108
244	" "	2	S½SW	1870-02-18		A3 G108
293	CUMMINGS, Norman	4	E½NW	1872-07-01		A1 F
294	" "	4	NESW	1872-07-01		A1

ID	Individual in Patent	Sec.	Sec. Part	Date Issued	Other Counties	For More Info . . .
251	DEARTH, Jacob	2	NESW	1874-08-01		A4
252	" "	2	S½NW	1874-08-01		A4
276	DEVER, Joseph M	6	S½NE	1869-09-01		A3 G327 F
277	" "	6	SENW	1869-09-01		A3 G327 F
276	DEVER, Rebecca F	6	S½NE	1869-09-01		A3 G327 F
277	" "	6	SENW	1869-09-01		A3 G327 F
216	DOANE, Clarissa	14	NE	1870-06-01		A3 G11
224	DOVE, Daniel G	30	E½SW	1875-02-10		A4
225	" "	30	N½SE	1875-02-10		A4
233	ELWELL, Elias	36	N½SW	1873-02-10		A4
302	ELWELL, Orlando C	24	E½NW	1878-06-13		A4
265	FINCH, John	36	W½NW	1872-04-05		A4
239	FRY, Ellen	2	N½SE	1870-02-18		A3 G109
240	" "	2	S½NE	1870-02-18		A3 G109
276	GLAZE, Sarah S	6	S½NE	1869-09-01		A3 G327 F
277	" "	6	SENW	1869-09-01		A3 G327 F
297	GRANADE, John A	14	S½SW	1869-06-15		A3 G219
297	GRANADE, William	14	S½SW	1869-06-15		A3 G219
297	HALL, Mary	14	S½SW	1869-06-15		A3 G219
286	HALL, Mary E	26	NESW	1874-08-01		A4 G76
287	" "	26	SENW	1874-08-01		A4 G76
276	HARNESS, James P	6	S½NE	1869-09-01		A3 G327 F
277	" "	6	SENW	1869-09-01		A3 G327 F
276	HARNESS, Susan E	6	S½NE	1869-09-01		A3 G327 F
277	" "	6	SENW	1869-09-01		A3 G327 F
266	HEMSWORTH, John	20	S½SE	1874-08-01		A4
212	HILLS, Charles T	4	SWSW	1872-03-20		A1 F
213	" "	8	NENE	1872-03-20		A1 F
311	HINMAN, William G	30	SWSW	1874-03-10		A1 F
306	HOVEY, Silas P	4	SESE	1873-05-15		A1 F
305	" "	30	NW	1885-01-07		A1 F
236	HUGHES, Frank	6	NESE	1877-04-25		A4
237	" "	6	NESW	1877-04-25		A4
238	" "	6	W½SE	1877-04-25		A4
248	INMAN, Ira A	24	N½NE	1879-11-25		A4
249	INMAN, Isaiah	36	W½NE	1873-02-10		A4
308	INMAN, Truman R	36	E½NE	1872-09-20		A4
291	JACKSON, Milton	36	E½NW	1872-09-20		A4
281	JOHNSON, Harley M	12	NWNE	1869-09-10		A1 G45 F
241	" "	2	N½NE	1870-02-18		A3 G110 F
239	" "	2	N½SE	1870-02-18		A3 G109
242	" "	2	NENW	1870-02-18		A3 G110 F
240	" "	2	S½NE	1870-02-18		A3 G109
243	" "	2	S½SE	1870-02-18		A3 G108
244	" "	2	S½SW	1870-02-18		A3 G108
259	KENNEDY, James	12	NW	1866-02-20		A3 G154 F
259	KING, Mary	12	NW	1866-02-20		A3 G154 F
286	KITCHEN, James	26	NESW	1874-08-01		A4 G76
287	" "	26	SENW	1874-08-01		A4 G76
296	LANE, Abraham	14	SE	1869-06-15		A3 G217
296	LANE, William E	14	SE	1869-06-15		A3 G217
259	LUDINGTON, James	12	NW	1866-02-20		A3 G154 F
263	" "	12	SW	1866-02-20		A3 G162 F
260	" "	18	NE	1866-02-20		A3 G161 F
262	" "	18	SE	1866-02-20		A3 G160
261	" "	8	SW	1866-02-20		A3 G148 F
254	" "	20	NWNW	1867-01-10		A1
255	" "	20	NWSE	1867-01-10		A1
256	" "	20	SENW	1867-01-10		A1
257	" "	8	E½SE	1867-01-10		A1 F R221
258	" "	18	NW	1867-02-01		A3 G150 F
264	" "	18	SW	1867-02-01		A3 G163 F
253	" "	2	NWNW	1869-09-10		A1 F
303	MALLET, Richmond D	30	NWSW	1881-10-19		A1 F
313	MCKENZIE, William	30	S½NE	1876-08-15		A4
226	MELENDY, David A	2	NWSW	1870-05-10		A1
227	" "	4	SESW	1870-05-10		A1
228	" "	6	SESE	1870-05-10		A1
229	" "	8	W½NW	1870-05-10		A1
217	MERRICK, Elliott T	20	N½NW	1869-07-01		A3 G17 C
218	" "	20	S½NE	1869-07-01		A3 G17
264	MITCHELL, David T	18	SW	1867-02-01		A3 G163 F
231	MONROE, Edwin	24	S½NE	1879-11-25		A4

ID	Individual in Patent	Sec.	Sec. Part	Date Issued	Other Counties	For More Info . . .
234	MONROE, Eugene	26	NENW	1881-05-03		A4
222	PATEN, William	14	N½NW	1870-06-01		A3 G18
223	" "	14	SENW	1870-06-01		A3 G18
208	PETERSON, Charles	20	NENE	1872-03-20		A1
209	" "	20	NESE	1872-03-20		A1
210	" "	4	NWSW	1872-03-20		A1 F
211	" "	4	W½NW	1872-03-20		A1
232	PETTIBONE, Edwin	26	E½SE	1873-02-10		A4
298	PILLSBURY, Oliver P	10	SESW	1869-06-15		A3 G218 F
299	" "	10	W½SE	1869-06-15		A3 G218 F
297	" "	14	S½SW	1869-06-15		A3 G219
296	" "	14	SE	1869-06-15		A3 G217
300	" "	4	N½SE	1869-06-15		A3 G218 F
301	" "	4	SWSE	1869-06-15		A3 G218 F
295	" "	10	NWSW	1869-09-10		A1 F
245	POTTER, Henry C	12	NWSE	1872-08-30		A1 G221 F
246	" "	12	SWNE	1872-08-30		A1 G221 F
241	PRESTON, David	2	N½NE	1870-02-18		A3 G110 F
242	" "	2	NENW	1870-02-18		A3 G110 F
205	RICE, Catherine	10	SWSW	1868-02-15		A1 F
206	" "	14	N½SW	1868-05-15		A3
207	" "	14	SWNW	1868-05-15		A3
203	RICHARDSON, Austin	12	NESE	1870-08-10		A1 G226 F
203	RICHARDSON, James C	12	NESE	1870-08-10		A1 G226 F
250	ROBINSON, Issacher N	6	NWNW	1872-07-01		A1 F
247	ROBISON, Henry M	22	E½SE	1877-03-01		A4
304	ROOT, Samuel	22	NE	1875-10-20		A4
262	SAWYER, Polly L	18	SE	1866-02-20		A3 G160
280	SMITH, Canton	12	SENE	1870-05-02		A1 G46 F
241	SOEVYN, John	2	N½NE	1870-02-18		A3 G110 F
242	" "	2	NENW	1870-02-18		A3 G110 F
292	SOPER, Mortimer	24	W½NW	1884-12-20		A4
307	SPAULDING, Silas	36	S½SE	1875-10-20		A4
260	TARR, Mary	18	NE	1866-02-20		A3 G161 F
276	THOMPSON, Albert C	6	S½NE	1869-09-01		A3 G327 F
277	" "	6	SENW	1869-09-01		A3 G327 F
261	TICHENOR, Sarah L A	8	SW	1866-02-20		A3 G148 F
283	TUCK, George F	32	E½SE	1904-09-16		A4 G293
284	" "	32	SENE	1904-09-16		A4 G293
283	TUCK, Lizzie M	32	E½SE	1904-09-16		A4 G293
284	" "	32	SENE	1904-09-16		A4 G293
288	VAN WILTENBURG, MICHAEL	20	E½SW	1872-07-01		A1
289	" "	20	SWNW	1872-07-01		A1
290	" "	30	N½NE	1872-07-01		A1
263	WAKE,	12	SW	1866-02-20		A3 G162 F
245	WEBBER, William L	12	NWSE	1872-08-30		A1 G221 F
246	" "	12	SWNE	1872-08-30		A1 G221 F
264	WEDD, William	18	SW	1867-02-01		A3 G163 F
202	WHIPPLE, Amos W	22	W½SE	1876-06-30		A4
285	WHIPPLE, Luther	24	N½SE	1875-08-20		A4
309	WHIPPLE, W H	26	N½NE	1874-08-01		A4
310	WHIPPLE, Walter L	12	S½SE	1876-01-05		A4 F
314	WHIPPLE, William	24	S½SE	1876-06-30		A4
259	WILLIAMS, Josephine	12	NW	1866-02-20		A3 G154 F
270	WOOD, John L	29	W½SW	1869-09-01		A3 C
276	" "	6	S½NE	1869-09-01		A3 G327 F
277	" "	6	SENW	1869-09-01		A3 G327 F
272	" "	4	SENE	1869-11-30		A1 F
273	" "	6	N½NE	1869-11-30		A1 F
274	" "	6	NENW	1869-11-30		A1 F
275	" "	8	E½NW	1869-11-30		A1 F
267	" "	10	N	1870-05-02		A1 F
268	" "	10	NESW	1870-05-02		A1 F
271	" "	34	SWNW	1870-05-02		A1
269	" "	20	W½SW	1870-09-10		A3

Patent Map

T16-N R12-W
Michigan-Toledo Strip Meridian

Map Group 3

Township Statistics

Parcels Mapped	:	113
Number of Patents	:	89
Number of Individuals	:	98
Patentees Identified	:	71
Number of Surnames	:	75
Multi-Patentee Parcels	:	40
Oldest Patent Date	:	2/20/1866
Most Recent Patent	:	10/29/1970
Block/Lot Parcels	:	1
Parcels Re - Issued	:	1
Parcels that Overlap	:	0
Cities and Towns	:	0
Cemeteries	:	2

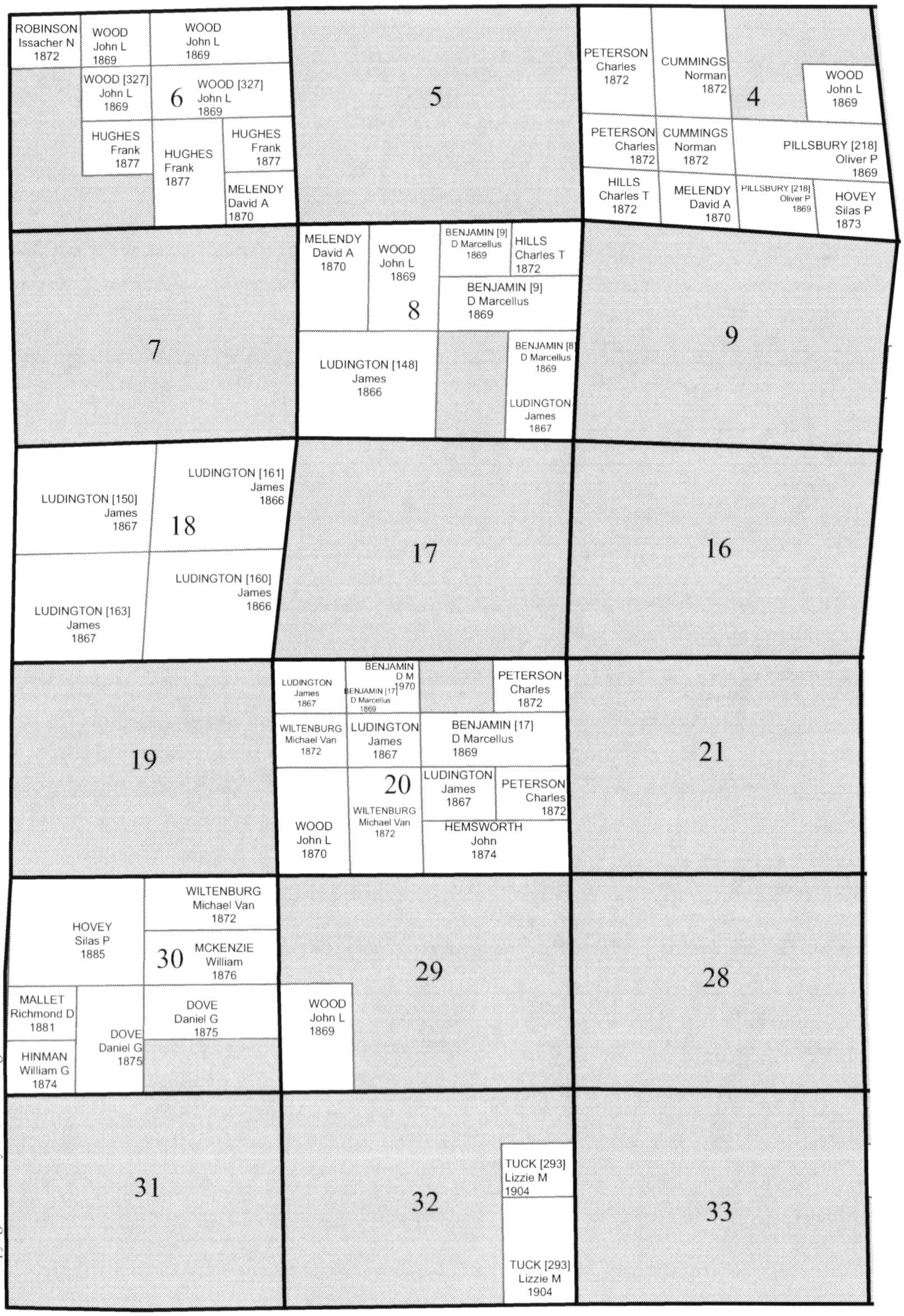

3

LUDINGTON James 1869
JOHNSON [110] Harley M 1870
JOHNSON [110] Harley M 1870
DEARTH Jacob 1874
2
JOHNSON [109] Harley M 1870
MELENDY David A 1870
DEARTH Jacob 1874
JOHNSON [109] Harley M 1870
JOHNSON [108] Harley M 1870
JOHNSON [108] Harley M 1870

1

Lots-Sec. 10
N WOOD, John L 1870
10
PILLSBURY Oliver P 1869
WOOD John L 1870
RICE Catherine 1868
PILLSBURY [218] Oliver P 1869
PILLSBURY [218] Oliver P 1869

11

COOK [45] Josiah M 1869
COOK Josiah M 1868
LUDINGTON [154] James 1866
POTTER [221] Henry C 1872
COOK [46] Josiah M 1870
12
POTTER [221] Henry C 1872
RICHARDSON [226] Austin 1870
LUDINGTON [162] James 1866
WHIPPLE Walter L 1876

15

BENJAMIN [18] D Marcellus 1870
BENJAMIN [11] D Marcellus 1870
RICE Catherine 1868
BENJAMIN [18] D Marcellus 1870
RICE Catherine 1868
14
PILLSBURY [217] Oliver P 1869
PILLSBURY [219] Oliver P 1869

13

ROOT Samuel 1875
22
WHIPPLE Amos W 1876
ROBISON Henry M 1877

23

SOPER Mortimer 1884
ELWELL Orlando C 1878
INMAN Ira A 1879
24
MONROE Edwin 1879
BRITTON Christopher H 1873
WHIPPLE Luther 1875
CONKLIN [37] Catharine 1884
WHIPPLE William 1876

27

MONROE Eugene 1881
WHIPPLE W H 1874
CONKLIN [38] Frank 1884
HALL [76] Mary E 1874
CONKLIN William H 1877
HALL [76] Mary E 1874
26
CHILDS Joshua G 1877
PETTIBONE Edwin 1873

25

WOOD John L 1870
34

35

FINCH John 1872
JACKSON Milton 1872
INMAN Isaiah 1873
INMAN Truman R 1872
ELWELL Elias 1873
36
CHAPMAN Justus 1873
BEATON Duncan 1875
SPAULDING Silas 1875

Helpful Hints

1. This Map's INDEX can be found on the preceding pages.
2. Refer to Map "C" to see where this Township lies within Newaygo County, Michigan.
3. Numbers within square brackets [ ] denote a multi-patentee land parcel (multi-owner). Refer to Appendix "C" for a full list of members in this group.
4. Areas that look to be crowded with Patentees usually indicate multiple sales of the same parcel (Re-issues) or Overlapping parcels. See this Township's Index for an explanation of these and other circumstances that might explain "odd" groupings of Patentees on this map.

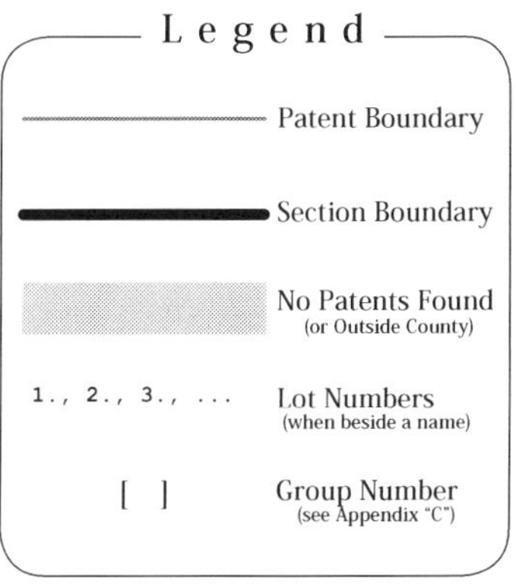

Scale: Section = 1 mile X 1 mile
(generally, with some exceptions)

Road Map

T16-N R12-W
Michigan-Toledo Strip Meridian

Map Group 3

Cities & Towns

None

Cemeteries

Curtice Cemetery
Whipple Cemetery

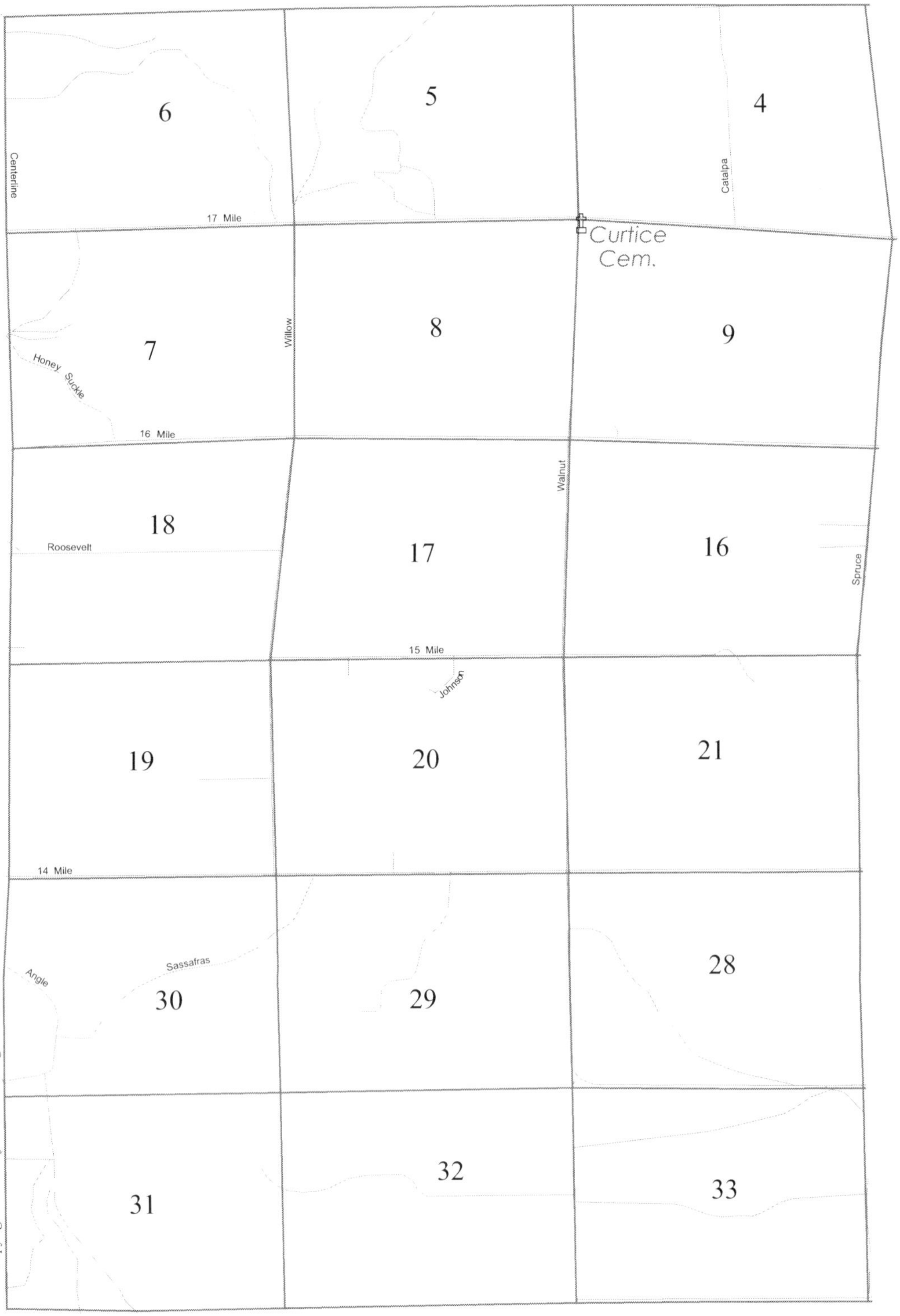

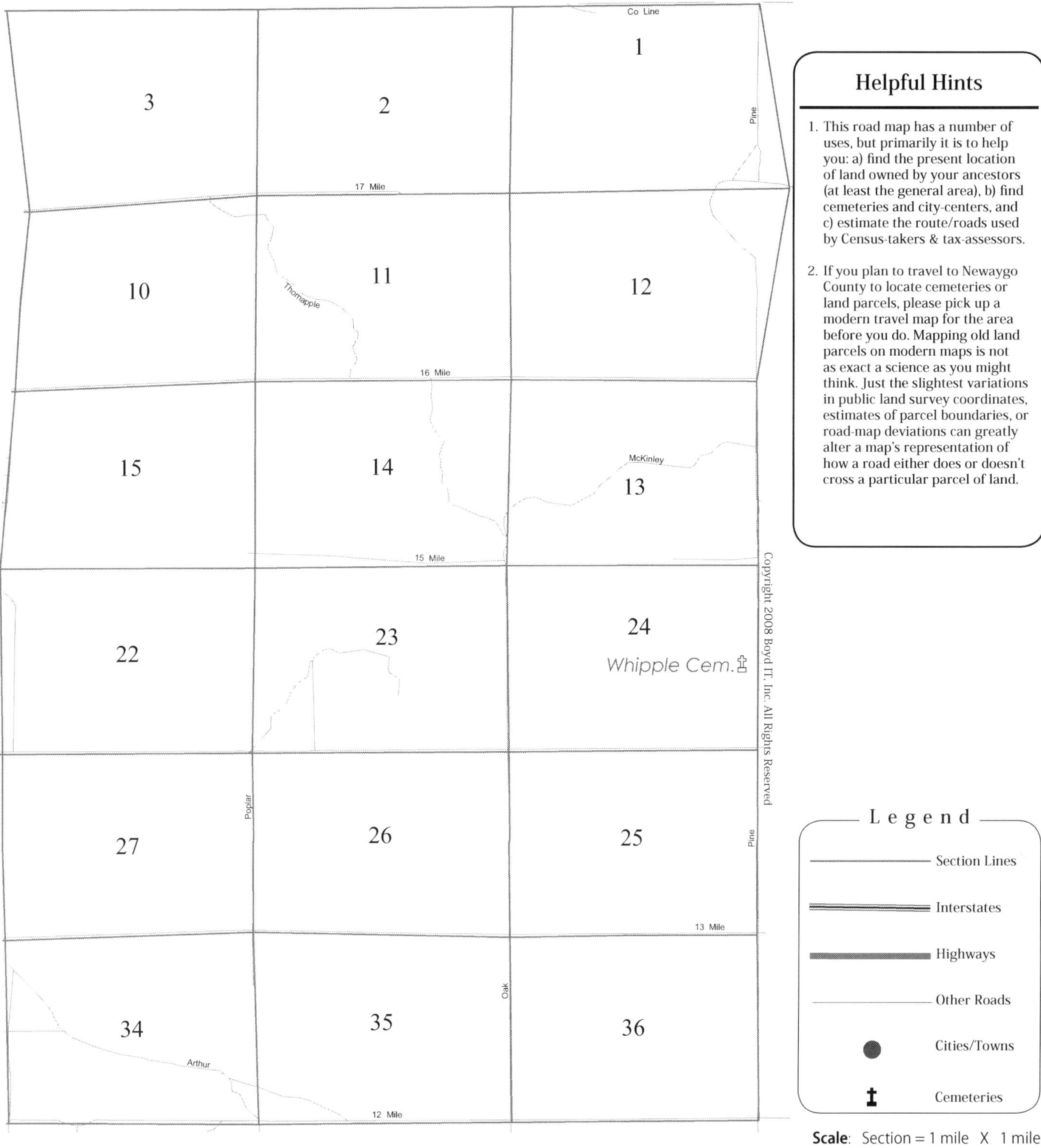

Helpful Hints

1. This road map has a number of uses, but primarily it is to help you: a) find the present location of land owned by your ancestors (at least the general area), b) find cemeteries and city-centers, and c) estimate the route/roads used by Census-takers & tax-assessors.
2. If you plan to travel to Newaygo County to locate cemeteries or land parcels, please pick up a modern travel map for the area before you do. Mapping old land parcels on modern maps is not as exact a science as you might think. Just the slightest variations in public land survey coordinates, estimates of parcel boundaries, or road-map deviations can greatly alter a map's representation of how a road either does or doesn't cross a particular parcel of land.

Scale: Section = 1 mile X 1 mile
(generally, with some exceptions)

Historical Map

T16-N R12-W
Michigan-Toledo Strip Meridian

Map Group 3

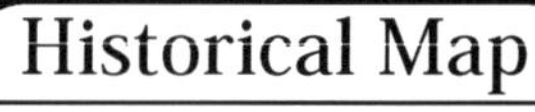

Cities & Towns

None

Cemeteries

Curtice Cemetery
Whipple Cemetery

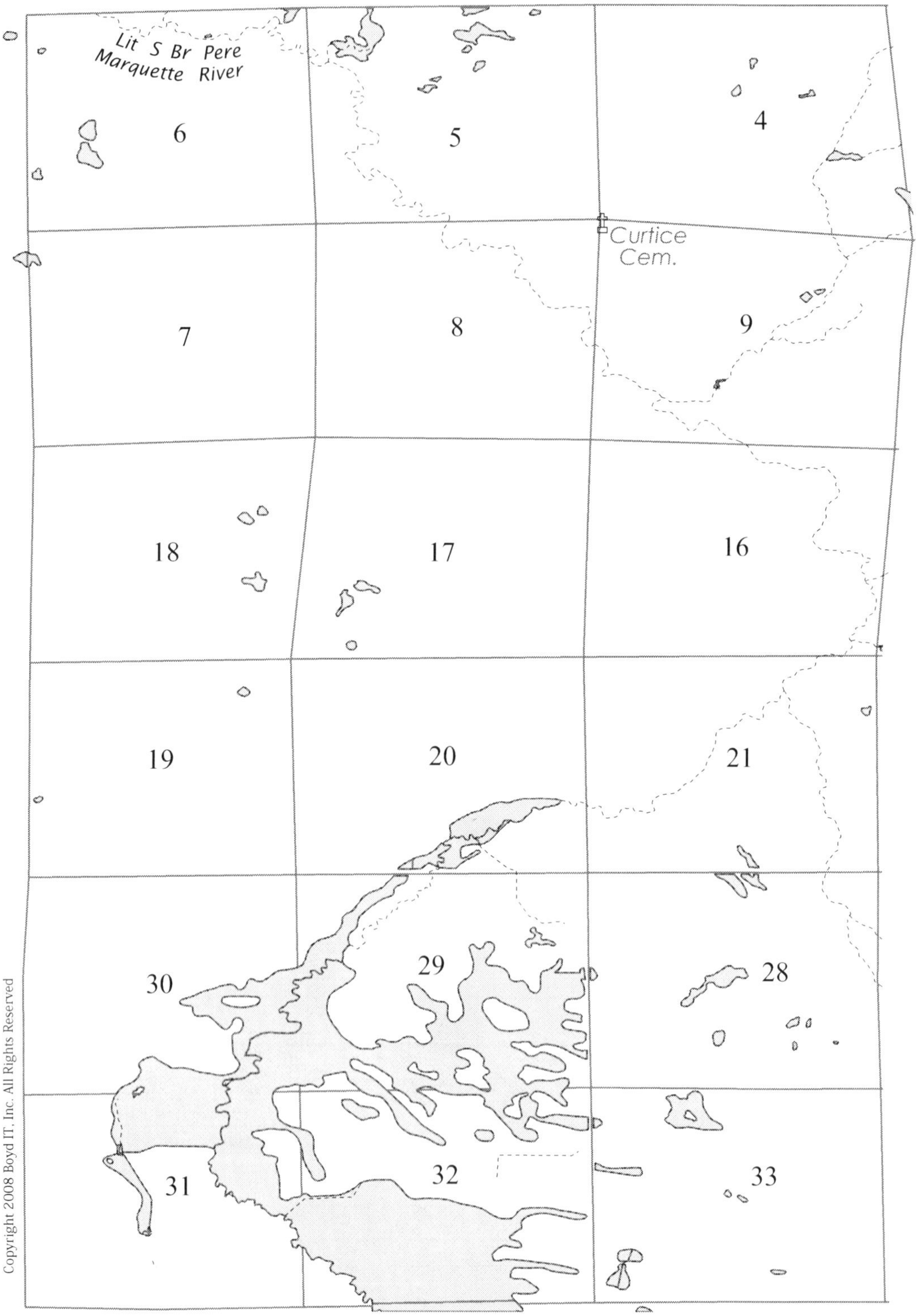

Lit S Br Pere Marquette River
6
5
4
Curtice Cem.
7
8
9
18
17
16
19
20
21
30
29
28
31
32
33

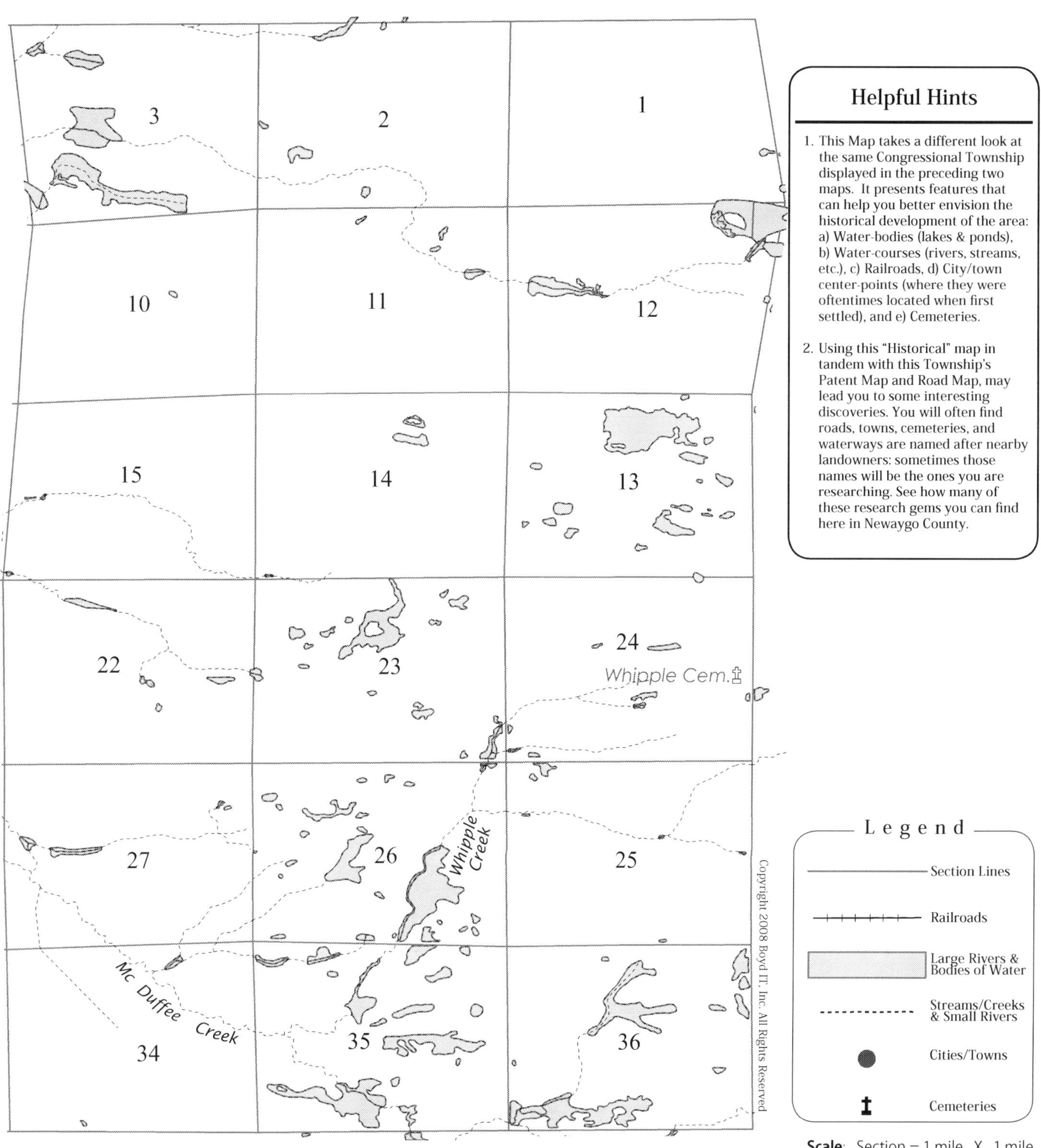

Helpful Hints

1. This Map takes a different look at the same Congressional Township displayed in the preceding two maps. It presents features that can help you better envision the historical development of the area: a) Water-bodies (lakes & ponds), b) Water-courses (rivers, streams, etc.), c) Railroads, d) City/town center-points (where they were oftentimes located when first settled), and e) Cemeteries.

2. Using this "Historical" map in tandem with this Township's Patent Map and Road Map, may lead you to some interesting discoveries. You will often find roads, towns, cemeteries, and waterways are named after nearby landowners: sometimes those names will be the ones you are researching. See how many of these research gems you can find here in Newaygo County.

Scale: Section = 1 mile X 1 mile
(there are some exceptions)

Map Group 4: Index to Land Patents

Township 16-North Range 11-West (Michigan-Toledo Strip)

After you locate an individual in this Index, take note of the Section and Section Part then proceed to the Land Patent map on the pages immediately following. You should have no difficulty locating the corresponding parcel of land.

The "For More Info" Column will lead you to more information about the underlying Patents. See the *Legend* at right, and the "How to Use this Book" chapter, for more information.

LEGEND

"For More Info . . . " column

A = Authority (Legislative Act, See Appendix "A")
B = Block or Lot (location in Section unknown)
C = Cancelled Patent
F = Fractional Section
G = Group (Multi-Patentee Patent, see Appendix "C")
V = Overlaps another Parcel
R = Re-Issued (Parcel patented more than once)

(A & G items require you to look in the Appendixes referred to above. All other Letter-designations followed by a number require you to locate line-items in this index that possess the ID number found after the letter).

ID	Individual in Patent	Sec.	Sec. Part	Date Issued	Other Counties	For More Info . . .
429	AITKEN, James	10	W½SW	1872-04-05		A1 F
340	BADGEROW, Clarissa	6	NWNW	1878-06-13		A4 F
404	BARB, Ruth	32	SWNE	1859-08-03		A3 G122
405	" "	32	W½SE	1859-08-03		A3 G122
337	BARSTOW, Charles R	10	NWSE	1870-08-10		A1 F
336	" "	10	E½SW	1872-04-05		A1 F
478	BARTON, Samuel	32	S½NW	1884-12-20		A4
342	BENJAMIN, D Marcellus	18	SW	1870-06-01		A3 G10 F
496	BEVIER, William N	2	N½NW	1869-11-01		A4 F
367	BLACK, Franklin	12	NE	1857-02-20		A3
473	BLACK, Peter	1	NWNE	1858-05-01		A1 F
472	" "	1	NENE	1859-08-10		A3 F
474	" "	1	S½NE	1859-08-10		A3 F
492	BLISS, William C	2	W½NE	1869-11-01		A4 F
479	BOWER, Samuel	20	W½SW	1880-11-20		A4 F
315	BOWMAN, Absalom A	4	W½SE	1877-06-15		A4
421	BUZZLE, Gilbert	20	N½NW	1880-07-23		A4
329	CASE, Lucena	13	SESW	1859-08-10		A3 G169
330	" "	13	W½SW	1859-08-10		A3 G169
475	CHAPIN, Richard B	2	E½NE	1869-11-01		A4 F
342	CHASE, Tryphena	18	SW	1870-06-01		A3 G10 F
463	CHILD, Nathan	12	SE	1857-02-20		A3
443	COLE, John J	30	S½NW	1872-04-05		A4 F
460	CONLEY, Mary	6	E½NW	1875-11-10		A4 F
341	COOK, Cornelius	2	N½SW	1872-09-20		A4
362	COOK, Ezra J	12	SESW	1859-08-10		A3
363	" "	12	W½SW	1859-08-10		A3
355	COUNTRIMAN, Edward	18	E½SE	1880-12-10		A4 F
357	CRUM, Eli H	12	NESW	1871-11-01		A4 F
465	CUMINGS, Norman	6	SWNW	1870-07-15		A1 F
426	DAVENPORT, Henry	22	N½NE	1873-05-15		A1 F
437	DAVENPORT, Jesse L	14	N½SW	1877-11-20		A4 F
493	DAVENPORT, William	14	NE	1858-05-01		A1
458	DAVIS, Marion	10	E½NW	1872-09-20		A4
459	DAVIS, Martin	8	SWNE	1890-09-03		A4
464	DAVIS, Nathan	10	W½NW	1873-04-10		A4
491	DAVIS, Warren	4	E½SE	1873-04-10		A4
360	DECKER, Eugene	28	W½SW	1871-05-01		A4 F
433	DELAHOUSSAYE, Gustave	8	N½NW	1871-02-20		A3 G155
434	" "	8	NWNE	1871-02-20		A3 G155
358	DIRSTEIN, Elias	13	SE	1855-12-15		A1
359	" "	24	NE	1855-12-15		A1
438	DOCHERTY, John	32	N½NE	1875-02-10		A4
494	DUBOIS, William H	10	E½NE	1871-11-01		A4
430	DUFFY, James	20	S½SE	1873-05-20		A4 F
327	DUTCHER, Benjamin F	24	N½SE	1873-02-10		A4

ID	Individual in Patent	Sec.	Sec. Part	Date Issued	Other Counties	For More Info . . .
433	ELMS, George O	8	N½NW	1871-02-20		A3 G155
434	" "	8	NWNE	1871-02-20		A3 G155
364	FURRY, Francis	4	E½SW	1874-06-15		A4
365	" "	4	NWSW	1874-06-15		A4 F
366	" "	4	SWNW	1874-06-15		A4 F
486	GARD, Squire	6	E½NE	1874-08-01		A4 F
440	GILL, John	12	NENW	1858-01-15		A3
441	" "	12	W½NW	1858-01-15		A3
392	GILLILAND, Elizabeth	33	S½SW	1859-08-03		A3 G127
393	" "	33	SWSE	1859-08-03		A3 G127
431	GREENFIELD, James F	20	N½NE	1876-03-20		A4
442	GREENFIELD, John	20	N½SE	1872-09-20		A4
419	HALL, George P	28	E½NE	1871-05-01		A4 F
316	HAMILTON, Addison R	14	NWSE	1858-01-15		A3
317	" "	14	S½SE	1858-01-15		A3
318	" "	23	NENE	1858-01-15		A3
319	" "	24	N½NW	1858-01-15		A3
320	" "	24	S½NW	1858-05-01		A1
321	" "	23	NWNE	1860-10-01		A3 G80
322	" "	23	S½NE	1860-10-01		A3 G80
477	HANCOCK, Russell F	32	N½SW	1875-10-20		A4
457	HAWKINS, Maria	2	S½NW	1870-05-02		A4
428	HAYWOOD, Isaac	8	S½NW	1877-06-15		A4
484	HEALD, Horatio N	22	E½SE	1858-05-01		A1 G314
480	" "	10	SWSE	1859-08-10		A3 G313
481	" "	15	N½NE	1859-08-10		A3 G313
482	" "	23	W½NW	1859-08-10		A3 G313
483	" "	23	W½SW	1859-08-10		A3 G313
420	HEATH, George W	28	E½NW	1876-12-30		A4 F
334	HIGBE, Charles	13	S½NE	1858-05-01		A1
332	" "	1	NESW	1859-08-10		A3
333	" "	1	W½SW	1859-08-10		A3
361	HOLE, Even B	14	S½SW	1878-06-13		A4 F
390	IVES, Chauncey P	32	E½SE	1859-08-03		A3 G140
391	" "	32	SENE	1859-08-03		A3 G140
404	" "	32	SWNE	1859-08-03		A3 G122
405	" "	32	W½SE	1859-08-03		A3 G122
380	" "	33	E½SE	1859-08-03		A3 G121
394	" "	33	N½NW	1859-08-03		A3 G137
381	" "	33	N½SW	1859-08-03		A3 G121
396	" "	33	NENE	1859-08-03		A3 G132
395	" "	33	NWNE	1859-08-03		A3 G137
382	" "	33	NWSE	1859-08-03		A3 G121
402	" "	33	S½NW	1859-08-03		A3 G133
392	" "	33	S½SW	1859-08-03		A3 G127
383	" "	33	SENE	1859-08-03		A3 G121
403	" "	33	SWNE	1859-08-03		A3 G133
393	" "	33	SWSE	1859-08-03		A3 G127
406	" "	34	E½NW	1859-08-03		A3 G134
407	" "	34	NESW	1859-08-03		A3 G134
384	" "	34	SENE	1859-08-03		A3 G121
385	" "	34	SESW	1859-08-03		A3 G121
386	" "	34	W½NE	1859-08-03		A3 G121
397	" "	34	W½NW	1859-08-03		A3 G132
387	" "	34	W½SW	1859-08-03		A3 G121
388	" "	36	NESW	1859-08-03		A3 G121
389	" "	36	S½NW	1859-08-03		A3 G121
400	" "	36	S½SE	1859-08-03		A3 G131
401	" "	36	SESW	1859-08-03		A3 G131
398	" "	26	E½SW	1859-08-10		A3 G136
370	" "	26	SESE	1859-08-10		A3 G121
399	" "	26	SWSW	1859-08-10		A3 G136
371	" "	26	W½SE	1859-08-10		A3 G121
372	" "	27	E½NE	1859-08-10		A3 G121
374	" "	27	NENW	1859-08-10		A3 G121
375	" "	27	NESE	1859-08-10		A3 G121
376	" "	27	SESE	1859-08-10		A3 G121
378	" "	27	W½NE	1859-08-10		A3 G121
379	" "	27	W½SE	1859-08-10		A3 G121
368	" "	23	W½SE	1860-09-03		A3 G121
369	" "	26	NWNE	1860-09-03		A3 G121
373	" "	27	E½SW	1865-10-20		A3 G121
377	" "	27	SWSW	1865-10-20		A3 G121

ID	Individual in Patent	Sec.	Sec. Part	Date Issued	Other Counties	For More Info . . .
408	IVES, Chauncy P	26	E½NW	1859-08-10		A3 G144
410	" "	26	NWSW	1859-08-10		A3 G145
409	" "	26	SWNE	1859-08-10		A3 G144
411	" "	26	W½NW	1859-08-10		A3 G145
487	JARVIS, Thomas J	18	N½NE	1877-03-01		A4 F
335	KEELEAN, Charles	30	S½NE	1879-11-25		A4
415	KENDALL, George	24	SWSE	1856-03-10		A1
416	KITCHEN, George	30	N½SW	1875-10-20		A4 F
325	LACKEY, Amasa	20	S½NW	1875-10-20		A4
462	LACKEY, Moses H	18	S½NE	1875-10-20		A4
400	LANNING, Mary	36	S½SE	1859-08-03		A3 G131
401	" "	36	SESW	1859-08-03		A3 G131
433	LAVERGNE, Alexandre	8	N½NW	1871-02-20		A3 G155
434	" "	8	NWNE	1871-02-20		A3 G155
390	LEONARD, Frederick B	32	E½SE	1859-08-03		A3 G140
391	" "	32	SENE	1859-08-03		A3 G140
404	" "	32	SWNE	1859-08-03		A3 G122
405	" "	32	W½SE	1859-08-03		A3 G122
380	" "	33	E½SE	1859-08-03		A3 G121
394	" "	33	N½NW	1859-08-03		A3 G137
381	" "	33	N½SW	1859-08-03		A3 G121
396	" "	33	NENE	1859-08-03		A3 G132
395	" "	33	NWNE	1859-08-03		A3 G137
382	" "	33	NWSE	1859-08-03		A3 G121
402	" "	33	S½NW	1859-08-03		A3 G133
392	" "	33	S½SW	1859-08-03		A3 G127
383	" "	33	SENE	1859-08-03		A3 G121
403	" "	33	SWNE	1859-08-03		A3 G133
393	" "	33	SWSE	1859-08-03		A3 G127
406	" "	34	E½NW	1859-08-03		A3 G134
407	" "	34	NESW	1859-08-03		A3 G134
384	" "	34	SENE	1859-08-03		A3 G121
385	" "	34	SESW	1859-08-03		A3 G121
386	" "	34	W½NE	1859-08-03		A3 G121
397	" "	34	W½NW	1859-08-03		A3 G132
387	" "	34	W½SW	1859-08-03		A3 G121
388	" "	36	NESW	1859-08-03		A3 G121
389	" "	36	S½NW	1859-08-03		A3 G121
400	" "	36	S½SE	1859-08-03		A3 G131
401	" "	36	SESW	1859-08-03		A3 G131
408	" "	26	E½NW	1859-08-10		A3 G144
398	" "	26	E½SW	1859-08-10		A3 G136
410	" "	26	NWSW	1859-08-10		A3 G145
370	" "	26	SESE	1859-08-10		A3 G121
409	" "	26	SWNE	1859-08-10		A3 G144
399	" "	26	SWSW	1859-08-10		A3 G136
411	" "	26	W½NW	1859-08-10		A3 G145
371	" "	26	W½SE	1859-08-10		A3 G121
372	" "	27	E½NE	1859-08-10		A3 G121
374	" "	27	NENW	1859-08-10		A3 G121
375	" "	27	NESE	1859-08-10		A3 G121
376	" "	27	SESE	1859-08-10		A3 G121
378	" "	27	W½NE	1859-08-10		A3 G121
379	" "	27	W½SE	1859-08-10		A3 G121
368	" "	23	W½SE	1860-09-03		A3 G121
369	" "	26	NWNE	1860-09-03		A3 G121
373	" "	27	E½SW	1865-10-20		A3 G121
377	" "	27	SWSW	1865-10-20		A3 G121
461	LINCOLN, Melvin A	32	S½SW	1875-10-20		A4
356	LUCE, Eleazer	6	N½SE	1875-09-01		A4
432	LUDINGTON, James	6	W½SW	1870-08-10		A1 F
435	" "	6	S½SE	1871-02-20		A3 G158
433	" "	8	N½NW	1871-02-20		A3 G155
434	" "	8	NWNE	1871-02-20		A3 G155
480	LYON, James O	10	SWSE	1859-08-10		A3 G313
481	" "	15	N½NE	1859-08-10		A3 G313
482	" "	23	W½NW	1859-08-10		A3 G313
483	" "	23	W½SW	1859-08-10		A3 G313
484	LYONS, James O	22	E½SE	1858-05-01		A1 G314
329	MARSH, Carlos	13	SESW	1859-08-10		A3 G169
330	" "	13	W½SW	1859-08-10		A3 G169
423	MATTESON, Harvey	28	NWSE	1866-06-05		A1 F
424	" "	28	SWSE	1866-06-05		A1 F

ID	Individual in Patent	Sec.	Sec. Part	Date Issued	Other Counties	For More Info . . .
396	MCCLUNG, Jane	33	NENE	1859-08-03		A3 G132
397	" "	34	W½NW	1859-08-03		A3 G132
489	MERRITT, Titus	35	SW	1855-12-15		A1
495	MILLARD, William H	30	S½SW	1872-09-20		A4
402	MILLER, Phebe	33	S½NW	1859-08-03		A3 G133
403	" "	33	SWNE	1859-08-03		A3 G133
406	MILLER, Susannah	34	E½NW	1859-08-03		A3 G134
407	" "	34	NESW	1859-08-03		A3 G134
413	MISNER, Frederick	34	NENE	1870-07-15		A1 F
485	MOODY, Lucy	24	SW	1861-07-01		A3 G256
436	MOORE, James	4	E½NW	1875-02-10		A4 F
445	MOOTE, John	30	N½NW	1873-06-10		A4 F
476	NASON, Robert H	4	NE	1870-06-20		A1 F
323	ORN, Albert N	30	E½SE	1876-12-30		A4
439	PARKS, John E	28	E½SE	1876-12-30		A4 F
456	PARMETER, Luther L	20	E½SW	1872-09-20		A4 F
344	PEARSON, Daniel K	8	SWSW	1872-03-20		A1 F
449	PERKINS, Joseph	30	W½SE	1872-04-05		A4
435	PLACKARD, Malinda	6	S½SE	1871-02-20		A3 G158
425	POTTER, Henry C	18	W½SE	1873-05-15		A1 G221 F
353	RANDALL, Earl D	11	NESE	1858-05-01		A1
354	" "	11	S½SE	1858-05-01		A1
453	REYNOLDS, Lemon D	13	NESW	1860-09-03		A3
454	" "	13	S½NW	1860-09-03		A3
338	RICHARDSON, Charles	8	SESW	1875-09-01		A4 F
339	" "	8	W½SE	1875-09-01		A4 F
485	ROGERS, Abigail	24	SW	1861-07-01		A3 G256
444	ROLSTONE, John M	14	NW	1858-05-01		A1
398	SAMMIS, Lydia	26	E½SW	1859-08-10		A3 G136
399	" "	26	SWSW	1859-08-10		A3 G136
394	SAMUEL, Frances	33	N½NW	1859-08-03		A3 G137
395	" "	33	NWNE	1859-08-03		A3 G137
414	SEAFORD, Frederick	30	N½NE	1877-06-04		A4
485	SECORD, Sidney	24	SW	1861-07-01		A3 G256
390	SIDERS, Ann	32	E½SE	1859-08-03		A3 G140
391	" "	32	SENE	1859-08-03		A3 G140
466	SLOSSON, Ozias J	1	SESW	1858-05-01		A1
467	" "	2	S½SW	1858-05-01		A1
468	" "	2	SE	1858-05-01		A1
469	" "	22	S½NE	1858-05-01		A1
470	" "	22	W½	1858-05-01		A1
471	" "	22	W½SE	1858-05-01		A1
417	SMITH, George M	1	E½SE	1857-02-20		A3
418	" "	1	SWSE	1857-02-20		A3
451	SMITH, James M	25	SENE	1859-08-03		A3 G287
452	" "	25	W½NE	1859-08-03		A3 G287
422	STAAB, Gottleib	11	SW	1858-05-01		A1
326	STEBBINS, Barnabas M	11	NW	1858-05-01		A1
324	STIMSON, Amasa D	28	E½SW	1875-10-20		A4
427	STONE, Henry L	28	W½NW	1868-02-15		A1 F
451	TENNY, Justus W	25	SENE	1859-08-03		A3 G287
452	" "	25	W½NE	1859-08-03		A3 G287
450	" "	25	NENE	1859-10-10		A1
446	TONER, John	10	E½SE	1877-06-15		A4 F
433	TRAHAN, Onezime	8	N½NW	1871-02-20		A3 G155
434	" "	8	NWNE	1871-02-20		A3 G155
447	VALLANCE, John	20	S½NE	1877-06-04		A4
488	VAN ALSTINE, THOMAS J	10	W½NE	1873-02-10		A4
455	VANDAWATERS, Lewis H	28	W½NE	1871-05-01		A4 F
352	VANDUSEN, Dennis F	8	E½SE	1873-02-10		A4 F
346	WARDWELL, Daniel	4	SWSW	1859-08-10		A3
348	" "	5	E½SE	1859-08-10		A3
349	" "	5	SWSE	1859-08-10		A3
350	" "	8	E½NE	1859-08-10		A3
351	" "	9	NWNW	1859-08-10		A3
345	" "	4	NWNW	1868-02-10		A3 F
347	" "	5	E½NE	1868-02-10		A3 F
497	WATERMAN, Zerial	25	SE	1857-03-10		A1
498	" "	36	N½NE	1858-05-01		A1
448	WEBBER, John	32	N½NW	1875-02-10		A4
425	WEBBER, William L	18	W½SE	1873-05-15		A1 G221 F
321	WEBSTER, Lucretia	23	NWNE	1860-10-01		A3 G80
322	" "	23	S½NE	1860-10-01		A3 G80

ID	Individual in Patent	Sec.	Sec. Part	Date Issued	Other Counties	For More Info . . .
331	WERT, Charles A	18	S½NW	1879-11-25		A4 F
412	WESTERBERG, Frederick B	6	E½SW	1876-02-10		A4
343	WHIPPLE, Daniel J	18	N½NW	1875-08-20		A4 F
410	WHITE, Alma	26	NWSW	1859-08-10		A3 G145
411	" "	26	W½NW	1859-08-10		A3 G145
484	WILCOX, Sextus N	22	E½SE	1858-05-01		A1 G314
480	" "	10	SWSE	1859-08-10		A3 G313
481	" "	15	N½NE	1859-08-10		A3 G313
482	" "	23	W½NW	1859-08-10		A3 G313
483	" "	23	W½SW	1859-08-10		A3 G313
490	WOODARD, Tracy L	24	SESE	1856-03-10		A1
328	YOUNGS, Benjamin	6	W½NE	1874-08-01		A4 F

Patent Map

T16-N R11-W
Michigan-Toledo Strip Meridian

Map Group 4

Township Statistics

Parcels Mapped	:	184
Number of Patents	:	137
Number of Individuals	:	125
Patentees Identified	:	114
Number of Surnames	:	112
Multi-Patentee Parcels	:	61
Oldest Patent Date	:	12/15/1855
Most Recent Patent	:	9/3/1890
Block/Lot Parcels	:	0
Parcels Re - Issued	:	0
Parcels that Overlap	:	0
Cities and Towns	:	1
Cemeteries	:	0

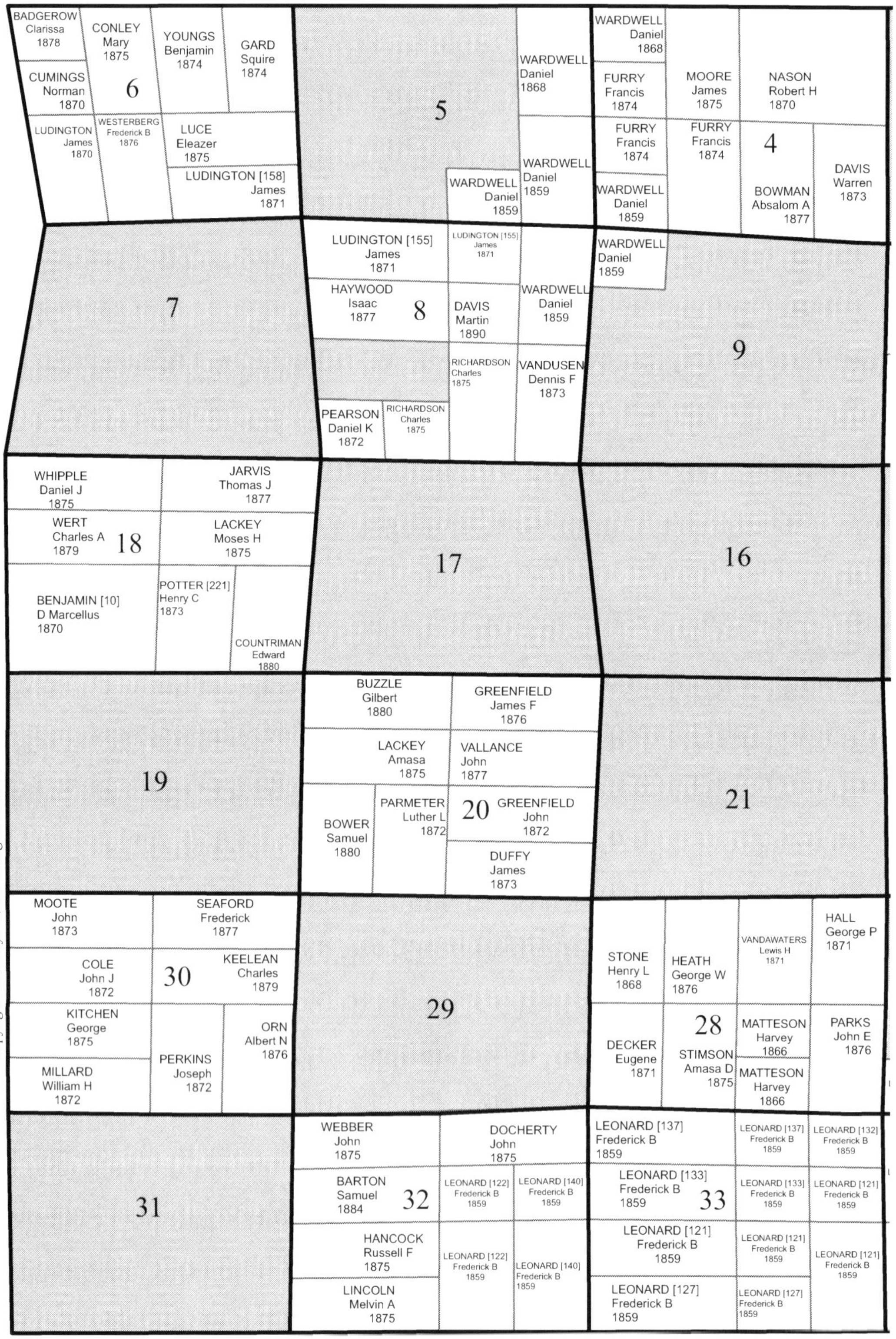

3

BEVIER
William N
1869

CHAPIN
Richard B
1869

HAWKINS
Maria
1870

BLISS
William C
1869

COOK
Cornelius
1872

2

SLOSSON
Ozias J
1858

SLOSSON
Ozias J
1858

BLACK
Peter
1858

BLACK
Peter
1859

1

BLACK
Peter
1859

HIGBE
Charles
1859

SMITH
George M
1857

HIGBE
Charles
1859

SLOSSON
Ozias J
1858

SMITH
George M
1857

DAVIS
Nathan
1873

DAVIS
Marion
1872

10

ALSTINE
Thomas J Van
1873

DUBOIS
William H
1871

AITKEN
James
1872

BARSTOW
Charles R
1872

BARSTOW
Charles R
1870

TONER
John
1877

WILCOX [313]
Sextus N
1859

STEBBINS
Barnabas M
1858

11

STAAB
Gottleib
1858

RANDALL
Earl D
1858

RANDALL
Earl D
1858

GILL
John
1858

GILL
John
1858

BLACK
Franklin
1857

12

CRUM
Eli H
1871

CHILD
Nathan
1857

COOK
Ezra J
1859

COOK
Ezra J
1859

WILCOX [313]
Sextus N
1859

15

ROLSTONE
John M
1858

14

DAVENPORT
William
1858

DAVENPORT
Jesse L
1877

HAMILTON
Addison R
1858

HOLE
Even B
1878

HAMILTON
Addison R
1858

REYNOLDS
Lemon D
1860

13

HIGBE
Charles
1858

REYNOLDS
Lemon D
1860

DIRSTEIN
Elias
1855

MARSH [169]
Carlos
1859

MARSH [169]
Carlos
1859

SLOSSON
Ozias J
1858

22

DAVENPORT
Henry
1873

SLOSSON
Ozias J
1858

SLOSSON
Ozias J
1858

WILCOX [314]
Sextus N
1858

WILCOX [313]
Sextus N
1859

WILCOX [313]
Sextus N
1859

HAMILTON [80]
Addison R
1860

HAMILTON
Addison R
1858

HAMILTON [80]
Addison R
1860

23

LEONARD [121]
Frederick B
1860

HAMILTON
Addison R
1858

HAMILTON
Addison R
1858

DIRSTEIN
Elias
1855

24

SECORD [256]
Sidney
1861

DUTCHER
Benjamin F
1873

KENDALL
George
1856

WOODARD
Tracy L
1856

LEONARD [121]
Frederick B
1859

LEONARD [121]
Frederick B
1859

LEONARD [121]
Frederick B
1859

27

LEONARD [121]
Frederick B
1859

LEONARD [121]
Frederick B
1859

LEONARD [121]
Frederick B
1859

LEONARD [121]
Frederick B
1865

LEONARD [121]
Frederick B
1865

LEONARD [145]
Frederick B
1859

LEONARD [144]
Frederick B
1859

LEONARD [145]
Frederick B
1859

26

LEONARD [136]
Frederick B
1859

LEONARD [136]
Frederick B
1859

LEONARD [121]
Frederick B
1860

LEONARD [144]
Frederick B
1859

LEONARD [121]
Frederick B
1859

LEONARD [121]
Frederick B
1859

TENNY
Justus W
1859

TENNY [287]
Justus W
1859

TENNY [287]
Justus W
1859

25

WATERMAN
Zerial
1857

LEONARD [132]
Frederick B
1859

LEONARD [134]
Frederick B
1859

LEONARD [121]
Frederick B
1859

MISNER
Frederick
1870

LEONARD [121]
Frederick B
1859

LEONARD [134]
Frederick B
1859

34

LEONARD [121]
Frederick B
1859

LEONARD [121]
Frederick B
1859

35

MERRITT
Titus
1855

WATERMAN
Zerial
1858

LEONARD [121]
Frederick B
1859

36

LEONARD [121]
Frederick B
1859

LEONARD [131]
Frederick B
1859

LEONARD [131]
Frederick B
1859

Helpful Hints

1. This Map's INDEX can be found on the preceding pages.
2. Refer to Map "C" to see where this Township lies within Newaygo County, Michigan.
3. Numbers within square brackets [ ] denote a multi-patentee land parcel (multi-owner). Refer to Appendix "C" for a full list of members in this group.
4. Areas that look to be crowded with Patentees usually indicate multiple sales of the same parcel (Re-issues) or Overlapping parcels. See this Township's Index for an explanation of these and other circumstances that might explain "odd" groupings of Patentees on this map.

Legend

Patent Boundary

Section Boundary

No Patents Found (or Outside County)

1., 2., 3., ... Lot Numbers (when beside a name)

[ ] Group Number (see Appendix "C")

Scale: Section = 1 mile X 1 mile (generally, with some exceptions)

Road Map

T16-N R11-W
Michigan-Toledo Strip Meridian

Map Group 4

Cities & Towns

Hawkins

Cemeteries

None

6
5
4
Pine
Dogwood
Smiley
17 Mile
7
8
9
16 Mile
18
17
16
Locust
15 Mile
19
20
21
Elm
Cypress
14 Mile
Pine
30
29
28
13 Mile
31
32
33
Hemlock
12 Mile

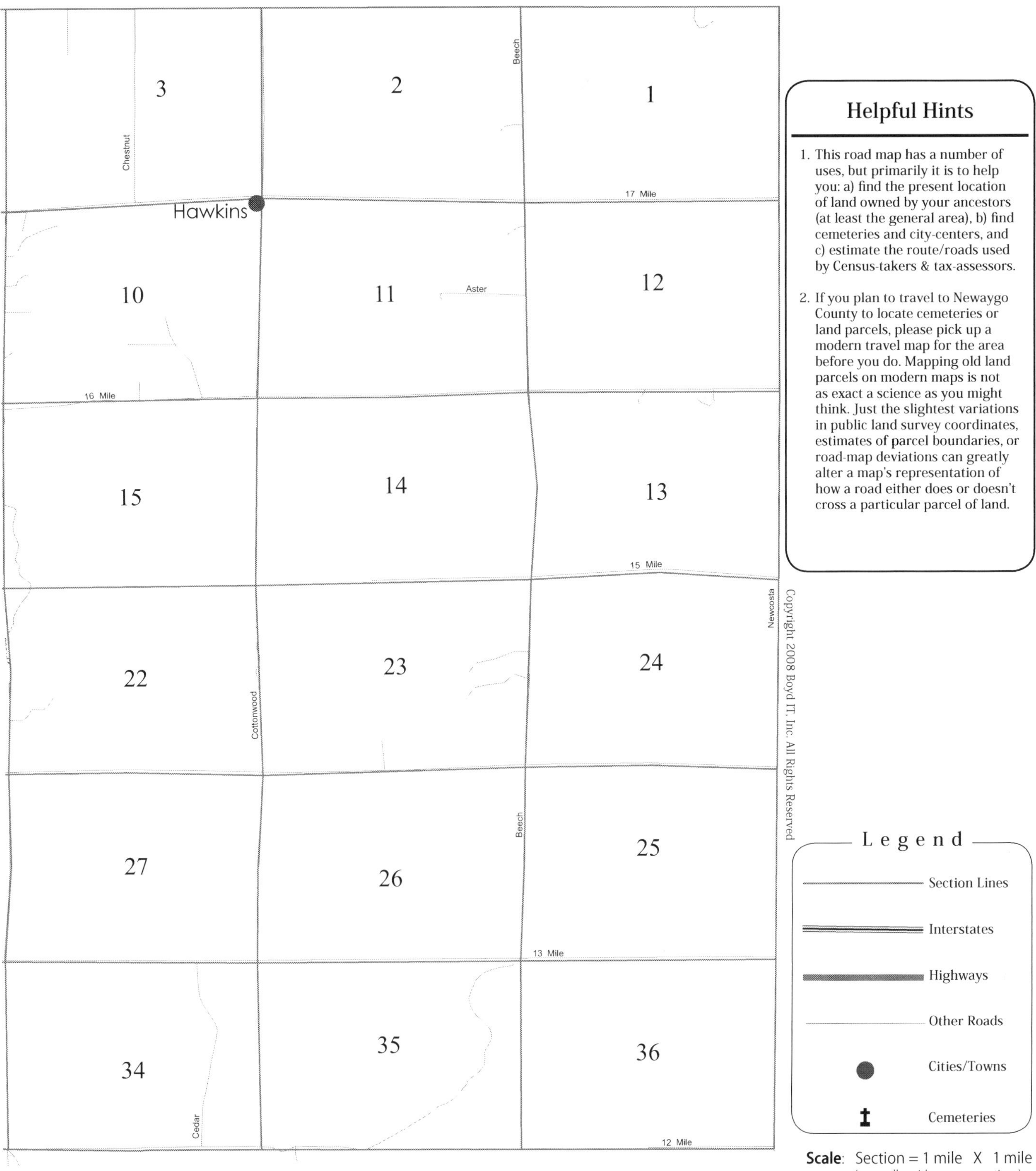
3
2
1
Beech
Chestnut
17 Mile
Hawkins
10
11
Aster
12
16 Mile
15
14
13
15 Mile
Newcosta
22
23
24
Cottonwood
27
26
Beech
25
13 Mile
34
35
36
Cedar
12 Mile
Helpful Hints
1. This road map has a number of uses, but primarily it is to help you: a) find the present location of land owned by your ancestors (at least the general area), b) find cemeteries and city-centers, and c) estimate the route/roads used by Census-takers & tax-assessors.
2. If you plan to travel to Newaygo County to locate cemeteries or land parcels, please pick up a modern travel map for the area before you do. Mapping old land parcels on modern maps is not as exact a science as you might think. Just the slightest variations in public land survey coordinates, estimates of parcel boundaries, or road-map deviations can greatly alter a map's representation of how a road either does or doesn't cross a particular parcel of land.
Copyright 2008 Boyd IT, Inc. All Rights Reserved
Legend
Section Lines
Interstates
Highways
Other Roads
Cities/Towns
Cemeteries

Scale: Section = 1 mile X 1 mile
(generally, with some exceptions)

T16-N R11-W
Michigan-Toledo Strip Meridian

Map Group 4

Cities & Towns
Hawkins

Cemeteries
None

6 5 4

Pease Creek

7 8 9

18 17 16

Whipple Lake

19 20 21

30 29 28

Mc Duffee Creek

31 32 33

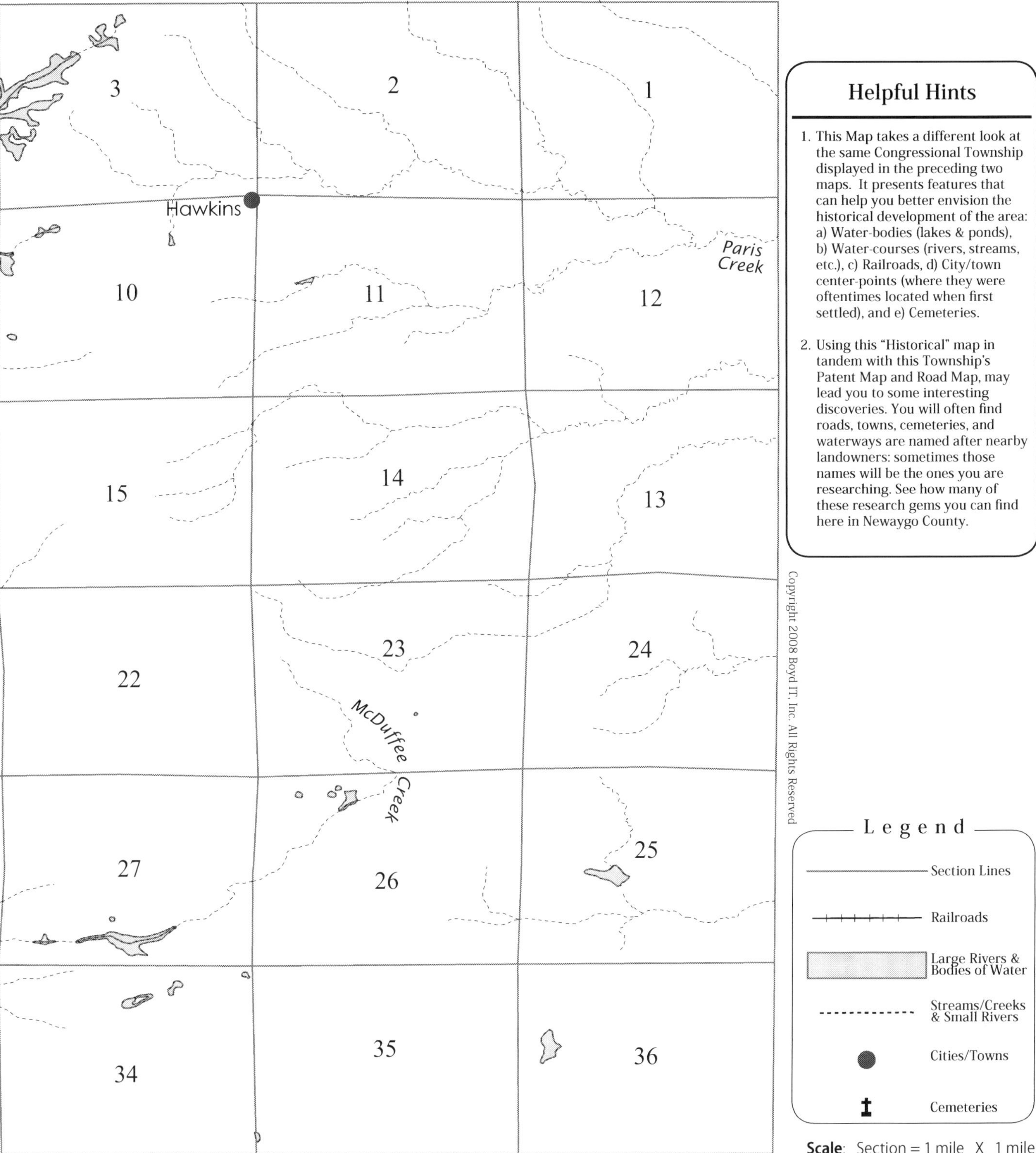

Helpful Hints

1. This Map takes a different look at the same Congressional Township displayed in the preceding two maps. It presents features that can help you better envision the historical development of the area: a) Water-bodies (lakes & ponds), b) Water-courses (rivers, streams, etc.), c) Railroads, d) City/town center-points (where they were oftentimes located when first settled), and e) Cemeteries.

2. Using this "Historical" map in tandem with this Township's Patent Map and Road Map, may lead you to some interesting discoveries. You will often find roads, towns, cemeteries, and waterways are named after nearby landowners: sometimes those names will be the ones you are researching. See how many of these research gems you can find here in Newaygo County.

Scale: Section = 1 mile X 1 mile
(there are some exceptions)

Map Group 5: Index to Land Patents

Township 15-North Range 14-West (Michigan-Toledo Strip)

After you locate an individual in this Index, take note of the Section and Section Part then proceed to the Land Patent map on the pages immediately following. You should have no difficulty locating the corresponding parcel of land.

The "For More Info" Column will lead you to more information about the underlying Patents. See the *Legend* at right, and the "How to Use this Book" chapter, for more information.

LEGEND

"For More Info . . . " column

- **A** = Authority (Legislative Act, See Appendix "A")
- **B** = Block or Lot (location in Section unknown)
- **C** = Cancelled Patent
- **F** = Fractional Section
- **G** = Group (Multi-Patentee Patent, see Appendix "C")
- **V** = Overlaps another Parcel
- **R** = Re-Issued (Parcel patented more than once)

(A & G items require you to look in the Appendixes referred to above. All other Letter-designations followed by a number require you to locate line-items in this index that possess the ID number found after the letter).

ID	Individual in Patent	Sec.	Sec. Part	Date Issued	Other Counties	For More Info . . .
521	COOPER, Joel M	28	E½NW	1863-10-01		A3 G68
522	" "	28	W½NE	1863-10-01		A3 G68
535	CRAWFORD, Francis	22	S½SW	1869-09-01		A3 G265
536	" "	22	SWSE	1869-09-01		A3 G265
526	CREPIN, Ernest E	34	2	1880-03-05		A1 G84
516	CROSS, Ira B	4	SWSE	1869-09-10		A1
515	" "	4	SW	1875-04-20		A4
525	EAEGLE, John	6	N½SW	1870-05-02		A1 F
503	GIDDINGS, Barzillai	30	NE	1869-11-01		A4
521	GIDDINGS, Jane	28	E½NW	1863-10-01		A3 G68
522	" "	28	W½NE	1863-10-01		A3 G68
521	GIDDINGS, June	28	E½NW	1863-10-01		A3 G68
522	" "	28	W½NE	1863-10-01		A3 G68
513	GORDON, Goodien S	31	E½SW	1858-01-15		A3 F
514	" "	31	NWSE	1858-01-15		A3
508	GRAY, Edgar L	14	NWNW	1866-04-03		A1
499	GUDGELL, Van Buren	28	E½NE	1868-07-20		A3 G260
526	HEALD, Joseph	34	2	1880-03-05		A1 G84
504	KIEFER, Herman	2	N½NE	1868-12-01		A3 G273 F
505	" "	2	NWSE	1869-09-10		A1 G273
517	KNAPP, Ira	30	N½SE	1869-11-01		A4
518	" "	30	NESW	1869-11-01		A4
519	" "	30	SESE	1869-11-01		A4
537	KNOWLES, Thomas J	30	NW	1875-02-10		A4 F
504	LICHTENBERG, Gustav B	2	N½NE	1868-12-01		A3 G273 F
505	" "	2	NWSE	1869-09-10		A1 G273
507	MELENDY, David A	20	SESE	1870-05-10		A1
538	MITCHELL, William W	22	SESE	1871-02-01		A1
502	MUDGE, Andrew	6	NW	1875-04-20		A4
526	MURPHY, Simon J	34	2	1880-03-05		A1 G84
531	NELSON, Roselia	2	SENE	1905-06-30		A4
524	PAINTER, Jesse D	4	SWNW	1869-09-10		A1
523	" "	26	W½NW	1878-12-30		A4
506	PALMER, Chandler	31	SWNE	1870-07-15		A1
533	REWALT, Catharine	6	S½SE	1869-09-01		A3 G268 F
534	" "	6	SESW	1869-09-01		A3 G268 F
535	ROWE, Mary	22	S½SW	1869-09-01		A3 G265
536	" "	22	SWSE	1869-09-01		A3 G265
499	SKINNER, Adolphus L	28	E½NE	1868-07-20		A3 G260
535	STEVENSON, Thomas G	22	S½SW	1869-09-01		A3 G265
536	" "	22	SWSE	1869-09-01		A3 G265
533	" "	6	S½SE	1869-09-01		A3 G268 F
534	" "	6	SESW	1869-09-01		A3 G268 F
504	STROH, Bernhard	2	N½NE	1868-12-01		A3 G273 F
505	" "	2	NWSE	1869-09-10		A1 G273
510	STUART, Euphemia A	30	NWSW	1876-02-10		A4 F

ID	Individual in Patent	Sec.	Sec. Part	Date Issued	Other Counties	For More Info . . .
500	SWEAT, Allen	8	E½NW	1875-08-20		A4
501	" "	8	NWNW	1875-08-20		A4
529	TOWER, Osmond S	26	NWSE	1871-02-01		A1
530	" "	26	SENW	1871-02-01		A1
520	TURNER, James M	2	SWNE	1872-03-20		A1
532	WEBSTER, Solon	20	SWSW	1863-12-05		A1
509	WELLS, Eliza	6	SWSW	1870-05-02		A1 F
527	WELLS, Mary	6	NWNE	1873-02-10		A4 F
528	" "	6	S½NE	1873-02-10		A4
521	WHITE, John	28	E½NW	1863-10-01		A3 G68
522	" "	28	W½NE	1863-10-01		A3 G68
512	WILSON, Gilbert F	34	SE	1873-05-15		A1 F
511	WILSON, Gilbert F D	8	NE	1869-09-01		A3

Patent Map

T15-N R14-W
Michigan-Toledo Strip Meridian

Map Group 5

Township Statistics

Parcels Mapped	:	40
Number of Patents	:	31
Number of Individuals	:	38
Patentees Identified	:	28
Number of Surnames	:	34
Multi-Patentee Parcels	:	10
Oldest Patent Date	:	1/15/1858
Most Recent Patent	:	6/30/1905
Block/Lot Parcels	:	1
Parcels Re - Issued	:	0
Parcels that Overlap	:	0
Cities and Towns	:	1
Cemeteries	:	0

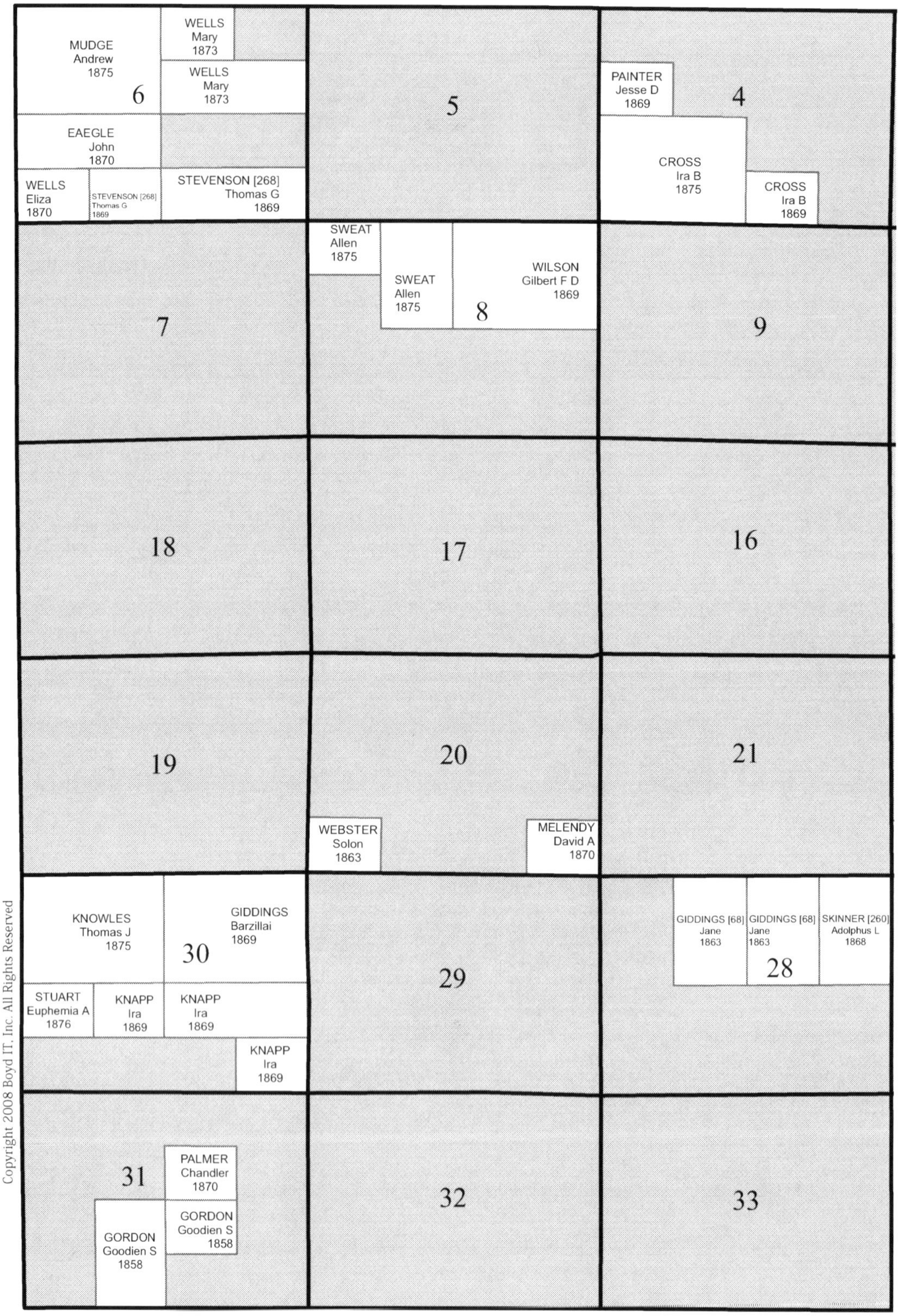

MUDGE Andrew 1875
WELLS Mary 1873
WELLS Mary 1873
6
EAEGLE John 1870
WELLS Eliza 1870
STEVENSON [268] Thomas G 1869
STEVENSON [268] Thomas G 1869
5
PAINTER Jesse D 1869
4
CROSS Ira B 1875
CROSS Ira B 1869
7
SWEAT Allen 1875
SWEAT Allen 1875
WILSON Gilbert F D 1869
8
9
18
17
16
19
20
21
WEBSTER Solon 1863
MELENDY David A 1870
KNOWLES Thomas J 1875
GIDDINGS Barzillai 1869
30
STUART Euphemia A 1876
KNAPP Ira 1869
KNAPP Ira 1869
KNAPP Ira 1869
29
GIDDINGS [68] Jane 1863
GIDDINGS [68] Jane 1863
SKINNER [260] Adolphus L 1868
28
31
PALMER Chandler 1870
GORDON Goodien S 1858
GORDON Goodien S 1858
32
33

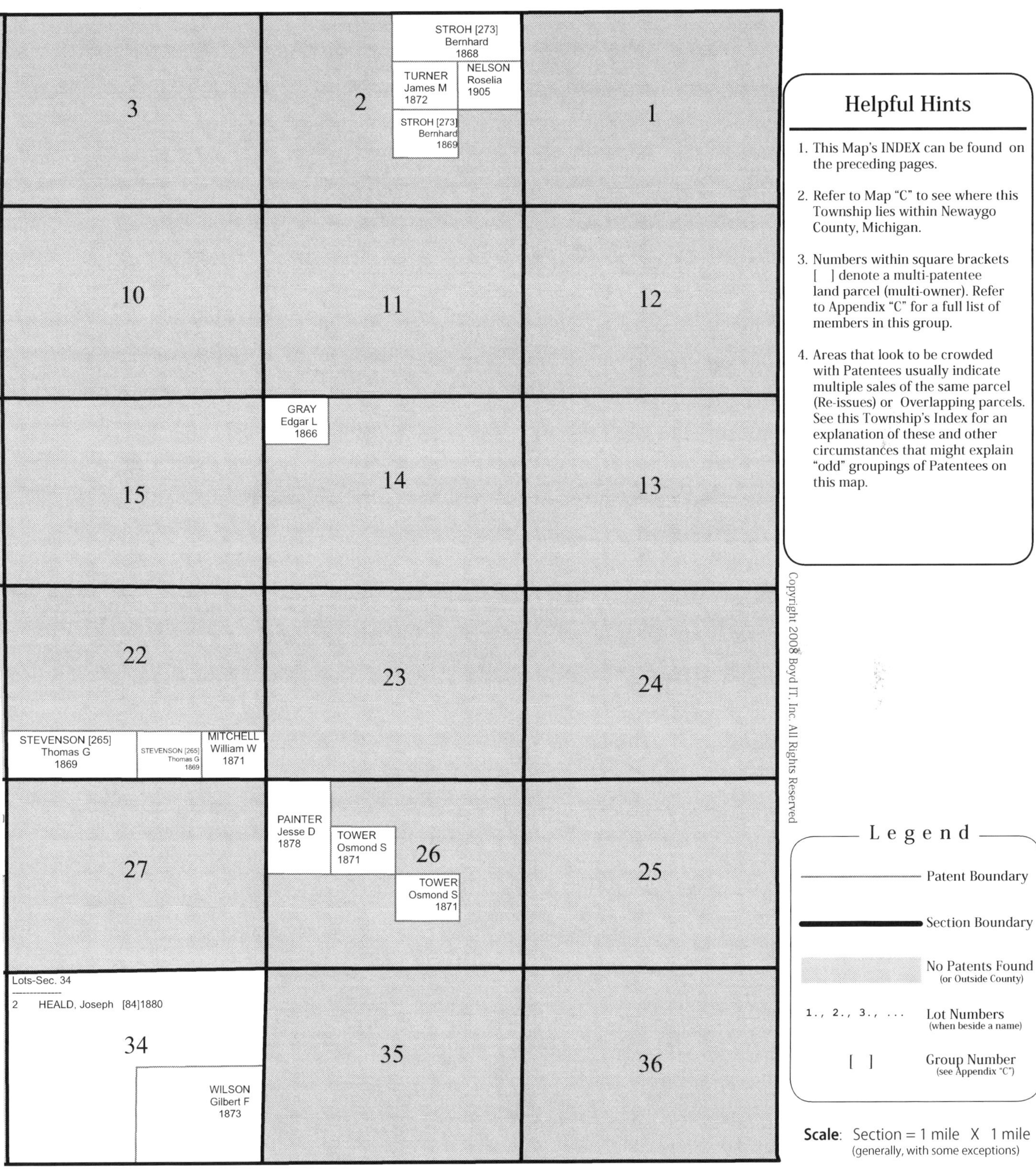
3
2
1
STROH [273]
Bernhard
1868
TURNER
James M
1872
NELSON
Roselia
1905
STROH [273]
Bernhard
1869
10
11
12
GRAY
Edgar L
1866
15
14
13
22
23
24
STEVENSON [265]
Thomas G
1869
STEVENSON [265]
Thomas G
1869
MITCHELL
William W
1871
PAINTER
Jesse D
1878
TOWER
Osmond S
1871
TOWER
Osmond S
1871
27
26
25
Lots-Sec. 34
2 HEALD, Joseph [84]1880
34
35
36
WILSON
Gilbert F
1873
Helpful Hints
1. This Map's INDEX can be found on the preceding pages.
2. Refer to Map "C" to see where this Township lies within Newaygo County, Michigan.
3. Numbers within square brackets [ ] denote a multi-patentee land parcel (multi-owner). Refer to Appendix "C" for a full list of members in this group.
4. Areas that look to be crowded with Patentees usually indicate multiple sales of the same parcel (Re-issues) or Overlapping parcels. See this Township's Index for an explanation of these and other circumstances that might explain "odd" groupings of Patentees on this map.
Copyright 2008 Boyd IT, Inc. All Rights Reserved
Legend
Patent Boundary
Section Boundary
No Patents Found
(or Outside County)
1., 2., 3., ...
Lot Numbers
(when beside a name)
[ ]
Group Number
(see Appendix "C")
Scale: Section = 1 mile X 1 mile
(generally, with some exceptions)

Road Map

T15-N R14-W
Michigan-Toledo Strip Meridian

Map Group 5

Cities & Towns

Volney

Cemeteries

None

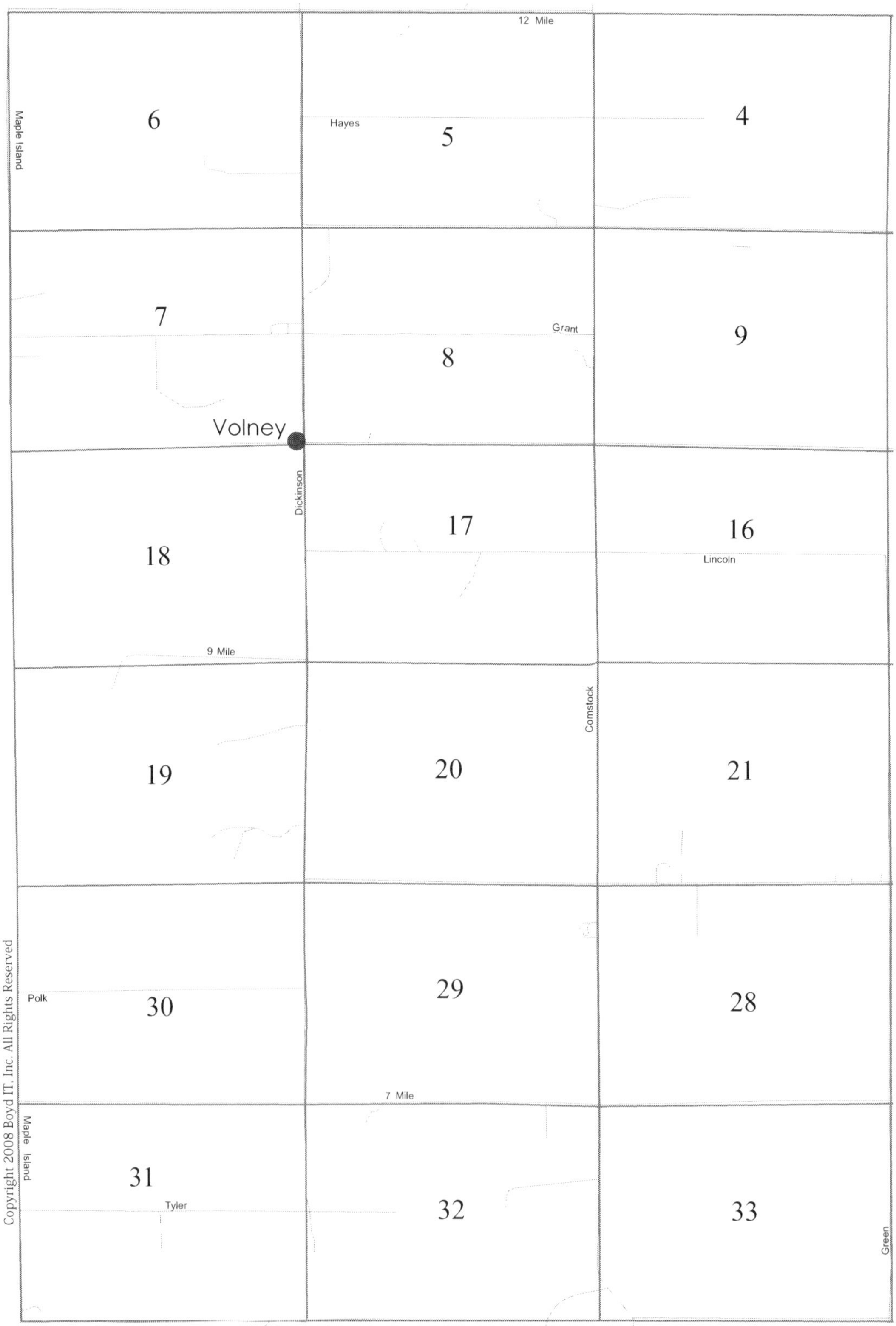

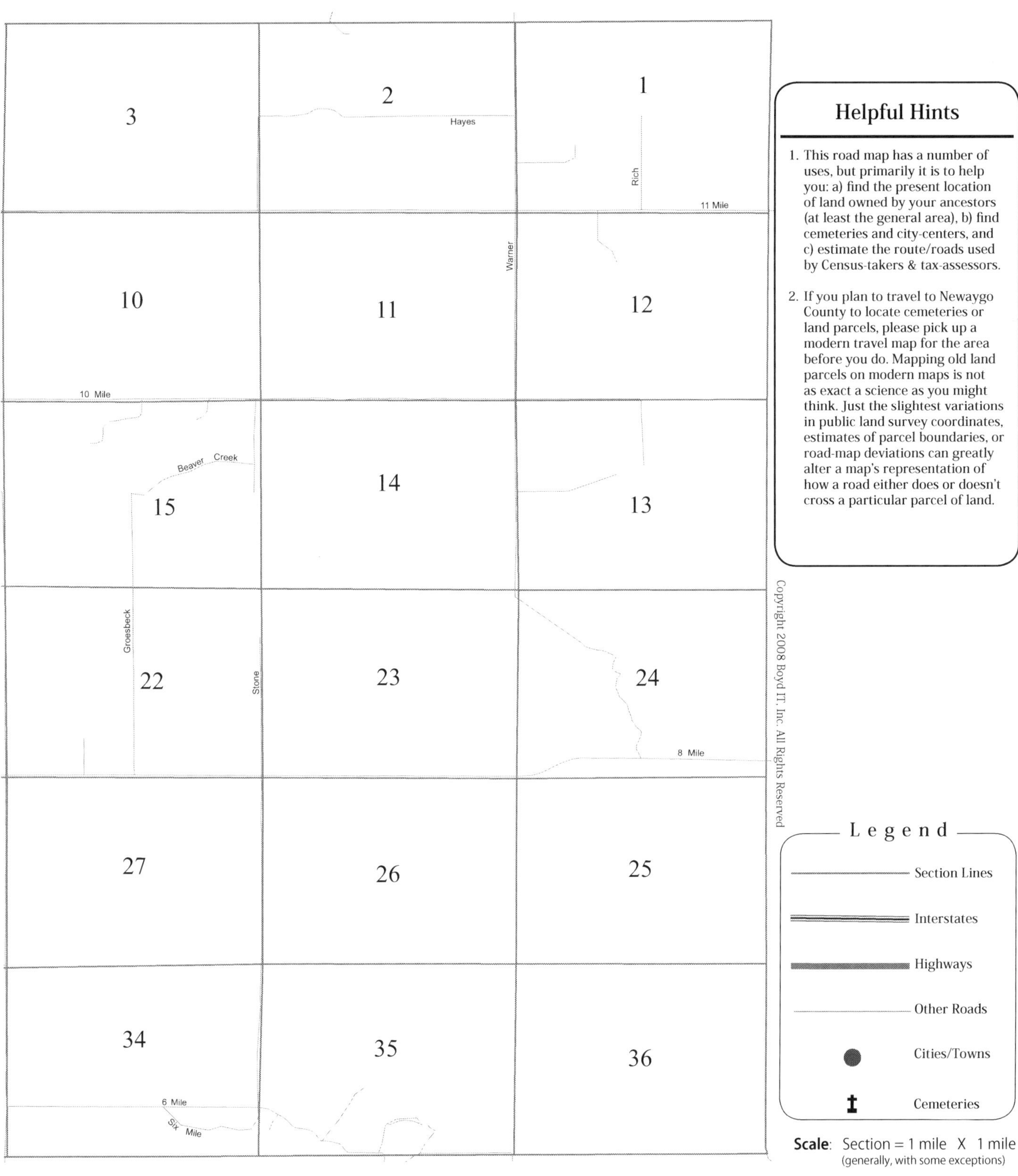
3
2
1
Hayes
Rich
11 Mile
Warner
10
11
12
10 Mile
Beaver Creek
14
15
13
Groesbeck
Stone
22
23
24
8 Mile
27
26
25
34
35
36
6 Mile
Six Mile
Helpful Hints
1. This road map has a number of uses, but primarily it is to help you: a) find the present location of land owned by your ancestors (at least the general area), b) find cemeteries and city-centers, and c) estimate the route/roads used by Census-takers & tax-assessors.
2. If you plan to travel to Newaygo County to locate cemeteries or land parcels, please pick up a modern travel map for the area before you do. Mapping old land parcels on modern maps is not as exact a science as you might think. Just the slightest variations in public land survey coordinates, estimates of parcel boundaries, or road-map deviations can greatly alter a map's representation of how a road either does or doesn't cross a particular parcel of land.
Copyright 2008 Boyd IT, Inc. All Rights Reserved
Legend
Section Lines
Interstates
Highways
Other Roads
Cities/Towns
Cemeteries
Scale: Section = 1 mile X 1 mile
(generally, with some exceptions)

Historical Map

T15-N R14-W
Michigan-Toledo Strip Meridian

Map Group 5

Cities & Towns

Volney

Cemeteries

None

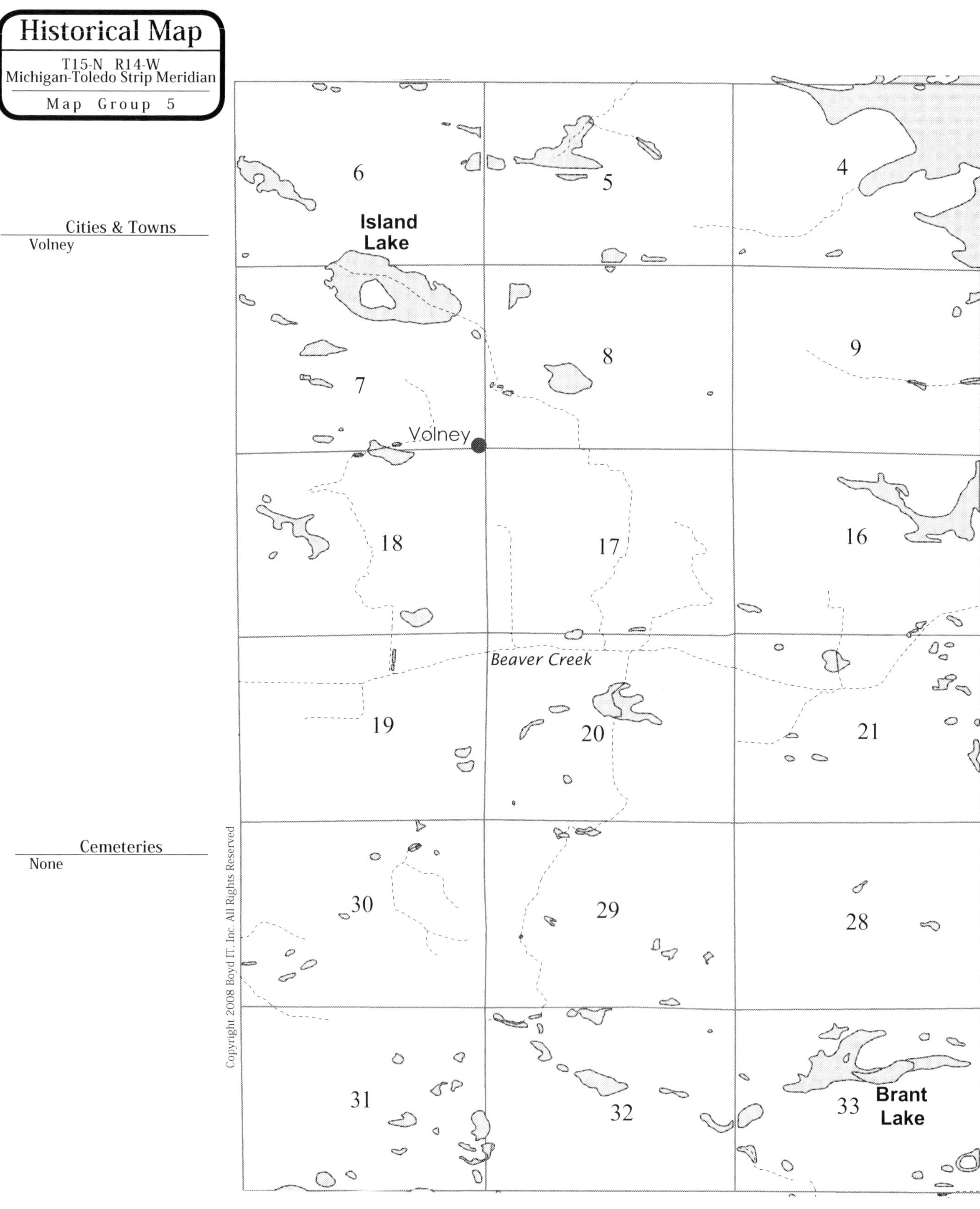

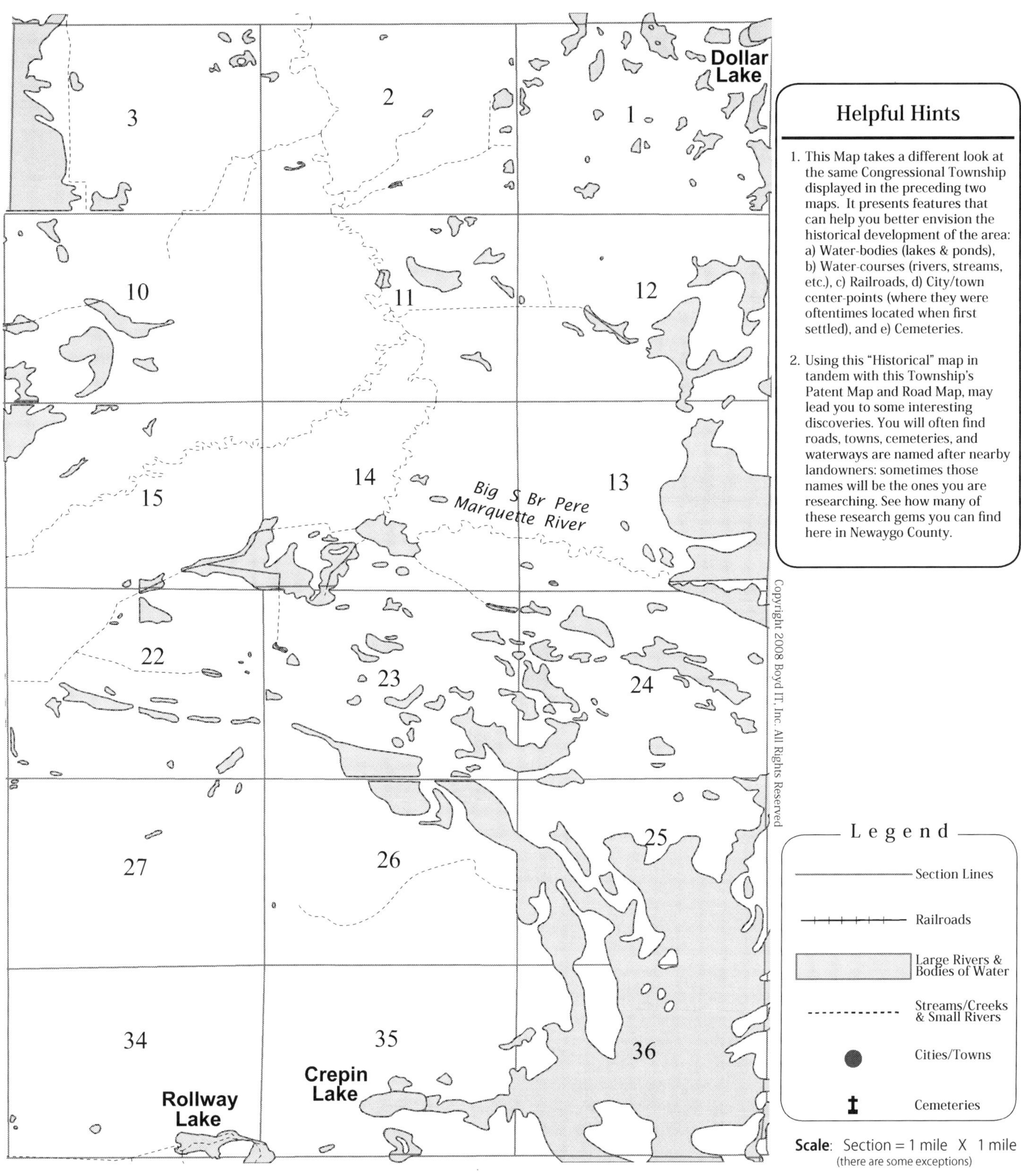
Dollar Lake
3
2
1
10
11
12
15
14
13
Big S Br Pere Marquette River
22
23
24
27
26
25
34
35
36
Rollway Lake
Crepin Lake
Helpful Hints
1. This Map takes a different look at the same Congressional Township displayed in the preceding two maps. It presents features that can help you better envision the historical development of the area: a) Water-bodies (lakes & ponds), b) Water-courses (rivers, streams, etc.), c) Railroads, d) City/town center-points (where they were oftentimes located when first settled), and e) Cemeteries.
2. Using this "Historical" map in tandem with this Township's Patent Map and Road Map, may lead you to some interesting discoveries. You will often find roads, towns, cemeteries, and waterways are named after nearby landowners: sometimes those names will be the ones you are researching. See how many of these research gems you can find here in Newaygo County.
Legend
Section Lines
Railroads
Large Rivers & Bodies of Water
Streams/Creeks & Small Rivers
Cities/Towns
Cemeteries
Scale: Section = 1 mile X 1 mile
(there are some exceptions)

Map Group 6: Index to Land Patents

Township 15-North Range 13-West (Michigan-Toledo Strip)

After you locate an individual in this Index, take note of the Section and Section Part then proceed to the Land Patent map on the pages immediately following. You should have no difficulty locating the corresponding parcel of land.

The "For More Info" Column will lead you to more information about the underlying Patents. See the *Legend* at right, and the "How to Use this Book" chapter, for more information.

LEGEND

"For More Info . . . " column

A = Authority (Legislative Act, See Appendix "A")
B = Block or Lot (location in Section unknown)
C = Cancelled Patent
F = Fractional Section
G = Group (Multi-Patentee Patent, see Appendix "C")
V = Overlaps another Parcel
R = Re-Issued (Parcel patented more than once)

(A & G items require you to look in the Appendixes referred to above. All other Letter-designations followed by a number require you to locate line-items in this index that possess the ID number found after the letter).

ID	Individual in Patent	Sec.	Sec. Part	Date Issued	Other Counties	For More Info . . .
543	BELL, Chauncey S	14	SENE	1874-03-10		A1
544	" "	14	SENW	1874-03-10		A1
545	" "	14	W½NE	1874-03-10		A1
555	BOLDMAN, Jacob	24	SE	1880-06-30		A4
541	BROWN, Augustus L	34	N½NE	1868-07-20		A3 G259
576	CHRISTIAN, Sarah	8	E½NE	1867-01-15		A3 G206
577	" "	8	SWNE	1867-01-15		A3 G206
559	DINGMAN, Jarret	24	NE	1877-03-01		A4
578	DUNGAN, Sarah	32	E½NE	1867-01-15		A3 G207
567	DUNN, Susannah	14	N½NW	1869-09-01		A3 G325
541	FORSHAY, David F	34	N½NE	1868-07-20		A3 G259
571	GOODALL, Eliza B	18	E½NE	1867-02-01		A3 G208
572	" "	18	NWNE	1867-02-01		A3 G208
568	HANCOCK, George W	14	E½SE	1869-09-01		A3 G326
568	HANCOCK, William H	14	E½SE	1869-09-01		A3 G326
573	HARRIS, William S	20	S½SE	1867-01-15		A3 G211
579	" "	8	W½NW	1867-01-15		A3 G209
569	HARRISON, Mary A	32	E½NW	1871-07-15		A3 G291
570	" "	32	SWNW	1871-07-15		A3 G291
580	JOHNSON, William W	26	SWNW	1872-04-05		A1
557	LESUEUR, Napoleon B	8	E½NW	1869-07-01		A3 G157
558	" "	8	NWNE	1869-07-01		A3 G157
557	LUDINGTON, James	8	E½NW	1869-07-01		A3 G157
558	" "	8	NWNE	1869-07-01		A3 G157
556	" "	17	SWNW	1869-09-10		A1
574	MCCLAIN, Mary	32	E½SW	1867-02-01		A3 G210
575	" "	32	SWSW	1867-02-01		A3 G210
565	MCFARLAN, James	24	N½SW	1869-09-01		A3 G332
566	" "	24	S½NW	1869-09-01		A3 G332
573	PAGE, Stephen F	20	S½SE	1867-01-15		A3 G211
578	" "	32	E½NE	1867-01-15		A3 G207
576	" "	8	E½NE	1867-01-15		A3 G206
577	" "	8	SWNE	1867-01-15		A3 G206
579	" "	8	W½NW	1867-01-15		A3 G209
571	" "	18	E½NE	1867-02-01		A3 G208
572	" "	18	NWNE	1867-02-01		A3 G208
574	" "	32	E½SW	1867-02-01		A3 G210
575	" "	32	SWSW	1867-02-01		A3 G210
573	RESSEGINE, Charles E	20	S½SE	1867-01-15		A3 G211
578	" "	32	E½NE	1867-01-15		A3 G207
576	" "	8	E½NE	1867-01-15		A3 G206
577	" "	8	SWNE	1867-01-15		A3 G206
579	" "	8	W½NW	1867-01-15		A3 G209
571	" "	18	E½NE	1867-02-01		A3 G208
572	" "	18	NWNE	1867-02-01		A3 G208
574	" "	32	E½SW	1867-02-01		A3 G210

ID	Individual in Patent	Sec.	Sec. Part	Date Issued	Other Counties	For More Info . . .
575	RESSEGINE, Charles E (Cont'd)	32	SWSW	1867-02-01		A3 G210
569	SEAMAN, Oliver	32	E½NW	1871-07-15		A3 G291
570	" "	32	SWNW	1871-07-15		A3 G291
541	SKINNER, Adolphus L	34	N½NE	1868-07-20		A3 G259
539	" "	26	SE	1938-02-18		A2
540	" "	26	SW	1939-03-24		A2
546	SQUIER, David W	10	2	1867-01-10		A1
547	" "	10	3	1867-01-10		A1
548	" "	10	4	1867-01-10		A1
549	" "	10	SWSW	1867-01-10		A1
569	TOWER, Osmond S	32	E½NW	1871-07-15		A3 G291
570	" "	32	SWNW	1871-07-15		A3 G291
565	WARREN, James M	24	N½SW	1869-09-01		A3 G332
566	" "	24	S½NW	1869-09-01		A3 G332
542	WILSON, Andrew	32	NWSW	1882-10-20		A4
550	WILSON, Gilbert F	24	NENW	1871-05-01		A1
551	" "	24	S½SW	1871-11-15		A1
552	" "	26	E½NW	1871-11-15		A1
553	" "	26	NWNE	1871-11-15		A1
554	" "	26	NWNW	1872-03-20		A1
576	WINN, William	8	E½NE	1867-01-15		A3 G206
577	" "	8	SWNE	1867-01-15		A3 G206
573	WITHEROW, John	20	S½SE	1867-01-15		A3 G211
573	WITHEROW, John H	20	S½SE	1867-01-15		A3 G211
579	" "	8	W½NW	1867-01-15		A3 G209
568	WOOD, John L	14	E½SE	1869-09-01		A3 G326
567	" "	14	N½NW	1869-09-01		A3 G325
565	" "	24	N½SW	1869-09-01		A3 G332
566	" "	24	S½NW	1869-09-01		A3 G332
560	" "	10	1	1870-05-02		A1
561	" "	14	SW	1870-05-02		A1
562	" "	14	W½SE	1870-05-02		A1
563	" "	26	E½NE	1870-05-02		A1
564	" "	26	SWNE	1870-05-02		A1

Patent Map

T15-N R13-W
Michigan-Toledo Strip Meridian

Map Group 6

Township Statistics

Parcels Mapped	:	42
Number of Patents	:	28
Number of Individuals	:	31
Patentees Identified	:	22
Number of Surnames	:	28
Multi-Patentee Parcels	:	18
Oldest Patent Date	:	1/10/1867
Most Recent Patent	:	3/24/1939
Block/Lot Parcels	:	4
Parcels Re - Issued	:	0
Parcels that Overlap	:	0
Cities and Towns	:	2
Cemeteries	:	1

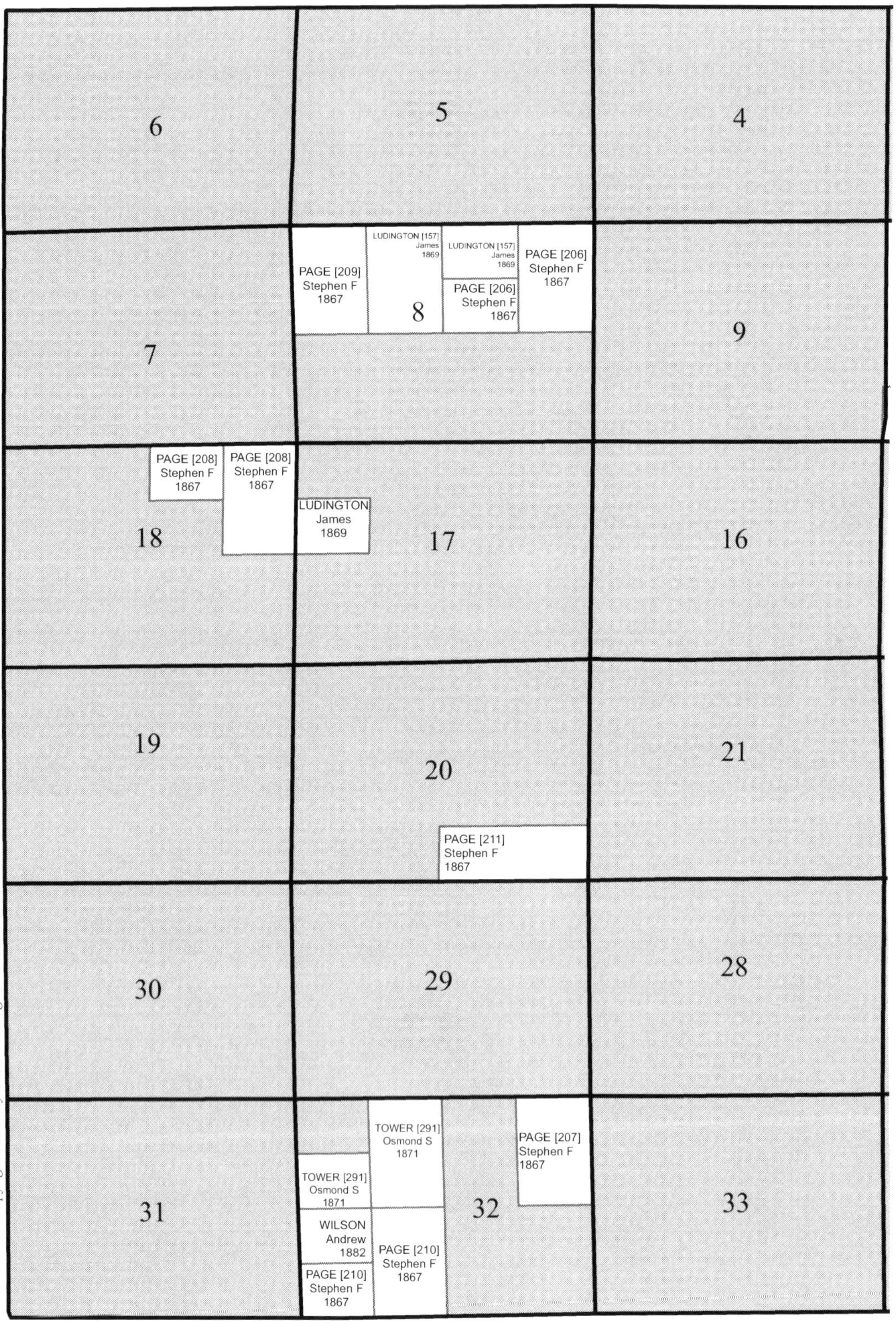

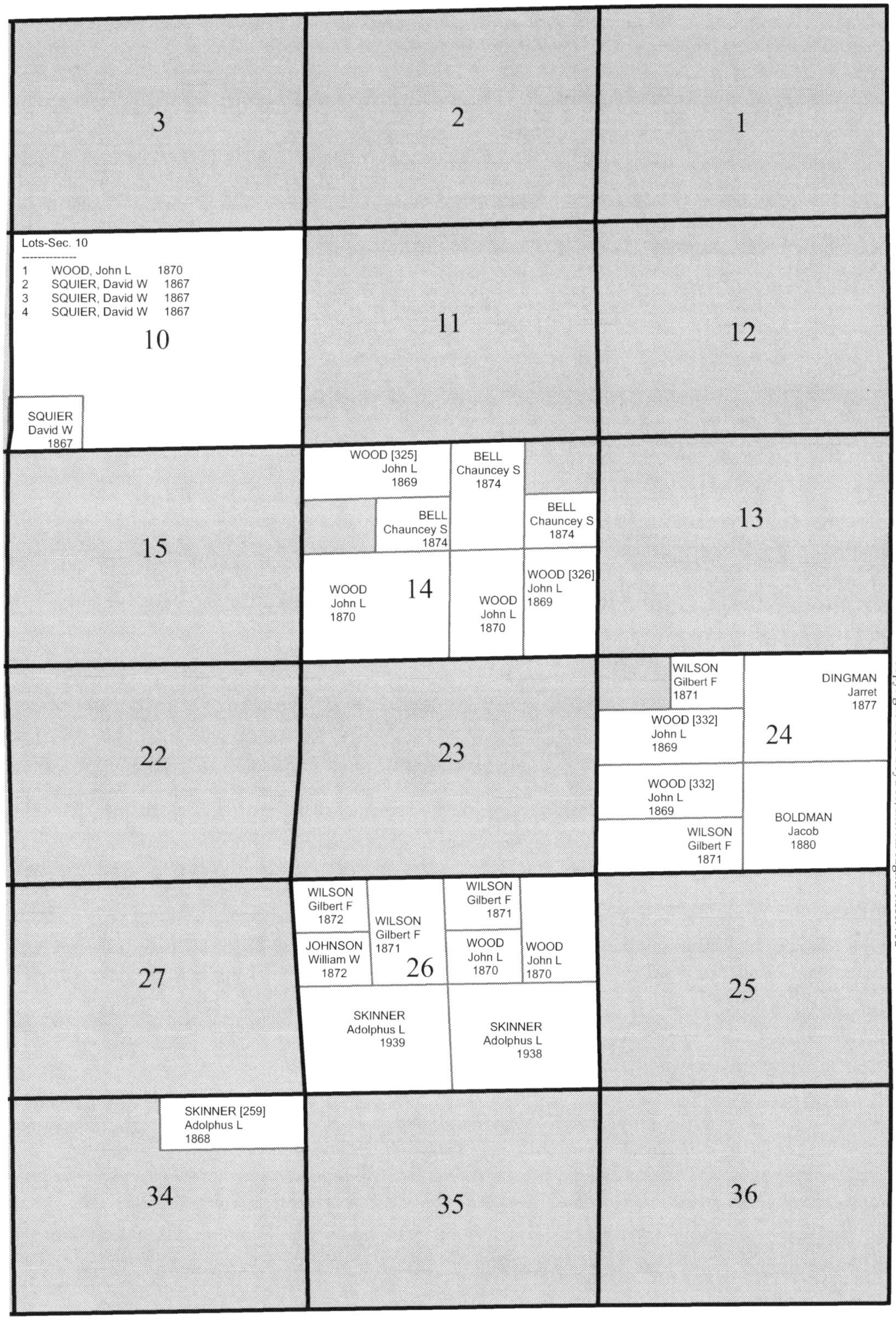

3
2
1

Lots-Sec. 10

1 WOOD, John L 1870
2 SQUIER, David W 1867
3 SQUIER, David W 1867
4 SQUIER, David W 1867

10

SQUIER David W 1867

11
12

WOOD [325] John L 1869
BELL Chauncey S 1874
BELL Chauncey S 1874
BELL Chauncey S 1874
WOOD John L 1870
14
WOOD John L 1870
WOOD [326] John L 1869

15
13

22
23

WILSON Gilbert F 1871
DINGMAN Jarret 1877
WOOD [332] John L 1869
24
WOOD [332] John L 1869
WILSON Gilbert F 1871
BOLDMAN Jacob 1880

27

WILSON Gilbert F 1872
WILSON Gilbert F 1871
WILSON Gilbert F 1871
JOHNSON William W 1872
26
WOOD John L 1870
WOOD John L 1870
SKINNER Adolphus L 1939
SKINNER Adolphus L 1938

25

SKINNER [259] Adolphus L 1868

34
35
36

Helpful Hints

1. This Map's INDEX can be found on the preceding pages.
2. Refer to Map "C" to see where this Township lies within Newaygo County, Michigan.
3. Numbers within square brackets [ ] denote a multi-patentee land parcel (multi-owner). Refer to Appendix "C" for a full list of members in this group.
4. Areas that look to be crowded with Patentees usually indicate multiple sales of the same parcel (Re-issues) or Overlapping parcels. See this Township's Index for an explanation of these and other circumstances that might explain "odd" groupings of Patentees on this map.

Legend

Patent Boundary

Section Boundary

No Patents Found (or Outside County)

1., 2., 3., ... Lot Numbers (when beside a name)

[ ] Group Number (see Appendix "C")

Scale: Section = 1 mile X 1 mile (generally, with some exceptions)

Road Map

T15-N R13-W
Michigan-Toledo Strip Meridian

Map Group 6

Cities & Towns

Brohman
Woodland Park

Cemeteries

Hillers Cemetery

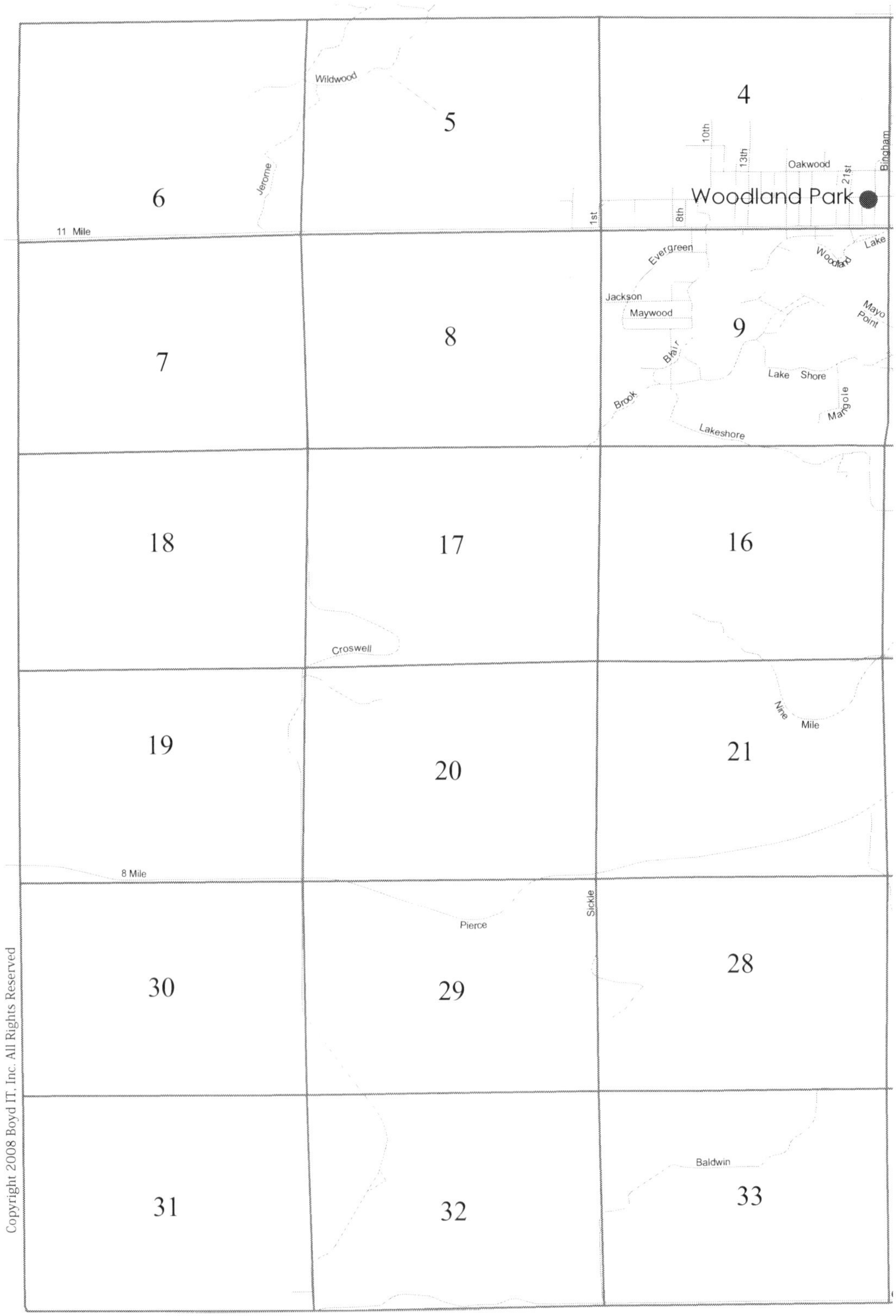

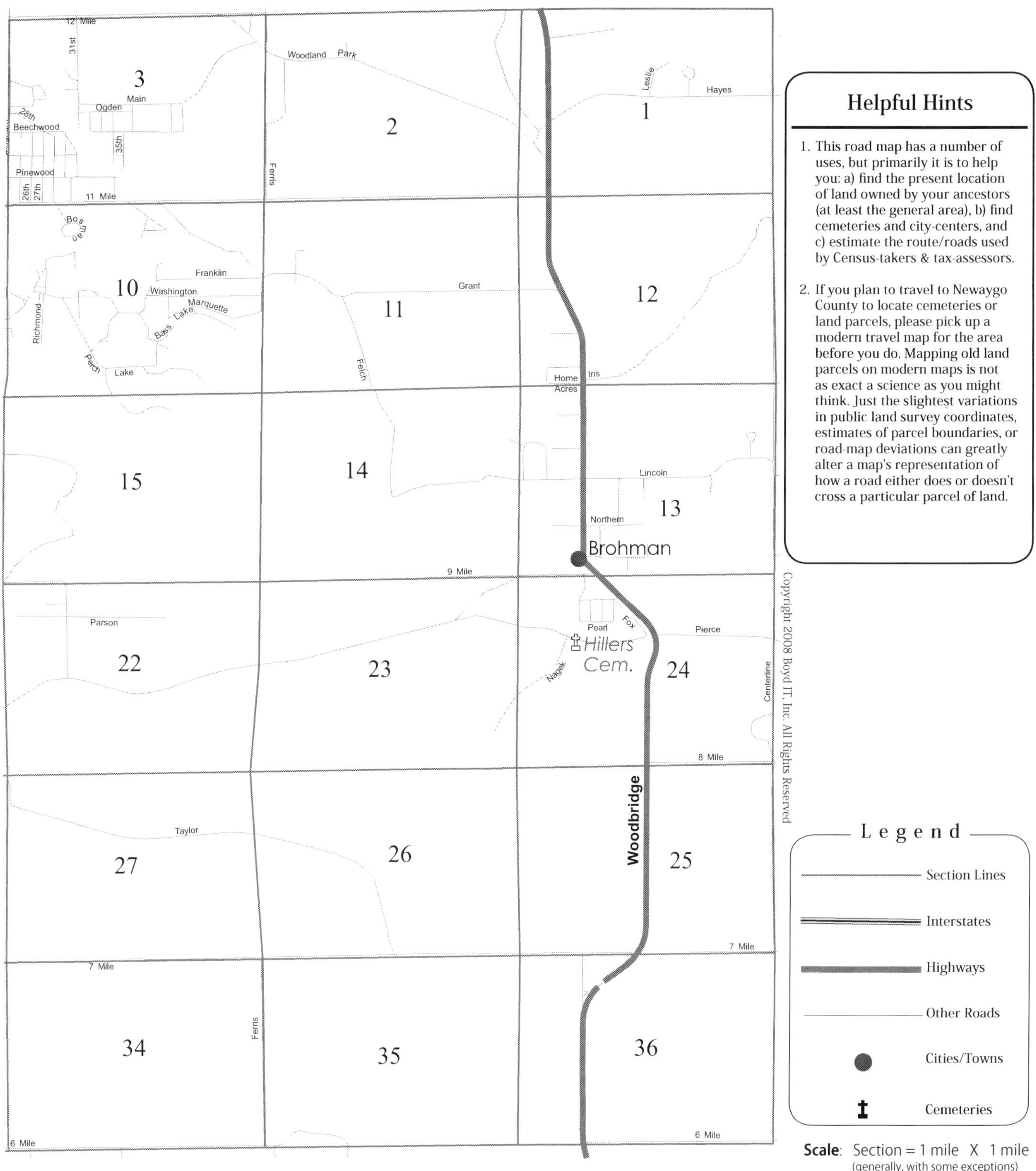

Helpful Hints

1. This road map has a number of uses, but primarily it is to help you: a) find the present location of land owned by your ancestors (at least the general area), b) find cemeteries and city-centers, and c) estimate the route/roads used by Census-takers & tax-assessors.

2. If you plan to travel to Newaygo County to locate cemeteries or land parcels, please pick up a modern travel map for the area before you do. Mapping old land parcels on modern maps is not as exact a science as you might think. Just the slightest variations in public land survey coordinates, estimates of parcel boundaries, or road-map deviations can greatly alter a map's representation of how a road either does or doesn't cross a particular parcel of land.

Scale: Section = 1 mile X 1 mile (generally, with some exceptions)

Historical Map

T15-N R13-W
Michigan-Toledo Strip Meridian

Map Group 6

Cities & Towns

Brohman
Woodland Park

Cemeteries

Hillers Cemetery

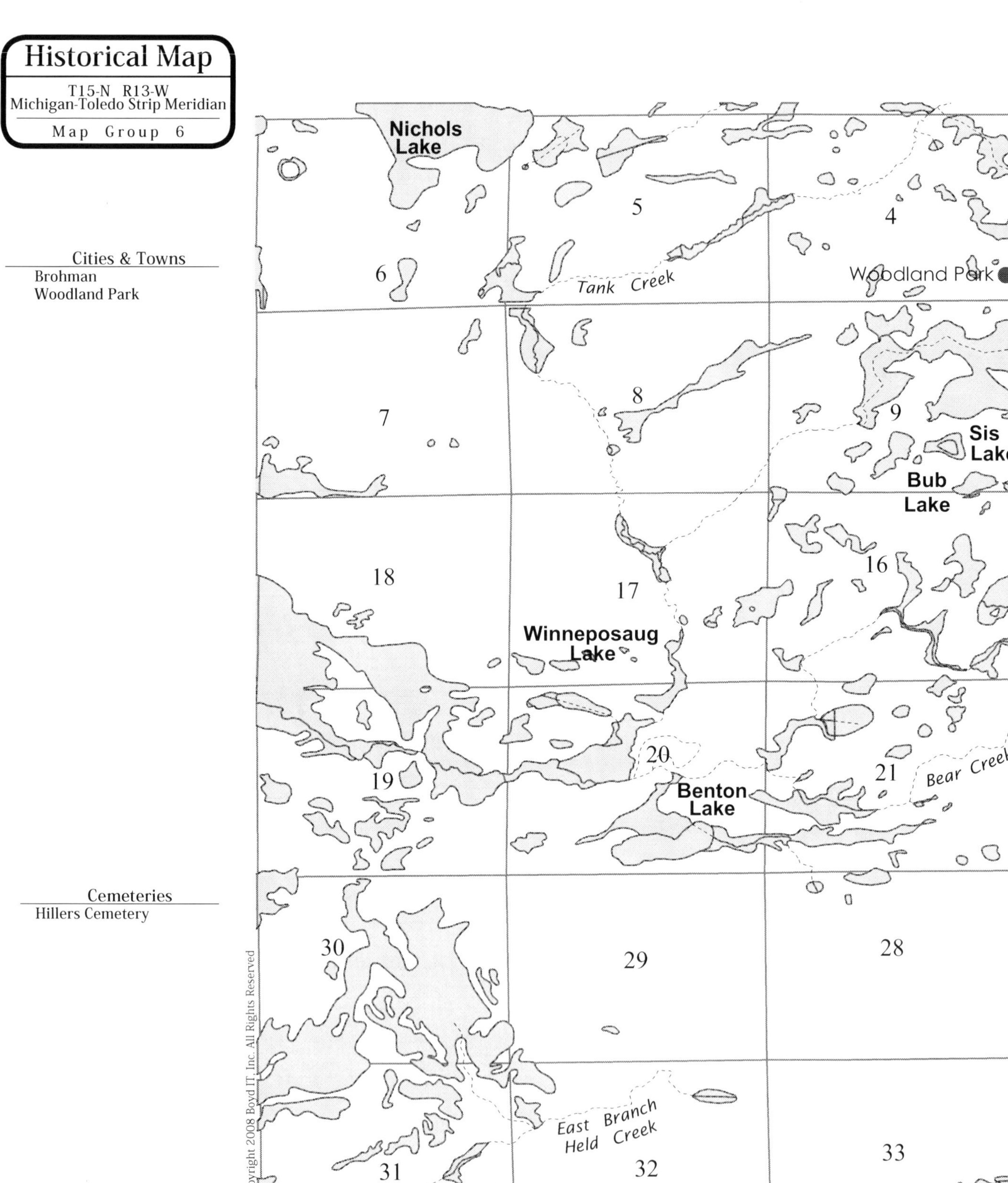

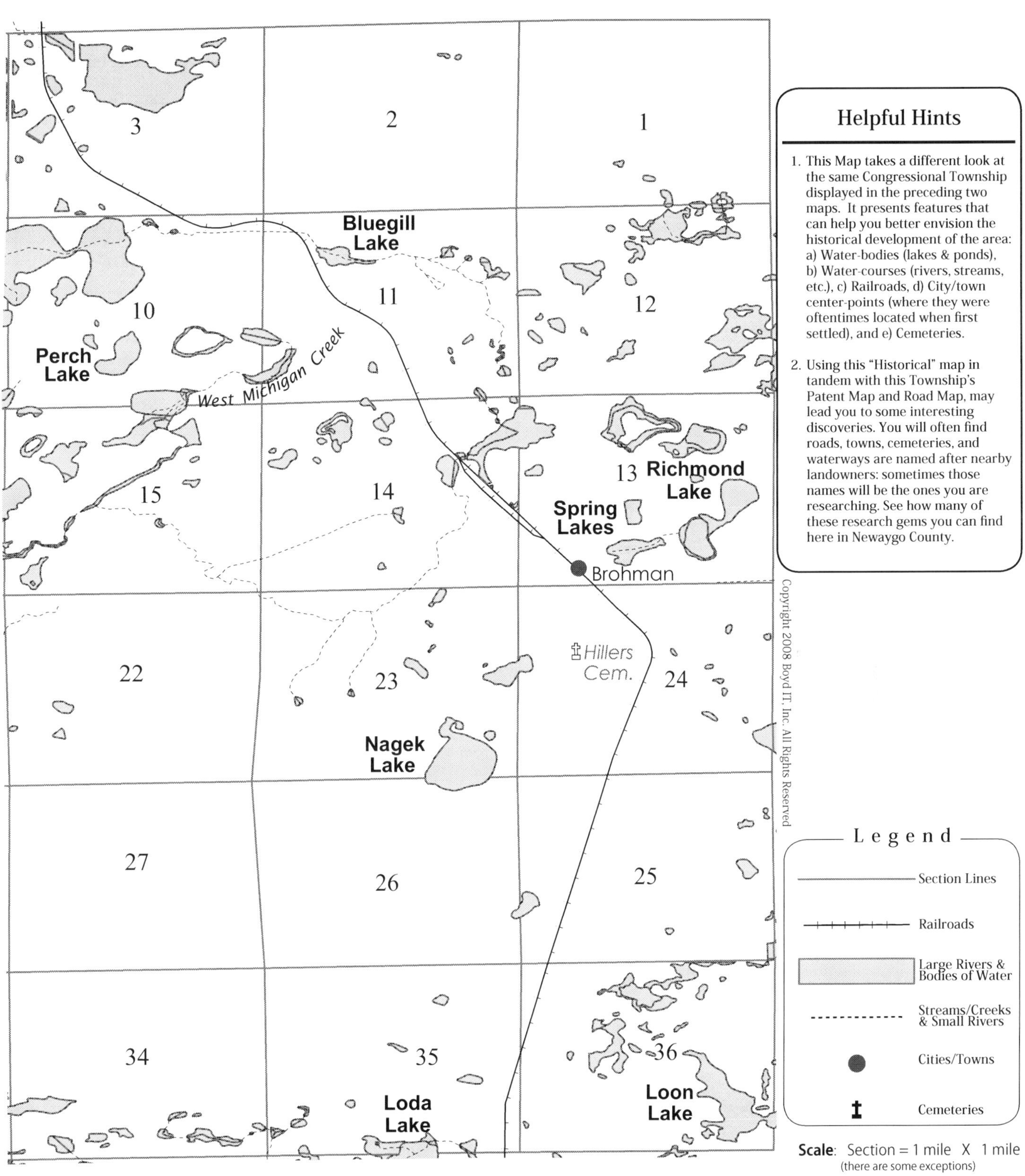

Helpful Hints

1. This Map takes a different look at the same Congressional Township displayed in the preceding two maps. It presents features that can help you better envision the historical development of the area: a) Water-bodies (lakes & ponds), b) Water-courses (rivers, streams, etc.), c) Railroads, d) City/town center-points (where they were oftentimes located when first settled), and e) Cemeteries.

2. Using this "Historical" map in tandem with this Township's Patent Map and Road Map, may lead you to some interesting discoveries. You will often find roads, towns, cemeteries, and waterways are named after nearby landowners: sometimes those names will be the ones you are researching. See how many of these research gems you can find here in Newaygo County.

Map Group 7: Index to Land Patents

Township 15-North Range 12-West (Michigan-Toledo Strip)

After you locate an individual in this Index, take note of the Section and Section Part then proceed to the Land Patent map on the pages immediately following. You should have no difficulty locating the corresponding parcel of land.

The "For More Info" Column will lead you to more information about the underlying Patents. See the *Legend* at right, and the "How to Use this Book" chapter, for more information.

LEGEND

"For More Info . . . " column

A = Authority (Legislative Act, See Appendix "A")
B = Block or Lot (location in Section unknown)
C = Cancelled Patent
F = Fractional Section
G = Group (Multi-Patentee Patent, see Appendix "C")
V = Overlaps another Parcel
R = Re-Issued (Parcel patented more than once)

(A & G items require you to look in the Appendixes referred to above. All other Letter-designations followed by a number require you to locate line-items in this index that possess the ID number found after the letter).

ID	Individual in Patent	Sec.	Sec. Part	Date Issued	Other Counties	For More Info . . .
590	BELL, Darwin G	14	NWSE	1885-01-07		A1 G32
590	CARLSON, Charles M	14	NWSE	1885-01-07		A1 G32
589	CHICK, Charles H	4	NWSW	1885-01-07		A1
607	COLLINS, David	20	NENW	1889-12-31		A1 G214
608	DAVIS, Stephen V	14	W½NE	1955-05-02		A1
595	EASTMAN, George	30	NWNW	1868-02-15		A1 G167 F
609	FALES, Thomas E	2	N½SE	1874-08-01		A4
595	HEFFERAN, Thomas	30	NWNW	1868-02-15		A1 G167 F
610	HINMAN, William G	10	NESE	1881-10-19		A1
591	IVES, Chauncey P	13	S½	1855-12-15		A1 G121
592	" "	24		1855-12-15		A1 G121
593	" "	25		1855-12-15		A1 G121
594	" "	36	E½	1855-12-15		A1 G121
596	JENKINS, Hunnewell	2	W½NE	1878-06-13		A4 F
581	KIEFER, Herman	10	S½NE	1868-12-01		A3 G273
582	" "	10	SENW	1868-12-01		A3 G273
583	" "	2	N½SW	1868-12-01		A3 G274
584	" "	6	NENE	1868-12-01		A3 G275 F
588	" "	6	NW	1868-12-01		A3 G277
585	" "	6	W½NE	1868-12-01		A3 G275 F
586	" "	8	S½NE	1868-12-01		A3 G276
587	" "	8	SENW	1868-12-01		A3 G276
591	LEONARD, Frederick B	13	S½	1855-12-15		A1 G121
592	" "	24		1855-12-15		A1 G121
593	" "	25		1855-12-15		A1 G121
594	" "	36	E½	1855-12-15		A1 G121
588	LICHTENBERG, Gustav	6	NW	1868-12-01		A3 G277
581	LICHTENBERG, Gustav B	10	S½NE	1868-12-01		A3 G273
582	" "	10	SENW	1868-12-01		A3 G273
583	" "	2	N½SW	1868-12-01		A3 G274
584	" "	6	NENE	1868-12-01		A3 G275 F
585	" "	6	W½NE	1868-12-01		A3 G275 F
586	" "	8	S½NE	1868-12-01		A3 G276
587	" "	8	SENW	1868-12-01		A3 G276
595	LULL, Hiram	30	NWNW	1868-02-15		A1 G167 F
583	MATHERS, Nancy	2	N½SW	1868-12-01		A3 G274
606	MILLER, Robert J	2	E½NE	1875-02-10		A4
607	PARKER, Samuel E	20	NENW	1889-12-31		A1 G214
583	PEAT, James	2	N½SW	1868-12-01		A3 G274
588	PRESTON, William E	6	NW	1868-12-01		A3 G277
584	PROBASCO, Mary	6	NENE	1868-12-01		A3 G275 F
585	" "	6	W½NE	1868-12-01		A3 G275 F
584	PROBASCO, Uzzet H	6	NENE	1868-12-01		A3 G275 F
585	" "	6	W½NE	1868-12-01		A3 G275 F
588	SIMMS, Juliet Ann	6	NW	1868-12-01		A3 G277
611	SMITH, William	6	SENE	1877-03-01		A4

ID	Individual in Patent	Sec.	Sec. Part	Date Issued	Other Counties	For More Info . . .
581	STROH, Bernhard	10	S½NE	1868-12-01		A3 G273
582	" "	10	SENW	1868-12-01		A3 G273
583	" "	2	N½SW	1868-12-01		A3 G274
584	" "	6	NENE	1868-12-01		A3 G275 F
588	" "	6	NW	1868-12-01		A3 G277
585	" "	6	W½NE	1868-12-01		A3 G275 F
586	" "	8	S½NE	1868-12-01		A3 G276
587	" "	8	SENW	1868-12-01		A3 G276
583	TUTTLE, Elias W	2	N½SW	1868-12-01		A3 G274
597	WOOD, John L	10	NWNW	1870-05-02		A1
598	" "	14	E½NE	1870-05-02		A1 F
599	" "	14	E½SE	1870-05-02		A1 F
600	" "	14	SWSE	1870-05-02		A1 F
601	" "	22	W½SW	1870-05-02		A1
602	" "	26	E½	1870-05-02		A1
603	" "	26	E½SW	1870-05-02		A1
604	" "	26	NW	1870-05-02		A1
605	" "	26	NWSW	1870-05-02		A1
586	WRIGHT, Mary	8	S½NE	1868-12-01		A3 G276
587	" "	8	SENW	1868-12-01		A3 G276

Patent Map

T15-N R12-W
Michigan-Toledo Strip Meridian

Map Group 7

Township Statistics

Parcels Mapped	:	31
Number of Patents	:	23
Number of Individuals	:	29
Patentees Identified	:	17
Number of Surnames	:	27
Multi-Patentee Parcels	:	15
Oldest Patent Date	:	12/15/1855
Most Recent Patent	:	5/2/1955
Block/Lot Parcels	:	0
Parcels Re - Issued	:	0
Parcels that Overlap	:	0
Cities and Towns	:	1
Cemeteries	:	0

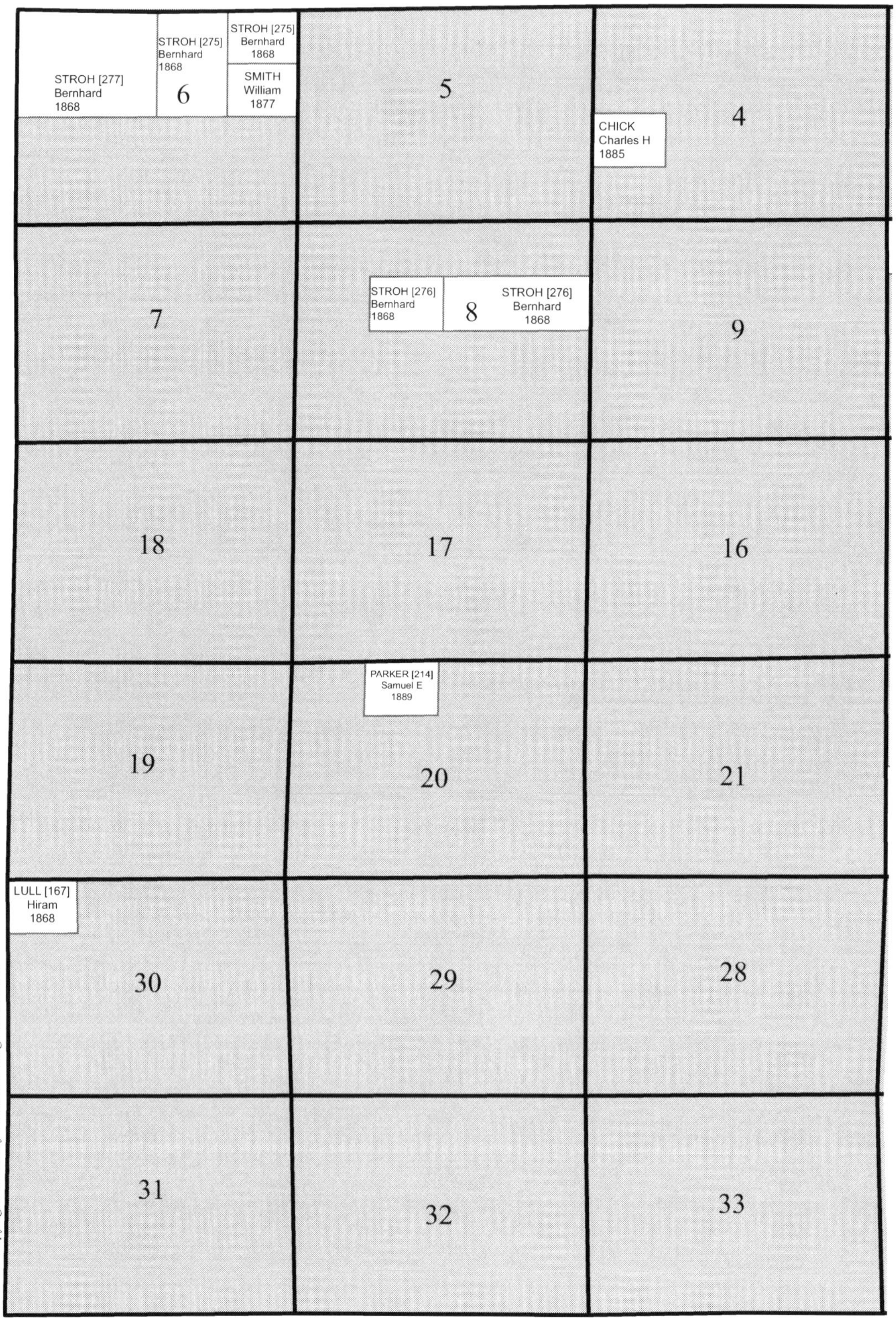

STROH [277] Bernhard 1868
STROH [275] Bernhard 1868
STROH [275] Bernhard 1868
6
SMITH William 1877
5
4
CHICK Charles H 1885
7
STROH [276] Bernhard 1868
8
STROH [276] Bernhard 1868
9
18
17
16
PARKER [214] Samuel E 1889
19
20
21
LULL [167] Hiram 1868
30
29
28
31
32
33

Helpful Hints

1. This Map's INDEX can be found on the preceding pages.
2. Refer to Map "C" to see where this Township lies within Newaygo County, Michigan.
3. Numbers within square brackets [ ] denote a multi-patentee land parcel (multi-owner). Refer to Appendix "C" for a full list of members in this group.
4. Areas that look to be crowded with Patentees usually indicate multiple sales of the same parcel (Re-issues) or Overlapping parcels. See this Township's Index for an explanation of these and other circumstances that might explain "odd" groupings of Patentees on this map.

Legend

- Patent Boundary
- Section Boundary
- No Patents Found (or Outside County)
- 1., 2., 3., ... Lot Numbers (when beside a name)
- [ ] Group Number (see Appendix "C")

Scale: Section = 1 mile X 1 mile
(generally, with some exceptions)

Road Map

T15-N R12-W
Michigan-Toledo Strip Meridian

Map Group 7

Cities & Towns

Woodville

Cemeteries

None

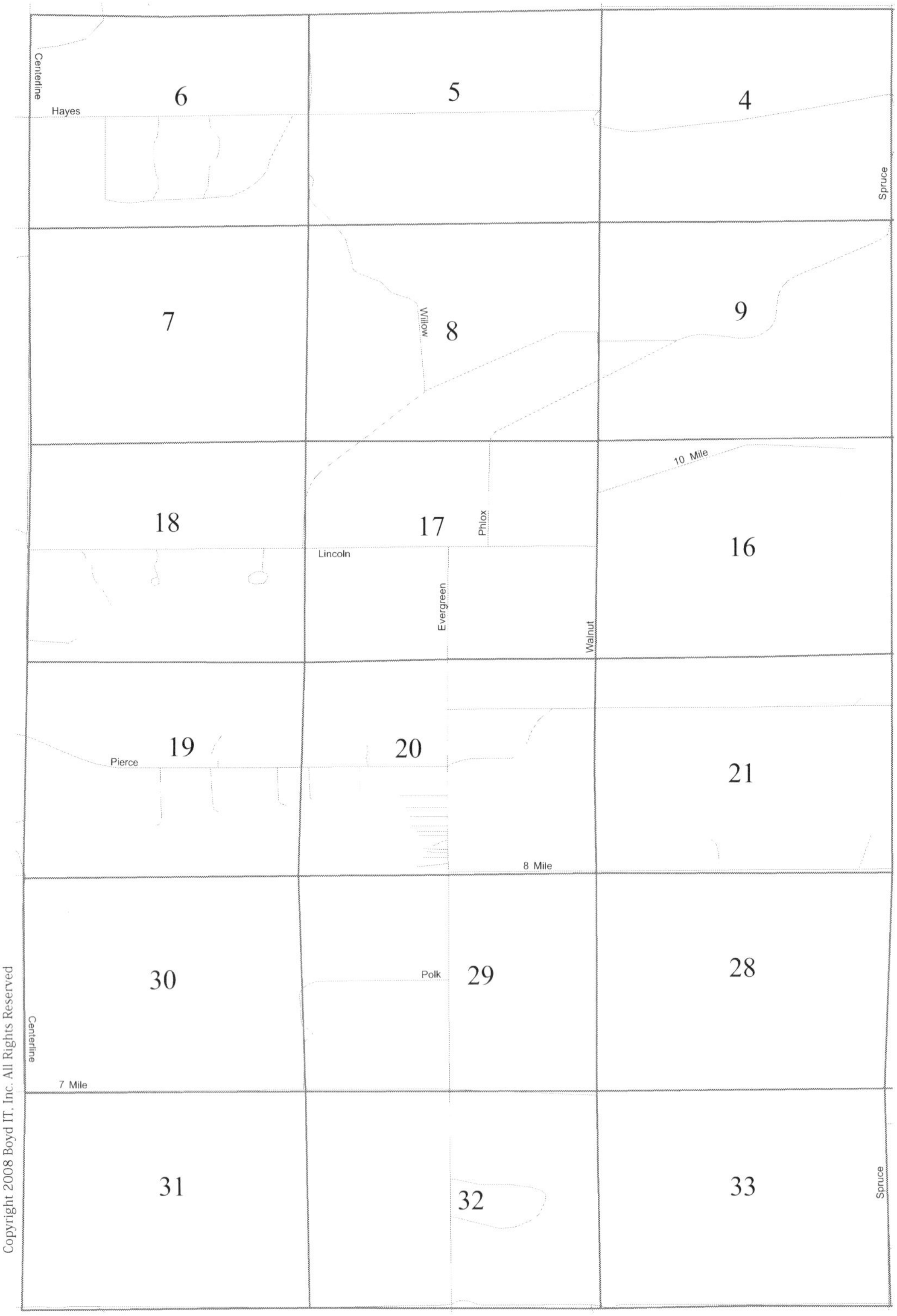

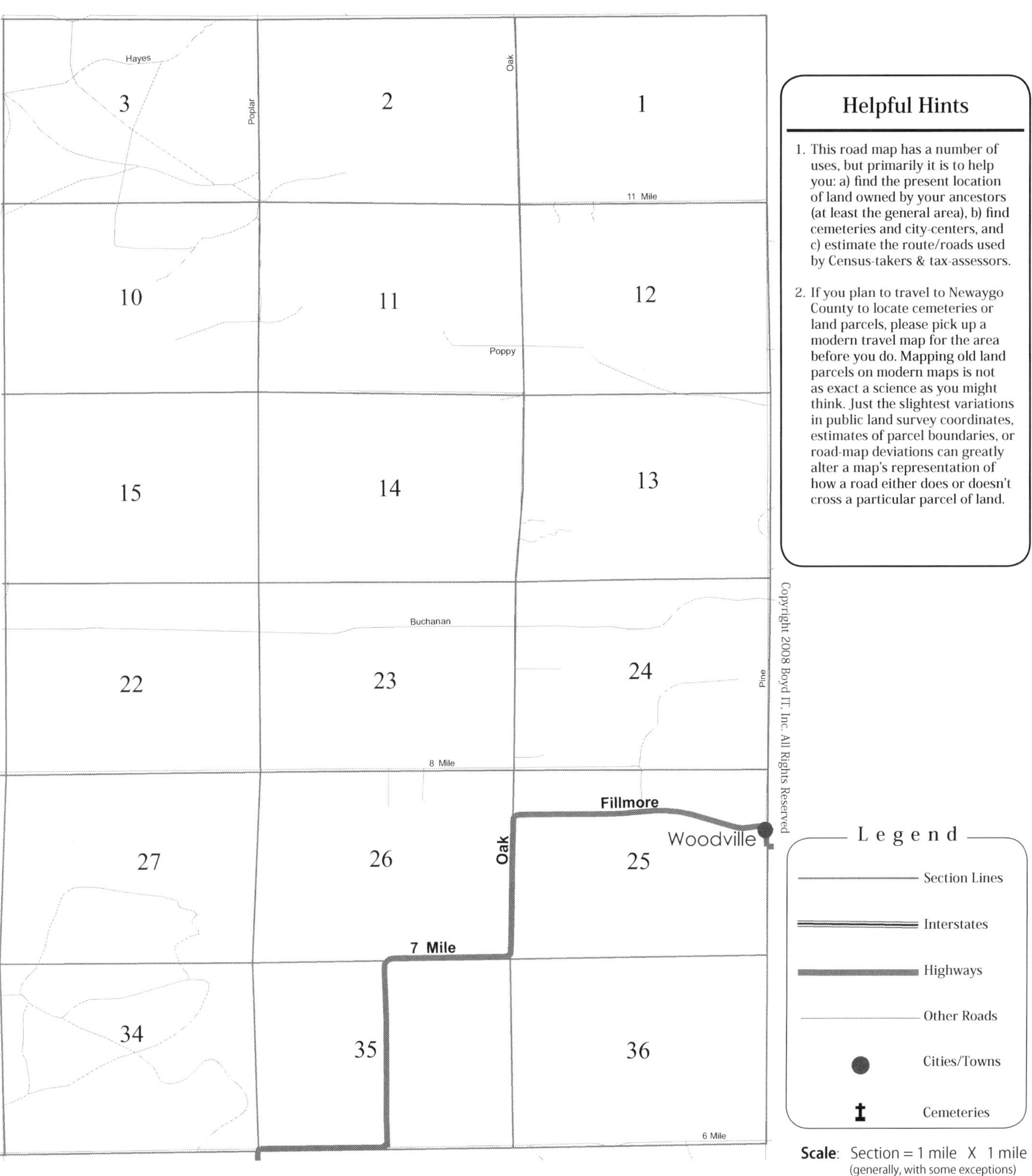

Helpful Hints

1. This road map has a number of uses, but primarily it is to help you: a) find the present location of land owned by your ancestors (at least the general area), b) find cemeteries and city-centers, and c) estimate the route/roads used by Census-takers & tax-assessors.

2. If you plan to travel to Newaygo County to locate cemeteries or land parcels, please pick up a modern travel map for the area before you do. Mapping old land parcels on modern maps is not as exact a science as you might think. Just the slightest variations in public land survey coordinates, estimates of parcel boundaries, or road-map deviations can greatly alter a map's representation of how a road either does or doesn't cross a particular parcel of land.

Historical Map

T15-N R12-W
Michigan-Toledo Strip Meridian

Map Group 7

Cities & Towns
Woodville

Cemeteries
None

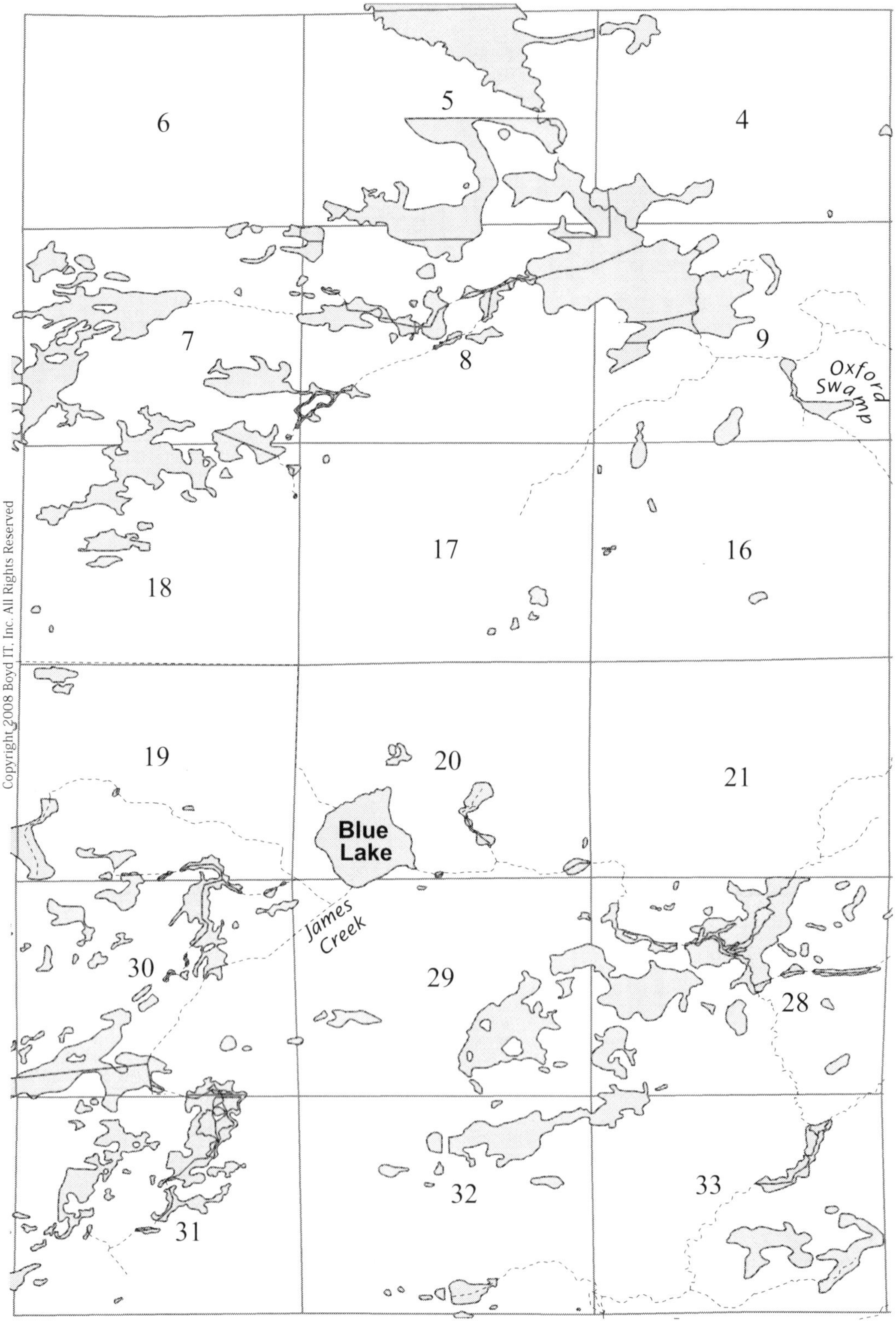

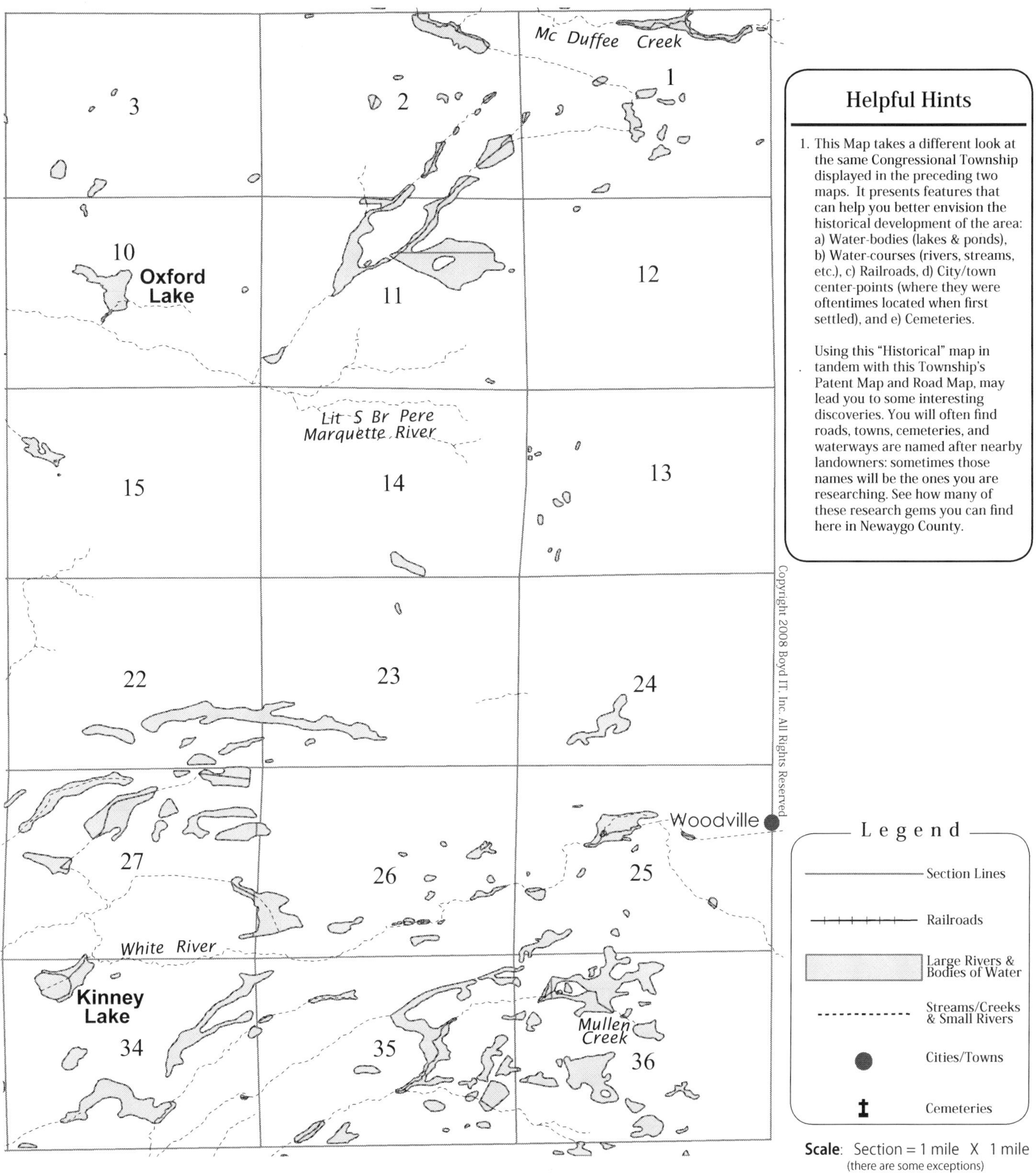

Helpful Hints

1. This Map takes a different look at the same Congressional Township displayed in the preceding two maps. It presents features that can help you better envision the historical development of the area: a) Water-bodies (lakes & ponds), b) Water-courses (rivers, streams, etc.), c) Railroads, d) City/town center-points (where they were oftentimes located when first settled), and e) Cemeteries.

   Using this "Historical" map in tandem with this Township's Patent Map and Road Map, may lead you to some interesting discoveries. You will often find roads, towns, cemeteries, and waterways are named after nearby landowners: sometimes those names will be the ones you are researching. See how many of these research gems you can find here in Newaygo County.

Scale: Section = 1 mile X 1 mile
(there are some exceptions)

Map Group 8: Index to Land Patents

Township 15-North Range 11-West (Michigan-Toledo Strip)

After you locate an individual in this Index, take note of the Section and Section Part then proceed to the Land Patent map on the pages immediately following. You should have no difficulty locating the corresponding parcel of land.

The "For More Info" Column will lead you to more information about the underlying Patents. See the *Legend* at right, and the "How to Use this Book" chapter, for more information.

LEGEND

"For More Info . . . " column

A = Authority (Legislative Act, See Appendix "A")
B = Block or Lot (location in Section unknown)
C = Cancelled Patent
F = Fractional Section
G = Group (Multi-Patentee Patent, see Appendix "C")
V = Overlaps another Parcel
R = Re-Issued (Parcel patented more than once)

(A & G items require you to look in the Appendixes referred to above. All other Letter-designations followed by a number require you to locate line-items in this index that possess the ID number found after the letter).

ID	Individual in Patent	Sec.	Sec. Part	Date Issued	Other Counties	For More Info . . .
749	BALL, John	24	SE	1855-03-01		A1
750	" "	25	E½	1855-03-01		A1
751	" "	36	E½	1855-03-01		A1
669	BALL, Malinda C	18	W½NW	1870-06-01		A3 G14 F
744	BARTON, George	26	N½SW	1873-02-10		A4
797	BARTON, Willard	32	E½SE	1873-02-10		A4 F
798	" "	32	S½NE	1873-02-10		A4 F
656	BEAZLEY, Martha E	11	E½SW	1859-08-03		A3 G92
657	" "	11	SENW	1859-08-03		A3 G92
742	BEDIENT, Eunice	31	NESW	1859-08-10		A3 G297 F
743	" "	31	W½SW	1859-08-10		A3 G297 F
662	BENJAMIN, D M	18	SENE	1870-05-10		A1 F
663	" "	6	SWSW	1870-05-10		A1 F
664	" "	8	SWNW	1870-05-10		A1
666	BENJAMIN, D Marcellus	18	E½NW	1870-06-01		A3 G13 F
667	" "	18	N½NE	1870-06-01		A3 G13 F
668	" "	18	SWNE	1870-06-01		A3 G13 F
669	" "	18	W½NW	1870-06-01		A3 G14 F
670	" "	6	S½SE	1870-06-01		A3 G15
671	" "	6	SESW	1870-06-01		A3 G15
665	" "	8	N½NE	1870-06-01		A3 G16
616	BENNETT, Alfred J	6	W½NE	1875-02-10		A4 F
732	BENNETT, Mary	12	SENW	1859-08-03		A3 G123
733	" "	12	W½NE	1859-08-03		A3 G123
777	BROWN, John W	12	NENW	1875-02-10		A4
741	BRUNSON, Rebecca	1	N½NE	1859-08-10		A3 G120 F
771	BUSH, John J	8	SESW	1870-06-01		A3 G86
772	" "	8	W½SE	1870-06-01		A3 G86
773	" "	8	N½SW	1871-07-15		A3 G87
774	" "	8	SWSW	1871-07-15		A3 G87
673	BUTTON, Demetrius	26	E½SE	1873-02-10		A4 F
757	CLARK, Lafred L	13	S½	1855-12-15		A1 G59
758	" "	13	S½NE	1855-12-15		A1 G59
759	" "	13	S½NW	1855-12-15		A1 G59
760	" "	14	S½NE	1855-12-15		A1 G59
761	" "	14	S½NW	1855-12-15		A1 G59
762	" "	14	SE	1855-12-15		A1 G59
763	" "	21	S½SW	1855-12-15		A1 G59
764	" "	23	NE	1855-12-15		A1 G59
765	" "	23	S½	1855-12-15		A1 G59
766	" "	24	N½	1855-12-15		A1 G59
767	" "	24	SW	1855-12-15		A1 G59
768	" "	28	N½NW	1855-12-15		A1 G59
778	CONKLIN, Joseph	34	NWSW	1883-08-01		A4
746	CUDABACK, Harvey	32	N½SW	1860-09-03		A3 G48
747	" "	32	SESW	1860-09-03		A3 G48

ID	Individual in Patent	Sec.	Sec. Part	Date Issued	Other Counties	For More Info . . .
748	CUDABACK, Harvey (Cont'd)	32	SWSE	1860-09-03		A3 G48
752	CUDABACK, John D	28	N½SW	1860-09-03		A3
753	" "	28	S½NW	1860-09-03		A3
757	ELY, John J	13	S½	1855-12-15		A1 G59
758	" "	13	S½NE	1855-12-15		A1 G59
759	" "	13	S½NW	1855-12-15		A1 G59
760	" "	14	S½NE	1855-12-15		A1 G59
761	" "	14	S½NW	1855-12-15		A1 G59
762	" "	14	SE	1855-12-15		A1 G59
763	" "	21	S½SW	1855-12-15		A1 G59
764	" "	23	NE	1855-12-15		A1 G59
765	" "	23	S½	1855-12-15		A1 G59
766	" "	24	N½	1855-12-15		A1 G59
767	" "	24	SW	1855-12-15		A1 G59
768	" "	28	N½NW	1855-12-15		A1 G59
617	EWING, Benjamin L	6	N½NW	1877-04-05		A4 F
780	EWING, Newton	6	S½NW	1877-04-05		A4 F
612	EYCK, Abraham Ten	32	E½NW	1873-05-15		A1 F
613	" "	32	SWNW	1873-05-15		A1 F
654	FARINHOLT, Maria	10	W½SE	1859-08-03		A3 G93
655	" "	15	NWNE	1859-08-03		A3 G93
773	FERRISS, Lucy Maria	8	N½SW	1871-07-15		A3 G87
774	" "	8	SWSW	1871-07-15		A3 G87
642	FISCHER, Angelles	4	E½SE	1859-08-03		A3 G97
643	" "	9	NENE	1859-08-03		A3 G97
656	FOGG, Elzer	11	E½SW	1859-08-03		A3 G92
657	" "	11	SENW	1859-08-03		A3 G92
781	FORD, Oliver B	12	S½SE	1855-12-15		A1
782	" "	12	S½SW	1855-12-15		A1
783	" "	13	N½NE	1855-12-15		A1
784	" "	13	N½NW	1855-12-15		A1
785	" "	35	S½	1855-12-15		A1
786	" "	36	W½	1855-12-15		A1
669	GASTON, Mary J	18	W½NW	1870-06-01		A3 G14 F
669	GASTON, William S	18	W½NW	1870-06-01		A3 G14 F
650	GATEWOOD, Rhoda	11	N½NW	1859-08-03		A3 G98 C R736
736	" "	11	N½NW	1859-08-03		A3 G126 R650
651	" "	2	SWSW	1859-08-03		A3 G98 C R737
737	" "	2	SWSW	1859-08-03		A3 G126 R651
666	HALL, Rebecca	18	E½NW	1870-06-01		A3 G13 F
667	" "	18	N½NE	1870-06-01		A3 G13 F
668	" "	18	SWNE	1870-06-01		A3 G13 F
618	HATFIELD, Caleb	34	NENE	1875-04-20		A4
754	HATFIELD, John E	26	SWSW	1874-04-01		A4
771	HILDRETH, John P	8	SESW	1870-06-01		A3 G86
772	" "	8	W½SE	1870-06-01		A3 G86
773	" "	8	N½SW	1871-07-15		A3 G87
775	" "	8	NESE	1871-07-15		A3 G88
776	" "	8	S½NE	1871-07-15		A3 G88
774	" "	8	SWSW	1871-07-15		A3 G87
644	HOLLOWAY, Joanna	10	N½NE	1859-08-03		A3 G99
645	" "	10	NENW	1859-08-03		A3 G99
658	HOUSTON, Nancy	14	N½NW	1859-08-03		A3 G94
659	" "	14	NWNE	1859-08-03		A3 G94
669	HUNTER, Noble W	18	W½NW	1870-06-01		A3 G14 F
669	HUNTER, Sarah	18	W½NW	1870-06-01		A3 G14 F
670	HUSTON, Tabitha	6	S½SE	1870-06-01		A3 G15
671	" "	6	SESW	1870-06-01		A3 G15
726	HUTCHERSON, Elizabeth	4	N½SW	1859-08-03		A3 G129
727	" "	4	NWSE	1859-08-03		A3 G129
693	IVES, Chauncey P	19		1855-12-15		A1 G121 F
711	" "	30		1855-12-15		A1 G121 F
712	" "	31	N	1855-12-15		A1 G121 F
692	" "	18	S½	1856-03-10		A1 G121 F
684	" "	17	E½SW	1858-01-15		A3 G121
685	" "	17	N½NE	1858-01-15		A3 G121
686	" "	17	NENW	1858-01-15		A3 G121
687	" "	17	NWSW	1858-01-15		A3 G121
688	" "	17	S½NE	1858-01-15		A3 G121
689	" "	17	SENW	1858-01-15		A3 G121
690	" "	17	SESE	1858-01-15		A3 G121
691	" "	17	W½NW	1858-01-15		A3 G121
696	" "	20	E½NE	1858-01-15		A3 G121

ID	Individual in Patent	Sec.	Sec. Part	Date Issued	Other Counties	For More Info . . .
697	IVES, Chauncey P (Cont'd)	20	N½SE	1858-01-15		A3 G121
698	" "	20	NESW	1858-01-15		A3 G121
699	" "	20	SESW	1858-01-15		A3 G121
700	" "	20	SWNW	1858-01-15		A3 G121
701	" "	20	W½SW	1858-01-15		A3 G121
702	" "	21	E½NW	1858-01-15		A3 G121
703	" "	21	NESW	1858-01-15		A3 G121
704	" "	21	NWSE	1858-01-15		A3 G121
705	" "	21	NWSW	1858-01-15		A3 G121
706	" "	21	W½NE	1858-01-15		A3 G121
707	" "	21	W½NW	1858-01-15		A3 G121
734	" "	29		1858-01-15		A3 G138
708	" "	29	N½NW	1858-01-15		A3 G121 V734
735	" "	29	N½SE	1858-01-15		A3 G138 V734
709	" "	29	NWSW	1858-01-15		A3 G121 V734
710	" "	29	S½NW	1858-01-15		A3 G121 V734
713	" "	31	SESE	1858-01-15		A3 G121
714	" "	31	W½SE	1858-01-15		A3 G121
717	" "	5	E½SE	1858-01-15		A3 G121
718	" "	5	E½SW	1858-01-15		A3 G121
719	" "	5	SENE	1858-01-15		A3 G121
720	" "	5	SENW	1858-01-15		A3 G121
721	" "	5	SWNE	1858-01-15		A3 G121
722	" "	5	SWNW	1858-01-15		A3 G121
723	" "	5	W½SE	1858-01-15		A3 G121
724	" "	5	W½SW	1858-01-15		A3 G121
725	" "	8	SESE	1858-01-15		A3 G121
619	" "	10	E½SW	1859-08-03		A3 G96
644	" "	10	N½NE	1859-08-03		A3 G99
645	" "	10	NENW	1859-08-03		A3 G99
620	" "	10	NESE	1859-08-03		A3 G96
621	" "	10	NWSW	1859-08-03		A3 G96
622	" "	10	S½NE	1859-08-03		A3 G96
652	" "	10	SENW	1859-08-03		A3 G103
623	" "	10	SWSW	1859-08-03		A3 G96
653	" "	10	W½NW	1859-08-03		A3 G103
654	" "	10	W½SE	1859-08-03		A3 G93
656	" "	11	E½SW	1859-08-03		A3 G92
650	" "	11	N½NW	1859-08-03		A3 G98 C R736
736	" "	11	N½NW	1859-08-03		A3 G126 R650
676	" "	11	N½SE	1859-08-03		A3 G121 R677
676	" "	11	N½SE	1859-08-03		A3 G121 C R677
677	" "	11	N½SE	1859-08-03		A3 G121 R676
677	" "	11	N½SE	1859-08-03		A3 G121 C R676
624	" "	11	S½NE	1859-08-03		A3 G96 C R678
678	" "	11	S½NE	1859-08-03		A3 G121 R624
646	" "	11	S½SE	1859-08-03		A3 G101
657	" "	11	SENW	1859-08-03		A3 G92
660	" "	11	SWNW	1859-08-03		A3 G95
661	" "	11	W½SW	1859-08-03		A3 G95
679	" "	12	N½SE	1859-08-03		A3 G121
680	" "	12	NESW	1859-08-03		A3 G121
681	" "	12	NWSW	1859-08-03		A3 G121 R682
681	" "	12	NWSW	1859-08-03		A3 G121 C R682
682	" "	12	NWSW	1859-08-03		A3 G121 R681
682	" "	12	NWSW	1859-08-03		A3 G121 C R681
732	" "	12	SENW	1859-08-03		A3 G123
625	" "	12	SWNW	1859-08-03		A3 G96 C R683
683	" "	12	SWNW	1859-08-03		A3 G121 R625
733	" "	12	W½NE	1859-08-03		A3 G123
658	" "	14	N½NW	1859-08-03		A3 G94
647	" "	14	NENE	1859-08-03		A3 G101
659	" "	14	NWNE	1859-08-03		A3 G94
626	" "	15	1	1859-08-03		A3 G96
627	" "	15	2	1859-08-03		A3 G96
655	" "	15	NWNE	1859-08-03		A3 G93
728	" "	2	E½NW	1859-08-03		A3 G139 F
740	" "	2	N½NE	1859-08-03		A3 G143 F
694	" "	2	N½SE	1859-08-03		A3 G121
695	" "	2	NESW	1859-08-03		A3 G121
729	" "	2	NWNW	1859-08-03		A3 G139 F
730	" "	2	S½SE	1859-08-03		A3 G142
731	" "	2	SESW	1859-08-03		A3 G142

ID	Individual in Patent	Sec.	Sec. Part	Date Issued	Other Counties	For More Info . . .
651	IVES, Chauncey P (Cont'd) (Cont'd)	2	SWSW	1859-08-03		A3 G98 C R737
737	" "	2	SWSW	1859-08-03		A3 G126 R651
642	" "	4	E½SE	1859-08-03		A3 G97
648	" "	4	N½NE	1859-08-03		A3 G100 F
738	" "	4	N½NW	1859-08-03		A3 G141 F
726	" "	4	N½SW	1859-08-03		A3 G129
727	" "	4	NWSE	1859-08-03		A3 G129
628	" "	4	S½NW	1859-08-03		A3 G96
715	" "	4	S½SW	1859-08-03		A3 G121
649	" "	4	SENE	1859-08-03		A3 G100 F
629	" "	4	SWNE	1859-08-03		A3 G96
716	" "	4	SWSE	1859-08-03		A3 G121
630	" "	5	N½NW	1859-08-03		A3 G96 F
739	" "	5	NENE	1859-08-03		A3 G141 F
631	" "	5	NWNE	1859-08-03		A3 G96 F
632	" "	9	E½SE	1859-08-03		A3 G96
633	" "	9	N½NW	1859-08-03		A3 G96
634	" "	9	N½SW	1859-08-03		A3 G96
643	" "	9	NENE	1859-08-03		A3 G97
635	" "	9	NWNE	1859-08-03		A3 G96
636	" "	9	NWSE	1859-08-03		A3 G96
637	" "	9	S½SW	1859-08-03		A3 G96 R638
638	" "	9	S½SW	1859-08-03		A3 G96 R637
639	" "	9	SENE	1859-08-03		A3 G96
640	" "	9	SWNE	1859-08-03		A3 G96
641	" "	9	SWSE	1859-08-03		A3 G96
742	IVES, Chauncy P	31	NESW	1859-08-10		A3 G297 F
743	" "	31	W½SW	1859-08-10		A3 G297 F
669	JACOBS, John C	18	W½NW	1870-06-01		A3 G14 F
665	JOHNSON, Nehemiah	8	N½NE	1870-06-01		A3 G16
796	JOHNSON, Wellington	34	S½SW	1880-11-20		A4 F
660	JONES, William T	11	SWNW	1859-08-03		A3 G95
661	" "	11	W½SW	1859-08-03		A3 G95
793	LANGFORD, Rosalia	34	NENW	1878-06-13		A4 F
794	" "	34	NWNE	1878-06-13		A4 F
614	LAWRENCE, Alexander	28	N½SE	1874-04-01		A4
615	" "	28	SWNE	1874-04-01		A4
787	LEACH, Paul A	8	E½NW	1866-11-10		A3 G116
788	" "	8	NWNW	1866-11-10		A3 G116
670	LENNEN, Peter	6	S½SE	1870-06-01		A3 G15
671	" "	6	SESW	1870-06-01		A3 G15
693	LEONARD, Frederick B	19		1855-12-15		A1 G121 F
711	" "	30		1855-12-15		A1 G121 F
712	" "	31	N	1855-12-15		A1 G121 F
692	" "	18	S½	1856-03-10		A1 G121 F
684	" "	17	E½SW	1858-01-15		A3 G121
685	" "	17	N½NE	1858-01-15		A3 G121
686	" "	17	NENW	1858-01-15		A3 G121
687	" "	17	NWSW	1858-01-15		A3 G121
688	" "	17	S½NE	1858-01-15		A3 G121
689	" "	17	SENW	1858-01-15		A3 G121
690	" "	17	SESE	1858-01-15		A3 G121
691	" "	17	W½NW	1858-01-15		A3 G121
696	" "	20	E½NE	1858-01-15		A3 G121
697	" "	20	N½SE	1858-01-15		A3 G121
698	" "	20	NESW	1858-01-15		A3 G121
699	" "	20	SESW	1858-01-15		A3 G121
700	" "	20	SWNW	1858-01-15		A3 G121
701	" "	20	W½SW	1858-01-15		A3 G121
702	" "	21	E½NW	1858-01-15		A3 G121
703	" "	21	NESW	1858-01-15		A3 G121
704	" "	21	NWSE	1858-01-15		A3 G121
705	" "	21	NWSW	1858-01-15		A3 G121
706	" "	21	W½NE	1858-01-15		A3 G121
707	" "	21	W½NW	1858-01-15		A3 G121
734	" "	29		1858-01-15		A3 G138
708	" "	29	N½NW	1858-01-15		A3 G121 V734
735	" "	29	N½SE	1858-01-15		A3 G138 V734
709	" "	29	NWSW	1858-01-15		A3 G121 V734
710	" "	29	S½NW	1858-01-15		A3 G121 V734
713	" "	31	SESE	1858-01-15		A3 G121
714	" "	31	W½SE	1858-01-15		A3 G121
717	" "	5	E½SE	1858-01-15		A3 G121

ID	Individual in Patent	Sec.	Sec. Part	Date Issued	Other Counties	For More Info . . .
718	LEONARD, Frederick B (Cont'd)	5	E½SW	1858-01-15		A3 G121
719	" "	5	SENE	1858-01-15		A3 G121
720	" "	5	SENW	1858-01-15		A3 G121
721	" "	5	SWNE	1858-01-15		A3 G121
722	" "	5	SWNW	1858-01-15		A3 G121
723	" "	5	W½SE	1858-01-15		A3 G121
724	" "	5	W½SW	1858-01-15		A3 G121
725	" "	8	SESE	1858-01-15		A3 G121
619	" "	10	E½SW	1859-08-03		A3 G96
644	" "	10	N½NE	1859-08-03		A3 G99
645	" "	10	NENW	1859-08-03		A3 G99
620	" "	10	NESE	1859-08-03		A3 G96
621	" "	10	NWSW	1859-08-03		A3 G96
622	" "	10	S½NE	1859-08-03		A3 G96
623	" "	10	SWSW	1859-08-03		A3 G96
654	" "	10	W½SE	1859-08-03		A3 G93
656	" "	11	E½SW	1859-08-03		A3 G92
650	" "	11	N½NW	1859-08-03		A3 G98 C R736
736	" "	11	N½NW	1859-08-03		A3 G126 R650
676	" "	11	N½SE	1859-08-03		A3 G121 R677
676	" "	11	N½SE	1859-08-03		A3 G121 C R677
677	" "	11	N½SE	1859-08-03		A3 G121 R676
677	" "	11	N½SE	1859-08-03		A3 G121 C R676
624	" "	11	S½NE	1859-08-03		A3 G96 C R678
678	" "	11	S½NE	1859-08-03		A3 G121 R624
646	" "	11	S½SE	1859-08-03		A3 G101
657	" "	11	SENW	1859-08-03		A3 G92
660	" "	11	SWNW	1859-08-03		A3 G95
661	" "	11	W½SW	1859-08-03		A3 G95
679	" "	12	N½SE	1859-08-03		A3 G121
680	" "	12	NESW	1859-08-03		A3 G121
681	" "	12	NWSW	1859-08-03		A3 G121 R682
681	" "	12	NWSW	1859-08-03		A3 G121 C R682
682	" "	12	NWSW	1859-08-03		A3 G121 R681
682	" "	12	NWSW	1859-08-03		A3 G121 C R681
732	" "	12	SENW	1859-08-03		A3 G123
625	" "	12	SWNW	1859-08-03		A3 G96 C R683
683	" "	12	SWNW	1859-08-03		A3 G121 R625
733	" "	12	W½NE	1859-08-03		A3 G123
658	" "	14	N½NW	1859-08-03		A3 G94
647	" "	14	NENE	1859-08-03		A3 G101
659	" "	14	NWNE	1859-08-03		A3 G94
626	" "	15	1	1859-08-03		A3 G96
627	" "	15	2	1859-08-03		A3 G96
655	" "	15	NWNE	1859-08-03		A3 G93
728	" "	2	E½NW	1859-08-03		A3 G139 F
740	" "	2	N½NE	1859-08-03		A3 G143 F
694	" "	2	N½SE	1859-08-03		A3 G121
695	" "	2	NESW	1859-08-03		A3 G121
729	" "	2	NWNW	1859-08-03		A3 G139 F
730	" "	2	S½SE	1859-08-03		A3 G142
731	" "	2	SESW	1859-08-03		A3 G142
651	" "	2	SWSW	1859-08-03		A3 G98 C R737
737	" "	2	SWSW	1859-08-03		A3 G126 R651
642	" "	4	E½SE	1859-08-03		A3 G97
648	" "	4	N½NE	1859-08-03		A3 G100 F
738	" "	4	N½NW	1859-08-03		A3 G141 F
726	" "	4	N½SW	1859-08-03		A3 G129
727	" "	4	NWSE	1859-08-03		A3 G129
628	" "	4	S½NW	1859-08-03		A3 G96
715	" "	4	S½SW	1859-08-03		A3 G121
649	" "	4	SENE	1859-08-03		A3 G100 F
629	" "	4	SWNE	1859-08-03		A3 G96
716	" "	4	SWSE	1859-08-03		A3 G121
630	" "	5	N½NW	1859-08-03		A3 G96 F
739	" "	5	NENE	1859-08-03		A3 G141 F
631	" "	5	NWNE	1859-08-03		A3 G96 F
632	" "	9	E½SE	1859-08-03		A3 G96
633	" "	9	N½NW	1859-08-03		A3 G96
634	" "	9	N½SW	1859-08-03		A3 G96
643	" "	9	NENE	1859-08-03		A3 G97
635	" "	9	NWNE	1859-08-03		A3 G96
636	" "	9	NWSE	1859-08-03		A3 G96

ID	Individual in Patent	Sec.	Sec. Part	Date Issued	Other Counties	For More Info . . .
637	LEONARD, Frederick B (Cont'd) (Cont'd)	9	S½SW	1859-08-03		A3 G96 R638
638	" "	9	S½SW	1859-08-03		A3 G96 R637
639	" "	9	SENE	1859-08-03		A3 G96
640	" "	9	SWNE	1859-08-03		A3 G96
641	" "	9	SWSE	1859-08-03		A3 G96
741	" "	1	N½NE	1859-08-10		A3 G120 F
742	" "	31	NESW	1859-08-10		A3 G297 F
743	" "	31	W½SW	1859-08-10		A3 G297 F
773	MANLEY, Franklin Norman	8	N½SW	1871-07-15		A3 G87
774	" "	8	SWSW	1871-07-15		A3 G87
773	MANLEY, Lucy Maria	8	N½SW	1871-07-15		A3 G87
774	" "	8	SWSW	1871-07-15		A3 G87
652	MARTIN, Frederick P	10	SENW	1859-08-03		A3 G103
653	" "	10	W½NW	1859-08-03		A3 G103
799	MCDUFFIE, William	6	N½SW	1877-04-05		A4 F
746	MCNITT, Catharine H	32	N½SW	1860-09-03		A3 G48
747	" "	32	SESW	1860-09-03		A3 G48
748	" "	32	SWSE	1860-09-03		A3 G48
669	MILLER, David M	18	W½NW	1870-06-01		A3 G14 F
669	MILLER, John W	18	W½NW	1870-06-01		A3 G14 F
669	MILLER, Nancy E	18	W½NW	1870-06-01		A3 G14 F
669	MILLER, Susanah	18	W½NW	1870-06-01		A3 G14 F
769	NORTHROP, John O	15	3	1855-12-15		A1
770	" "	15	SWSW	1855-12-15		A1
795	PAGE, Stephen F	28	1	1858-05-01		A1
675	PHELPS, Fitch	26	S½NE	1872-03-20		A1 F
648	PITTS, Nancy	4	N½NE	1859-08-03		A3 G100 F
649	" "	4	SENE	1859-08-03		A3 G100 F
665	PRESTON, W E	8	N½NE	1870-06-01		A3 G16
646	PULLER, Mary A	11	S½SE	1859-08-03		A3 G101
647	" "	14	NENE	1859-08-03		A3 G101
674	RAMSEY, Edwin J	26	W½SE	1876-09-06		A4 F
757	RAYNSFORD, Frederick	13	S½	1855-12-15		A1 G59
758	" "	13	S½NE	1855-12-15		A1 G59
759	" "	13	S½NW	1855-12-15		A1 G59
760	" "	14	S½NE	1855-12-15		A1 G59
761	" "	14	S½NW	1855-12-15		A1 G59
762	" "	14	SE	1855-12-15		A1 G59
763	" "	21	S½SW	1855-12-15		A1 G59
764	" "	23	NE	1855-12-15		A1 G59
765	" "	23	S½	1855-12-15		A1 G59
766	" "	24	N½	1855-12-15		A1 G59
767	" "	24	SW	1855-12-15		A1 G59
768	" "	28	N½NW	1855-12-15		A1 G59
775	RUSH, John J	8	NESE	1871-07-15		A3 G88
776	" "	8	S½NE	1871-07-15		A3 G88
734	SELLEARS, Nancy	29		1858-01-15		A3 G138
735	" "	29	N½SE	1858-01-15		A3 G138 V734
728	SHOWARD, Lucy	2	E½NW	1859-08-03		A3 G139 F
729	" "	2	NWNW	1859-08-03		A3 G139 F
738	SKELTON, Sally	4	N½NW	1859-08-03		A3 G141 F
739	" "	5	NENE	1859-08-03		A3 G141 F
730	SOUTHWORTH, Lucy	2	S½SE	1859-08-03		A3 G142
731	" "	2	SESW	1859-08-03		A3 G142
740	SPARKS, Sarah L	2	N½NE	1859-08-03		A3 G143 F
779	SPAULDING, Joseph	6	N½SE	1875-02-10		A4
672	SWAIN, Daniel T	6	E½NE	1879-11-25		A4 F
742	WARREN, George B	31	NESW	1859-08-10		A3 G297 F
743	" "	31	W½SW	1859-08-10		A3 G297 F
745	WASHBURN, George	34	SENW	1883-09-15		A4 F
787	WILLARD, David	8	E½NW	1866-11-10		A3 G116
788	" "	8	NWNW	1866-11-10		A3 G116
789	WOOD, Ransom E	15	E½SW	1858-01-15		A3
790	" "	28	S½SE	1858-01-15		A3
791	" "	28	SESW	1858-01-15		A3
792	" "	29	E½NE	1858-01-15		A3 V734
670	WRENN, William B	6	S½SE	1870-06-01		A3 G15
671	" "	6	SESW	1870-06-01		A3 G15
755	WRIGHT, John G	11	N½NE	1855-12-15		A1
756	" "	12	NWNW	1855-12-15		A1

Patent Map

T15-N R11-W
Michigan-Toledo Strip Meridian

Map Group 8

Township Statistics

Parcels Mapped	:	188
Number of Patents	:	111
Number of Individuals	:	82
Patentees Identified	:	60
Number of Surnames	:	67
Multi-Patentee Parcels	:	141
Oldest Patent Date	:	3/1/1855
Most Recent Patent	:	9/15/1883
Block/Lot Parcels	:	5
Parcels Re - Issued	:	7
Parcels that Overlap	:	5
Cities and Towns	:	0
Cemeteries	:	1

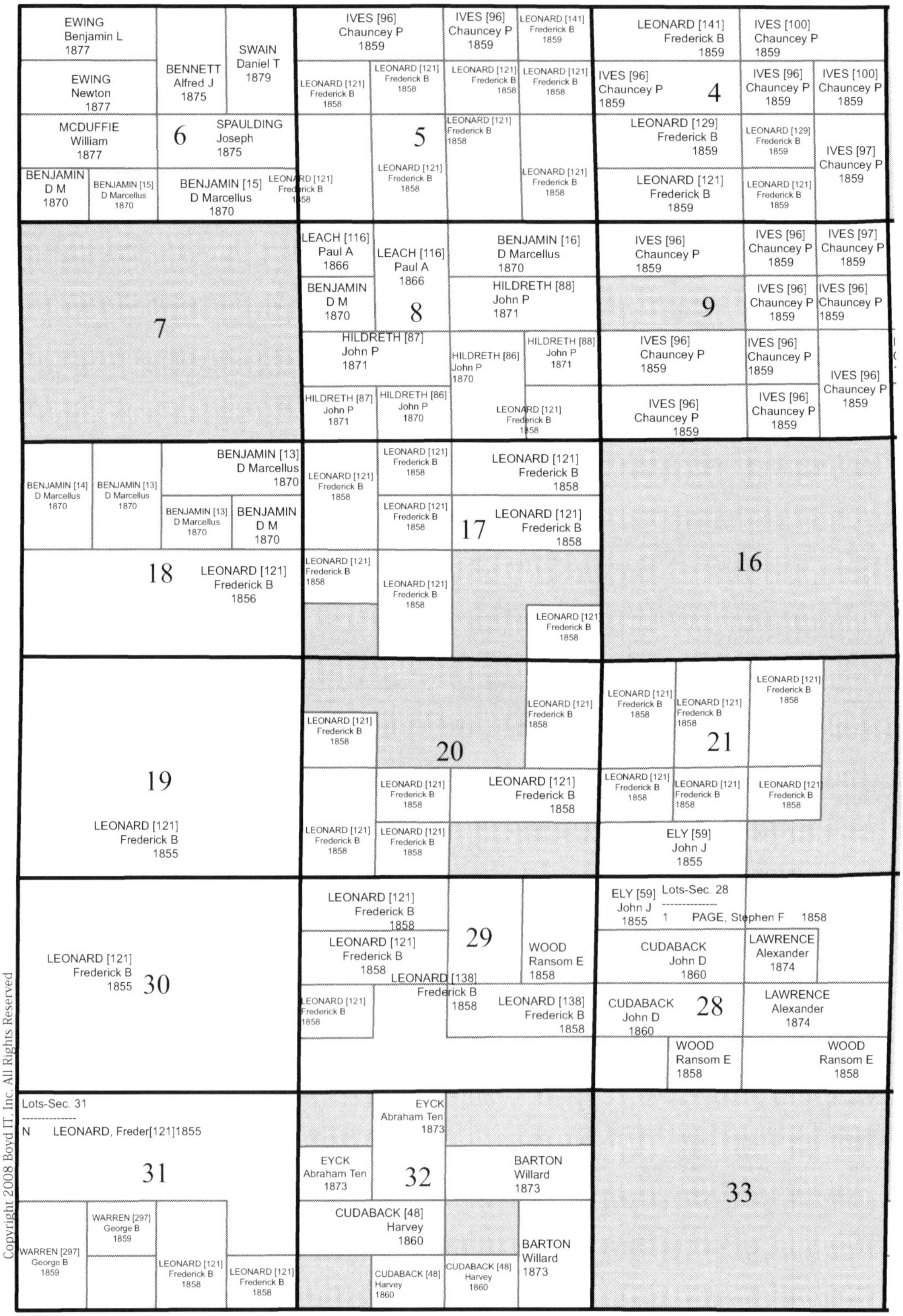

6
EWING Benjamin L 1877
EWING Newton 1877
BENNETT Alfred J 1875
SWAIN Daniel T 1879
MCDUFFIE William 1877
SPAULDING Joseph 1875
BENJAMIN D M 1870
BENJAMIN [15] D Marcellus 1870
BENJAMIN [15] D Marcellus 1870
LEONARD [121] Frederick B 1858

5
IVES [96] Chauncey P 1859
IVES [96] Chauncey P 1859
LEONARD [141] Frederick B 1859
LEONARD [121] Frederick B 1858
LEONARD [121] Frederick B 1858
LEONARD [121] Frederick B 1858
LEONARD [121] Frederick B 1858
LEONARD [121] Frederick B 1858
LEONARD [121] Frederick B 1858
LEONARD [121] Frederick B 1858

4
LEONARD [141] Frederick B 1859
IVES [100] Chauncey P 1859
IVES [96] Chauncey P 1859
IVES [96] Chauncey P 1859
IVES [100] Chauncey P 1859
LEONARD [129] Frederick B 1859
LEONARD [129] Frederick B 1859
IVES [97] Chauncey P 1859
LEONARD [121] Frederick B 1859
LEONARD [121] Frederick B 1859

7

8
LEACH [116] Paul A 1866
LEACH [116] Paul A 1866
BENJAMIN [16] D Marcellus 1870
BENJAMIN D M 1870
HILDRETH [88] John P 1871
HILDRETH [87] John P 1871
HILDRETH [86] John P 1870
HILDRETH [88] John P 1871
HILDRETH [87] John P 1871
HILDRETH [86] John P 1870
LEONARD [121] Frederick B 1858

9
IVES [96] Chauncey P 1859
IVES [96] Chauncey P 1859
IVES [97] Chauncey P 1859
IVES [96] Chauncey P 1859
IVES [96] Chauncey P 1859
IVES [96] Chauncey P 1859
IVES [96] Chauncey P 1859
IVES [96] Chauncey P 1859
IVES [96] Chauncey P 1859
IVES [96] Chauncey P 1859

18
BENJAMIN [13] D Marcellus 1870
BENJAMIN [14] D Marcellus 1870
BENJAMIN [13] D Marcellus 1870
BENJAMIN [13] D Marcellus 1870
BENJAMIN D M 1870
LEONARD [121] Frederick B 1856

17
LEONARD [121] Frederick B 1858
LEONARD [121] Frederick B 1858
LEONARD [121] Frederick B 1858
LEONARD [121] Frederick B 1858
LEONARD [121] Frederick B 1858
LEONARD [121] Frederick B 1858
LEONARD [121] Frederick B 1858
LEONARD [121] Frederick B 1858

16

19
LEONARD [121] Frederick B 1855

20
LEONARD [121] Frederick B 1858
LEONARD [121] Frederick B 1858
LEONARD [121] Frederick B 1858
LEONARD [121] Frederick B 1858
LEONARD [121] Frederick B 1858
LEONARD [121] Frederick B 1858

21
LEONARD [121] Frederick B 1858
LEONARD [121] Frederick B 1858
LEONARD [121] Frederick B 1858
LEONARD [121] Frederick B 1858
LEONARD [121] Frederick B 1858
LEONARD [121] Frederick B 1858
ELY [59] John J 1855

30
LEONARD [121] Frederick B 1855

29
LEONARD [121] Frederick B 1858
LEONARD [121] Frederick B 1858
WOOD Ransom E 1858
LEONARD [138] Frederick B 1858
LEONARD [138] Frederick B 1858
LEONARD [121] Frederick B 1858

28
ELY [59] John J 1855
Lots-Sec. 28
1 PAGE, Stephen F 1858
CUDABACK John D 1860
LAWRENCE Alexander 1874
CUDABACK John D 1860
LAWRENCE Alexander 1874
WOOD Ransom E 1858
WOOD Ransom E 1858

31
Lots-Sec. 31
N LEONARD, Freder[121]1855
WARREN [297] George B 1859
WARREN [297] George B 1859
LEONARD [121] Frederick B 1858
LEONARD [121] Frederick B 1858

32
EYCK Abraham Ten 1873
EYCK Abraham Ten 1873
BARTON Willard 1873
CUDABACK [48] Harvey 1860
BARTON Willard 1873
CUDABACK [48] Harvey 1860
CUDABACK [48] Harvey 1860

33

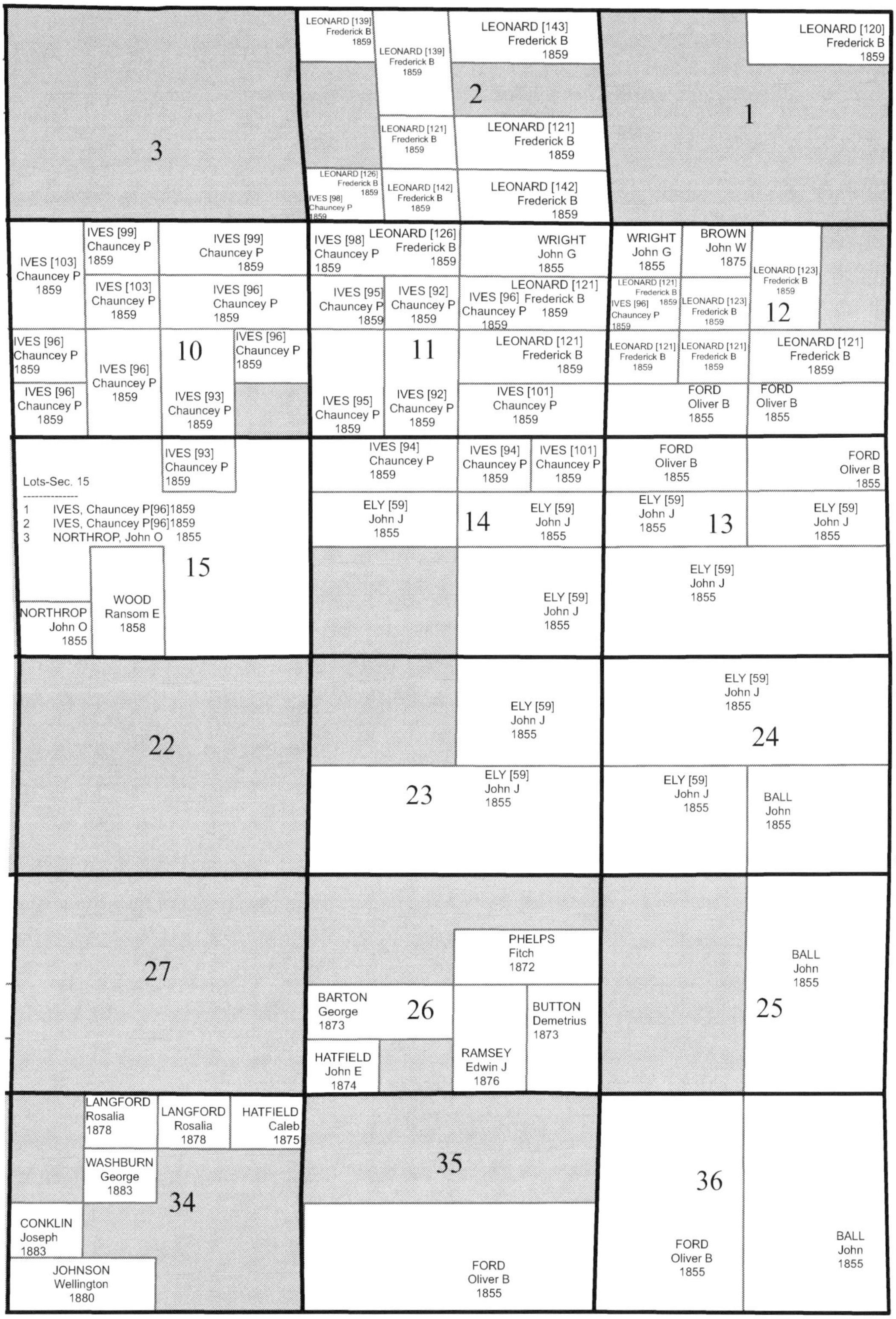

3

LEONARD [139] Frederick B 1859
LEONARD [139] Frederick B 1859
LEONARD [143] Frederick B 1859
2
LEONARD [121] Frederick B 1859
LEONARD [121] Frederick B 1859
LEONARD [126] Frederick B 1859
IVES [98] Chauncey P 1859
LEONARD [142] Frederick B 1859
LEONARD [142] Frederick B 1859

LEONARD [120] Frederick B 1859
1

IVES [103] Chauncey P 1859
IVES [99] Chauncey P 1859
IVES [99] Chauncey P 1859
IVES [103] Chauncey P 1859
IVES [96] Chauncey P 1859
IVES [96] Chauncey P 1859
IVES [96] Chauncey P 1859
10
IVES [96] Chauncey P 1859
IVES [96] Chauncey P 1859
IVES [93] Chauncey P 1859

IVES [98] Chauncey P 1859
LEONARD [126] Frederick B 1859
WRIGHT John G 1855
IVES [95] Chauncey P 1859
IVES [92] Chauncey P 1859
LEONARD [121] Frederick B 1859
IVES [96] Chauncey P 1859
11
LEONARD [121] Frederick B 1859
IVES [95] Chauncey P 1859
IVES [92] Chauncey P 1859
IVES [101] Chauncey P 1859

WRIGHT John G 1855
BROWN John W 1875
LEONARD [123] Frederick B 1859
LEONARD [121] Frederick B 1859
IVES [96] Chauncey P 1859
LEONARD [123] Frederick B 1859
12
LEONARD [121] Frederick B 1859
LEONARD [121] Frederick B 1859
LEONARD [121] Frederick B 1859
FORD Oliver B 1855
FORD Oliver B 1855

IVES [93] Chauncey P 1859
Lots-Sec. 15
1 IVES, Chauncey P[96]1859
2 IVES, Chauncey P[96]1859
3 NORTHROP, John O 1855
15
WOOD Ransom E 1858
NORTHROP John O 1855

IVES [94] Chauncey P 1859
IVES [94] Chauncey P 1859
IVES [101] Chauncey P 1859
ELY [59] John J 1855
14
ELY [59] John J 1855
ELY [59] John J 1855

FORD Oliver B 1855
FORD Oliver B 1855
ELY [59] John J 1855
13
ELY [59] John J 1855
ELY [59] John J 1855

22

ELY [59] John J 1855
23
ELY [59] John J 1855

ELY [59] John J 1855
24
ELY [59] John J 1855
BALL John 1855

27

PHELPS Fitch 1872
BARTON George 1873
26
BUTTON Demetrius 1873
HATFIELD John E 1874
RAMSEY Edwin J 1876

BALL John 1855
25

LANGFORD Rosalia 1878
LANGFORD Rosalia 1878
HATFIELD Caleb 1875
WASHBURN George 1883
34
CONKLIN Joseph 1883
JOHNSON Wellington 1880

35
FORD Oliver B 1855

36
FORD Oliver B 1855
BALL John 1855

Helpful Hints

1. This Map's INDEX can be found on the preceding pages.
2. Refer to Map "C" to see where this Township lies within Newaygo County, Michigan.
3. Numbers within square brackets [ ] denote a multi-patentee land parcel (multi-owner). Refer to Appendix "C" for a full list of members in this group.
4. Areas that look to be crowded with Patentees usually indicate multiple sales of the same parcel (Re-issues) or Overlapping parcels. See this Township's Index for an explanation of these and other circumstances that might explain "odd" groupings of Patentees on this map.

Legend

Patent Boundary
Section Boundary
No Patents Found (or Outside County)
1., 2., 3., ... Lot Numbers (when beside a name)
[ ] Group Number (see Appendix "C")

Scale: Section = 1 mile X 1 mile (generally, with some exceptions)

Road Map

T15-N R11-W
Michigan-Toledo Strip Meridian

Map Group 8

Cities & Towns

None

Cemeteries

Hungerford Cemetery

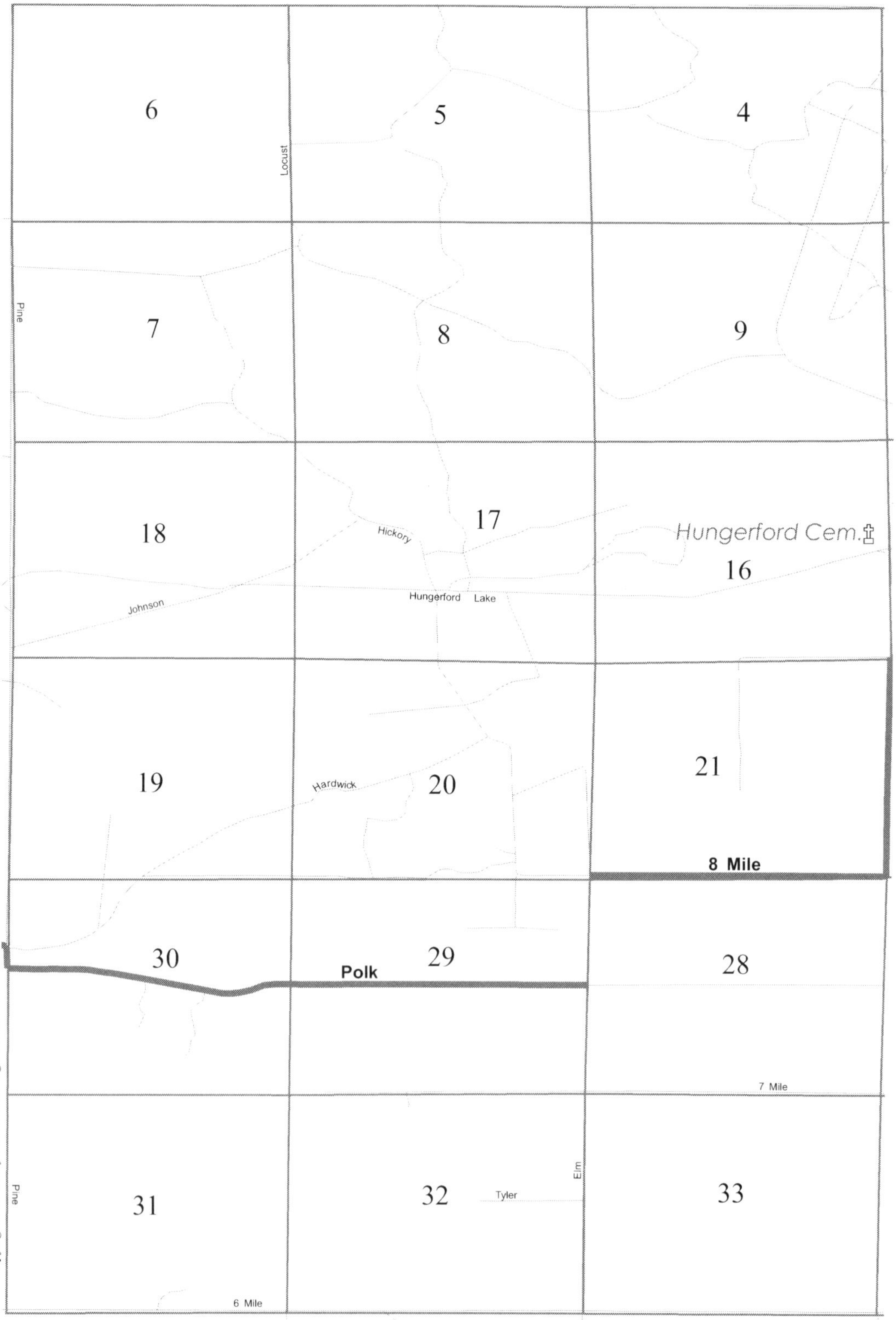

6
5
4
Locust
Pine
7
8
9
18
Hickory
17
Hungerford Cem.
16
Johnson
Hungerford Lake
19
Hardwick
20
21
8 Mile
30
Polk
29
28
7 Mile
Pine
31
32
Tyler
Elm
33
6 Mile

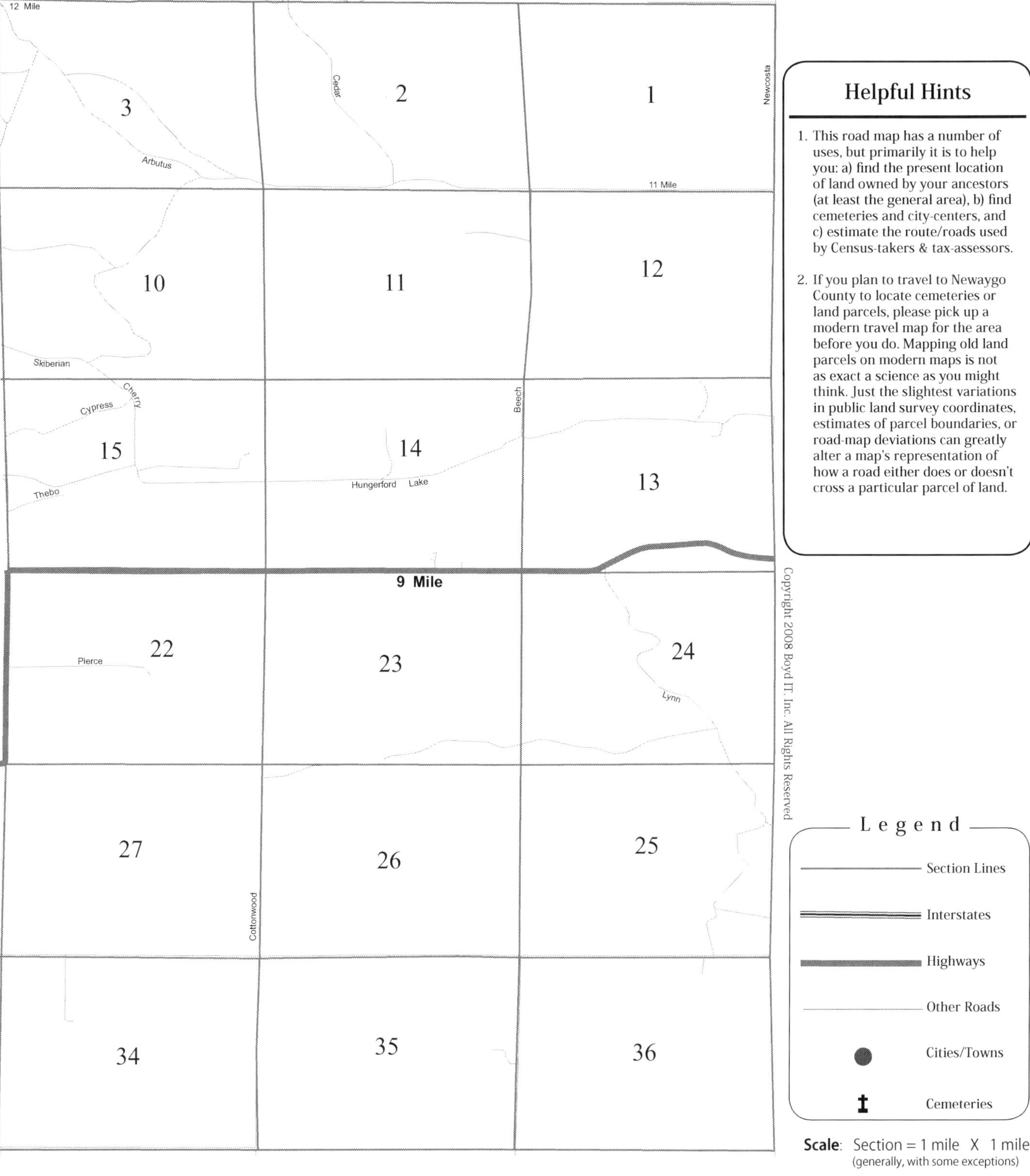

Helpful Hints

1. This road map has a number of uses, but primarily it is to help you: a) find the present location of land owned by your ancestors (at least the general area), b) find cemeteries and city-centers, and c) estimate the route/roads used by Census-takers & tax-assessors.

2. If you plan to travel to Newaygo County to locate cemeteries or land parcels, please pick up a modern travel map for the area before you do. Mapping old land parcels on modern maps is not as exact a science as you might think. Just the slightest variations in public land survey coordinates, estimates of parcel boundaries, or road-map deviations can greatly alter a map's representation of how a road either does or doesn't cross a particular parcel of land.

Cities & Towns
None

Cemeteries
Hungerford Cemetery

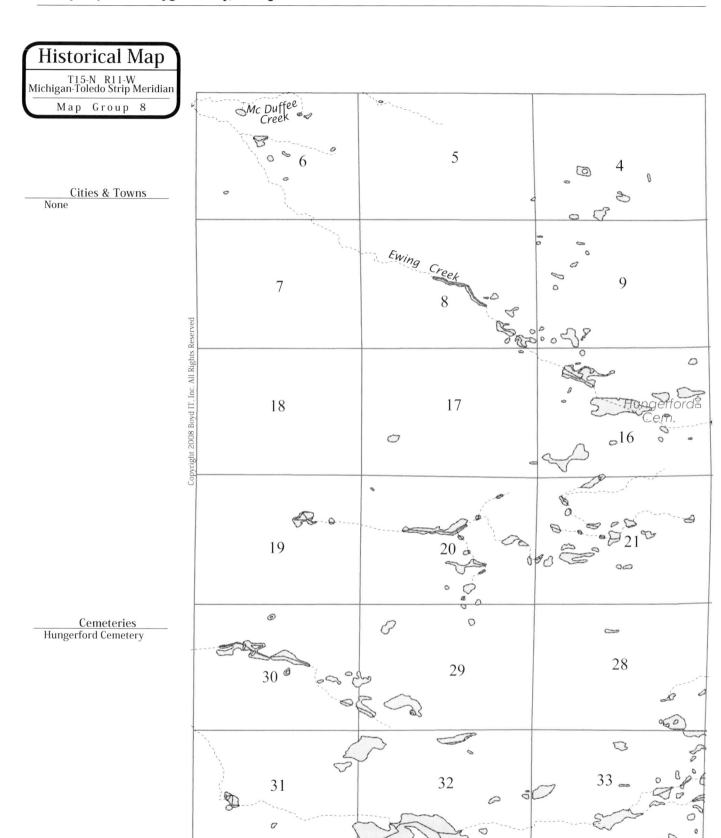

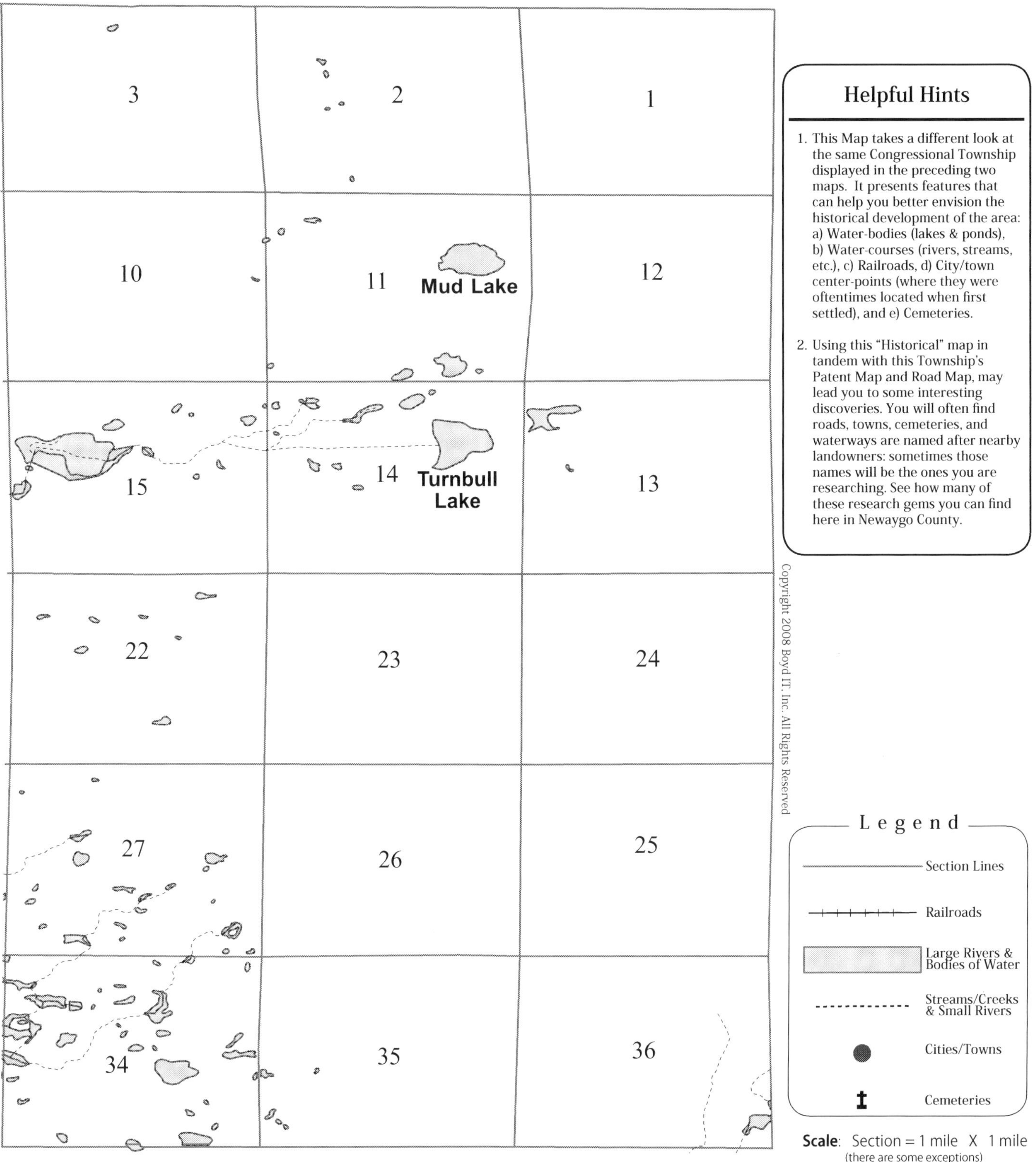

Helpful Hints

1. This Map takes a different look at the same Congressional Township displayed in the preceding two maps. It presents features that can help you better envision the historical development of the area: a) Water-bodies (lakes & ponds), b) Water-courses (rivers, streams, etc.), c) Railroads, d) City/town center-points (where they were oftentimes located when first settled), and e) Cemeteries.

2. Using this "Historical" map in tandem with this Township's Patent Map and Road Map, may lead you to some interesting discoveries. You will often find roads, towns, cemeteries, and waterways are named after nearby landowners: sometimes those names will be the ones you are researching. See how many of these research gems you can find here in Newaygo County.

Scale: Section = 1 mile X 1 mile
(there are some exceptions)

Map Group 9: Index to Land Patents

Township 14-North Range 14-West (Michigan-Toledo Strip)

After you locate an individual in this Index, take note of the Section and Section Part then proceed to the Land Patent map on the pages immediately following. You should have no difficulty locating the corresponding parcel of land.

The "For More Info" Column will lead you to more information about the underlying Patents. See the *Legend* at right, and the "How to Use this Book" chapter, for more information.

LEGEND

"For More Info . . . " column

A = Authority (Legislative Act, See Appendix "A")
B = Block or Lot (location in Section unknown)
C = Cancelled Patent
F = Fractional Section
G = Group (Multi-Patentee Patent, see Appendix "C")
V = Overlaps another Parcel
R = Re-Issued (Parcel patented more than once)

(A & G items require you to look in the Appendixes referred to above. All other Letter-designations followed by a number require you to locate line-items in this index that possess the ID number found after the letter).

ID	Individual in Patent	Sec.	Sec. Part	Date Issued	Other Counties	For More Info . . .
903	AVERY, Newell	19	SWSE	1861-07-01		A3 G3
904	" "	30	E½NW	1861-07-01		A3 G3
905	" "	30	NWNE	1861-07-01		A3 G3
953	BALLINGER, John T	19	W½NW	1860-10-01		A3 G111 F
953	BALLINGER, Sarah Ann	19	W½NW	1860-10-01		A3 G111 F
928	BARNHARD, Simon	33	E½SW	1858-05-01		A1
929	" "	33	W½SE	1858-05-01		A1
947	BEAN, Emery O	35	N½NW	1862-11-01		A3 G183
948	" "	35	NWNE	1862-11-01		A3 G183
800	BEERS, Almon	31	SW	1859-08-03		A3 F
865	BINGHAM, John	28	E½SE	1858-05-01		A1
828	BRIGGS, Edward L	10	SESW	1865-10-10		A1
931	BROWN, Stephen	5	SW	1863-05-20		A3 G30
913	BRUCE, Samuel C	26	SENE	1859-10-10		A1
855	BUICK, James	34	E½NW	1857-03-10		A1
856	" "	34	NE	1857-03-10		A1
829	BULL, Elijah G	34	W½NW	1858-05-01		A1
891	BULL, M D	33	E½SE	1857-03-10		A1
892	" "	34	SW	1857-03-10		A1
956	CILLEY, Susan	28	W½SW	1860-09-03		A3 G289
957	" "	33	W½NW	1860-09-03		A3 G289
878	COOK, John P	24	N½SE	1859-08-10		A3 G44
879	" "	24	SWNE	1859-08-10		A3 G44
874	" "	25	E½SW	1859-08-10		A3
875	" "	25	SWSW	1859-08-10		A3
876	" "	36	E½SE	1859-08-10		A3
877	" "	36	SWSE	1859-08-10		A3
967	COOPER, Sarah	14	SESW	1863-03-20		A3 G303
968	" "	14	W½NE	1863-03-20		A3 G303
885	CREPIN, Ernest E	2	NWSE	1880-03-05		A1 G84
919	CROFOOT, Silas D	35	NESE	1859-10-10		A1
920	" "	35	SENE	1859-10-10		A1
921	" "	36	NWSW	1859-10-10		A1
922	" "	36	SWNW	1859-10-10		A1
804	DAKE, Aruna	35	NESW	1859-10-10		A1
805	" "	35	SENW	1859-10-10		A1
889	DAKE, Judah B	35	NWSE	1860-12-01		A1
890	" "	35	SWNE	1860-12-01		A1
942	DAKE, Talcott P	35	NWSW	1859-10-10		A1
943	" "	35	SWNW	1859-10-10		A1
836	DICKISON, Frederick	22	NWSE	1860-10-01		A3 G52
837	" "	22	S½SE	1860-10-01		A3 G52
838	" "	23	SWSW	1860-10-01		A3 G52
844	DOWLING, George E	11	W½NE	1869-09-10		A1
845	" "	11	W½SE	1869-09-10		A1
959	DUNLAP, William	29	SE	1859-08-10		A3

ID	Individual in Patent	Sec.	Sec. Part	Date Issued	Other Counties	For More Info . . .
857	DUNNING, James W	18	SWSW	1867-01-10		A1 F
818	EDDY, Daniel B	28	NENW	1860-09-01		A1
819	" "	28	NWNE	1860-09-01		A1
893	EDDY, Martin A	17	E½SE	1860-09-01		A1
894	" "	20	NENE	1860-09-01		A1
945	EDDY, Thomas	33	NENW	1860-12-01		A1
866	ELLIOTT, John	33	W½SW	1856-03-10		A1
846	FLANDERS, George	5	S½NE	1872-01-01		A4
847	" "	5	S½NW	1872-01-01		A4
914	FORBES, Samuel	25	SE	1859-10-10		A1
806	GRANGER, Austin	34	SE	1859-08-03		A3
903	GROVENBERRY, Mary	19	SWSE	1861-07-01		A3 G3
904	" "	30	E½NW	1861-07-01		A3 G3
905	" "	30	NWNE	1861-07-01		A3 G3
932	HALL, Stephen C	13	NE	1862-11-01		A3
938	" "	14	N½SE	1863-05-20		A3 G77
939	" "	14	SENE	1863-05-20		A3 G77
935	" "	24	SENW	1863-06-05		A1
936	" "	13	SWSW	1864-09-15		A3 G78
937	" "	14	SESE	1864-09-15		A3 G78
933	" "	13	NESW	1879-04-15		A1
934	" "	13	SENW	1879-04-15		A1
832	HARRINGTON, Eliphalet	33	NE	1858-05-01		A1
831	" "	23	NESW	1863-06-05		A1
830	" "	22	NWNE	1864-11-01		A1
860	HARRINGTON, Jasper	22	SWSW	1860-10-01		A1
861	" "	28	E½NE	1860-10-01		A1
883	HEALD, Joseph	21	NWSE	1862-02-10		A3
884	" "	21	SWNE	1862-02-10		A3
882	" "	21	NWNE	1864-11-01		A1
885	" "	2	NWSE	1880-03-05		A1 G84
842	HERRICK, Gamaliel	6	SWNW	1858-05-01		A1 F
843	" "	7	NWNW	1858-05-01		A1 F
840	HERRICK, Gamaliel E	6	NESE	1858-05-01		A1
841	" "	6	W½SW	1858-05-01		A1 F
916	HIGGS, Benjamin	28	S½NW	1861-10-10		A3 G224
917	" "	28	SWNE	1861-10-10		A3 G224
916	HIGGS, Jackson	28	S½NW	1861-10-10		A3 G224
917	" "	28	SWNE	1861-10-10		A3 G224
853	HILES, Jacob	5	SE	1869-11-01		A4
949	HOLMES, Varrick	35	S½SE	1858-01-15		A3
951	HOSKIN, William A	30	SW	1859-10-10		A1 F
927	HOVEY, Silas P	6	NWNW	1874-03-10		A1
925	" "	10	SESE	1875-01-05		A1
926	" "	14	NENW	1875-01-05		A1
915	HOWE, Samuel	27	SW	1858-05-01		A1
817	JOHNSON, Charles	10	W½NW	1866-11-10		A3 G106
811	" "	11	NWNW	1867-01-10		A1
814	" "	6	SESE	1867-01-10		A1
815	" "	8	NENW	1867-01-10		A1
816	" "	9	NESE	1867-01-10		A1
812	" "	2	NWNE	1868-02-15		A1 F
813	" "	6	SENE	1868-02-15		A1
810	" "	10	SWSE	1869-09-10		A1
952	JOHNSON, William A	19	NWSW	1860-10-01		A1 F
953	" "	19	W½NW	1860-10-01		A3 G111 F
835	LEWIS, Frank	33	SENW	1872-09-20		A4
911	LEWIS, Richard	27	NWSE	1861-04-01		A1
900	MACOMBER, Nathaniel D	27	NW	1857-03-10		A1
899	" "	22	E½SW	1861-04-01		A1
867	MANNING, John	20	NWSE	1869-11-01		A4
868	" "	20	S½SE	1869-11-01		A4
869	" "	21	SWSW	1869-11-01		A4
871	MANSFIELD, John	15	NWNW	1861-12-10		A1
870	" "	10	SWSW	1869-11-01		A4
872	" "	9	S½SE	1869-11-01		A4
897	MANSFIELD, Miles	20	E½SW	1869-11-01		A4
898	" "	29	N½NW	1869-11-01		A4
912	MANSFIELD, Samantha	29	NE	1856-03-10		A1
839	MATTESON, Freeman	26	SW	1855-11-08		A3 G170
873	MAYNARD, John	27	NE	1858-05-01		A1
817	MCCRACKEN, Otho	10	W½NW	1866-11-10		A3 G106
906	MCGHAN, Porter	4	N½SE	1873-02-10		A4

ID	Individual in Patent	Sec.	Sec. Part	Date Issued	Other Counties	For More Info . . .
907	MCGHAN, Porter (Cont'd)	4	SENE	1873-02-10		A4
947	MERRITT, Titus	35	N½NW	1862-11-01		A3 G183
948	" "	35	NWNE	1862-11-01		A3 G183
854	MILLER, Jacob	36	SENE	1859-10-10		A1
848	MILLIS, George H	23	SWSE	1858-05-01		A1
849	" "	26	NENW	1858-05-01		A1
850	" "	26	NWNE	1858-05-01		A1
895	MILLIS, Martin	27	E½SE	1858-05-01		A1
896	" "	27	SWSE	1858-05-01		A1
923	MILLIS, Silas	26	SENW	1858-05-01		A1
924	" "	26	W½NW	1858-05-01		A1
885	MURPHY, Simon J	2	NWSE	1880-03-05		A1 G84
820	NELSON, David B	20	E½NW	1859-10-10		A1
833	NORTH, Elisha S	18	S½NW	1869-11-01		A4
888	NORTH, Joseph	19	SENE	1862-05-15		A1
822	PAYNE, David	32	W½NE	1869-11-01		A4
821	" "	32	NWSE	1870-06-20		A1
886	PHILLIPS, Joseph M	28	E½SW	1857-02-20		A3
887	" "	28	W½SE	1857-02-20		A3
807	PRICE, Bartholomew W	31	SESE	1868-12-01		A3 G223
807	PRICE, John L	31	SESE	1868-12-01		A3 G223
807	PRICE, Parker C	31	SESE	1868-12-01		A3 G223
916	PRUYN, Samuel	28	S½NW	1861-10-10		A3 G224
917	" "	28	SWNE	1861-10-10		A3 G224
944	RANDOLPH, Theodore C	12	E½NE	1868-02-15		A1
862	RASSEDIR, Jeremiah	18	SESE	1869-11-01		A4
940	REDDIN, Sylvester	17	N½NW	1869-11-01		A4
941	" "	17	NWNE	1869-11-01		A4
958	ROBERTS, William D	21	W½NW	1857-04-02		A3
962	ROBERTS, William H	21	E½NW	1857-04-02		A3
863	ROSSEDIR, Jeremiah	17	SWSW	1862-08-15		A1
901	RUSSELL, Nathaniel I	29	SW	1857-03-10		A1
902	" "	30	SE	1857-03-10		A1
963	RUSSELL, William H	31	NE	1857-03-10		A1
964	" "	32	NW	1857-03-10		A1
965	" "	32	SWSW	1858-05-01		A1
808	SCOVILLE, Charles E	29	S½NW	1859-08-03		A3
809	" "	30	SENE	1859-08-03		A3
864	SKINNER, John A	30	W½NW	1876-12-30		A4 F
909	SLOCUM, Richard C	4	NENW	1869-11-01		A4 F
910	" "	4	NWNE	1869-11-01		A4 F
960	SLOCUM, William E	4	S½NW	1869-11-01		A4
961	" "	4	W½SW	1869-11-01		A4
859	SMITH, Jason	9	S½SW	1857-04-02		A3
858	" "	17	E½NE	1858-01-15		A3
802	SPENCER, Andrew J	26	NWSE	1860-12-01		A1
803	" "	26	SWNE	1860-12-01		A1
880	STANLEY, John	24	SESE	1859-10-10		A1
881	" "	25	NENE	1859-10-10		A1
908	STANLEY, Reuben T	23	N½SE	1861-12-10		A1
946	STANLEY, Thomas	25	S½NE	1860-12-01		A1
878	STORMS, Mary	24	N½SE	1859-08-10		A3 G44
879	" "	24	SWNE	1859-08-10		A3 G44
931	STUDLEY, Susan	5	SW	1863-05-20		A3 G30
938	THOMPSON, Samuel C	14	N½SE	1863-05-20		A3 G77
939	" "	14	SENE	1863-05-20		A3 G77
936	THORP, Lucy	13	SWSW	1864-09-15		A3 G78
937	" "	14	SESE	1864-09-15		A3 G78
956	TINDALL, William A	28	W½SW	1860-09-03		A3 G289
954	" "	32	N½SW	1860-09-03		A3
955	" "	32	SESW	1860-09-03		A3
957	" "	33	W½NW	1860-09-03		A3 G289
823	WARD, David	3	1	1853-11-01		A1
824	" "	7	NESW	1858-01-15		A3
825	" "	7	NWSE	1858-01-15		A3
826	" "	7	SENE	1858-01-15		A3
827	" "	8	SWNW	1858-01-15		A3
836	WASHBURN, Deborah	22	NWSE	1860-10-01		A3 G52
837	" "	22	S½SE	1860-10-01		A3 G52
838	" "	23	SWSW	1860-10-01		A3 G52
851	WELLES, Henry W	23	S½NW	1858-01-15		A3
852	" "	8	N½SW	1858-01-15		A3
967	WESTON, William	14	SESW	1863-03-20		A3 G303

ID	Individual in Patent	Sec.	Sec. Part	Date Issued	Other Counties	For More Info . . .
968	WESTON, William (Cont'd)	14	W½NE	1863-03-20		A3 G303
839	WHEELER, Suphronia	26	SW	1855-11-08		A3 G170
930	WILDER, Spencer	35	S½SW	1859-08-10		A3
950	WILDER, Willard	36	S½SW	1858-05-01		A1 F
918	WILLETS, Samuel R	26	NESE	1860-09-01		A1
801	WILSON, Alonzo	31	NW	1859-08-03		A3 F
834	WINSTON, Ephraim	21	SENE	1869-11-01		A4
966	WOOD, William W	31	W½SE	1859-08-10		A3

Patent Map

T14-N R14-W
Michigan-Toledo Strip Meridian

Map Group 9

Township Statistics

Parcels Mapped	:	169
Number of Patents	:	120
Number of Individuals	:	107
Patentees Identified	:	95
Number of Surnames	:	83
Multi-Patentee Parcels	:	26
Oldest Patent Date	:	11/1/1853
Most Recent Patent	:	3/5/1880
Block/Lot Parcels	:	1
Parcels Re - Issued	:	0
Parcels that Overlap	:	0
Cities and Towns	:	2
Cemeteries	:	1

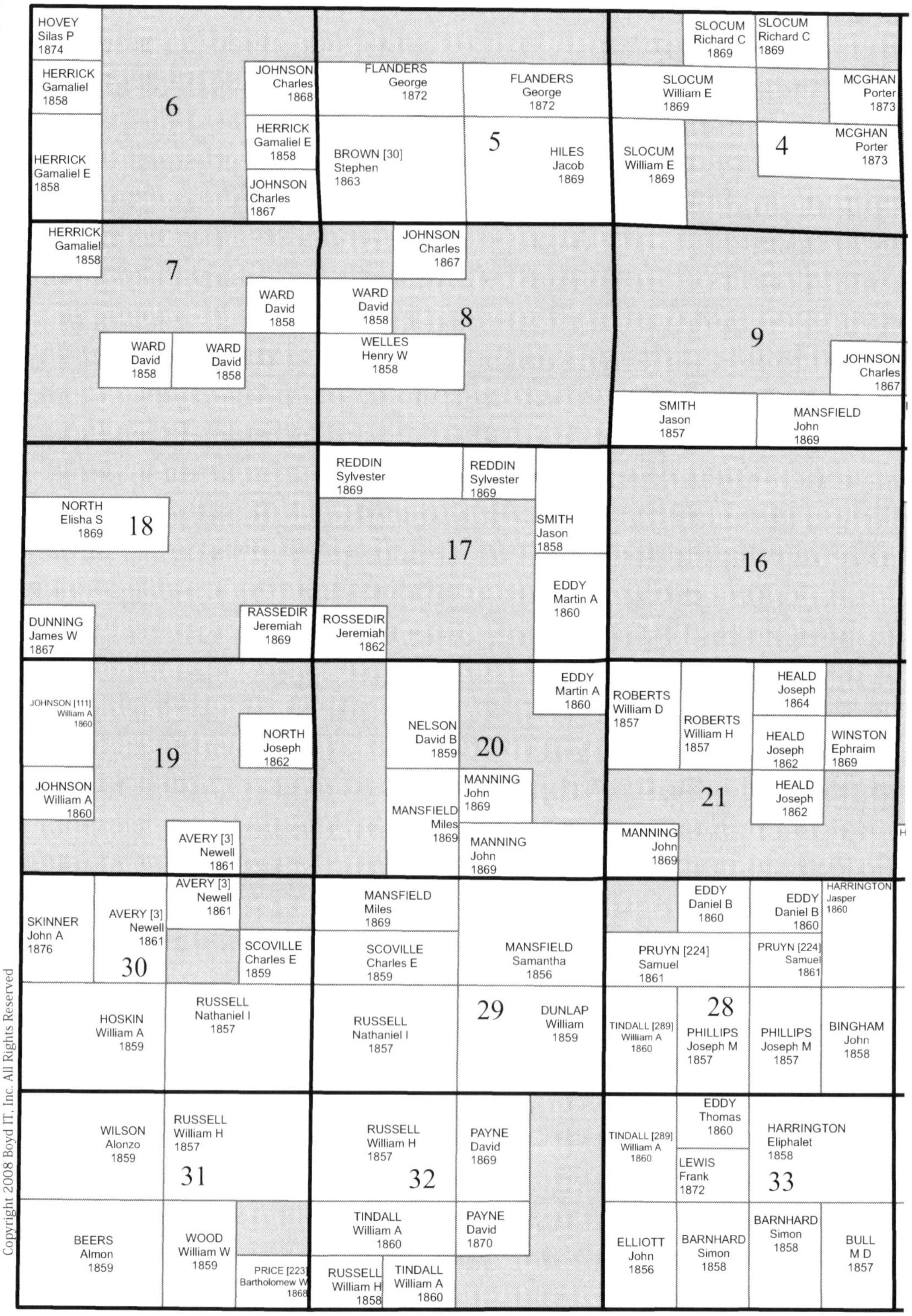

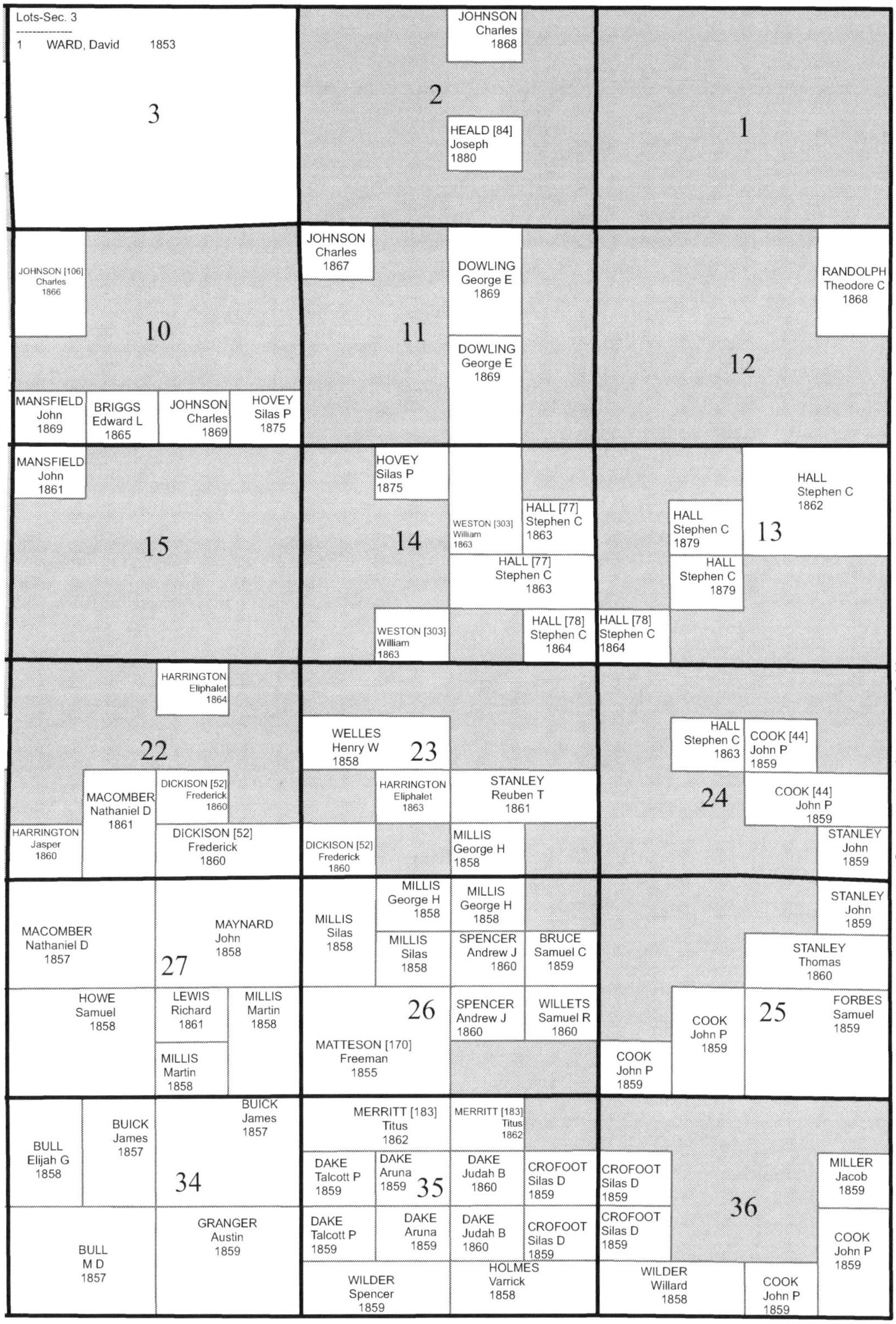

Lots-Sec. 3
1 WARD, David 1853

3
JOHNSON Charles 1868
2
HEALD [84] Joseph 1880
1

JOHNSON [106] Charles 1866
10
MANSFIELD John 1869
BRIGGS Edward L 1865
JOHNSON Charles 1869
HOVEY Silas P 1875
JOHNSON Charles 1867
11
DOWLING George E 1869
DOWLING George E 1869
RANDOLPH Theodore C 1868
12

MANSFIELD John 1861
15
HOVEY Silas P 1875
14
WESTON [303] William 1863
HALL [77] Stephen C 1863
HALL [77] Stephen C 1863
WESTON [303] William 1863
HALL [78] Stephen C 1864
HALL [78] Stephen C 1864
HALL Stephen C 1879
HALL Stephen C 1879
HALL Stephen C 1862
13

HARRINGTON Eliphalet 1864
22
MACOMBER Nathaniel D 1861
DICKISON [52] Frederick 1860
HARRINGTON Jasper 1860
DICKISON [52] Frederick 1860
WELLES Henry W 1858
23
HARRINGTON Eliphalet 1863
STANLEY Reuben T 1861
DICKISON [52] Frederick 1860
MILLIS George H 1858
HALL Stephen C 1863
COOK [44] John P 1859
24
COOK [44] John P 1859
STANLEY John 1859

MACOMBER Nathaniel D 1857
MAYNARD John 1858
27
HOWE Samuel 1858
LEWIS Richard 1861
MILLIS Martin 1858
MILLIS Martin 1858
MILLIS Silas 1858
MILLIS George H 1858
MILLIS George H 1858
MILLIS Silas 1858
SPENCER Andrew J 1860
BRUCE Samuel C 1859
26
SPENCER Andrew J 1860
WILLETS Samuel R 1860
MATTESON [170] Freeman 1855
STANLEY John 1859
STANLEY Thomas 1860
25
FORBES Samuel 1859
COOK John P 1859
COOK John P 1859

BULL Elijah G 1858
BUICK James 1857
BUICK James 1857
34
BULL M D 1857
GRANGER Austin 1859
MERRITT [183] Titus 1862
MERRITT [183] Titus 1862
DAKE Talcott P 1859
DAKE Aruna 1859
35
DAKE Judah B 1860
CROFOOT Silas D 1859
DAKE Talcott P 1859
DAKE Aruna 1859
DAKE Judah B 1860
CROFOOT Silas D 1859
WILDER Spencer 1859
HOLMES Varrick 1858
CROFOOT Silas D 1859
CROFOOT Silas D 1859
36
MILLER Jacob 1859
COOK John P 1859
WILDER Willard 1858
COOK John P 1859

Helpful Hints

1. This Map's INDEX can be found on the preceding pages.
2. Refer to Map "C" to see where this Township lies within Newaygo County, Michigan.
3. Numbers within square brackets [ ] denote a multi-patentee land parcel (multi-owner). Refer to Appendix "C" for a full list of members in this group.
4. Areas that look to be crowded with Patentees usually indicate multiple sales of the same parcel (Re-issues) or Overlapping parcels. See this Township's Index for an explanation of these and other circumstances that might explain "odd" groupings of Patentees on this map.

Legend

Patent Boundary
Section Boundary
No Patents Found (or Outside County)
1., 2., 3., ... Lot Numbers (when beside a name)
[ ] Group Number (see Appendix "C")

Scale: Section = 1 mile X 1 mile
(generally, with some exceptions)

Road Map

T14-N R14-W
Michigan-Toledo Strip Meridian

Map Group 9

Cities & Towns

Aetna
Huber

Cemeteries

Bull Cemetery

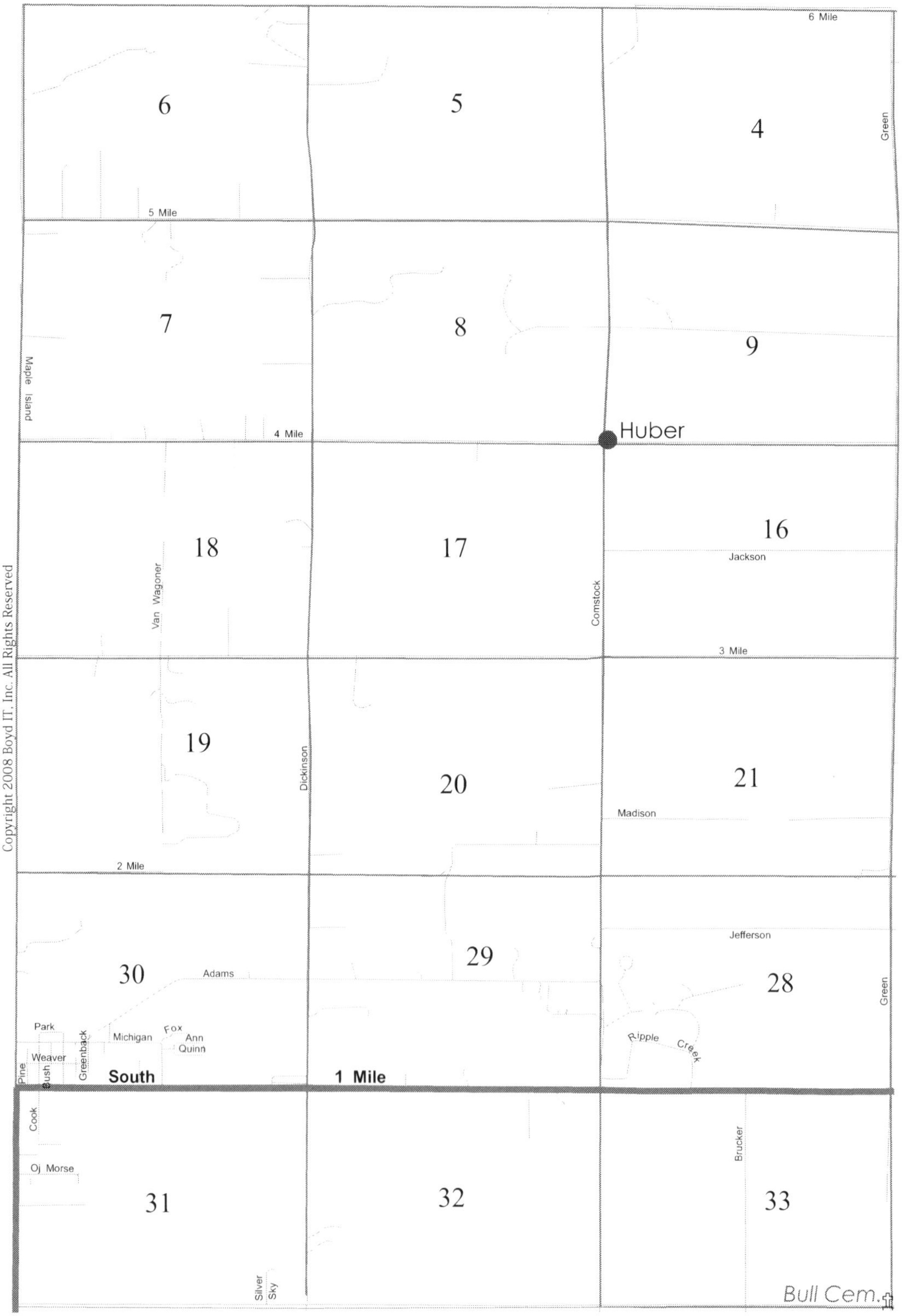

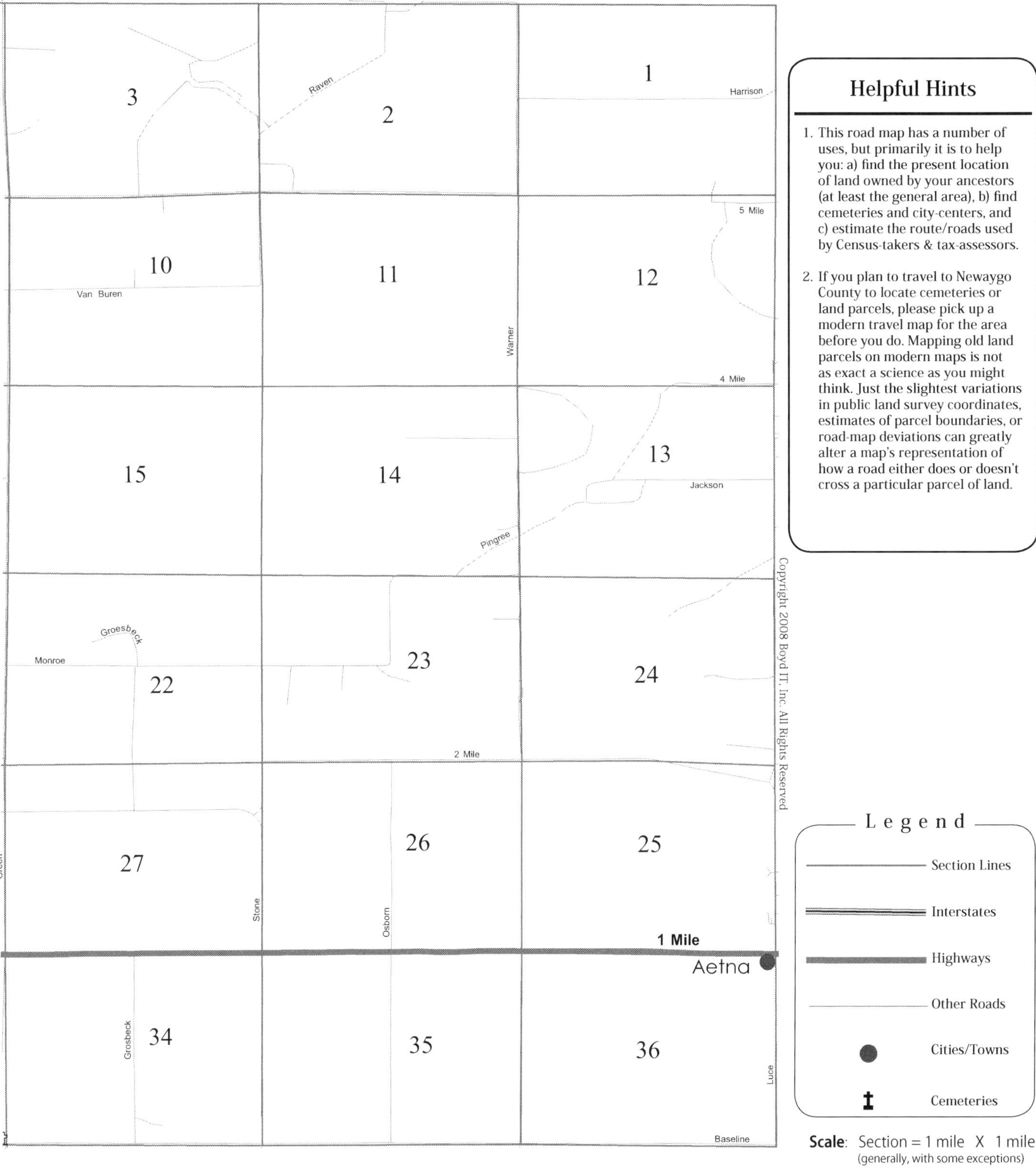
1
2
3
Raven
Harrison
5 Mile
10
11
12
Van Buren
Warner
4 Mile
13
14
15
Jackson
Pingree
22
23
24
Groesbeck
Monroe
2 Mile
25
26
27
Stone
Osborn
1 Mile
Aetna
34
35
36
Grosbeck
Luce
Baseline
Copyright 2008 Boyd IT, Inc. All Rights Reserved
Helpful Hints
1. This road map has a number of uses, but primarily it is to help you: a) find the present location of land owned by your ancestors (at least the general area), b) find cemeteries and city-centers, and c) estimate the route/roads used by Census-takers & tax-assessors.
2. If you plan to travel to Newaygo County to locate cemeteries or land parcels, please pick up a modern travel map for the area before you do. Mapping old land parcels on modern maps is not as exact a science as you might think. Just the slightest variations in public land survey coordinates, estimates of parcel boundaries, or road-map deviations can greatly alter a map's representation of how a road either does or doesn't cross a particular parcel of land.
Legend
Section Lines
Interstates
Highways
Other Roads
Cities/Towns
Cemeteries

Scale: Section = 1 mile X 1 mile
(generally, with some exceptions)

Historical Map

T14-N R14-W
Michigan-Toledo Strip Meridian

Map Group 9

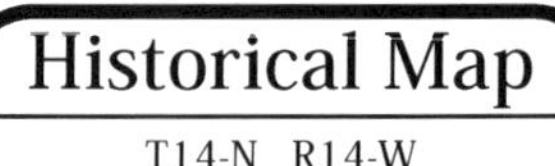

Cities & Towns
- Aetna
- Huber

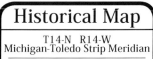

Cemeteries
- Bull Cemetery

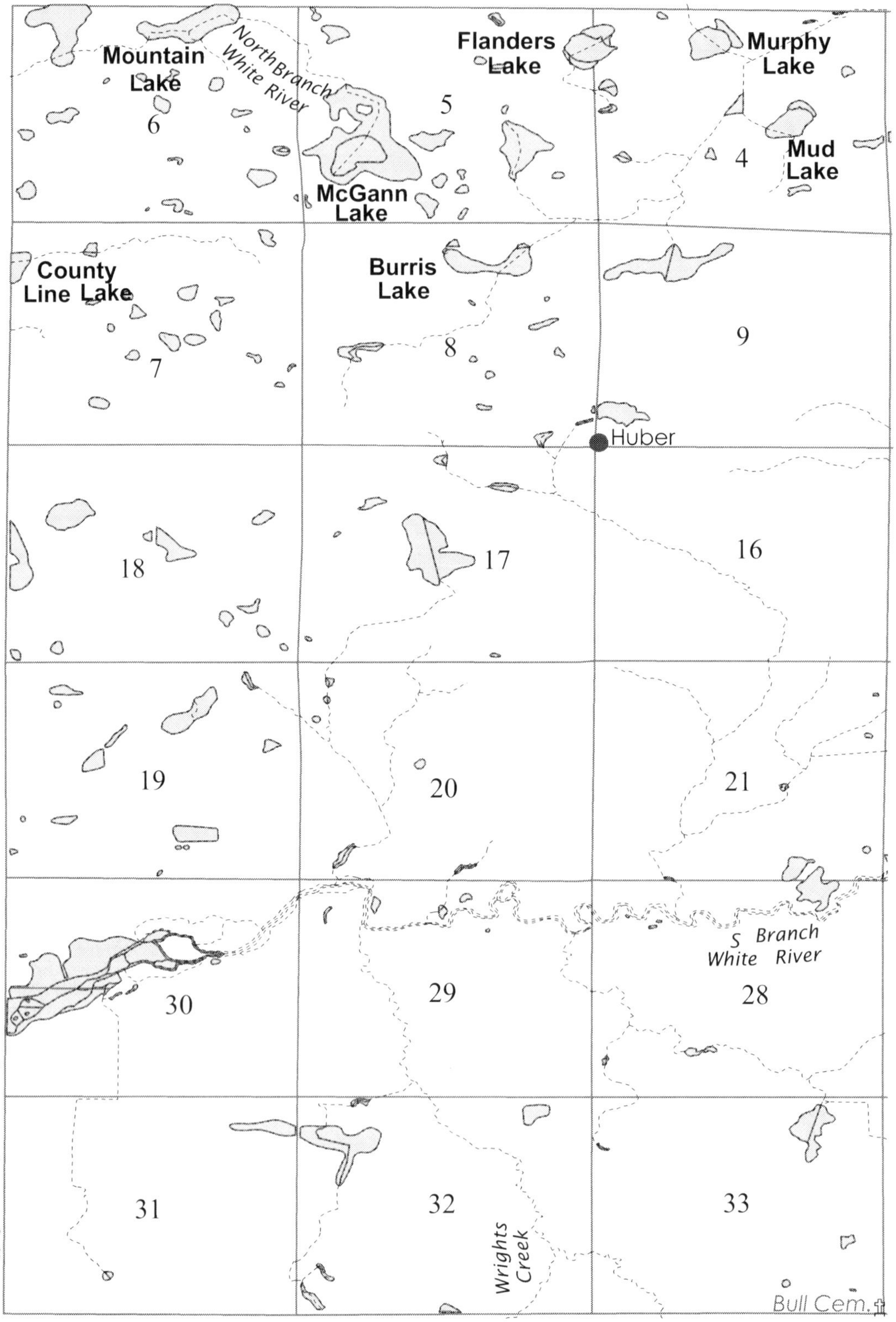

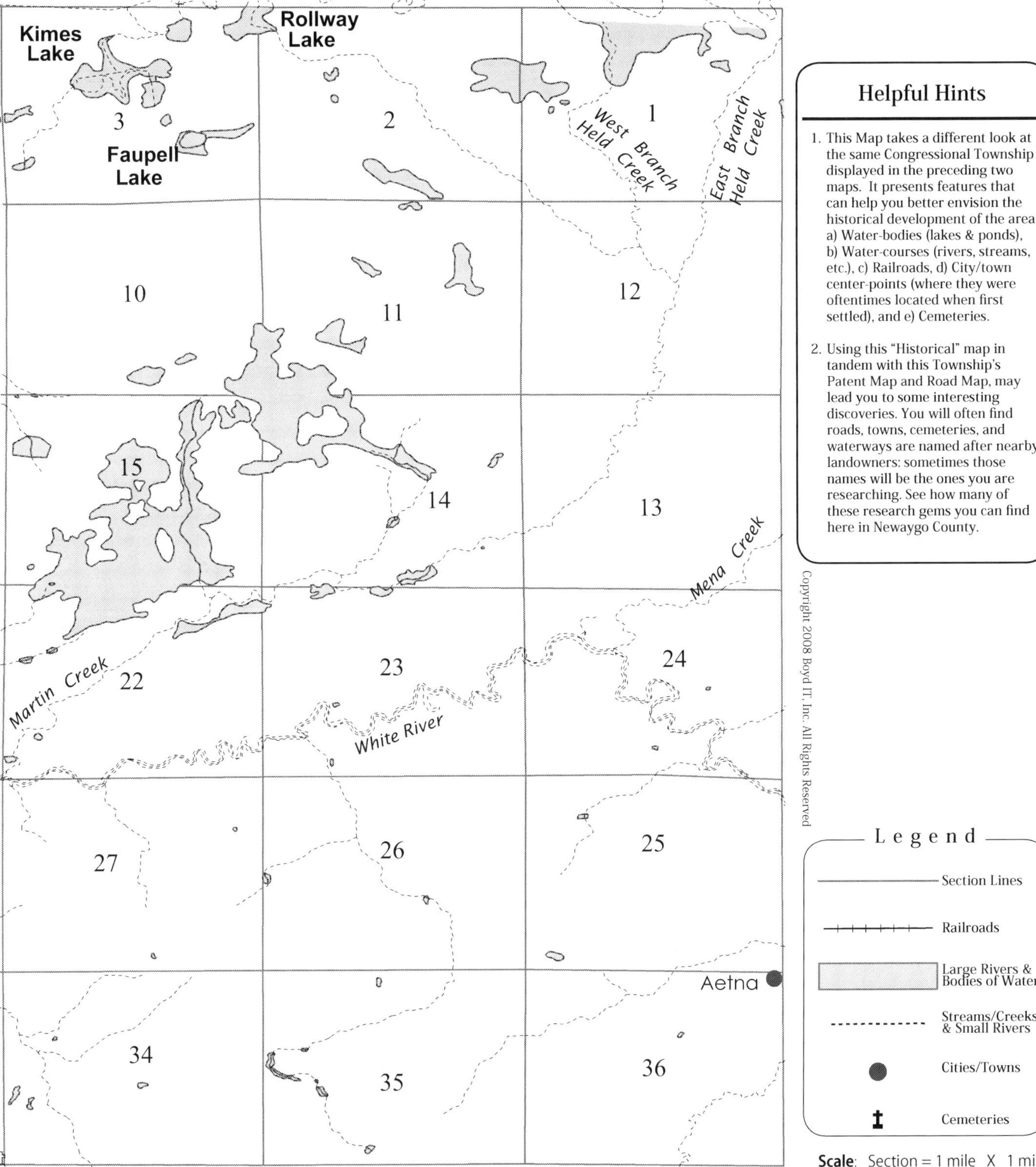

Helpful Hints

1. This Map takes a different look at the same Congressional Township displayed in the preceding two maps. It presents features that can help you better envision the historical development of the area: a) Water-bodies (lakes & ponds), b) Water-courses (rivers, streams, etc.), c) Railroads, d) City/town center-points (where they were oftentimes located when first settled), and e) Cemeteries.

2. Using this "Historical" map in tandem with this Township's Patent Map and Road Map, may lead you to some interesting discoveries. You will often find roads, towns, cemeteries, and waterways are named after nearby landowners: sometimes those names will be the ones you are researching. See how many of these research gems you can find here in Newaygo County.

Scale: Section = 1 mile X 1 mile
(there are some exceptions)

Map Group 10: Index to Land Patents

Township 14-North Range 13-West (Michigan-Toledo Strip)

After you locate an individual in this Index, take note of the Section and Section Part then proceed to the Land Patent map on the pages immediately following. You should have no difficulty locating the corresponding parcel of land.

The "For More Info" Column will lead you to more information about the underlying Patents. See the *Legend* at right, and the "How to Use this Book" chapter, for more information.

LEGEND

"For More Info . . . " column

A = Authority (Legislative Act, See Appendix "A")
B = Block or Lot (location in Section unknown)
C = Cancelled Patent
F = Fractional Section
G = Group (Multi-Patentee Patent, see Appendix "C")
V = Overlaps another Parcel
R = Re-Issued (Parcel patented more than once)

(A & G items require you to look in the Appendixes referred to above. All other Letter-designations followed by a number require you to locate line-items in this index that possess the ID number found after the letter).

ID	Individual in Patent	Sec.	Sec. Part	Date Issued	Other Counties	For More Info . . .
1086	ADAMS, Abigail	28	NESE	1866-11-10		A3 G305
1087	" "	28	SESW	1866-11-10		A3 G305
1088	" "	28	W½SE	1866-11-10		A3 G305
1056	ALLEY, Samuel M	23	NESW	1867-01-10		A1 F
1057	" "	24	SESE	1867-01-10		A1
1072	ANDERSON, William A	30	SWNE	1865-10-10		A1
991	ARNOLD, Susan H	18	S½SE	1864-02-10		A3 G283
992	" "	18	SESW	1864-02-10		A3 G283 F
1039	BENDER, John C	12	S½SE	1867-02-01		A3 G57
999	BLAZO, Jonathan	20	S½NW	1864-02-10		A3 G185 F
999	BLAZO, William A	20	S½NW	1864-02-10		A3 G185 F
1047	BRIGHAM, Orlando S	27	S½SE	1855-12-15		A1 G26
1048	" "	27	S½SW	1855-12-15		A1 G26
1049	" "	28	SESE	1855-12-15		A1 G26
1050	" "	33	NE	1855-12-15		A1 G26
1051	" "	34	W½NW	1855-12-15		A1 G26
994	CHICK, Charles H	30	NESE	1885-01-07		A1 G285
999	CLARK, Susan J	20	S½NW	1864-02-10		A3 G185 F
1064	CLENLEY, Martha	6	E½NE	1868-02-10		A3 G212 F
1065	" "	6	E½SE	1868-02-10		A3 G212
1059	COCHRAN, Fanny	25	SWSW	1868-02-10		A3 G191
1060	" "	26	NESE	1868-02-10		A3 G191 F
1061	" "	26	S½SE	1868-02-10		A3 G191 F
1002	COOK, John P	17	E½SE	1859-08-10		A3
1003	" "	20	NENE	1859-08-10		A3
1004	" "	20	SENE	1859-08-10		A3
1005	" "	20	W½NE	1859-08-10		A3
1006	" "	21	N½NE	1859-08-10		A3
1026	" "	21	NENW	1859-08-10		A3 G40
1007	" "	21	NESE	1859-08-10		A3
1024	" "	21	NWSE	1859-08-10		A3 G42
1025	" "	21	S½NE	1859-08-10		A3 G42
1008	" "	21	SESE	1859-08-10		A3
1009	" "	21	SWSE	1859-08-10		A3
1027	" "	21	W½NW	1859-08-10		A3 G40
1010	" "	22	N½NE	1859-08-10		A3
1011	" "	22	N½SW	1859-08-10		A3
1012	" "	22	NENW	1859-08-10		A3
1013	" "	22	NWNW	1859-08-10		A3
1014	" "	22	S½SW	1859-08-10		A3
1022	" "	27	N½NW	1859-08-10		A3 G41
1015	" "	27	S½NW	1859-08-10		A3
1023	" "	28	NENE	1859-08-10		A3 G41
1016	" "	28	SENE	1859-08-10		A3
1017	" "	28	W½NE	1859-08-10		A3
1018	" "	30	W½SW	1859-08-10		A3 F

ID	Individual in Patent	Sec.	Sec. Part	Date Issued	Other Counties	For More Info . . .
1019	COOK, John P (Cont'd)	31	NENW	1859-08-10		A3
1020	" "	31	W½NE	1859-08-10		A3
1021	" "	31	W½NW	1859-08-10		A3 F
1026	EARLY, Sarah	21	NENW	1859-08-10		A3 G40
1027	" "	21	W½NW	1859-08-10		A3 G40
1039	ELDRIDGE, Lorenzo	12	S½SE	1867-02-01		A3 G57
1039	EUT, William	12	S½SE	1867-02-01		A3 G57
999	FERRAN, Jane	20	S½NW	1864-02-10		A3 G185 F
1058	FORBES, Samuel M	19	NENW	1867-01-10		A1
1029	FRANKLIN, George W	26	SWNW	1869-09-10		A1 G263 F
989	GAMBLE, Sarah	21	N½SW	1864-02-10		A3 G284 F
990	" "	21	SENW	1864-02-10		A3 G284 F
1039	GARNER, Cyrus C	12	S½SE	1867-02-01		A3 G57
1039	GARNER, Ranyon	12	S½SE	1867-02-01		A3 G57
1040	GORING, Lucretia A	28	SENW	1863-09-05		A1
1062	HALL, Stephen C	32	S½NE	1863-01-10		A3 G79 F
1063	" "	33	S½NW	1863-01-10		A3 G79
1090	HARDEN, Julia	34	SESW	1866-11-10		A3 G304
1091	" "	34	SWSE	1866-11-10		A3 G304
1022	HILL, Elizabeth	27	N½NW	1859-08-10		A3 G41
1023	" "	28	NENE	1859-08-10		A3 G41
1086	JOHNSON, Charles	28	NESE	1866-11-10		A3 G305
1087	" "	28	SESW	1866-11-10		A3 G305
1088	" "	28	W½SE	1866-11-10		A3 G305
974	" "	23	SWSW	1867-02-01		A3 F
975	" "	26	NWNW	1867-02-01		A3 F
1089	" "	36	SESE	1867-02-01		A3 G307
972	" "	19	NESW	1868-02-15		A1 F
973	" "	20	NWSE	1868-02-15		A1 F
976	" "	14	NWNW	1869-09-10		A1 G107 F
1029	" "	26	SWNW	1869-09-10		A1 G263 F
993	LEWIS, Frank	18	NWNW	1868-02-15		A1 F
1089	LYNN, Mary W	36	SESE	1867-02-01		A3 G307
1024	MABIE, Margaret	21	NWSE	1859-08-10		A3 G42
1025	" "	21	S½NE	1859-08-10		A3 G42
1090	MERRICK, Elliott T	34	SESW	1866-11-10		A3 G304
1091	" "	34	SWSE	1866-11-10		A3 G304
995	MILES, James H	23	NWSW	1863-12-05		A1 G184 F
999	" "	20	S½NW	1864-02-10		A3 G185 F
996	" "	25	N½SW	1866-02-20		A3 G184
997	" "	25	NWSE	1866-02-20		A3 G184
1000	" "	25	S½NE	1866-02-20		A3 G186
1001	" "	25	SENW	1866-02-20		A3 G186
998	" "	25	SWNW	1866-02-20		A3 G184
995	MILES, William	23	NWSW	1863-12-05		A1 G184 F
999	" "	20	S½NW	1864-02-10		A3 G185 F
996	" "	25	N½SW	1866-02-20		A3 G184
997	" "	25	NWSE	1866-02-20		A3 G184
1000	" "	25	S½NE	1866-02-20		A3 G186
1001	" "	25	SENW	1866-02-20		A3 G186
998	" "	25	SWNW	1866-02-20		A3 G184
1000	MINK, Margaret	25	S½NE	1866-02-20		A3 G186
1001	" "	25	SENW	1866-02-20		A3 G186
1059	MITCHELL, Samuel	25	SWSW	1868-02-10		A3 G191
1060	" "	26	NESE	1868-02-10		A3 G191 F
1061	" "	26	S½SE	1868-02-10		A3 G191 F
1064	PAGE, Stephen F	6	E½NE	1868-02-10		A3 G212 F
1065	" "	6	E½SE	1868-02-10		A3 G212
978	PETERSON, Charles	18	SWSW	1863-12-05		A1 F
979	" "	28	SWNW	1863-12-05		A1
980	" "	29	SESE	1863-12-05		A1
981	" "	33	NENW	1867-01-10		A1
982	" "	34	NENW	1867-01-10		A1
983	" "	34	NWNE	1867-01-10		A1
976	" "	14	NWNW	1869-09-10		A1 G107 F
977	" "	18	NENW	1872-03-20		A1
984	" "	36	SWNE	1872-03-20		A1
1064	RISSEGUIE, Charles E	6	E½NE	1868-02-10		A3 G212 F
1065	" "	6	E½SE	1868-02-10		A3 G212
1052	RUMSEY, Peter	28	N½SW	1865-02-10		A3
1038	SIBLEY, Anna	22	S½NW	1866-05-01		A3 G292
1044	SMITH, Mary	24	SESW	1864-02-10		A3 G346
1045	" "	24	SWSE	1864-02-10		A3 G346

ID	Individual in Patent	Sec.	Sec. Part	Date Issued	Other Counties	For More Info . . .
1046	SMITH, Mary (Cont'd)	25	NENW	1864-02-10		A3 G346
1028	STANLEY, John	19	W½SW	1872-04-05		A4 F
1066	STANLEY, Sylvester	31	NENE	1861-12-10		A1 F
1067	" "	32	NWNW	1861-12-10		A1 F
1071	STANLEY, Thomas	30	W½NW	1860-12-01		A1 F
1069	STANLEY, Thomas B	30	NENW	1860-09-01		A1 F
1068	" "	29	NWNW	1864-11-01		A1
1070	" "	30	SENW	1865-10-10		A1
1029	STEBBINS, Joseph D	26	SWNW	1869-09-10		A1 G263 F
985	STEVENS, Edmund	31	SENE	1900-07-30		A4
1055	SVANO, Peter	26	SENW	1867-01-10		A1 F
991	SWAIN, Elisha R	18	S½SE	1864-02-10		A3 G283
992	" "	18	SESW	1864-02-10		A3 G283 F
989	" "	21	N½SW	1864-02-10		A3 G284 F
990	" "	21	SENW	1864-02-10		A3 G284 F
986	" "	25	SESE	1867-01-10		A1
987	" "	36	NENE	1867-01-10		A1
988	" "	36	NWNE	1867-01-10		A1
994	TAYLOR, James B	30	NESE	1885-01-07		A1 G285
1022	THOMPSON, J E	27	N½NW	1859-08-10		A3 G41
1023	" "	28	NENE	1859-08-10		A3 G41
1031	TOWNSEND, Larmon B	26	NE	1871-10-10		A1 F
1032	" "	26	NENW	1871-10-10		A1 F
1033	" "	26	NWSE	1871-10-10		A1 F
1034	" "	36	NESE	1871-10-10		A1
1035	" "	36	SENE	1871-10-10		A1
1036	" "	36	SESW	1871-10-10		A1
1037	" "	36	SWSE	1871-10-10		A1
1030	" "	14	SENW	1871-11-15		A1 F
1038	TROTT, Levi L	22	S½NW	1866-05-01		A3 G292
1062	TUTHILL, Mehitable	32	S½NE	1863-01-10		A3 G79 F
1063	" "	33	S½NW	1863-01-10		A3 G79
1053	VANO, Peter S	24	N½SE	1867-02-01		A3
1054	" "	24	N½SW	1867-02-01		A3
969	WARREN, Chancellor	30	E½SW	1860-10-01		A1 F
970	" "	30	SESE	1860-10-01		A1
971	" "	30	W½SE	1860-10-01		A1
1074	WESTON, William	34	NENE	1863-03-20		A3
1075	" "	34	NESE	1863-03-20		A3 C R1076
1077	" "	34	S½NE	1863-03-20		A3
1078	" "	34	SENW	1863-03-20		A3
1079	" "	35	N½NE	1863-03-20		A3
1080	" "	35	N½NW	1863-03-20		A3
1081	" "	35	N½SW	1863-03-20		A3 C R1082
1083	" "	35	S½NW	1863-03-20		A3
1084	" "	35	SENE	1863-03-20		A3
1085	" "	35	SWNE	1863-03-20		A3
1073	" "	33	NESW	1863-06-05		A1 F
1076	" "	34	NESE	1864-01-06		A3 R1075
1082	" "	35	N½SW	1864-01-06		A3 R1081
1086	" "	28	NESE	1866-11-10		A3 G305
1087	" "	28	SESW	1866-11-10		A3 G305
1088	" "	28	W½SE	1866-11-10		A3 G305
1090	" "	34	SESW	1866-11-10		A3 G304
1091	" "	34	SWSE	1866-11-10		A3 G304
1089	" "	36	SESE	1867-02-01		A3 G307
1047	WHEELER, Silas	27	S½SE	1855-12-15		A1 G26
1048	" "	27	S½SW	1855-12-15		A1 G26
1049	" "	28	SESE	1855-12-15		A1 G26
1050	" "	33	NE	1855-12-15		A1 G26
1051	" "	34	W½NW	1855-12-15		A1 G26
999	WOODMAN, Horatio	20	S½NW	1864-02-10		A3 G185 F
1041	YOUNG, Martin B	23	SESE	1864-02-10		A3
1044	" "	24	SESW	1864-02-10		A3 G346
1045	" "	24	SWSE	1864-02-10		A3 G346
1042	" "	24	SWSW	1864-02-10		A3
1046	" "	25	NENW	1864-02-10		A3 G346
1043	" "	25	NWNW	1864-02-10		A3

Patent Map

T14-N R13-W
Michigan-Toledo Strip Meridian

Map Group 10

Township Statistics

Parcels Mapped	:	123
Number of Patents	:	74
Number of Individuals	:	60
Patentees Identified	:	42
Number of Surnames	:	54
Multi-Patentee Parcels	:	43
Oldest Patent Date	:	12/15/1855
Most Recent Patent	:	7/30/1900
Block/Lot Parcels	:	0
Parcels Re - Issued	:	2
Parcels that Overlap	:	0
Cities and Towns	:	1
Cemeteries	:	1

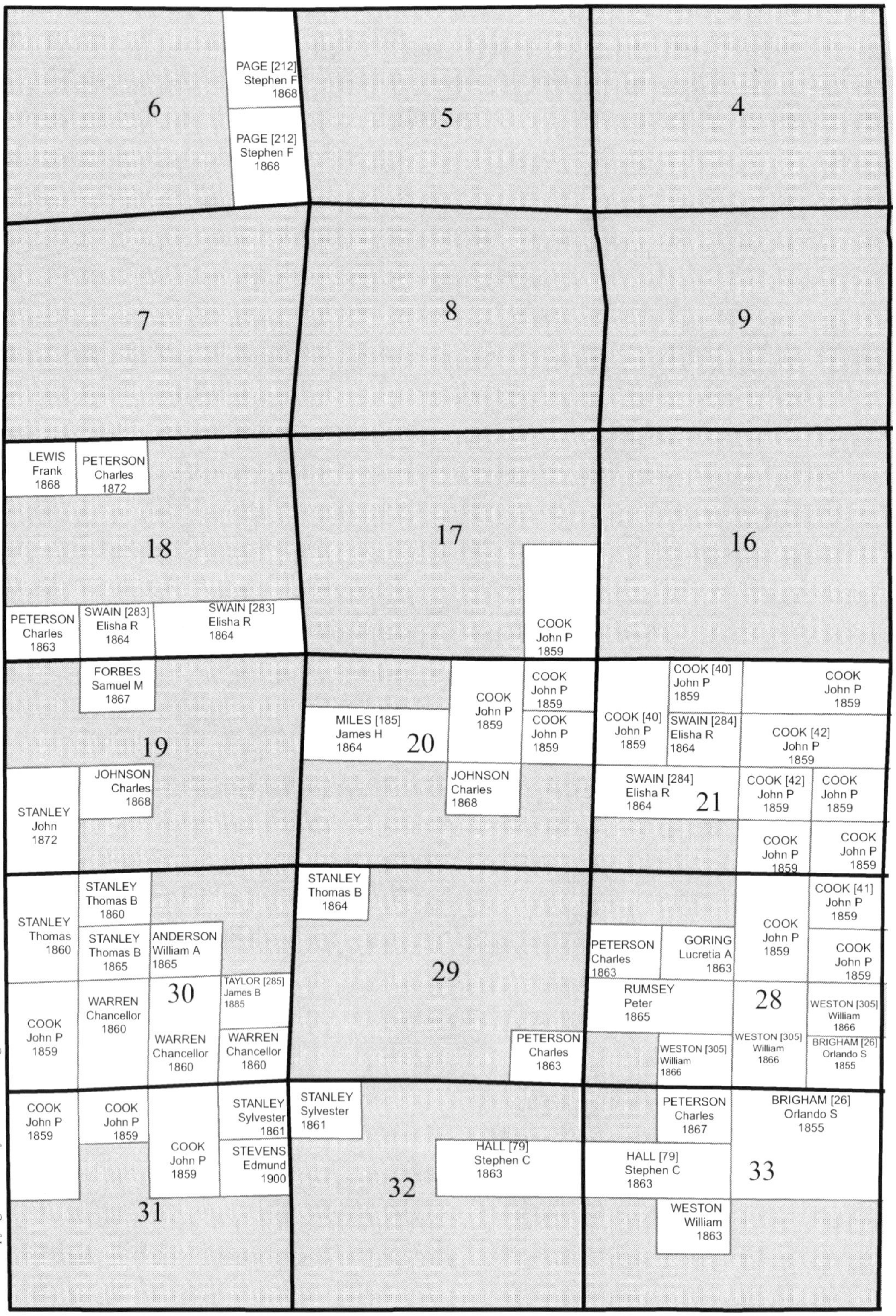

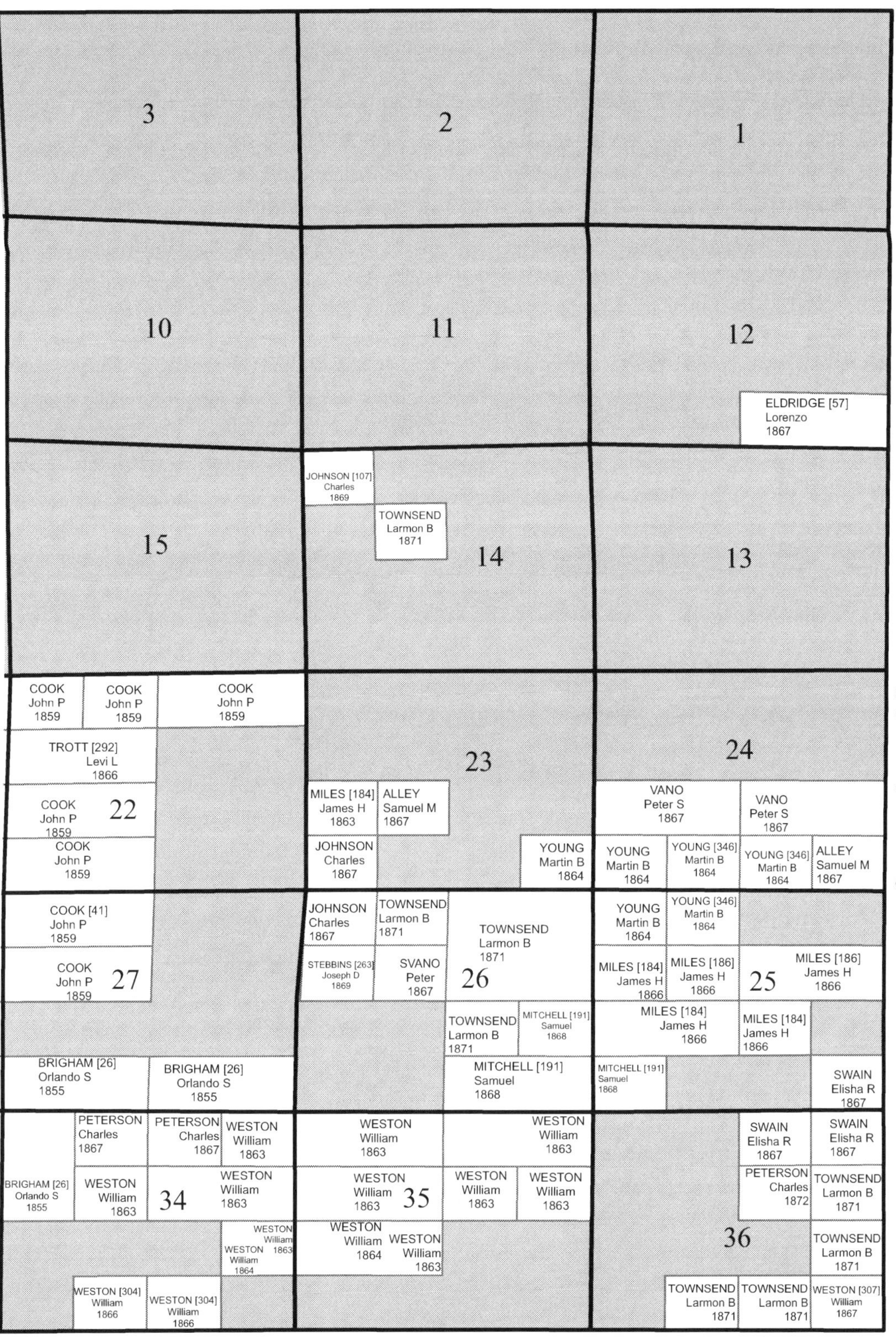

Helpful Hints

1. This Map's INDEX can be found on the preceding pages.
2. Refer to Map "C" to see where this Township lies within Newaygo County, Michigan.
3. Numbers within square brackets [ ] denote a multi-patentee land parcel (multi-owner). Refer to Appendix "C" for a full list of members in this group.
4. Areas that look to be crowded with Patentees usually indicate multiple sales of the same parcel (Re-issues) or Overlapping parcels. See this Township's Index for an explanation of these and other circumstances that might explain "odd" groupings of Patentees on this map.

Legend

- Patent Boundary
- Section Boundary
- No Patents Found (or Outside County)
- 1., 2., 3., ... Lot Numbers (when beside a name)
- [ ] Group Number (see Appendix "C")

Scale: Section = 1 mile X 1 mile (generally, with some exceptions)

Road Map

T14-N R13-W
Michigan-Toledo Strip Meridian

Map Group 10

Cities & Towns

Ramona

Cemeteries

Lincoln Cemetery

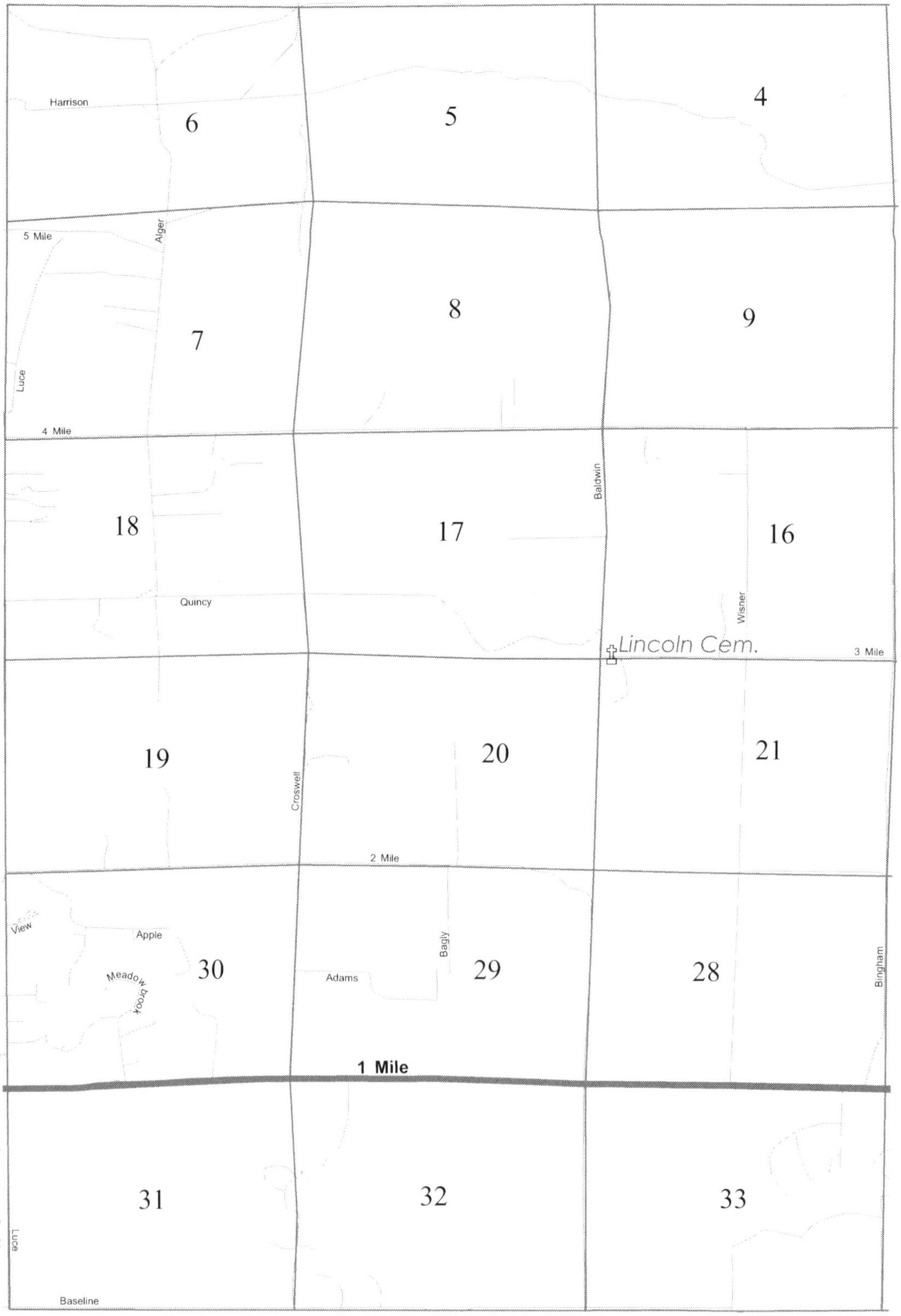

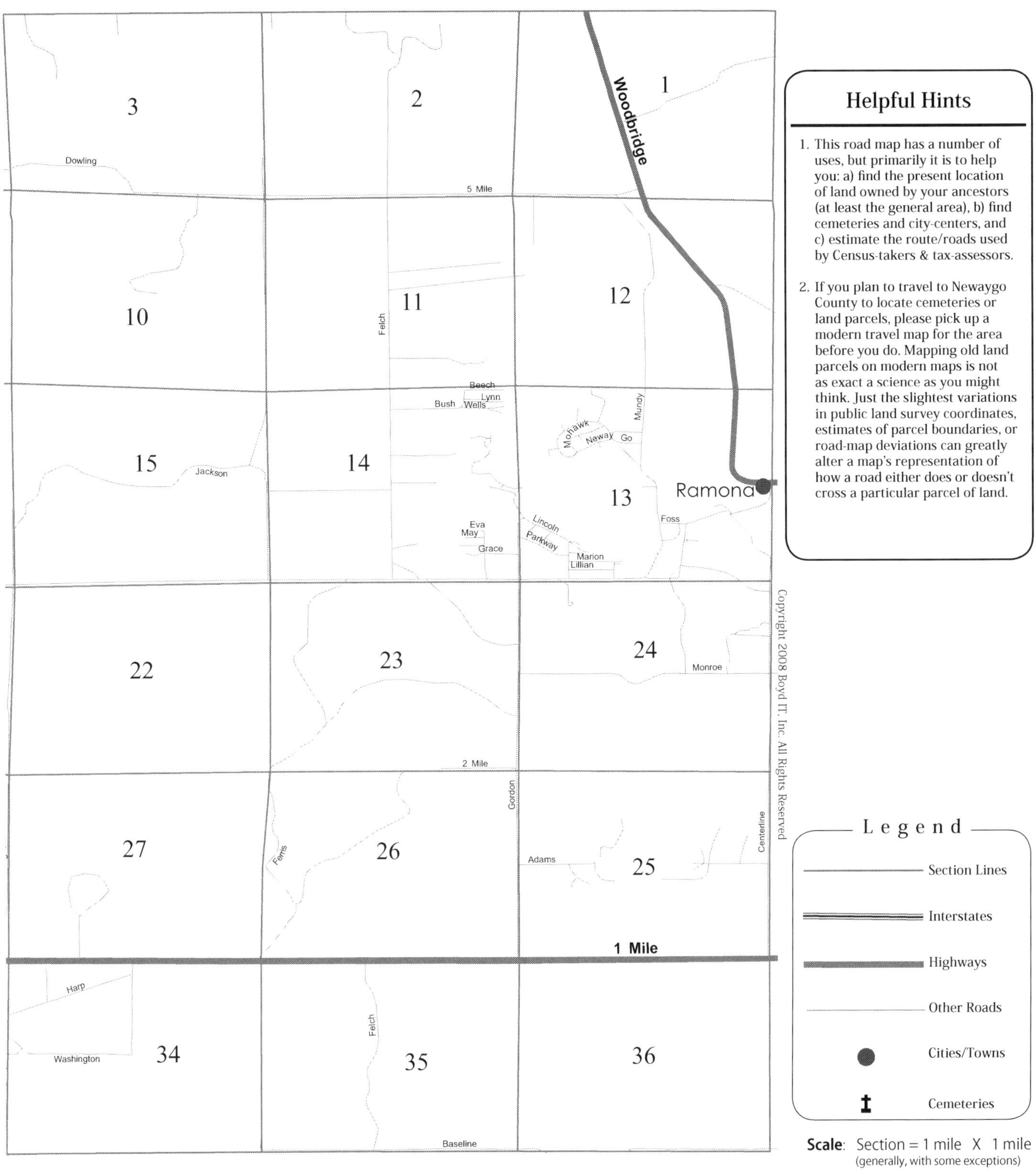
3
2
1
Woodbridge
Dowling
5 Mile
10
11
12
Felch
15
14
13
Jackson
Beech
Lynn
Bush
Wells
Mundy
Mohawk
Neway
Go
Ramona
Foss
Eva
May
Grace
Lincoln
Parkway
Marion
Lillian
22
23
24
Monroe
2 Mile
Gordon
27
26
25
Ferns
Adams
Centerline
1 Mile
Harp
Washington
34
35
36
Felch
Baseline
Copyright 2008 Boyd IT, Inc. All Rights Reserved
Helpful Hints
1. This road map has a number of uses, but primarily it is to help you: a) find the present location of land owned by your ancestors (at least the general area), b) find cemeteries and city-centers, and c) estimate the route/roads used by Census-takers & tax-assessors.
2. If you plan to travel to Newaygo County to locate cemeteries or land parcels, please pick up a modern travel map for the area before you do. Mapping old land parcels on modern maps is not as exact a science as you might think. Just the slightest variations in public land survey coordinates, estimates of parcel boundaries, or road-map deviations can greatly alter a map's representation of how a road either does or doesn't cross a particular parcel of land.
Legend
Section Lines
Interstates
Highways
Other Roads
Cities/Towns
Cemeteries
Scale: Section = 1 mile X 1 mile
(generally, with some exceptions)

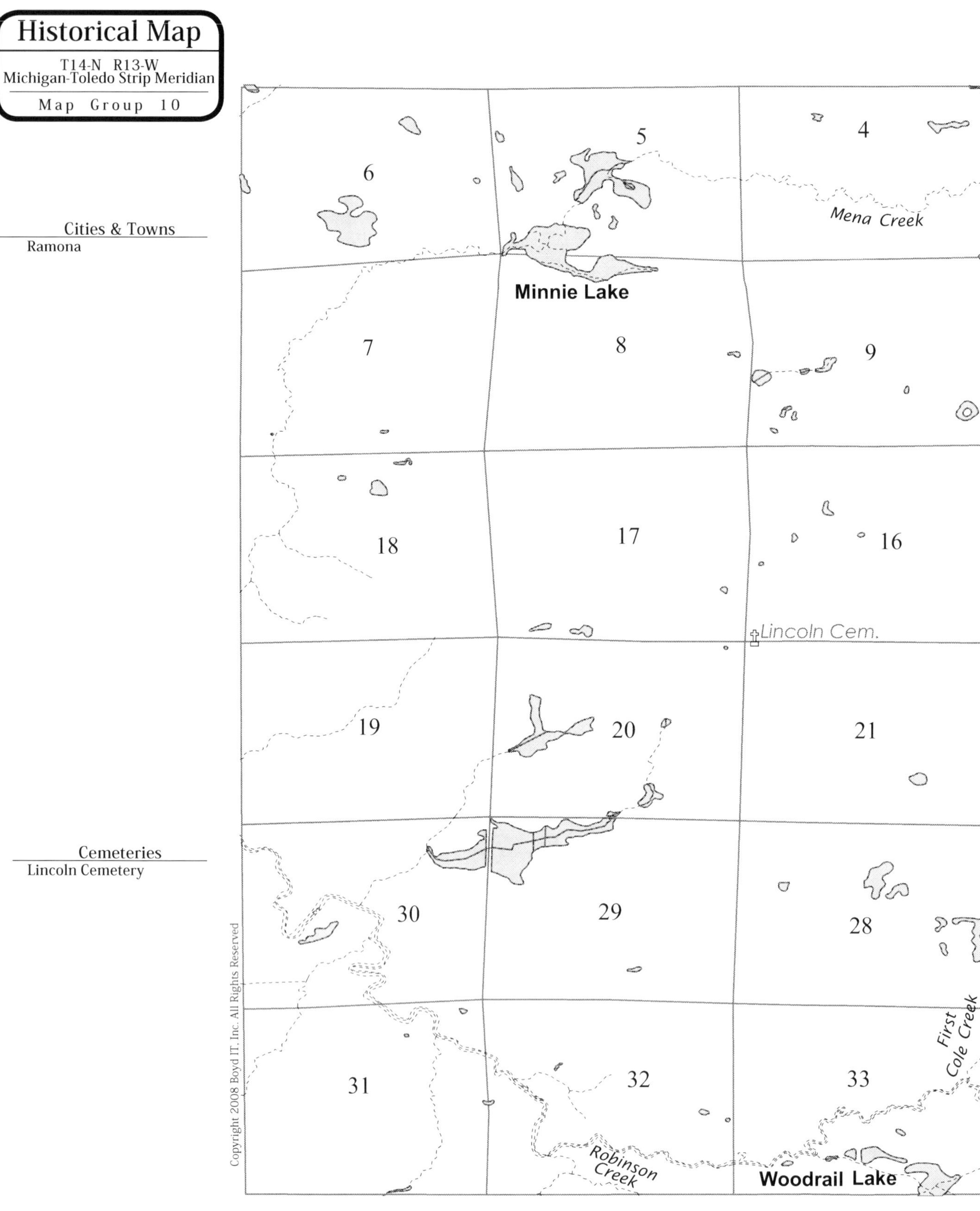
Historical Map
T14-N R13-W
Michigan-Toledo Strip Meridian
Map Group 10
Cities & Towns
Ramona
Cemeteries
Lincoln Cemetery
6
5
4
Mena Creek
Minnie Lake
7
8
9
18
17
16
Lincoln Cem.
19
20
21
30
29
28
31
32
33
First Cole Creek
Robinson Creek
Woodrail Lake
Copyright 2008 Boyd IT, Inc. All Rights Reserved

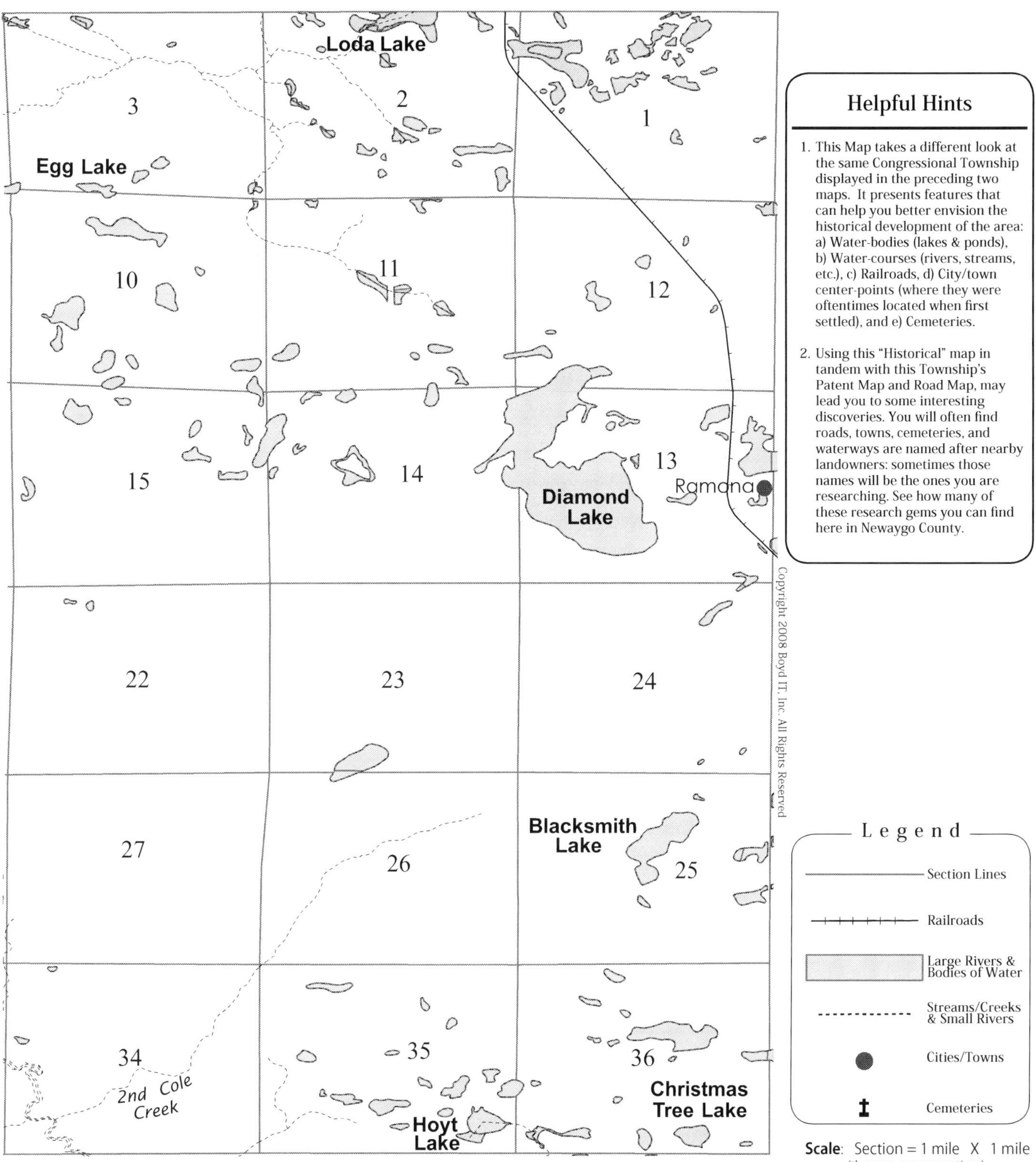

Helpful Hints

1. This Map takes a different look at the same Congressional Township displayed in the preceding two maps. It presents features that can help you better envision the historical development of the area: a) Water-bodies (lakes & ponds), b) Water-courses (rivers, streams, etc.), c) Railroads, d) City/town center-points (where they were oftentimes located when first settled), and e) Cemeteries.

2. Using this "Historical" map in tandem with this Township's Patent Map and Road Map, may lead you to some interesting discoveries. You will often find roads, towns, cemeteries, and waterways are named after nearby landowners: sometimes those names will be the ones you are researching. See how many of these research gems you can find here in Newaygo County.

Legend

- Section Lines
- Railroads
- Large Rivers & Bodies of Water
- Streams/Creeks & Small Rivers
- Cities/Towns
- Cemeteries

Scale: Section = 1 mile X 1 mile
(there are some exceptions)

Map Group 11: Index to Land Patents

Township 14-North Range 12-West (Michigan-Toledo Strip)

After you locate an individual in this Index, take note of the Section and Section Part then proceed to the Land Patent map on the pages immediately following. You should have no difficulty locating the corresponding parcel of land.

The "For More Info" Column will lead you to more information about the underlying Patents. See the *Legend* at right, and the "How to Use this Book" chapter, for more information.

LEGEND

"For More Info . . . " column

A = Authority (Legislative Act, See Appendix "A")
B = Block or Lot (location in Section unknown)
C = Cancelled Patent
F = Fractional Section
G = Group (Multi-Patentee Patent, see Appendix "C")
V = Overlaps another Parcel
R = Re-Issued (Parcel patented more than once)

(A & G items require you to look in the Appendixes referred to above. All other Letter-designations followed by a number require you to locate line-items in this index that possess the ID number found after the letter).

ID	Individual in Patent	Sec.	Sec. Part	Date Issued	Other Counties	For More Info . . .
1172	ALLEY, Samuel M	4	NWNW	1867-05-01		A1 F
1171	" "	2	W½SW	1871-11-15		A1
1159	AVERY, Newell	18	E½NW	1870-05-02		A1 G5
1160	" "	18	SWSE	1870-05-02		A1 G5
1158	" "	2	E½SW	1870-05-02		A1 G4
1161	" "	8	NESE	1870-05-02		A1 G5
1162	" "	8	SENE	1870-05-02		A1 G5
1165	AYER, Delila	31	SWNE	1867-02-01		A3 G294
1166	" "	31	W½SE	1867-02-01		A3 G294
1182	BROWN, Silvester	18	NE	1866-02-20		A3 G29
1123	CLAY, Joseph G	30	NESW	1868-07-20		A3 G165
1124	" "	30	S½NE	1868-07-20		A3 G165
1125	" "	30	SENW	1868-07-20		A3 G165
1123	CLAY, Nancy	30	NESW	1868-07-20		A3 G165
1124	" "	30	S½NE	1868-07-20		A3 G165
1125	" "	30	SENW	1868-07-20		A3 G165
1123	CLAY, William	30	NESW	1868-07-20		A3 G165
1124	" "	30	S½NE	1868-07-20		A3 G165
1125	" "	30	SENW	1868-07-20		A3 G165
1093	COMSTOCK, Charles C	22	SWSW	1855-12-15		A1
1094	" "	27	NWNW	1855-12-15		A1
1095	" "	28	E½NW	1855-12-15		A1
1096	" "	28	NENE	1855-12-15		A1
1097	" "	28	SW	1855-12-15		A1
1098	" "	28	SWNW	1855-12-15		A1
1099	" "	28	W½NE	1855-12-15		A1
1100	" "	29	E½SE	1855-12-15		A1
1101	" "	29	SENE	1855-12-15		A1
1102	" "	32	NENE	1855-12-15		A1
1103	" "	33	NW	1855-12-15		A1
1092	" "	22	N½NW	1859-08-10		A3
1144	COOK, John P	20	SESE	1870-06-20		A1
1165	CRITCHLOW, John J	31	SWNE	1867-02-01		A3 G294
1166	" "	31	W½SE	1867-02-01		A3 G294
1113	DARLING, Henry	27	NWSW	1856-03-10		A1
1114	" "	36	E½SE	1857-02-20		A3
1115	" "	36	NWSE	1857-02-20		A3
1116	" "	36	S½SW	1857-02-20		A3
1117	" "	36	SWSE	1857-02-20		A3
1182	DOUGLAS, Ann E	18	NE	1866-02-20		A3 G29
1118	EASTMAN, George	18	E½SE	1868-02-15		A1 G164
1119	" "	20	W½NW	1868-02-15		A1 G164
1126	" "	8	NENW	1868-02-15		A1 G167
1120	" "	8	S½SW	1868-02-15		A1 G164
1121	" "	8	SWSE	1868-02-15		A1 G164
1122	" "	8	W½NW	1868-02-15		A1 G164

ID	Individual in Patent	Sec.	Sec. Part	Date Issued	Other Counties	For More Info . . .
1123	EASTMAN, George (Cont'd)	30	NESW	1868-07-20		A3 G165
1124	" "	30	S½NE	1868-07-20		A3 G165
1125	" "	30	SENW	1868-07-20		A3 G165
1169	EASTMAN, Samuel	26	SESW	1861-12-10		A1
1170	" "	26	SWSE	1861-12-10		A1
1183	EASTMAN, Simon	26	N½SE	1861-04-01		A1
1184	" "	26	S½NE	1861-04-01		A1
1148	ELDREDGE, Lorenzo	22	S½SE	1866-09-01		A1
1149	" "	31	SWSW	1866-09-01		A1
1147	ELDRIDGE, Lorenza	32	NESE	1866-04-03		A1
1156	ELDRIDGE, Lorenzo	32	NENW	1866-01-10		A3 G58 C
1157	" "	32	NWNE	1866-01-10		A3 G58 C
1150	" "	18	NWNW	1866-04-03		A1 F
1151	" "	22	SESW	1866-04-03		A1
1152	" "	30	NWSW	1866-04-03		A1 F
1154	" "	8	SESE	1866-04-03		A1
1153	" "	8	SENW	1866-11-10		A3
1155	" "	8	W½NE	1866-11-10		A3
1109	FERRY, Edward P	28	NWNW	1868-06-10		A1
1107	" "	24	E½SE	1868-12-01		A3
1108	" "	24	NWSE	1868-12-01		A3
1185	" "	32	SESE	1872-04-05		A1 G62
1185	FERRY, Thomas W	32	SESE	1872-04-05		A1 G62
1141	GOOCH, John	2	NW	1878-06-13		A4 F
1165	GOULD, John	31	SWNE	1867-02-01		A3 G294
1166	" "	31	W½SE	1867-02-01		A3 G294
1142	GROVESTEEN, John M	36	SENE	1870-05-10		A1
1104	GUSTROUS, John	24	N½NW	1868-02-15		A1 G105
1105	" "	26	N½NE	1868-02-15		A1 G105
1143	HAGERMANN, Charles	18	NWSE	1867-05-01		A1 G188
1139	HARPER, John S	8	N½SW	1871-02-20		A3 G290
1140	" "	8	NWSE	1871-02-20		A3 G290
1159	HEALD, Joseph	18	E½NW	1870-05-02		A1 G5
1160	" "	18	SWSE	1870-05-02		A1 G5
1161	" "	8	NESE	1870-05-02		A1 G5
1162	" "	8	SENE	1870-05-02		A1 G5
1126	HEFFERAN, Thomas	8	NENW	1868-02-15		A1 G167
1168	HOBLER, Ruth	4	SWNW	1867-05-01		A1
1189	JOHNSON, Charles	14	W½SE	1866-11-10		A3 G310
1188	" "	22	N½NE	1866-11-10		A3 G308
1104	" "	24	N½NW	1868-02-15		A1 G105
1105	" "	26	N½NE	1868-02-15		A1 G105
1118	LULL, Hiram	18	E½SE	1868-02-15		A1 G164
1119	" "	20	W½NW	1868-02-15		A1 G164
1126	" "	8	NENW	1868-02-15		A1 G167
1120	" "	8	S½SW	1868-02-15		A1 G164
1121	" "	8	SWSE	1868-02-15		A1 G164
1122	" "	8	W½NW	1868-02-15		A1 G164
1123	" "	30	NESW	1868-07-20		A3 G165
1124	" "	30	S½NE	1868-07-20		A3 G165
1125	" "	30	SENW	1868-07-20		A3 G165
1131	MILES, James H	25	SESW	1855-11-08		A3 G187
1132	" "	25	SWSE	1855-11-08		A3 G187
1134	" "	36	E½NW	1855-11-08		A3 G187
1130	" "	25	SESE	1855-12-15		A1 G187
1133	" "	26	SESE	1855-12-15		A1 G187
1135	" "	36	N½NE	1855-12-15		A1 G187
1127	" "	25	NESE	1856-03-10		A1
1128	" "	20	N½SE	1864-02-10		A3 G184
1129	" "	20	SWSE	1864-02-10		A3 G184
1136	" "	30	SWNW	1866-02-20		A3 G186 F
1131	MILES, William	25	SESW	1855-11-08		A3 G187
1132	" "	25	SWSE	1855-11-08		A3 G187
1134	" "	36	E½NW	1855-11-08		A3 G187
1130	" "	25	SESE	1855-12-15		A1 G187
1133	" "	26	SESE	1855-12-15		A1 G187
1135	" "	36	N½NE	1855-12-15		A1 G187
1128	" "	20	N½SE	1864-02-10		A3 G184
1129	" "	20	SWSE	1864-02-10		A3 G184
1136	" "	30	SWNW	1866-02-20		A3 G186 F
1143	MILLER, John	18	NWSE	1867-05-01		A1 G188
1136	MINK, Margaret	30	SWNW	1866-02-20		A3 G186 F
1173	MITCHELL, Samuel	23	E½SW	1857-02-20		A3 G192

ID	Individual in Patent	Sec.	Sec. Part	Date Issued	Other Counties	For More Info . . .
1174	MITCHELL, Samuel (Cont'd)	24	N½SW	1857-02-20		A3 G192
1175	" "	24	S½SW	1857-02-20		A3 G192
1176	" "	24	SENW	1857-02-20		A3 G192
1177	" "	24	SWSE	1857-02-20		A3 G192
1178	" "	25	NENW	1857-02-20		A3 G192
1179	" "	25	NWNE	1857-02-20		A3 G192
1146	MORGAN, Lester C	18	SWNW	1872-03-20		A1
1111	MOSES, Henry C	26	NW	1860-11-10		A3
1112	" "	34	NE	1861-07-01		A3
1159	MURPHY, Simon J	18	E½NW	1870-05-02		A1 G5
1160	" "	18	SWSE	1870-05-02		A1 G5
1158	" "	2	E½SW	1870-05-02		A1 G4
1161	" "	8	NESE	1870-05-02		A1 G5
1162	" "	8	SENE	1870-05-02		A1 G5
1173	NICHOLS, James	23	E½SW	1857-02-20		A3 G192
1174	" "	24	N½SW	1857-02-20		A3 G192
1175	" "	24	S½SW	1857-02-20		A3 G192
1176	" "	24	SENW	1857-02-20		A3 G192
1177	" "	24	SWSE	1857-02-20		A3 G192
1178	" "	25	NENW	1857-02-20		A3 G192
1179	" "	25	NWNE	1857-02-20		A3 G192
1106	PATTERSON, David	26	N½SW	1871-06-15		A4
1181	PEARSON, Daniel K	20	E½NW	1871-10-10		A1 G315
1180	" "	10	NWNE	1871-11-15		A1 G315
1156	REASMON, Magdalene	32	NENW	1866-01-10		A3 G58 C
1157	" "	32	NWNE	1866-01-10		A3 G58 C
1131	SAUNDERS, Isaac M	25	SESW	1855-11-08		A3 G187
1132	" "	25	SWSE	1855-11-08		A3 G187
1134	" "	36	E½NW	1855-11-08		A3 G187
1130	" "	25	SESE	1855-12-15		A1 G187
1133	" "	26	SESE	1855-12-15		A1 G187
1135	" "	36	N½NE	1855-12-15		A1 G187
1186	SIBLEY, William H	32	SESW	1871-10-10		A1
1187	" "	32	W½SW	1871-10-10		A1
1167	SVANO, Peter	30	SESW	1867-01-10		A1
1139	TAYLOR, Royal	8	N½SW	1871-02-20		A3 G290
1140	" "	8	NWSE	1871-02-20		A3 G290
1137	TINKHAM, John F	28	NWSE	1869-09-10		A1
1138	" "	36	NWSW	1869-09-10		A1
1139	" "	8	N½SW	1871-02-20		A3 G290
1140	" "	8	NWSE	1871-02-20		A3 G290
1145	TOWNSEND, Larmon B	30	SWSW	1871-10-10		A1 F
1163	VANO, Peter S	31	E½SW	1867-02-01		A3
1164	" "	31	SENW	1867-02-01		A3
1165	" "	31	SWNE	1867-02-01		A3 G294
1166	" "	31	W½SE	1867-02-01		A3 G294
1159	WELCH, John	18	E½NW	1870-05-02		A1 G5
1160	" "	18	SWSE	1870-05-02		A1 G5
1161	" "	8	NESE	1870-05-02		A1 G5
1162	" "	8	SENE	1870-05-02		A1 G5
1189	WESTON, William	14	W½SE	1866-11-10		A3 G310
1188	" "	22	N½NE	1866-11-10		A3 G308
1181	WILCOX, Sextus N	20	E½NW	1871-10-10		A1 G315
1180	" "	10	NWNE	1871-11-15		A1 G315
1189	WILLARD, David	14	W½SE	1866-11-10		A3 G310
1188	" "	22	N½NE	1866-11-10		A3 G308
1110	WILSON, Gilbert F	8	NENE	1871-05-01		A1

Patent Map

T14-N R12-W
Michigan-Toledo Strip Meridian

Map Group 11

Township Statistics

Parcels Mapped	:	98
Number of Patents	:	73
Number of Individuals	:	55
Patentees Identified	:	42
Number of Surnames	:	48
Multi-Patentee Parcels	:	45
Oldest Patent Date	:	11/8/1855
Most Recent Patent	:	6/13/1878
Block/Lot Parcels	:	0
Parcels Re - Issued	:	0
Parcels that Overlap	:	0
Cities and Towns	:	0
Cemeteries	:	1

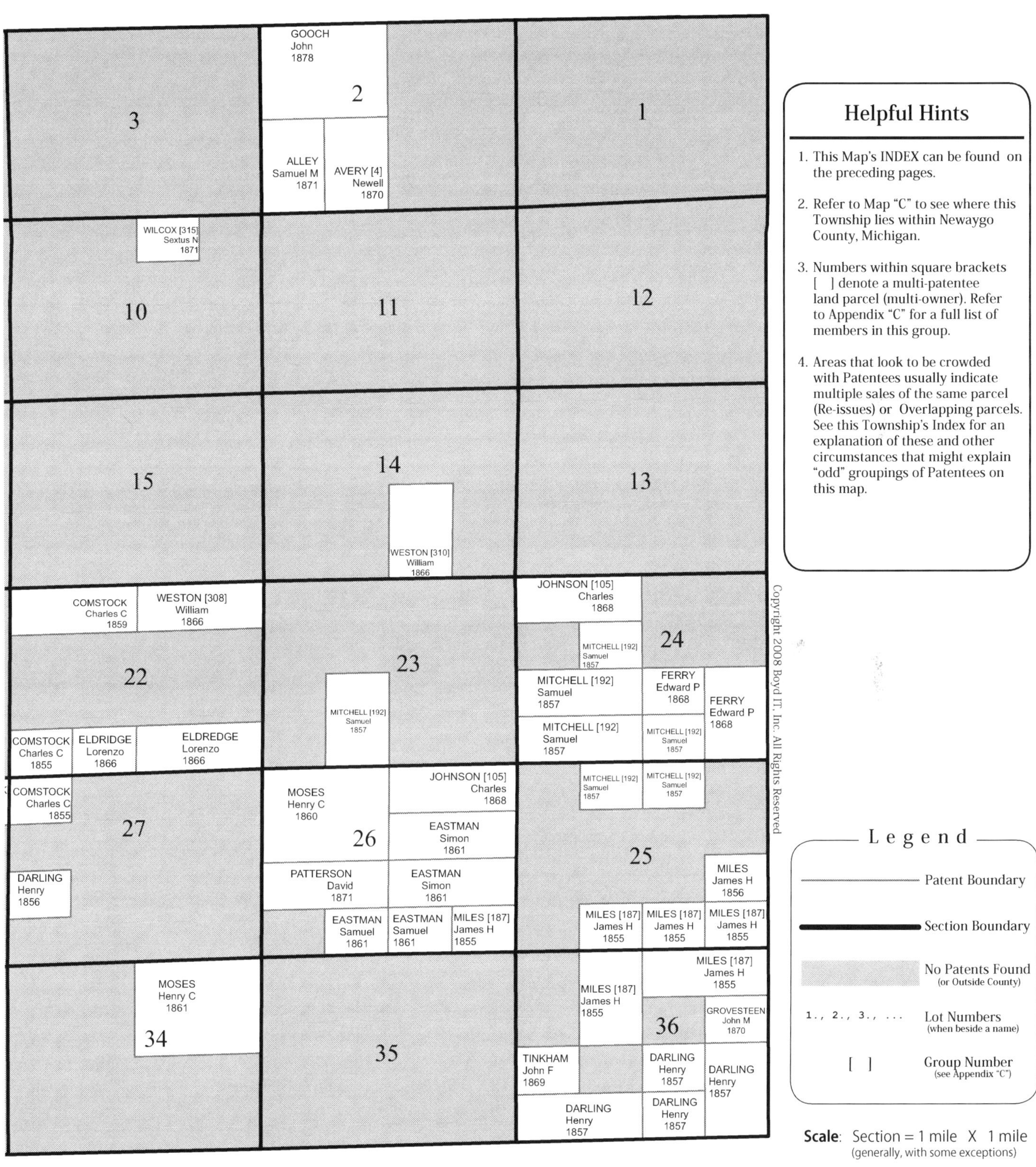

Helpful Hints

1. This Map's INDEX can be found on the preceding pages.
2. Refer to Map "C" to see where this Township lies within Newaygo County, Michigan.
3. Numbers within square brackets [ ] denote a multi-patentee land parcel (multi-owner). Refer to Appendix "C" for a full list of members in this group.
4. Areas that look to be crowded with Patentees usually indicate multiple sales of the same parcel (Re-issues) or Overlapping parcels. See this Township's Index for an explanation of these and other circumstances that might explain "odd" groupings of Patentees on this map.

Legend

- Patent Boundary
- Section Boundary
- No Patents Found (or Outside County)
- 1., 2., 3., ... Lot Numbers (when beside a name)
- [ ] Group Number (see Appendix "C")

Scale: Section = 1 mile X 1 mile (generally, with some exceptions)

Road Map

T14-N R12-W
Michigan-Toledo Strip Meridian

Map Group 11

Cities & Towns

None

Cemeteries

Amish Cemetery

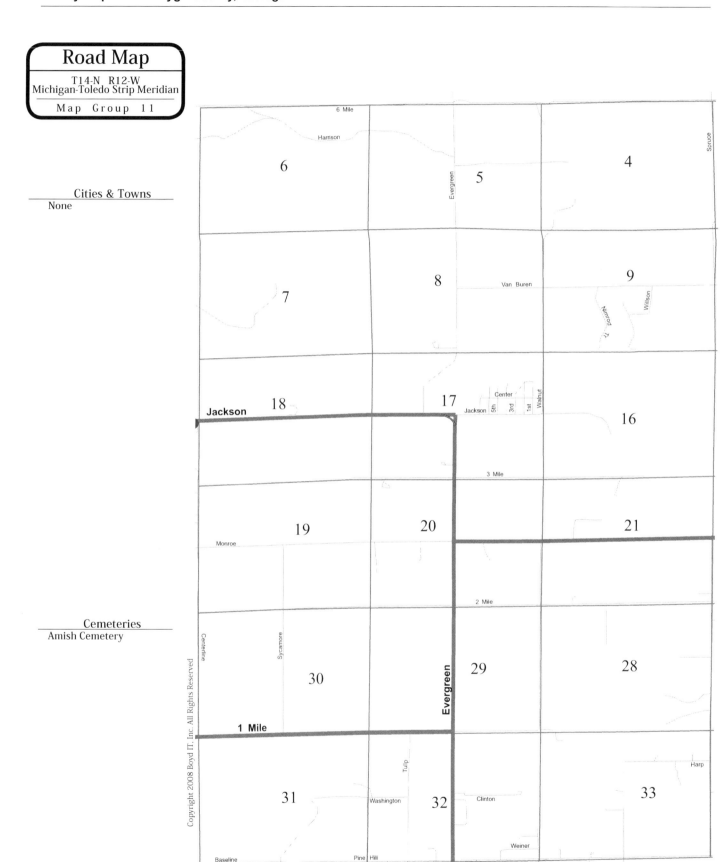

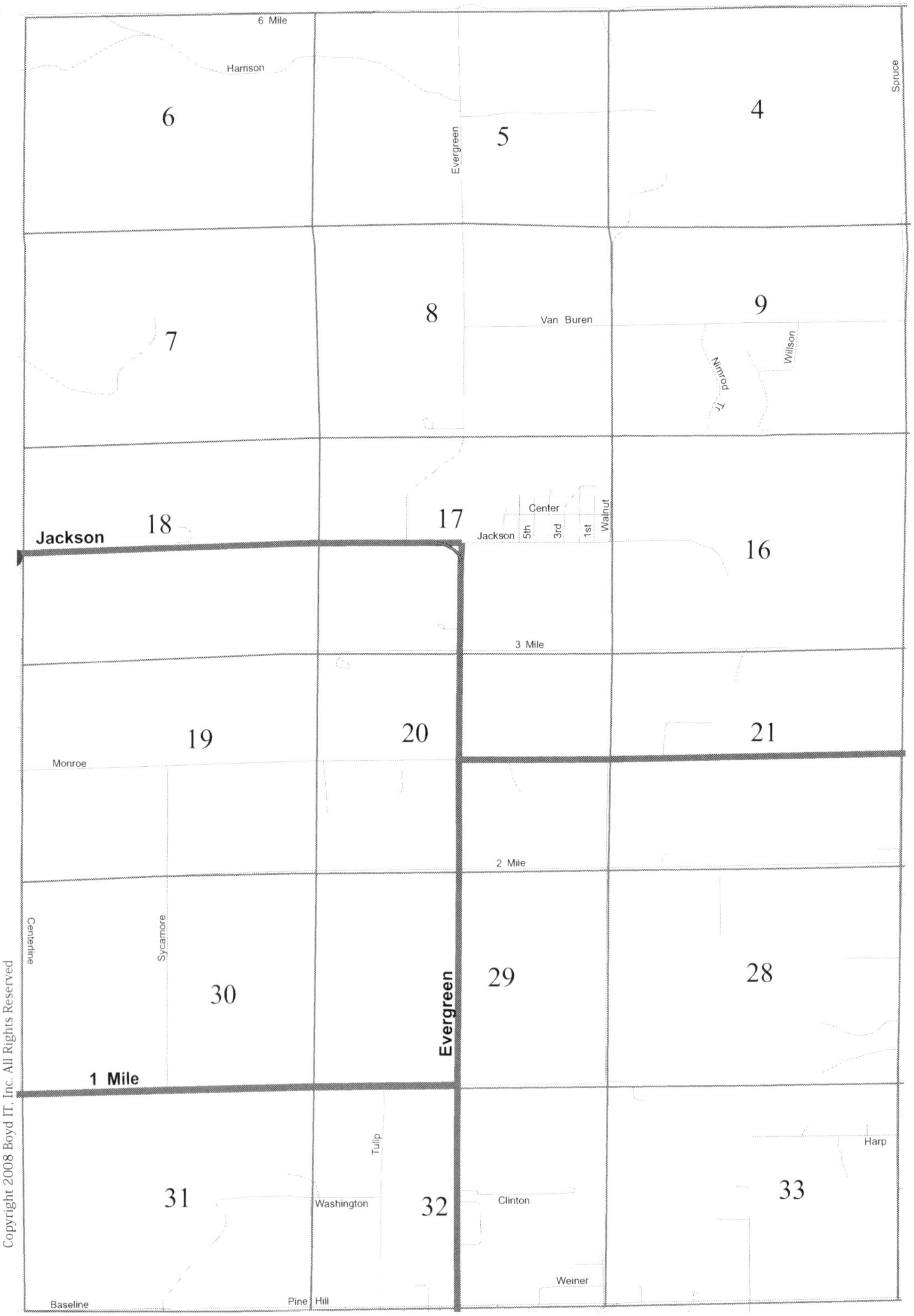

6 Mile
Harrison
Spruce
Evergreen
Van Buren
Nimrod Tr.
Willson
Center
Jackson
5th
3rd
1st
Walnut
3 Mile
Monroe
2 Mile
Centerline
Sycamore
Evergreen
1 Mile
Tulip
Harp
Washington
Clinton
Weiner
Baseline
Pine Hill
6 5 4 7 8 9 18 17 16 19 20 21 30 29 28 31 32 33

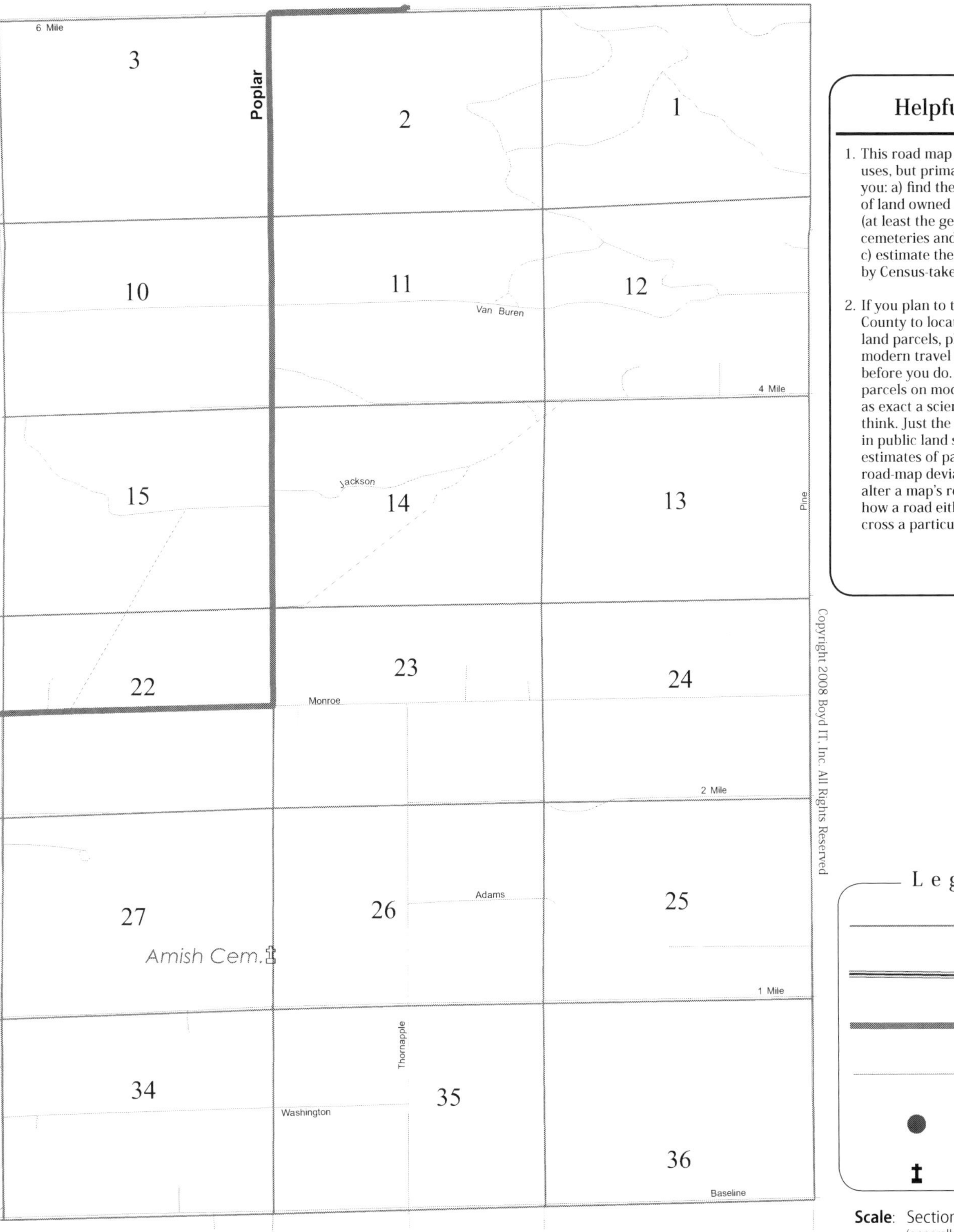

Helpful Hints

1. This road map has a number of uses, but primarily it is to help you: a) find the present location of land owned by your ancestors (at least the general area), b) find cemeteries and city-centers, and c) estimate the route/roads used by Census-takers & tax-assessors.

2. If you plan to travel to Newaygo County to locate cemeteries or land parcels, please pick up a modern travel map for the area before you do. Mapping old land parcels on modern maps is not as exact a science as you might think. Just the slightest variations in public land survey coordinates, estimates of parcel boundaries, or road-map deviations can greatly alter a map's representation of how a road either does or doesn't cross a particular parcel of land.

Legend

- Section Lines
- Interstates
- Highways
- Other Roads
- Cities/Towns
- Cemeteries

Scale: Section = 1 mile X 1 mile
(generally, with some exceptions)

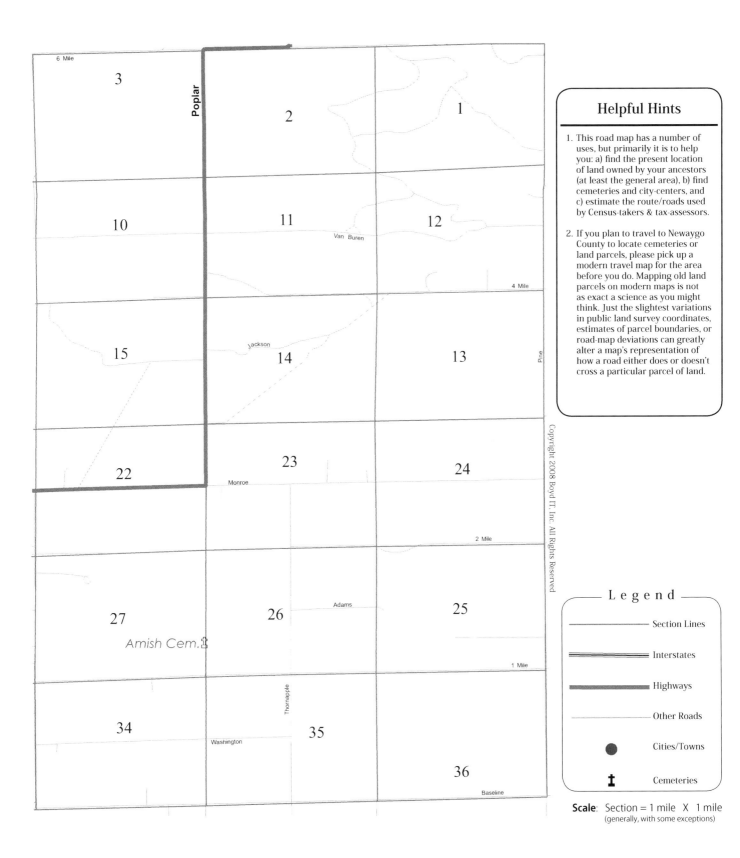

Historical Map

T14-N R12-W
Michigan-Toledo Strip Meridian

Map Group 11

Cities & Towns
None

Cemeteries
Amish Cemetery

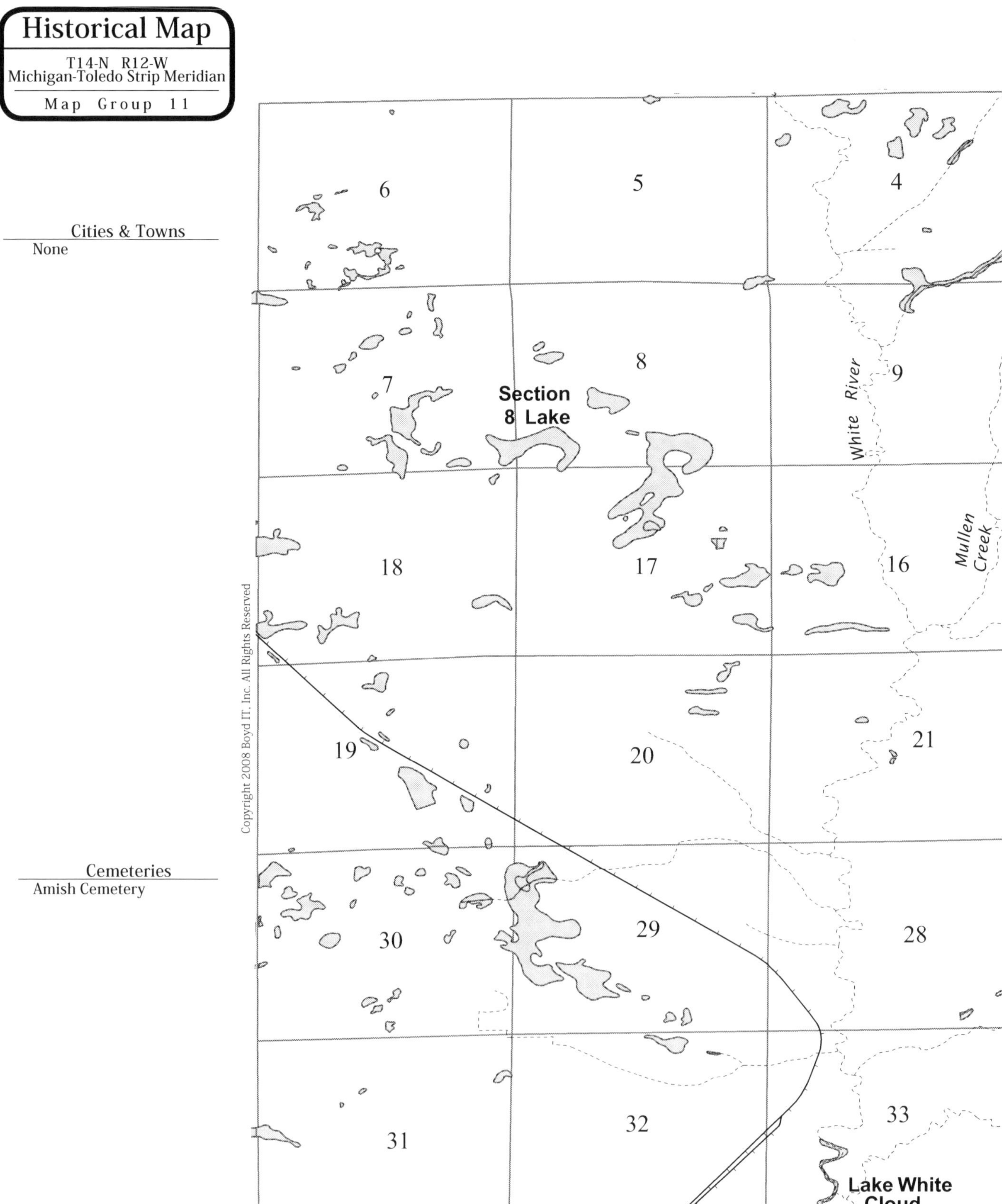

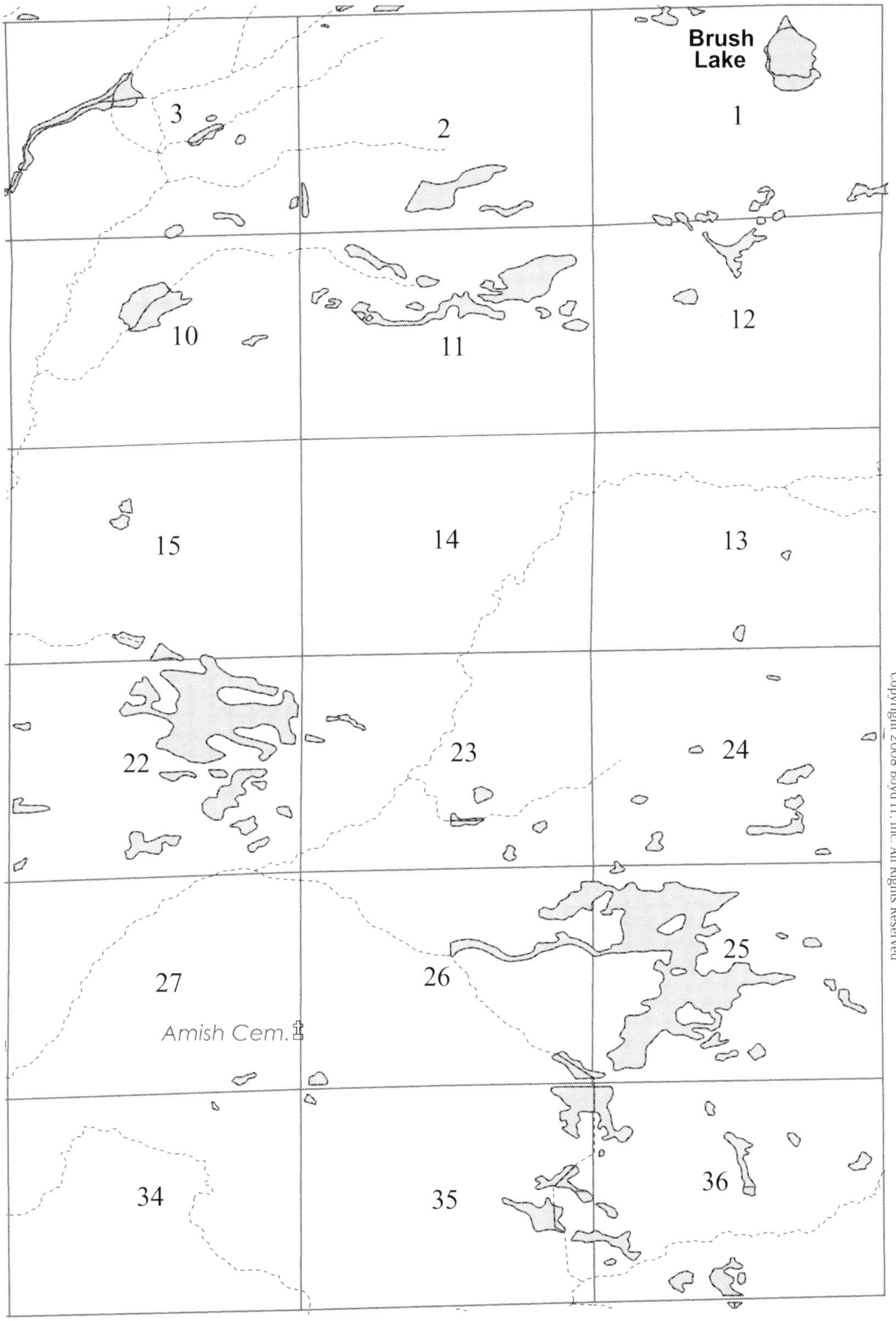

Brush Lake

3 2 1

10 11 12

15 14 13

22 23 24

27 26 25

Amish Cem.

34 35 36

Helpful Hints

1. This Map takes a different look at the same Congressional Township displayed in the preceding two maps. It presents features that can help you better envision the historical development of the area: a) Water-bodies (lakes & ponds), b) Water-courses (rivers, streams, etc.), c) Railroads, d) City/town center-points (where they were oftentimes located when first settled), and e) Cemeteries.

2. Using this "Historical" map in tandem with this Township's Patent Map and Road Map, may lead you to some interesting discoveries. You will often find roads, towns, cemeteries, and waterways are named after nearby landowners: sometimes those names will be the ones you are researching. See how many of these research gems you can find here in Newaygo County.

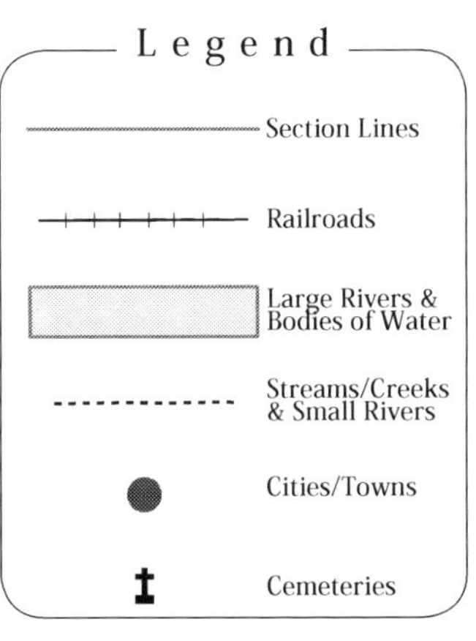

Scale: Section = 1 mile X 1 mile
(there are some exceptions)

Map Group 12: Index to Land Patents

Township 14-North Range 11-West (Michigan-Toledo Strip)

After you locate an individual in this Index, take note of the Section and Section Part then proceed to the Land Patent map on the pages immediately following. You should have no difficulty locating the corresponding parcel of land.

The "For More Info" Column will lead you to more information about the underlying Patents. See the *Legend* at right, and the "How to Use this Book" chapter, for more information.

LEGEND

"For More Info . . . " column

A = Authority (Legislative Act, See Appendix "A")
B = Block or Lot (location in Section unknown)
C = Cancelled Patent
F = Fractional Section
G = Group (Multi-Patentee Patent, see Appendix "C")
V = Overlaps another Parcel
R = Re-Issued (Parcel patented more than once)

(A & G items require you to look in the Appendixes referred to above. All other Letter-designations followed by a number require you to locate line-items in this index that possess the ID number found after the letter).

ID	Individual in Patent	Sec.	Sec. Part	Date Issued	Other Counties	For More Info . . .
1337	ALLEY, Samuel M	22	NW	1866-11-10		A3 G1
1304	ASHLEY, Samuel M	22	E½SW	1866-04-03		A1 G39
1314	BALL, John	1	SWNE	1855-03-01		A1
1315	" "	12	N½SE	1855-03-01		A1
1316	" "	12	SWSE	1855-03-01		A1
1197	BENDER, John C	12	E½SW	1867-02-01		A3 G203
1304	BENNETT, William	22	E½SW	1866-04-03		A1 G39
1266	BOWMAN, Mary	7	E½NE	1858-01-15		A3 G124
1267	" "	8	SWNW	1858-01-15		A3 G124
1192	BOYD, Rufus	26	E½SE	1855-12-15		A1 G261
1219	BUCK, Elias B	36	S½SE	1882-03-20		A4
1206	CARTER, Maria	13	S½SW	1859-08-03		A3 G102
1304	COOK, James M	22	E½SW	1866-04-03		A1 G39
1341	CRARY, Mehitabel	4	N½SW	1860-10-01		A3 G47
1342	" "	4	S½NW	1860-10-01		A3 G47 F
1341	CRARY, Stephen	4	N½SW	1860-10-01		A3 G47
1342	" "	4	S½NW	1860-10-01		A3 G47 F
1220	DANIEL, Elias	4	N½NW	1860-10-01		A3 G50 F
1221	" "	4	NWNE	1860-10-01		A3 G50 F
1220	DANIEL, Susanna	4	N½NW	1860-10-01		A3 G50 F
1221	" "	4	NWNE	1860-10-01		A3 G50 F
1225	DOUGLASS, Everett	32	NESW	1867-01-10		A1
1226	" "	32	W½SW	1867-01-10		A1
1264	EANES, Jane T	5	NWSW	1858-01-15		A3 G125
1265	" "	5	W½NW	1858-01-15		A3 G125 F
1197	EDWARDS, Phineas	12	E½SW	1867-02-01		A3 G203
1348	FOWTER, Alvah	36	NENE	1851-05-01		A1 G262
1223	FRY, Elmer	34	S½SE	1880-12-10		A4
1224	" "	34	S½SW	1880-12-10		A4
1305	GIBBS, James M	28	NESE	1869-09-10		A1
1195	GOLLADAY, David	14	E½NE	1867-02-01		A3 G204
1196	" "	14	NWNE	1867-02-01		A3 G204
1201	GOOCH, Benjamin F	36	N½SE	1858-05-01		A1
1202	" "	36	SENE	1858-05-01		A1
1324	GOOCH, Nathan W	36	E½NW	1854-06-15		A1
1325	" "	36	SESW	1854-06-15		A1
1260	GRAHAM, Catharine	4	SWSW	1858-01-15		A3 G128
1261	" "	5	S½SE	1858-01-15		A3 G128
1313	GREEN, Jesse R	24	W½SW	1875-10-20		A4
1351	GREEN, William J	26	NENE	1879-11-25		A4
1217	HARTZER, Edward H	34	NWSE	1879-11-25		A4
1218	" "	34	W½NE	1879-11-25		A4
1340	HEALD, Horatio N	33	S½NE	1854-06-15		A1 G314
1338	" "	31	S½NW	1854-09-15		A1 G314 F
1339	" "	31	SW	1854-09-15		A1 G314 F
1195	HOYT, Benjamin	14	E½NE	1867-02-01		A3 G204

ID	Individual in Patent	Sec.	Sec. Part	Date Issued	Other Counties	For More Info . . .
1196	HOYT, Benjamin (Cont'd)	14	NWNE	1867-02-01		A3 G204
1228	HULL, Francis B	26	E½SW	1878-06-13		A4
1229	" "	26	W½SE	1878-06-13		A4
1318	HUZZEY, Susannah	19	SENE	1857-02-20		A3 G147
1319	" "	20	NWSW	1857-02-20		A3 G147
1320	" "	20	S½NW	1857-02-20		A3 G147
1230	IVES, Chauncey P	1	E½SW	1858-01-15		A3 G121
1231	" "	1	NWSW	1858-01-15		A3 G121
1232	" "	1	SWSW	1858-01-15		A3 G121
1233	" "	10	E½NW	1858-01-15		A3 G121
1234	" "	10	NWNW	1858-01-15		A3 G121
1235	" "	10	SWNW	1858-01-15		A3 G121
1262	" "	11	E½SE	1858-01-15		A3 G130
1263	" "	11	NWSE	1858-01-15		A3 G130
1236	" "	11	SESW	1858-01-15		A3 G121
1237	" "	11	W½SW	1858-01-15		A3 G121
1238	" "	13	N½SW	1858-01-15		A3 G121
1239	" "	13	NWSE	1858-01-15		A3 G121
1240	" "	2	N½SE	1858-01-15		A3 G121
1241	" "	23	E½NW	1858-01-15		A3 G121
1242	" "	23	NENE	1858-01-15		A3 G121
1243	" "	23	SWNW	1858-01-15		A3 G121
1244	" "	23	W½NE	1858-01-15		A3 G121
1245	" "	4	SESW	1858-01-15		A3 G121
1260	" "	4	SWSW	1858-01-15		A3 G128
1246	" "	4	W½SE	1858-01-15		A3 G121
1268	" "	5	E½NW	1858-01-15		A3 G135 F
1247	" "	5	E½SW	1858-01-15		A3 G121
1269	" "	5	NWNE	1858-01-15		A3 G135 F
1264	" "	5	NWSW	1858-01-15		A3 G125
1261	" "	5	S½SE	1858-01-15		A3 G128
1248	" "	5	SWSW	1858-01-15		A3 G121
1265	" "	5	W½NW	1858-01-15		A3 G125 F
1266	" "	7	E½NE	1858-01-15		A3 G124
1249	" "	7	NENW	1858-01-15		A3 G121
1250	" "	7	SENW	1858-01-15		A3 G121
1251	" "	7	W½NE	1858-01-15		A3 G121
1252	" "	7	W½NW	1858-01-15		A3 G121 F
1253	" "	8	E½NW	1858-01-15		A3 G121
1254	" "	8	NWNW	1858-01-15		A3 G121
1267	" "	8	SWNW	1858-01-15		A3 G124
1255	" "	9	E½NE	1858-01-15		A3 G121
1256	" "	9	N½NW	1858-01-15		A3 G121
1257	" "	9	NWNE	1858-01-15		A3 G121
1258	" "	9	S½NW	1858-01-15		A3 G121
1259	" "	9	SWNE	1858-01-15		A3 G121
1206	" "	13	S½SW	1859-08-03		A3 G102
1270	" "	19	E½NW	1859-08-15		A3 G300
1271	" "	19	SWNW	1859-08-15		A3 G299 F
1272	" "	19	W½SW	1859-08-15		A3 G299 F
1273	" "	30	NWNW	1859-08-15		A3 G299 F
1276	" "	30	SWNW	1859-08-15		A3 G298 F
1277	" "	30	W½SW	1859-08-15		A3 G298 F
1278	" "	31	NWNW	1859-08-15		A3 G298 F
1274	" "	12	SWNW	1859-12-01		A3 G298
1275	" "	12	W½SW	1859-12-01		A3 G298
1352	JAY, William	24	E½SW	1875-10-20		A4
1343	JOHNSON, Peter	14	N½NW	1871-11-15		A1 G237
1214	JONES, Elizabeth E	14	N½SE	1857-02-20		A3 G246
1198	JUDSON, Zerah	14	NESW	1867-02-01		A3 G205
1199	" "	14	SENW	1867-02-01		A3 G205
1200	" "	14	SWNE	1867-02-01		A3 G205
1279	KENDALL, George	20	N½SE	1856-03-10		A1
1280	" "	21	SESE	1856-03-10		A1
1281	" "	21	SW	1856-03-10		A1
1282	" "	21	W½SE	1856-03-10		A1
1283	" "	22	W½SW	1856-03-10		A1
1284	" "	27	N½SW	1856-03-10		A1
1285	" "	27	NW	1856-03-10		A1
1286	" "	27	NWSE	1856-03-10		A1
1287	" "	27	SESW	1856-03-10		A1
1288	" "	27	W½NE	1856-03-10		A1
1289	" "	28	N½NE	1856-03-10		A1

ID	Individual in Patent	Sec.	Sec. Part	Date Issued	Other Counties	For More Info . . .
1290	KENDALL, George (Cont'd)	28	N½SW	1856-03-10		A1
1291	" "	28	NENW	1856-03-10		A1
1292	" "	28	NWSE	1856-03-10		A1
1293	" "	28	S½NE	1856-03-10		A1
1294	" "	28	S½NW	1856-03-10		A1
1295	" "	34	NENE	1856-03-10		A1
1296	" "	34	NESE	1856-03-10		A1
1297	" "	35	NWNW	1856-03-10		A1 R1298
1297	" "	35	NWNW	1856-03-10		A1 C R1298
1298	" "	35	NWNW	1856-03-10		A1 R1297
1298	" "	35	NWNW	1856-03-10		A1 C R1297
1300	" "	35	SWSE	1856-03-10		A1 R1301
1300	" "	35	SWSE	1856-03-10		A1 C R1301
1301	" "	35	SWSE	1856-03-10		A1 R1300
1301	" "	35	SWSE	1856-03-10		A1 C R1300
1299	" "	35	S½SW	1857-02-20		A3
1262	KING, Eunice P	11	E½SE	1858-01-15		A3 G130
1263	" "	11	NWSE	1858-01-15		A3 G130
1215	LASHER, Mary	13	S½NW	1857-02-20		A3 G247
1216	" "	13	SWNE	1857-02-20		A3 G247
1222	LAWRENCE, John	12	SENW	1867-01-10		A1 G320
1230	LEONARD, Frederick B	1	E½SW	1858-01-15		A3 G121
1231	" "	1	NWSW	1858-01-15		A3 G121
1232	" "	1	SWSW	1858-01-15		A3 G121
1233	" "	10	E½NW	1858-01-15		A3 G121
1234	" "	10	NWNW	1858-01-15		A3 G121
1235	" "	10	SWNW	1858-01-15		A3 G121
1262	" "	11	E½SE	1858-01-15		A3 G130
1263	" "	11	NWSE	1858-01-15		A3 G130
1236	" "	11	SESW	1858-01-15		A3 G121
1237	" "	11	W½SW	1858-01-15		A3 G121
1238	" "	13	N½SW	1858-01-15		A3 G121
1239	" "	13	NWSE	1858-01-15		A3 G121
1240	" "	2	N½SE	1858-01-15		A3 G121
1241	" "	23	E½NW	1858-01-15		A3 G121
1242	" "	23	NENE	1858-01-15		A3 G121
1243	" "	23	SWNW	1858-01-15		A3 G121
1244	" "	23	W½NE	1858-01-15		A3 G121
1245	" "	4	SESW	1858-01-15		A3 G121
1260	" "	4	SWSW	1858-01-15		A3 G128
1246	" "	4	W½SE	1858-01-15		A3 G121
1268	" "	5	E½NW	1858-01-15		A3 G135 F
1247	" "	5	E½SW	1858-01-15		A3 G121
1269	" "	5	NWNE	1858-01-15		A3 G135 F
1264	" "	5	NWSW	1858-01-15		A3 G125
1261	" "	5	S½SE	1858-01-15		A3 G128
1248	" "	5	SWSW	1858-01-15		A3 G121
1265	" "	5	W½NW	1858-01-15		A3 G125 F
1266	" "	7	E½NE	1858-01-15		A3 G124
1249	" "	7	NENW	1858-01-15		A3 G121
1250	" "	7	SENW	1858-01-15		A3 G121
1251	" "	7	W½NE	1858-01-15		A3 G121
1252	" "	7	W½NW	1858-01-15		A3 G121 F
1253	" "	8	E½NW	1858-01-15		A3 G121
1254	" "	8	NWNW	1858-01-15		A3 G121
1267	" "	8	SWNW	1858-01-15		A3 G124
1255	" "	9	E½NE	1858-01-15		A3 G121
1256	" "	9	N½NW	1858-01-15		A3 G121
1257	" "	9	NWNE	1858-01-15		A3 G121
1258	" "	9	S½NW	1858-01-15		A3 G121
1259	" "	9	SWNE	1858-01-15		A3 G121
1206	" "	13	S½SW	1859-08-03		A3 G102
1270	" "	19	E½NW	1859-08-15		A3 G300
1271	" "	19	SWNW	1859-08-15		A3 G299 F
1272	" "	19	W½SW	1859-08-15		A3 G299 F
1273	" "	30	NWNW	1859-08-15		A3 G299 F
1276	" "	30	SWNW	1859-08-15		A3 G298 F
1277	" "	30	W½SW	1859-08-15		A3 G298 F
1278	" "	31	NWNW	1859-08-15		A3 G298 F
1274	" "	12	SWNW	1859-12-01		A3 G298
1275	" "	12	W½SW	1859-12-01		A3 G298
1318	LOVELL, Louis S	19	SENE	1857-02-20		A3 G147
1319	" "	20	NWSW	1857-02-20		A3 G147

ID	Individual in Patent	Sec.	Sec. Part	Date Issued	Other Counties	For More Info . . .
1320	LOVELL, Louis S (Cont'd)	20	S½NW	1857-02-20		A3 G147
1344	LULL, Walter	1	SESE	1854-06-15		A1
1345	" "	12	NENE	1854-06-15		A1
1346	" "	2	S½NE	1855-11-01		A1
1347	" "	4	E½SE	1855-11-01		A1
1207	LUTZ, Christian	36	NWNW	1883-08-01		A4
1197	LYKINE, John	12	E½SW	1867-02-01		A3 G203
1306	LYONS, James O	28	SWSW	1854-06-15		A1
1307	" "	32	N½SE	1854-06-15		A1
1308	" "	32	S½NE	1854-06-15		A1
1309	" "	32	SESE	1854-06-15		A1
1310	" "	33	S½	1854-06-15		A1
1340	" "	33	S½NE	1854-06-15		A1 G314
1311	" "	33	S½NW	1854-06-15		A1
1312	" "	34	NWSW	1854-06-15		A1
1338	" "	31	S½NW	1854-09-15		A1 G314 F
1339	" "	31	SW	1854-09-15		A1 G314 F
1353	MCCOY, William	36	NESW	1876-01-20		A4
1303	MILES, James H	8	NE	1855-11-08		A3 G187
1303	MILES, William	8	NE	1855-11-08		A3 G187
1271	MILLIMAN, Eunice M	19	SWNW	1859-08-15		A3 G299 F
1272	" "	19	W½SW	1859-08-15		A3 G299 F
1273	" "	30	NWNW	1859-08-15		A3 G299 F
1321	MORRIS, Robert W	25	N½NW	1864-12-15		A1 G236
1322	" "	26	NWNE	1864-12-15		A1 G236
1323	" "	34	S½NW	1864-12-15		A1 G236
1205	NEWTON, Charles O	34	SENE	1880-12-10		A4
1208	NORTHROP, John O	10	NESW	1857-02-20		A3 G241
1209	" "	10	W½SW	1857-02-20		A3 G241
1210	" "	13	N½NW	1857-02-20		A3 G241
1211	" "	13	NWNE	1857-02-20		A3 G241
1215	" "	13	S½NW	1857-02-20		A3 G247
1216	" "	13	SWNE	1857-02-20		A3 G247
1214	" "	14	N½SE	1857-02-20		A3 G246
1212	" "	24	E½NW	1857-02-20		A3 G241
1213	" "	24	NWNE	1857-02-20		A3 G241
1326	NORTHROP, Nelson W	10	SENE	1857-02-20		A3
1327	" "	10	W½NE	1857-02-20		A3
1328	" "	15	SW	1857-02-20		A3
1331	" "	2	E½SW	1857-02-20		A3 G202
1332	" "	2	SWSW	1857-02-20		A3 G202
1329	" "	29	W½SE	1857-02-20		A3
1330	" "	32	NWNE	1857-02-20		A3
1197	PADDOCK, Augustus	12	E½SW	1867-02-01		A3 G203
1195	" "	14	E½NE	1867-02-01		A3 G204
1198	" "	14	NESW	1867-02-01		A3 G205
1196	" "	14	NWNE	1867-02-01		A3 G204
1199	" "	14	SENW	1867-02-01		A3 G205
1200	" "	14	SWNE	1867-02-01		A3 G205
1193	" "	2	S½SE	1867-05-01		A1
1194	" "	2	SWNW	1867-05-01		A1
1349	PAGE, Wellington C	26	S½NE	1873-05-15		A1
1350	" "	26	SWNW	1873-05-15		A1
1354	PAYNE, William	26	SENW	1869-09-10		A1
1268	RAYBORNE, Sally	5	E½NW	1858-01-15		A3 G135 F
1269	" "	5	NWNE	1858-01-15		A3 G135 F
1270	REARDON, Betsey	19	E½NW	1859-08-15		A3 G300
1227	REYNOLDS, Floyd	18	N½SE	1885-01-07		A1
1203	ROGERS, Calvin S	24	NWSE	1866-09-01		A1
1204	" "	24	SWNE	1874-02-20		A4
1321	RYERSON, Martin	25	N½NW	1864-12-15		A1 G236
1322	" "	26	NWNE	1864-12-15		A1 G236
1323	" "	34	S½NW	1864-12-15		A1 G236
1343	RYERSON, Tunis	14	N½NW	1871-11-15		A1 G237
1208	SANFORD, Ebenezer	10	NESW	1857-02-20		A3 G241
1209	" "	10	W½SW	1857-02-20		A3 G241
1210	" "	13	N½NW	1857-02-20		A3 G241
1211	" "	13	NWNE	1857-02-20		A3 G241
1215	" "	13	S½NW	1857-02-20		A3 G247
1216	" "	13	SWNE	1857-02-20		A3 G247
1214	" "	14	N½SE	1857-02-20		A3 G246
1212	" "	24	E½NW	1857-02-20		A3 G241
1213	" "	24	NWNE	1857-02-20		A3 G241

ID	Individual in Patent	Sec.	Sec. Part	Date Issued	Other Counties	For More Info . . .
1303	SAUNDERS, Isaac M	8	NE	1855-11-08		A3 G187
1190	SLATER, Alanson	34	N½NW	1861-12-10		A1
1191	SMITH, Arabut F	25	NWSW	1855-12-15		A1
1192	" "	26	E½SE	1855-12-15		A1 G261
1302	SMITH, Henry S	36	SWSW	1854-06-15		A1
1348	SMITH, Warren	36	NENE	1851-05-01		A1 G262
1331	SPAIDS, Clarisa	2	E½SW	1857-02-20		A3 G202
1332	" "	2	SWSW	1857-02-20		A3 G202
1317	SPENCER, Laban	24	NESE	1855-11-01		A1
1198	STEVENS, Edward	14	NESW	1867-02-01		A3 G205
1199	" "	14	SENW	1867-02-01		A3 G205
1200	" "	14	SWNE	1867-02-01		A3 G205
1333	TRACY, Philander	25	SENE	1854-06-15		A1
1335	" "	25	SWSE	1854-06-15		A1
1336	" "	36	NWNE	1854-06-15		A1
1334	" "	25	SWNE	1854-09-15		A1
1337	VARNUM, Mercy	22	NW	1866-11-10		A3 G1
1206	WARREN, George B	13	S½SW	1859-08-03		A3 G102
1270	" "	19	E½NW	1859-08-15		A3 G300
1271	" "	19	SWNW	1859-08-15		A3 G299 F
1272	" "	19	W½SW	1859-08-15		A3 G299 F
1273	" "	30	NWNW	1859-08-15		A3 G299 F
1276	" "	30	SWNW	1859-08-15		A3 G298 F
1277	" "	30	W½SW	1859-08-15		A3 G298 F
1278	" "	31	NWNW	1859-08-15		A3 G298 F
1274	" "	12	SWNW	1859-12-01		A3 G298
1275	" "	12	W½SW	1859-12-01		A3 G298
1340	WILCOX, Sextus N	33	S½NE	1854-06-15		A1 G314
1338	" "	31	S½NW	1854-09-15		A1 G314 F
1339	" "	31	SW	1854-09-15		A1 G314 F
1355	WILSON, William R	4	E½NE	1873-05-15		A1 F
1356	" "	4	SWNE	1873-05-15		A1 F
1222	WOOD, Eliphalet	12	SENW	1867-01-10		A1 G320

Patent Map

T14-N R11-W
Michigan-Toledo Strip Meridian

Map Group 12

Township Statistics

Parcels Mapped	:	167
Number of Patents	:	106
Number of Individuals	:	78
Patentees Identified	:	59
Number of Surnames	:	69
Multi-Patentee Parcels	:	87
Oldest Patent Date	:	5/1/1851
Most Recent Patent	:	1/7/1885
Block/Lot Parcels	:	0
Parcels Re - Issued	:	2
Parcels that Overlap	:	0
Cities and Towns	:	0
Cemeteries	:	1

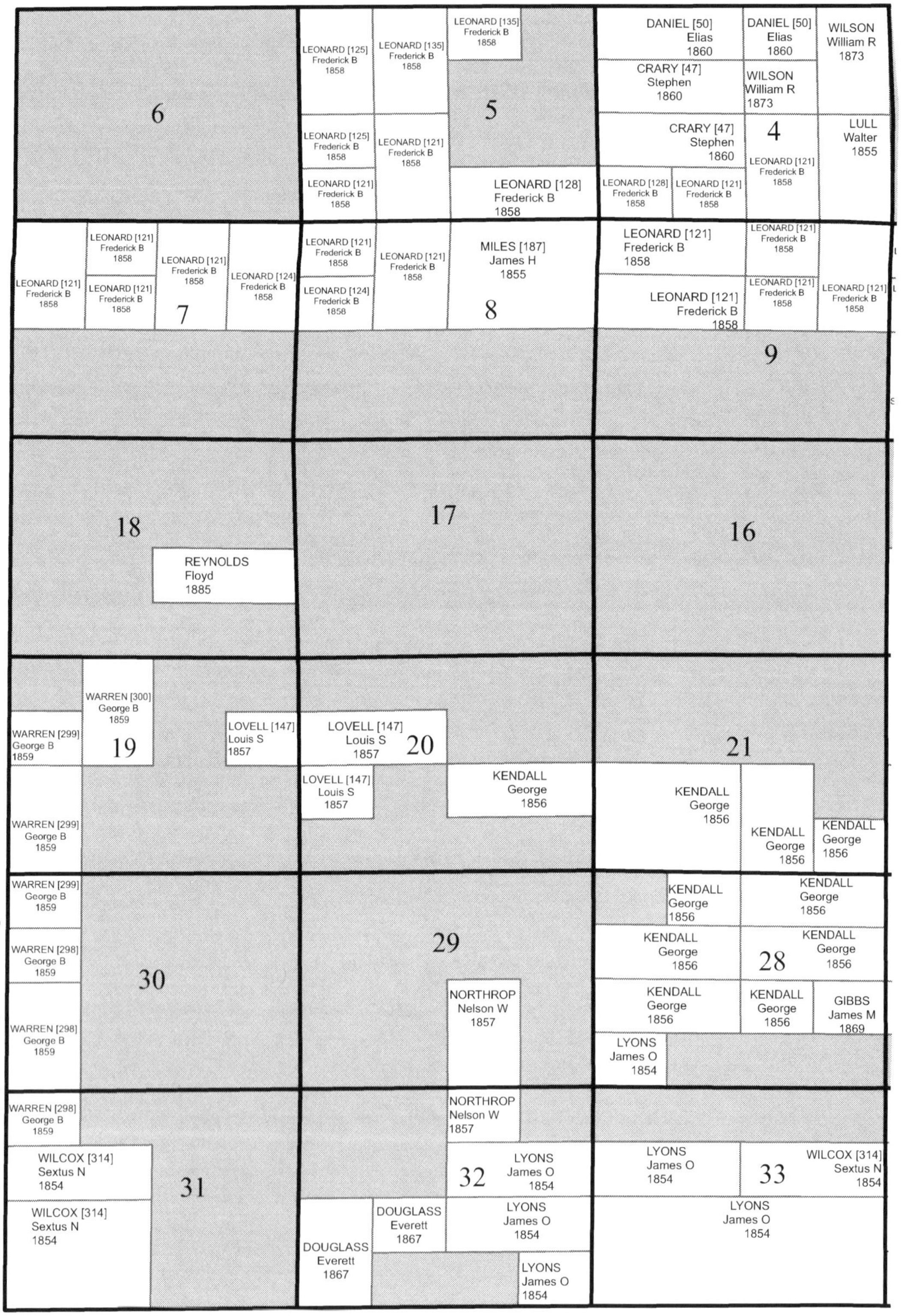

6

LEONARD [125] Frederick B 1858
LEONARD [135] Frederick B 1858
LEONARD [135] Frederick B 1858
5
LEONARD [125] Frederick B 1858
LEONARD [121] Frederick B 1858
LEONARD [121] Frederick B 1858
LEONARD [128] Frederick B 1858

DANIEL [50] Elias 1860
DANIEL [50] Elias 1860
WILSON William R 1873
CRARY [47] Stephen 1860
WILSON William R 1873
CRARY [47] Stephen 1860
4
LULL Walter 1855
LEONARD [121] Frederick B 1858
LEONARD [128] Frederick B 1858
LEONARD [121] Frederick B 1858

LEONARD [121] Frederick B 1858
LEONARD [121] Frederick B 1858
LEONARD [121] Frederick B 1858
LEONARD [124] Frederick B 1858
LEONARD [121] Frederick B 1858
7

LEONARD [121] Frederick B 1858
LEONARD [121] Frederick B 1858
MILES [187] James H 1855
LEONARD [124] Frederick B 1858
8

LEONARD [121] Frederick B 1858
LEONARD [121] Frederick B 1858
LEONARD [121] Frederick B 1858
LEONARD [121] Frederick B 1858
LEONARD [121] Frederick B 1858
9

18
REYNOLDS Floyd 1885
17
16

WARREN [300] George B 1859
WARREN [299] George B 1859
19
LOVELL [147] Louis S 1857
WARREN [299] George B 1859

LOVELL [147] Louis S 1857
20
LOVELL [147] Louis S 1857
KENDALL George 1856

21
KENDALL George 1856
KENDALL George 1856
KENDALL George 1856

WARREN [299] George B 1859
WARREN [298] George B 1859
30
WARREN [298] George B 1859

29
NORTHROP Nelson W 1857

KENDALL George 1856
KENDALL George 1856
KENDALL George 1856
KENDALL George 1856
28
KENDALL George 1856
KENDALL George 1856
GIBBS James M 1869
LYONS James O 1854

WARREN [298] George B 1859
WILCOX [314] Sextus N 1854
31
WILCOX [314] Sextus N 1854

NORTHROP Nelson W 1857
LYONS James O 1854
32
DOUGLASS Everett 1867
LYONS James O 1854
DOUGLASS Everett 1867
LYONS James O 1854

LYONS James O 1854
33
WILCOX [314] Sextus N 1854
LYONS James O 1854

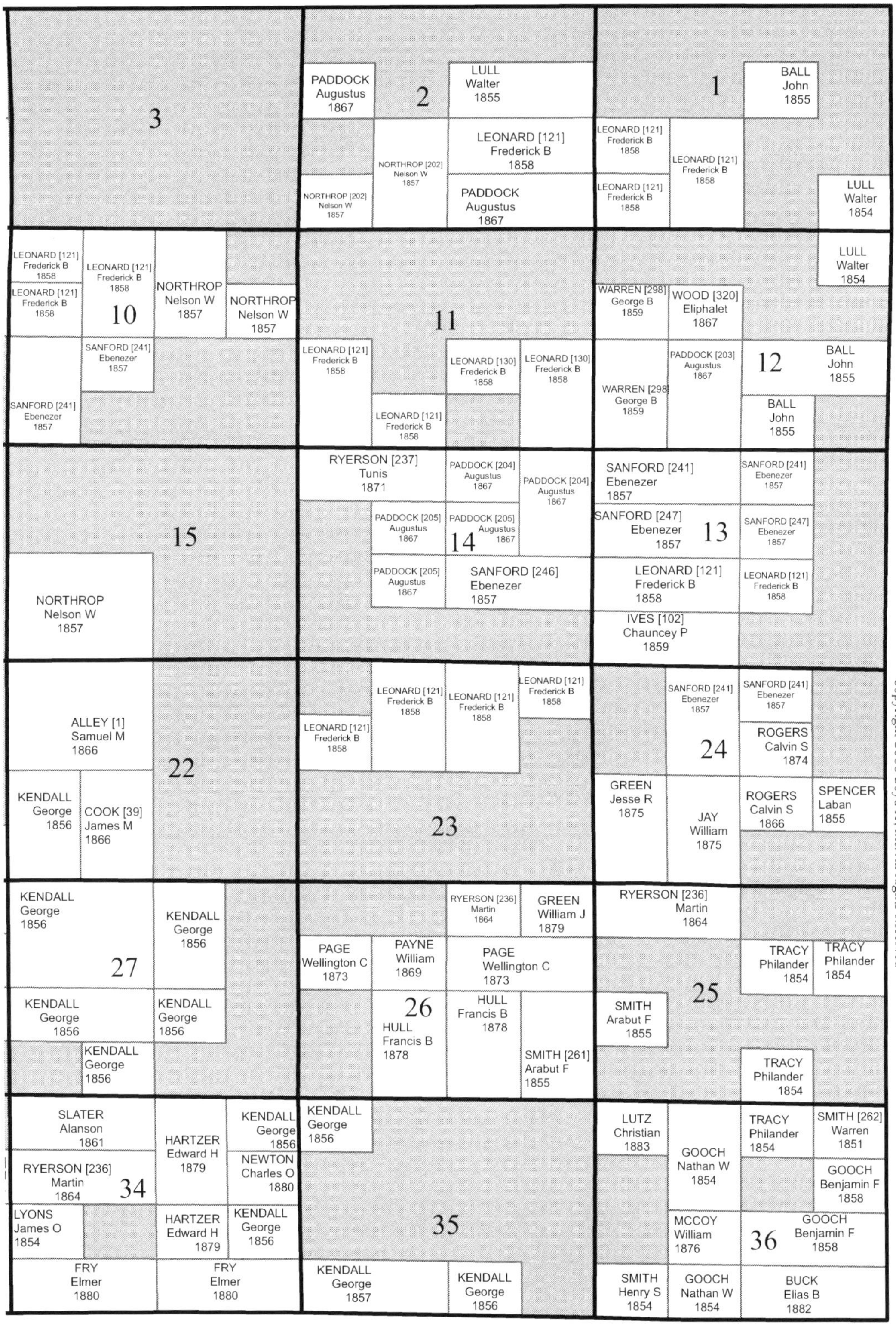

Helpful Hints

1. This Map's INDEX can be found on the preceding pages.
2. Refer to Map "C" to see where this Township lies within Newaygo County, Michigan.
3. Numbers within square brackets [ ] denote a multi-patentee land parcel (multi-owner). Refer to Appendix "C" for a full list of members in this group.
4. Areas that look to be crowded with Patentees usually indicate multiple sales of the same parcel (Re-issues) or Overlapping parcels. See this Township's Index for an explanation of these and other circumstances that might explain "odd" groupings of Patentees on this map.

Legend

- Patent Boundary
- Section Boundary
- No Patents Found (or Outside County)
- 1., 2., 3., ... Lot Numbers (when beside a name)
- [ ] Group Number (see Appendix "C")

Scale: Section = 1 mile X 1 mile (generally, with some exceptions)

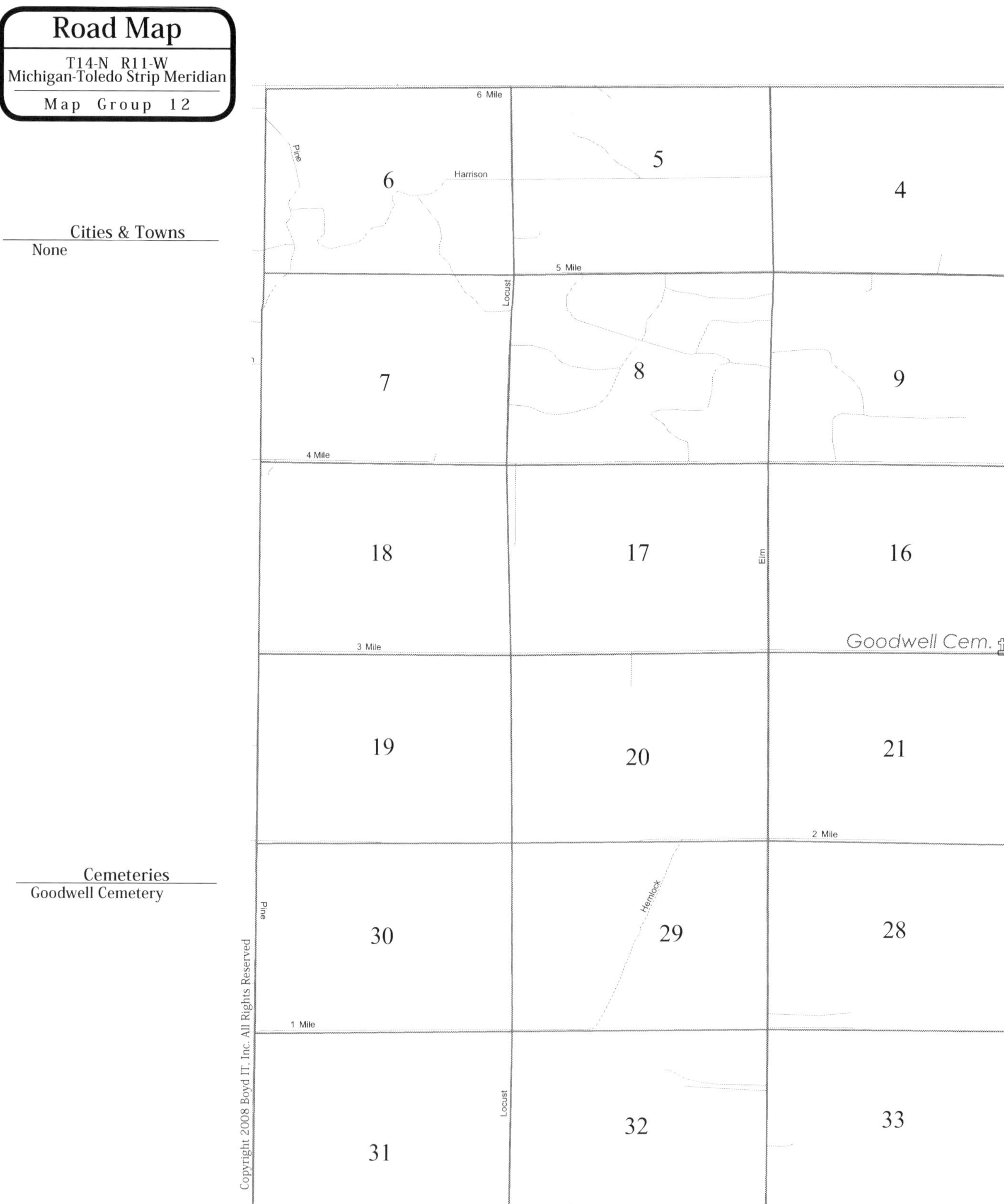
Road Map
T14-N R11-W
Michigan-Toledo Strip Meridian
Map Group 12
Cities & Towns
None
Cemeteries
Goodwell Cemetery
6 Mile
Pine
Harrison
6
5
4
Cypress
5 Mile
Locust
7
8
9
4 Mile
18
17
Elm
16
3 Mile
Goodwell Cem.
19
20
21
2 Mile
Pine
Hemlock
30
29
28
1 Mile
Locust
31
32
33
Baseline

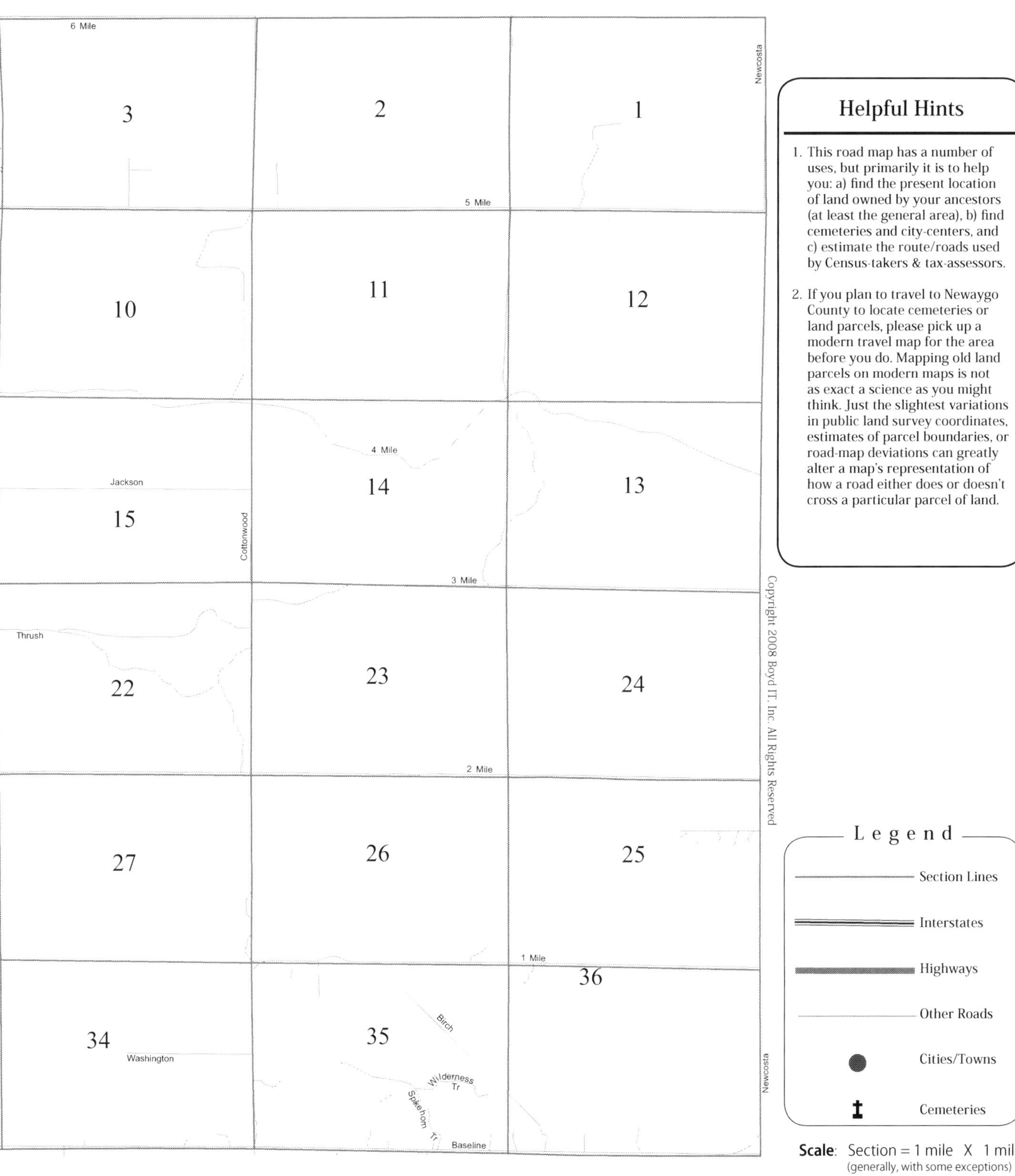

Helpful Hints

1. This road map has a number of uses, but primarily it is to help you: a) find the present location of land owned by your ancestors (at least the general area), b) find cemeteries and city-centers, and c) estimate the route/roads used by Census-takers & tax-assessors.

2. If you plan to travel to Newaygo County to locate cemeteries or land parcels, please pick up a modern travel map for the area before you do. Mapping old land parcels on modern maps is not as exact a science as you might think. Just the slightest variations in public land survey coordinates, estimates of parcel boundaries, or road-map deviations can greatly alter a map's representation of how a road either does or doesn't cross a particular parcel of land.

Legend

- Section Lines
- Interstates
- Highways
- Other Roads
- Cities/Towns
- Cemeteries

Scale: Section = 1 mile X 1 mile
(generally, with some exceptions)

Historical Map

T14-N R11-W
Michigan-Toledo Strip Meridian

Map Group 12

Cities & Towns

None

Cemeteries

Goodwell Cemetery

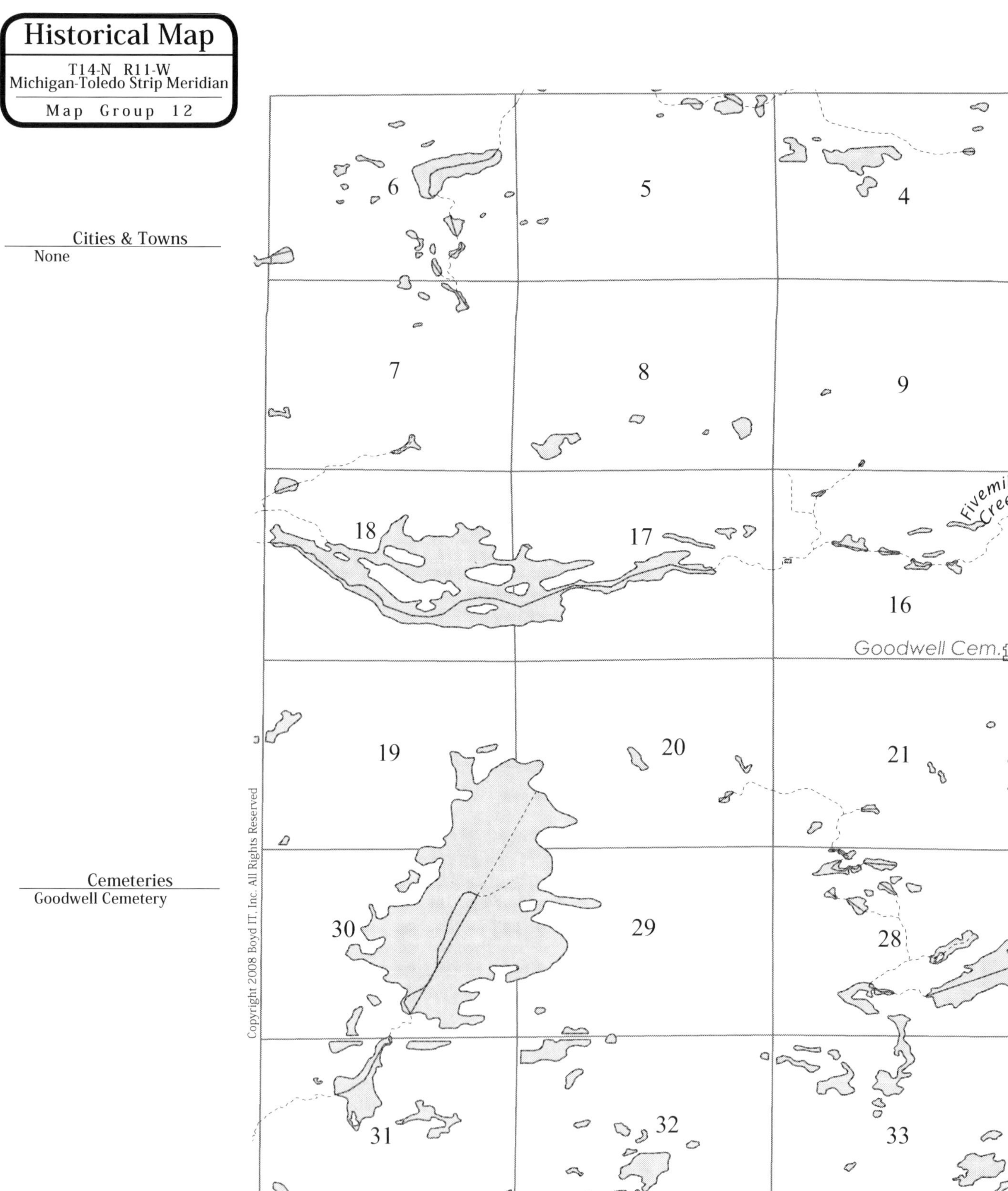

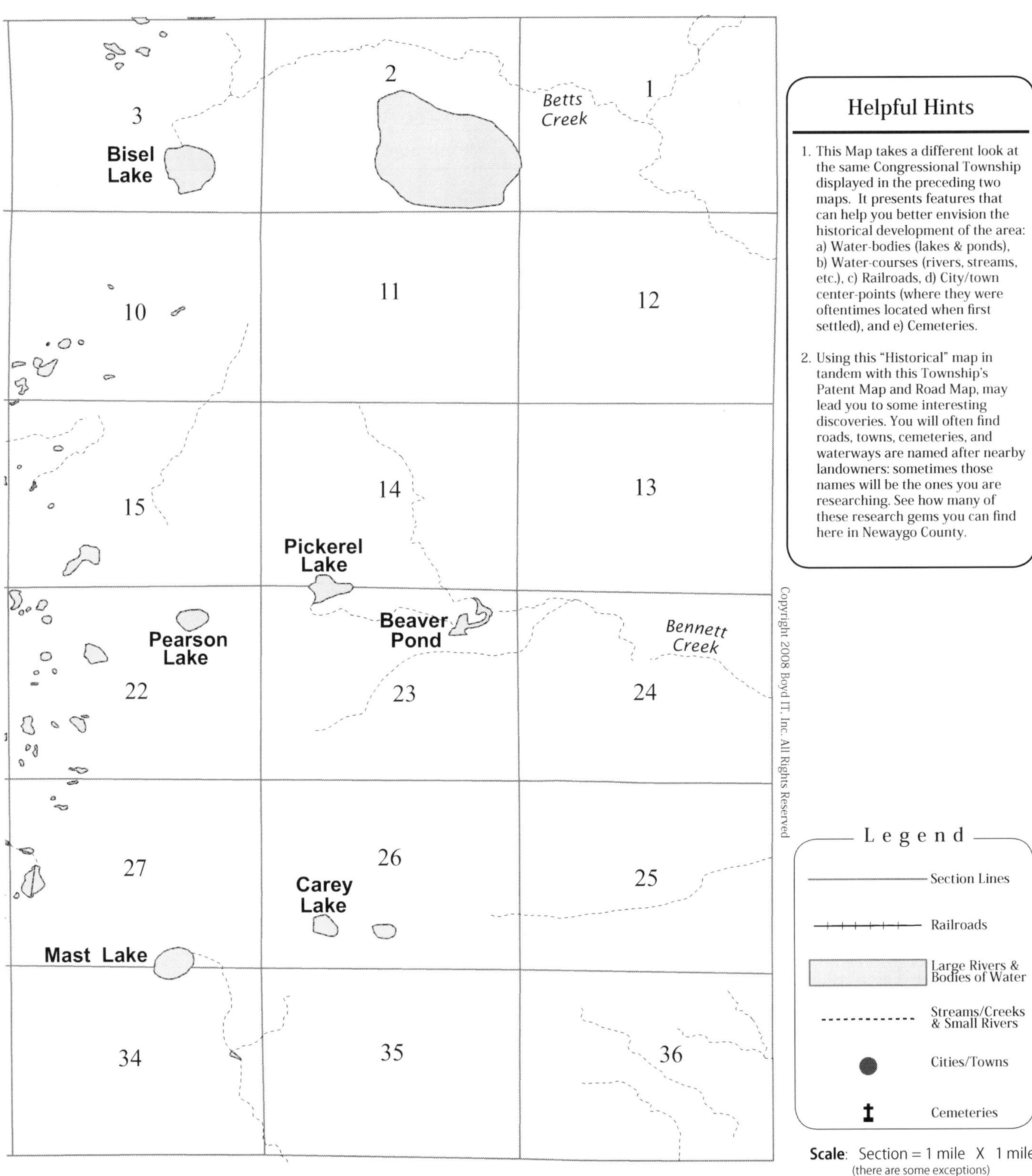

3
Bisel Lake
2
Betts Creek
1
10
11
12
15
14
13
Pickerel Lake
Beaver Pond
Pearson Lake
Bennett Creek
22
23
24
27
26
25
Carey Lake
Mast Lake
34
35
36
Helpful Hints
1. This Map takes a different look at the same Congressional Township displayed in the preceding two maps. It presents features that can help you better envision the historical development of the area: a) Water-bodies (lakes & ponds), b) Water-courses (rivers, streams, etc.), c) Railroads, d) City/town center-points (where they were oftentimes located when first settled), and e) Cemeteries.
2. Using this "Historical" map in tandem with this Township's Patent Map and Road Map, may lead you to some interesting discoveries. You will often find roads, towns, cemeteries, and waterways are named after nearby landowners: sometimes those names will be the ones you are researching. See how many of these research gems you can find here in Newaygo County.
Legend
Section Lines
Railroads
Large Rivers & Bodies of Water
Streams/Creeks & Small Rivers
Cities/Towns
Cemeteries

Scale: Section = 1 mile X 1 mile
(there are some exceptions)

Map Group 13: Index to Land Patents

Township 13-North Range 14-West (Michigan-Toledo Strip)

After you locate an individual in this Index, take note of the Section and Section Part then proceed to the Land Patent map on the pages immediately following. You should have no difficulty locating the corresponding parcel of land.

The "For More Info" Column will lead you to more information about the underlying Patents. See the *Legend* at right, and the "How to Use this Book" chapter, for more information.

LEGEND

"For More Info . . . " column

A = Authority (Legislative Act, See Appendix "A")
B = Block or Lot (location in Section unknown)
C = Cancelled Patent
F = Fractional Section
G = Group (Multi-Patentee Patent, see Appendix "C")
V = Overlaps another Parcel
R = Re-Issued (Parcel patented more than once)

(A & G items require you to look in the Appendixes referred to above. All other Letter-designations followed by a number require you to locate line-items in this index that possess the ID number found after the letter).

ID	Individual in Patent	Sec.	Sec. Part	Date Issued	Other Counties	For More Info . . .
1574	ALBERTSON, Sylvanus	31	E½SE	1855-11-08		A3
1575	" "	32	W½SW	1855-11-08		A3
1386	ALLEN, John S	17	E½NW	1859-08-03		A3 G71
1387	" "	17	NWNE	1859-08-03		A3 G71
1362	AMOS, Alfred	30	SE	1860-09-01		A1
1388	BALLOU, Chauncey P	25	1	1856-03-10		A1
1389	" "	25	2	1856-03-10		A1 C R1511
1390	" "	25	3	1856-03-10		A1 C R1395
1391	" "	25	SWNE	1856-03-10		A1
1467	BARNHARD, Jacob	4	SE	1858-05-01		A1
1572	BARNHARD, Simon	4	E½SW	1857-03-10		A1
1576	BOWLEY, Polly	30	E½SW	1868-02-10		A3 G64 F
1577	" "	30	SWSW	1868-02-10		A3 G64 F
1578	" "	31	NWNW	1868-02-10		A3 G64 F
1531	BOWMAN, Martin V	24	SWSE	1858-05-01		A1
1434	BRIGGS, George N	12	S½NW	1874-04-01		A4
1435	" "	12	SWNE	1874-04-01		A4
1593	BRIGGS, Willard	12	E½SW	1871-11-01		A4
1594	" "	12	W½SE	1871-11-01		A4
1606	BRIGGS, William S	13	NW	1870-05-02		A4
1476	BROOKS, John A	25	S½SW	1859-08-10		A3
1477	" "	36	3	1859-08-10		A3
1478	BROTHERTON, John	32	E½NE	1857-03-10		A1
1479	" "	33	W½NW	1857-03-10		A1
1551	BUCK, Robert T	13	SESW	1875-07-01		A4
1552	" "	24	N½NE	1875-07-01		A4
1553	" "	24	NENW	1875-07-01		A4
1392	BUGGS, Chester M	11	NENE	1869-11-01		A4
1393	" "	12	N½NW	1869-11-01		A4
1394	" "	12	NWNE	1869-11-01		A4
1567	CAIRNS, Elizabeth	20	SWNE	1855-11-08		A3 G232
1568	" "	20	W½SE	1855-11-08		A3 G232
1414	CARPENTER, Anthony W	19	SE	1865-10-20		A3 G33
1372	CARPENTER, Asa	8	S½NW	1858-05-01		A1
1414	CARPENTER, Ebenezer S	19	SE	1865-10-20		A3 G33
1414	CARPENTER, George W	19	SE	1865-10-20		A3 G33
1502	CARPENTER, John R	31	NE	1857-02-20		A3
1602	CLARK, William P	23	N½SW	1871-02-01		A4
1603	" "	23	W½SE	1871-02-01		A4
1462	COGSWELL, Isaac H	29	N½SW	1858-05-01		A1
1463	" "	29	S½NW	1858-05-01		A1
1464	" "	29	SE	1858-05-01		A1
1541	COLBURN, Oliver C	18	NENE	1856-03-10		A1
1437	COLLINS, Henry A	21	E½NE	1860-12-01		A1
1438	" "	21	NESE	1860-12-01		A1
1494	COOK, John P	22	W½NE	1859-08-10		A3

ID	Individual in Patent	Sec.	Sec. Part	Date Issued	Other Counties	For More Info . . .
1495	COOK, John P (Cont'd)	23	E½NW	1859-08-10		A3
1497	" "	34	N½SE	1859-08-10		A3
1498	" "	34	NESW	1859-08-10		A3
1499	" "	34	S½SE	1859-08-10		A3
1500	" "	34	SESW	1859-08-10		A3
1496	" "	30	NW	1859-08-15		A3 F
1501	" "	24	W½SW	1865-10-20		A3 G43
1370	CRESSMAN, Andrew J	5	N½SE	1857-04-02		A3
1371	" "	5	SENE	1857-04-02		A3
1483	CROY, John G	1	W½SE	1866-01-10		A3
1366	CURTICE, Alphonzo	14	N½SW	1873-06-10		A4
1559	CURTICE, Sheldon W	22	E½SW	1873-06-10		A4
1560	" "	22	NWSW	1873-06-10		A4
1441	DARLING, Henry	2	E½SW	1857-02-20		A3
1442	" "	2	NESE	1857-02-20		A3
1443	" "	2	NWSE	1857-02-20		A3
1444	" "	2	S½NE	1857-02-20		A3 F
1445	" "	2	W½SW	1857-02-20		A3
1446	" "	22	E½NE	1857-02-20		A3
1447	" "	23	W½NW	1857-02-20		A3
1449	" "	3	SESE	1857-02-20		A3
1448	" "	3	N½SE	1862-08-01		A3
1450	" "	3	SWSE	1862-08-01		A3
1480	DARLING, John	26	SESE	1861-04-01		A1
1532	DARLING, Mary	5	E½SW	1858-01-15		A3
1533	" "	5	SWSE	1858-01-15		A3
1482	DICKINSON, John F	34	NE	1858-05-01		A1
1561	DICKINSON, Sherman S	7	NW	1860-03-01		A1 F
1455	DOBSON, Hiram	3	W½NW	1859-10-10		A1 F
1473	DOUD, Jason	8	SW	1858-05-01		A1
1469	DOYLE, James	35	NW	1857-03-10		A1
1487	DRAGOO, John J	20	NWSW	1872-01-01		A4
1358	DUNFEE, Abner	3	SW	1859-08-10		A3
1376	EDDY, Benjamin F	36	NWNW	1859-10-10		A1 C
1377	" "	36	W½NW	1861-07-01		A3
1529	EDDY, Martin A	21	E½SW	1869-11-01		A4 V1365, 1369
1530	" "	21	SWSE	1869-11-01		A4 V1555
1481	ELLIOTT, John	4	W½NW	1856-03-10		A1 F
1460	EMBREE, Isaac	19	S½NW	1869-11-01		A4 F
1461	" "	19	W½NE	1869-11-01		A4 F
1398	FARNHAM, Daniel S	20	S½SW	1875-12-20		A4
1399	" "	29	N½NW	1875-12-20		A4
1470	FORBES, James	30	NE	1869-11-01		A4
1576	FOWLER, Thomas	30	E½SW	1868-02-10		A3 G64 F
1577	" "	30	SWSW	1868-02-10		A3 G64 F
1578	" "	31	NWNW	1868-02-10		A3 G64 F
1459	FOX, Irwin C	30	NWSW	1872-01-01		A4 F
1458	GOOCH, Horace N	8	W½SE	1858-05-01		A1
1457	" "	8	SESE	1860-09-01		A1
1385	GOODRICH, Chauncey	7	W½NW	1856-03-10		A1
1386	" "	17	E½NW	1859-08-03		A3 G71
1387	" "	17	NWNE	1859-08-03		A3 G71
1359	GRACEY, Alexander	14	NW	1869-03-01		A4
1417	GRAY, Edgar L	6	NW	1859-08-03		A3 F
1451	HATHERLEY, Henry	28	SESE	1858-05-01		A1
1580	HERENDEEN, Thomas	31	SWSW	1857-03-10		A1 F
1587	HERENDEEN, Welcome	32	SESE	1857-03-10		A1
1514	HETSLER, Joseph	28	NESW	1870-10-01		A4
1515	" "	28	NWSE	1870-10-01		A4
1516	" "	28	SENW	1870-10-01		A4
1415	HEWES, Edgar J	24	E½SW	1867-01-10		A1
1416	" "	24	NWSE	1867-01-10		A1
1418	HEWES, Edgar P	25	NESW	1867-05-01		A1
1365	HILL, Alpheus G	21	N½SW	1855-12-15		A1 V1529
1592	HOLMES, Susan	25	E½NE	1857-04-02		A3 G278
1406	HOPKINS, David	1	E½SW	1861-12-05		A1
1539	HOPKINS, Nelson R	2	NENE	1858-05-01		A1 F
1407	HOW, David	14	NE	1878-12-30		A4
1600	HUNT, William N	13	N½SW	1871-11-01		A4
1601	" "	14	N½SE	1871-11-01		A4
1378	ISH, Benjamin	31	E½NW	1857-03-10		A1
1379	" "	31	N½SW	1857-03-10		A1 F
1380	" "	31	SWNW	1857-03-10		A1 F

ID	Individual in Patent	Sec.	Sec. Part	Date Issued	Other Counties	For More Info . . .
1547	JACKLIN, Robert	26	SWSE	1872-09-20		A4
1548	" "	35	NWNE	1872-09-20		A4
1456	JENNE, Horace C	5	NW	1859-10-10		A1 F
1512	JEWELL, Joseph B	23	S½SW	1858-05-01		A1
1513	" "	26	NW	1858-05-01		A1
1421	JONES, Edward N	5	SESE	1856-03-10		A1
1420	" "	4	W½SW	1859-10-10		A1
1395	JOSLIN, Daniel R	25	3	1857-03-10		A1 R1390
1396	" "	26	1	1857-03-10		A1
1397	" "	26	2	1857-03-10		A1
1507	KELLEY, John S	33	W½SE	1857-03-10		A1
1432	KENDALL, George	34	NENW	1856-03-10		A1
1431	" "	29	S½SW	1858-05-01		A1
1430	KLETT, George A	18	NWSW	1860-12-01		A1
1556	LAKE, Erastus	27	NENW	1855-11-08		A3 G114
1557	" "	27	S½NW	1855-11-08		A3 G114
1424	" "	18	NW	1860-09-03		A3
1554	LAKE, Samuel	21	SESE	1855-11-08		A3
1555	" "	21	W½SE	1855-11-08		A3 V1530
1556	" "	27	NENW	1855-11-08		A3 G114
1557	" "	27	S½NW	1855-11-08		A3 G114
1426	LEVI, Ezra S	33	E½NW	1858-05-01		A1
1427	" "	33	SW	1858-05-01		A1
1484	LEWIS, John H	8	N½NE	1858-05-01		A1
1485	" "	8	N½NW	1858-05-01		A1
1452	MACK, Henry	18	SENE	1860-10-01		A1
1453	" "	18	W½NE	1860-10-01		A1
1491	MANNING, John	17	E½NE	1860-09-01		A1
1492	" "	17	SWNE	1860-09-01		A1
1598	MARTIN, William	20	NESW	1859-10-10		A1
1599	" "	20	NW	1859-10-10		A1
1471	MCCLURE, James	15	NWSE	1869-11-01		A4
1472	" "	15	SWNE	1869-11-01		A4
1419	MCKENZIE, Edward D	22	NW	1873-06-10		A4
1428	MILLER, Frederick	1	SWSW	1860-09-01		A1
1429	" "	2	SESE	1860-09-01		A1
1433	MILLER, George	25	NWNE	1858-05-01		A1
1493	MILLER, John	10	NENE	1864-11-01		A1
1488	MILLER, John J	10	NWNE	1859-10-10		A1
1489	" "	10	S½NE	1859-10-10		A1
1490	" "	11	SWNW	1859-10-10		A1
1543	MILLER, Orrin A	11	N½SW	1860-09-03		A3 G189
1544	" "	11	SESW	1860-09-03		A3 G189
1543	MILLER, Samuel	11	N½SW	1860-09-03		A3 G189
1544	" "	11	SESW	1860-09-03		A3 G189
1440	MOE, Henry C	19	N½NW	1858-05-01		A1 F
1367	MORELL, Alvah J	35	NESW	1857-03-10		A1
1381	MORTON, Bernard E	6	NESW	1861-12-05		A1 F
1408	MOSHER, David	1	NWSW	1861-04-01		A1
1409	" "	2	SWSE	1872-01-01		A4
1584	OBRIEN, Thomas	13	E½NE	1870-05-02		A4
1585	" "	13	NESE	1870-05-02		A4
1536	OLDS, Mortimer	8	S½NE	1858-05-01		A1
1535	" "	8	NESE	1861-12-10		A1
1604	PARKER, William	15	N½SW	1869-11-01		A4
1605	" "	15	S½NW	1869-11-01		A4
1465	PARSHALL, Isaac R	13	W½NE	1873-04-10		A4
1466	" "	13	W½SE	1873-04-10		A4
1528	PRESTON, Margaret	9	NWNE	1856-03-10		A1
1527	" "	9	NENE	1857-03-10		A1
1563	PRESTON, Shinar	9	SENE	1860-06-01		A1
1562	" "	10	NESW	1861-04-01		A1
1375	PRICE, Bartholomew W	6	E½NE	1868-12-01		A3 G223
1375	PRICE, John L	6	E½NE	1868-12-01		A3 G223
1375	PRICE, Parker C	6	E½NE	1868-12-01		A3 G223
1486	PRINGLE, John H	27	SW	1858-05-01		A1
1525	PUTNAM, Lucina	25	SENW	1858-05-01		A1
1524	" "	25	N½NW	1859-08-10		A3
1526	" "	25	SWNW	1859-08-10		A3
1503	REED, John	6	SESW	1857-02-20		A3 F
1504	" "	6	W½SW	1857-02-20		A3 F
1520	REED, Lewis	11	SE	1873-04-10		A4
1569	REED, Silvanus	4	E½NE	1856-03-10		A1 F

ID	Individual in Patent	Sec.	Sec. Part	Date Issued	Other Counties	For More Info . . .
1570	REED, Silvanus (Cont'd)	4	E½NW	1857-03-10		A1 F
1571	" "	4	W½NE	1857-03-10		A1 F
1412	RICHARDSON, Ebenezer	5	N½NE	1861-04-01		A1
1413	" "	5	SWNE	1882-11-20		A1
1410	ROBBINS, David	1	S½NE	1860-09-03		A3 G227 F
1411	" "	1	SENW	1860-09-03		A3 G227 F
1410	ROBBINS, Hepzibah	1	S½NE	1860-09-03		A3 G227 F
1411	" "	1	SENW	1860-09-03		A3 G227 F
1549	ROBINSON, Robert	32	E½SW	1857-02-20		A3
1550	" "	32	W½SE	1857-02-20		A3
1436	RODES, George	34	S½NW	1857-03-10		A1
1505	ROOKE, John	7	E½SW	1858-05-01		A1
1506	" "	7	W½SW	1858-05-01		A1 F
1564	RUSHMORE, Silas	20	E½SE	1855-11-08		A3
1565	" "	20	SENE	1855-11-08		A3
1567	" "	20	SWNE	1855-11-08		A3 G232
1568	" "	20	W½SE	1855-11-08		A3 G232
1566	" "	29	NE	1855-11-08		A3
1517	SANBORN, Joseph	10	N½SE	1860-09-03		A3
1518	" "	10	SESE	1860-09-03		A3
1519	" "	15	NENE	1860-09-03		A3
1607	SAVAGE, William	27	NE	1855-12-15		A1
1608	" "	28	NENW	1855-12-15		A1
1609	" "	28	W½NW	1855-12-15		A1
1534	SCOTT, Melvin W	6	SE	1858-05-01		A1
1474	SELFRIDGE, Jerome W	17	SW	1858-05-01		A1
1475	" "	17	W½SE	1858-05-01		A1
1439	SHAW, Henry B	33	NE	1859-10-10		A1
1558	SHAW, Samuel	17	E½SE	1860-09-01		A1
1610	SINE, William	35	W½SW	1857-03-10		A1
1468	SLAGHT, Jacob	6	W½NE	1858-05-01		A1 F
1374	SMITH, Barlow	11	SENW	1875-09-20		A4
1422	SMITH, Eleazer	31	SESW	1857-03-10		A1
1423	" "	31	W½SE	1857-03-10		A1
1363	SOULE, Alfred W	15	NESE	1862-03-10		A1
1364	" "	15	SENE	1862-03-10		A1
1501	STEVENSON, James L	24	W½SW	1865-10-20		A3 G43
1425	STOCKING, Adeline M	26	NE	1861-11-01		A3 G272
1425	STOCKING, Erastus P	26	NE	1861-11-01		A3 G272
1425	STOCKING, Jared W	26	NE	1861-11-01		A3 G272
1357	STONE, Aaron C	2	NWNE	1860-12-01		A1 F
1537	STONE, Myron	26	SW	1860-06-01		A1
1579	STUART, Thomas H	36	SE	1857-03-10		A1
1591	STUART, Wilkes L	36	SENW	1856-03-10		A1 F
1588	" "	35	S½NE	1857-03-10		A1
1589	" "	35	SESW	1857-03-10		A1
1590	" "	35	W½SE	1857-03-10		A1
1592	" "	25	E½NE	1857-04-02		A3 G278
1373	TANNER, Asher	27	SE	1858-05-01		A1
1384	TIBBITTS, Chancey	7	NE	1860-10-01		A1
1581	TINDALL, Thomas J	21	W½NW	1860-09-03		A3
1582	" "	28	NESE	1860-10-01		A1
1583	" "	28	SWSW	1860-10-01		A1
1586	TINDOLL, Thomas	22	SE	1860-11-10		A3
1508	TOBY, John	9	S½SE	1860-09-03		A3
1509	" "	9	SESW	1860-09-03		A3
1454	UPTON, Henry	28	NE	1855-12-15		A1
1360	WALKER, Alexander W	9	NW	1860-06-01		A1
1361	" "	9	W½SW	1860-06-01		A1
1573	WALKER, Solomon V	5	W½SW	1860-06-01		A1
1501	WALKER, William L	24	W½SW	1865-10-20		A3 G43
1510	WALLACE, John	3	E½NW	1856-03-10		A1 F
1511	WATERS, Jonas	25	2	1861-12-10		A1 R1389
1521	WATERS, Lucas	9	NESW	1858-01-15		A3
1522	" "	9	NWSE	1858-01-15		A3
1523	" "	9	SWNE	1858-01-15		A3
1501	WATSON, Robert	24	W½SW	1865-10-20		A3 G43
1403	WEAVER, Daniel	35	E½SE	1857-03-10		A1
1405	" "	36	SW	1857-03-10		A1
1400	" "	25	NWSW	1866-05-01		A3
1401	" "	26	NESE	1866-05-01		A3
1402	" "	26	NWSE	1866-06-05		A1
1404	" "	35	NENE	1866-06-05		A1

ID	Individual in Patent	Sec.	Sec. Part	Date Issued	Other Counties	For More Info . . .
1545	WEAVER, Philip H	32	NW	1857-03-10		A1
1546	" "	32	W½NE	1857-03-10		A1
1382	WHITE, Cada	19	SW	1860-09-03		A3 G311 F
1382	WHITE, Jane	19	SW	1860-09-03		A3 G311 F
1368	WHITEHEAD, Amos	2	NW	1858-05-01		A1 F
1369	WILCOX, Amos	21	S½SW	1857-03-10		A1 V1529
1383	WILCOX, Caleb	7	SE	1858-05-01		A1
1595	WILDER, Willard	1	N½NE	1857-03-10		A1 F
1596	" "	1	N½NW	1857-03-10		A1 F
1597	" "	1	SWNW	1858-05-01		A1 F
1542	WISWELL, Orin	32	NESE	1860-09-01		A1
1538	WRIGHT, Nathaniel	15	NWNW	1891-11-02		A4
1540	WRIGHT, Nelson	18	SWSW	1859-10-10		A1

Patent Map

T13-N R14-W
Michigan-Toledo Strip Meridian

Map Group 13

Township Statistics

Parcels Mapped	:	254
Number of Patents	:	176
Number of Individuals	:	156
Patentees Identified	:	145
Number of Surnames	:	116
Multi-Patentee Parcels	:	19
Oldest Patent Date	:	11/8/1855
Most Recent Patent	:	11/2/1891
Block/Lot Parcels	:	8
Parcels Re - Issued	:	2
Parcels that Overlap	:	5
Cities and Towns	:	2
Cemeteries	:	3

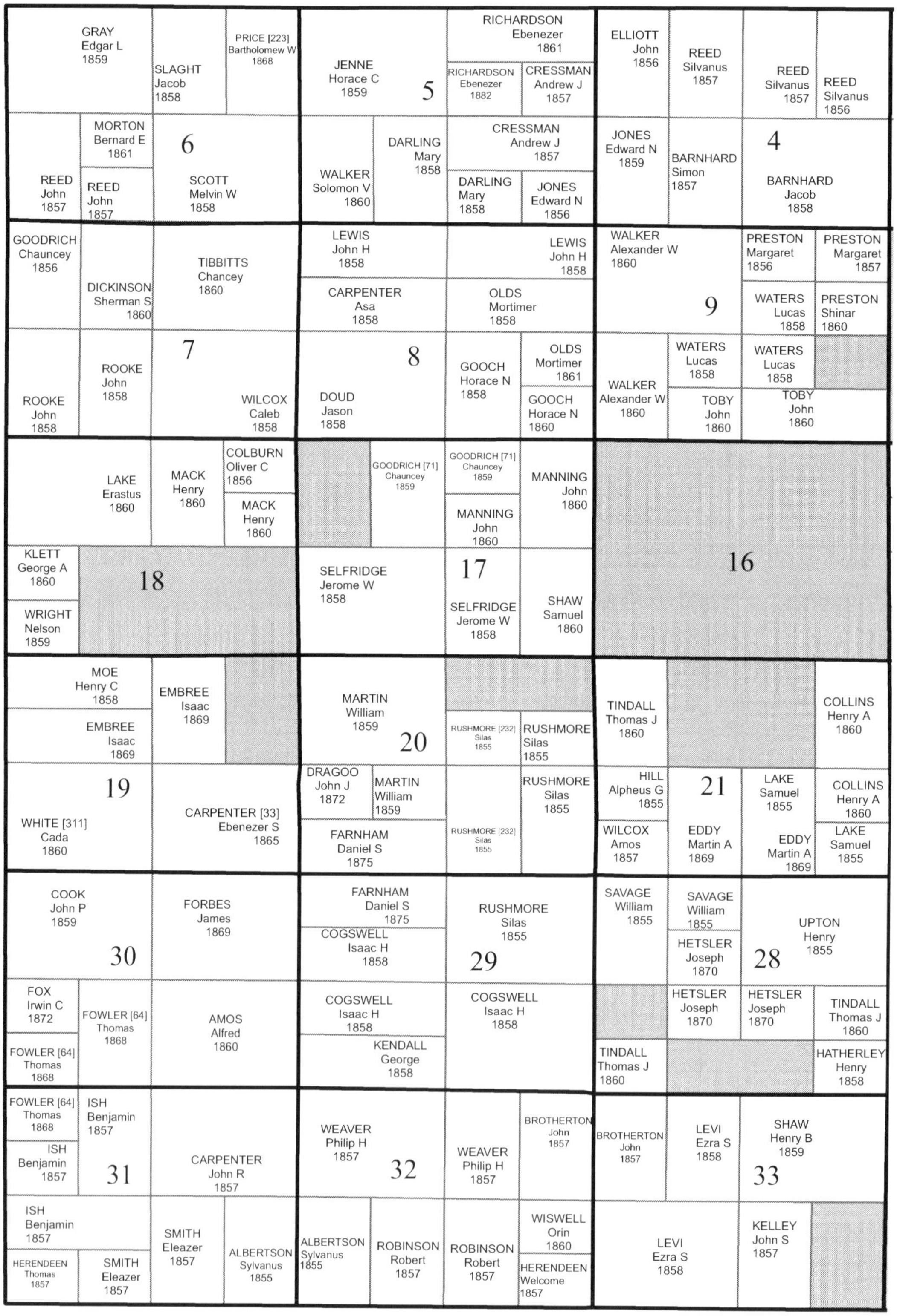

6
GRAY Edgar L 1859
SLAGHT Jacob 1858
PRICE [223] Bartholomew W 1868
MORTON Bernard E 1861
REED John 1857
REED John 1857
SCOTT Melvin W 1858

5
JENNE Horace C 1859
RICHARDSON Ebenezer 1861
RICHARDSON Ebenezer 1882
CRESSMAN Andrew J 1857
WALKER Solomon V 1860
DARLING Mary 1858
CRESSMAN Andrew J 1857
DARLING Mary 1858
JONES Edward N 1856

4
ELLIOTT John 1856
REED Silvanus 1857
REED Silvanus 1857
REED Silvanus 1856
JONES Edward N 1859
BARNHARD Simon 1857
BARNHARD Jacob 1858

7
GOODRICH Chauncey 1856
DICKINSON Sherman S 1860
TIBBITTS Chancey 1860
ROOKE John 1858
ROOKE John 1858
WILCOX Caleb 1858

8
LEWIS John H 1858
LEWIS John H 1858
CARPENTER Asa 1858
OLDS Mortimer 1858
DOUD Jason 1858
GOOCH Horace N 1858
OLDS Mortimer 1861
GOOCH Horace N 1860

9
WALKER Alexander W 1860
PRESTON Margaret 1856
PRESTON Margaret 1857
WATERS Lucas 1858
PRESTON Shinar 1860
WALKER Alexander W 1860
WATERS Lucas 1858
WATERS Lucas 1858
TOBY John 1860
TOBY John 1860

18
LAKE Erastus 1860
MACK Henry 1860
COLBURN Oliver C 1856
MACK Henry 1860
KLETT George A 1860
WRIGHT Nelson 1859

17
GOODRICH [71] Chauncey 1859
GOODRICH [71] Chauncey 1859
MANNING John 1860
MANNING John 1860
SELFRIDGE Jerome W 1858
SELFRIDGE Jerome W 1858
SHAW Samuel 1860

16

19
MOE Henry C 1858
EMBREE Isaac 1869
EMBREE Isaac 1869
WHITE [311] Cada 1860
CARPENTER [33] Ebenezer S 1865

20
MARTIN William 1859
RUSHMORE [232] Silas 1855
RUSHMORE Silas 1855
DRAGOO John J 1872
MARTIN William 1859
FARNHAM Daniel S 1875
RUSHMORE [232] Silas 1855
RUSHMORE Silas 1855

21
TINDALL Thomas J 1860
COLLINS Henry A 1860
HILL Alpheus G 1855
LAKE Samuel 1855
COLLINS Henry A 1860
WILCOX Amos 1857
EDDY Martin A 1869
EDDY Martin A 1869
LAKE Samuel 1855

30
COOK John P 1859
FORBES James 1869
FOX Irwin C 1872
FOWLER [64] Thomas 1868
AMOS Alfred 1860
FOWLER [64] Thomas 1868

29
FARNHAM Daniel S 1875
COGSWELL Isaac H 1858
RUSHMORE Silas 1855
COGSWELL Isaac H 1858
COGSWELL Isaac H 1858
KENDALL George 1858

28
SAVAGE William 1855
SAVAGE William 1855
HETSLER Joseph 1870
UPTON Henry 1855
HETSLER Joseph 1870
HETSLER Joseph 1870
TINDALL Thomas J 1860
TINDALL Thomas J 1860
HATHERLEY Henry 1858

31
FOWLER [64] Thomas 1868
ISH Benjamin 1857
ISH Benjamin 1857
CARPENTER John R 1857
ISH Benjamin 1857
SMITH Eleazer 1857
ALBERTSON Sylvanus 1855
HERENDEEN Thomas 1857
SMITH Eleazer 1857

32
WEAVER Philip H 1857
WEAVER Philip H 1857
BROTHERTON John 1857
ALBERTSON Sylvanus 1855
ROBINSON Robert 1857
ROBINSON Robert 1857
WISWELL Orin 1860
HERENDEEN Welcome 1857

33
BROTHERTON John 1857
LEVI Ezra S 1858
SHAW Henry B 1859
LEVI Ezra S 1858
KELLEY John S 1857

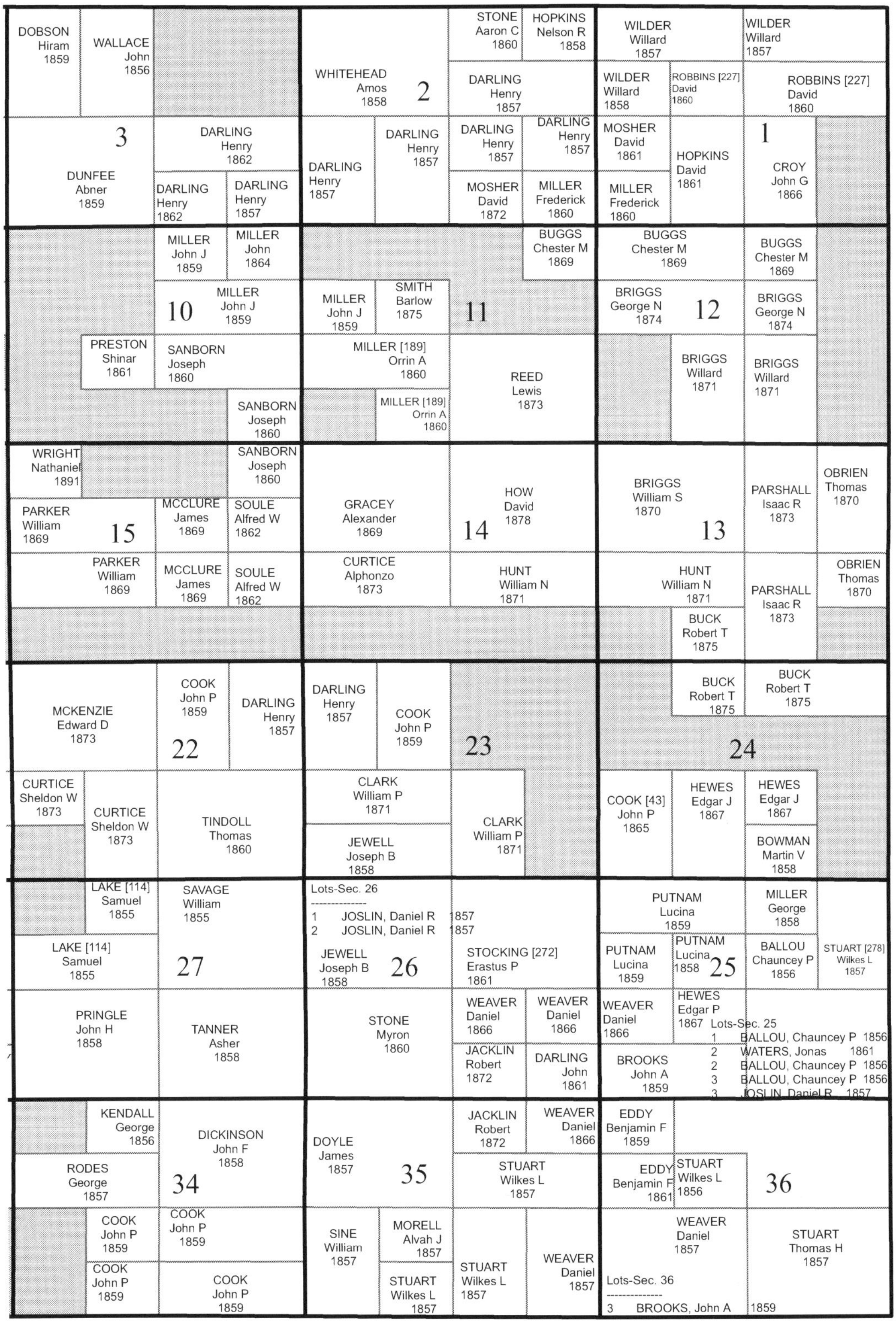

3
DOBSON Hiram 1859
WALLACE John 1856
DARLING Henry 1862
DUNFEE Abner 1859
DARLING Henry 1862
DARLING Henry 1857

2
WHITEHEAD Amos 1858
STONE Aaron C 1860
HOPKINS Nelson R 1858
DARLING Henry 1857
DARLING Henry 1857
DARLING Henry 1857
DARLING Henry 1857
DARLING Henry 1857
MOSHER David 1872
MILLER Frederick 1860

1
WILDER Willard 1857
WILDER Willard 1857
WILDER Willard 1858
ROBBINS [227] David 1860
ROBBINS [227] David 1860
MOSHER David 1861
HOPKINS David 1861
CROY John G 1866
MILLER Frederick 1860

10
MILLER John J 1859
MILLER John 1864
MILLER John J 1859
PRESTON Shinar 1861
SANBORN Joseph 1860
SANBORN Joseph 1860

11
BUGGS Chester M 1869
MILLER John J 1859
SMITH Barlow 1875
MILLER [189] Orrin A 1860
MILLER [189] Orrin A 1860
REED Lewis 1873

12
BUGGS Chester M 1869
BUGGS Chester M 1869
BRIGGS George N 1874
BRIGGS George N 1874
BRIGGS Willard 1871
BRIGGS Willard 1871

15
WRIGHT Nathaniel 1891
SANBORN Joseph 1860
PARKER William 1869
MCCLURE James 1869
SOULE Alfred W 1862
PARKER William 1869
MCCLURE James 1869
SOULE Alfred W 1862

14
GRACEY Alexander 1869
HOW David 1878
CURTICE Alphonzo 1873
HUNT William N 1871

13
BRIGGS William S 1870
PARSHALL Isaac R 1873
OBRIEN Thomas 1870
HUNT William N 1871
PARSHALL Isaac R 1873
OBRIEN Thomas 1870
BUCK Robert T 1875

22
MCKENZIE Edward D 1873
COOK John P 1859
DARLING Henry 1857
CURTICE Sheldon W 1873
CURTICE Sheldon W 1873
TINDOLL Thomas 1860

23
DARLING Henry 1857
COOK John P 1859
CLARK William P 1871
JEWELL Joseph B 1858
CLARK William P 1871

24
BUCK Robert T 1875
BUCK Robert T 1875
COOK [43] John P 1865
HEWES Edgar J 1867
HEWES Edgar J 1867
BOWMAN Martin V 1858

27
LAKE [114] Samuel 1855
SAVAGE William 1855
LAKE [114] Samuel 1855
PRINGLE John H 1858
TANNER Asher 1858

26
Lots-Sec. 26
1 JOSLIN, Daniel R 1857
2 JOSLIN, Daniel R 1857
JEWELL Joseph B 1858
STOCKING [272] Erastus P 1861
STONE Myron 1860
WEAVER Daniel 1866
WEAVER Daniel 1866
JACKLIN Robert 1872
DARLING John 1861

25
PUTNAM Lucina 1859
MILLER George 1858
PUTNAM Lucina 1859
PUTNAM Lucina 1858
BALLOU Chauncey P 1856
STUART [278] Wilkes L 1857
WEAVER Daniel 1866
HEWES Edgar P 1867
BROOKS John A 1859
Lots-Sec. 25
1 BALLOU, Chauncey P 1856
2 WATERS, Jonas 1861
2 BALLOU, Chauncey P 1856
3 BALLOU, Chauncey P 1856
3 JOSLIN, Daniel R 1857

34
KENDALL George 1856
DICKINSON John F 1858
RODES George 1857
COOK John P 1859
COOK John P 1859
COOK John P 1859
COOK John P 1859

35
DOYLE James 1857
JACKLIN Robert 1872
WEAVER Daniel 1866
STUART Wilkes L 1857
SINE William 1857
MORELL Alvah J 1857
STUART Wilkes L 1857
STUART Wilkes L 1857
WEAVER Daniel 1857

36
EDDY Benjamin F 1859
EDDY Benjamin F 1861
STUART Wilkes L 1856
WEAVER Daniel 1857
STUART Thomas H 1857
Lots-Sec. 36
3 BROOKS, John A 1859

Helpful Hints

1. This Map's INDEX can be found on the preceding pages.
2. Refer to Map "C" to see where this Township lies within Newaygo County, Michigan.
3. Numbers within square brackets [ ] denote a multi-patentee land parcel (multi-owner). Refer to Appendix "C" for a full list of members in this group.
4. Areas that look to be crowded with Patentees usually indicate multiple sales of the same parcel (Re-issues) or Overlapping parcels. See this Township's Index for an explanation of these and other circumstances that might explain "odd" groupings of Patentees on this map.

Legend

Patent Boundary
Section Boundary
No Patents Found (or Outside County)
1., 2., 3., ... Lot Numbers (when beside a name)
[ ] Group Number (see Appendix "C")

Scale: Section = 1 mile X 1 mile (generally, with some exceptions)

Road Map

T13-N R14-W
Michigan-Toledo Strip Meridian

Map Group 13

Cities & Towns

Dayton Center
Fremont

Cemeteries

Clark Cemetery
Dayton Center Cemetery
Evans Cemetery

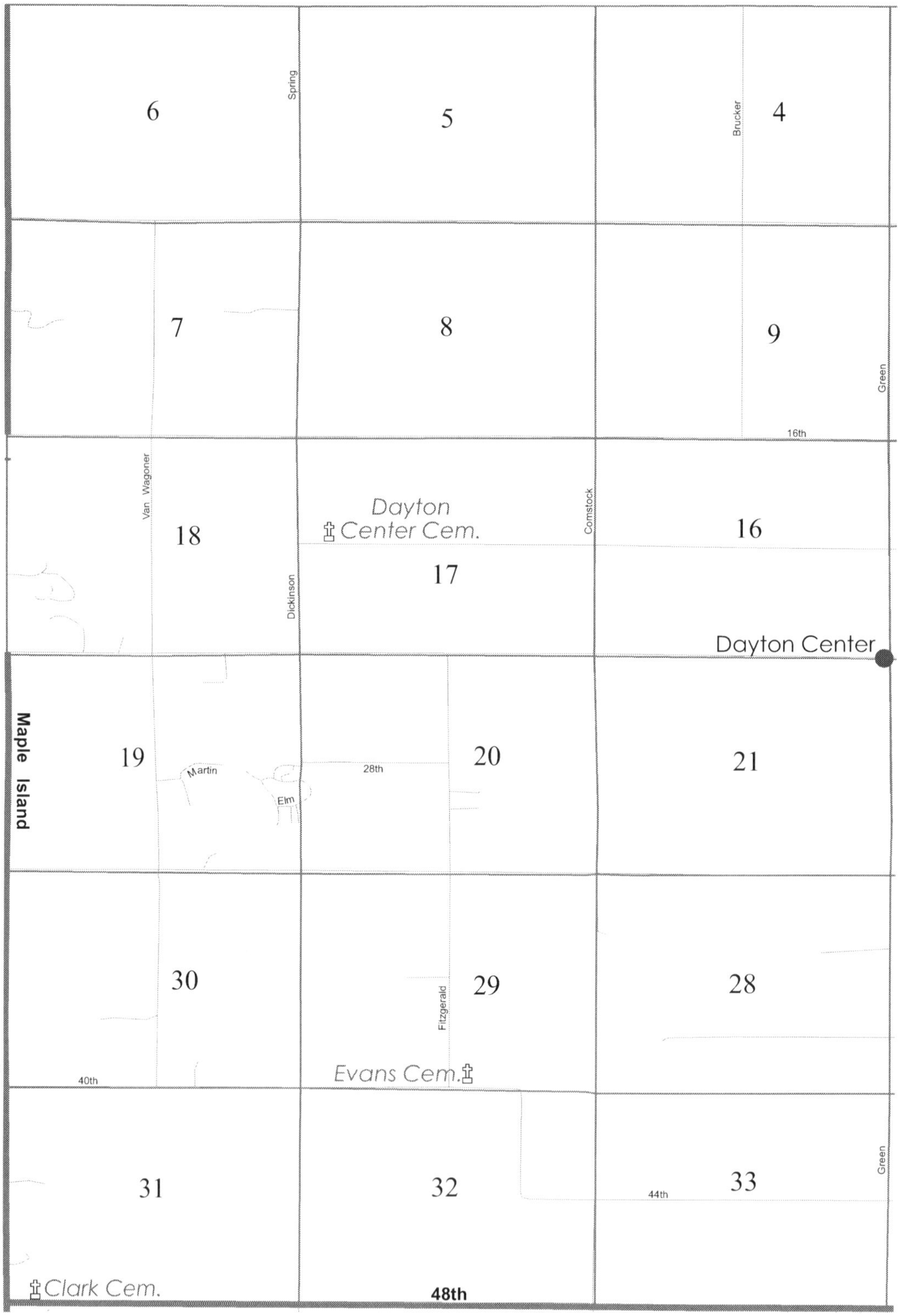

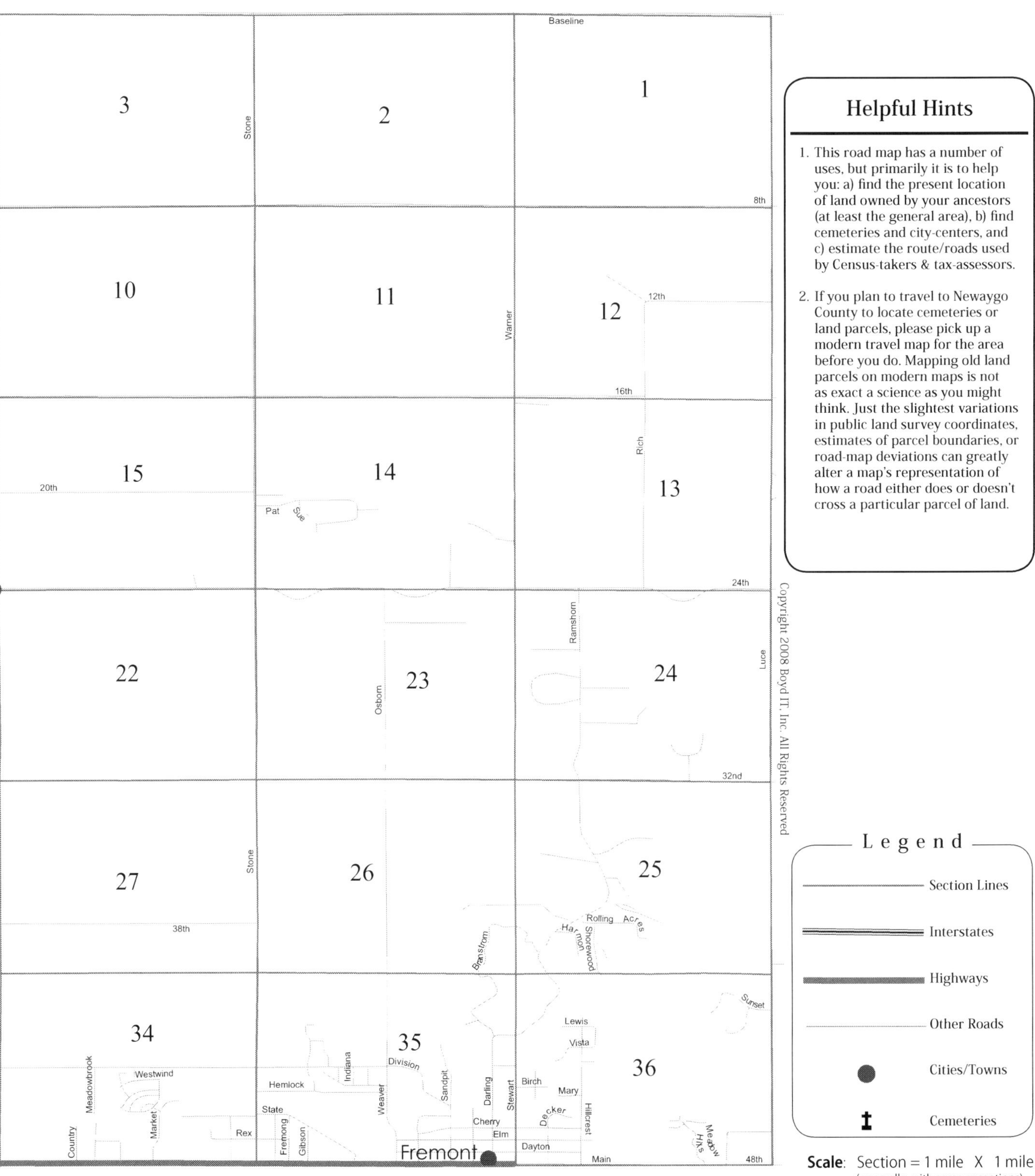

Helpful Hints

1. This road map has a number of uses, but primarily it is to help you: a) find the present location of land owned by your ancestors (at least the general area), b) find cemeteries and city-centers, and c) estimate the route/roads used by Census-takers & tax-assessors.
2. If you plan to travel to Newaygo County to locate cemeteries or land parcels, please pick up a modern travel map for the area before you do. Mapping old land parcels on modern maps is not as exact a science as you might think. Just the slightest variations in public land survey coordinates, estimates of parcel boundaries, or road-map deviations can greatly alter a map's representation of how a road either does or doesn't cross a particular parcel of land.

Historical Map

T13-N R14-W
Michigan-Toledo Strip Meridian

Map Group 13

Cities & Towns
- Dayton Center
- Fremont

Cemeteries
- Clark Cemetery
- Dayton Center Cemetery
- Evans Cemetery

6 5 4
Wrights Creek
7 8 9
18 17 16
Dayton Center Cem.
Dayton Center
19 20 21
Martin Lake
Brayden Creek
30 29 28
Dragod Creek
Cushman Creek
Evans Cem.
Evans Lake
31 32 33
Clark Cem.

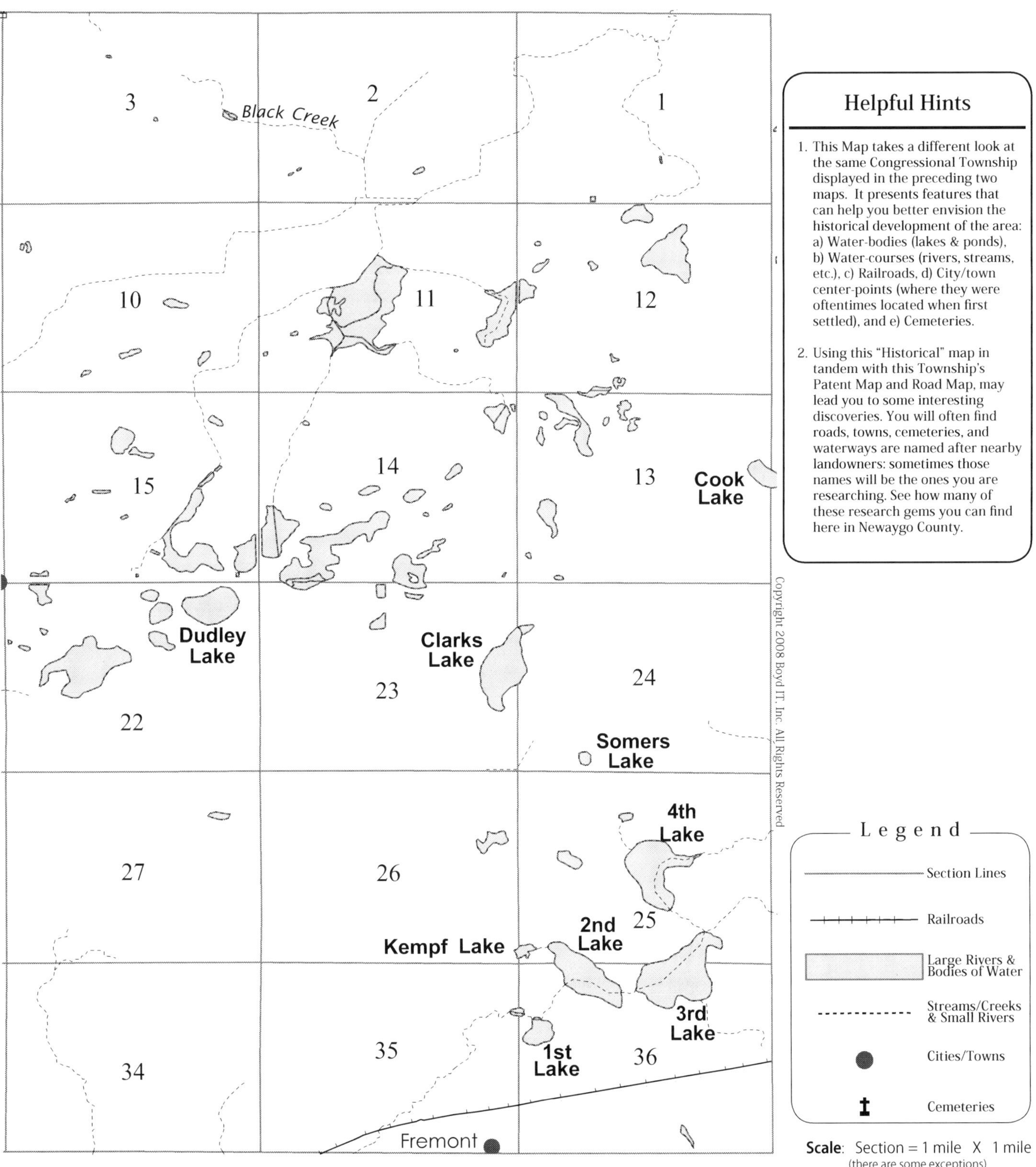

Helpful Hints

1. This Map takes a different look at the same Congressional Township displayed in the preceding two maps. It presents features that can help you better envision the historical development of the area: a) Water-bodies (lakes & ponds), b) Water-courses (rivers, streams, etc.), c) Railroads, d) City/town center-points (where they were oftentimes located when first settled), and e) Cemeteries.

2. Using this "Historical" map in tandem with this Township's Patent Map and Road Map, may lead you to some interesting discoveries. You will often find roads, towns, cemeteries, and waterways are named after nearby landowners: sometimes those names will be the ones you are researching. See how many of these research gems you can find here in Newaygo County.

Scale: Section = 1 mile X 1 mile
(there are some exceptions)

Map Group 14: Index to Land Patents

Township 13-North Range 13-West (Michigan-Toledo Strip)

After you locate an individual in this Index, take note of the Section and Section Part then proceed to the Land Patent map on the pages immediately following. You should have no difficulty locating the corresponding parcel of land.

The "For More Info" Column will lead you to more information about the underlying Patents. See the *Legend* at right, and the "How to Use this Book" chapter, for more information.

LEGEND

"For More Info . . . " column

A = Authority (Legislative Act, See Appendix "A")
B = Block or Lot (location in Section unknown)
C = Cancelled Patent
F = Fractional Section
G = Group (Multi-Patentee Patent, see Appendix "C")
V = Overlaps another Parcel
R = Re-Issued (Parcel patented more than once)

(A & G items require you to look in the Appendixes referred to above. All other Letter-designations followed by a number require you to locate line-items in this index that possess the ID number found after the letter).

ID	Individual in Patent	Sec.	Sec. Part	Date Issued	Other Counties	For More Info . . .
1719	ANDERSON, Patience	6	S½NW	1863-05-20		A3 G2 F
1612	ARMS, Lewis L	34	4	1854-10-05		A1 G35
1613	" "	36	NE	1854-10-05		A1 G35
1614	" "	36	S½	1854-10-05		A1 G35
1615	" "	36	SENW	1854-10-05		A1 G35
1719	AVERY, Newell	6	S½NW	1863-05-20		A3 G2 F
1697	" "	24	NENW	1872-11-06		A1 G302
1703	" "	24	W½NW	1872-11-06		A1 G83
1681	BALL, John	1	E½SW	1855-03-01		A1
1682	" "	1	SE	1855-03-01		A1
1683	" "	1	SENE	1855-03-01		A1
1684	" "	1	SWSW	1855-03-01		A1
1685	" "	12	NE	1855-03-01		A1
1686	" "	12	NENW	1855-03-01		A1
1687	" "	12	NESE	1855-03-01		A1
1637	BALLOU, Chauncey P	30	SWSW	1856-03-10		A1 C F R1700
1635	BAMBER, Robert	1	N½NW	1866-01-10		A3 G216 F
1636	" "	1	NWNE	1866-01-10		A3 G216 F
1702	BELL, Joseph	19	NENW	1873-05-15		A1
1722	BRIGHAM, Orlando S	9	1	1855-12-15		A1 G26
1723	" "	9	N½SW	1855-12-15		A1 G26
1724	" "	9	NWSE	1855-12-15		A1 G26
1725	" "	9	SWNW	1855-12-15		A1 G26
1678	BROOKS, John A	33	N½SE	1855-11-08		A3
1680	" "	33	SWSE	1855-11-08		A3
1679	" "	33	SESE	1856-03-10		A1
1732	BRUBAKER, Phares S	24	SESE	1870-07-15		A1
1733	" "	24	N½SE	1871-02-20		A3 G31
1734	" "	24	N½SW	1871-02-20		A3 G31
1660	CADY, Susannah	15	E½SW	1857-02-20		A3 G249
1661	" "	15	NWSW	1857-02-20		A3 G249
1677	CHAFFEE, Elanor	20	NE	1860-09-03		A3 G34
1677	CHAFFEE, Joel S	20	NE	1860-09-03		A3 G34
1756	CHEENEY, Damon E	10	1	1855-03-01		A1 G341
1757	" "	10	2	1855-03-01		A1 G341
1758	" "	10	3	1855-03-01		A1 G341
1759	" "	3	NWNW	1855-03-01		A1 G341 F
1760	" "	4	E½NW	1855-03-01		A1 G341
1761	" "	4	N½SE	1855-03-01		A1 G341
1762	" "	4	NE	1855-03-01		A1 G341
1612	CHENEY, Albert N	34	4	1854-10-05		A1 G35
1613	" "	36	NE	1854-10-05		A1 G35
1614	" "	36	S½	1854-10-05		A1 G35
1615	" "	36	SENW	1854-10-05		A1 G35
1674	COWLES, Jason	17	NWNW	1860-11-10		A3
1675	" "	17	S½NW	1860-11-10		A3

ID	Individual in Patent	Sec.	Sec. Part	Date Issued	Other Counties	For More Info . . .
1676	COWLES, Jason (Cont'd)	18	SENE	1860-11-10		A3
1776	DAVIS, John G	7	SENE	1866-11-10		A3 G306 C R1777
1778	" "	7	W½NE	1866-11-10		A3 G306 C R1779
1777	" "	7	SENE	1868-06-26		A3 G306 R1776
1779	" "	7	W½NE	1868-06-26		A3 G306 R1778
1704	DEWOLF, Joseph P	31	NW	1862-05-15		A1 F
1663	EWERS, Sarah	18	SESE	1858-01-15		A3 G243
1664	" "	19	E½NE	1858-01-15		A3 G243
1688	FORD, John	32	E½NE	1870-05-02		A4
1666	FRENCH, Sarah	17	E½NE	1860-11-10		A3 G198
1667	" "	17	SWNE	1860-11-10		A3 G198
1668	" "	8	SESE	1860-11-10		A3 G198
1707	GATES, Lucius	31	SE	1857-03-10		A1
1708	GETTY, Henry H	21	NENE	1873-05-15		A1 G233 F
1662	GREGORY, Mary	33	S½SW	1858-01-15		A3 G244
1690	GROVESTEEN, John M	12	SESE	1867-01-10		A1
1691	" "	13	N½SW	1867-02-01		A3 G73
1692	" "	13	SWNW	1867-02-01		A3 G73
1693	" "	23	NW	1868-07-20		A3 G74 C
1623	GUSTROUS, John	12	NWSE	1868-02-15		A1 G105
1624	" "	12	SENW	1868-02-15		A1 G105
1693	HARRIS, Mary	23	NW	1868-07-20		A3 G74 C
1697	HEALD, Joseph	24	NENW	1872-11-06		A1 G302
1703	" "	24	W½NW	1872-11-06		A1 G83
1689	HERINGTON, John L	30	E½NW	1858-05-01		A1
1670	HERSHBERGER, Jacob B	24	E½NE	1871-04-01		A1
1671	" "	24	SENW	1871-04-01		A1
1708	HILLS, Charles T	21	NENE	1873-05-15		A1 G233 F
1718	HINDES, Moses S	32	NWSE	1859-10-10		A1
1768	HOLMES, Susan	30	W½NW	1857-04-02		A3 G278 F
1726	HOPKINS, Orrin W	19	SESE	1875-07-01		A4
1727	" "	30	NENE	1875-07-01		A4
1769	HOWE, William	25	E½NE	1860-10-01		A3
1770	" "	25	NESE	1860-10-01		A3
1771	" "	25	SESE	1860-10-01		A3
1772	" "	25	W½SE	1860-10-01		A3
1754	JACKLIN, Robert	20	4	1861-12-10		A1
1701	JEWELL, Joseph B	20	NENW	1873-05-15		A1 G104
1774	JOHNSON, Charles	10	4	1866-11-10		A3 G309
1775	" "	10	5	1866-11-10		A3 G309
1776	" "	7	SENE	1866-11-10		A3 G306 C R1777
1778	" "	7	W½NE	1866-11-10		A3 G306 C R1779
1780	" "	1	NENE	1867-02-01		A3 G307
1623	" "	12	NWSE	1868-02-15		A1 G105
1624	" "	12	SENW	1868-02-15		A1 G105
1777	" "	7	SENE	1868-06-26		A3 G306 R1776
1779	" "	7	W½NE	1868-06-26		A3 G306 R1778
1665	LEWIS, Frank	5	SWSE	1865-10-10		A1
1780	LYNN, Mary W	1	NENE	1867-02-01		A3 G307
1705	MAHAN, Lambert	19	NESE	1861-04-01		A1
1706	" "	20	NWSW	1861-04-01		A1
1672	MALLERY, James B	31	SW	1857-03-10		A1 F
1622	MERWIN, Betsy N	28	W½SW	1855-12-15		A1
1646	MERWIN, Henry	15	E½SE	1857-02-20		A3 G248
1660	" "	15	E½SW	1857-02-20		A3 G249
1647	" "	15	NW	1857-02-20		A3 G248
1648	" "	15	NWSE	1857-02-20		A3 G248
1661	" "	15	NWSW	1857-02-20		A3 G249
1649	" "	15	SWSE	1857-02-20		A3 G248
1650	" "	15	W½NE	1857-02-20		A3 G248
1651	" "	22	E½SW	1857-02-20		A3 G248
1652	" "	22	NE	1857-02-20		A3 G248
1653	" "	22	W½SE	1857-02-20		A3 G248
1654	" "	29	S½SW	1857-02-20		A3 G248
1655	" "	29	SWSE	1857-02-20		A3 G248
1656	" "	32	N½NW	1857-02-20		A3 G248
1657	" "	32	NWNE	1857-02-20		A3 G248
1658	" "	32	S½NW	1857-02-20		A3 G248
1659	" "	32	SWNE	1857-02-20		A3 G248
1669	MERWIN, Henry N	28	E½SW	1855-12-15		A1
1720	MERWIN, Noble W	29	N½SE	1855-12-15		A1
1721	" "	29	SESE	1855-12-15		A1
1709	MORRIS, Robert W	22	E½SE	1854-10-05		A1 G236

ID	Individual in Patent	Sec.	Sec. Part	Date Issued	Other Counties	For More Info . . .
1710	MORRIS, Robert W (Cont'd)	23	SW	1854-10-05		A1 G236
1711	" "	23	W½SE	1854-10-05		A1 G236
1712	" "	26	N½	1854-10-05		A1 G236
1713	" "	26	SW	1854-10-05		A1 G236
1714	" "	26	W½SE	1854-10-05		A1 G236
1715	" "	34	7	1854-10-05		A1 G236
1716	" "	34	E½NE	1854-10-05		A1 G236
1717	" "	35	N½NW	1854-10-05		A1 G236
1666	MOSES, Henry C	17	E½NE	1860-11-10		A3 G198
1667	" "	17	SWNE	1860-11-10		A3 G198
1668	" "	8	SESE	1860-11-10		A3 G198
1733	MOSS, Charles N	24	N½SE	1871-02-20		A3 G31
1734	" "	24	N½SW	1871-02-20		A3 G31
1733	MOSS, Elizabeth	24	N½SE	1871-02-20		A3 G31
1734	" "	24	N½SW	1871-02-20		A3 G31
1701	MULDER, Kornelius	20	NENW	1873-05-15		A1 G104
1703	MURPHY, Simon J	24	W½NW	1872-11-06		A1 G83
1691	NEAL, Aurelia C	13	N½SW	1867-02-01		A3 G73
1692	" "	13	SWNW	1867-02-01		A3 G73
1767	NININGER, Valentine	20	NWNW	1862-05-15		A1
1646	NORTHROP, John O	15	E½SE	1857-02-20		A3 G248
1660	" "	15	E½SW	1857-02-20		A3 G249
1647	" "	15	NW	1857-02-20		A3 G248
1648	" "	15	NWSE	1857-02-20		A3 G248
1661	" "	15	NWSW	1857-02-20		A3 G249
1649	" "	15	SWSE	1857-02-20		A3 G248
1650	" "	15	W½NE	1857-02-20		A3 G248
1651	" "	22	E½SW	1857-02-20		A3 G248
1652	" "	22	NE	1857-02-20		A3 G248
1653	" "	22	W½SE	1857-02-20		A3 G248
1654	" "	29	S½SW	1857-02-20		A3 G248
1655	" "	29	SWSE	1857-02-20		A3 G248
1656	" "	32	N½NW	1857-02-20		A3 G248
1657	" "	32	NWNE	1857-02-20		A3 G248
1658	" "	32	S½NW	1857-02-20		A3 G248
1659	" "	32	SWNE	1857-02-20		A3 G248
1638	" "	17	SE	1858-01-15		A3 G241
1639	" "	17	SW	1858-01-15		A3 G241
1663	" "	18	SESE	1858-01-15		A3 G243
1640	" "	18	SWSE	1858-01-15		A3 G241
1664	" "	19	E½NE	1858-01-15		A3 G243
1641	" "	19	W½NE	1858-01-15		A3 G241
1642	" "	28	S½NW	1858-01-15		A3 G241
1643	" "	33	E½NW	1858-01-15		A3 G241
1662	" "	33	S½SW	1858-01-15		A3 G244
1644	" "	33	SWNE	1858-01-15		A3 G241
1645	" "	33	W½NW	1858-01-15		A3 G241
1694	ODELL, John	20	2	1861-12-10		A1
1695	" "	20	3	1861-12-10		A1
1696	" "	20	S½NW	1861-12-10		A1
1728	PECK, Peter	20	1	1870-05-02		A4
1729	" "	20	NESE	1870-05-02		A4 F
1730	" "	29	3	1870-05-02		A4
1731	" "	29	4	1870-05-02		A4
1755	PELTON, Abagail	23	NE	1868-10-01		A3 G215 C
1755	PELTON, Ephraim	23	NE	1868-10-01		A3 G215 C
1693	PELTON, Rollin H	23	NW	1868-07-20		A3 G74 C
1755	" "	23	NE	1868-10-01		A3 G215 C
1627	PETERSON, Charles	4	W½SW	1864-02-10		A3
1628	" "	5	NESE	1864-02-10		A3
1632	" "	8	NENE	1864-02-10		A3
1633	" "	9	E½NW	1864-02-10		A3
1634	" "	9	NWNW	1864-02-10		A3
1629	" "	5	SESW	1865-10-10		A1
1625	" "	4	NESW	1865-11-01		A1
1631	" "	7	NENE	1865-11-01		A1
1635	" "	1	N½NW	1866-01-10		A3 G216 F
1636	" "	1	NWNE	1866-01-10		A3 G216 F
1626	" "	4	S½SE	1867-01-10		A1
1630	" "	5	SWSW	1868-02-15		A1
1765	REED, Silvanus	32	NESE	1857-03-10		A1
1766	" "	32	S½SE	1857-03-10		A1
1733	REED, William A	24	N½SE	1871-02-20		A3 G31

ID	Individual in Patent	Sec.	Sec. Part	Date Issued	Other Counties	For More Info . . .
1734	REED, William A (Cont'd)	24	N½SW	1871-02-20		A3 G31
1709	RYERSON, Martin	22	E½SE	1854-10-05		A1 G236
1710	" "	23	SW	1854-10-05		A1 G236
1711	" "	23	W½SE	1854-10-05		A1 G236
1712	" "	26	N½	1854-10-05		A1 G236
1713	" "	26	SW	1854-10-05		A1 G236
1714	" "	26	W½SE	1854-10-05		A1 G236
1715	" "	34	7	1854-10-05		A1 G236
1716	" "	34	E½NE	1854-10-05		A1 G236
1717	" "	35	N½NW	1854-10-05		A1 G236
1708	" "	21	NENE	1873-05-15		A1 G233 F
1646	SANFORD, Ebenezer	15	E½SE	1857-02-20		A3 G248
1660	" "	15	E½SW	1857-02-20		A3 G249
1647	" "	15	NW	1857-02-20		A3 G248
1648	" "	15	NWSE	1857-02-20		A3 G248
1661	" "	15	NWSW	1857-02-20		A3 G249
1649	" "	15	SWSE	1857-02-20		A3 G248
1650	" "	15	W½NE	1857-02-20		A3 G248
1651	" "	22	E½SW	1857-02-20		A3 G248
1652	" "	22	NE	1857-02-20		A3 G248
1653	" "	22	W½SE	1857-02-20		A3 G248
1654	" "	29	S½SW	1857-02-20		A3 G248
1655	" "	29	SWSE	1857-02-20		A3 G248
1656	" "	32	N½NW	1857-02-20		A3 G248
1657	" "	32	NWNE	1857-02-20		A3 G248
1658	" "	32	S½NW	1857-02-20		A3 G248
1659	" "	32	SWNE	1857-02-20		A3 G248
1638	" "	17	SE	1858-01-15		A3 G241
1639	" "	17	SW	1858-01-15		A3 G241
1663	" "	18	SESE	1858-01-15		A3 G243
1640	" "	18	SWSE	1858-01-15		A3 G241
1664	" "	19	E½NE	1858-01-15		A3 G243
1641	" "	19	W½NE	1858-01-15		A3 G241
1642	" "	28	S½NW	1858-01-15		A3 G241
1643	" "	33	E½NW	1858-01-15		A3 G241
1662	" "	33	S½SW	1858-01-15		A3 G244
1644	" "	33	SWNE	1858-01-15		A3 G241
1645	" "	33	W½NW	1858-01-15		A3 G241
1618	SKEELS, Amos K	30	E½SE	1860-09-01		A1
1619	" "	30	SENE	1860-09-01		A1
1620	" "	19	E½SW	1861-09-12		A3 G258 F
1621	" "	19	W½SE	1861-09-12		A3 G258
1768	STUART, Wilkes L	30	W½NW	1857-04-02		A3 G278 F
1673	TURNER, James M	4	SESW	1872-04-05		A1
1611	UPTON, Adonijah E	18	NESE	1865-10-10		A1
1620	WARREN, Persis	19	E½SW	1861-09-12		A3 G258 F
1621	" "	19	W½SE	1861-09-12		A3 G258
1698	WATERS, Jonas	30	E½SW	1858-05-01		A1 F
1699	" "	30	NWSW	1858-05-01		A1
1700	" "	30	SWSW	1859-10-10		A1 F R1637
1617	WATSON, Amasa B	32	SW	1855-11-08		A3 G301
1616	" "	31	NE	1857-02-20		A3
1697	WELCH, John	24	NENW	1872-11-06		A1 G302
1773	WESTON, William	2	NENE	1863-09-01		A1 F
1774	" "	10	4	1866-11-10		A3 G309
1775	" "	10	5	1866-11-10		A3 G309
1776	" "	7	SENE	1866-11-10		A3 G306 C R1777
1778	" "	7	W½NE	1866-11-10		A3 G306 C R1779
1780	" "	1	NENE	1867-02-01		A3 G307
1777	" "	7	SENE	1868-06-26		A3 G306 R1776
1779	" "	7	W½NE	1868-06-26		A3 G306 R1778
1617	WHALEN, Elizabeth	32	SW	1855-11-08		A3 G301
1722	WHEELER, Silas	9	1	1855-12-15		A1 G26
1723	" "	9	N½SW	1855-12-15		A1 G26
1724	" "	9	NWSE	1855-12-15		A1 G26
1725	" "	9	SWNW	1855-12-15		A1 G26
1756	WHEELOCK, Addison P	10	1	1855-03-01		A1 G341
1757	" "	10	2	1855-03-01		A1 G341
1758	" "	10	3	1855-03-01		A1 G341
1759	" "	3	NWNW	1855-03-01		A1 G341 F
1760	" "	4	E½NW	1855-03-01		A1 G341
1761	" "	4	N½SE	1855-03-01		A1 G341
1762	" "	4	NE	1855-03-01		A1 G341

ID	Individual in Patent	Sec.	Sec. Part	Date Issued	Other Counties	For More Info . . .
1763	WILCOX, Sextus N	35	SESW	1854-06-15		A1
1764	" "	35	SWSE	1854-06-15		A1
1735	WOOD, Ransom E	21	1	1855-12-15		A1
1736	" "	21	2	1855-12-15		A1
1737	" "	21	3	1855-12-15		A1
1738	" "	22	1	1855-12-15		A1
1739	" "	22	2	1855-12-15		A1
1740	" "	27	1	1855-12-15		A1
1741	" "	27	2	1855-12-15		A1
1742	" "	27	3	1855-12-15		A1
1743	" "	27	4	1855-12-15		A1
1744	" "	28	1	1855-12-15		A1
1745	" "	28	2	1855-12-15		A1
1746	" "	28	3	1855-12-15		A1
1747	" "	33	1	1855-12-15		A1
1748	" "	34	1	1855-12-15		A1
1749	" "	34	2	1855-12-15		A1
1750	" "	34	3	1855-12-15		A1
1751	" "	34	5	1855-12-15		A1
1752	" "	34	6	1855-12-15		A1
1753	" "	34	W½NW	1855-12-15		A1
1756	WOOD, Sarell	10	1	1855-03-01		A1 G341
1757	" "	10	2	1855-03-01		A1 G341
1758	" "	10	3	1855-03-01		A1 G341
1759	" "	3	NWNW	1855-03-01		A1 G341 F
1760	" "	4	E½NW	1855-03-01		A1 G341
1761	" "	4	N½SE	1855-03-01		A1 G341
1762	" "	4	NE	1855-03-01		A1 G341
1774	WOODMAN, Horatio	10	4	1866-11-10		A3 G309
1775	" "	10	5	1866-11-10		A3 G309

Patent Map

T13-N R13-W
Michigan-Toledo Strip Meridian

Map Group 14

Township Statistics

Parcels Mapped	:	170
Number of Patents	:	102
Number of Individuals	:	81
Patentees Identified	:	63
Number of Surnames	:	72
Multi-Patentee Parcels	:	81
Oldest Patent Date	:	6/15/1854
Most Recent Patent	:	7/1/1875
Block/Lot Parcels	:	32
Parcels Re - Issued	:	3
Parcels that Overlap	:	0
Cities and Towns	:	2
Cemeteries	:	0

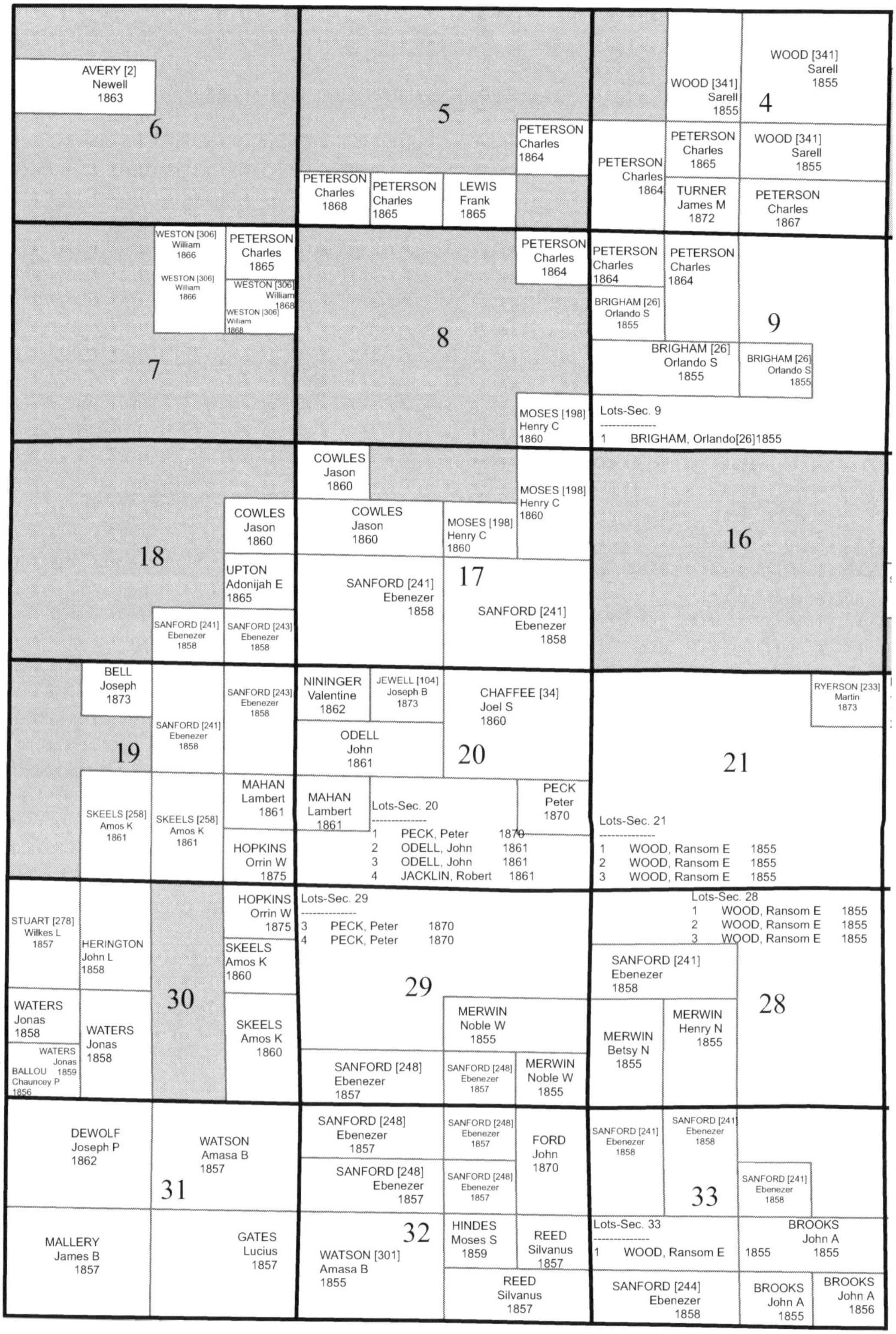

6
AVERY [2] Newell 1863

5
PETERSON Charles 1864
PETERSON Charles 1868
PETERSON Charles 1865
LEWIS Frank 1865

4
WOOD [341] Sarell 1855
WOOD [341] Sarell 1855
PETERSON Charles 1865
WOOD [341] Sarell 1855
PETERSON Charles 1864
TURNER James M 1872
PETERSON Charles 1867

7
WESTON [306] William 1866
WESTON [306] William 1866
PETERSON Charles 1865
WESTON [306] William 1868
WESTON [306] William 1868

8
PETERSON Charles 1864
MOSES [198] Henry C 1860

9
PETERSON Charles 1864
PETERSON Charles 1864
BRIGHAM [26] Orlando S 1855
BRIGHAM [26] Orlando S 1855
BRIGHAM [26] Orlando S 1855
Lots-Sec. 9
1 BRIGHAM, Orlando[26]1855

18
COWLES Jason 1860
UPTON Adonijah E 1865
SANFORD [241] Ebenezer 1858
SANFORD [243] Ebenezer 1858

17
COWLES Jason 1860
COWLES Jason 1860
MOSES [198] Henry C 1860
MOSES [198] Henry C 1860
SANFORD [241] Ebenezer 1858
SANFORD [241] Ebenezer 1858

16

19
BELL Joseph 1873
SANFORD [241] Ebenezer 1858
SANFORD [243] Ebenezer 1858
SKEELS [258] Amos K 1861
SKEELS [258] Amos K 1861
MAHAN Lambert 1861
HOPKINS Orrin W 1875

20
NININGER Valentine 1862
JEWELL [104] Joseph B 1873
CHAFFEE [34] Joel S 1860
ODELL John 1861
MAHAN Lambert 1861
PECK Peter 1870
Lots-Sec. 20
1 PECK, Peter 1870
2 ODELL, John 1861
3 ODELL, John 1861
4 JACKLIN, Robert 1861

21
RYERSON [233] Martin 1873
Lots-Sec. 21
1 WOOD, Ransom E 1855
2 WOOD, Ransom E 1855
3 WOOD, Ransom E 1855

30
STUART [278] Wilkes L 1857
HERINGTON John L 1858
HOPKINS Orrin W 1875
SKEELS Amos K 1860
WATERS Jonas 1858
WATERS Jonas 1858
WATERS Jonas 1859
BALLOU Chauncey P 1856
SKEELS Amos K 1860

29
Lots-Sec. 29
3 PECK, Peter 1870
4 PECK, Peter 1870
MERWIN Noble W 1855
SANFORD [248] Ebenezer 1857
SANFORD [248] Ebenezer 1857
MERWIN Noble W 1855

28
Lots-Sec. 28
1 WOOD, Ransom E 1855
2 WOOD, Ransom E 1855
3 WOOD, Ransom E 1855
SANFORD [241] Ebenezer 1858
MERWIN Betsy N 1855
MERWIN Henry N 1855

31
DEWOLF Joseph P 1862
WATSON Amasa B 1857
MALLERY James B 1857
GATES Lucius 1857

32
SANFORD [248] Ebenezer 1857
SANFORD [248] Ebenezer 1857
FORD John 1870
SANFORD [248] Ebenezer 1857
SANFORD [248] Ebenezer 1857
HINDES Moses S 1859
REED Silvanus 1857
WATSON [301] Amasa B 1855
REED Silvanus 1857

33
SANFORD [241] Ebenezer 1858
SANFORD [241] Ebenezer 1858
SANFORD [241] Ebenezer 1858
Lots-Sec. 33
1 WOOD, Ransom E
BROOKS John A 1855
SANFORD [244] Ebenezer 1858
BROOKS John A 1855
BROOKS John A 1856

Helpful Hints

1. This Map's INDEX can be found on the preceding pages.
2. Refer to Map "C" to see where this Township lies within Newaygo County, Michigan.
3. Numbers within square brackets [ ] denote a multi-patentee land parcel (multi-owner). Refer to Appendix "C" for a full list of members in this group.
4. Areas that look to be crowded with Patentees usually indicate multiple sales of the same parcel (Re-issues) or Overlapping parcels. See this Township's Index for an explanation of these and other circumstances that might explain "odd" groupings of Patentees on this map.

Legend

- Patent Boundary
- Section Boundary
- No Patents Found (or Outside County)
- 1., 2., 3., ... Lot Numbers (when beside a name)
- [ ] Group Number (see Appendix "C")

Scale: Section = 1 mile X 1 mile (generally, with some exceptions)

Road Map

T13-N R13-W
Michigan-Toledo Strip Meridian

Map Group 14

Cities & Towns
Jugville
Wooster

Cemeteries
None

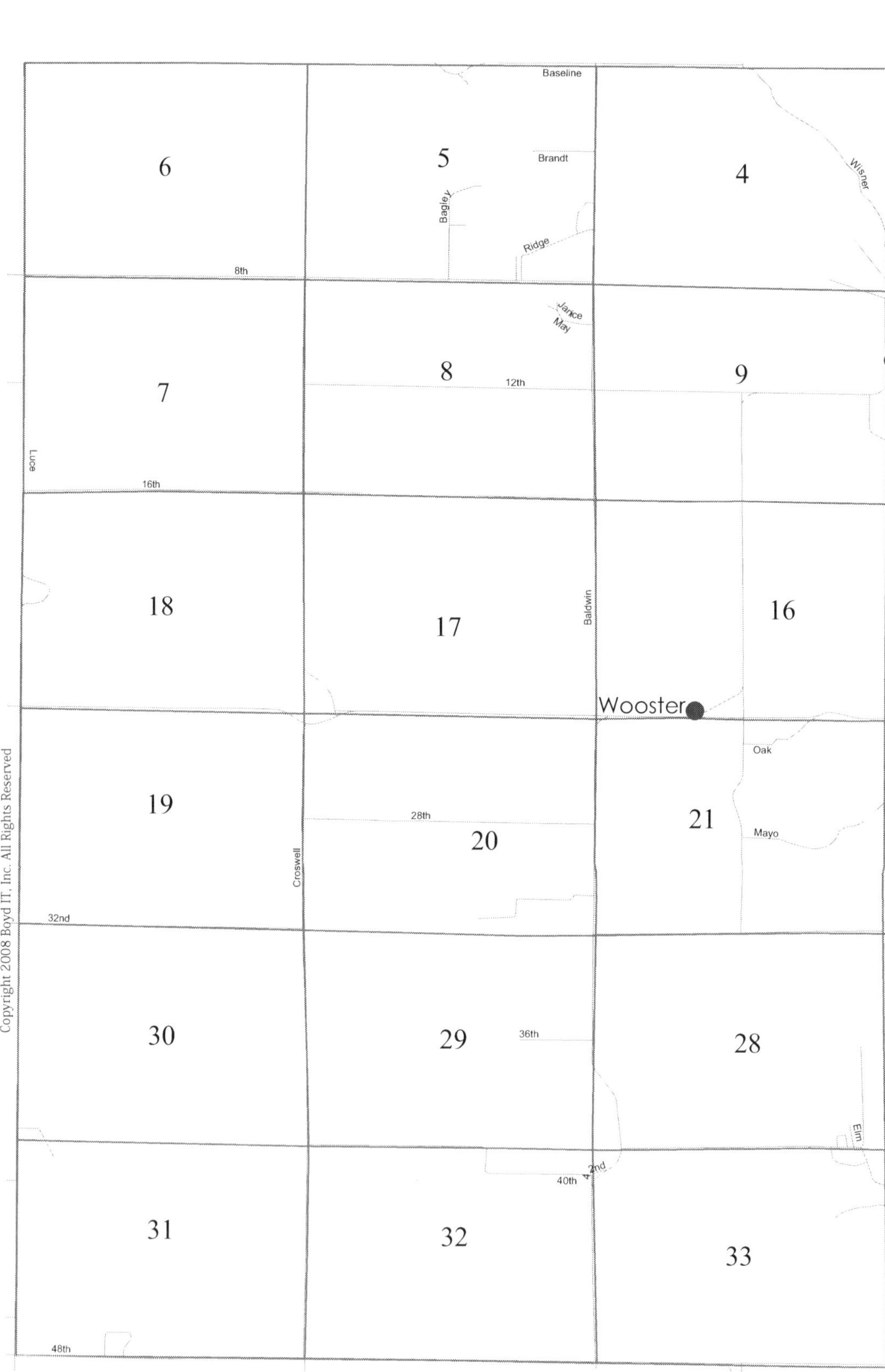

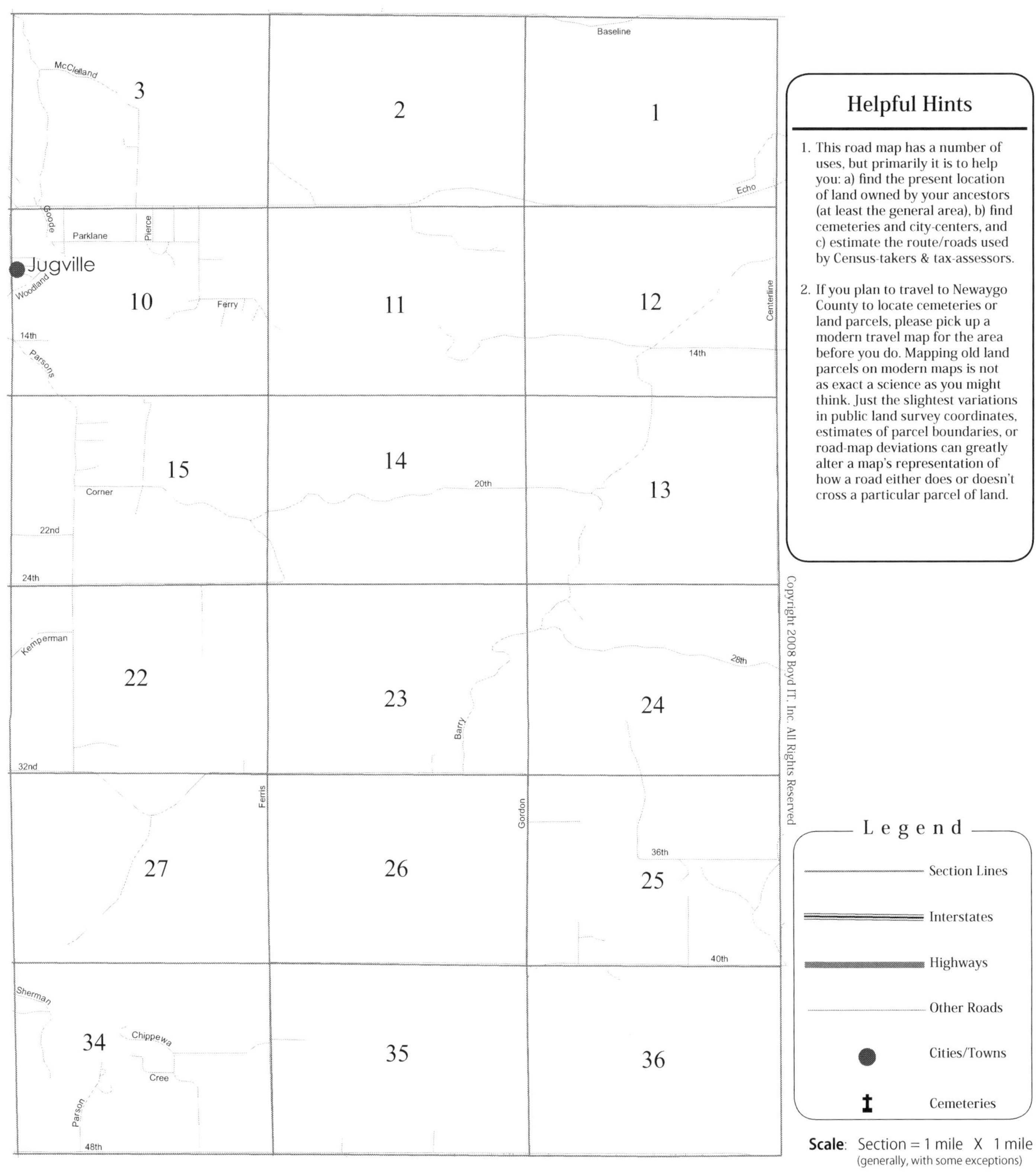

Helpful Hints

1. This road map has a number of uses, but primarily it is to help you: a) find the present location of land owned by your ancestors (at least the general area), b) find cemeteries and city-centers, and c) estimate the route/roads used by Census-takers & tax-assessors.

2. If you plan to travel to Newaygo County to locate cemeteries or land parcels, please pick up a modern travel map for the area before you do. Mapping old land parcels on modern maps is not as exact a science as you might think. Just the slightest variations in public land survey coordinates, estimates of parcel boundaries, or road-map deviations can greatly alter a map's representation of how a road either does or doesn't cross a particular parcel of land.

Legend

- Section Lines
- Interstates
- Highways
- Other Roads
- Cities/Towns
- Cemeteries

Scale: Section = 1 mile X 1 mile
(generally, with some exceptions)

Cities & Towns

Jugville
Wooster

Cemeteries

None

6
5
Woodrail Lake
4
Robinson Creek
Peterson Lake
Blackberry Lake
7
8
9
18
17
16
Dutch Lake
Wooster
Crystal Lake
19
20
21
Peck Lake
Mud Lake
28
30
29
Ford Lake
31
32
33

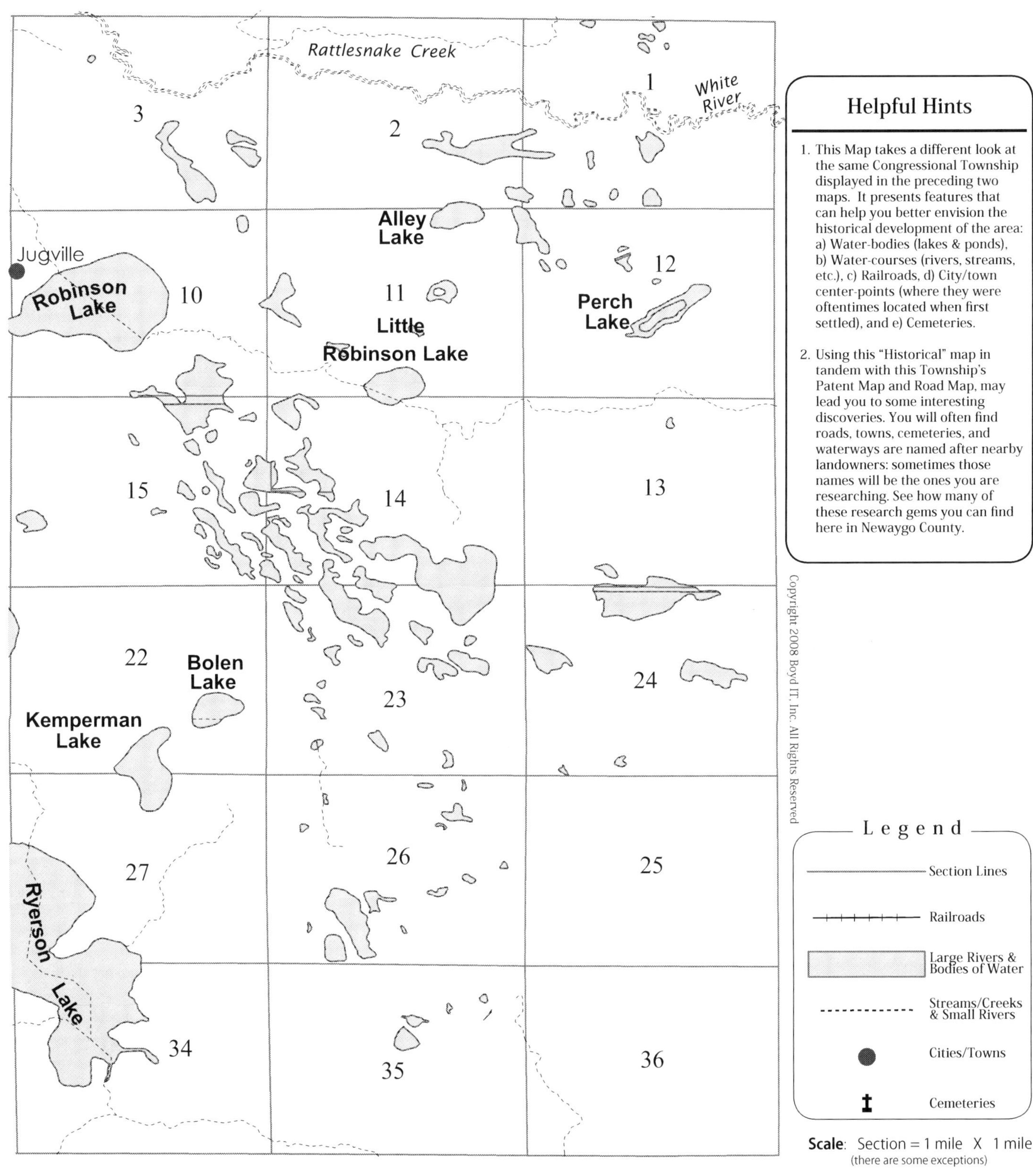

Helpful Hints

1. This Map takes a different look at the same Congressional Township displayed in the preceding two maps. It presents features that can help you better envision the historical development of the area: a) Water-bodies (lakes & ponds), b) Water-courses (rivers, streams, etc.), c) Railroads, d) City/town center-points (where they were oftentimes located when first settled), and e) Cemeteries.

2. Using this "Historical" map in tandem with this Township's Patent Map and Road Map, may lead you to some interesting discoveries. You will often find roads, towns, cemeteries, and waterways are named after nearby landowners: sometimes those names will be the ones you are researching. See how many of these research gems you can find here in Newaygo County.

Scale: Section = 1 mile X 1 mile
(there are some exceptions)

Map Group 15: Index to Land Patents

Township 13-North Range 12-West (Michigan-Toledo Strip)

After you locate an individual in this Index, take note of the Section and Section Part then proceed to the Land Patent map on the pages immediately following. You should have no difficulty locating the corresponding parcel of land.

The "For More Info" Column will lead you to more information about the underlying Patents. See the *Legend* at right, and the "How to Use this Book" chapter, for more information.

LEGEND

"For More Info . . . " column

A = Authority (Legislative Act, See Appendix "A")
B = Block or Lot (location in Section unknown)
C = Cancelled Patent
F = Fractional Section
G = Group (Multi-Patentee Patent, see Appendix "C")
V = Overlaps another Parcel
R = Re-Issued (Parcel patented more than once)

(A & G items require you to look in the Appendixes referred to above. All other Letter-designations followed by a number require you to locate line-items in this index that possess the ID number found after the letter).

ID	Individual in Patent	Sec.	Sec. Part	Date Issued	Other Counties	For More Info . . .
1928	ALLEY, George	6	N½NW	1866-11-10		A3 G21 F
1929	" "	8	SWNE	1866-11-10		A3 G22
1930	" "	8	W½SE	1866-11-10		A3 G22
1931	" "	4	SWNE	1867-01-10		A1 G23
1928	ALLEY, James	6	N½NW	1866-11-10		A3 G21 F
1929	" "	8	SWNE	1866-11-10		A3 G22
1930	" "	8	W½SE	1866-11-10		A3 G22
1931	" "	4	SWNE	1867-01-10		A1 G23
1928	ALLEY, Samuel M	6	N½NW	1866-11-10		A3 G21 F
1929	" "	8	SWNE	1866-11-10		A3 G22
1930	" "	8	W½SE	1866-11-10		A3 G22
1931	" "	4	SWNE	1867-01-10		A1 G23
1884	AVERY, Newell	18	W½SW	1872-11-06		A1 G83 F
1903	BADGEROW, Reuben	22	S½SW	1873-04-10		A4
1904	" "	22	SWSE	1873-04-10		A4
1856	BALDWIN, Joel A	13	E½SW	1858-05-01		A1
1857	" "	13	SWSW	1858-05-01		A1
1858	" "	15	NWNE	1859-10-10		A1
1859	BALL, John	15	SWNE	1855-03-01		A1
1860	" "	18	W½NW	1855-03-01		A1
1861	" "	3	SWSW	1855-03-01		A1
1862	" "	4	S½	1855-03-01		A1
1863	" "	6	S½NW	1855-03-01		A1
1864	" "	6	W½SW	1855-03-01		A1
1865	" "	7	E½NE	1855-03-01		A1
1866	" "	7	E½SE	1855-03-01		A1
1867	" "	7	W½NW	1855-03-01		A1
1868	" "	7	W½SW	1855-03-01		A1
1869	" "	8	W½	1855-03-01		A1
1870	" "	9	W½NE	1855-03-01		A1
1871	" "	9	W½SE	1855-03-01		A1
1954	BARRON, Mary	30	NWSE	1860-10-01		A3 G89
1955	" "	30	S½NE	1860-10-01		A3 G89
1807	BARTON, Charles	25	SWSE	1856-03-10		A1
1805	" "	25	NWSE	1857-03-10		A1
1806	" "	25	SESE	1857-03-10		A1
1910	BARTON, Samuel	36	NENE	1857-03-10		A1
1911	" "	36	NWNE	1857-03-10		A1
1912	BARTON, Samuel C	13	NESE	1852-03-10		A1
1928	BENNETT, William	6	N½NW	1866-11-10		A3 G21 F
1929	" "	8	SWNE	1866-11-10		A3 G22
1930	" "	8	W½SE	1866-11-10		A3 G22
1931	" "	4	SWNE	1867-01-10		A1 G23
1850	BESHER, Cornelia	17	NESW	1866-11-10		A3 G230
1851	" "	17	NWSE	1866-11-10		A3 G230
1852	" "	17	SENW	1866-11-10		A3 G230

ID	Individual in Patent	Sec.	Sec. Part	Date Issued	Other Counties	For More Info . . .
1853	BESHER, Cornelia (Cont'd)	17	SWNE	1866-11-10		A3 G230
1808	BIGELOW, Cyrus	21	SWSE	1855-12-15		A1
1811	BIGELOW, Czar J	33	NENW	1856-03-10		A1
1809	" "	28	NESW	1870-05-02		A4
1810	" "	28	SWSE	1870-05-02		A4
1830	BOWEN, Anson	2	E½SW	1869-09-10		A1 G54
1831	" "	2	N½SE	1869-09-10		A1 G54
1932	BOWEN, William	24	SWSE	1857-03-10		A1
1933	" "	25	E½NW	1857-03-10		A1
1934	" "	25	W½NE	1857-03-10		A1
1848	BUSH, James C	20	SWNW	1868-06-10		A1
1803	CALHOUN, Benjamin W	20	NE	1873-02-10		A4
1849	CAVENDAR, James	22	N½NE	1858-05-01		A1
1914	CHIPMAN, Samuel S	26	SW	1858-05-01		A1
1872	COLE, John	14	N½	1857-03-10		A1
1890	CONKWRIGHT, Lydia P	24	SESE	1855-11-01		A1
1913	CONKWRIGHT, Samuel	25	NESE	1857-03-10		A1
1837	COOK, Hiram	36	NW	1874-08-01		A4
1847	COOK, James B	13	SWSE	1856-03-10		A1
1802	COOLBAUGH, Benjamin H	34	SWNW	1869-11-30		A1
1855	CROFOOT, James P	28	N½SE	1893-01-07		A4
1899	CROFOOT, Ner	34	SESE	1857-03-10		A1
1900	" "	34	SWSE	1873-02-10		A4
1792	CROMAN, Abram	29	E½SW	1858-05-01		A1
1793	" "	29	W½SE	1858-05-01		A1
1935	DICKINSON, William	22	SESE	1857-03-10		A1
1936	" "	23	S½SW	1857-03-10		A1
1937	" "	23	SWSE	1857-03-10		A1
1938	" "	26	N½NW	1857-03-10		A1
1825	DOUGLASS, Everett	25	NWSW	1857-03-10		A1
1826	" "	25	SWNW	1857-03-10		A1
1827	" "	26	NE	1857-03-10		A1
1828	" "	26	NESE	1857-03-10		A1
1829	" "	26	NWSE	1857-03-10		A1
1830	" "	2	E½SW	1869-09-10		A1 G54
1831	" "	2	N½SE	1869-09-10		A1 G54
1838	DUNN, Hannah	8	E½NE	1868-02-10		A3 G166
1839	" "	8	E½SE	1868-02-10		A3 G166
1838	EASTMAN, George	8	E½NE	1868-02-10		A3 G166
1839	" "	8	E½SE	1868-02-10		A3 G166
1833	" "	8	NWNE	1869-09-10		A1
1881	FURGERSON, Joseph	25	E½SW	1857-03-10		A1
1882	" "	25	SWSW	1857-03-10		A1
1883	" "	26	S½SE	1857-03-10		A1
1920	GODFREY, Solomon	12	NESW	1856-03-10		A1
1919	" "	11	SESE	1857-03-10		A1
1921	" "	12	SENW	1857-03-10		A1
1922	" "	12	SWNW	1857-03-10		A1
1923	" "	12	W½SW	1857-03-10		A1
1794	GRAVES, Alfred	34	SENE	1870-05-02		A4
1834	GRAVES, Gideon D	32	NWSE	1865-10-10		A1
1901	GRAVES, Peter W	20	NESE	1876-05-15		A4
1902	" "	20	W½SE	1876-05-15		A4
1873	GROVESTEEN, John M	30	NENE	1873-05-15		A1
1791	HALL, Charlotte	31	W½NE	1861-11-01		A3 G91
1956	HARRIS, William J	14	W½SW	1857-03-10		A1
1957	" "	15	E½SE	1857-03-10		A1
1928	HASKELL, Nathaniel B	6	N½NW	1866-11-10		A3 G21 F
1929	" "	8	SWNE	1866-11-10		A3 G22
1930	" "	8	W½SE	1866-11-10		A3 G22
1931	" "	4	SWNE	1867-01-10		A1 G23
1884	HEALD, Joseph	18	W½SW	1872-11-06		A1 G83 F
1952	HEATH, Elizabeth	30	E½NW	1860-10-01		A3 G90 F
1953	" "	30	NESW	1860-10-01		A3 G90 F
1905	HEATON, Robert	23	E½NE	1857-03-10		A1
1906	" "	23	E½SE	1857-03-10		A1
1907	" "	24	N½NW	1857-03-10		A1
1908	" "	32	SESW	1866-06-05		A1
1926	HEATON, Thomas	12	SESW	1858-05-01		A1
1927	" "	13	N½NW	1858-05-01		A1
1878	HOWE, Johnson	21	SESW	1871-02-01		A4
1879	" "	28	E½NW	1871-02-01		A4
1880	" "	28	SWNW	1871-02-01		A4

ID	Individual in Patent	Sec.	Sec. Part	Date Issued	Other Counties	For More Info . . .
1940	HOWE, William	29	W½SW	1860-10-01		A3
1952	" "	30	E½NW	1860-10-01		A3 G90 F
1941	" "	30	NESE	1860-10-01		A3
1953	" "	30	NESW	1860-10-01		A3 G90 F
1954	" "	30	NWSE	1860-10-01		A3 G89
1955	" "	30	S½NE	1860-10-01		A3 G89
1942	" "	30	S½SE	1860-10-01		A3
1943	" "	30	SESW	1860-10-01		A3 F
1944	" "	30	W½SW	1860-10-01		A3 F
1946	" "	31	E½NW	1860-10-01		A3 F
1947	" "	31	NENE	1860-10-01		A3
1949	" "	31	W½NW	1860-10-01		A3 F
1945	" "	31	1	1861-12-05		A3
1948	" "	31	SENE	1861-12-05		A3
1950	" "	32	1	1861-12-05		A3
1951	" "	32	W½NW	1861-12-05		A3
1782	HUBBARD, Abel B	15	NWSW	1856-03-10		A1
1783	" "	15	SWNW	1856-03-10		A1
1784	" "	23	E½NW	1857-03-10		A1
1785	" "	23	W½NE	1857-03-10		A1
1786	HUBBARD, Abijah	28	SWSW	1858-05-01		A1
1787	" "	29	E½SE	1858-05-01		A1
1788	" "	31	W½SE	1858-05-01		A1 C
1789	" "	33	NWNW	1858-05-01		A1
1790	" "	33	SWNW	1861-04-01		A1
1791	" "	31	W½NE	1861-11-01		A3 G91
1898	KNOX, Charles A	7	W½NE	1866-09-01		A1 G220
1929	KONKEL, Jacob	8	SWNE	1866-11-10		A3 G22
1930	" "	8	W½SE	1866-11-10		A3 G22
1815	LAWRENCE, John	17	NWSW	1867-01-10		A1 G320
1816	" "	17	SWNW	1867-01-10		A1 G320
1817	" "	17	SWSE	1867-01-10		A1 G320
1799	LOGAN, Andrew	26	S½NW	1876-11-03		A4
1889	LOVELL, Louis S	15	NENW	1858-05-01		A1
1838	LULL, Hiram	8	E½NE	1868-02-10		A3 G166
1839	" "	8	E½SE	1868-02-10		A3 G166
1835	MANROW, Harry	21	NE	1858-05-01		A1
1874	MCBRIDE, John	1	NENW	1849-04-05		A1 F
1876	" "	2	SESE	1849-04-05		A1
1875	" "	1	SWNE	1850-04-01		A1
1891	MELANCON, Maise	1	NWNE	1849-04-05		A1
1845	MILLS, James A	13	NWSW	1857-03-10		A1
1846	" "	13	S½NW	1857-03-10		A1
1812	MONROE, Daniel S	29	SWNW	1863-12-05		A1
1813	" "	32	E½NW	1873-04-10		A4
1814	" "	32	N½NE	1873-04-10		A4
1909	MOORE, Robert	30	NWNE	1882-10-20		A4
1884	MURPHY, Simon J	18	W½SW	1872-11-06		A1 G83 F
1801	PADDOCK, Augustus	30	W½NW	1870-07-15		A1 F
1836	PALMER, Heman H	13	NWSE	1855-12-15		A1
1832	PEAK, Francis	15	W½SE	1857-03-10		A1
1915	PEARSON, Daniel K	4	SENE	1871-10-10		A1 G315
1795	PETERS, Alonson T	28	NE	1870-05-02		A4
1824	PIXLEY, Ephraim	20	SW	1874-02-20		A1
1898	PLATT, Nathan H	7	W½NE	1866-09-01		A1 G220
1800	PRATT, Angeline M	33	NWNE	1858-05-01		A1
1924	RANDOLPH, Theodore C	28	NWNW	1858-05-01		A1
1925	" "	29	NENE	1858-05-01		A1
1893	RAY, Mary E	34	NWSE	1890-02-04		A4
1894	" "	34	SENW	1890-02-04		A4
1895	" "	34	SWNE	1890-02-04		A4
1916	REED, Silvanus	21	NESW	1855-12-15		A1
1917	" "	36	SENE	1856-03-10		A1
1841	RIVERS, Israel	36	W½SW	1858-05-01		A1
1850	ROSS, James H	17	NESW	1866-11-10		A3 G230
1851	" "	17	NWSE	1866-11-10		A3 G230
1852	" "	17	SENW	1866-11-10		A3 G230
1853	" "	17	SWNE	1866-11-10		A3 G230
1850	SCHURCK, Morris B	17	NESW	1866-11-10		A3 G230
1851	" "	17	NWSE	1866-11-10		A3 G230
1852	" "	17	SENW	1866-11-10		A3 G230
1853	" "	17	SWNE	1866-11-10		A3 G230
1804	SHEAR, Calvin B	27	SE	1856-03-10		A1

ID	Individual in Patent	Sec.	Sec. Part	Date Issued	Other Counties	For More Info . . .
1939	SIBLEY, William H	4	NWNE	1871-10-10		A1 F
1958	SMITH, William	22	NW	1858-05-01		A1
1781	SWAIN, Aaron	1	NESE	1856-03-10		A1
1842	TERWILLIGER, Jacob A	22	NESE	1856-03-10		A1
1843	" "	22	S½NE	1856-03-10		A1
1844	" "	23	W½NW	1857-03-10		A1
1918	THAYER, Silvenus	15	E½NE	1857-03-10		A1
1877	TINKHAM, John T	20	SENW	1897-06-02		A1
1854	TURNER, James M	32	SENE	1872-04-05		A1
1818	UTLEY, Ephraim H	1	NESW	1856-03-10		A1
1823	" "	12	SWNE	1856-03-10		A1
1819	" "	1	NWSE	1857-03-10		A1
1820	" "	1	S½SE	1857-03-10		A1
1821	" "	12	N½NE	1857-03-10		A1
1822	" "	12	SENE	1857-03-10		A1
1840	VAN BRUNT, ISAAC	34	SW	1858-05-01		A1
1796	WHEELOCK, Alonzo A	15	S½SW	1858-01-15		A3
1797	" "	20	SESE	1858-01-15		A3
1798	" "	21	SWSW	1858-01-15		A3
1896	WHITE, Myron	23	N½SW	1857-03-10		A1
1897	" "	23	NWSE	1857-03-10		A1
1915	WILCOX, Sextus N	4	SENE	1871-10-10		A1 G315
1892	WILSON, Martin E	34	NESE	1858-05-01		A1
1815	WOOD, Eliphalet	17	NWSW	1867-01-10		A1 G320
1816	" "	17	SWNW	1867-01-10		A1 G320
1817	" "	17	SWSE	1867-01-10		A1 G320
1887	WOOD, Jotham	15	NESW	1856-03-10		A1
1888	" "	15	SENW	1856-03-10		A1
1885	" "	14	E½SW	1857-07-01		A1
1886	" "	14	SE	1857-07-01		A1

Patent Map

T13-N R12-W
Michigan-Toledo Strip Meridian

Map Group 15

Township Statistics

Parcels Mapped	:	178
Number of Patents	:	114
Number of Individuals	:	94
Patentees Identified	:	83
Number of Surnames	:	79
Multi-Patentee Parcels	:	23
Oldest Patent Date	:	4/5/1849
Most Recent Patent	:	6/2/1897
Block/Lot Parcels	:	2
Parcels Re - Issued	:	0
Parcels that Overlap	:	0
Cities and Towns	:	1
Cemeteries	:	2

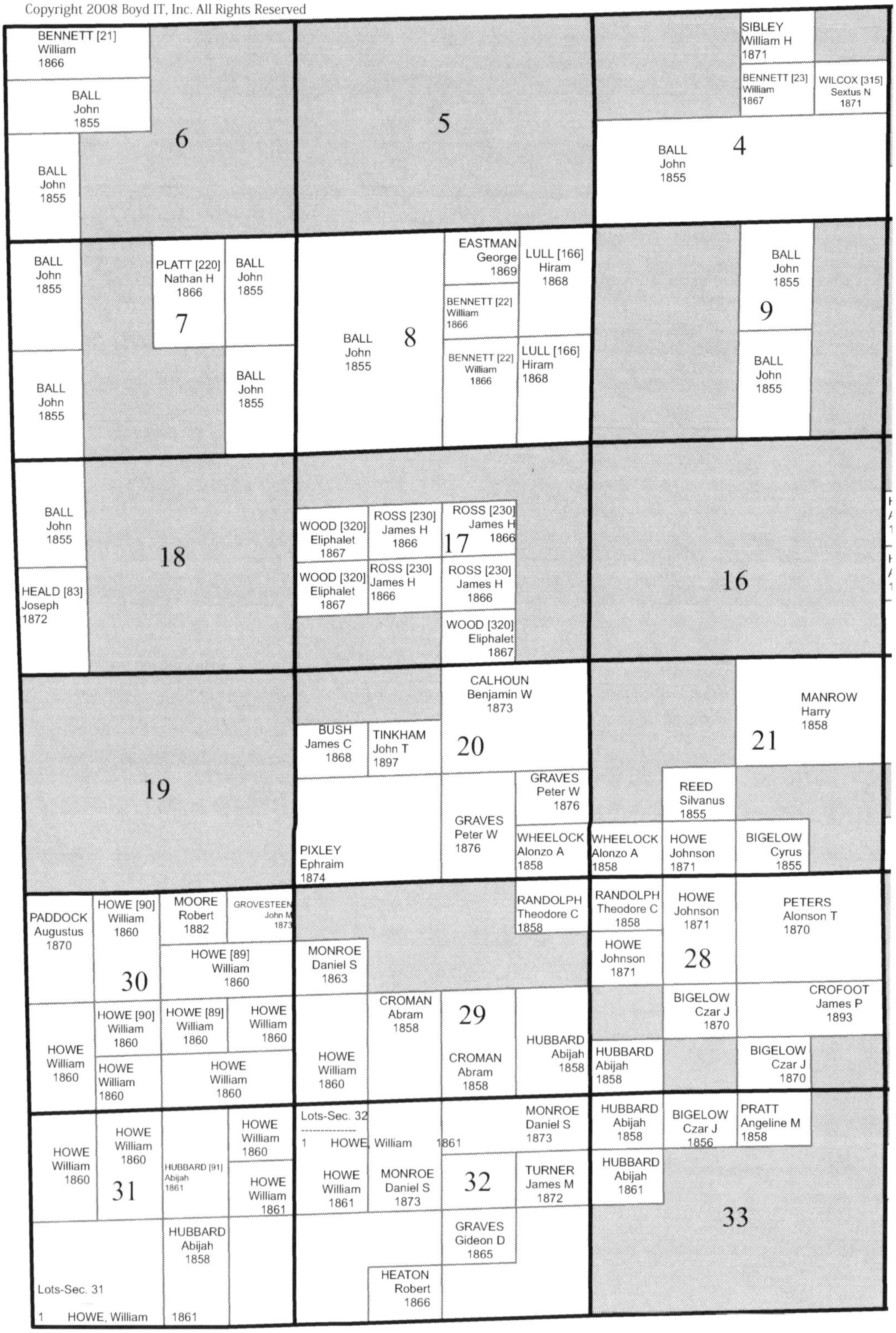

Helpful Hints

1. This Map's INDEX can be found on the preceding pages.
2. Refer to Map "C" to see where this Township lies within Newaygo County, Michigan.
3. Numbers within square brackets [ ] denote a multi-patentee land parcel (multi-owner). Refer to Appendix "C" for a full list of members in this group.
4. Areas that look to be crowded with Patentees usually indicate multiple sales of the same parcel (Re-issues) or Overlapping parcels. See this Township's Index for an explanation of these and other circumstances that might explain "odd" groupings of Patentees on this map.

Legend

- Patent Boundary
- Section Boundary
- No Patents Found (or Outside County)
- 1., 2., 3., ... Lot Numbers (when beside a name)
- [ ] Group Number (see Appendix "C")

Scale: Section = 1 mile X 1 mile (generally, with some exceptions)

Road Map

T13-N R12-W
Michigan-Toledo Strip Meridian

Map Group 15

Cities & Towns

White Cloud

Cemeteries

Big Prairie-Everett Cemetery
Prospect Hill Cemetery

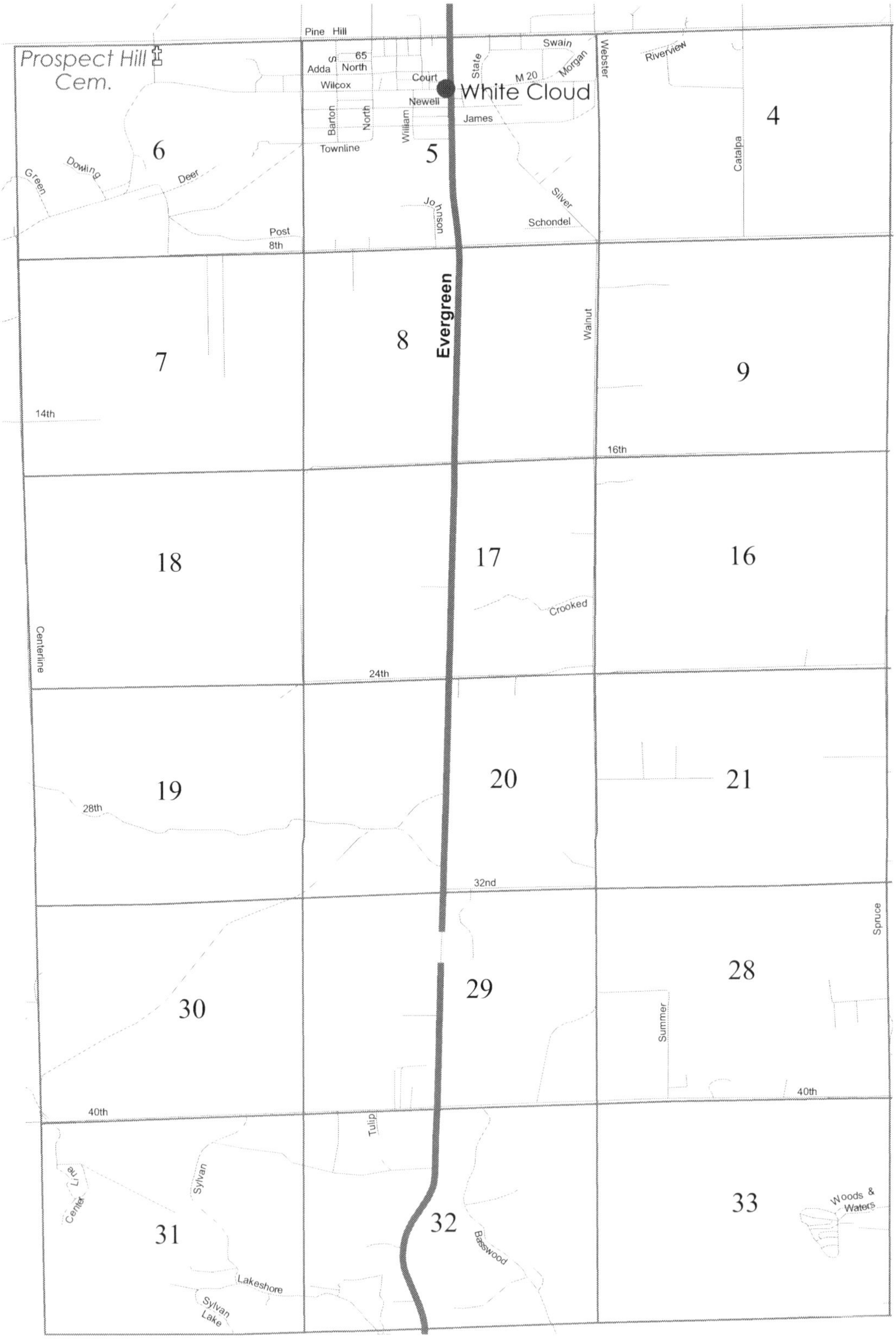

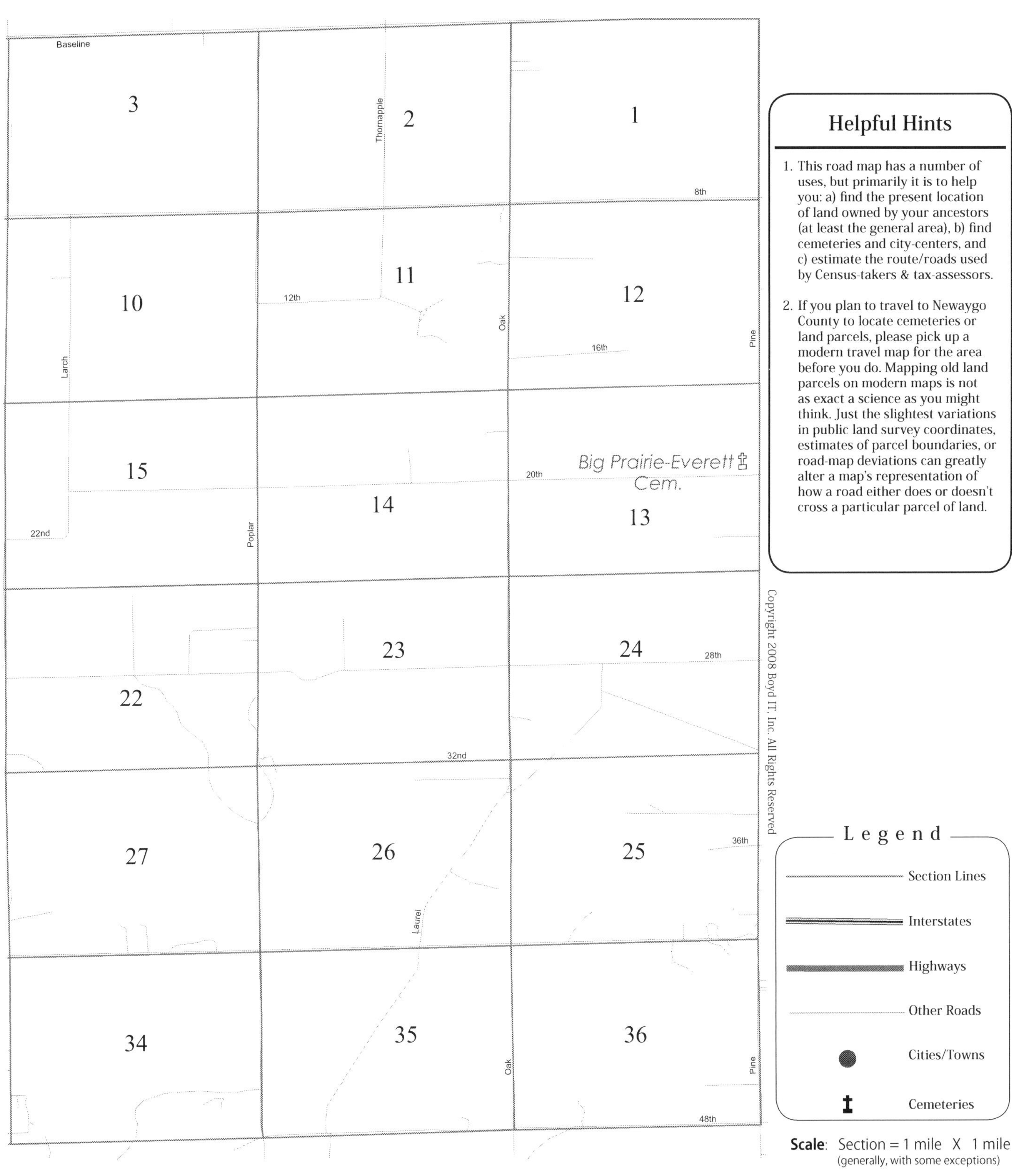
Baseline
3
Thornapple
2
1
8th
10
12th
11
Oak
12
16th
Pine
Larch
15
20th
Big Prairie-Everett Cem.
14
13
22nd
Poplar
23
24
28th
22
32nd
27
26
25
36th
Laurel
34
35
Oak
36
Pine
48th
Helpful Hints
1. This road map has a number of uses, but primarily it is to help you: a) find the present location of land owned by your ancestors (at least the general area), b) find cemeteries and city-centers, and c) estimate the route/roads used by Census-takers & tax-assessors.
2. If you plan to travel to Newaygo County to locate cemeteries or land parcels, please pick up a modern travel map for the area before you do. Mapping old land parcels on modern maps is not as exact a science as you might think. Just the slightest variations in public land survey coordinates, estimates of parcel boundaries, or road-map deviations can greatly alter a map's representation of how a road either does or doesn't cross a particular parcel of land.
Legend
Section Lines
Interstates
Highways
Other Roads
Cities/Towns
Cemeteries
Scale: Section = 1 mile X 1 mile
(generally, with some exceptions)

Historical Map

T13-N R12-W
Michigan-Toledo Strip Meridian

Map Group 15

Cities & Towns

White Cloud

Cemeteries

Big Prairie-Everett Cemetery
Prospect Hill Cemetery

Prospect Hill Cem.
White Cloud
Lake White Cloud
White River
Coolbough Creek
Twinwood Lake
Little Lake Placid
Sylvan Lake
Excelsior Lake

6 5 4
7 8 9
18 17 16
19 20 21
30 29 28
31 32 33

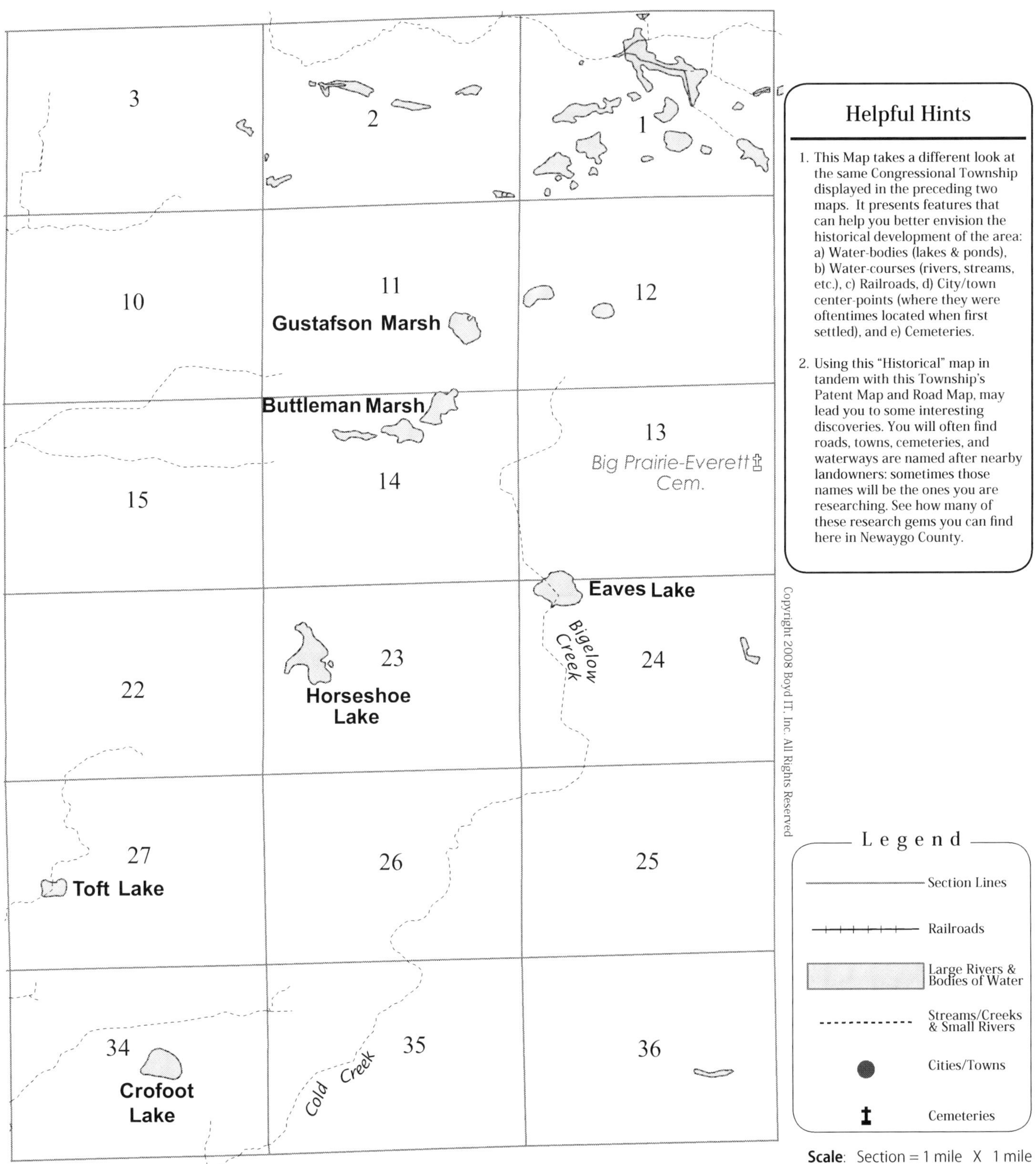
3
2
1
10
11
Gustafson Marsh
12
Buttleman Marsh
13
Big Prairie-Everett Cem.
15
14
Eaves Lake
Bigelow Creek
22
23
Horseshoe Lake
24
27
Toft Lake
26
25
34
Crofoot Lake
Cold Creek
35
36
Helpful Hints
1. This Map takes a different look at the same Congressional Township displayed in the preceding two maps. It presents features that can help you better envision the historical development of the area: a) Water-bodies (lakes & ponds), b) Water-courses (rivers, streams, etc.), c) Railroads, d) City/town center-points (where they were oftentimes located when first settled), and e) Cemeteries.
2. Using this "Historical" map in tandem with this Township's Patent Map and Road Map, may lead you to some interesting discoveries. You will often find roads, towns, cemeteries, and waterways are named after nearby landowners: sometimes those names will be the ones you are researching. See how many of these research gems you can find here in Newaygo County.
Legend
Section Lines
Railroads
Large Rivers & Bodies of Water
Streams/Creeks & Small Rivers
Cities/Towns
Cemeteries

Scale: Section = 1 mile X 1 mile
(there are some exceptions)

Map Group 16: Index to Land Patents

Township 13-North Range 11-West (Michigan-Toledo Strip)

After you locate an individual in this Index, take note of the Section and Section Part then proceed to the Land Patent map on the pages immediately following. You should have no difficulty locating the corresponding parcel of land.

The "For More Info" Column will lead you to more information about the underlying Patents. See the *Legend* at right, and the "How to Use this Book" chapter, for more information.

LEGEND

"For More Info . . . " column

A = Authority (Legislative Act, See Appendix "A")
B = Block or Lot (location in Section unknown)
C = Cancelled Patent
F = Fractional Section
G = Group (Multi-Patentee Patent, see Appendix "C")
V = Overlaps another Parcel
R = Re-Issued (Parcel patented more than once)

(A & G items require you to locate in the Appendixes referred to above. All other Letter-designations followed by a number require you to locate line-items in this index that possess the ID number found after the letter).

ID	Individual in Patent	Sec.	Sec. Part	Date Issued	Other Counties	For More Info . . .
2037	ALLEN, James	22	NWNE	1856-03-10		A1
2036	" "	15	6	1858-05-01		A1
2038	" "	22	SENW	1858-05-01		A1
2079	ALLERS, John H	4	SENE	1879-11-25		A4
2225	BALL, Daniel	12	3	1850-12-10		A1 G63
2226	" "	12	7	1850-12-10		A1 G63
2227	" "	24	2	1850-12-10		A1 G63
2228	" "	24	3	1850-12-10		A1 G63
1976	BARTON, Benjamin F	19	SWNW	1858-05-01		A1
2041	BARTON, James	17	NENW	1856-03-10		A1
2044	" "	8	SESW	1856-03-10		A1
2042	" "	28	NWNW	1858-05-01		A1
2043	" "	29	NENE	1858-05-01		A1
2045	" "	9	W½SW	1858-05-01		A1
2039	BARTON, James B	7	NESE	1856-03-10		A1
2040	" "	8	NWSW	1856-03-10		A1
2162	BARTON, Polly	19	NWNE	1852-11-01		A1
2172	BARTON, Samuel	31	NENW	1857-03-10		A1
2173	" "	31	NWNW	1857-03-10		A1 F
2230	BARTON, William	17	NENE	1856-03-10		A1
2231	" "	17	NWNE	1857-03-10		A1
2097	BATES, Joseph E	28	SWNW	1857-03-10		A1
1972	BONNEY, Alvah	29	NESE	1856-03-10		A1
2203	BONNEY, Walter	30	NESE	1854-10-05		A1
2204	BONNEY, Walter E	19	NWSE	1852-03-10		A1
2069	BRENNAN, John	32	6	1857-03-10		A1
2070	" "	32	NWNW	1857-03-10		A1
2068	BROOKS, John A	21	NESW	1857-03-10		A1
1998	BRUCE, Donald	31	SENW	1856-03-10		A1
2071	BUCK, John	22	NENE	1894-02-24		A4
2017	CARLISLE, Gamaliel	20	NWSE	1857-03-10		A1
1975	CARPENTER, Benjamin	34	NWNW	1868-02-15		A1
2077	CARPENTER, John G	29	1	1856-03-10		A1 R2087
2078	" "	32	5	1856-03-10		A1
2099	CARPENTER, Joseph W	32	1	1858-05-01		A1
2100	" "	32	2	1858-05-01		A1
2101	" "	33	1	1858-05-01		A1
2059	COLE, Jane E	19	NENW	1850-12-10		A1
2174	CONKWRIGHT, Samuel	19	SWSW	1854-09-15		A1 F
2150	COOK, Nelson P	2	NESW	1879-11-25		A4
2151	" "	2	NWSE	1879-11-25		A4
2152	" "	2	SENW	1879-11-25		A4
2153	" "	2	SWNE	1879-11-25		A4
1995	COOLEY, David R	34	SENW	1854-06-15		A1
2184	COULTER, John	14	E½SW	1871-02-20		A3 G75
2185	" "	14	W½SE	1871-02-20		A3 G75

ID	Individual in Patent	Sec.	Sec. Part	Date Issued	Other Counties	For More Info . . .
2046	CRABTREE, James	14	1	1878-06-13		A4
2047	" "	14	W½NW	1878-06-13		A4
2188	CULP, Christopher	32	4	1856-03-10		A1 G70
1982	DEAN, Charles R	10	NENE	1884-12-20		A4
2205	EASTMAN, Galen	12	SESE	1855-12-15		A1 G168
2206	" "	13	1	1855-12-15		A1 G168
2207	" "	14	SWSW	1855-12-15		A1 G168 F
2208	" "	22	5	1855-12-15		A1 G168
2209	" "	22	7	1855-12-15		A1 G168
2210	" "	22	8	1855-12-15		A1 G168
2211	" "	22	SENE	1855-12-15		A1 G168
2212	" "	23	3	1855-12-15		A1 G168
2213	" "	23	4	1855-12-15		A1 G168
2214	" "	23	5	1855-12-15		A1 G168 R1997
2215	" "	23	NESW	1855-12-15		A1 G168
2216	" "	23	NWSE	1855-12-15		A1 G168
2217	" "	23	SWNW	1855-12-15		A1 G168
2218	" "	27	NWNE	1855-12-15		A1 G168
2219	" "	27	NWNW	1855-12-15		A1 G168 F
2220	" "	28	2	1855-12-15		A1 G168
2221	" "	28	NENE	1855-12-15		A1 G168 F
2222	" "	28	SESE	1855-12-15		A1 G168
2223	" "	33	NESE	1855-12-15		A1 G168
2224	" "	34	NWSW	1855-12-15		A1 G168
2117	EASTMAN, George	1	3	1854-10-05		A1 G56
2118	" "	1	4	1854-10-05		A1 G56
2119	" "	1	SENW	1854-10-05		A1 G56
2120	" "	1	W½NW	1854-10-05		A1 G56 F
2121	" "	1	W½SW	1854-10-05		A1 G56
2122	" "	10	NWSE	1854-10-05		A1 G56
2123	" "	10	S½NE	1854-10-05		A1 G56
2124	" "	10	SESW	1854-10-05		A1 G56
2125	" "	11	1	1854-10-05		A1 G56
2126	" "	11	2	1854-10-05		A1 G56
2127	" "	11	E½NE	1854-10-05		A1 G56
2128	" "	11	N½NW	1854-10-05		A1 G56
2129	" "	11	NESW	1854-10-05		A1 G56
2130	" "	11	NWSE	1854-10-05		A1 G56
2131	" "	11	S½SW	1854-10-05		A1 G56
2132	" "	11	SWSE	1854-10-05		A1 G56
2133	" "	12	6	1854-10-05		A1 G56
2134	" "	14	E½NW	1854-10-05		A1 G56
2135	" "	14	NWNE	1854-10-05		A1 G56
2136	" "	15	3	1854-10-05		A1 G56
2137	" "	15	SENW	1854-10-05		A1 G56
2138	" "	2	E½NE	1854-10-05		A1 G56
2139	" "	2	E½SE	1854-10-05		A1 G56
2140	" "	2	SESW	1854-10-05		A1 G56
2141	" "	2	SWSE	1854-10-05		A1 G56
2018	" "	12	SWSW	1855-12-15		A1 G55 F
2117	EASTMAN, Mason	1	3	1854-10-05		A1 G56
2118	" "	1	4	1854-10-05		A1 G56
2119	" "	1	SENW	1854-10-05		A1 G56
2120	" "	1	W½NW	1854-10-05		A1 G56 F
2121	" "	1	W½SW	1854-10-05		A1 G56
2122	" "	10	NWSE	1854-10-05		A1 G56
2123	" "	10	S½NE	1854-10-05		A1 G56
2124	" "	10	SESW	1854-10-05		A1 G56
2125	" "	11	1	1854-10-05		A1 G56
2126	" "	11	2	1854-10-05		A1 G56
2127	" "	11	E½NE	1854-10-05		A1 G56
2128	" "	11	N½NW	1854-10-05		A1 G56
2129	" "	11	NESW	1854-10-05		A1 G56
2130	" "	11	NWSE	1854-10-05		A1 G56
2131	" "	11	S½SW	1854-10-05		A1 G56
2132	" "	11	SWSE	1854-10-05		A1 G56
2133	" "	12	6	1854-10-05		A1 G56
2134	" "	14	E½NW	1854-10-05		A1 G56
2135	" "	14	NWNE	1854-10-05		A1 G56
2136	" "	15	3	1854-10-05		A1 G56
2137	" "	15	SENW	1854-10-05		A1 G56
2138	" "	2	E½NE	1854-10-05		A1 G56
2139	" "	2	E½SE	1854-10-05		A1 G56

ID	Individual in Patent	Sec.	Sec. Part	Date Issued	Other Counties	For More Info . . .
2140	EASTMAN, Mason (Cont'd)	2	SESW	1854-10-05		A1 G56
2141	" "	2	SWSE	1854-10-05		A1 G56
2200	EASTMAN, Timothy	21	1	1855-12-15		A1
2201	" "	21	2	1855-12-15		A1
2202	" "	21	N½NW	1855-12-15		A1
2186	EDGCOMB, Silas	22	1	1883-03-10		A4
2187	" "	22	2	1883-03-10		A4
2233	EHLE, William	14	NENE	1879-11-25		A4
1980	EVANS, Bennoni	31	SESW	1850-12-10		A1
2199	FERRY, George F	26	NWSE	1852-11-01		A1 G61
2199	FERRY, Thomas G	26	NWSE	1852-11-01		A1 G61
2225	FOSTER, Wilder D	12	3	1850-12-10		A1 G63
2226	" "	12	7	1850-12-10		A1 G63
2227	" "	24	2	1850-12-10		A1 G63
2228	" "	24	3	1850-12-10		A1 G63
2098	FRANKLIN, Joseph	36	SW	1878-06-13		A4
2024	FRENCH, Henry	17	SWNE	1857-03-10		A1
2198	FRENCH, Susan	17	NWSE	1857-03-10		A1
1983	GAUWEILER, Frederick	26	NWSW	1852-11-01		A1 G112 C R2189
2050	GIBBS, James M	24	NWNW	1853-08-01		A1 F
2182	GLAZIER, Dexter P	4	SESE	1860-05-15		A3 G342
2183	" "	9	NENE	1860-05-15		A3 G342
2033	GODFREY, Isaac W	30	W½SW	1857-07-01		A1 F
2188	GODFREY, Solomon	32	4	1856-03-10		A1 G70
1999	GOODRICH, Egbertson	10	SESE	1854-06-15		A1
2000	" "	6	SENW	1856-03-10		A1 F
1974	HAIGHT, Ambrose	9	N½SE	1859-10-10		A1
2007	HAINES, Frank B	10	NESW	1876-01-20		A4
2008	" "	10	SWNW	1876-01-20		A4
2009	" "	10	W½SW	1876-01-20		A4
2184	HALCOMB, Seth	14	E½SW	1871-02-20		A3 G75
2185	" "	14	W½SE	1871-02-20		A3 G75
1973	HALL, Ambrose G	4	NESE	1860-09-01		A1
2013	HALL, Frederick	21	3	1856-03-10		A1
2107	HALL, Jotham	6	NESE	1861-12-10		A1
2014	HERTZER, G A	10	N½NW	1878-06-13		A4
2015	" "	10	NWNE	1878-06-13		A4
2016	" "	10	SENW	1878-06-13		A4
2106	HINDS, Michael	26	SENW	1852-03-10		A1 G271
2112	HOOKER, Lois M	12	2	1879-11-25		A4 R2114
2113	" "	12	SWNE	1879-11-25		A4 F
2114	HOOPER, Lois M	12	2	1877-11-20		A4 C R2112
2115	" "	12	SENW	1877-11-20		A4 C F
1991	HOUGHTON, David	3	E½SW	1874-04-10		A4
1992	" "	3	W½SE	1874-04-10		A4
1983	KAUFMAN, Christopher	26	NWSW	1852-11-01		A1 G112 C R2189
1986	KEENEY, Daniel	30	SWNW	1856-03-10		A1 F
2019	KENDALL, George	2	NWNW	1857-02-20		A3 F
2232	KIDD, William E	24	4	1868-02-15		A1 G113 F
2034	KIEFFER, Jacob	10	SWSE	1895-06-24		A4
2240	KIMBALL, William	20	S½SE	1855-12-15		A1
2241	" "	20	SESW	1855-12-15		A1
1981	LAFFERTY, Charles E	14	SESE	1883-09-15		A4
2242	LASLEY, William	34	NWNE	1852-03-10		A1
2234	LAVERTY, William H	30	E½NW	1857-03-10		A1
2243	LE BARON, WILLIAM	22	4	1879-11-10		A4
2244	" "	22	SWNE	1879-11-10		A4
2245	LE BARRON, WILLIAM	22	NENW	1880-11-20		A1
2028	LEWIS, Hiram	2	NENW	1875-10-20		A4
2029	" "	2	NWNE	1875-10-20		A4
2116	LOVELL, Louis S	8	S½SE	1857-02-20		A3
2179	LULL, Hiram	26	W½NW	1858-05-01		A1 G190
2180	" "	27	E½NE	1858-05-01		A1 G190
2205	LULL, Walter	12	SESE	1855-12-15		A1 G168
2206	" "	13	1	1855-12-15		A1 G168
2207	" "	14	SWSW	1855-12-15		A1 G168 F
2208	" "	22	5	1855-12-15		A1 G168
2209	" "	22	7	1855-12-15		A1 G168
2210	" "	22	8	1855-12-15		A1 G168
2211	" "	22	SENE	1855-12-15		A1 G168
2212	" "	23	3	1855-12-15		A1 G168
2213	" "	23	4	1855-12-15		A1 G168
2214	" "	23	5	1855-12-15		A1 G168 R1997

ID	Individual in Patent	Sec.	Sec. Part	Date Issued	Other Counties	For More Info . . .
2215	LULL, Walter (Cont'd)	23	NESW	1855-12-15		A1 G168
2216	" "	23	NWSE	1855-12-15		A1 G168
2217	" "	23	SWNW	1855-12-15		A1 G168
2218	" "	27	NWNE	1855-12-15		A1 G168
2219	" "	27	NWNW	1855-12-15		A1 G168 F
2220	" "	28	2	1855-12-15		A1 G168
2221	" "	28	NENE	1855-12-15		A1 G168 F
2222	" "	28	SESE	1855-12-15		A1 G168
2223	" "	33	NESE	1855-12-15		A1 G168
2224	" "	34	NWSW	1855-12-15		A1 G168
2054	LYONS, James O	4	N½NE	1854-06-15		A1 F
2055	" "	4	N½NW	1854-06-15		A1 F
2056	" "	5	NENE	1854-06-15		A1 F
2083	MCBRIDE, John	5	NWSE	1850-12-10		A1
2018	MCCAB, Owen	12	SWSW	1855-12-15		A1 G55 F
1964	MCCALL, Martha R	9	S½NE	1859-08-10		A3 G279
1965	" "	9	SENW	1859-08-10		A3 G279
2084	MCNIEL, John	36	S½SE	1879-11-25		A4
2085	MEIER, John	2	SWNW	1879-11-25		A4
2086	" "	2	W½SW	1879-11-25		A4
2189	MICHIGAN, State Of	26	NWSW	1951-05-25		A6 R1983
2048	MILES, James H	6	W½NW	1855-12-15		A1 G187 F
2049	" "	8	NENE	1855-12-15		A1 G187
2048	MILES, William	6	W½NW	1855-12-15		A1 G187 F
2049	" "	8	NENE	1855-12-15		A1 G187
2171	MITCHELL, Robert L	12	4	1858-05-01		A1
2177	MITCHELL, Samuel S	24	NESE	1856-03-10		A1
2178	" "	24	W½SE	1856-03-10		A1
2176	" "	13	2	1858-05-01		A1
2179	" "	26	W½NW	1858-05-01		A1 G190
2180	" "	27	E½NE	1858-05-01		A1 G190
1985	MOE, Craig B	21	SWSW	1856-03-10		A1
1984	" "	21	NWSW	1857-03-10		A1
2060	MORRISON, Jefferson	22	6	1854-10-05		A1
2061	" "	23	W½SW	1855-12-15		A1
2064	" "	26	E½NE	1855-12-15		A1
2065	" "	26	NESE	1855-12-15		A1
2062	" "	25	E½NW	1859-08-10		A3
2063	" "	25	W½NE	1859-08-10		A3
2087	MURRY, John	29	1	1856-03-10		A1 C R2077
2088	" "	31	SESE	1859-10-10		A1
2089	" "	32	9	1859-10-10		A1
2090	" "	32	S½SW	1859-10-10		A1
2157	NEVILLE, Patrick	30	S½SE	1856-03-10		A1
2158	" "	31	N½NE	1856-03-10		A1
2091	ONEIL, John	29	E½NW	1858-05-01		A1
2092	" "	29	NWNE	1858-05-01		A1
2144	ONEIL, Michael	4	SWNW	1859-10-10		A1
2145	" "	4	W½SW	1859-10-10		A1
2156	PAGE, Ozro N	29	SWNE	1858-05-01		A1
2190	PAGE, Stephen F	21	S½SE	1858-05-01		A1 F
2184	PRESTON, David	14	E½SW	1871-02-20		A3 G75
2185	" "	14	W½SE	1871-02-20		A3 G75
2175	PRUYN, Samuel	28	8	1856-03-10		A1
2066	RHYAN, Jeremiah	34	NENE	1852-03-10		A1 C
1996	RICE, David	34	NENW	1868-02-15		A1
2246	" "	36	N½SE	1868-06-10		A1 G225
2246	RICE, William	36	N½SE	1868-06-10		A1 G225
1979	ROGERS, Benjamin	6	NWNE	1860-10-01		A1 F
1978	" "	6	NENW	1865-10-10		A1 F
2146	RONAN, Michael	32	8	1856-03-10		A1
2159	RONAN, Patrick	31	S½NE	1857-03-10		A1
2032	ROSS, Hugh	32	3	1856-03-10		A1 C R1993
2147	ROWAN, Michael	31	NESE	1854-09-15		A1
2149	" "	32	NWSW	1854-09-15		A1
2148	" "	32	7	1857-07-01		A1
2067	RYAN, Jeremiah	34	SENE	1854-06-15		A1
2108	SAIEN, Lisidor	25	SESE	1859-08-10		A3
2109	" "	36	NENE	1859-08-10		A3
2110	" "	36	SENE	1859-08-10		A3
2111	" "	36	W½NE	1859-08-10		A3
1997	SAPP, Dexter T	23	5	1868-02-15		A1 F R2214
2232	" "	24	4	1868-02-15		A1 G113 F

ID	Individual in Patent	Sec.	Sec. Part	Date Issued	Other Counties	For More Info . . .
2048	SAUNDERS, Isaac M	6	W½NW	1855-12-15		A1 G187 F
2049	" "	8	NENE	1855-12-15		A1 G187
2026	SAVERCOOL, Henry	30	E½SW	1857-03-10		A1 F
2163	SAXTON, Reuben	25	E½NE	1856-03-10		A1
1969	SEELEY, Alexander M	20	W½NE	1856-03-10		A1
1968	" "	20	E½NW	1857-03-10		A1
2229	SHERMAN, William B	19	NWSW	1852-03-10		A1 F
2250	SHORTER, William	10	NESE	1903-01-31		A4
2022	SLADE, Harvey M	17	NESW	1856-03-10		A1
2023	" "	17	SWSE	1856-03-10		A1
2197	SLADE, Susan E	17	SESW	1855-12-15		A1
2010	SMITH, Franklin	28	7	1854-10-05		A1
2011	" "	28	9	1854-10-05		A1
2025	SMITH, Henry S	5	W½SW	1854-09-15		A1
2053	SMITH, James M	5	SENE	1856-03-10		A1
2051	" "	4	SESW	1860-06-01		A1
2052	" "	4	SWSE	1860-06-01		A1
2252	SMITH, William	34	SWSE	1871-11-01		A4
2251	" "	28	4	1880-03-05		A1
1971	SPENCER, Alva	31	SWSE	1853-11-01		A1
2235	SPES, William H	4	NESW	1860-06-01		A1
2236	" "	4	NWSE	1860-06-01		A1
2237	" "	4	SENW	1860-06-01		A1
2238	" "	4	SWNE	1860-06-01		A1
1970	STANLEY, Almond M	19	SENE	1854-06-15		A1
2106	STINGEL, Jost	26	SENW	1852-03-10		A1 G271
1987	SUTHERLAND, Daniel V	6	NENE	1880-11-20		A1 F
1988	" "	6	NWSE	1880-11-20		A1
1989	" "	6	S½NE	1880-11-20		A1
1963	SWAIN, Aaron	7	SWNW	1850-12-10		A1 F
1961	" "	6	W½SW	1856-03-10		A1
1962	" "	7	NWNW	1856-03-10		A1 F
1959	" "	20	NESW	1858-05-01		A1
1964	" "	9	S½NE	1859-08-10		A3 G279
1965	" "	9	SENW	1859-08-10		A3 G279
1960	" "	6	E½SW	1859-10-10		A1
2080	SWARTWOUT, John H	27	NESW	1854-09-15		A1
2081	" "	27	NWSE	1854-09-15		A1
2082	" "	35	N½SW	1854-09-15		A1
2247	SWITZER, William S	33	NENE	1856-03-10		A1
2003	TERRY, Emily	30	N½NE	1857-03-10		A1
2073	TIFT, John D	13	3	1859-10-10		A1
2074	" "	13	4	1859-10-10		A1
2075	" "	13	SENW	1859-10-10		A1
2076	" "	13	SWNE	1859-10-10		A1
2072	" "	12	5	1865-10-10		A1
2253	TIFT, William	23	6	1855-12-15		A1
2154	TOWER, Osmond S	12	1	1871-11-15		A1 R2035
2155	" "	24	5	1871-11-15		A1 F
1966	TOWNE, Albert	26	NENW	1907-04-17		A4
2160	TRACY, Philander	1	SESE	1859-10-10		A1
2161	" "	12	E½NE	1859-10-10		A1
1977	TRASK, Benjamin F	20	NESE	1857-03-10		A1
2035	TRIPP, Jairus W	12	1	1870-05-10		A1 R2154
2001	TRUFONT, Emery	24	E½SW	1871-11-15		A1
2002	" "	24	SWSW	1871-11-15		A1
2239	TUBBS, William H	30	S½NE	1857-03-10		A1
1993	TUCKER, David N	32	3	1858-05-01		A1 R2032
1994	" "	33	NWSW	1858-05-01		A1
2093	TUCKER, John	33	SESE	1859-10-10		A1
2094	" "	34	S½SW	1859-10-10		A1
2004	UTLEY, Ephraim H	15	4	1854-09-15		A1
2020	UTLEY, George	8	NENW	1854-09-15		A1
2027	UTLEY, Henry	7	E½NE	1854-09-15		A1
2181	UTLEY, Sarah	7	W½SW	1850-04-01		A1 F
2248	UTLEY, William S	7	NENW	1856-03-10		A1
2249	" "	7	NWNE	1856-03-10		A1
2021	WART, Gilbert M	31	SWNW	1857-07-01		A1 F
2030	WATERS, Hiram	20	NENE	1856-03-10		A1
2031	" "	20	SENE	1856-03-10		A1
2195	WATERS, Stephen	29	SWNW	1854-09-15		A1
2192	" "	21	NE	1856-03-10		A1 F
2193	" "	21	SENW	1856-03-10		A1

ID	Individual in Patent	Sec.	Sec. Part	Date Issued	Other Counties	For More Info . . .
2194	WATERS, Stephen (Cont'd)	21	SWNW	1856-03-10		A1
2191	" "	15	5	1858-05-01		A1
2096	WEBSTER, John	22	NWNW	1854-09-15		A1 F
2095	" "	11	NWNE	1856-03-10		A1
2166	WEBSTER, Rila	21	SESW	1856-03-10		A1
2169	" "	28	NENW	1856-03-10		A1
2164	" "	21	4	1858-05-01		A1 F
2165	" "	21	NWSE	1858-05-01		A1 F
2167	" "	28	5	1858-05-01		A1
2168	" "	28	6	1858-05-01		A1
2170	" "	28	SENW	1858-05-01		A1 F
2005	WEIDMAN, Evan	24	1	1876-01-05		A4
2006	" "	24	S½NE	1876-01-05		A4
1967	WESTGATE, Alden	19	SESW	1856-03-10		A1 F
2057	WHITE, James	29	E½SW	1858-05-01		A1
2058	" "	29	W½SE	1858-05-01		A1
2142	WHITE, Mathew	3	N½NW	1859-10-10		A1 F
2143	" "	3	SENW	1859-10-10		A1 F
1990	WHITNEY, David H	34	NESW	1868-02-15		A1
2196	WILSON, Stephen	20	W½SW	1854-06-15		A1
2182	WOOD, Sarell	4	SESE	1860-05-15		A3 G342
2183	" "	9	NENE	1860-05-15		A3 G342
2102	YERKES, Joseph	13	7	1856-03-10		A1
2103	" "	13	8	1856-03-10		A1
2104	" "	9	NWNE	1856-03-10		A1
2105	" "	9	SWNW	1856-03-10		A1
2012	YOUNG, Frederick H	24	NENE	1873-05-15		A1

Patent Map

T13-N R11-W
Michigan-Toledo Strip Meridian

Map Group 16

Township Statistics

Parcels Mapped	:	295
Number of Patents	:	205
Number of Individuals	:	157
Patentees Identified	:	145
Number of Surnames	:	120
Multi-Patentee Parcels	:	66
Oldest Patent Date	:	4/1/1850
Most Recent Patent	:	5/25/1951
Block/Lot Parcels	:	65
Parcels Re - Issued	:	6
Parcels that Overlap	:	0
Cities and Towns	:	4
Cemeteries	:	0

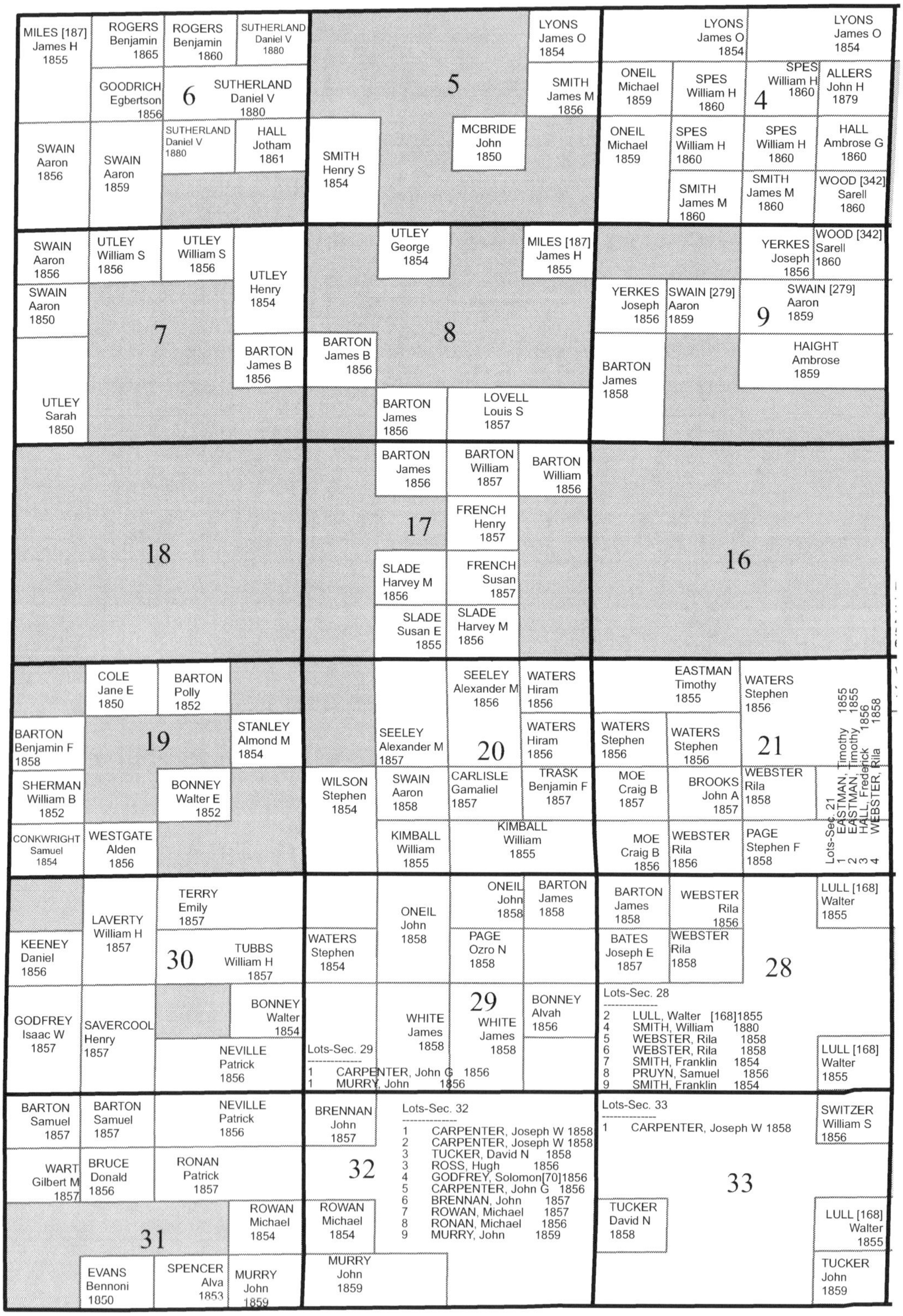

Helpful Hints

1. This Map's INDEX can be found on the preceding pages.
2. Refer to Map "C" to see where this Township lies within Newaygo County, Michigan.
3. Numbers within square brackets [ ] denote a multi-patentee land parcel (multi-owner). Refer to Appendix "C" for a full list of members in this group.
4. Areas that look to be crowded with Patentees usually indicate multiple sales of the same parcel (Re-issues) or Overlapping parcels. See this Township's Index for an explanation of these and other circumstances that might explain "odd" groupings of Patentees on this map.

Legend

- Patent Boundary
- Section Boundary
- No Patents Found (or Outside County)
- 1., 2., 3., ... Lot Numbers (when beside a name)
- [ ] Group Number (see Appendix "C")

Scale: Section = 1 mile X 1 mile (generally, with some exceptions)

Road Map

T13-N R11-W
Michigan-Toledo Strip Meridian

Map Group 16

Cities & Towns

Big Bend
Big Prairie
Oxbow
Oxbow Park

Cemeteries

None

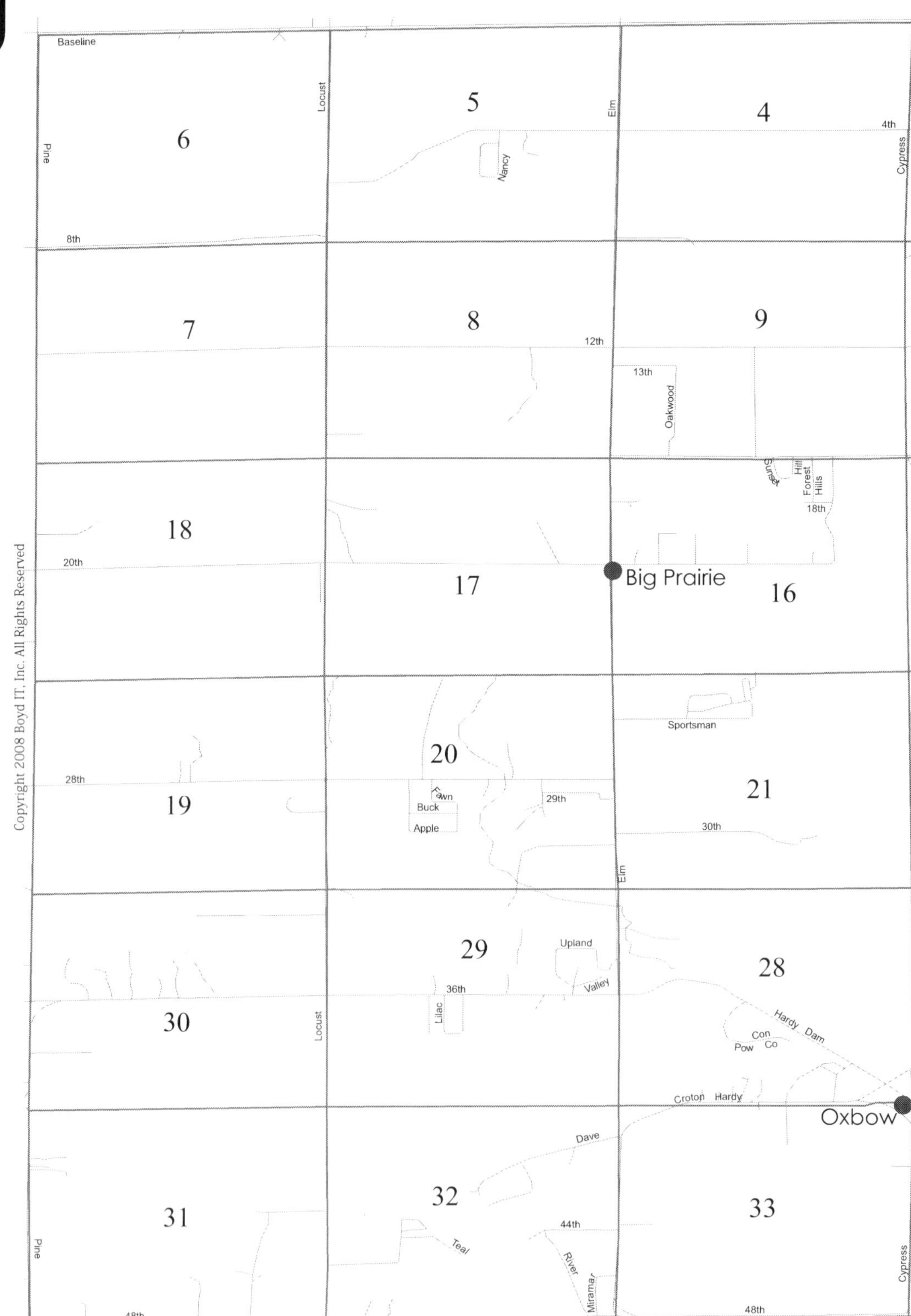

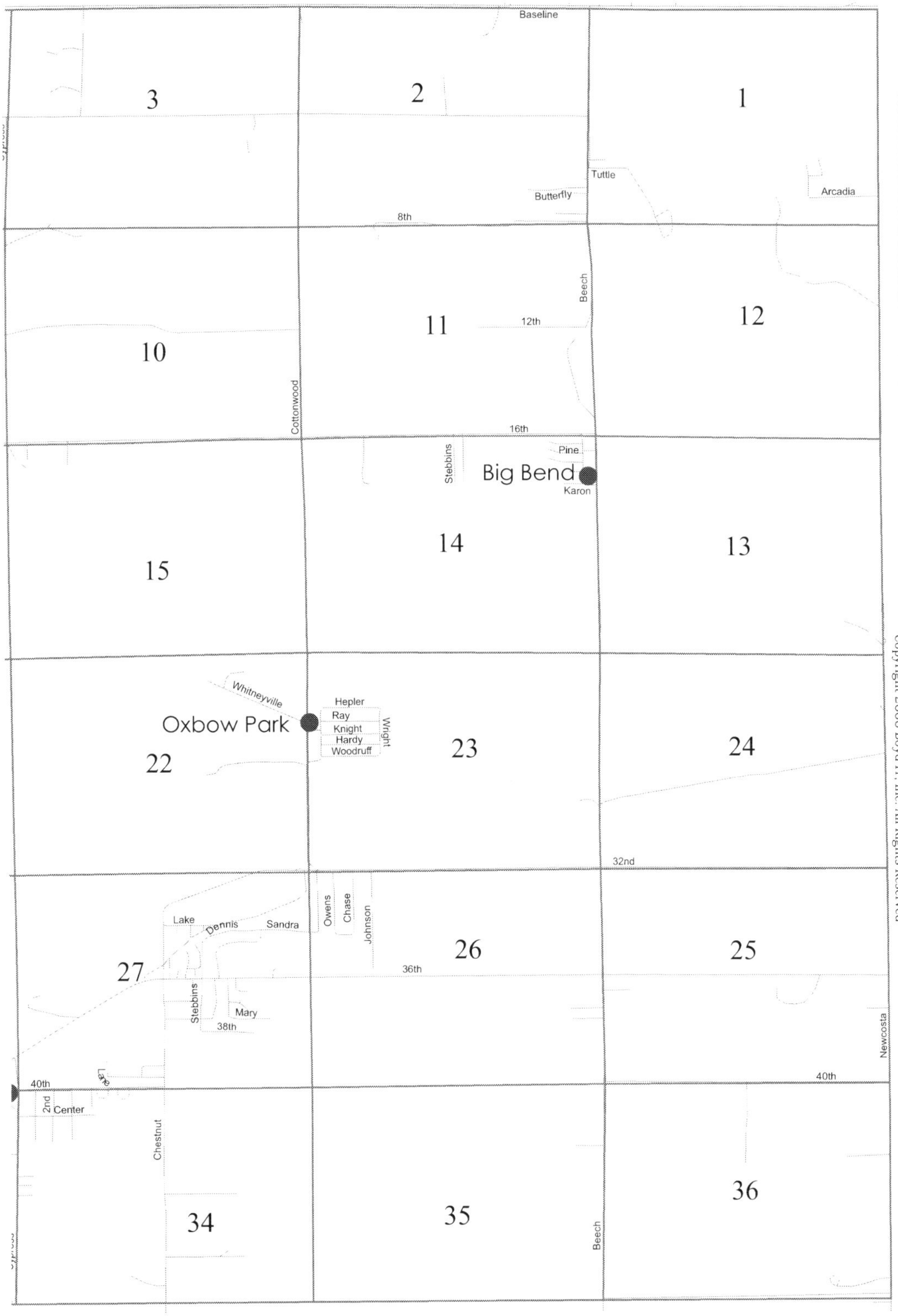

Baseline
3
2
1
Tuttle
Butterfly
Arcadia
8th
Beech
11
12th
12
10
Cottonwood
16th
Pine
Stebbins
Big Bend
Karon
14
13
15
Whitneyville
Oxbow Park
Hepler
Ray
Knight
Hardy
Woodruff
Wright
23
24
22
32nd
Lake
Dennis
Sandra
Owens
Chase
Johnson
26
25
27
36th
Stebbins
Mary
38th
Newcosta
40th
Lake
40th
2nd
Center
Chestnut
36
34
35
Beech

Helpful Hints

1. This road map has a number of uses, but primarily it is to help you: a) find the present location of land owned by your ancestors (at least the general area), b) find cemeteries and city-centers, and c) estimate the route/roads used by Census-takers & tax-assessors.

2. If you plan to travel to Newaygo County to locate cemeteries or land parcels, please pick up a modern travel map for the area before you do. Mapping old land parcels on modern maps is not as exact a science as you might think. Just the slightest variations in public land survey coordinates, estimates of parcel boundaries, or road-map deviations can greatly alter a map's representation of how a road either does or doesn't cross a particular parcel of land.

Legend
Section Lines
Interstates
Highways
Other Roads
Cities/Towns
Cemeteries

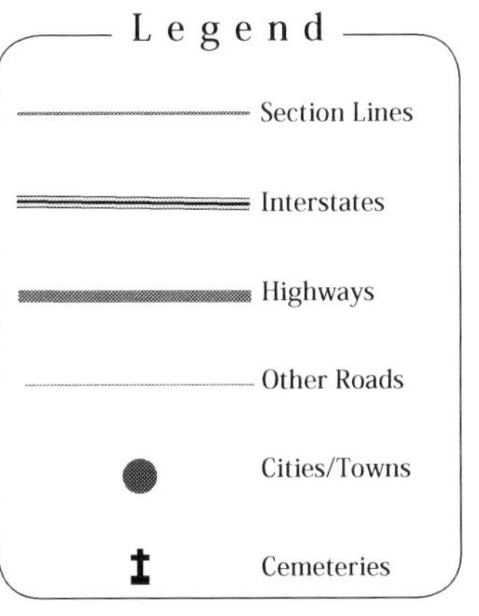

Scale: Section = 1 mile X 1 mile
(generally, with some exceptions)

Historical Map

T13-N R11-W
Michigan-Toledo Strip Meridian

Map Group 16

Cities & Towns

- Big Bend
- Big Prairie
- Oxbow
- Oxbow Park

Cemeteries

None

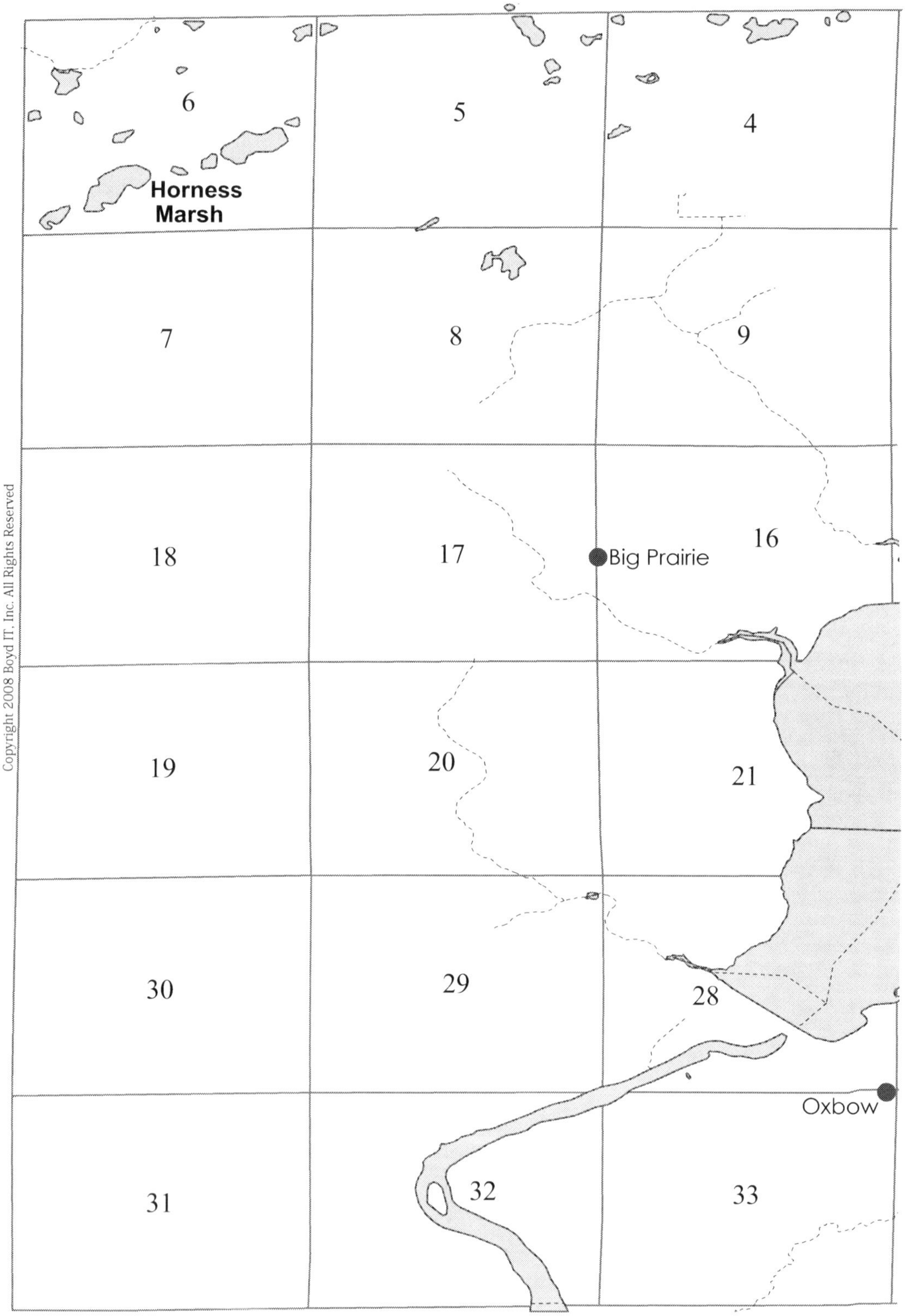

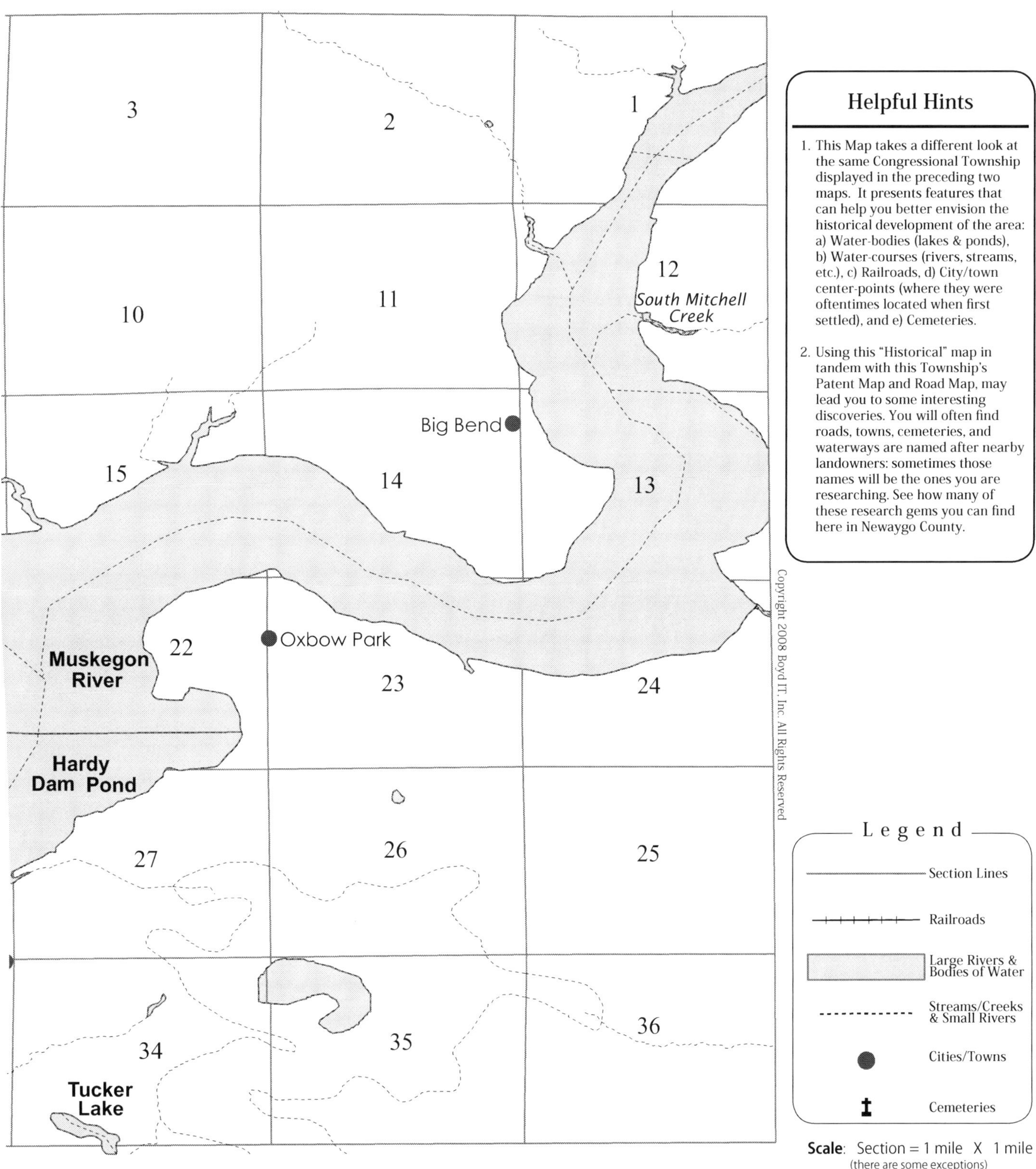

Helpful Hints

1. This Map takes a different look at the same Congressional Township displayed in the preceding two maps. It presents features that can help you better envision the historical development of the area: a) Water-bodies (lakes & ponds), b) Water-courses (rivers, streams, etc.), c) Railroads, d) City/town center-points (where they were oftentimes located when first settled), and e) Cemeteries.

2. Using this "Historical" map in tandem with this Township's Patent Map and Road Map, may lead you to some interesting discoveries. You will often find roads, towns, cemeteries, and waterways are named after nearby landowners: sometimes those names will be the ones you are researching. See how many of these research gems you can find here in Newaygo County.

Legend

- Section Lines
- Railroads
- Large Rivers & Bodies of Water
- Streams/Creeks & Small Rivers
- Cities/Towns
- Cemeteries

Scale: Section = 1 mile X 1 mile
(there are some exceptions)

Map Group 17: Index to Land Patents

Township 12-North Range 14-West (Michigan-Toledo Strip)

After you locate an individual in this Index, take note of the Section and Section Part then proceed to the Land Patent map on the pages immediately following. You should have no difficulty locating the corresponding parcel of land.

The "For More Info" Column will lead you to more information about the underlying Patents. See the *Legend* at right, and the "How to Use this Book" chapter, for more information.

LEGEND

"For More Info . . . " column

A = Authority (Legislative Act, See Appendix "A")
B = Block or Lot (location in Section unknown)
C = Cancelled Patent
F = Fractional Section
G = Group (Multi-Patentee Patent, see Appendix "C")
V = Overlaps another Parcel
R = Re-Issued (Parcel patented more than once)

(A & G items require you to look in the Appendixes referred to above. All other Letter-designations followed by a number require you to locate line-items in this index that possess the ID number found after the letter).

ID	Individual in Patent	Sec.	Sec. Part	Date Issued	Other Counties	For More Info . . .
2384	ALEXANDER, Jedediah	3	W½NW	1855-12-15		A1 F
2292	ASHCRAFT, Daniel	15	SW	1868-02-10		A3
2411	BALDWIN, Lewis M	31	E½SW	1860-09-03		A3
2388	BALL, John	34	S½SE	1854-09-15		A1
2387	" "	25	SESE	1858-01-15		A3
2432	BEEG, O Saw O	1	SESW	1857-07-01		A1
2283	BELDEN, Burton S	33	SWSW	1869-11-01		A4
2404	BELL, Jonathan	7	SESW	1861-04-01		A1 F
2405	" "	7	SWSE	1861-04-01		A1
2415	BIRCHARD, W H	35	SENW	1857-02-20		A3 G146
2416	" "	35	W½NW	1857-02-20		A3 G146
2378	BIRDSELL, Isaac C	13	SWNW	1872-04-05		A4
2379	" "	13	W½SW	1872-04-05		A4
2380	" "	14	SENE	1872-04-05		A4
2373	BLAIR, Henry M	35	E½SE	1875-11-10		A4
2348	BLANCHARD, John C	9	N½SE	1868-12-01		A3 G245
2349	" "	9	SESE	1868-12-01		A3 G245
2343	BRIGGS, Catherine	9	W½NE	1857-02-20		A3 G242
2470	CASTLE, Truman L	31	SWSW	1861-12-05		A1 F
2478	CLARK, William	29	SE	1873-02-10		A4
2270	CRADIT, Amos	6	W½NW	1858-05-01		A1 F
2454	CRAWFORD, Samuel F	31	E½NW	1873-02-10		A4
2455	" "	31	S½NE	1873-02-10		A4
2465	CURDY, Thomas	31	SE	1860-09-03		A3
2422	DE MOO, ME SHE MIN	1	SENW	1855-12-15		A1
2381	DOBE, Isabell	18	N½NW	1861-07-01		A3 F
2382	" "	7	SWSW	1861-07-01		A3 F
2375	DUBOIS, Henry W	29	NWSW	1889-12-31		A1
2370	EASTMAN, Harvey	29	E½SW	1863-10-01		A3
2371	" "	29	SWSW	1863-10-01		A3
2372	" "	32	NWNW	1863-10-01		A3
2276	EDDY, Benjamin F	6	S½SW	1860-09-03		A3 F
2277	" "	7	N½NW	1860-09-03		A3 F
2310	ELTING, Evelina	9	SENW	1857-02-20		A3 G240
2311	" "	9	W½NW	1857-02-20		A3 G240
2403	ELY, Phebe	22	NW	1863-05-20		A3 G286
2294	FARNHAM, Daniel S	7	NESE	1868-02-15		A1
2313	GAYLORD, Irwin B	11	NW	1855-12-15		A1 G238 C
2312	" "	11	NE	1857-01-06		A1 G238
2314	" "	12	SE	1857-03-10		A1 G238
2419	GETTY, Henry H	22	NENE	1866-11-10		A3 G234
2420	" "	23	E½NW	1866-11-10		A3 G234
2421	" "	23	NWNW	1866-11-10		A3 G234
2385	GIBB, John B	2	NWNW	1859-10-10		A1 F
2386	" "	3	NENE	1859-10-10		A1 F
2447	GLASS, Reuben	33	W½NE	1860-10-01		A3

ID	Individual in Patent	Sec.	Sec. Part	Date Issued	Other Counties	For More Info . . .
2448	GLASS, Reuben (Cont'd)	33	W½SE	1860-10-01		A3
2437	GO, Pe	1	SWNW	1857-07-01		A1
2350	GRAY, Edgar L	36	S½SE	1865-11-01		A1
2260	GUOM, Ah Gee She	3	3	1856-05-15		A1
2376	HASCALL, Herbert A	28	NWSE	1860-10-01		A3
2377	" "	28	S½SE	1860-10-01		A3
2417	HASCALL, Lucien A	33	E½NE	1860-10-01		A3 G82
2418	" "	34	W½NW	1860-10-01		A3 G82
2348	HAYWARD, Ruth	9	N½SE	1868-12-01		A3 G245
2349	" "	9	SESE	1868-12-01		A3 G245
2364	HESS, George H	31	SESE	1863-12-05		A1 C
2479	HICKS, William	5	NE	1859-08-10		A3 F
2419	HILLS, Charles T	22	NENE	1866-11-10		A3 G234
2420	" "	23	E½NW	1866-11-10		A3 G234
2421	" "	23	NWNW	1866-11-10		A3 G234
2399	HINE, John	12	NESW	1856-03-10		A1 G199
2400	" "	12	SESW	1857-04-02		A3 G199
2401	" "	12	W½SW	1857-04-02		A3 G199
2293	HOWELL, Daniel C	15	SE	1868-02-15		A1
2368	HULL, Guernsey	32	NESE	1861-12-10		A1
2369	" "	32	SENE	1861-12-10		A1
2427	HUNT, Miles B	4	NESE	1857-07-01		A1 F
2428	" "	4	W½SE	1857-07-01		A1 F
2274	JOHNSON, Arnold	28	SESW	1861-04-01		A1
2275	" "	33	NENW	1861-04-01		A1
2471	KAKE, Wah Be Ka	2	2	1857-07-01		A1
2290	KEMP, Christoph	32	S½SE	1860-09-01		A1
2392	KEMP, John N	32	NWSE	1861-04-01		A1
2365	KENDALL, George	22	S½SE	1856-03-10		A1
2355	KENNE, Elias G	10	SWSW	1855-03-01		A1 G264
2357	" "	28	NESE	1855-03-01		A1 G264
2358	" "	28	SENE	1855-03-01		A1 G264
2359	" "	8	SESE	1855-03-01		A1 G264
2360	" "	9	S½SW	1855-03-01		A1 G264
2361	" "	9	SWSE	1855-03-01		A1 G264
2356	" "	17	NENE	1855-05-01		A1 G264
2419	KIMBALL, Orson W	22	NENE	1866-11-10		A3 G234
2420	" "	23	E½NW	1866-11-10		A3 G234
2421	" "	23	NWNW	1866-11-10		A3 G234
2390	LANCASTER, John	30	NENW	1884-05-10		A4
2391	" "	30	NWNE	1884-05-10		A4
2389	LIFER, John C	22	W½NE	1861-12-10		A1
2423	LINDEN, Menno	24	NESW	1870-05-02		A1
2424	LINDON, Menno	24	SESW	1878-12-30		A4
2425	" "	24	W½SW	1878-12-30		A4
2467	LORDAN, Thomas	4	N½NE	1859-08-10		A3 F
2468	" "	4	SWNE	1859-08-10		A3 F
2469	LORDON, Thomas	4	SENE	1879-11-25		A4
2412	LOVELL, Louis S	34	N½SE	1857-02-20		A3
2413	" "	35	N½NE	1857-02-20		A3
2414	" "	35	NENW	1857-02-20		A3
2415	" "	35	SENW	1857-02-20		A3 G146
2416	" "	35	W½NW	1857-02-20		A3 G146
2352	MARKLE, Elias	28	SWSW	1859-10-10		A1
2353	" "	32	NENE	1859-10-10		A1
2354	" "	33	W½NW	1859-10-10		A1
2351	MARTIN, Edward A	5	E½NW	1856-03-10		A1 F
2280	MARTIN, Hannah	31	NWSW	1862-08-01		A3 G179 F R2278
2281	" "	31	W½NW	1862-08-01		A3 G179 F R2279
2278	" "	31	NWSW	1862-11-01		A3 G178 F R2280
2279	" "	31	W½NW	1862-11-01		A3 G178 F R2281
2278	MARTIN, Marion	31	NWSW	1862-11-01		A3 G178 F R2280
2279	" "	31	W½NW	1862-11-01		A3 G178 F R2281
2280	MARTIN, Marson	31	NWSW	1862-08-01		A3 G179 F R2278
2281	" "	31	W½NW	1862-08-01		A3 G179 F R2279
2449	MARTIN, Richard A	4	N½NW	1855-12-15		A1 F
2451	" "	4	SWNW	1855-12-15		A1 F
2450	" "	4	SENW	1856-03-10		A1 F
2362	MATHEW, Frederick	32	E½NW	1861-12-05		A1
2363	" "	32	W½NE	1861-12-05		A1
2452	MAZE, Sally	6	N½SE	1855-12-15		A1
2273	MCGUIRE, Archibold	18	NWSW	1861-04-01		A1 F
2254	MCQUEEN, Aaron J	8	E½SW	1871-11-01		A4

ID	Individual in Patent	Sec.	Sec. Part	Date Issued	Other Counties	For More Info . . .
2255	MCQUEEN, Aaron J (Cont'd)	8	NWSW	1871-11-01		A4
2256	" "	8	SWSE	1871-11-01		A4
2434	MEE, Pa Paw	3	1	1857-07-01		A1
2435	" "	3	2	1857-07-01		A1
2280	MERCHANT, Benjamin P	31	NWSW	1862-08-01		A3 G179 F R2278
2281	" "	31	W½NW	1862-08-01		A3 G179 F R2279
2278	" "	31	NWSW	1862-11-01		A3 G178 F R2280
2279	" "	31	W½NW	1862-11-01		A3 G178 F R2281
2296	MERWIN, Henry	21	N½NW	1857-02-20		A3 G239
2297	" "	21	N½SW	1857-02-20		A3 G239
2298	" "	21	NENE	1857-02-20		A3 G239
2299	" "	21	S½SW	1857-02-20		A3 G239
2300	" "	21	SENW	1857-02-20		A3 G239
2301	" "	21	SWNW	1857-02-20		A3 G239
2302	" "	21	W½NE	1857-02-20		A3 G239
2344	" "	34	NE	1857-02-20		A3 G251
2303	" "	5	N½SE	1857-02-20		A3 G239
2304	" "	5	NESW	1857-02-20		A3 G239
2345	" "	5	S½SE	1857-02-20		A3 G250
2305	" "	5	S½SW	1857-02-20		A3 G239
2306	" "	8	N½NE	1857-02-20		A3 G239
2307	" "	8	NENW	1857-02-20		A3 G239
2308	" "	8	S½NE	1857-02-20		A3 G239
2309	" "	8	SENW	1857-02-20		A3 G239
2310	" "	9	SENW	1857-02-20		A3 G240
2311	" "	9	W½NW	1857-02-20		A3 G240
2393	" "	11	2	1859-08-10		A3 G201
2394	" "	11	E½SE	1859-08-10		A3 G201
2395	" "	23	E½SE	1859-08-10		A3 G201
2396	" "	23	NWSW	1859-08-10		A3 G201
2397	" "	23	S½SW	1859-08-10		A3 G201
2398	" "	23	SWSE	1859-08-10		A3 G201
2476	MILLER, John D	23	W½NE	1868-02-10		A3 G343
2466	MOORE, Thomas L	23	SWNW	1865-10-10		A1
2438	NO, Puck Ah Naw Ba	2	NESE	1857-03-10		A1
2291	NORTHROP, Cogswell R	15	NW	1869-11-01		A4
2399	NORTHROP, John O	12	NESW	1856-03-10		A1 G199
2318	" "	14	E½SE	1857-02-20		A3 G241
2341	" "	14	NESW	1857-02-20		A3 G252
2342	" "	14	W½SW	1857-02-20		A3 G252
2296	" "	21	N½NW	1857-02-20		A3 G239
2297	" "	21	N½SW	1857-02-20		A3 G239
2298	" "	21	NENE	1857-02-20		A3 G239
2299	" "	21	S½SW	1857-02-20		A3 G239
2300	" "	21	SENW	1857-02-20		A3 G239
2301	" "	21	SWNW	1857-02-20		A3 G239
2302	" "	21	W½NE	1857-02-20		A3 G239
2322	" "	23	NENE	1857-02-20		A3 G241
2323	" "	23	SENE	1857-02-20		A3 G241
2324	" "	24	W½NW	1857-02-20		A3 G241
2325	" "	26	E½NE	1857-02-20		A3 G241
2326	" "	26	E½NW	1857-02-20		A3 G241
2327	" "	26	NESE	1857-02-20		A3 G241
2328	" "	26	NESW	1857-02-20		A3 G241
2329	" "	26	NWSE	1857-02-20		A3 G241
2330	" "	26	W½NE	1857-02-20		A3 G241
2331	" "	26	W½NW	1857-02-20		A3 G241
2333	" "	27	SENE	1857-02-20		A3 G241
2344	" "	34	NE	1857-02-20		A3 G251
2303	" "	5	N½SE	1857-02-20		A3 G239
2304	" "	5	NESW	1857-02-20		A3 G239
2345	" "	5	S½SE	1857-02-20		A3 G250
2305	" "	5	S½SW	1857-02-20		A3 G239
2306	" "	8	N½NE	1857-02-20		A3 G239
2307	" "	8	NENW	1857-02-20		A3 G239
2308	" "	8	S½NE	1857-02-20		A3 G239
2309	" "	8	SENW	1857-02-20		A3 G239
2310	" "	9	SENW	1857-02-20		A3 G240
2343	" "	9	W½NE	1857-02-20		A3 G242
2311	" "	9	W½NW	1857-02-20		A3 G240
2400	" "	12	SESW	1857-04-02		A3 G199
2401	" "	12	W½SW	1857-04-02		A3 G199
2319	" "	14	SESW	1857-04-02		A3 G241

ID	Individual in Patent	Sec.	Sec. Part	Date Issued	Other Counties	For More Info . . .
2320	NORTHROP, John O (Cont'd)	14	W½SE	1857-04-02		A3 G241
2321	" "	21	SE	1858-01-15		A3 G241
2346	" "	22	N½SE	1858-01-15		A3 G254
2347	" "	22	N½SW	1858-01-15		A3 G254
2315	" "	10	2	1859-08-10		A3 G241
2316	" "	10	NWSW	1859-08-10		A3 G241
2317	" "	10	SESW	1859-08-10		A3 G241
2393	" "	11	2	1859-08-10		A3 G201
2394	" "	11	E½SE	1859-08-10		A3 G201
2395	" "	23	E½SE	1859-08-10		A3 G201
2396	" "	23	NWSW	1859-08-10		A3 G201
2397	" "	23	S½SW	1859-08-10		A3 G201
2398	" "	23	SWSE	1859-08-10		A3 G201
2332	" "	26	W½SW	1859-08-10		A3 G241
2334	" "	27	SESE	1859-08-10		A3 G241
2335	" "	3	NENW	1859-08-10		A3 G241 F
2336	" "	3	NWNE	1859-08-10		A3 G241 F
2337	" "	33	SESE	1859-08-10		A3 G241
2338	" "	34	W½SW	1859-08-10		A3 G241
2339	" "	8	N½SE	1868-12-01		A3 G241
2348	" "	9	N½SE	1868-12-01		A3 G245
2340	" "	9	N½SW	1868-12-01		A3 G241
2349	" "	9	SESE	1868-12-01		A3 G245
2263	ORTON, Alanson F	14	SENW	1855-12-15		A1
2261	" "	10	3	1857-03-10		A1
2262	" "	10	4	1857-03-10		A1
2264	" "	14	SWNW	1857-03-10		A1
2265	" "	15	NE	1857-03-10		A1
2366	PETER, George	11	1	1858-05-01		A1
2266	PIGEON, Alexander	12	NW	1857-03-10		A1
2439	PUNK-E-NOB-BI-NO,	2	SESE	1857-03-10		A1
2440	" "	2	W½SE	1857-03-10		A1
2287	PUTNAM, Charles	10	1	1857-03-10		A1
2288	" "	4	1	1857-03-10		A1
2289	" "	9	1	1857-03-10		A1
2463	QUOT, Te Tan Wan O	1	SWSW	1855-12-15		A1
2409	REED, Joseph	28	NWNW	1872-11-06		A1
2462	RIBLET, Solomon K	21	SENE	1868-02-15		A1
2296	ROBERTS, William	21	N½NW	1857-02-20		A3 G239
2297	" "	21	N½SW	1857-02-20		A3 G239
2298	" "	21	NENE	1857-02-20		A3 G239
2299	" "	21	S½SW	1857-02-20		A3 G239
2300	" "	21	SENW	1857-02-20		A3 G239
2301	" "	21	SWNW	1857-02-20		A3 G239
2302	" "	21	W½NE	1857-02-20		A3 G239
2303	" "	5	N½SE	1857-02-20		A3 G239
2304	" "	5	NESW	1857-02-20		A3 G239
2345	" "	5	S½SE	1857-02-20		A3 G250
2305	" "	5	S½SW	1857-02-20		A3 G239
2306	" "	8	N½NE	1857-02-20		A3 G239
2307	" "	8	NENW	1857-02-20		A3 G239
2308	" "	8	S½NE	1857-02-20		A3 G239
2309	" "	8	SENW	1857-02-20		A3 G239
2310	" "	9	SENW	1857-02-20		A3 G240
2311	" "	9	W½NW	1857-02-20		A3 G240
2257	ROSENBERGER, Adam	29	E½NE	1870-10-01		A4
2258	" "	29	SENW	1870-10-01		A4
2259	" "	29	SWNE	1870-10-01		A4
2480	RUFRECHT, William	28	NENE	1870-11-01		A1
2481	RUPRECHT, William	28	NENW	1864-11-01		A1
2419	RYERSON, Martin	22	NENE	1866-11-10		A3 G234
2420	" "	23	E½NW	1866-11-10		A3 G234
2421	" "	23	NWNW	1866-11-10		A3 G234
2284	SAGE, Caleb	11	3	1857-03-10		A1
2285	" "	11	4	1857-03-10		A1
2286	" "	14	N½NW	1857-03-10		A1
2313	SANFORD, Ebenezer	11	NW	1855-12-15		A1 G238 C
2312	" "	11	NE	1857-01-06		A1 G238
2318	" "	14	E½SE	1857-02-20		A3 G241
2341	" "	14	NESW	1857-02-20		A3 G252
2342	" "	14	W½SW	1857-02-20		A3 G252
2296	" "	21	N½NW	1857-02-20		A3 G239
2297	" "	21	N½SW	1857-02-20		A3 G239

ID	Individual in Patent	Sec.	Sec. Part	Date Issued	Other Counties	For More Info . . .
2298	SANFORD, Ebenezer (Cont'd)	21	NENE	1857-02-20		A3 G239
2299	" "	21	S½SW	1857-02-20		A3 G239
2300	" "	21	SENW	1857-02-20		A3 G239
2301	" "	21	SWNW	1857-02-20		A3 G239
2302	" "	21	W½NE	1857-02-20		A3 G239
2322	" "	23	NENE	1857-02-20		A3 G241
2323	" "	23	SENE	1857-02-20		A3 G241
2324	" "	24	W½NW	1857-02-20		A3 G241
2325	" "	26	E½NE	1857-02-20		A3 G241
2326	" "	26	E½NW	1857-02-20		A3 G241
2327	" "	26	NESE	1857-02-20		A3 G241
2328	" "	26	NESW	1857-02-20		A3 G241
2329	" "	26	NWSE	1857-02-20		A3 G241
2330	" "	26	W½NE	1857-02-20		A3 G241
2331	" "	26	W½NW	1857-02-20		A3 G241
2333	" "	27	SENE	1857-02-20		A3 G241
2344	" "	34	NE	1857-02-20		A3 G251
2303	" "	5	N½SE	1857-02-20		A3 G239
2304	" "	5	NESW	1857-02-20		A3 G239
2345	" "	5	S½SE	1857-02-20		A3 G250
2305	" "	5	S½SW	1857-02-20		A3 G239
2306	" "	8	N½NE	1857-02-20		A3 G239
2307	" "	8	NENW	1857-02-20		A3 G239
2308	" "	8	S½NE	1857-02-20		A3 G239
2309	" "	8	SENW	1857-02-20		A3 G239
2310	" "	9	SENW	1857-02-20		A3 G240
2343	" "	9	W½NE	1857-02-20		A3 G242
2311	" "	9	W½NW	1857-02-20		A3 G240
2314	" "	12	SE	1857-03-10		A1 G238
2319	" "	14	SESW	1857-04-02		A3 G241
2320	" "	14	W½SE	1857-04-02		A3 G241
2321	" "	21	SE	1858-01-15		A3 G241
2346	" "	22	N½SE	1858-01-15		A3 G254
2347	" "	22	N½SW	1858-01-15		A3 G254
2315	" "	10	2	1859-08-10		A3 G241
2316	" "	10	NWSW	1859-08-10		A3 G241
2317	" "	10	SESW	1859-08-10		A3 G241
2393	" "	11	2	1859-08-10		A3 G201
2394	" "	11	E½SE	1859-08-10		A3 G201
2395	" "	23	E½SE	1859-08-10		A3 G201
2396	" "	23	NWSW	1859-08-10		A3 G201
2397	" "	23	S½SW	1859-08-10		A3 G201
2398	" "	23	SWSE	1859-08-10		A3 G201
2332	" "	26	W½SW	1859-08-10		A3 G241
2334	" "	27	SESE	1859-08-10		A3 G241
2335	" "	3	NENW	1859-08-10		A3 G241 F
2336	" "	3	NWNE	1859-08-10		A3 G241 F
2337	" "	33	SESE	1859-08-10		A3 G241
2338	" "	34	W½SW	1859-08-10		A3 G241
2339	" "	8	N½SE	1868-12-01		A3 G241
2348	" "	9	N½SE	1868-12-01		A3 G245
2340	" "	9	N½SW	1868-12-01		A3 G241
2349	" "	9	SESE	1868-12-01		A3 G245
2482	SAVAGE, William	6	E½NW	1855-12-15		A1 F
2483	" "	6	NE	1855-12-15		A1 F
2484	" "	9	NENW	1855-12-15		A1
2431	SE, Ne Con Ne Pe Nah	3	SENW	1857-07-01		A1
2426	SHARAR, Michael	22	SENE	1861-12-10		A1
2410	SHE, Ke Wa Ah	1	NWNW	1855-12-15		A1
2344	SHEARMAN, Elizabeth	34	NE	1857-02-20		A3 G251
2355	SHERMAN, Alonzo	10	SWSW	1855-03-01		A1 G264
2357	" "	28	NESE	1855-03-01		A1 G264
2358	" "	28	SENE	1855-03-01		A1 G264
2359	" "	8	SESE	1855-03-01		A1 G264
2360	" "	9	S½SW	1855-03-01		A1 G264
2361	" "	9	SWSE	1855-03-01		A1 G264
2356	" "	17	NENE	1855-05-01		A1 G264
2464	SKEELS, Theron N	6	N½SW	1860-09-01		A1 F
2473	SMITH, Welman	14	SWNE	1880-06-30		A4
2485	SMITH, William	12	E½NE	1857-07-01		A1
2429	SNYDER, Moses H	18	S½NW	1861-12-05		A1
2271	SQUIER, Andrew T	27	SWSW	1863-08-01		A1
2272	" "	34	SESW	1863-08-01		A1

ID	Individual in Patent	Sec.	Sec. Part	Date Issued	Other Counties	For More Info . . .
2280	STANLEY, Thomas B	31	NWSW	1862-08-01		A3 G179 F R2278
2281	" "	31	W½NW	1862-08-01		A3 G179 F R2279
2278	" "	31	NWSW	1862-11-01		A3 G178 F R2280
2279	" "	31	W½NW	1862-11-01		A3 G178 F R2281
2341	STAUDT, Anna	14	NESW	1857-02-20		A3 G252
2342	" "	14	W½SW	1857-02-20		A3 G252
2430	STEINER, Narzis	32	SESW	1861-12-10		A1
2419	STEVENS, Ezra	22	NENE	1866-11-10		A3 G234
2420	" "	23	E½NW	1866-11-10		A3 G234
2421	" "	23	NWNW	1866-11-10		A3 G234
2355	STEVENS, Fitz H	10	SWSW	1855-03-01		A1 G264
2357	" "	28	NESE	1855-03-01		A1 G264
2358	" "	28	SENE	1855-03-01		A1 G264
2359	" "	8	SESE	1855-03-01		A1 G264
2360	" "	9	S½SW	1855-03-01		A1 G264
2361	" "	9	SWSE	1855-03-01		A1 G264
2356	" "	17	NENE	1855-05-01		A1 G264
2280	STEWART, John R	31	NWSW	1862-08-01		A3 G179 F R2278
2281	" "	31	W½NW	1862-08-01		A3 G179 F R2279
2278	" "	31	NWSW	1862-11-01		A3 G178 F R2280
2279	" "	31	W½NW	1862-11-01		A3 G178 F R2281
2477	STUART, Wilkes L	2	N½NE	1857-03-10		A1
2367	TAYLOR, George	3	NESE	1903-01-31		A1
2403	TENANT, Jonas L	22	NW	1863-05-20		A3 G286
2456	TIBBITS, Shepard	2	NENW	1855-12-15		A1
2282	TIBBITTS, Benjamin	8	NWNW	1867-01-10		A1
2457	TIBBITTS, Shepard	2	1	1856-03-10		A1
2458	" "	2	NESW	1856-03-10		A1 F
2460	" "	2	SWNE	1856-03-10		A1
2461	" "	3	S½NE	1856-03-10		A1
2459	" "	2	S½NW	1857-03-10		A1
2267	TINDALL, Alva A	33	NESE	1885-01-07		A1
2383	TITUS, James H	17	NWNE	1876-12-30		A4
2433	TUSK, Pa Ko	1	NWSW	1857-07-01		A1
2374	UPTON, Henry	1	E½	1857-03-10		A1
2436	WAH, Pay Min Ah	2	SENE	1855-12-15		A1
2445	WALTERHOUSE, Thomas S	30	E½SE	1866-05-01		A3 G339
2446	" "	30	SWSE	1866-05-01		A3 G339
2268	WATSON, Amasa B	11	SWSE	1857-02-20		A3
2269	" "	14	NWNE	1857-02-20		A3
2472	WAU-BA-TO,	1	NESW	1857-03-10		A1
2295	WEAVER, Daniel	1	NENW	1857-03-10		A1
2417	WEBB, Nancy	33	E½NE	1860-10-01		A3 G82
2418	" "	34	W½NW	1860-10-01		A3 G82
2453	WILLIAMS, Samuel E	25	NWNW	1857-03-10		A1
2346	WOOD, Lydia	22	N½SE	1858-01-15		A3 G254
2347	" "	22	N½SW	1858-01-15		A3 G254
2443	WOOD, Ransom E	29	SWNW	1866-04-03		A1
2445	" "	30	E½SE	1866-05-01		A3 G339
2446	" "	30	SWSE	1866-05-01		A3 G339
2441	" "	23	NESW	1866-06-05		A1
2442	" "	23	NWSE	1866-06-05		A1
2444	" "	30	SWSW	1866-06-05		A1 F
2476	WOOD, Wesley F	23	W½NE	1868-02-10		A3 G343
2474	" "	14	NENE	1868-02-15		A1
2475	" "	34	NESW	1868-02-15		A1
2402	YUNG, John	32	NESW	1861-04-01		A1
2406	ZERLANT, Joseph A	33	E½SW	1871-06-15		A4
2407	" "	33	NWSW	1871-06-15		A4
2408	" "	33	SENW	1871-06-15		A4

Patent Map

T12-N R14-W
Michigan-Toledo Strip Meridian

Map Group 17

Township Statistics

Parcels Mapped	:	232
Number of Patents	:	153
Number of Individuals	:	128
Patentees Identified	:	115
Number of Surnames	:	116
Multi-Patentee Parcels	:	85
Oldest Patent Date	:	9/15/1854
Most Recent Patent	:	1/31/1903
Block/Lot Parcels	:	15
Parcels Re - Issued	:	2
Parcels that Overlap	:	0
Cities and Towns	:	2
Cemeteries	:	2

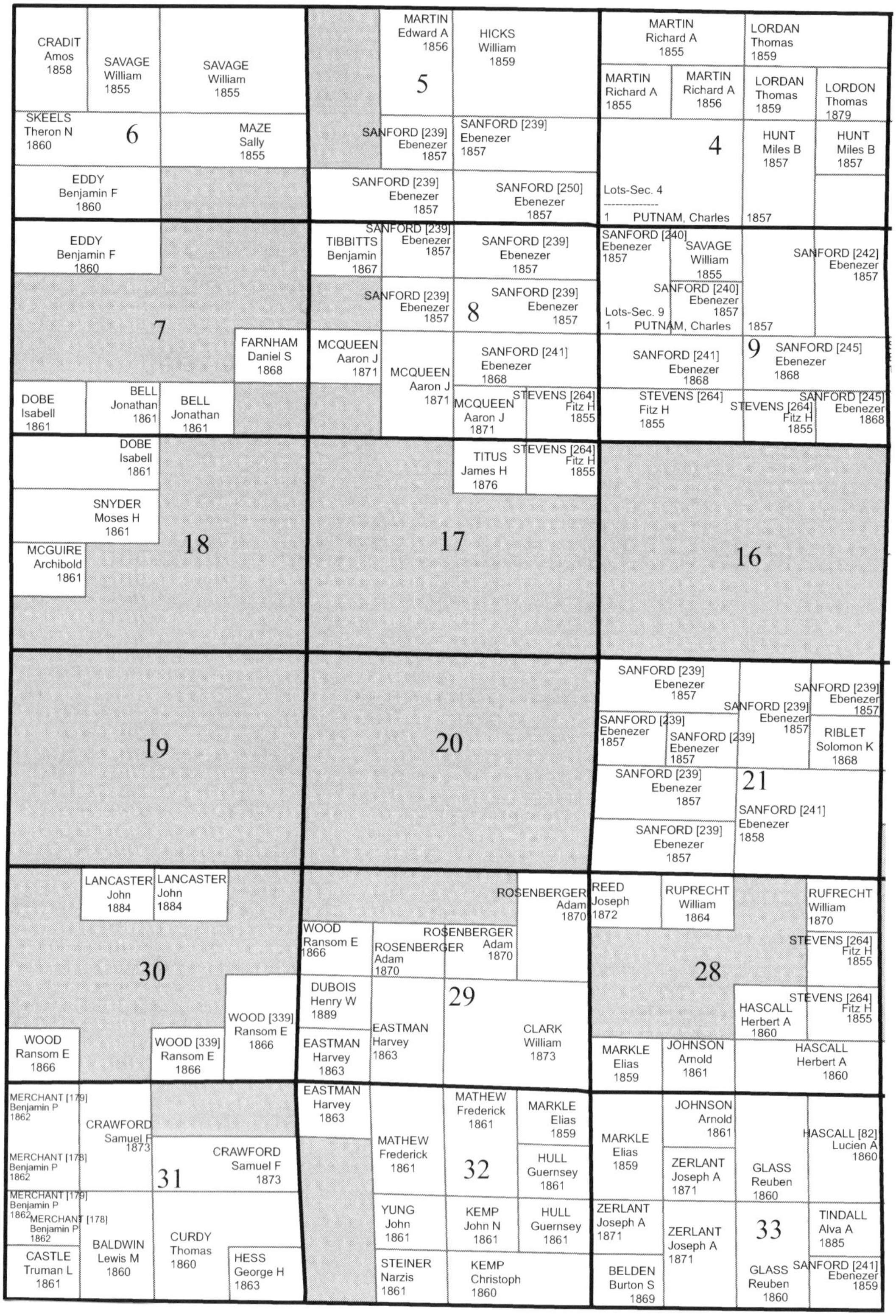

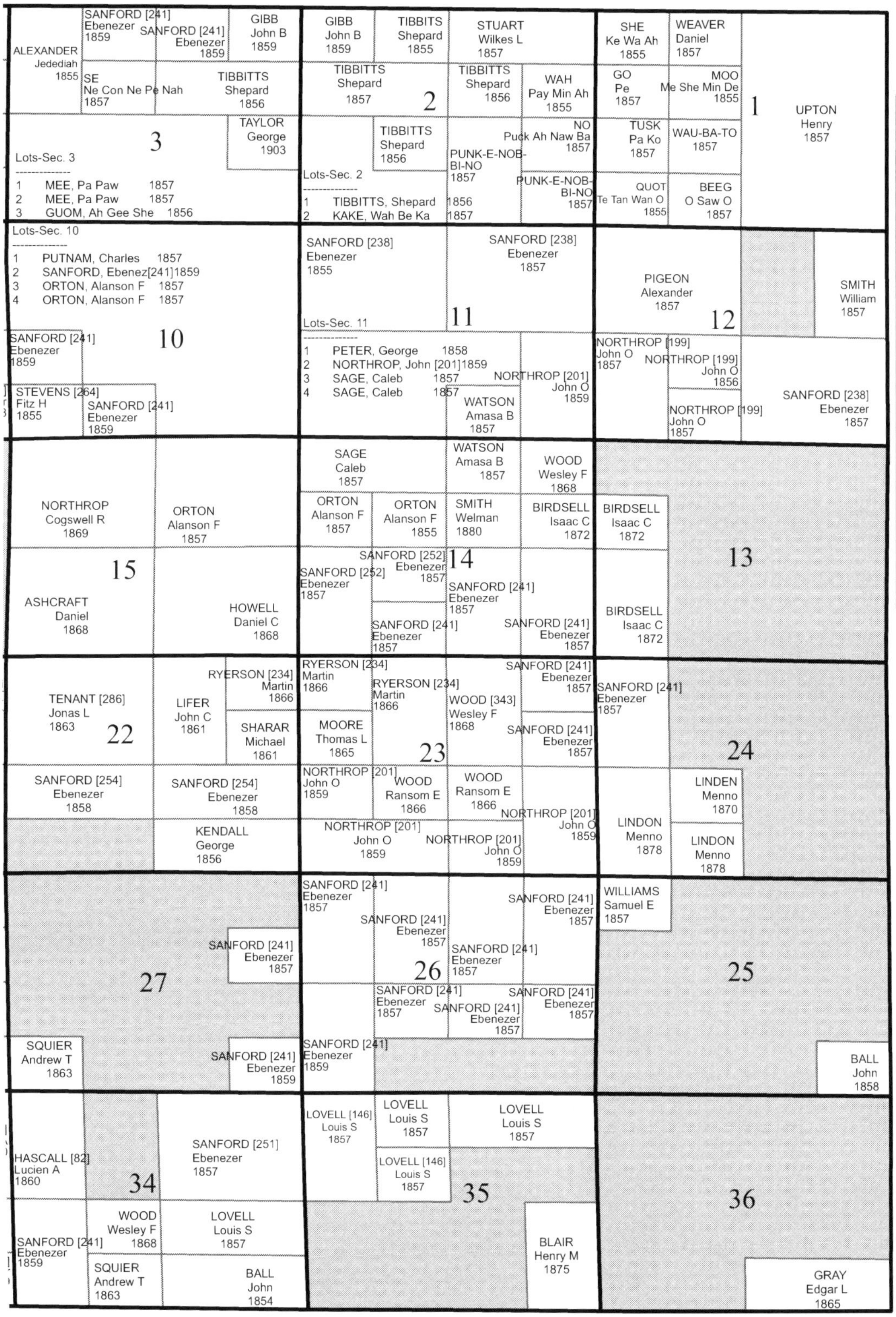

SANFORD [241]
Ebenezer
1859
SANFORD [241]
Ebenezer
1859
GIBB
John B
1859
ALEXANDER
Jedediah
1855
SE
Ne Con Ne Pe Nah
1857
TIBBITTS
Shepard
1856
TAYLOR
George
1903
3
Lots-Sec. 3
----
1 MEE, Pa Paw 1857
2 MEE, Pa Paw 1857
3 GUOM, Ah Gee She 1856

GIBB
John B
1859
TIBBITS
Shepard
1855
STUART
Wilkes L
1857
TIBBITTS
Shepard
1857
TIBBITTS
Shepard
1856
WAH
Pay Min Ah
1855
2
TIBBITTS
Shepard
1856
NO
Puck Ah Naw Ba
1857
PUNK-E-NOB-
BI-NO
1857
PUNK-E-NOB-
BI-NO
1857
Lots-Sec. 2
----
1 TIBBITTS, Shepard 1856
2 KAKE, Wah Be Ka 1857

SHE
Ke Wa Ah
1855
WEAVER
Daniel
1857
GO
Pe
1857
MOO
Me She Min De
1855
1
UPTON
Henry
1857
TUSK
Pa Ko
1857
WAU-BA-TO
1857
QUOT
Te Tan Wan O
1855
BEEG
O Saw O
1857

Lots-Sec. 10
----
1 PUTNAM, Charles 1857
2 SANFORD, Ebenez[241]1859
3 ORTON, Alanson F 1857
4 ORTON, Alanson F 1857
SANFORD [241]
Ebenezer
1859
10
STEVENS [264]
Fitz H
1855
SANFORD [241]
Ebenezer
1859

SANFORD [238]
Ebenezer
1855
SANFORD [238]
Ebenezer
1857
Lots-Sec. 11
11
----
1 PETER, George 1858
2 NORTHROP, John [201]1859
3 SAGE, Caleb 1857
4 SAGE, Caleb 1857
NORTHROP [201]
John O
1859
WATSON
Amasa B
1857

PIGEON
Alexander
1857
12
SMITH
William
1857
NORTHROP [199]
John O
1857
NORTHROP [199]
John O
1856
NORTHROP [199]
John O
1857
SANFORD [238]
Ebenezer
1857

NORTHROP
Cogswell R
1869
ORTON
Alanson F
1857
15
ASHCRAFT
Daniel
1868
HOWELL
Daniel C
1868

SAGE
Caleb
1857
WATSON
Amasa B
1857
WOOD
Wesley F
1868
ORTON
Alanson F
1857
ORTON
Alanson F
1855
SMITH
Welman
1880
BIRDSELL
Isaac C
1872
SANFORD [252]
Ebenezer
1857
14
SANFORD [252]
Ebenezer
1857
SANFORD [241]
Ebenezer
1857
SANFORD [241]
Ebenezer
1857
SANFORD [241]
Ebenezer
1857

BIRDSELL
Isaac C
1872
13
BIRDSELL
Isaac C
1872

TENANT [286]
Jonas L
1863
22
RYERSON [234]
Martin
1866
LIFER
John C
1861
SHARAR
Michael
1861
SANFORD [254]
Ebenezer
1858
SANFORD [254]
Ebenezer
1858
KENDALL
George
1856

RYERSON [234]
Martin
1866
RYERSON [234]
Martin
1866
SANFORD [241]
Ebenezer
1857
WOOD [343]
Wesley F
1868
MOORE
Thomas L
1865
23
SANFORD [241]
Ebenezer
1857
NORTHROP [201]
John O
1859
WOOD
Ransom E
1866
WOOD
Ransom E
1866
NORTHROP [201]
John O
1859
NORTHROP [201]
John O
1859
NORTHROP [201]
John O
1859

SANFORD [241]
Ebenezer
1857
24
LINDEN
Menno
1870
LINDON
Menno
1878
LINDON
Menno
1878

27
SANFORD [241]
Ebenezer
1857
SQUIER
Andrew T
1863
SANFORD [241]
Ebenezer
1859

SANFORD [241]
Ebenezer
1857
SANFORD [241]
Ebenezer
1857
SANFORD [241]
Ebenezer
1857
SANFORD [241]
Ebenezer
1857
26
SANFORD [241]
Ebenezer
1857
SANFORD [241]
Ebenezer
1857
SANFORD [241]
Ebenezer
1857
SANFORD [241]
Ebenezer
1859

WILLIAMS
Samuel E
1857
25
BALL
John
1858

HASCALL [82]
Lucien A
1860
34
SANFORD [251]
Ebenezer
1857
WOOD
Wesley F
1868
LOVELL
Louis S
1857
SANFORD [241]
Ebenezer
1859
SQUIER
Andrew T
1863
BALL
John
1854

LOVELL [146]
Louis S
1857
LOVELL
Louis S
1857
LOVELL
Louis S
1857
LOVELL [146]
Louis S
1857
35
BLAIR
Henry M
1875

36
GRAY
Edgar L
1865

Helpful Hints

1. This Map's INDEX can be found on the preceding pages.
2. Refer to Map "C" to see where this Township lies within Newaygo County, Michigan.
3. Numbers within square brackets [ ] denote a multi-patentee land parcel (multi-owner). Refer to Appendix "C" for a full list of members in this group.
4. Areas that look to be crowded with Patentees usually indicate multiple sales of the same parcel (Re-issues) or Overlapping parcels. See this Township's Index for an explanation of these and other circumstances that might explain "odd" groupings of Patentees on this map.

Legend

Patent Boundary

Section Boundary

No Patents Found (or Outside County)

1., 2., 3., ... Lot Numbers (when beside a name)

[ ] Group Number (see Appendix "C")

Scale: Section = 1 mile X 1 mile (generally, with some exceptions)

Road Map

T12-N R14-W
Michigan-Toledo Strip Meridian

Map Group 17

Cities & Towns

Reeman
Sitka

Cemeteries

Reeman Cemetery
Saint Michaels Cemetery

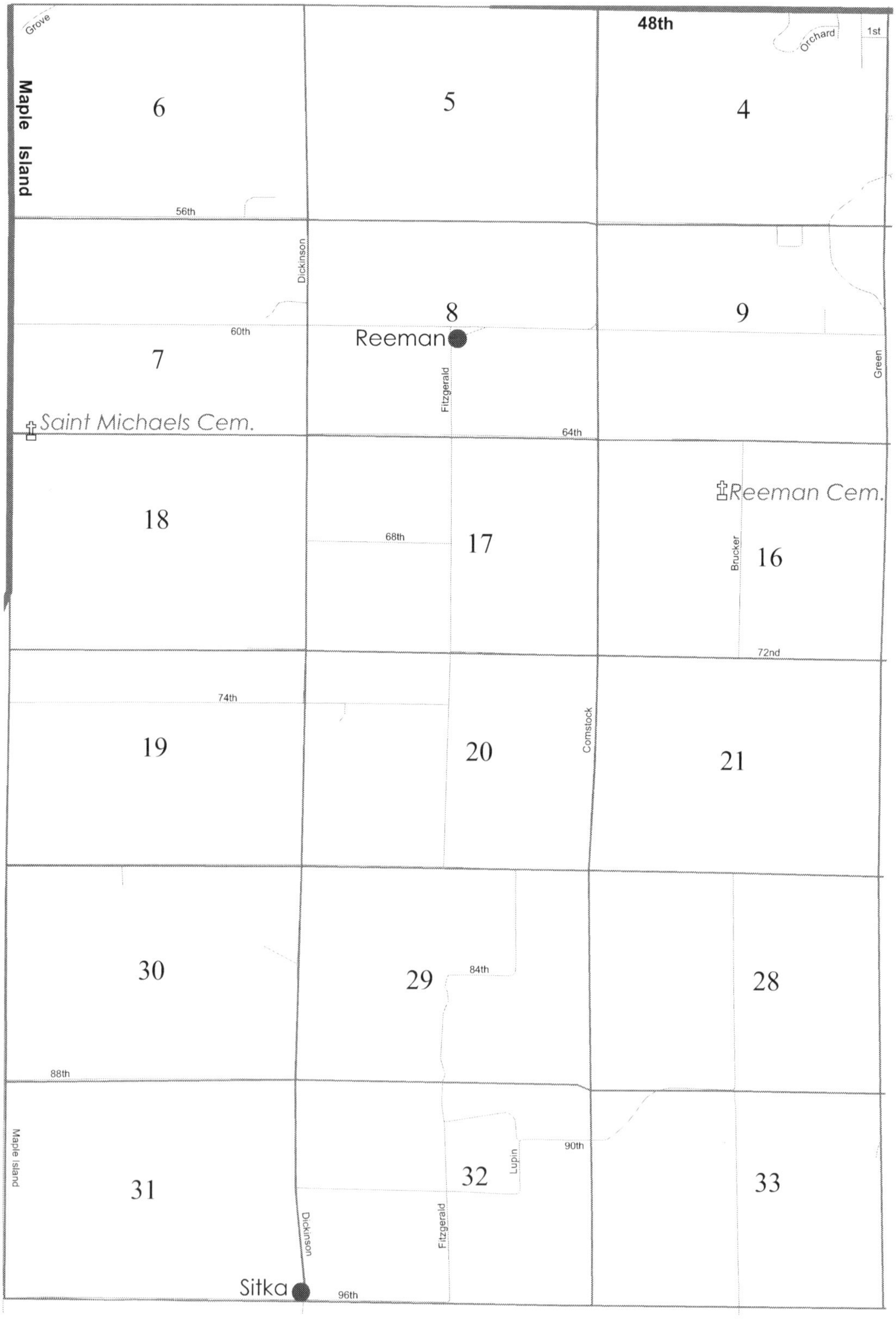

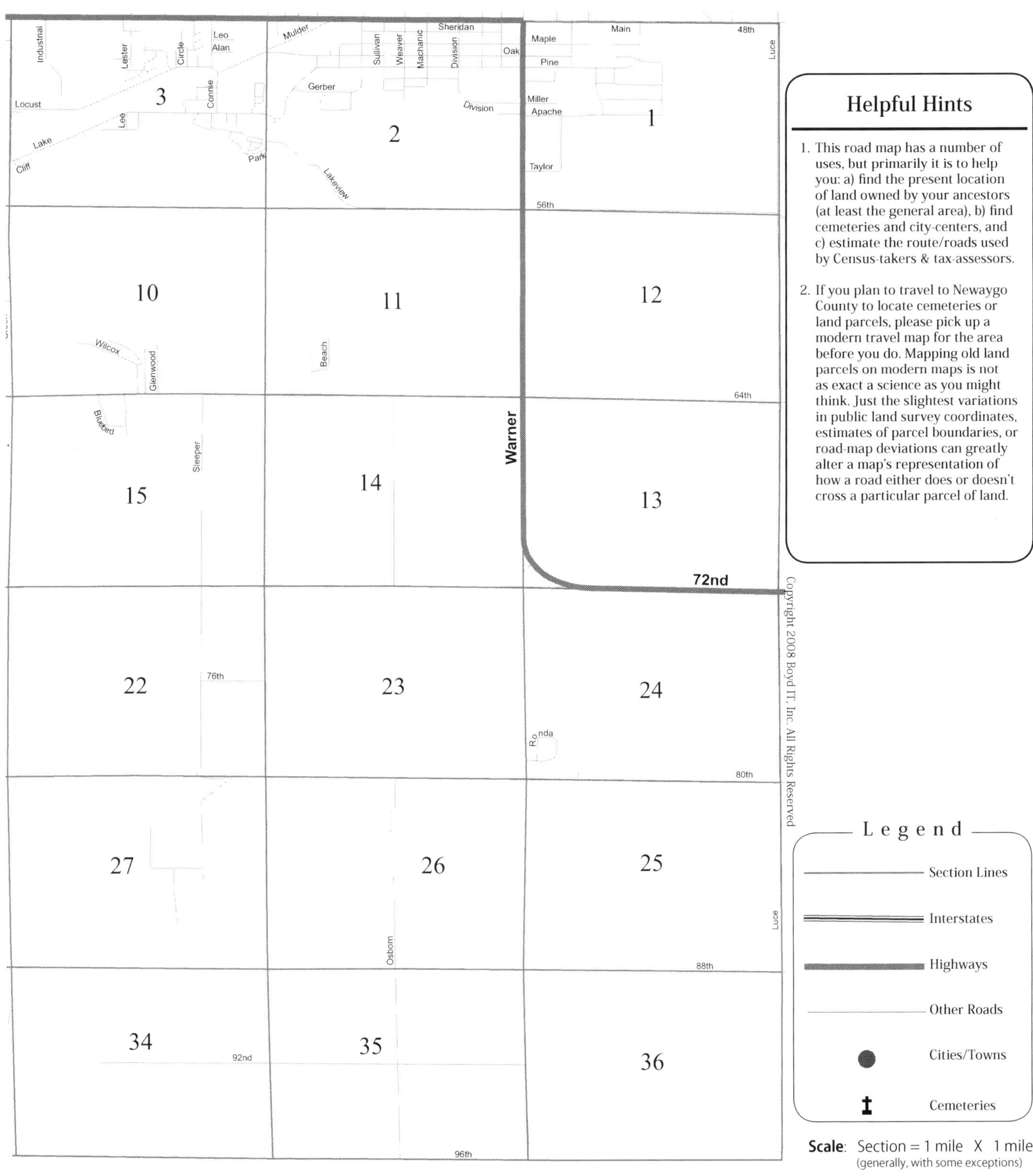

Helpful Hints

1. This road map has a number of uses, but primarily it is to help you: a) find the present location of land owned by your ancestors (at least the general area), b) find cemeteries and city-centers, and c) estimate the route/roads used by Census-takers & tax-assessors.

2. If you plan to travel to Newaygo County to locate cemeteries or land parcels, please pick up a modern travel map for the area before you do. Mapping old land parcels on modern maps is not as exact a science as you might think. Just the slightest variations in public land survey coordinates, estimates of parcel boundaries, or road-map deviations can greatly alter a map's representation of how a road either does or doesn't cross a particular parcel of land.

Legend

- Section Lines
- Interstates
- Highways
- Other Roads
- Cities/Towns
- Cemeteries

Scale: Section = 1 mile X 1 mile
(generally, with some exceptions)

Cities & Towns
Reeman
Sitka

Cemeteries
Reeman Cemetery
Saint Michaels Cemetery

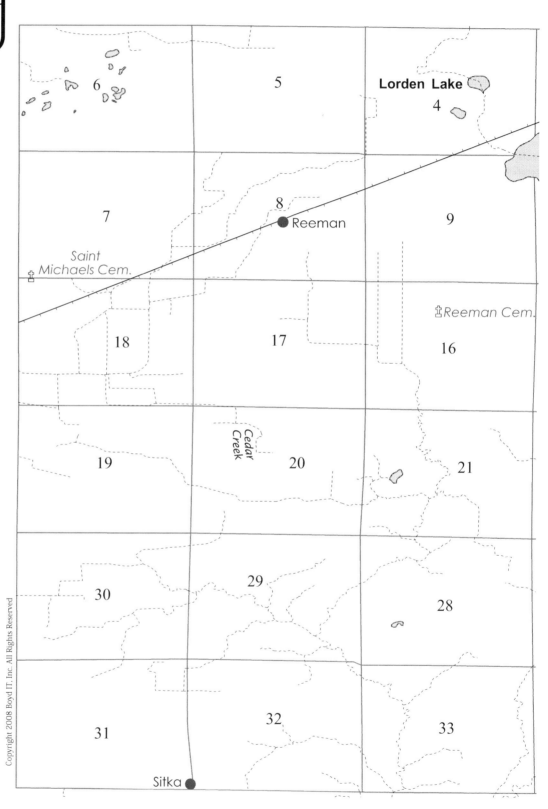

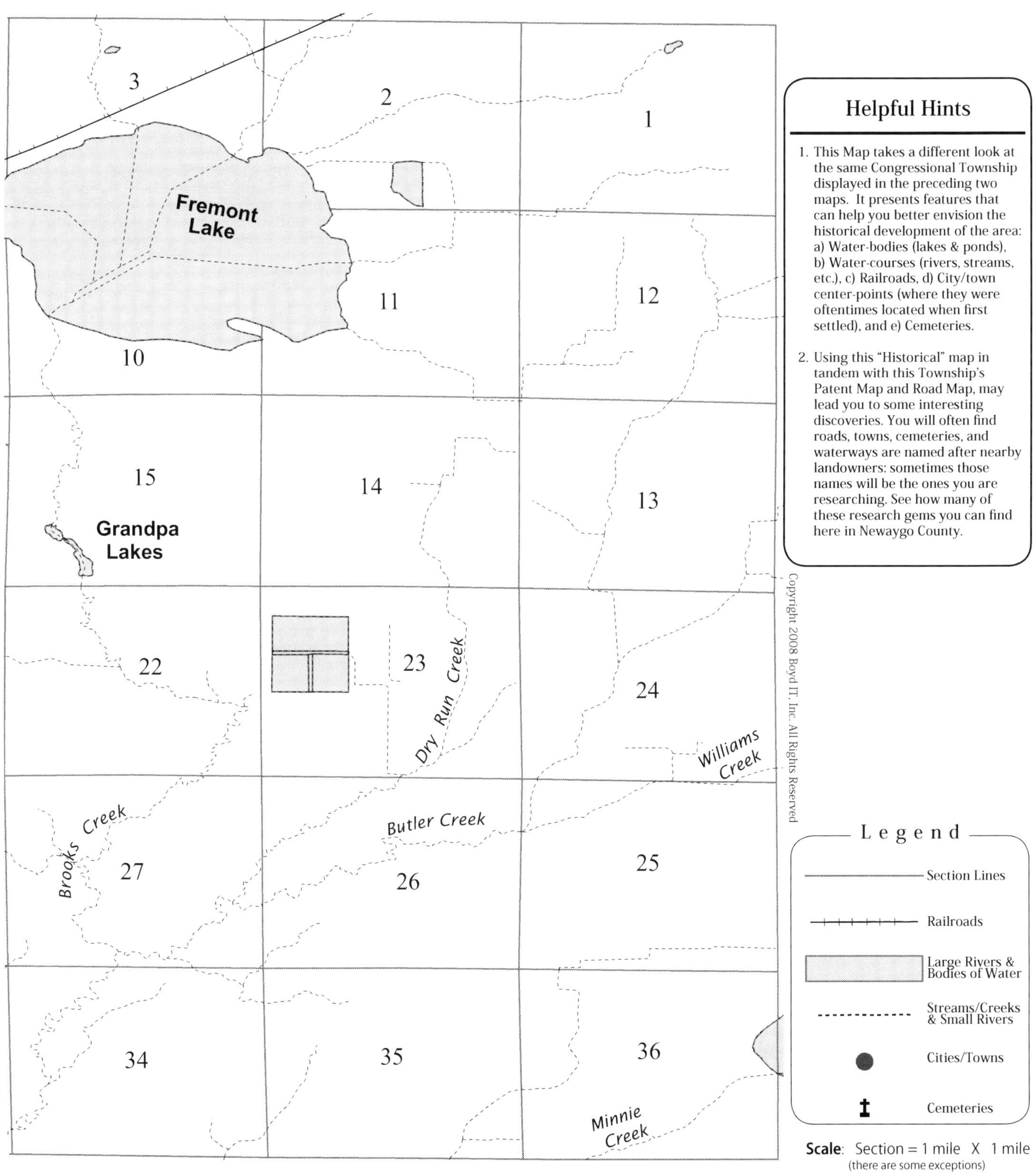

Helpful Hints

1. This Map takes a different look at the same Congressional Township displayed in the preceding two maps. It presents features that can help you better envision the historical development of the area: a) Water-bodies (lakes & ponds), b) Water-courses (rivers, streams, etc.), c) Railroads, d) City/town center-points (where they were oftentimes located when first settled), and e) Cemeteries.

2. Using this "Historical" map in tandem with this Township's Patent Map and Road Map, may lead you to some interesting discoveries. You will often find roads, towns, cemeteries, and waterways are named after nearby landowners: sometimes those names will be the ones you are researching. See how many of these research gems you can find here in Newaygo County.

Map Group 18: Index to Land Patents

Township 12-North Range 13-West (Michigan-Toledo Strip)

After you locate an individual in this Index, take note of the Section and Section Part then proceed to the Land Patent map on the pages immediately following. You should have no difficulty locating the corresponding parcel of land.

The "For More Info" Column will lead you to more information about the underlying Patents. See the *Legend* at right, and the "How to Use this Book" chapter, for more information.

LEGEND

"For More Info . . . " column

- **A** = Authority (Legislative Act, See Appendix "A")
- **B** = Block or Lot (location in Section unknown)
- **C** = Cancelled Patent
- **F** = Fractional Section
- **G** = Group (Multi-Patentee Patent, see Appendix "C")
- **V** = Overlaps another Parcel
- **R** = Re-Issued (Parcel patented more than once)

(A & G items require you to look in the Appendixes referred to above. All other Letter-designations followed by a number require you to locate line-items in this index that possess the ID number found after the letter).

ID	Individual in Patent	Sec.	Sec. Part	Date Issued	Other Counties	For More Info . . .
2664	ADAMS, Warren P	24	1	1867-01-10		A1 R2532
2665	" "	24	2	1867-01-10		A1 R2569
2633	ANDREWS, Samuel A	33	SWSW	1853-11-01		A1 F
2552	BALFOUR, James	17	E½NE	1857-03-10		A1
2553	" "	8	E½SE	1857-03-10		A1
2576	BALL, John	24	NESE	1851-05-01		A1
2578	" "	28	N½NE	1854-09-15		A1
2577	" "	26	SESW	1858-01-15		A3
2579	" "	30	SWSW	1858-01-15		A3 F
2580	" "	31	W½NW	1858-01-15		A3 F
2581	" "	35	2	1858-01-15		A3
2582	" "	35	3	1858-01-15		A3
2655	BELDEN, Sarah E	31	SWSW	1865-11-01		A1 F
2567	BENNETT, Jerome	26	5	1858-05-01		A1
2568	BENNETT, Jerome P	36	W½NW	1858-05-01		A1 F
2613	BRITTON, Mary M	8	SESW	1865-10-10		A1
2570	BROOKS, John A	24	5	1841-11-10		A1
2571	" "	24	6	1841-11-10		A1
2572	" "	24	7	1849-04-05		A1
2569	" "	24	2	1852-03-10		A1 R2665
2565	BROWN, Elsey	35	7	1860-09-03		A3 G257
2566	" "	35	SESE	1860-09-03		A3 G257
2548	BUTLER, Hiram	8	NENW	1857-03-10		A1
2549	" "	8	NWSW	1857-03-10		A1
2550	" "	8	W½NW	1857-03-10		A1
2532	COLE, Franklin	24	1	1852-03-10		A1 R2664
2511	CRANDELL, Charles	7	SW	1857-03-10		A1 F
2588	CROSSMAN, John S	12	3	1859-10-10		A1
2589	" "	12	4	1859-10-10		A1
2590	" "	12	S½NW	1859-10-10		A1 F
2591	DANA, Josiah P	32	NENE	1858-05-01		A1
2592	" "	33	3	1858-05-01		A1
2593	" "	33	NESW	1858-05-01		A1
2637	DAVIS, Mary	30	NWSE	1866-02-20		A3 G255
2638	" "	30	SENW	1866-02-20		A3 G255
2639	" "	30	SWNE	1866-02-20		A3 G255
2555	DEANE, James M	19	SESW	1863-03-20		A3 G51
2556	" "	19	SWSE	1863-03-20		A3 G51
2629	DENSLOW, Polly	36	1	1858-01-15		A3 G333
2630	DUELL, Reuben	7	NE	1857-03-10		A1
2666	EDMUNDS, William	7	SE	1857-03-10		A1
2487	FAIRCHILDES, Albert H	23	N½NE	1857-02-20		A3
2488	" "	23	SWNE	1857-02-20		A3
2505	FURMAN, Ashley B	34	6	1851-05-01		A1
2504	" "	24	4	1853-11-01		A1
2506	" "	35	6	1854-06-15		A1

ID	Individual in Patent	Sec.	Sec. Part	Date Issued	Other Counties	For More Info . . .
2507	FURMAN, Ashley B (Cont'd)	35	NESW	1854-06-15		A1
2503	" "	12	S½NE	1855-12-15		A1 F
2573	GIBB, John B	18	SWSW	1871-02-01		A4 F
2574	" "	19	NWSW	1871-02-01		A4
2575	" "	19	W½NW	1871-02-01		A4
2585	GILBERT, John	26	6	1854-10-05		A1 G69
2585	GILBERT, Joseph	26	6	1854-10-05		A1 G69
2585	GILBERT, William	26	6	1854-10-05		A1 G69
2667	" "	35	1	1857-03-10		A1
2524	GRAY, Edgar L	31	NWNE	1866-04-03		A1
2525	" "	5	SESE	1870-05-10		A1
2554	HAMENT, James	6	SW	1855-12-15		A1 F
2656	HEALD, Horatio N	10	NESW	1854-06-15		A1 G314
2657	" "	10	NWSE	1854-06-15		A1 G314
2658	" "	11	SWSW	1854-06-15		A1 G314
2659	" "	2	3	1854-06-15		A1 G314
2660	" "	3	SWSW	1854-06-15		A1 G314
2661	" "	4	SESE	1854-06-15		A1 G314
2616	HENNESSY, Patrick	6	W½NE	1857-03-10		A1 F
2533	HERRINGTON, Franklin	6	E½NW	1857-03-10		A1 F
2536	HESS, George H	31	SESE	1864-05-28		A1
2587	HINE, John	17	NW	1857-02-20		A3 G200
2631	HOWLETT, Robert	17	E½SW	1854-10-05		A1
2632	" "	8	W½SE	1854-10-05		A1
2617	JOHNSON, Peter	31	NENW	1865-10-10		A1
2537	KENDALL, George	12	1	1855-12-15		A1
2538	" "	12	2	1855-12-15		A1
2539	" "	5	NWSW	1857-03-10		A1
2540	" "	5	S½SW	1857-03-10		A1
2541	KENDULL, George	23	SESE	1854-06-15		A1 F
2542	" "	24	9	1854-06-15		A1
2543	" "	24	NWNW	1854-06-15		A1
2583	KIMBELL, John E	11	2	1859-10-10		A1
2584	" "	11	3	1859-10-10		A1
2671	KIMBELL, William	11	SWNE	1860-12-01		A1
2670	" "	10	NESE	1861-12-05		A1
2586	KNICKERBOCKER, John H	34	10	1854-09-15		A1
2618	LANBAUGH, Peter	17	N½SE	1864-11-01		A1
2528	LAWRENCE, John	1	3	1867-01-10		A1 G320 F
2529	" "	1	S	1867-01-10		A1 G320 F
2530	" "	14	NWNE	1867-01-10		A1 G320
2594	LOVELL, Louis S	20	SENE	1857-02-20		A3
2595	" "	21	N½SW	1857-02-20		A3
2596	" "	21	NWSE	1857-02-20		A3
2597	" "	21	S½NW	1857-02-20		A3
2559	LYON, James O	2	5	1854-06-15		A1 F
2560	" "	2	N½NW	1854-06-15		A1 F
2561	" "	3	SESW	1854-06-15		A1
2656	LYONS, James O	10	NESW	1854-06-15		A1 G314
2657	" "	10	NWSE	1854-06-15		A1 G314
2658	" "	11	SWSW	1854-06-15		A1 G314
2659	" "	2	3	1854-06-15		A1 G314
2660	" "	3	SWSW	1854-06-15		A1 G314
2661	" "	4	SESE	1854-06-15		A1 G314
2551	MALLERY, James B	6	W½NW	1857-03-10		A1 F
2557	MARTIN, James M	32	1	1857-03-10		A1
2558	" "	33	4	1857-03-10		A1
2526	MAYBEE, Electa	26	1	1854-06-15		A1
2527	" "	26	2	1854-06-15		A1
2635	MCCUNE, Samuel	5	W½NW	1856-03-10		A1
2636	" "	6	E½NE	1856-03-10		A1 F
2516	MILLER, Dennis	28	N½SW	1873-02-10		A4
2517	" "	28	S½NW	1873-02-10		A4
2663	MOORE, Thomas D	22	NWNW	1865-11-01		A1
2600	MORRIS, Robert W	21	S½SW	1854-06-15		A1 G236
2601	" "	27	NWNW	1854-06-15		A1 G236
2602	" "	32	2	1854-06-15		A1 G236
2603	" "	32	NESW	1854-06-15		A1 G236
2604	" "	34	7	1854-06-15		A1 G236
2599	" "	14	NENW	1854-10-05		A1 G236
2605	" "	4	E½SW	1854-10-05		A1 G236
2606	" "	4	SWNW	1854-10-05		A1 G236
2607	" "	4	SWSE	1854-10-05		A1 G236

ID	Individual in Patent	Sec.	Sec. Part	Date Issued	Other Counties	For More Info . . .
2608	MORRIS, Robert W (Cont'd)	5	NESE	1854-10-05		A1 G236
2609	" "	8	NENE	1854-10-05		A1 G236
2610	" "	9	N½SE	1854-10-05		A1 G236
2611	" "	9	S½NE	1854-10-05		A1 G236
2612	" "	9	S½NW	1854-10-05		A1 G236
2619	MOSHER, Philip	17	W½SW	1857-07-01		A1
2620	" "	18	E½SE	1857-07-01		A1
2621	" "	18	SWSE	1857-07-01		A1
2622	" "	19	N½NE	1857-07-01		A1
2623	" "	20	NWNW	1857-07-01		A1
2662	NEWELL, Theodore	19	NESW	1868-02-15		A1 R2598
2587	NORTHROP, John O	17	NW	1857-02-20		A3 G200
2519	" "	20	N½SW	1857-02-20		A3 G241
2520	" "	20	SWNW	1857-02-20		A3 G241
2518	" "	17	W½NE	1858-01-15		A3 G241
2521	" "	23	NWSW	1858-01-15		A3 G241
2522	" "	23	S½NW	1858-01-15		A3 G241
2523	" "	4	N½NE	1858-01-15		A3 G241 F
2672	PEACOCK, William	32	SWSW	1868-02-15		A1
2614	PLATT, Merit S	19	S½NE	1855-11-08		A3
2615	" "	19	SENW	1855-11-08		A3
2499	ROOT, Anson	4	E½NW	1870-05-02		A4 F
2500	" "	4	NWNW	1870-05-02		A4 F
2562	ROOT, James	4	NESE	1870-05-02		A4
2563	" "	4	SENE	1870-05-02		A4
2648	ROSE, Samuel	22	SESW	1854-06-15		A1
2643	" "	21	N½NE	1854-10-05		A1
2654	" "	9	S½SE	1854-10-05		A1
2640	" "	10	SENW	1855-12-15		A1
2641	" "	10	SWNE	1855-12-15		A1
2642	" "	15	NWNW	1855-12-15		A1
2646	" "	22	NENW	1855-12-15		A1
2650	" "	22	SWSW	1855-12-15		A1
2644	" "	21	NESE	1856-03-10		A1
2645	" "	21	S½NE	1856-03-10		A1
2647	" "	22	NWSW	1856-03-10		A1
2653	" "	35	NENE	1856-03-10		A1
2651	" "	27	SE	1858-05-01		A1 R2544 V2513
2652	" "	27	SWSW	1858-05-01		A1
2649	" "	22	SWSE	1863-05-15		A1
2600	RYERSON, Martin	21	S½SW	1854-06-15		A1 G236
2601	" "	27	NWNW	1854-06-15		A1 G236
2602	" "	32	2	1854-06-15		A1 G236
2603	" "	32	NESW	1854-06-15		A1 G236
2604	" "	34	7	1854-06-15		A1 G236
2599	" "	14	NENW	1854-10-05		A1 G236
2605	" "	4	E½SW	1854-10-05		A1 G236
2606	" "	4	SWNW	1854-10-05		A1 G236
2607	" "	4	SWSE	1854-10-05		A1 G236
2608	" "	5	NESE	1854-10-05		A1 G236
2609	" "	8	NENE	1854-10-05		A1 G236
2610	" "	9	N½SE	1854-10-05		A1 G236
2611	" "	9	S½NE	1854-10-05		A1 G236
2612	" "	9	S½NW	1854-10-05		A1 G236
2598	SANDS, Louis	19	NESW	1864-11-01		A1 R2662
2519	SANFORD, Ebenezer	20	N½SW	1857-02-20		A3 G241
2520	" "	20	SWNW	1857-02-20		A3 G241
2518	" "	17	W½NE	1858-01-15		A3 G241
2521	" "	23	NWSW	1858-01-15		A3 G241
2522	" "	23	S½NW	1858-01-15		A3 G241
2523	" "	4	N½NE	1858-01-15		A3 G241 F
2637	SANFORD, Samuel R	30	NWSE	1866-02-20		A3 G255
2638	" "	30	SENW	1866-02-20		A3 G255
2639	" "	30	SWNE	1866-02-20		A3 G255
2501	SCHOONOVER, Archibald	30	E½SW	1879-11-10		A4
2502	" "	30	NWSW	1879-11-10		A4
2534	SCHWEITZER, George E	19	SWSW	1884-12-05		A4 F
2535	" "	30	W½NW	1884-12-05		A4 F
2547	SCOFIELD, Henry	18	NWNW	1857-03-10		A1 F
2544	SHAW, George	27	SE	1868-06-10		A1 C F R2651
2565	SIMONS, James V	35	7	1860-09-03		A3 G257
2566	" "	35	SESE	1860-09-03		A3 G257
2508	SMITH, Canton	34	8	1854-09-15		A1

ID	Individual in Patent	Sec.	Sec. Part	Date Issued	Other Counties	For More Info . . .
2509	SMITH, Canton (Cont'd)	34	9	1854-09-15		A1
2510	" "	34	NWNW	1854-09-15		A1
2531	SMITH, Erastus	18	SENE	1872-04-05		A4
2677	SMITH, William	7	NW	1857-07-01		A1
2555	STILWELL, Sherman	19	SESW	1863-03-20		A3 G51
2556	" "	19	SWSE	1863-03-20		A3 G51
2512	STONE, Charles	6	SE	1857-03-10		A1
2673	STRONG, William S	34	2	1854-10-05		A1
2674	" "	34	3	1854-10-05		A1
2675	" "	34	4	1854-10-05		A1
2676	" "	35	NWSW	1854-10-05		A1
2564	TAGUASON, James	35	5	1852-11-01		A1
2489	TROWBRIDGE, Alva	33	1	1854-09-15		A1
2486	UPTON, Adenijah E	1	SE	1867-01-10		A1 F
2587	WATERHOUSE, Ruth	17	NW	1857-02-20		A3 G200
2496	WATSON, Amasa	4	NWSE	1855-12-15		A1
2497	" "	4	SWNE	1855-12-15		A1
2490	WATSON, Amasa B	1	5	1854-06-15		A1
2491	" "	2	1	1854-06-15		A1
2492	" "	2	2	1854-06-15		A1
2494	" "	8	W½NE	1857-02-20		A3
2493	" "	5	W½SE	1857-03-10		A1
2495	" "	9	SW	1858-01-15		A3
2545	WEAVER, George	17	S½SE	1857-03-10		A1
2546	" "	20	N½NE	1857-03-10		A1
2668	WELLES, William J	25	1	1854-06-15		A1
2669	" "	25	SWNW	1855-11-01		A1
2513	WHITMAN, Chauncey	27	NWSE	1865-11-01		A1 V2651
2514	" "	27	SWNE	1865-11-01		A1
2515	" "	33	2	1868-02-15		A1 C
2656	WILCOX, Sextus N	10	NESW	1854-06-15		A1 G314
2657	" "	10	NWSE	1854-06-15		A1 G314
2658	" "	11	SWSW	1854-06-15		A1 G314
2659	" "	2	3	1854-06-15		A1 G314
2660	" "	3	SWSW	1854-06-15		A1 G314
2661	" "	4	SESE	1854-06-15		A1 G314
2634	WILLIAMS, Samuel E	19	NWSE	1873-05-15		A1
2528	WOOD, Eliphalet	1	3	1867-01-10		A1 G320 F
2529	" "	1	S	1867-01-10		A1 G320 F
2530	" "	14	NWNE	1867-01-10		A1 G320
2624	WOOD, Ransom E	3	N½NE	1855-12-15		A1 F
2625	" "	3	N½SW	1858-01-15		A3
2626	" "	3	S½NE	1858-01-15		A3
2627	" "	3	SENW	1858-01-15		A3
2628	" "	3	SWNW	1858-01-15		A3
2629	" "	36	1	1858-01-15		A3 G333
2498	WUTCH, An So	26	SWSW	1866-06-05		A1 F

Patent Map

T12-N R13-W
Michigan-Toledo Strip Meridian

Map Group 18

Township Statistics

Parcels Mapped	:	192
Number of Patents	:	133
Number of Individuals	:	89
Patentees Identified	:	79
Number of Surnames	:	79
Multi-Patentee Parcels	:	39
Oldest Patent Date	:	11/10/1841
Most Recent Patent	:	12/5/1884
Block/Lot Parcels	:	47
Parcels Re - Issued	:	4
Parcels that Overlap	:	2
Cities and Towns	:	1
Cemeteries	:	1

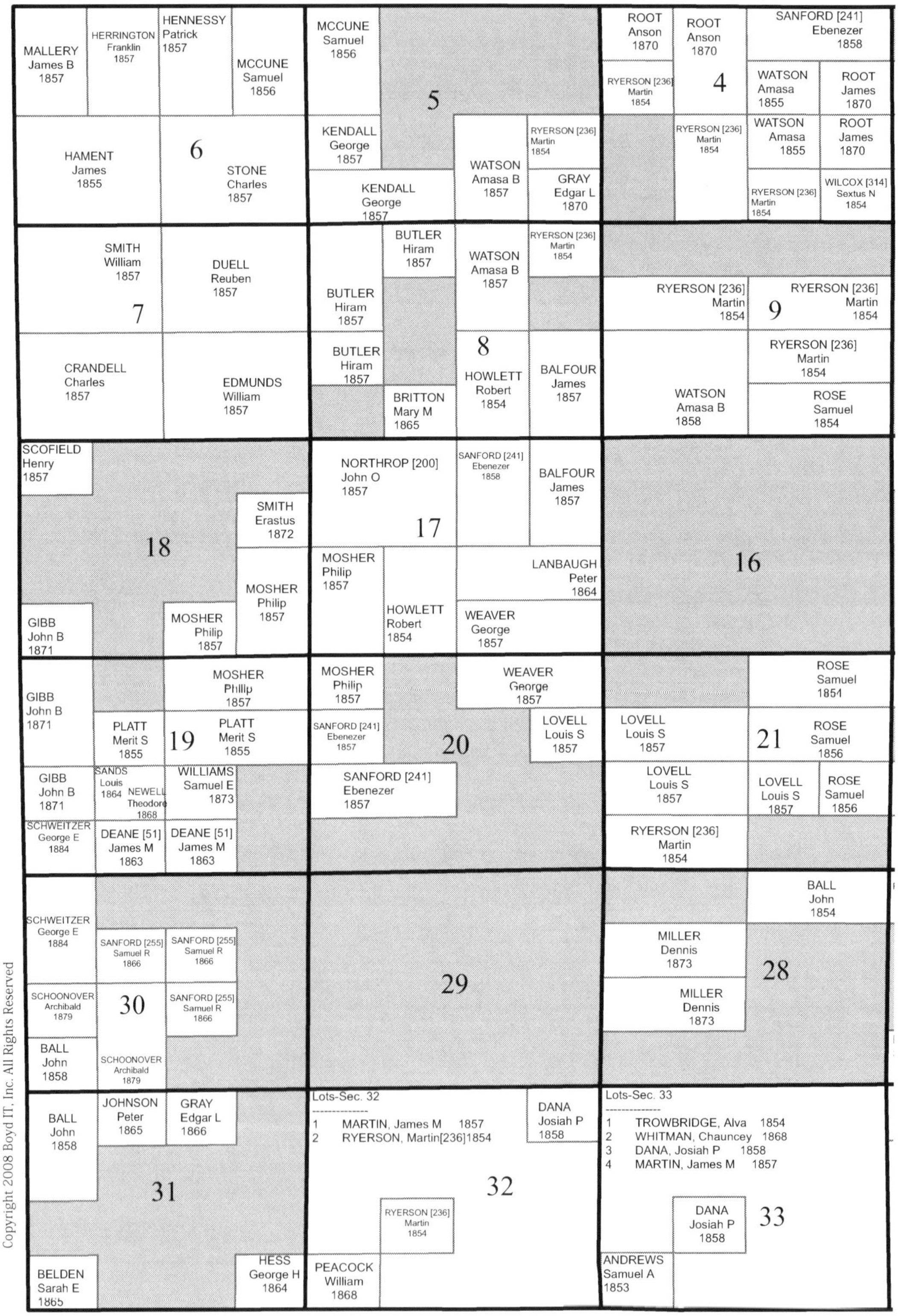

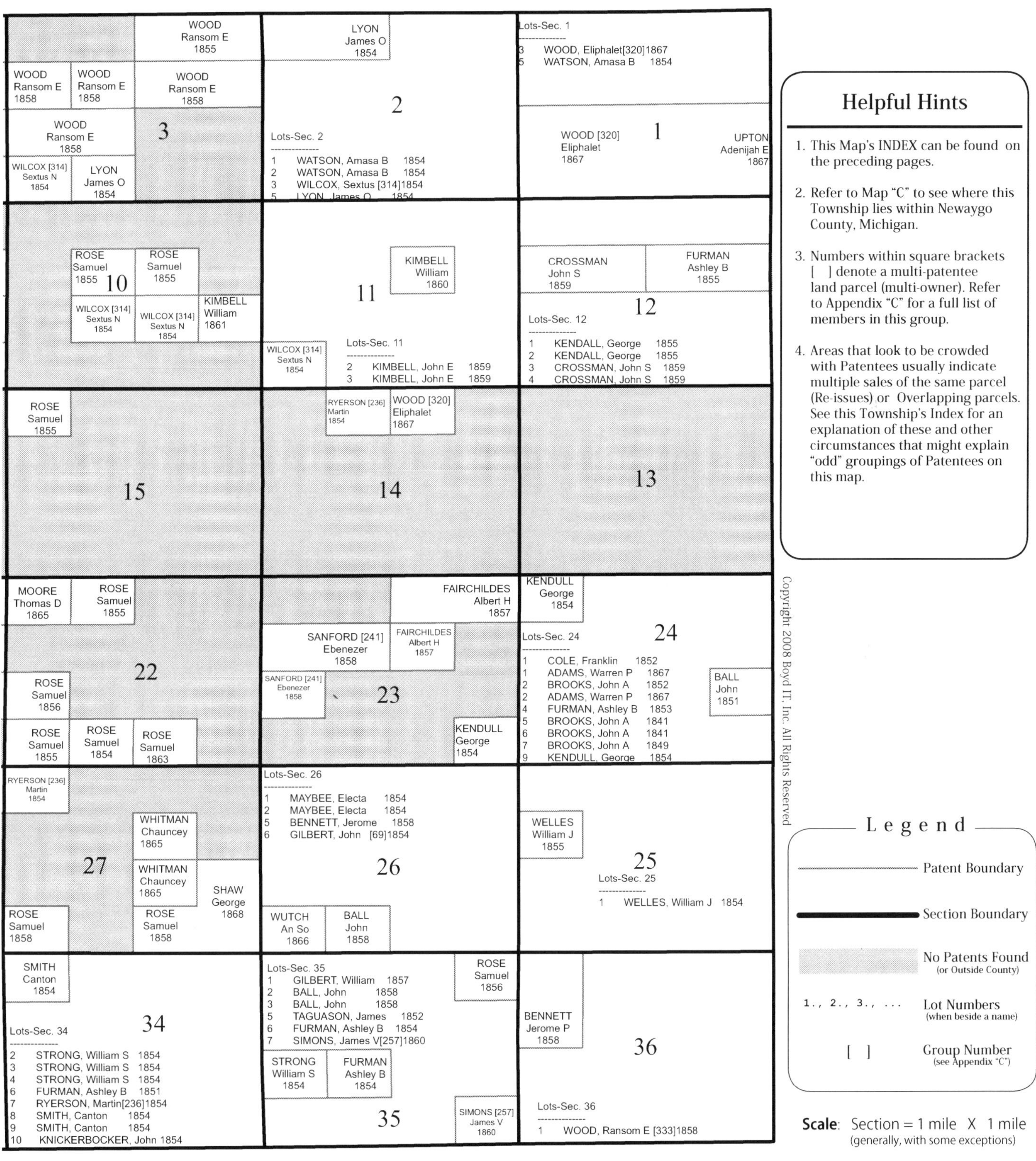
WOOD Ransom E 1855
WOOD Ransom E 1858
WOOD Ransom E 1858
WOOD Ransom E 1858
WOOD Ransom E 1858
3
WILCOX [314] Sextus N 1854
LYON James O 1854
LYON James O 1854
2
Lots-Sec. 2
1 WATSON, Amasa B 1854
2 WATSON, Amasa B 1854
3 WILCOX, Sextus [314]1854
5 LYON, James O 1854
Lots-Sec. 1
3 WOOD, Eliphalet[320]1867
5 WATSON, Amasa B 1854
WOOD [320] Eliphalet 1867
1
UPTON Adenijah E 1867
ROSE Samuel 1855
10
ROSE Samuel 1855
WILCOX [314] Sextus N 1854
WILCOX [314] Sextus N 1854
KIMBELL William 1861
KIMBELL William 1860
11
WILCOX [314] Sextus N 1854
Lots-Sec. 11
2 KIMBELL, John E 1859
3 KIMBELL, John E 1859
CROSSMAN John S 1859
FURMAN Ashley B 1855
12
Lots-Sec. 12
1 KENDALL, George 1855
2 KENDALL, George 1855
3 CROSSMAN, John S 1859
4 CROSSMAN, John S 1859
ROSE Samuel 1855
15
RYERSON [236] Martin 1854
WOOD [320] Eliphalet 1867
14
13
MOORE Thomas D 1865
ROSE Samuel 1855
22
ROSE Samuel 1856
ROSE Samuel 1855
ROSE Samuel 1854
ROSE Samuel 1863
FAIRCHILDES Albert H 1857
SANFORD [241] Ebenezer 1858
FAIRCHILDES Albert H 1857
SANFORD [241] Ebenezer 1858
23
KENDULL George 1854
KENDULL George 1854
24
Lots-Sec. 24
1 COLE, Franklin 1852
1 ADAMS, Warren P 1867
2 BROOKS, John A 1852
2 ADAMS, Warren P 1867
4 FURMAN, Ashley B 1853
5 BROOKS, John A 1841
6 BROOKS, John A 1841
7 BROOKS, John A 1849
9 KENDULL, George 1854
BALL John 1851
RYERSON [236] Martin 1854
WHITMAN Chauncey 1865
27
WHITMAN Chauncey 1865
SHAW George 1868
ROSE Samuel 1858
ROSE Samuel 1858
Lots-Sec. 26
1 MAYBEE, Electa 1854
2 MAYBEE, Electa 1854
5 BENNETT, Jerome 1858
6 GILBERT, John [69]1854
26
WUTCH An So 1866
BALL John 1858
WELLES William J 1855
25
Lots-Sec. 25
1 WELLES, William J 1854
SMITH Canton 1854
34
Lots-Sec. 34
2 STRONG, William S 1854
3 STRONG, William S 1854
4 STRONG, William S 1854
6 FURMAN, Ashley B 1851
7 RYERSON, Martin[236]1854
8 SMITH, Canton 1854
9 SMITH, Canton 1854
10 KNICKERBOCKER, John 1854
Lots-Sec. 35
1 GILBERT, William 1857
2 BALL, John 1858
3 BALL, John 1858
5 TAGUASON, James 1852
6 FURMAN, Ashley B 1854
7 SIMONS, James V[257]1860
ROSE Samuel 1856
STRONG William S 1854
FURMAN Ashley B 1854
35
SIMONS [257] James V 1860
BENNETT Jerome P 1858
36
Lots-Sec. 36
1 WOOD, Ransom E [333]1858
Helpful Hints
1. This Map's INDEX can be found on the preceding pages.
2. Refer to Map "C" to see where this Township lies within Newaygo County, Michigan.
3. Numbers within square brackets [ ] denote a multi-patentee land parcel (multi-owner). Refer to Appendix "C" for a full list of members in this group.
4. Areas that look to be crowded with Patentees usually indicate multiple sales of the same parcel (Re-issues) or Overlapping parcels. See this Township's Index for an explanation of these and other circumstances that might explain "odd" groupings of Patentees on this map.
Copyright 2008 Boyd IT, Inc. All Rights Reserved
Legend
Patent Boundary
Section Boundary
No Patents Found (or Outside County)
1., 2., 3., ... Lot Numbers (when beside a name)
[ ] Group Number (see Appendix "C")

Scale: Section = 1 mile X 1 mile (generally, with some exceptions)

Road Map

T12-N R13-W
Michigan-Toledo Strip Meridian

Map Group 18

Cities & Towns
Bishop

Cemeteries
Saint Marks Cemetery

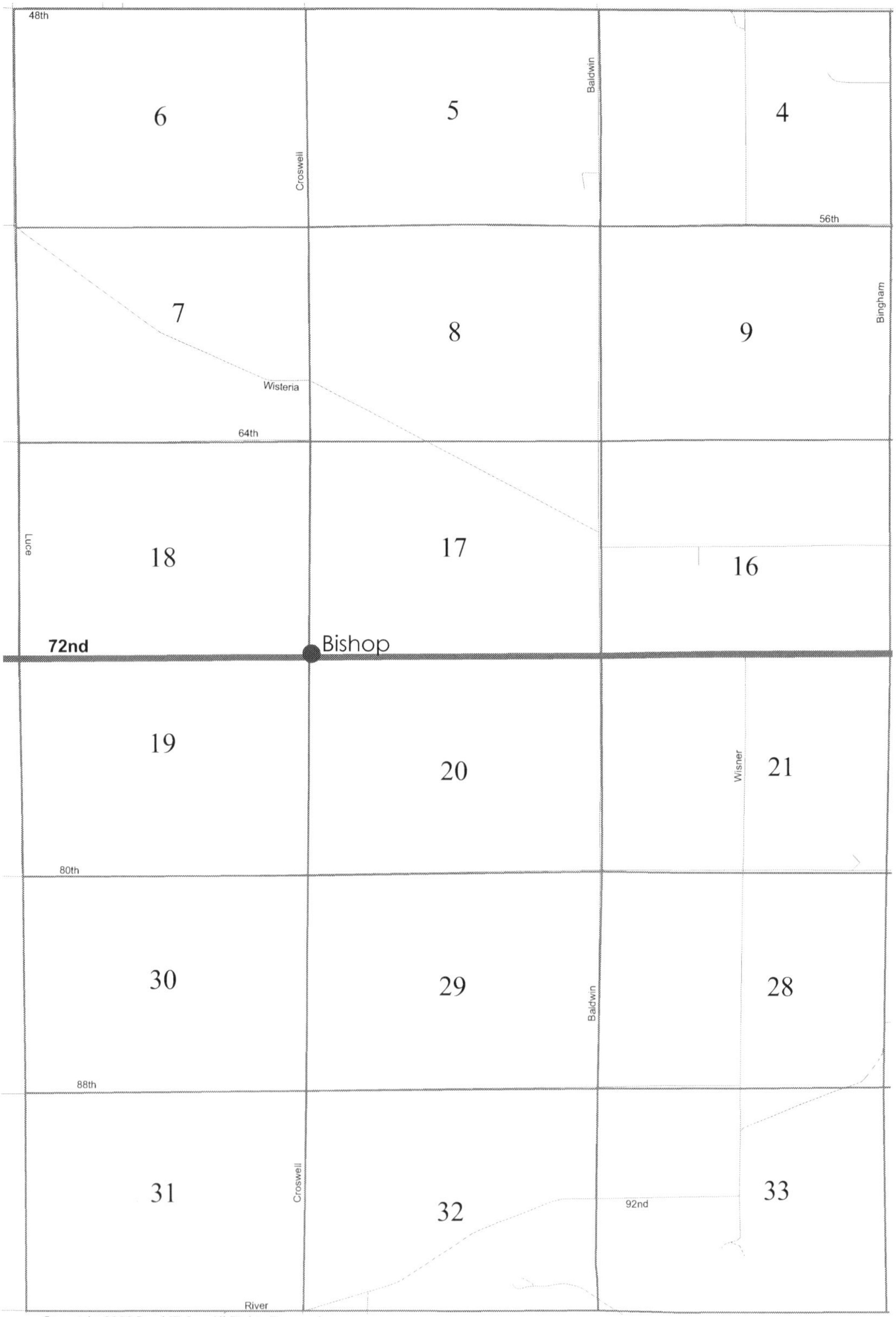

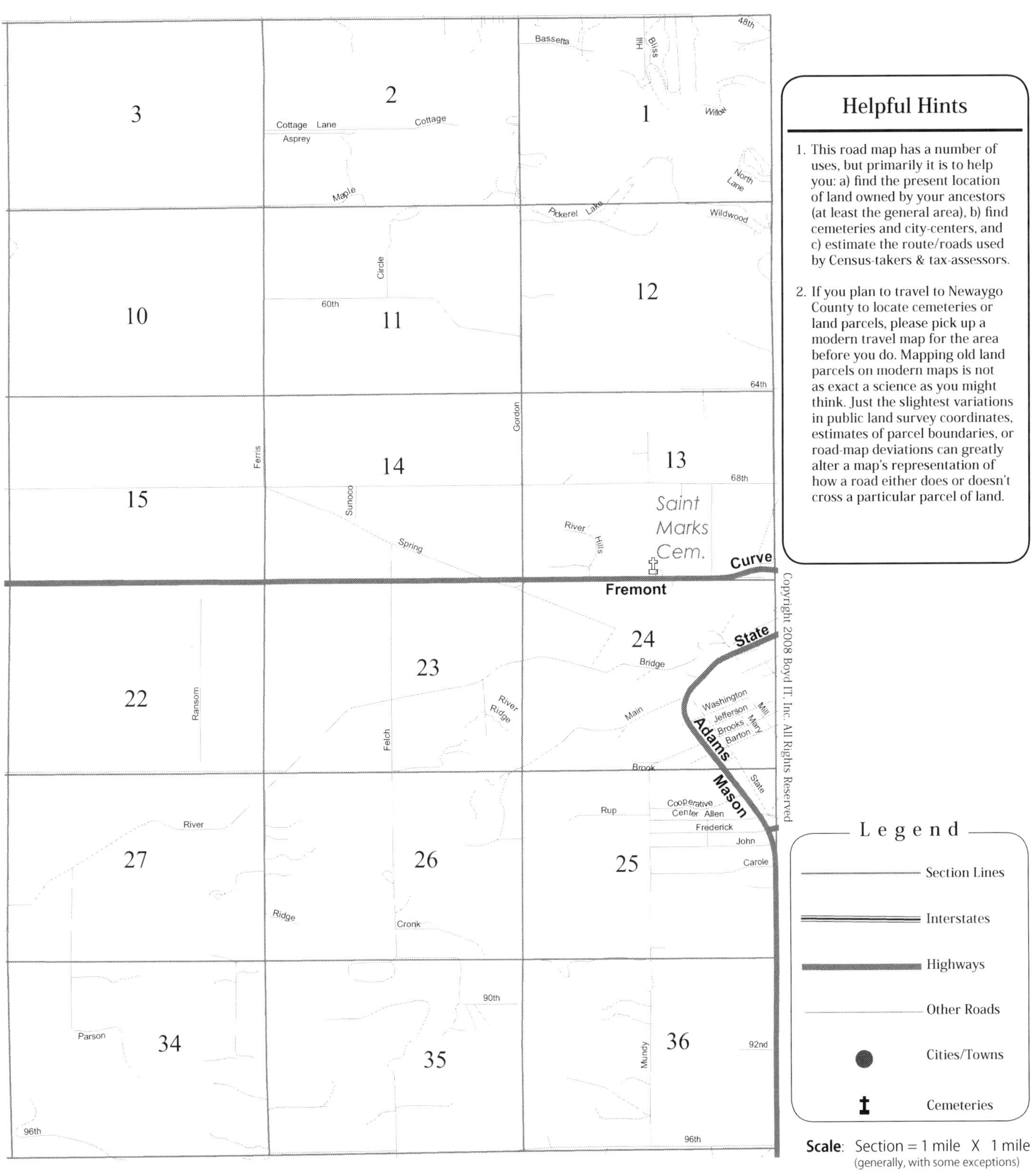
3
2
1
Cottage Lane
Cottage
Asprey
Maple
Bassetta
Hill
Bliss
48th
Willow
North Lane
Pickerel Lake
Wildwood
10
11
12
Circle
60th
64th
15
14
13
Ferris
Gordon
Sunoco
Spring
68th
River
Hills
Saint Marks Cem.
Curve
Fremont
22
23
24
Ransom
Felch
River Ridge
Bridge
State
Main
Washington
Jefferson
Brooks
Barton
Mill
Mary
Adams
Brook
Mason
State
27
26
25
River
Ridge
Cronk
Rup
Cooperative
Center
Allen
Frederick
John
Carole
34
35
36
Parson
90th
Mundy
92nd
96th
96th
Copyright 2008 Boyd IT, Inc. All Rights Reserved
Helpful Hints
1. This road map has a number of uses, but primarily it is to help you: a) find the present location of land owned by your ancestors (at least the general area), b) find cemeteries and city-centers, and c) estimate the route/roads used by Census-takers & tax-assessors.
2. If you plan to travel to Newaygo County to locate cemeteries or land parcels, please pick up a modern travel map for the area before you do. Mapping old land parcels on modern maps is not as exact a science as you might think. Just the slightest variations in public land survey coordinates, estimates of parcel boundaries, or road-map deviations can greatly alter a map's representation of how a road either does or doesn't cross a particular parcel of land.
Legend
Section Lines
Interstates
Highways
Other Roads
Cities/Towns
Cemeteries
Scale: Section = 1 mile X 1 mile
(generally, with some exceptions)

Historical Map

T12-N R13-W
Michigan-Toledo Strip Meridian

Map Group 18

Cities & Towns
Bishop

Cemeteries
Saint Marks Cemetery

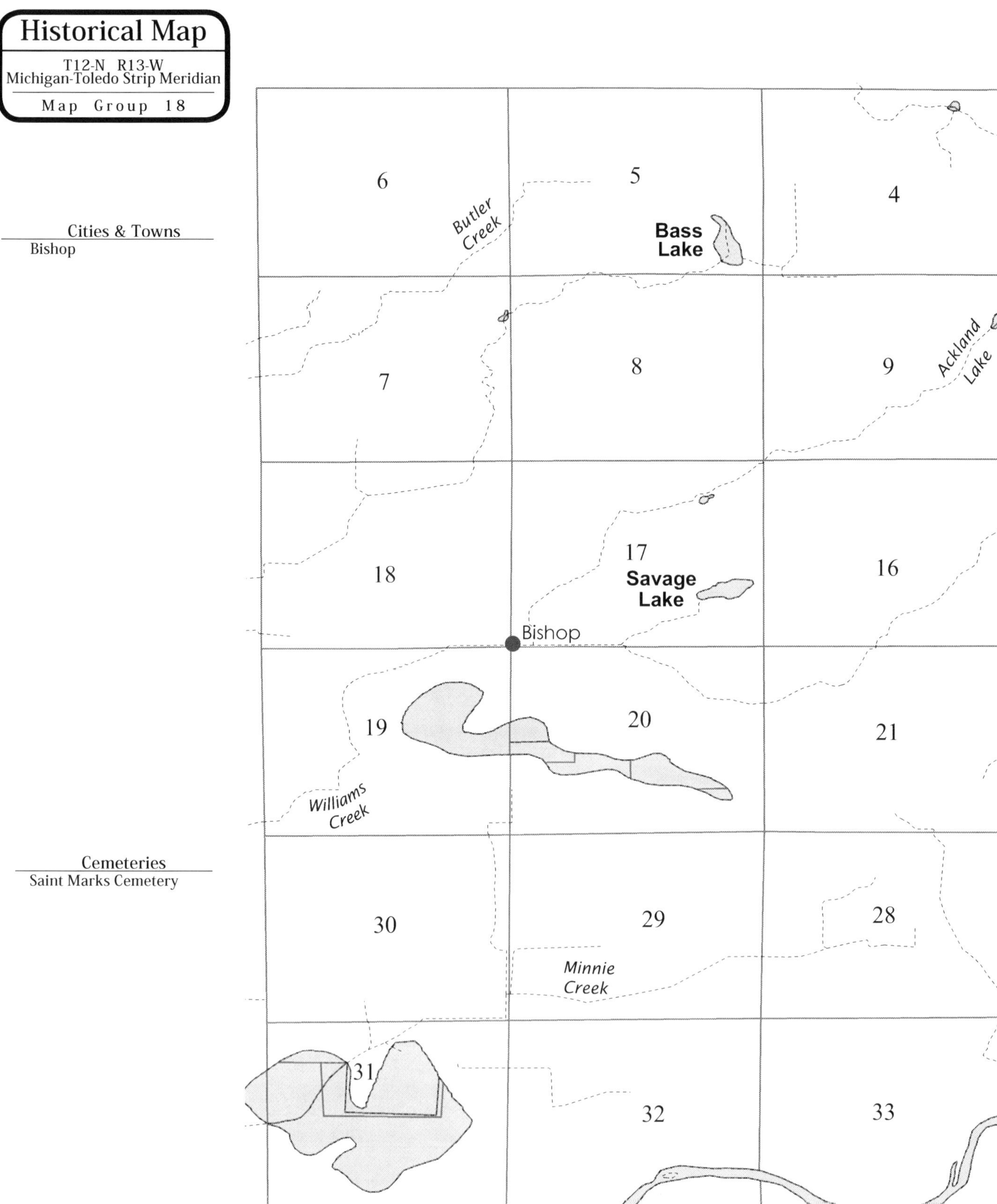

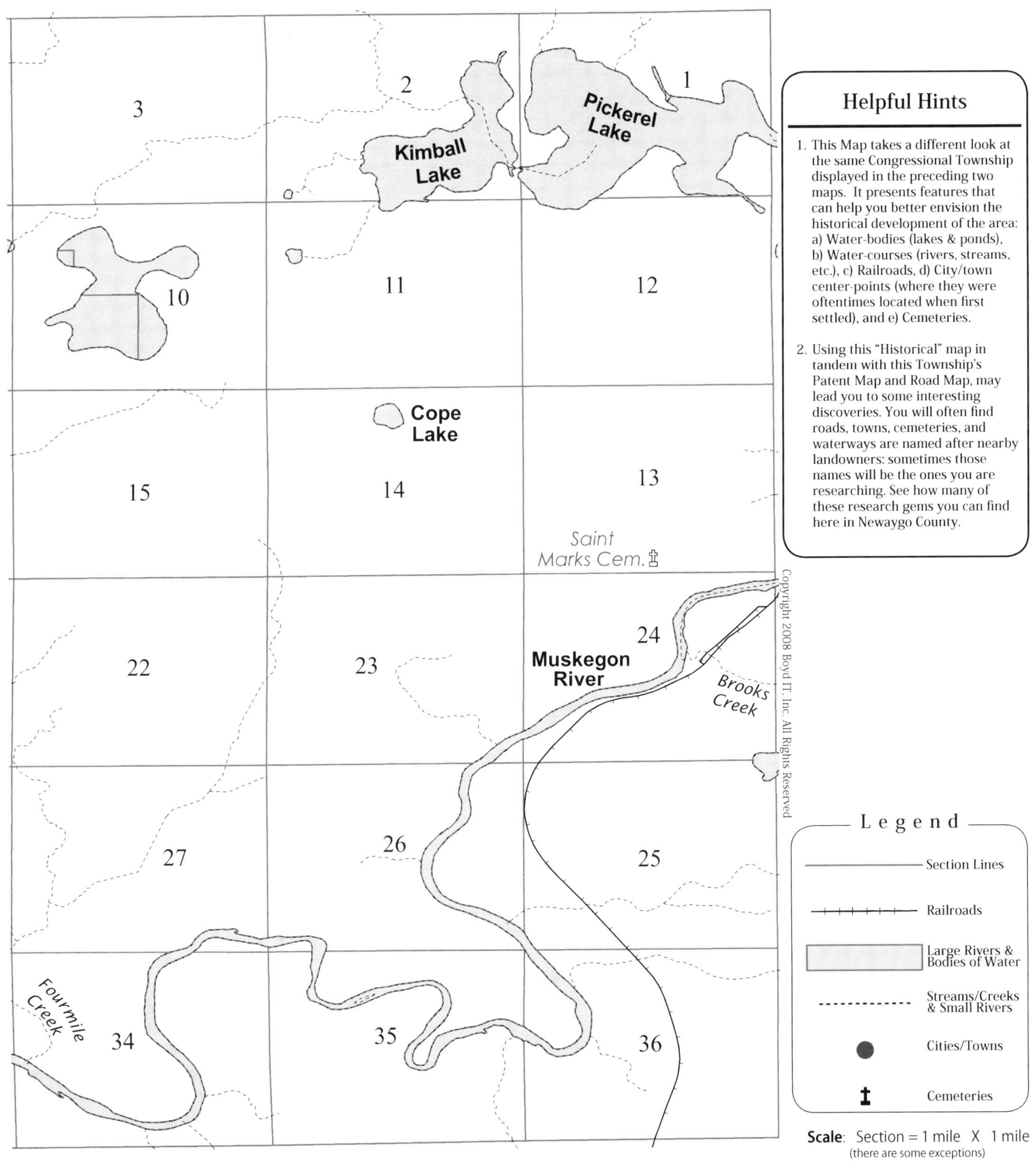

Helpful Hints

1. This Map takes a different look at the same Congressional Township displayed in the preceding two maps. It presents features that can help you better envision the historical development of the area: a) Water-bodies (lakes & ponds), b) Water-courses (rivers, streams, etc.), c) Railroads, d) City/town center-points (where they were oftentimes located when first settled), and e) Cemeteries.

2. Using this "Historical" map in tandem with this Township's Patent Map and Road Map, may lead you to some interesting discoveries. You will often find roads, towns, cemeteries, and waterways are named after nearby landowners: sometimes those names will be the ones you are researching. See how many of these research gems you can find here in Newaygo County.

Legend

- Section Lines
- Railroads
- Large Rivers & Bodies of Water
- Streams/Creeks & Small Rivers
- Cities/Towns
- Cemeteries

Scale: Section = 1 mile X 1 mile
(there are some exceptions)

Map Group 19: Index to Land Patents

Township 12-North Range 12-West (Michigan-Toledo Strip)

After you locate an individual in this Index, take note of the Section and Section Part then proceed to the Land Patent map on the pages immediately following. You should have no difficulty locating the corresponding parcel of land.

The "For More Info" Column will lead you to more information about the underlying Patents. See the *Legend* at right, and the "How to Use this Book" chapter, for more information.

LEGEND

"For More Info . . . " column

- **A** = Authority (Legislative Act, See Appendix "A")
- **B** = Block or Lot (location in Section unknown)
- **C** = Cancelled Patent
- **F** = Fractional Section
- **G** = Group (Multi-Patentee Patent, see Appendix "C")
- **V** = Overlaps another Parcel
- **R** = Re-Issued (Parcel patented more than once)

(A & G items require you to look in the Appendixes referred to above. All other Letter-designations followed by a number require you to locate line-items in this index that possess the ID number found after the letter).

ID	Individual in Patent	Sec.	Sec. Part	Date Issued	Other Counties	For More Info . . .
2684	ARMS, Lewis L	24	2	1854-09-15		A1 G35
2685	" "	24	3	1854-09-15		A1 G35
2686	" "	26	NWNW	1854-09-15		A1 G35 F
2687	" "	6	SWSE	1855-12-15		A1 G36
2788	AUGERINE, John	4	SENE	1872-04-05		A1
2789	BALL, John	14	7	1856-03-10		A1
2774	BARNHARD, Jacob	19	NESE	1854-06-15		A1
2834	BARNHARD, Simon	3	SWNE	1852-03-10		A1
2807	BARNUM, Linus	15	N½NW	1858-05-01		A1
2838	BEMENT, Theodore W	28	2	1882-03-20		A4
2839	" "	28	3	1882-03-20		A4
2771	BENNETT, Jacob B	22	4	1866-06-05		A1 R2701
2772	" "	27	2	1866-06-05		A1
2773	" "	27	3	1866-06-05		A1
2775	BERRY, James P	22	6	1858-05-01		A1 F
2776	" "	22	NESE	1858-05-01		A1 F
2722	BIGELOW, Czar J	22	7	1854-06-15		A1
2727	BIGELOW, Daniel L	17	SWSE	1850-12-10		A1
2728	" "	20	1	1854-06-15		A1
2725	" "	17	NWNE	1855-12-15		A1
2726	" "	17	SESE	1855-12-15		A1
2779	BISBEE, Jasper E	26	SW	1872-04-05		A4
2820	BISBEE, Nahum A	26	NE	1869-11-01		A4
2787	BROOKS, John A	20	2	1848-06-01		A1 G28
2783	" "	19	4	1850-12-10		A1
2782	" "	19	1	1853-11-01		A1
2781	" "	18	SESE	1854-06-15		A1
2784	" "	21	1	1854-06-15		A1
2785	" "	23	NWSE	1854-06-15		A1
2786	" "	27	NWNW	1855-11-01		A1
2742	CASS, Esra	10	W½NE	1871-05-01		A4
2819	CHARLOE, Mitchell	15	SWNE	1860-06-01		A1
2684	CHENEY, Albert N	24	2	1854-09-15		A1 G35
2685	" "	24	3	1854-09-15		A1 G35
2686	" "	26	NWNW	1854-09-15		A1 G35 F
2687	" "	6	SWSE	1855-12-15		A1 G36
2825	CHURCH, Ortha S	1	NESE	1851-05-01		A1
2723	CLAY, D T	32	SE	1879-04-15		A1 F
2713	COLE, Charles L	24	7	1857-07-01		A1
2714	" "	24	8	1857-07-01		A1
2715	" "	25	1	1857-07-01		A1
2833	COOK, Silas	34	NW	1879-11-25		A4
2843	COOK, William C	34	SE	1878-06-13		A4
2823	CROFOOT, Norman L	10	E½NE	1857-03-10		A1
2683	CULVER, Albert B	27	4	1868-02-15		A1 C F
2745	CURTIS, Frank L	28	SESE	1870-07-15		A1 F

ID	Individual in Patent	Sec.	Sec. Part	Date Issued	Other Counties	For More Info . . .
2690	DAVIS, Alice	10	NWSE	1857-03-10		A1
2791	DAVIS, John	11	SWNW	1853-11-01		A1
2790	" "	10	NESE	1854-06-15		A1
2845	DECKER, William D	1	SESW	1850-04-01		A1
2844	" "	1	NESW	1850-12-10		A1
2846	" "	1	SWSW	1850-12-10		A1
2799	DICKERSON, Wallace W	6	SENW	1870-08-10		A1 G228
2854	EDMONSON, William P	10	SWSE	1874-08-01		A4
2762	FRISBY, George M	26	NWSE	1876-03-20		A4
2780	FULLMER, Jeremiah	10	SW	1868-10-01		A3 G65
2703	FURMAN, Ashley B	7	W½NW	1855-12-15		A1
2704	" "	7	W½SW	1855-12-15		A1 F
2702	" "	5	W½SW	1859-12-01		A3
2792	GILBERT, John	4	E½SW	1874-02-20		A4
2793	" "	4	SWSW	1874-02-20		A4
2780	GOODRIDGE, Charles	10	SW	1868-10-01		A3 G65
2815	HART, Martin	26	1	1869-11-01		A4
2816	" "	26	2	1869-11-01		A4
2817	" "	26	SENW	1869-11-01		A4 F
2769	HASCALL, Herbert A	36	NWSE	1860-10-01		A3 G81
2770	" "	36	W½NE	1860-10-01		A3 G81
2821	HIGBEE, Nelson	36	NENW	1851-05-01		A1
2717	HILLS, Charles T	14	SWSW	1880-03-05		A1 F
2718	" "	24	6	1880-03-05		A1
2847	HOWE, William	5	1	1860-10-01		A3
2848	" "	5	2	1860-10-01		A3
2849	" "	5	SENW	1860-10-01		A3 F
2850	" "	8	SWNE	1867-01-10		A1
2766	HYDE, Hannibal	12	W½NW	1848-06-01		A1
2777	IRONS, James W	36	W½NW	1857-03-10		A1
2778	" "	36	W½SW	1857-03-10		A1
2748	KENDALL, George	28	1	1854-06-15		A1
2749	" "	28	4	1854-06-15		A1
2750	" "	28	SWSW	1854-06-15		A1 F
2747	" "	27	N½NE	1856-03-10		A1
2746	" "	18	W½NE	1857-03-10		A1
2751	KENDULL, George	18	NESW	1854-06-15		A1
2752	" "	29	1	1854-06-15		A1
2753	" "	29	2	1854-06-15		A1
2754	" "	29	SESE	1854-06-15		A1
2755	" "	30	W½NW	1854-06-15		A1 F
2756	" "	30	W½SW	1854-06-15		A1 F
2757	" "	31	1	1854-06-15		A1
2758	" "	31	SW	1854-06-15		A1 F
2759	" "	32	1	1854-06-15		A1
2760	" "	32	2	1854-06-15		A1
2761	" "	33	3	1854-06-15		A1
2808	KETCHUM, Lorin E	4	NWSE	1857-03-10		A1
2851	LASLEY, William	14	4	1841-11-10		A1
2852	" "	22	1	1841-11-10		A1
2853	" "	22	2	1841-11-10		A1
2735	LAWRENCE, John	8	E½SW	1866-11-10		A3 G321
2736	" "	8	N½SE	1866-11-10		A3 G321
2734	" "	5	NENW	1867-01-10		A1 G320 F
2763	LESTER, George W	24	5	1860-10-01		A3
2764	" "	24	NWSW	1860-10-01		A3
2795	LEWIS, John	10	E½NW	1871-05-01		A4
2796	" "	10	SWNW	1871-05-01		A4
2809	LOVELL, Louis S	33	2	1856-03-10		A1
2797	MCBRIDE, John	2	SESE	1849-04-05		A1
2812	MELANCON, Maise	11	NENE	1849-02-01		A1
2811	" "	1	SWSE	1850-04-01		A1
2787	MERRILL, Isaac D	20	2	1848-06-01		A1 G28
2831	METEVY, Samuel	11	NWNE	1853-08-01		A1
2830	MORGAN, Samuel F	34	SW	1868-02-10		A3 G194
2832	MOYE, Samuel	21	9	1855-11-01		A1
2794	MUNDY, John H	14	NWNW	1857-03-10		A1
2719	NICHOLS, Chauncey H	36	SESW	1857-03-10		A1
2720	" "	36	SWSE	1857-03-10		A1
2741	NICHOLS, Erastus G	25	SE	1857-03-10		A1
2798	NIEGLESON, John	15	E½NE	1841-11-10		A1
2822	NORTHROP, Nelson W	8	SWSE	1867-01-10		A1
2680	ORTON, Alonson F	30	E½NE	1858-01-15		A3 G281

ID	Individual in Patent	Sec.	Sec. Part	Date Issued	Other Counties	For More Info . . .
2681	ORTON, Alonson F (Cont'd)	5	E½SW	1858-01-15		A3 G281
2678	" "	5	S½SE	1858-01-15		A3 G280
2679	" "	8	NWNE	1858-01-15		A3 G280
2678	ORTON, Henry F	5	S½SE	1858-01-15		A3 G280
2679	" "	8	NWNE	1858-01-15		A3 G280
2680	ORTON, Henry J	30	E½NE	1858-01-15		A3 G281
2681	" "	5	E½SW	1858-01-15		A3 G281
2810	ORTON, Lydia A	8	NENE	1885-01-07		A1
2705	PADDOCK, Augustus	4	NWNW	1867-01-10		A1 F
2706	" "	4	NWSW	1867-01-10		A1
2707	" "	5	NWSE	1867-01-10		A1
2708	" "	8	SESE	1870-08-10		A1
2767	PALMER, Harriet C	12	E½NW	1850-04-01		A1
2829	PEIRCE, Richard	34	NE	1869-11-01		A4
2709	PENNOYER, Augustus	18	W½SW	1841-11-10		A1 F
2710	" "	19	2	1841-11-10		A1
2711	" "	19	3	1841-11-10		A1
2712	" "	20	3	1841-11-10		A1
2732	PLATT, Eli	14	3	1854-10-05		A1 F
2733	" "	14	NENW	1854-10-05		A1 F
2830	PORTER, Abigail	34	SW	1868-02-10		A3 G194
2700	PRATT, Angeline M	22	3	1858-05-01		A1
2701	" "	22	4	1858-05-01		A1 R2771
2813	PRESTON, Margaret	2	NESE	1852-03-10		A1
2814	" "	2	W½SE	1852-03-10		A1
2743	PRUDDEN, Ezra	26	E½SE	1861-07-01		A3
2744	" "	26	SWSE	1861-07-01		A3
2837	REED, Sylvanus	1	S½NE	1850-04-01		A1
2836	" "	1	NWSE	1850-12-10		A1
2688	REEVES, Albert	36	E½NE	1860-09-01		A1
2689	" "	36	E½SE	1860-09-01		A1
2835	RIBLET, Solomon K	4	NWNE	1885-01-07		A1 F
2799	ROCHESTER, John W	6	SENW	1870-08-10		A1 G228
2735	ROGERS, Effy	8	E½SW	1866-11-10		A3 G321
2736	" "	8	N½SE	1866-11-10		A3 G321
2735	ROGERS, William C	8	E½SW	1866-11-10		A3 G321
2736	" "	8	N½SE	1866-11-10		A3 G321
2824	SEAMAN, Oliver H	22	E½NE	1855-12-15		A1 F
2826	SEAMAN, Peter	10	NWNW	1854-10-05		A1
2827	" "	22	NWNE	1857-07-01		A1
2716	SLADE, Charles P	11	E½SW	1857-03-10		A1
2724	SLADE, Daniel G	11	W½SW	1858-05-01		A1
2721	SMITH, Clark W	1	NWNE	1857-03-10		A1 F
2855	SMITH, William	20	6	1854-09-15		A1
2856	" "	30	W½NE	1855-12-15		A1
2801	SPENCER, Labin	24	1	1858-05-01		A1
2818	STAILER, Michael	12	SENE	1852-03-10		A1
2840	STIMSON, Thomas D	13	SESE	1857-03-10		A1
2738	STODDARD, Emery D	21	SESW	1865-10-10		A1
2739	" "	21	SWSE	1865-10-10		A1
2740	" "	28	NWNE	1865-10-10		A1
2828	SURRARRER, Ransom	23	4	1854-06-15		A1
2680	SWAIN, Aaron	30	E½NE	1858-01-15		A3 G281
2681	" "	5	E½SW	1858-01-15		A3 G281
2678	" "	5	S½SE	1858-01-15		A3 G280
2679	" "	8	NWNE	1858-01-15		A3 G280
2806	THOMPSON, Levi J	10	SESE	1856-03-10		A1
2765	TRIPP, Gideon B	36	SENW	1864-11-01		A1
2802	TRIPP, Laney	1	SESE	1850-12-10		A1
2803	" "	12	NENE	1850-12-10		A1
2691	TROWBRIDGE, Alva	6	2	1854-10-05		A1
2804	TRUDE, Leonard L	4	E½SE	1874-08-01		A4
2805	" "	4	SWSE	1874-08-01		A4
2682	UPTON, Adonijah E	8	SENE	1868-02-15		A1
2800	WARANGASOE, Joseph	14	8	1848-02-01		A1
2768	WARTROUS, Harry S	36	NESW	1885-12-07		A1
2692	WATSON, Amasa B	22	11	1854-06-15		A1
2693	" "	22	5	1854-06-15		A1
2694	" "	23	1	1854-06-15		A1
2695	" "	23	2	1854-06-15		A1
2696	" "	23	5	1854-06-15		A1
2697	" "	23	6	1854-06-15		A1
2698	" "	27	N	1854-06-15		A1 F

ID	Individual in Patent	Sec.	Sec. Part	Date Issued	Other Counties	For More Info . . .
2699	WATSON, Amasa B (Cont'd)	27	NENE	1854-06-15		A1 F
2687	WELLES, William P	6	SWSE	1855-12-15		A1 G36
2780	WHITNEY, Brazill H	10	SW	1868-10-01		A3 G65
2730	WHITNEY, David H	13	SENE	1855-12-15		A1
2729	" "	13	NESE	1856-03-10		A1
2841	WIGGINS, Thomas J	14	5	1855-03-01		A1
2842	" "	14	6	1855-03-01		A1
2769	WILLIAMS, Ann	36	NWSE	1860-10-01		A3 G81
2770	" "	36	W½NE	1860-10-01		A3 G81
2737	WILSON, Elizabeth	11	SENE	1850-12-10		A1
2735	WOOD, Eliphalet	8	E½SW	1866-11-10		A3 G321
2736	" "	8	N½SE	1866-11-10		A3 G321
2734	" "	5	NENW	1867-01-10		A1 G320 F
2731	WOODRUFF, David	1	NWSW	1851-05-01		A1

Patent Map

T12-N R12-W
Michigan-Toledo Strip Meridian

Map Group 19

Township Statistics

Parcels Mapped	:	179
Number of Patents	:	137
Number of Individuals	:	109
Patentees Identified	:	99
Number of Surnames	:	94
Multi-Patentee Parcels	:	17
Oldest Patent Date	:	11/10/1841
Most Recent Patent	:	12/7/1885
Block/Lot Parcels	:	58
Parcels Re - Issued	:	1
Parcels that Overlap	:	0
Cities and Towns	:	1
Cemeteries	:	0

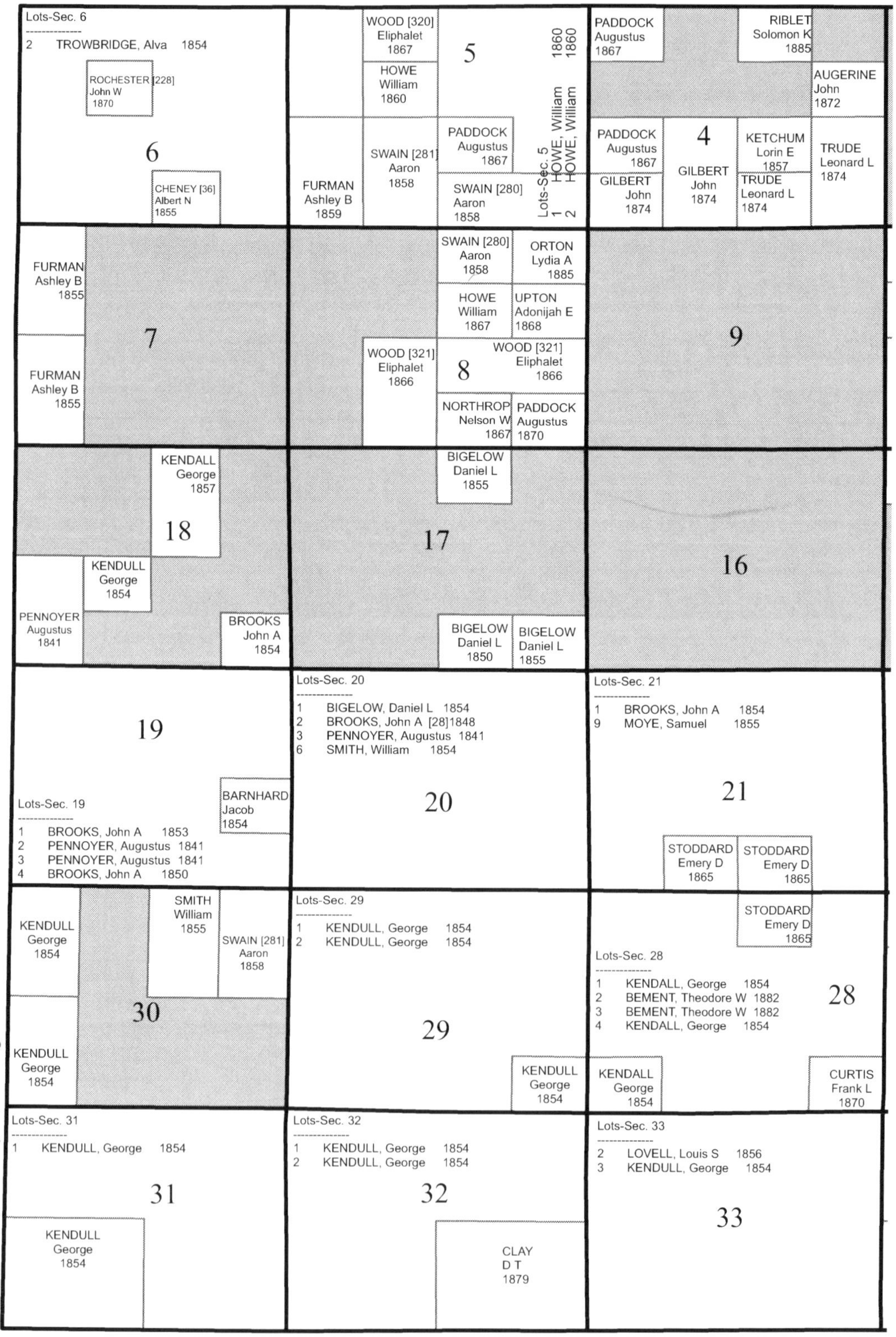

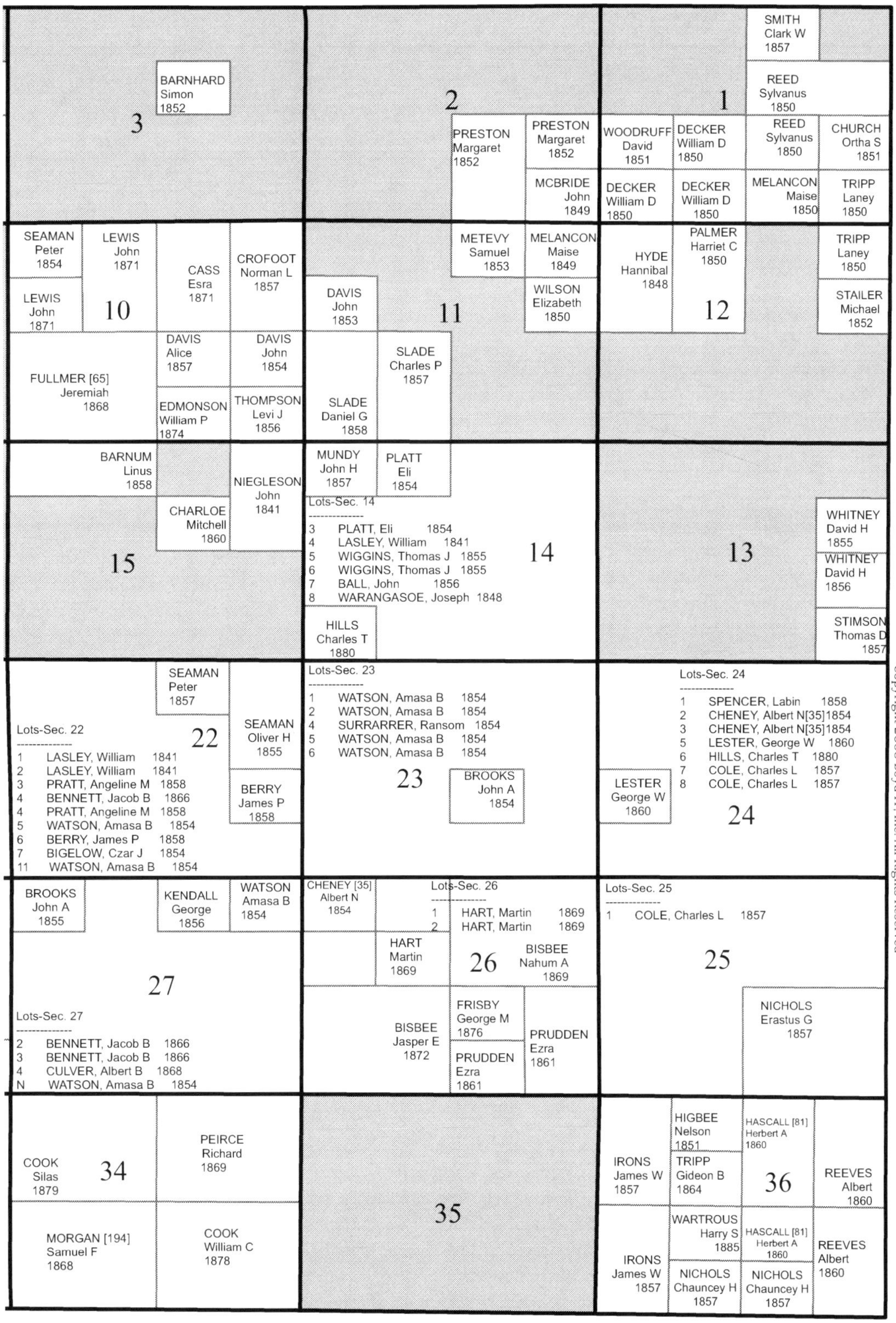

Helpful Hints

1. This Map's INDEX can be found on the preceding pages.
2. Refer to Map "C" to see where this Township lies within Newaygo County, Michigan.
3. Numbers within square brackets [ ] denote a multi-patentee land parcel (multi-owner). Refer to Appendix "C" for a full list of members in this group.
4. Areas that look to be crowded with Patentees usually indicate multiple sales of the same parcel (Re-issues) or Overlapping parcels. See this Township's Index for an explanation of these and other circumstances that might explain "odd" groupings of Patentees on this map.

Legend

- Patent Boundary
- Section Boundary
- No Patents Found (or Outside County)
- 1., 2., 3., ... Lot Numbers (when beside a name)
- [ ] Group Number (see Appendix "C")

Scale: Section = 1 mile X 1 mile (generally, with some exceptions)

Road Map

T12-N R12-W
Michigan-Toledo Strip Meridian

Map Group 19

Cities & Towns

Newaygo

Cemeteries

None

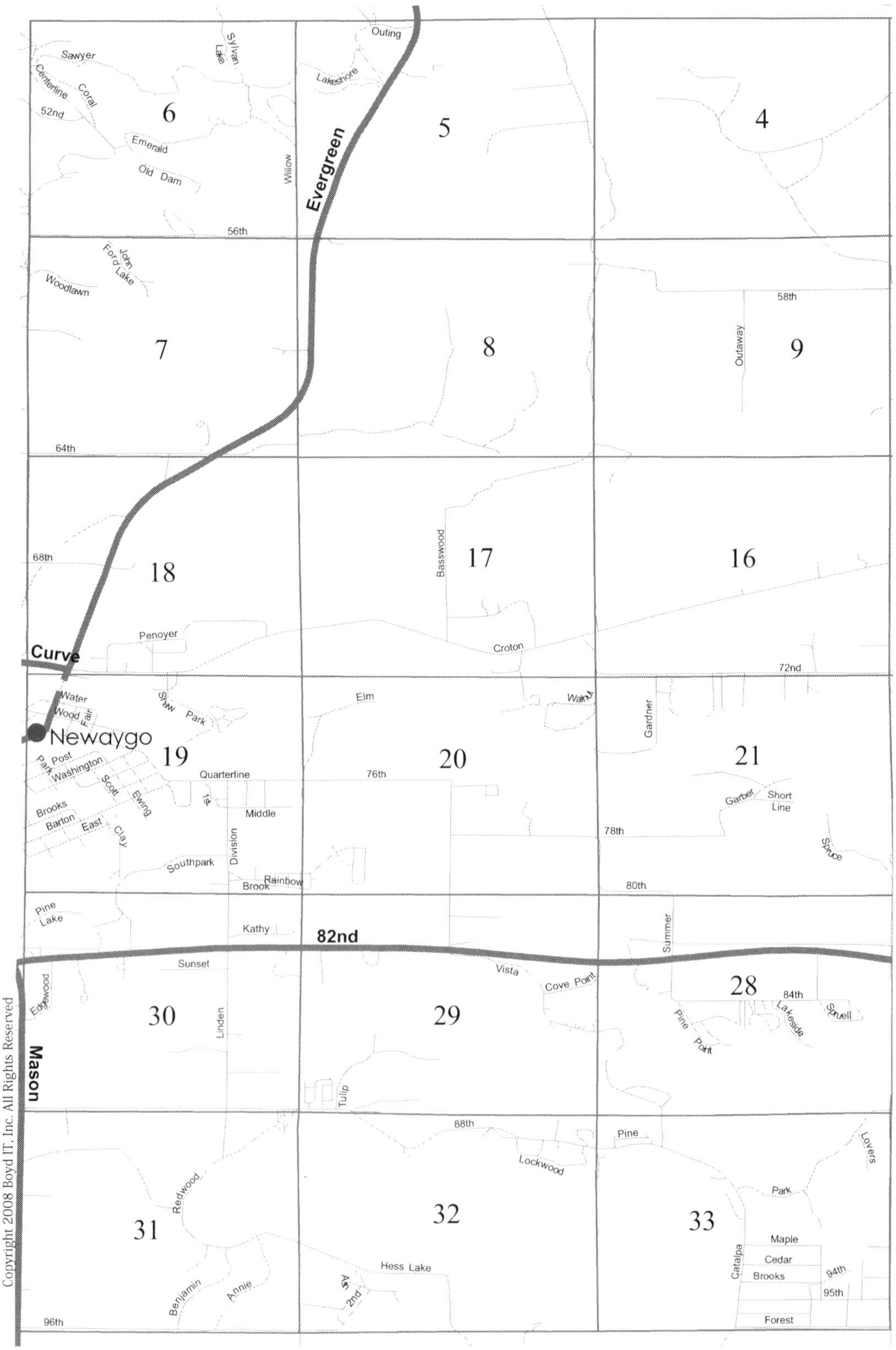

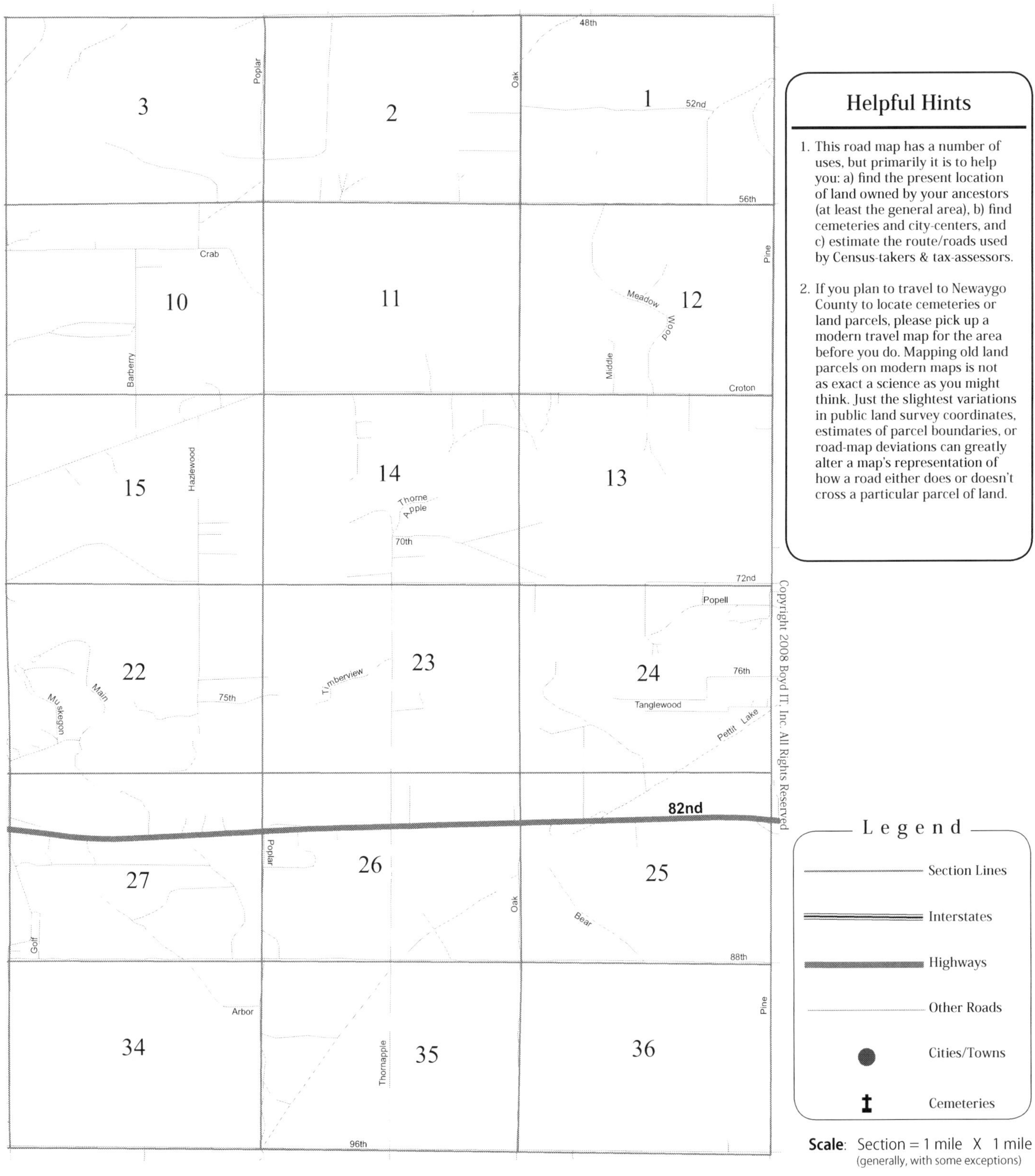

Helpful Hints

1. This road map has a number of uses, but primarily it is to help you: a) find the present location of land owned by your ancestors (at least the general area), b) find cemeteries and city-centers, and c) estimate the route/roads used by Census-takers & tax-assessors.

2. If you plan to travel to Newaygo County to locate cemeteries or land parcels, please pick up a modern travel map for the area before you do. Mapping old land parcels on modern maps is not as exact a science as you might think. Just the slightest variations in public land survey coordinates, estimates of parcel boundaries, or road-map deviations can greatly alter a map's representation of how a road either does or doesn't cross a particular parcel of land.

Scale: Section = 1 mile X 1 mile
(generally, with some exceptions)

Cities & Towns

Newaygo

Cemeteries

None

Emerald Lake
Sylvan Lake
Ibeys Lake
6
5
4
John Ford Lake
7
8
9
Penover Creek
Bigelow Creek
18
17
16
Penover Lake
Newaygo
Muskegon River
Brooks Creek
19
20
21
June Lake
30
Butterfield Lake
29
28
Brooks Lake
32
31
Hess Lake
33

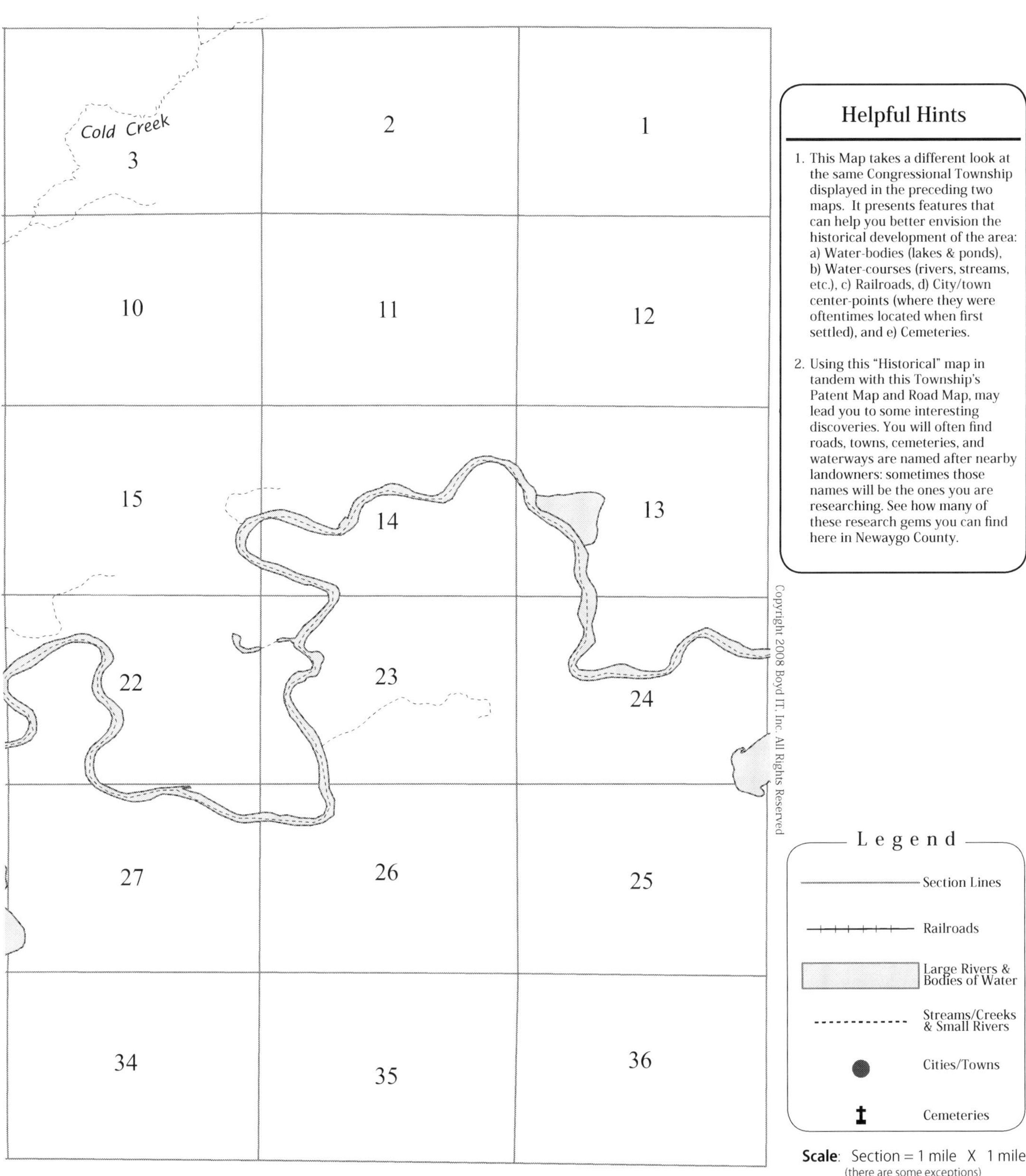

Helpful Hints

1. This Map takes a different look at the same Congressional Township displayed in the preceding two maps. It presents features that can help you better envision the historical development of the area: a) Water-bodies (lakes & ponds), b) Water-courses (rivers, streams, etc.), c) Railroads, d) City/town center-points (where they were oftentimes located when first settled), and e) Cemeteries.

2. Using this "Historical" map in tandem with this Township's Patent Map and Road Map, may lead you to some interesting discoveries. You will often find roads, towns, cemeteries, and waterways are named after nearby landowners: sometimes those names will be the ones you are researching. See how many of these research gems you can find here in Newaygo County.

Map Group 20: Index to Land Patents

Township 12-North Range 11-West (Michigan-Toledo Strip)

After you locate an individual in this Index, take note of the Section and Section Part then proceed to the Land Patent map on the pages immediately following. You should have no difficulty locating the corresponding parcel of land.

The "For More Info" Column will lead you to more information about the underlying Patents. See the *Legend* at right, and the "How to Use this Book" chapter, for more information.

LEGEND

"For More Info . . . " column

A = Authority (Legislative Act, See Appendix "A")
B = Block or Lot (location in Section unknown)
C = Cancelled Patent
F = Fractional Section
G = Group (Multi-Patentee Patent, see Appendix "C")
V = Overlaps another Parcel
R = Re-Issued (Parcel patented more than once)

(A & G items require you to look in the Appendixes referred to above. All other Letter-designations followed by a number require you to locate line-items in this index that possess the ID number found after the letter).

ID	Individual in Patent	Sec.	Sec. Part	Date Issued	Other Counties	For More Info . . .
3041	ANDREWS, Samuel B	14	W½NW	1857-03-10		A1
3042	" "	15	SESE	1857-03-10		A1
2868	ARMS, Lewis L	31	E½SW	1855-12-15		A1 G36
2920	BACKARD, George	14	E½NE	1854-09-15		A1
2921	" "	14	SWNE	1854-09-15		A1
2925	BACKART, George	25	NESE	1854-09-15		A1
2926	" "	5	2	1854-09-15		A1
2922	" "	17	NWSW	1855-12-15		A1
2924	" "	18	NESE	1855-12-15		A1
2927	" "	9	SESE	1855-12-15		A1
2928	" "	9	SESW	1855-12-15		A1
2923	" "	18	7	1856-03-10		A1
2929	BACKHART, George	5	SW	1854-09-15		A1 F R3028
3081	BARTON, William	5	NENW	1855-11-01		A1 F
3091	BEAN, William W	22	NESE	1859-10-10		A1
3092	" "	22	SESE	1860-09-03		A3
3093	" "	23	W½SW	1860-09-03		A3
3039	BENNETT, Sally	27	S½NW	1856-03-10		A1 F
3040	BENNITT, Sally	27	N½SW	1856-03-10		A1
2861	BILLS, Abel	36	SWSE	1854-09-15		A1
2858	" "	30	3	1857-03-10		A1
2859	" "	30	NWSE	1857-03-10		A1
2860	" "	30	S½NE	1857-03-10		A1
3054	BLACKWELL, Thomas J	26	E½SE	1858-05-01		A1
3055	" "	26	NENW	1858-05-01		A1
3056	" "	26	S½NE	1858-05-01		A1
2869	BLANCHARD, Allen	22	SWSW	1858-05-01		A1
2870	" "	27	NWNW	1858-05-01		A1
2886	BOHNE, Charles L	18	6	1841-11-10		A1
2887	" "	7	2	1841-11-10		A1
2888	" "	8	SW	1841-11-10		A1
2889	" "	8	W½SE	1841-11-10		A1
2974	BORDEN, John D	25	NWNE	1856-03-10		A1
3049	BORDEN, Susan	25	SESE	1855-12-15		A1
2973	BOTSFORD, Jerome A	9	W½SW	1858-05-01		A1
2909	BRUCE, Donald	6	NESW	1849-04-15		A1
2952	BURKE, James H	29	NWNW	1858-05-01		A1
3014	BUSH, Levi M	19	1	1859-10-10		A1
3015	" "	19	2	1859-10-10		A1
2998	CADY, Joseph	22	NENW	1862-08-01		A3
2999	" "	22	W½NW	1862-08-01		A3
3082	CALLAR, William	23	SENE	1858-05-01		A1
3083	" "	24	SWNW	1858-05-01		A1
2879	CARPENTER, Asa P	6	NENW	1853-11-01		A1
2907	CAVENDER, Dennis	29	W½SE	1858-05-01		A1
2908	" "	32	1	1871-02-01		A4

ID	Individual in Patent	Sec.	Sec. Part	Date Issued	Other Counties	For More Info . . .
2868	CHENEY, Albert N	31	E½SW	1855-12-15		A1 G36
3061	COLVER, Timothy J	7	NWNW	1850-04-01		A1 F
2899	CRAM, David	21	NESW	1857-03-10		A1
2900	CULP, David	10	NESW	1854-06-15		A1
3045	DAGGETT, Simeon	13	SENE	1856-03-10		A1
2967	DAVIDSON, Miriam	29	W½NE	1859-08-10		A3 G195
2910	DELANO, Durfey H	15	N½NW	1856-03-10		A1
2911	" "	15	NENE	1856-03-10		A1
2912	" "	15	W½NE	1856-03-10		A1
2865	DOTY, Achsah M	30	NESW	1889-03-16		A4 G53
2865	DOTY, Edith B	30	NESW	1889-03-16		A4 G53
2865	DOTY, Enoch	30	NESW	1889-03-16		A4 G53
2865	DOTY, Rowena L	30	NESW	1889-03-16		A4 G53
3066	EASTMAN, Galen	15	NESW	1855-12-15		A1 G168
3067	" "	15	NWSE	1855-12-15		A1 G168
3068	" "	15	S½NW	1855-12-15		A1 G168
3069	" "	17	NWNE	1855-12-15		A1 G168
3070	" "	2	NWNW	1855-12-15		A1 G168 F
3071	" "	3	N½NW	1855-12-15		A1 G168 F
3072	" "	5	SESE	1855-12-15		A1 G168 F
3073	" "	8	2	1855-12-15		A1 G168
3074	" "	8	3	1855-12-15		A1 G168
3075	" "	8	E½SE	1855-12-15		A1 G168
2866	FINCH, Addison	23	NESW	1858-05-01		A1
2867	" "	23	SENW	1858-05-01		A1
3076	FINCH, Warren	23	SWNW	1857-03-10		A1
2939	FROST, George S	14	SWSE	1858-05-01		A1
2965	GARDNER, Anna	20	SWNE	1858-01-15		A3 G196
2966	" "	20	W½SE	1858-01-15		A3 G196
2919	GAUWEILER, Frederick	10	NWSW	1852-03-10		A1 G67
2968	GOODWILL, Jeremiah P	12	SENW	1923-02-19		A4
3077	GRIFFES, William A	36	NWSE	1870-07-15		A4
2949	GRIFFIN, Isaac	29	1	1859-10-10		A1
2950	" "	29	E½NW	1859-10-10		A1
2951	" "	29	NESW	1859-10-10		A1 F
3078	GRIFFIN, William A	19	3	1859-10-10		A1
3079	" "	19	E½SE	1859-10-10		A1
3080	" "	30	NENE	1859-10-10		A1
2901	GROW, David	20	NESW	1857-03-10		A1
2902	" "	20	SENW	1857-03-10		A1
2945	GROW, Henry	30	1	1856-03-10		A1
2944	" "	19	4	1857-03-10		A1
3053	HAIG, Thomas	21	SENW	1857-03-10		A1
3052	" "	21	S½NE	1859-10-10		A1
2976	HAIST, John	4	3	1855-11-01		A1
2977	" "	4	SWNE	1855-11-01		A1
2857	HALLOCK, Aaron E	35	N½NE	1870-05-02		A4
3085	HARRIES, William	1	NESW	1856-03-10		A1
3086	" "	1	W½SW	1856-03-10		A1
3087	" "	2	SESE	1856-03-10		A1
3036	HARRISON, Philip A	22	NE	1860-06-01		A1
3037	HART, Rescom	15	NWSW	1858-05-01		A1
3038	" "	21	NENE	1858-05-01		A1
3028	HIGBEE, Nelson	5	SW	1855-12-15		A1 F R2929
3029	" "	6	2	1855-12-15		A1
2948	HODGES, Ira	28	SWNE	1855-12-15		A1
2934	HOUSE, George	19	S½NE	1859-10-10		A1
2935	" "	20	NWSW	1859-10-10		A1
2936	" "	20	SWNW	1859-10-10		A1
3000	HOWSE, Joseph	36	S½NE	1857-03-10		A1
2895	HUDLER, Cornelius	28	N½NE	1856-03-10		A1
2896	" "	28	SENE	1856-03-10		A1
2954	HUGHES, James P	3	SENE	1855-12-15		A1
2947	JOACHIM, Herman	7	6	1841-11-10		A1
2882	JOHNSON, Calvin	10	NESE	1850-12-10		A1
3013	JONES, Levi	34	SENW	1860-09-01		A1
2919	KAUFMAN, Christopher	10	NWSW	1852-03-10		A1 G67
2871	KELLOGG, Alva	22	SESW	1871-02-01		A4
2872	" "	22	W½SE	1871-02-01		A4
3023	KLINE, Matthias T	17	NESW	1855-12-15		A1
3001	KNISS, Joseph	22	N½SW	1858-05-01		A1
3022	KRICK, Mary A	2	SWNE	1875-01-05		A1
3031	LALOTTE, Peter	7	SWNW	1855-11-01		A1 F

ID	Individual in Patent	Sec.	Sec. Part	Date Issued	Other Counties	For More Info . . .
3002	LAVANCE, Joseph N	2	NESW	1885-01-07		A1
2953	LEMAIRE, James	36	E½SE	1855-12-15		A1
2979	LOREE, John	23	NWSE	1856-03-10		A1
2980	" "	23	SESW	1856-03-10		A1
2978	" "	23	E½SE	1857-03-10		A1
2981	" "	23	SWSE	1857-03-10		A1
2982	LOSINGER, John	12	S½SE	1873-02-10		A4
3066	LULL, Walter	15	NESW	1855-12-15		A1 G168
3067	" "	15	NWSE	1855-12-15		A1 G168
3068	" "	15	S½NW	1855-12-15		A1 G168
3069	" "	17	NWNE	1855-12-15		A1 G168
3070	" "	2	NWNW	1855-12-15		A1 G168 F
3071	" "	3	N½NW	1855-12-15		A1 G168 F
3064	" "	4	4	1855-12-15		A1
3065	" "	4	NENE	1855-12-15		A1
3072	" "	5	SESE	1855-12-15		A1 G168 F
3073	" "	8	2	1855-12-15		A1 G168
3074	" "	8	3	1855-12-15		A1 G168
3075	" "	8	E½SE	1855-12-15		A1 G168
2986	LUNDY, John M	20	S½SW	1857-03-10		A1
3043	LUNDY, Silvester	29	2	1858-05-01		A1
3044	" "	29	SWNW	1858-05-01		A1
2983	LYON, John	26	E½SW	1872-04-05		A4
2984	" "	26	NWSE	1872-04-05		A4
2985	" "	26	SENW	1872-04-05		A4
3020	MARSH, Martin A	2	NWSE	1856-03-10		A1
2987	MCCALL, John	3	SWNW	1857-03-10		A1
2988	" "	4	SENE	1857-03-10		A1
2898	MILLER, Daniel	4	NESE	1851-05-01		A1
2897	" "	10	S½SE	1871-11-01		A4
2960	MORRISON, Jefferson	7	1	1853-11-01		A1
2957	" "	17	NENW	1854-10-05		A1
2958	" "	20	SENE	1855-12-15		A1
2961	" "	8	1	1855-12-15		A1
2962	" "	9	E½NW	1855-12-15		A1
2963	" "	9	NWNW	1855-12-15		A1
2959	" "	29	NENE	1857-03-10		A1
2965	" "	20	SWNE	1858-01-15		A3 G196
2966	" "	20	W½SE	1858-01-15		A3 G196
2964	" "	17	S½NW	1859-08-10		A3 G197
2967	" "	29	W½NE	1859-08-10		A3 G195
3084	MORRISON, William H	21	SESW	1856-03-10		A1
3030	MOSHER, Obed	26	N½NE	1860-03-01		A1
2941	MOST, Goodlove	13	N½SE	1859-07-01		A1
2885	NASON, Charles F	14	NENW	1869-09-10		A1
2875	NELLIS, Andrew	28	SWSW	1858-05-01		A1
2876	" "	29	SESE	1858-05-01		A1
2877	" "	32	NENE	1858-05-01		A1
2878	" "	33	NWNW	1858-05-01		A1
2964	PAGE, Almira Hellen	17	S½NW	1859-08-10		A3 G197
2874	PARDEE, Amaziah B	36	NW	1857-04-02		A3
2864	PITTS, Elizabeth	34	W½NW	1860-09-03		A3 G288
2989	PODOSZKIE, John	9	SWNE	1853-11-01		A1
2955	POMROY, James	30	SESW	1884-12-05		A4
2956	" "	30	W½SW	1884-12-05		A4 F
2881	POWERS, Benjamin F	3	NWNE	1854-06-15		A1 F
2880	" "	11	SESE	1855-12-15		A1
2990	PROBASCO, John	26	NWNW	1856-03-10		A1
2993	" "	26	SWSW	1856-03-10		A1
2995	" "	27	SESE	1856-03-10		A1
2991	" "	26	NWSW	1857-03-10		A1
2992	" "	26	SWNW	1857-03-10		A1
2994	" "	27	SENE	1857-03-10		A1
2937	QUIGLEY, George	1	W½SE	1866-04-03		A1
3019	QUIGLEY, Lysander	12	NESE	1856-03-10		A1
2938	RANK, George	2	N½NE	1874-03-10		A1
3088	RICE, William	1	E½NE	1850-12-10		A1 F
3089	" "	1	E½SE	1850-12-10		A1
3090	" "	11	NWNE	1850-12-10		A1
3032	RUSSELL, Peter M	24	NESW	1857-03-10		A1
3033	" "	24	SENW	1857-03-10		A1
3034	" "	24	SWNE	1857-03-10		A1
3035	" "	26	SWSE	1871-10-10		A1

ID	Individual in Patent	Sec.	Sec. Part	Date Issued	Other Counties	For More Info . . .
3062	RUSSELL, Tunis R	27	N½SE	1857-03-10		A1
3063	" "	27	SWNE	1857-03-10		A1
2970	RYAN, Jeremiah	6	NWSE	1850-04-01		A1
2972	" "	6	SWNE	1850-12-10		A1 F
2971	" "	6	SENE	1854-09-15		A1
2969	" "	6	NENE	1855-12-15		A1 F
2975	SAMPSON, John F	34	S½NE	1875-02-10		A4
2891	SAUNDERS, Chester P	30	2	1875-07-01		A4
2892	" "	30	S½NW	1875-07-01		A4 F
2996	SEEVERS, John	22	SENW	1883-06-07		A4
3027	SHALAH, Mitchell	8	NWNW	1841-11-10		A1 F
3003	SHUTTS, Josiah	34	SW	1873-05-20		A4
2890	SIMMONS, Charles W	36	SWSW	1870-07-15		A4
2883	SMITH, Charles C	34	N½NE	1871-11-01		A4
2884	" "	34	NENW	1871-11-01		A4
2917	SMITH, Franklin	14	SENW	1854-10-05		A1
2918	" "	9	SWNW	1854-10-05		A1
2862	SPEIRS, Abraham	30	4	1858-05-01		A1
2873	SPENCER, Alva	6	NWNE	1855-11-01		A1
2894	STEVENS, Clark	12	SWNW	1858-05-01		A1
2893	STEVENS, Clark H	14	NWNE	1856-03-10		A1
2943	STEVENS, Henry B	3	SWNE	1856-03-10		A1 F
2942	" "	12	W½SW	1857-03-10		A1
3004	STILES, Leroy R	25	N½SW	1856-03-10		A1
3005	" "	25	S½NW	1857-03-10		A1
3006	" "	25	SWSW	1858-05-01		A1
3051	STIMPSON, Thomas D	6	SENW	1853-08-01		A1 G270
3051	STIMSON, Thomas D	6	SENW	1853-08-01		A1 G270
2946	SWAYER, Henry	34	SE	1873-05-20		A4
2864	TERWILLIGER, Abram	34	W½NW	1860-09-03		A3 G288
3046	THOMAS, Solomon	28	N½NW	1858-05-01		A1
3047	" "	28	NESW	1858-05-01		A1
3048	" "	28	SENW	1858-05-01		A1
3007	TIFT, Leroy	31	1	1855-12-15		A1
3009	" "	32	3	1855-12-15		A1
3010	" "	32	4	1855-12-15		A1
3008	" "	32	2	1858-05-01		A1
3012	" "	32	NWSE	1858-05-01		A1
3011	" "	32	NW	1863-05-15		A1 F
3021	TIFT, Martin R	8	E½N½	1854-06-15		A1 F
2868	WELLES, William P	31	E½SW	1855-12-15		A1 G36
2916	WESTCOTT, Erasmus R	36	N½SW	1872-04-05		A4
3024	WHITE, Maurice	5	5	1859-10-10		A1
3025	" "	5	6	1859-10-10		A1
3026	" "	6	1	1859-10-10		A1
3059	WHITE, Thomas	6	SWSE	1856-03-10		A1
3060	" "	7	NENW	1856-03-10		A1
2903	WHITNEY, David H	18	4	1855-12-15		A1
2904	" "	18	5	1855-12-15		A1
2905	" "	19	NW	1855-12-15		A1 F
2906	" "	2	E½NW	1868-02-15		A1 F
3050	WILKIN, Thomas C	36	SESW	1859-08-03		A3
2913	WILLMER, Edmund	7	3	1857-03-10		A1
2914	" "	7	4	1857-03-10		A1
2915	" "	7	SENW	1857-03-10		A1
2940	WILSON, Gilbert F	19		1872-11-06		A1 F
3057	WILSON, Thomas P	2	NESE	1879-11-25		A1
3058	" "	2	SENE	1879-11-25		A1
2930	WONCH, George E	28	SESW	1871-02-01		A4
2863	WOOD, Abraham	12	NENW	1857-03-10		A1
2997	WOODFORD, Jonathan	11	SWNE	1858-05-01		A1
2931	WOODMAN, George	32	E½SE	1868-05-15		A3 G345
2932	" "	32	SESW	1868-05-15		A3 G345
2933	" "	32	SWSE	1868-05-15		A3 G345
2931	WRIGHT, George E	32	E½SE	1868-05-15		A3 G345
2932	" "	32	SESW	1868-05-15		A3 G345
2933	" "	32	SWSE	1868-05-15		A3 G345
3016	WRIGHT, Lewis E	28	SWNW	1855-12-15		A1
3017	" "	29	SENE	1855-12-15		A1
3018	" "	32	SENE	1863-09-01		A1
2931	WRIGHT, Susan	32	E½SE	1868-05-15		A3 G345
2932	" "	32	SESW	1868-05-15		A3 G345
2933	" "	32	SWSE	1868-05-15		A3 G345

Patent Map

T12-N R11-W
Michigan-Toledo Strip Meridian

Map Group 20

Township Statistics

Parcels Mapped	:	237
Number of Patents	:	175
Number of Individuals	:	135
Patentees Identified	:	125
Number of Surnames	:	116
Multi-Patentee Parcels	:	22
Oldest Patent Date	:	11/10/1841
Most Recent Patent	:	2/19/1923
Block/Lot Parcels	:	34
Parcels Re - Issued	:	1
Parcels that Overlap	:	0
Cities and Towns	:	4
Cemeteries	:	5

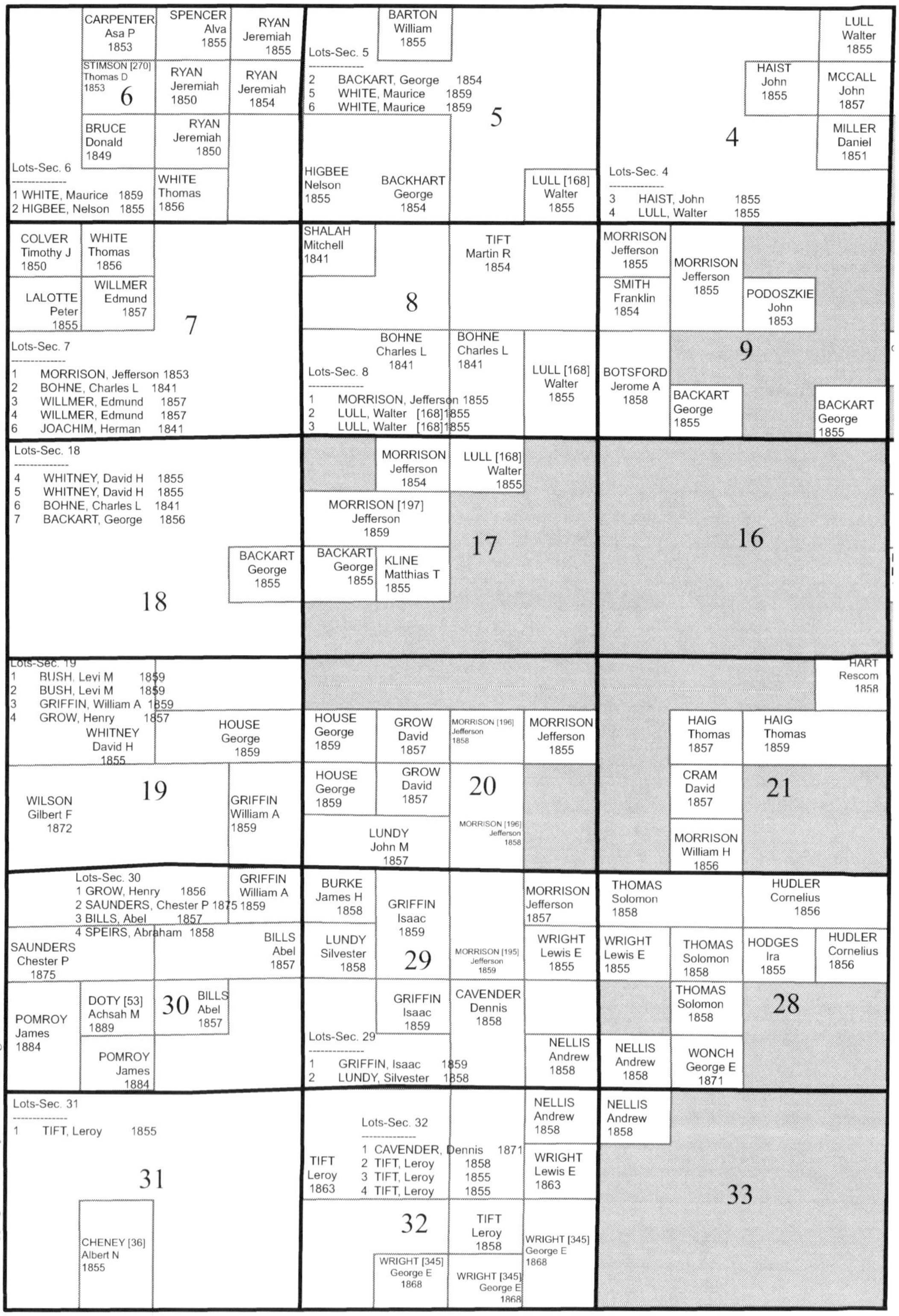

LULL [168] Walter 1855
POWERS Benjamin F 1854
LULL [168] Walter 1855
WHITNEY David H 1868
RANK George 1874
RICE William 1850
MCCALL John 1857
STEVENS Henry B 1856
HUGHES James P 1855
KRICK Mary A 1875
WILSON Thomas P 1879
3
2
1
LAVANCE Joseph N 1885
MARSH Martin A 1856
WILSON Thomas P 1879
HARRIES William 1856
HARRIES William 1856
HARRIES William 1856
QUIGLEY George 1866
RICE William 1850
RICE William 1850
WOOD Abraham 1857
WOODFORD Jonathan 1858
STEVENS Clark 1858
GOODWILL Jeremiah P 1923
10
11
12
GAUWEILER [67] Frederick 1852
CULP David 1854
JOHNSON Calvin 1850
QUIGLEY Lysander 1856
STEVENS Henry B 1857
MILLER Daniel 1871
POWERS Benjamin F 1855
LOSINGER John 1873
DELANO Durfey H 1856
DELANO Durfey H 1856
DELANO Durfey H 1856
NASON Charles F 1869
STEVENS Clark H 1856
BACKARD George 1854
ANDREWS Samuel B 1857
SMITH Franklin 1854
BACKARD George 1854
LULL [168] Walter 1855
15
DAGGETT Simeon 1856
HART Rescom 1858
LULL [168] Walter 1855
LULL [168] Walter 1855
14
13
MOST Goodlove 1859
ANDREWS Samuel B 1857
FROST George S 1858
CADY Joseph 1862
HARRISON Philip A 1860
CADY Joseph 1862
SEEVERS John 1883
22
FINCH Warren 1857
FINCH Addison 1858
23
CALLAR William 1858
CALLAR William 1858
RUSSELL Peter M 1857
RUSSELL Peter M 1857
KNISS Joseph 1858
BEAN William W 1859
BEAN William W 1860
FINCH Addison 1858
LOREE John 1856
RUSSELL Peter M 1857
24
KELLOGG Alva 1871
BLANCHARD Allen 1858
KELLOGG Alva 1871
BEAN William W 1860
LOREE John 1856
LOREE John 1857
LOREE John 1857
BLANCHARD Allen 1858
PROBASCO John 1856
BLACKWELL Thomas J 1858
MOSHER Obed 1860
BORDEN John D 1856
BENNETT Sally 1856
RUSSELL Tunis R 1857
PROBASCO John 1857
PROBASCO John 1857
LYON John 1872
26
BLACKWELL Thomas J 1858
STILES Leroy R 1857
25
BENNITT Sally 1856
27
RUSSELL Tunis R 1857
PROBASCO John 1857
LYON John 1872
LYON John 1872
BLACKWELL Thomas J 1858
STILES Leroy R 1856
BACKART George 1854
PROBASCO John 1856
PROBASCO John 1856
RUSSELL Peter M 1871
STILES Leroy R 1858
BORDEN Susan 1855
TERWILLIGER [288] Abram 1860
SMITH Charles C 1871
SMITH Charles C 1871
HALLOCK Aaron E 1870
PARDEE Amaziah B 1857
JONES Levi 1860
SAMPSON John F 1875
36
HOWSE Joseph 1857
34
35
WESTCOTT Erasmus R 1872
GRIFFES William A 1870
LEMAIRE James 1855
SHUTTS Josiah 1873
SWAYER Henry 1873
SIMMONS Charles W 1870
WILKIN Thomas C 1859
BILLS Abel 1854

Helpful Hints

1. This Map's INDEX can be found on the preceding pages.
2. Refer to Map "C" to see where this Township lies within Newaygo County, Michigan.
3. Numbers within square brackets [ ] denote a multi-patentee land parcel (multi-owner). Refer to Appendix "C" for a full list of members in this group.
4. Areas that look to be crowded with Patentees usually indicate multiple sales of the same parcel (Re-issues) or Overlapping parcels. See this Township's Index for an explanation of these and other circumstances that might explain "odd" groupings of Patentees on this map.

Legend

Patent Boundary
Section Boundary
No Patents Found (or Outside County)
1., 2., 3., ... Lot Numbers (when beside a name)
[ ] Group Number (see Appendix "C")

Scale: Section = 1 mile X 1 mile (generally, with some exceptions)

Road Map

T12-N R11-W
Michigan-Toledo Strip Meridian

Map Group 20

Cities & Towns

- Croton
- Croton Heights
- Riverview
- Tift Corner

Cemeteries

- Christian Plains Cemetery
- Croton Cemetery
- Gulp Cemetery
- Oak Grove Cemetery
- Prairie Cemetery

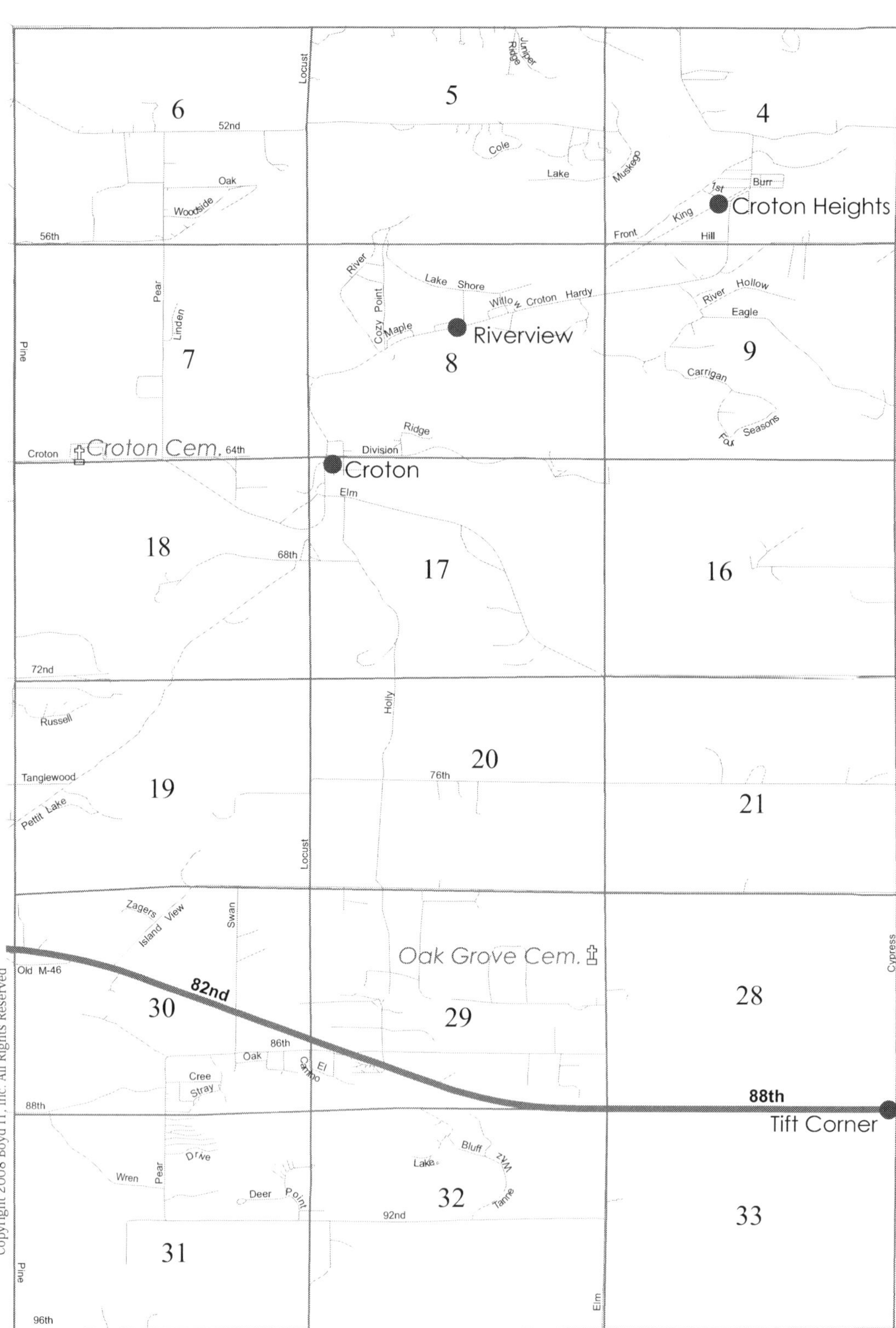

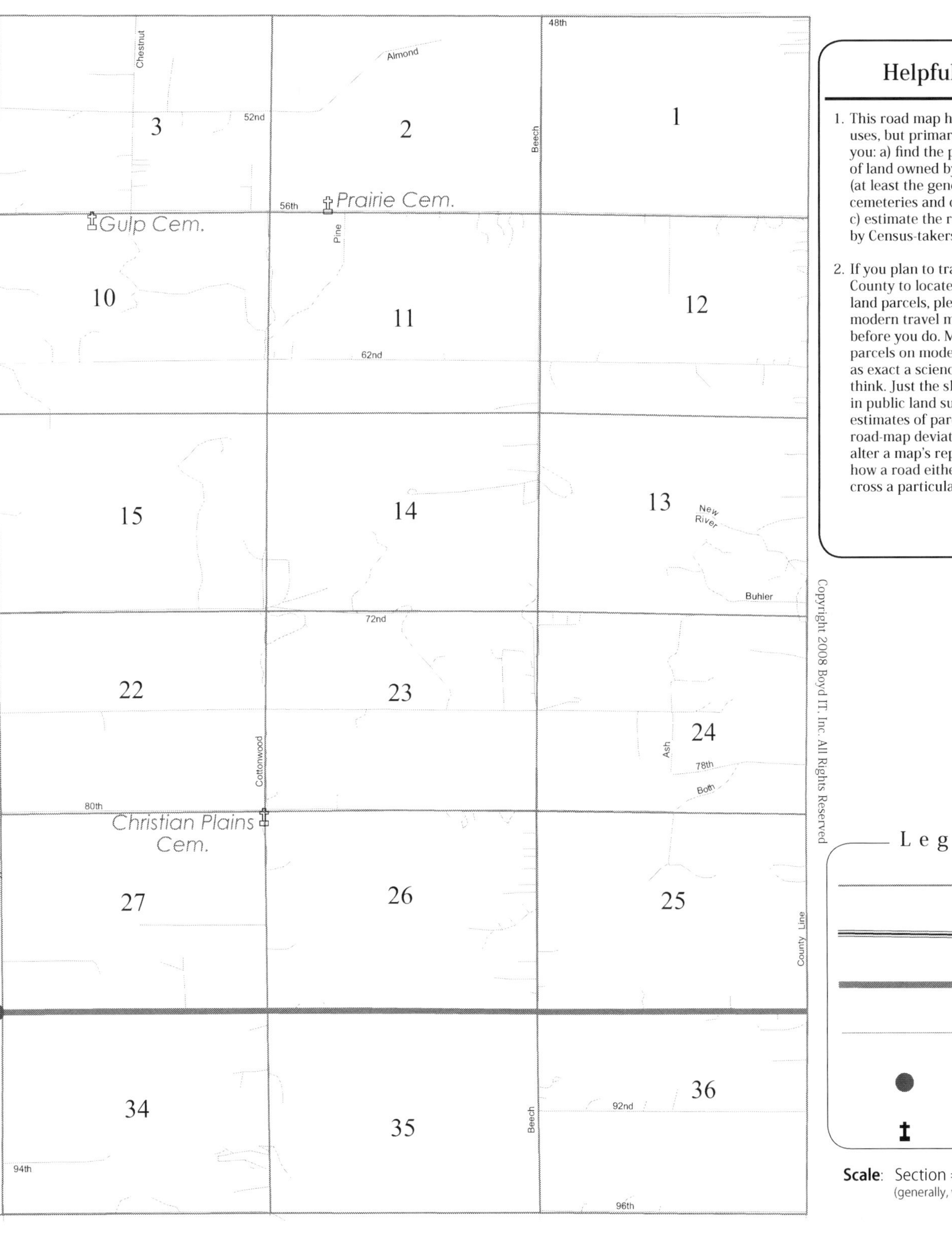

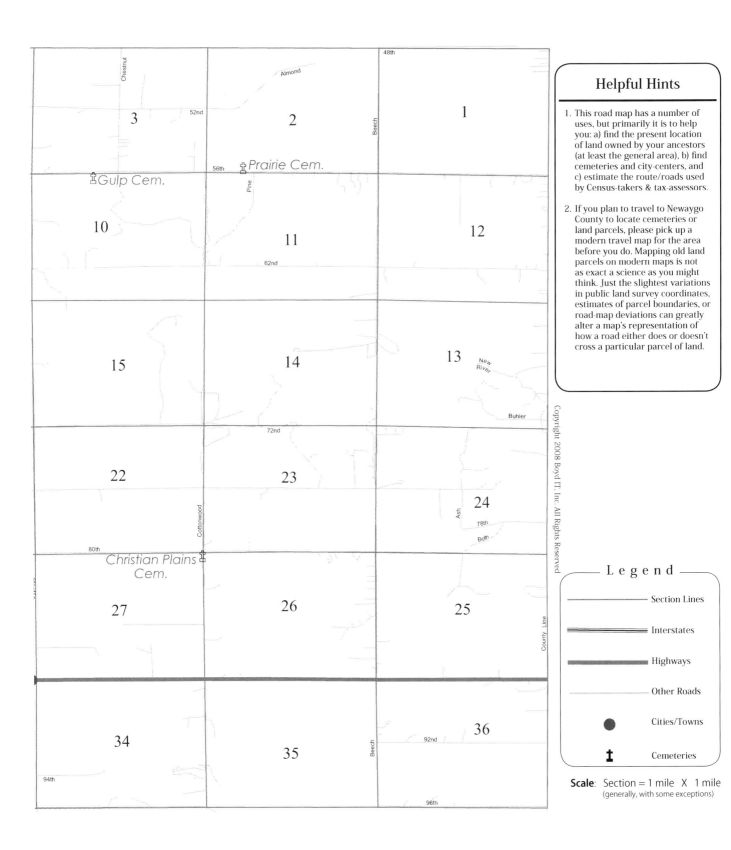

Helpful Hints

1. This road map has a number of uses, but primarily it is to help you: a) find the present location of land owned by your ancestors (at least the general area), b) find cemeteries and city-centers, and c) estimate the route/roads used by Census-takers & tax-assessors.

2. If you plan to travel to Newaygo County to locate cemeteries or land parcels, please pick up a modern travel map for the area before you do. Mapping old land parcels on modern maps is not as exact a science as you might think. Just the slightest variations in public land survey coordinates, estimates of parcel boundaries, or road-map deviations can greatly alter a map's representation of how a road either does or doesn't cross a particular parcel of land.

Legend

- Section Lines
- Interstates
- Highways
- Other Roads
- Cities/Towns
- Cemeteries

Scale: Section = 1 mile X 1 mile (generally, with some exceptions)

Historical Map

T12-N R11-W
Michigan-Toledo Strip Meridian

Map Group 20

Cities & Towns
- Croton
- Croton Heights
- Riverview
- Tift Corner

Cemeteries
- Christian Plains Cemetery
- Croton Cemetery
- Gulp Cemetery
- Oak Grove Cemetery
- Prairie Cemetery

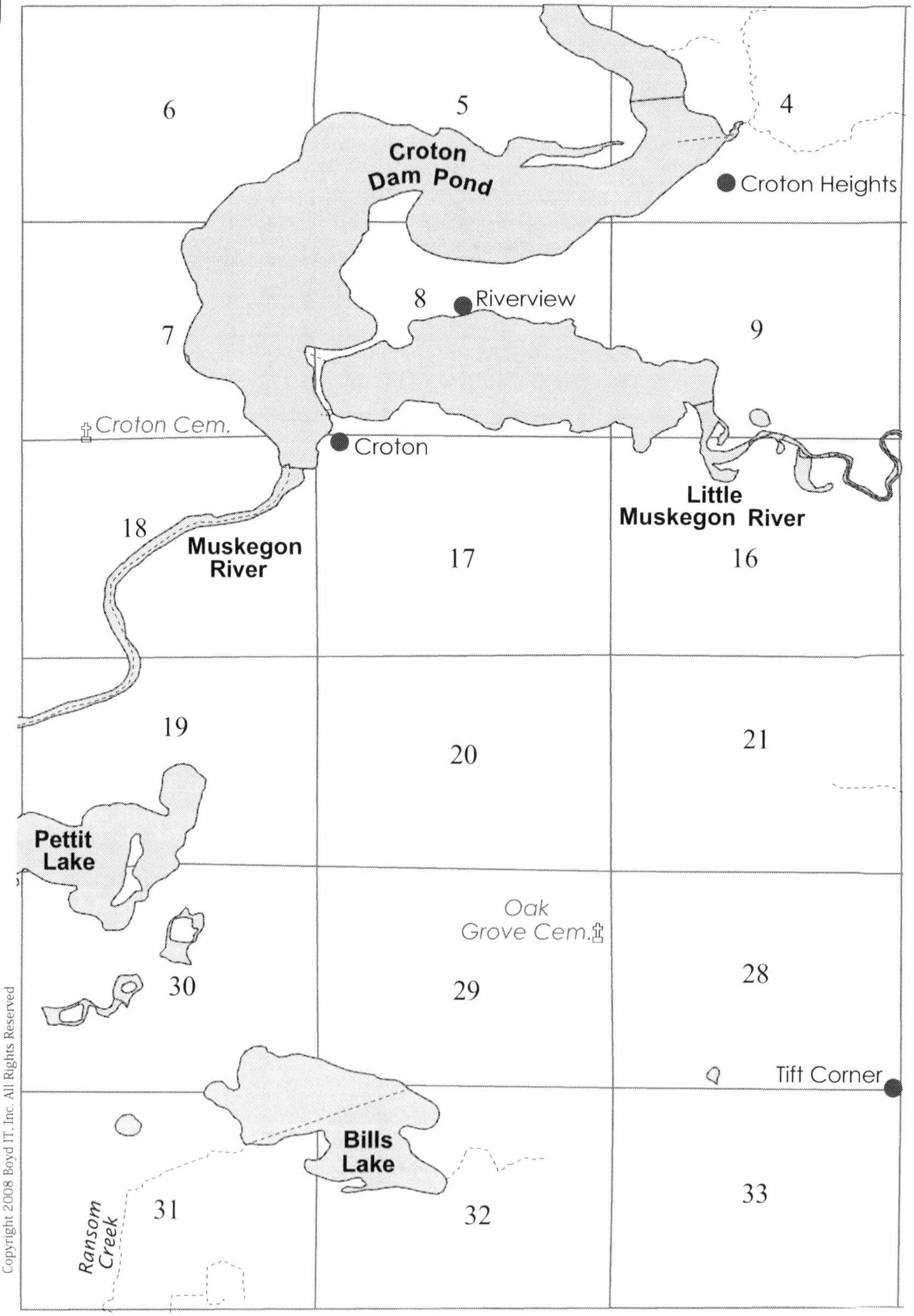

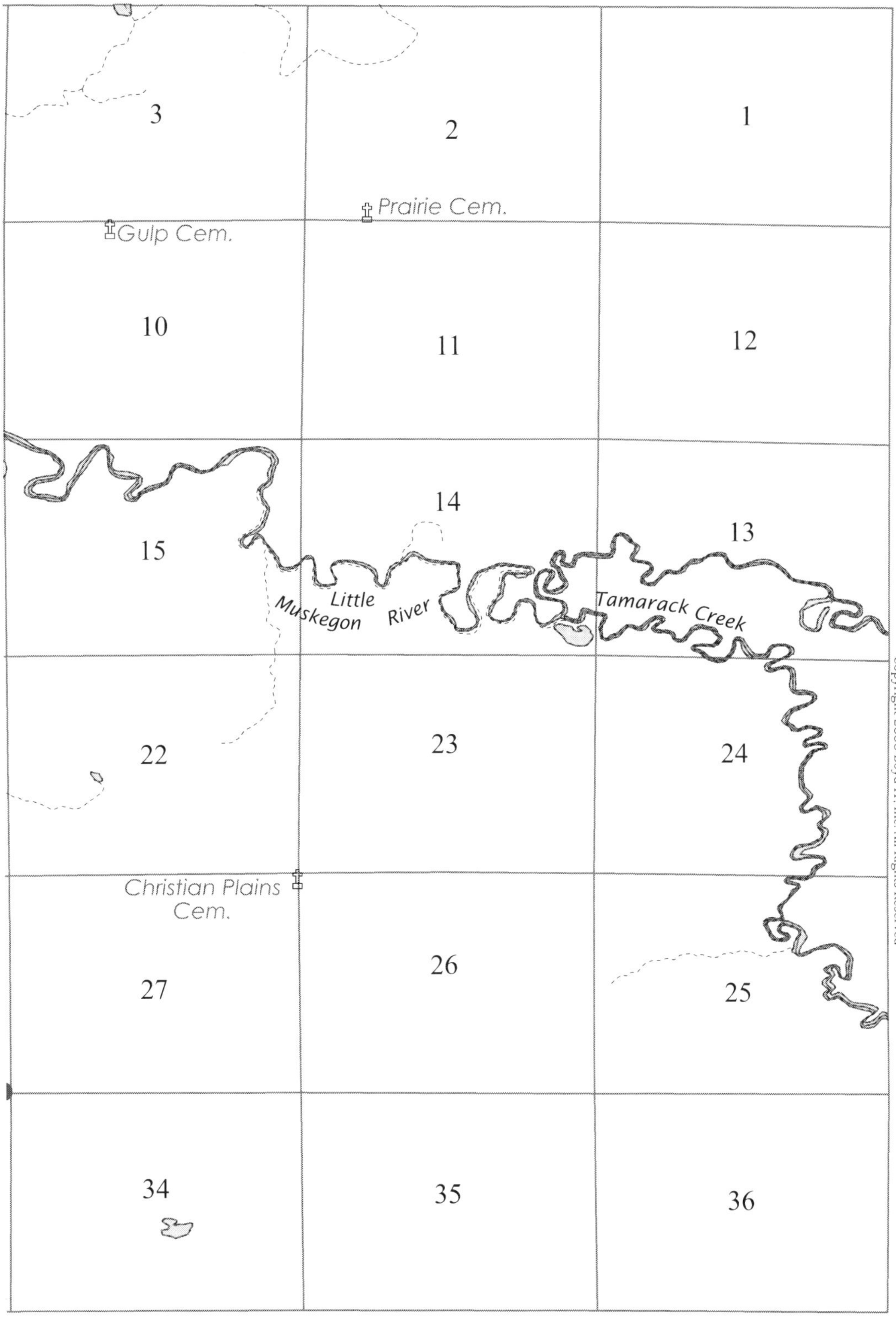

3
2
1
Prairie Cem.
Gulp Cem.
10
11
12
14
13
15
Little
Muskegon River
Tamarack Creek
22
23
24
Christian Plains
Cem.
26
27
25
34
35
36

Helpful Hints

1. This Map takes a different look at the same Congressional Township displayed in the preceding two maps. It presents features that can help you better envision the historical development of the area: a) Water-bodies (lakes & ponds), b) Water-courses (rivers, streams, etc.), c) Railroads, d) City/town center-points (where they were oftentimes located when first settled), and e) Cemeteries.
2. Using this "Historical" map in tandem with this Township's Patent Map and Road Map, may lead you to some interesting discoveries. You will often find roads, towns, cemeteries, and waterways are named after nearby landowners: sometimes those names will be the ones you are researching. See how many of these research gems you can find here in Newaygo County.

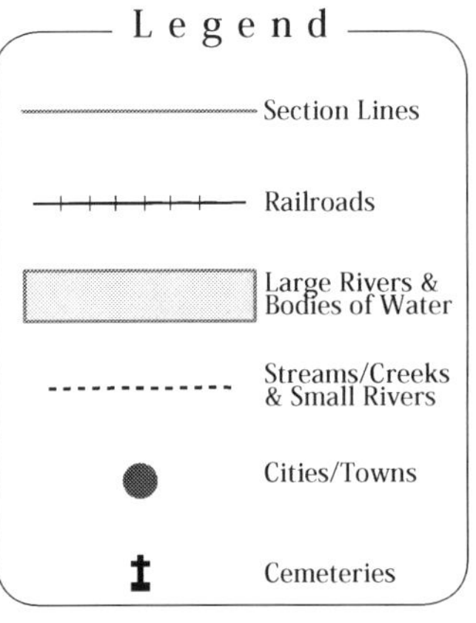

Scale: Section = 1 mile X 1 mile
(there are some exceptions)

Map Group 21: Index to Land Patents

Township 11-North Range 14-West (Michigan-Toledo Strip)

After you locate an individual in this Index, take note of the Section and Section Part then proceed to the Land Patent map on the pages immediately following. You should have no difficulty locating the corresponding parcel of land.

The "For More Info" Column will lead you to more information about the underlying Patents. See the *Legend* at right, and the "How to Use this Book" chapter, for more information.

LEGEND

"For More Info . . . " column

A = Authority (Legislative Act, See Appendix "A")
B = Block or Lot (location in Section unknown)
C = Cancelled Patent
F = Fractional Section
G = Group (Multi-Patentee Patent, see Appendix "C")
V = Overlaps another Parcel
R = Re-Issued (Parcel patented more than once)

(A & G items require you to look in the Appendixes referred to above. All other Letter-designations followed by a number require you to locate line-items in this index that possess the ID number found after the letter).

ID	Individual in Patent	Sec.	Sec. Part	Date Issued	Other Counties	For More Info . . .
3218	ACHENBACH, John	4	NESW	1875-03-22		A4
3219	" "	4	S½NW	1875-03-22		A4
3220	" "	5	SENE	1875-03-22		A4
3289	ACKLEY, Newton	11	SESW	1861-12-10		A1
3290	" "	11	SWSE	1861-12-10		A1
3111	AMES, Ares D	2	SWNE	1880-07-23		A4
3221	ANDRIE, John	26	NENW	1914-05-19		A6
3119	ANGEL, Betsey	20	7	1852-03-10		A1
3156	ATWATER, Edgar	21	SWSW	1877-06-04		A4
3208	BABCOCK, James	29	NWSW	1888-05-31		A4
3209	" "	29	SWNW	1888-05-31		A4
3223	BALL, John	11	W½NE	1854-09-15		A1
3229	" "	25	W½SE	1854-09-15		A1
3238	" "	9	NWSE	1854-09-15		A1
3239	" "	9	SWNE	1854-09-15		A1
3234	" "	33	E½SE	1855-03-01		A1
3235	" "	33	SWSE	1855-03-01		A1
3225	" "	15	6	1855-11-08		A3
3226	" "	15	7	1855-11-08		A3
3227	" "	15	8	1855-11-08		A3
3228	" "	15	9	1855-11-08		A3
3230	" "	30	10	1855-11-08		A3
3232	" "	30	9	1855-11-08		A3
3233	" "	30	NWSW	1855-11-08		A3
3222	" "	11	NWSE	1855-12-15		A1
3231	" "	30	11	1856-03-10		A1
3240	" "	14	3	1857-02-20		A3 G6
3241	" "	14	4	1857-02-20		A3 G6
3236	" "	36	E½SE	1858-01-15		A3
3237	" "	36	SWSE	1858-01-15		A3
3224	" "	15	5	1858-05-01		A1
3242	" "	17	NENW	1859-08-10		A3 G6
3243	" "	17	NWNE	1859-08-10		A3 G6
3244	" "	28	NESW	1859-08-10		A3 G6
3245	" "	28	NWSE	1859-08-10		A3 G6
3246	" "	29	E½SE	1859-08-10		A3 G6
3247	" "	29	SESW	1859-08-10		A3 G6
3248	" "	29	SWSE	1859-08-10		A3 G6
3120	BELDEN, Burton S	4	N½NW	1869-11-01		A4 F
3121	" "	5	NENE	1869-11-01		A4 F
3217	BROOKS, John A	13	2	1848-06-01		A1 G27
3216	" "	20	8	1849-04-05		A1
3327	BUMSTED, William H	7	S½SE	1868-02-10		A3 G231 V3313
3328	" "	7	SESW	1868-02-10		A3 G231
3312	CARR, Sarah	18	N½NE	1869-11-01		A4
3313	" "	7	SESE	1869-11-01		A4 V3327

ID	Individual in Patent	Sec.	Sec. Part	Date Issued	Other Counties	For More Info . . .
3314	CARR, Sarah (Cont'd)	8	SWSW	1869-11-01		A4
3327	CHAPMAN, Dwight P	7	S½SE	1868-02-10		A3 G231 V3313
3328	" "	7	SESW	1868-02-10		A3 G231
3177	COON, Egbert	1	SESE	1859-10-10		A1
3178	" "	1	SWNE	1859-10-10		A1
3195	COWN, George	30	4	1841-11-10		A1
3249	DAGAN, John	5	SESE	1852-03-10		A1 G49
3250	" "	8	NENE	1852-03-10		A1 G49
3206	DANA, Josiah P	24	NWNE	1854-06-15		A1 G182
3207	" "	24	W½SE	1854-06-15		A1 G182
3267	" "	12	6	1854-09-15		A1
3197	DE BOIS, GEORGE H	4	SWSE	1883-06-07		A4
3198	" "	9	NWNE	1883-06-07		A4
3320	DE BOIS, VICTOR	3	N½NE	1879-11-25		A4 F
3321	" "	3	SENW	1879-11-25		A4
3322	" "	3	SWNE	1879-11-25		A4
3199	DRAPER, George H	4	S½SW	1871-06-15		A4
3200	" "	9	N½NW	1871-06-15		A4
3130	DRESSER, Charles	5	NESW	1860-09-01		A1
3142	DRUHER, David	4	NWSW	1868-02-15		A1
3323	DUNN, William H	1	W½NW	1874-02-20		A4 F
3324	" "	2	NESE	1874-02-20		A4
3325	" "	2	SENE	1874-02-20		A4
3180	ECHTINAW, Ephraim	4	NWSE	1874-02-20		A4
3181	" "	4	SENE	1874-02-20		A4
3182	" "	4	W½NE	1874-02-20		A4 F
3196	EICHENLAUB, George	20	4	1850-12-10		A1
3110	ERRICKSON, Andrew	18	NWSW	1862-05-15		A1 F
3282	FENNER, Michael	7	N½NE	1873-02-10		A4
3269	GAY, Mace	14	5	1854-06-15		A1
3270	" "	14	6	1854-06-15		A1
3263	GEYASHE, Joseph Mash Shaw	21	1	1848-06-01		A1
3143	GRAHAM, David	9	SWNW	1876-02-10		A4
3210	GREY, James D	12	4	1860-10-01		A1
3268	HICKS, George W	29	E½NE	1911-02-20		A4 G85
3268	HICKS, Julia A	29	E½NE	1911-02-20		A4 G85
3257	HOPKINS, John W	29	NWSE	1852-11-01		A1
3258	" "	29	SWSW	1852-11-01		A1
3300	HOWLETT, Robert	1	NENE	1854-09-15		A1 F
3301	" "	1	W½SE	1854-09-15		A1
3302	" "	28	SENW	1854-09-15		A1
3303	" "	28	SWSW	1854-09-15		A1
3304	" "	30	SESE	1854-09-15		A1
3305	" "	31	NWNE	1854-09-15		A1
3306	" "	33	NWSE	1854-09-15		A1
3307	JIBSON, Robert	5	S½SW	1861-04-01		A1
3308	" "	5	SWSE	1861-04-01		A1
3309	" "	8	NWNE	1861-04-01		A1
3291	JOHNSON, Peter	17	SWNE	1854-06-15		A1
3292	" "	18	SENE	1855-03-01		A1
3293	" "	19	NESW	1855-12-15		A1
3294	" "	20	SWNW	1861-12-10		A1
3318	" "	3	NWNW	1864-11-01		A1 G237 F
3319	" "	4	NENE	1865-10-10		A1 G237 F
3287	JONES, Nathan W	8	N½SE	1874-02-20		A4
3288	" "	8	S½NE	1874-02-20		A4
3327	KINGSLEY, Thomas G	7	S½SE	1868-02-10		A3 G231 V3313
3328	" "	7	SESW	1868-02-10		A3 G231
3260	KOON, Joseph	3	NWSW	1874-03-10		A1
3261	" "	3	SWNW	1874-03-10		A1
3262	" "	4	NESE	1874-03-10		A1
3311	KUPRECHT, Rudolph	8	W½NW	1861-12-10		A1
3103	LACEY, Alice	28	NWSW	1912-08-22		A1
3104	" "	28	SWNW	1912-08-22		A1
3217	LASLEY, William	13	2	1848-06-01		A1 G27
3326	" "	15	4	1848-06-01		A1
3139	LEHMANN, Christiana	5	N½SE	1869-11-01		A4
3138	LETCH, Chauncey N	10	SESE	1875-09-01		A4
3140	MARSHALL, Christopher	7	NWNW	1862-03-10		A1 F
3213	MARSHALL, James	6	SESW	1862-05-15		A1
3214	" "	8	NESW	1873-02-10		A4
3215	" "	8	SENW	1873-02-10		A4
3310	MARSHALL, Robinson	18	NWNW	1862-05-15		A1 F

ID	Individual in Patent	Sec.	Sec. Part	Date Issued	Other Counties	For More Info . . .
3099	MARVIN, Alfred A	14	2	1852-03-10		A1
3186	MATHEW, Frank	6	NWSW	1859-10-10		A1 F
3185	" "	6	NESW	1860-09-01		A1
3187	" "	6	SWSW	1861-04-01		A1
3188	MATTHEW, Frank	2	NESW	1854-10-05		A1
3189	" "	2	NWNE	1854-10-05		A1 F
3190	" "	2	NWSE	1854-10-05		A1
3101	MAXIM, Alfred A	14	1	1850-12-10		A1
3102	" "	14	8	1850-12-10		A1
3100	" "	12	3	1854-06-15		A1
3251	MCINTOSH, John	19	W½SW	1841-11-10		A1
3252	" "	30	1	1841-11-10		A1
3253	" "	30	2	1841-11-10		A1
3254	" "	30	3	1841-11-10		A1
3211	MCKEE, James H	32	E½NW	1855-11-08		A3
3212	" "	32	NWNW	1855-11-08		A3
3240	" "	14	3	1857-02-20		A3 G6
3241	" "	14	4	1857-02-20		A3 G6
3242	" "	17	NENW	1859-08-10		A3 G6
3243	" "	17	NWNE	1859-08-10		A3 G6
3244	" "	28	NESW	1859-08-10		A3 G6
3245	" "	28	NWSE	1859-08-10		A3 G6
3246	" "	29	E½SE	1859-08-10		A3 G6
3247	" "	29	SESW	1859-08-10		A3 G6
3248	" "	29	SWSE	1859-08-10		A3 G6
3134	MCKIE, Charles	18	S½NW	1858-05-01		A1 F
3132	" "	18	NENW	1870-07-15		A4
3133	" "	18	NESW	1870-07-15		A4
3179	MERRILL, Elias W	13	NWNW	1850-12-10		A1 G180 F
3203	" "	14	SESE	1851-05-01		A1 G181
3205	" "	24	NWNW	1851-05-01		A1 G181
3206	" "	24	NWNE	1854-06-15		A1 G182
3207	" "	24	W½SE	1854-06-15		A1 G182
3204	" "	14	SWSE	1854-09-15		A1 G181 R3316
3179	MERRILL, Isaac D	13	NWNW	1850-12-10		A1 G180 F
3203	" "	14	SESE	1851-05-01		A1 G181
3205	" "	24	NWNW	1851-05-01		A1 G181
3206	" "	24	NWNE	1854-06-15		A1 G182
3207	" "	24	W½SE	1854-06-15		A1 G182
3204	" "	14	SWSE	1854-09-15		A1 G181 R3316
3259	MIZNER, Jonathan	10	NESW	1860-06-01		A1
3275	MORRIS, Robert	29	1	1849-04-05		A1 G235
3276	" "	29	2	1849-04-05		A1 G235
3277	MORRIS, Robert W	1	SENW	1851-05-01		A1 G236
3158	NORTON, Edwin A	23	NWNE	1844-09-15		A1
3163	" "	27	NWSW	1844-09-15		A1
3171	" "	33	N½SW	1844-09-15		A1
3172	" "	33	NE	1844-09-15		A1
3173	" "	33	NWNW	1844-09-15		A1
3174	" "	33	S½NW	1844-09-15		A1
3157	" "	21	SESW	1854-09-15		A1
3159	" "	24	E½NW	1854-09-15		A1
3160	" "	24	SWNE	1854-09-15		A1
3161	" "	24	SWNW	1854-09-15		A1
3162	" "	25	SENE	1854-09-15		A1
3164	" "	27	SESW	1854-09-15		A1
3165	" "	27	SWSE	1854-09-15		A1
3166	" "	28	NENW	1854-09-15		A1
3167	" "	28	NESE	1854-09-15		A1
3168	" "	28	S½SE	1854-09-15		A1
3169	" "	32	E½NE	1854-09-15		A1
3170	" "	32	N½SE	1854-09-15		A1
3175	" "	33	S½SW	1854-09-15		A1
3176	" "	34	NENW	1854-09-15		A1
3150	ORCUTT, Delbert F	17	SWSE	1903-06-12		A4
3095	ORTON, Alanson F	10	NESE	1856-03-10		A1 G282
3094	ORTON, Alonson F	11	S½NW	1857-04-02		A3 G281
3095	ORTON, Henry A	10	NESE	1856-03-10		A1 G282
3094	ORTON, Henry J	11	S½NW	1857-04-02		A3 G281
3144	OSTRANDER, David	8	SWSE	1869-11-30		A1
3149	OSTRANDER, Davis D	8	NWSW	1862-08-15		A1
3327	PARK, Erastus S	7	S½SE	1868-02-10		A3 G231 V3313
3328	" "	7	SESW	1868-02-10		A3 G231

ID	Individual in Patent	Sec.	Sec. Part	Date Issued	Other Counties	For More Info . . .
3327	PARK, Sarah A	7	S½SE	1868-02-10		A3 G231 V3313
3328	" "	7	SESW	1868-02-10		A3 G231
3191	PATTISON, Freaman W	17	SESE	1877-07-20		A4
3135	PAYSON, Charles	3	NESW	1859-10-10		A1
3136	PETERSON, Charles	11	SWSW	1860-09-01		A1
3297	PICHETTE, Placid	7	SENW	1873-02-10		A4
3151	PORTER, Dennis	10	SESW	1859-08-10		A3
3152	" "	10	W½SE	1859-08-10		A3
3201	PRENTICE, George W	9	NWSW	1904-10-17		A4
3153	PUTNAM, Dennis	26	SENW	1861-04-01		A1
3154	" "	34	NWNE	1912-11-11		A1
3317	QUICK, Thomas	18	S½SW	1852-11-01		A1 F
3192	RUPRECHT, Frederick	6	NWSE	1860-09-01		A1
3193	" "	6	SESE	1860-09-01		A1
3194	RUPRECHT, Friedrich	6	NESE	1859-10-10		A1
3327	RUPRECHT, William	7	S½SE	1868-02-10		A3 G231 V3313
3328	" "	7	SESW	1868-02-10		A3 G231
3271	RYERSON, Martin	30	13	1841-11-10		A1
3272	" "	30	6	1841-11-10		A1
3273	" "	30	7	1841-11-10		A1
3274	" "	30	8	1841-11-10		A1
3275	" "	29	1	1849-04-05		A1 G235
3276	" "	29	2	1849-04-05		A1 G235
3277	" "	1	SENW	1851-05-01		A1 G236
3318	RYERSON, Tunis	3	NWNW	1864-11-01		A1 G237 F
3319	" "	4	NENE	1865-10-10		A1 G237 F
3112	SACKS, August	5	NWSW	1859-10-10		A1
3141	SANBORN, Daniel	20	5	1850-12-10		A1
3295	SANBORN, Peter	2	NWNW	1854-06-15		A1
3296	" "	3	NENW	1854-06-15		A1 F
3315	SCHANK, Theron C	1	NENW	1875-11-10		A4
3283	SCOUGHTON, Michael	7	NESW	1867-01-10		A1
3316	SEARLES, Theron W	14	SWSE	1855-03-01		A1 C R3204
3106	SLATER, Amos	13	SENW	1858-05-01		A1
3105	" "	11	NESW	1869-09-10		A1
3129	SMITH, Canton	34	S½SE	1854-09-15		A1
3137	SMITH, Charles	21	5	1875-02-10		A4
3148	SQUIER, David W	31	NWSW	1860-10-01		A1 F
3146	" "	31	1	1861-04-01		A1
3147	" "	31	2	1861-04-01		A1
3145	" "	27	NESW	1865-10-10		A1
3299	SQUIER, Ransom P	6	NW	1861-04-01		A1 F
3097	ST PETER, ALEXANDER	20	3	1841-11-10		A1
3098	" "	21	6	1841-11-10		A1
3096	" "	20	2	1848-06-01		A1
3281	ST PETER, MARY A	29	3	1841-11-10		A1
3107	STAKER, Amos	13	NESW	1873-02-10		A4
3108	" "	13	NWSE	1873-02-10		A4
3109	" "	13	W½NE	1873-02-10		A4
3286	STEINER, Narzis	5	W½NE	1860-09-01		A1 F
3284	" "	5	NENW	1860-12-01		A1 F
3285	" "	5	S½NW	1860-12-01		A1
3131	STICKNEY, Charles E	10	SWSW	1874-04-01		A4
3264	STRONACH, Joseph	20	NENW	1845-06-01		A1
3123	SUTLIFF, Calvin A	12	1	1854-10-05		A1
3124	" "	12	2	1854-10-05		A1
3122	" "	1	NWNE	1865-11-01		A1 F
3126	" "	2	NENE	1865-11-01		A1 F
3128	" "	36	NENE	1865-11-01		A1
3125	" "	2	E½NW	1869-09-10		A1 F
3127	" "	2	SWSE	1871-11-15		A1
3095	SWAIN, Aaron	10	NESE	1856-03-10		A1 G282
3094	" "	11	S½NW	1857-04-02		A3 G281
3255	THOMPSON, John	8	NENW	1852-03-10		A1
3256	" "	8	SESW	1852-03-10		A1
3155	THURSTON, Earl B	27	N½SE	1906-08-16		A4
3183	TRENBLER, Francis L	30	5	1848-06-01		A1
3115	TROMBLY, Benjamin	12	NENE	1870-05-02		A4
3116	" "	12	W½NE	1870-05-02		A4
3184	TROMBLY, Francis	17	NWSE	1852-11-01		A1
3117	TROUNBLEY, Benjamin	2	SESE	1866-04-03		A1
3265	TROUTIER, Joseph	19	SESE	1850-04-01		A1
3202	WALTON, George W	20	6	1854-10-05		A1

ID	Individual in Patent	Sec.	Sec. Part	Date Issued	Other Counties	For More Info . . .
3249	WHITEHEAD, John	5	SESE	1852-03-10		A1 G49
3250	" "	8	NENE	1852-03-10		A1 G49
3113	WHITEMAN, Benjamin L	20	NESW	1852-03-10		A1 C
3118	WHITMAN, Benjamin	15	NWNW	1855-03-01		A1
3114	WHITMAN, Benjamin S	29	NESW	1970-05-13		A1
3278	WILLINS, Martin	7	NWSE	1872-07-01		A1
3279	WILLIUS, Martin	7	NESE	1861-04-01		A1
3280	" "	7	S½NE	1861-04-01		A1
3266	WISENFIELD, Joseph	31	NWNW	1865-10-10		A1 F
3298	WOOD, Ransom E	23	E½NE	1854-06-15		A1

Patent Map

T11-N R14-W
Michigan-Toledo Strip Meridian

Map Group 21

Township Statistics

Parcels Mapped	:	235
Number of Patents	:	174
Number of Individuals	:	118
Patentees Identified	:	111
Number of Surnames	:	98
Multi-Patentee Parcels	:	28
Oldest Patent Date	:	11/10/1841
Most Recent Patent	:	5/13/1970
Block/Lot Parcels	:	46
Parcels Re - Issued	:	1
Parcels that Overlap	:	2
Cities and Towns	:	1
Cemeteries	:	0

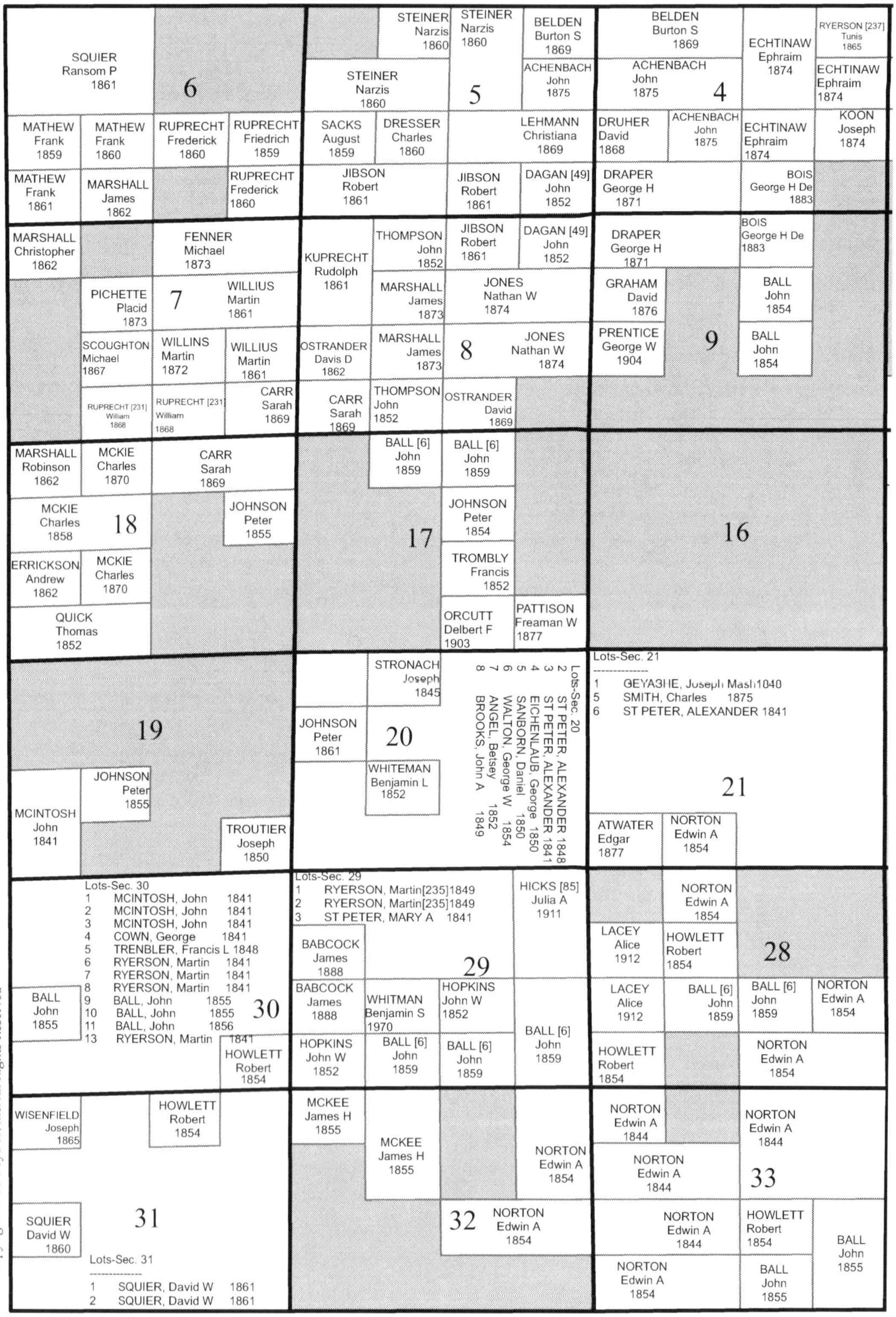

6
SQUIER Ransom P 1861
MATHEW Frank 1859
MATHEW Frank 1860
RUPRECHT Frederick 1860
RUPRECHT Friedrich 1859
MATHEW Frank 1861
MARSHALL James 1862
RUPRECHT Frederick 1860

5
STEINER Narzis 1860
STEINER Narzis 1860
BELDEN Burton S 1869
STEINER Narzis 1860
ACHENBACH John 1875
SACKS August 1859
DRESSER Charles 1860
LEHMANN Christiana 1869
JIBSON Robert 1861
JIBSON Robert 1861
DAGAN [49] John 1852

4
BELDEN Burton S 1869
RYERSON [237] Tunis 1865
ECHTINAW Ephraim 1874
ACHENBACH John 1875
ECHTINAW Ephraim 1874
DRUHER David 1868
ACHENBACH John 1875
ECHTINAW Ephraim 1874
KOON Joseph 1874
DRAPER George H 1871
BOIS George H De 1883

7
MARSHALL Christopher 1862
FENNER Michael 1873
PICHETTE Placid 1873
WILLIUS Martin 1861
SCOUGHTON Michael 1867
WILLINS Martin 1872
WILLIUS Martin 1861
CARR Sarah 1869
RUPRECHT [231] William 1868
RUPRECHT [231] William 1868

8
KUPRECHT Rudolph 1861
THOMPSON John 1852
JIBSON Robert 1861
DAGAN [49] John 1852
MARSHALL James 1873
JONES Nathan W 1874
OSTRANDER Davis D 1862
MARSHALL James 1873
JONES Nathan W 1874
CARR Sarah 1869
THOMPSON John 1852
OSTRANDER David 1869

9
DRAPER George H 1871
BOIS George H De 1883
GRAHAM David 1876
BALL John 1854
PRENTICE George W 1904
BALL John 1854

18
MARSHALL Robinson 1862
MCKIE Charles 1870
CARR Sarah 1869
MCKIE Charles 1858
JOHNSON Peter 1855
ERRICKSON Andrew 1862
MCKIE Charles 1870
QUICK Thomas 1852

17
BALL [6] John 1859
BALL [6] John 1859
JOHNSON Peter 1854
TROMBLY Francis 1852
ORCUTT Delbert F 1903
PATTISON Freaman W 1877

16

19
MCINTOSH John 1841
JOHNSON Peter 1855
TROUTIER Joseph 1850

20
STRONACH Joseph 1845
JOHNSON Peter 1861
WHITEMAN Benjamin L 1852

Lots-Sec. 20
2 ST PETER, ALEXANDER 1848
3 ST PETER, ALEXANDER 1841
4 EICHENLAUB, George 1850
5 SANBORN, Daniel 1850
6 WALTON, George W 1854
7 ANGEL, Betsey 1852
8 BROOKS, John A 1849

21
Lots-Sec. 21
1 GEYASHE, Joseph Mash1840
5 SMITH, Charles 1875
6 ST PETER, ALEXANDER 1841
ATWATER Edgar 1877
NORTON Edwin A 1854

30
Lots-Sec. 30
1 MCINTOSH, John 1841
2 MCINTOSH, John 1841
3 MCINTOSH, John 1841
4 COWN, George 1841
5 TRENBLER, Francis L 1848
6 RYERSON, Martin 1841
7 RYERSON, Martin 1841
8 RYERSON, Martin 1841
9 BALL, John 1855
10 BALL, John 1855
11 BALL, John 1856
13 RYERSON, Martin 1841
BALL John 1855
HOWLETT Robert 1854

29
Lots-Sec. 29
1 RYERSON, Martin[235]1849
2 RYERSON, Martin[235]1849
3 ST PETER, MARY A 1841
HICKS [85] Julia A 1911
BABCOCK James 1888
BABCOCK James 1888
WHITMAN Benjamin S 1970
HOPKINS John W 1852
BALL [6] John 1859
HOPKINS John W 1852
BALL [6] John 1859
BALL [6] John 1859

28
NORTON Edwin A 1854
LACEY Alice 1912
HOWLETT Robert 1854
LACEY Alice 1912
BALL [6] John 1859
BALL [6] John 1859
NORTON Edwin A 1854
HOWLETT Robert 1854
NORTON Edwin A 1854

31
WISENFIELD Joseph 1865
HOWLETT Robert 1854
SQUIER David W 1860
Lots-Sec. 31
1 SQUIER, David W 1861
2 SQUIER, David W 1861

32
MCKEE James H 1855
MCKEE James H 1855
NORTON Edwin A 1854
NORTON Edwin A 1854

33
NORTON Edwin A 1844
NORTON Edwin A 1844
NORTON Edwin A 1844
NORTON Edwin A 1844
HOWLETT Robert 1854
BALL John 1855
NORTON Edwin A 1854
BALL John 1855

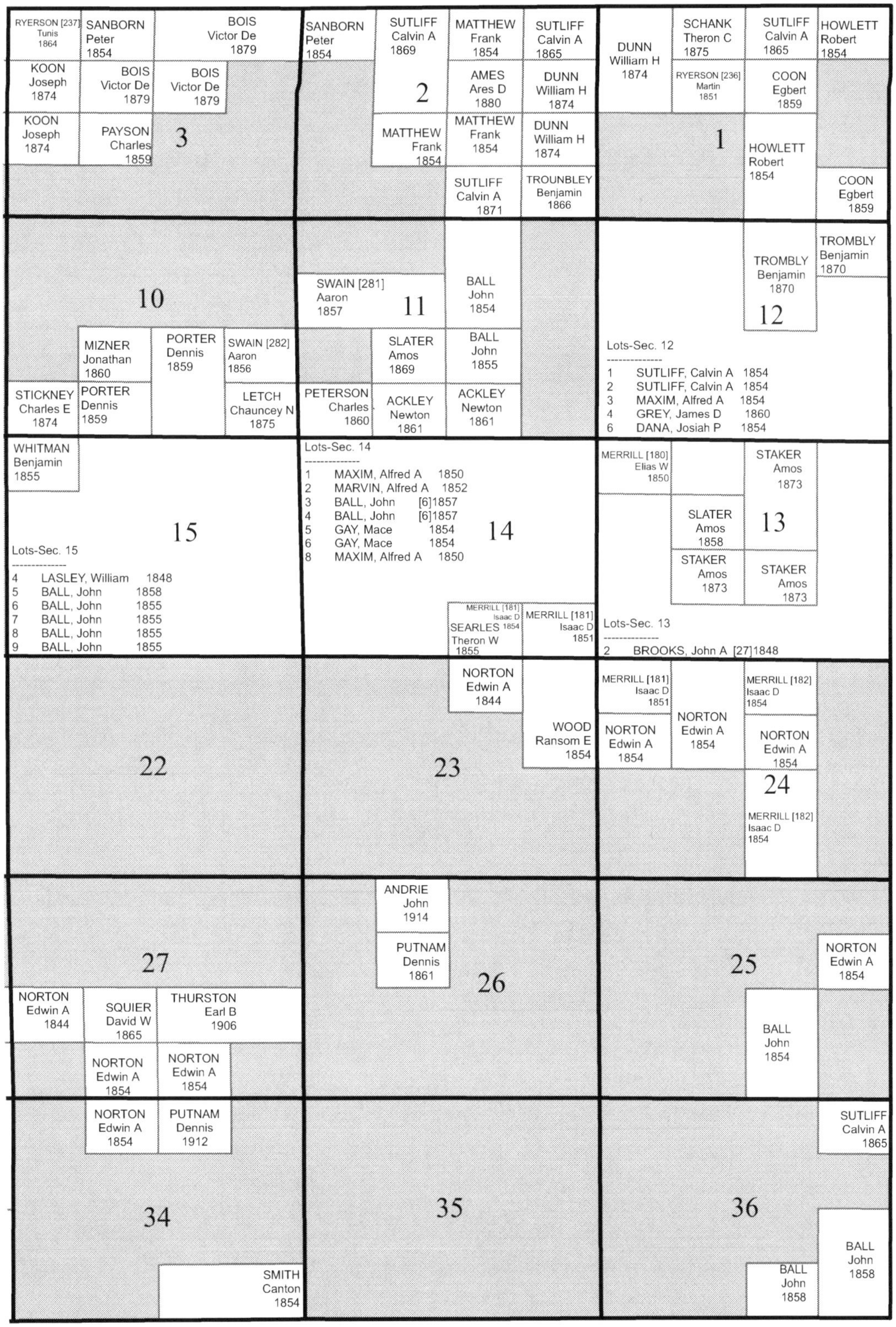

RYERSON [237] Tunis 1864
SANBORN Peter 1854
BOIS Victor De 1879
KOON Joseph 1874
BOIS Victor De 1879
BOIS Victor De 1879
KOON Joseph 1874
PAYSON Charles 1859
3
SANBORN Peter 1854
SUTLIFF Calvin A 1869
MATTHEW Frank 1854
SUTLIFF Calvin A 1865
AMES Ares D 1880
DUNN William H 1874
2
MATTHEW Frank 1854
MATTHEW Frank 1854
DUNN William H 1874
SUTLIFF Calvin A 1871
TROUNBLEY Benjamin 1866
DUNN William H 1874
SCHANK Theron C 1875
SUTLIFF Calvin A 1865
HOWLETT Robert 1854
RYERSON [236] Martin 1851
COON Egbert 1859
1
HOWLETT Robert 1854
COON Egbert 1859

10
MIZNER Jonathan 1860
PORTER Dennis 1859
SWAIN [282] Aaron 1856
STICKNEY Charles E 1874
PORTER Dennis 1859
LETCH Chauncey N 1875
SWAIN [281] Aaron 1857
11
BALL John 1854
SLATER Amos 1869
BALL John 1855
PETERSON Charles 1860
ACKLEY Newton 1861
ACKLEY Newton 1861
TROMBLY Benjamin 1870
TROMBLY Benjamin 1870
12

Lots-Sec. 12

1 SUTLIFF, Calvin A 1854
2 SUTLIFF, Calvin A 1854
3 MAXIM, Alfred A 1854
4 GREY, James D 1860
6 DANA, Josiah P 1854

WHITMAN Benjamin 1855
15

Lots-Sec. 15

4 LASLEY, William 1848
5 BALL, John 1858
6 BALL, John 1855
7 BALL, John 1855
8 BALL, John 1855
9 BALL, John 1855

Lots-Sec. 14

1 MAXIM, Alfred A 1850
2 MARVIN, Alfred A 1852
3 BALL, John [6]1857
4 BALL, John [6]1857
5 GAY, Mace 1854
6 GAY, Mace 1854
8 MAXIM, Alfred A 1850

14
MERRILL [181] Isaac D
SEARLES 1854 Theron W 1855
MERRILL [181] Isaac D 1851
MERRILL [180] Elias W 1850
STAKER Amos 1873
SLATER Amos 1858
13
STAKER Amos 1873
STAKER Amos 1873

Lots-Sec. 13

2 BROOKS, John A [27]1848

22
NORTON Edwin A 1844
WOOD Ransom E 1854
23
MERRILL [181] Isaac D 1851
NORTON Edwin A 1854
MERRILL [182] Isaac D 1854
NORTON Edwin A 1854
NORTON Edwin A 1854
24
MERRILL [182] Isaac D 1854

27
NORTON Edwin A 1844
SQUIER David W 1865
THURSTON Earl B 1906
NORTON Edwin A 1854
NORTON Edwin A 1854
ANDRIE John 1914
PUTNAM Dennis 1861
26
25
NORTON Edwin A 1854
BALL John 1854

NORTON Edwin A 1854
PUTNAM Dennis 1912
34
SMITH Canton 1854
35
36
SUTLIFF Calvin A 1865
BALL John 1858
BALL John 1858

Helpful Hints

1. This Map's INDEX can be found on the preceding pages.
2. Refer to Map "C" to see where this Township lies within Newaygo County, Michigan.
3. Numbers within square brackets [ ] denote a multi-patentee land parcel (multi-owner). Refer to Appendix "C" for a full list of members in this group.
4. Areas that look to be crowded with Patentees usually indicate multiple sales of the same parcel (Re-issues) or Overlapping parcels. See this Township's Index for an explanation of these and other circumstances that might explain "odd" groupings of Patentees on this map.

Legend

Patent Boundary
Section Boundary
No Patents Found (or Outside County)
1., 2., 3., ... Lot Numbers (when beside a name)
[ ] Group Number (see Appendix "C")

Scale: Section = 1 mile X 1 mile (generally, with some exceptions)

Road Map

T11-N R14-W
Michigan-Toledo Strip Meridian

Map Group 21

Cities & Towns

Bridgeton

Cemeteries

None

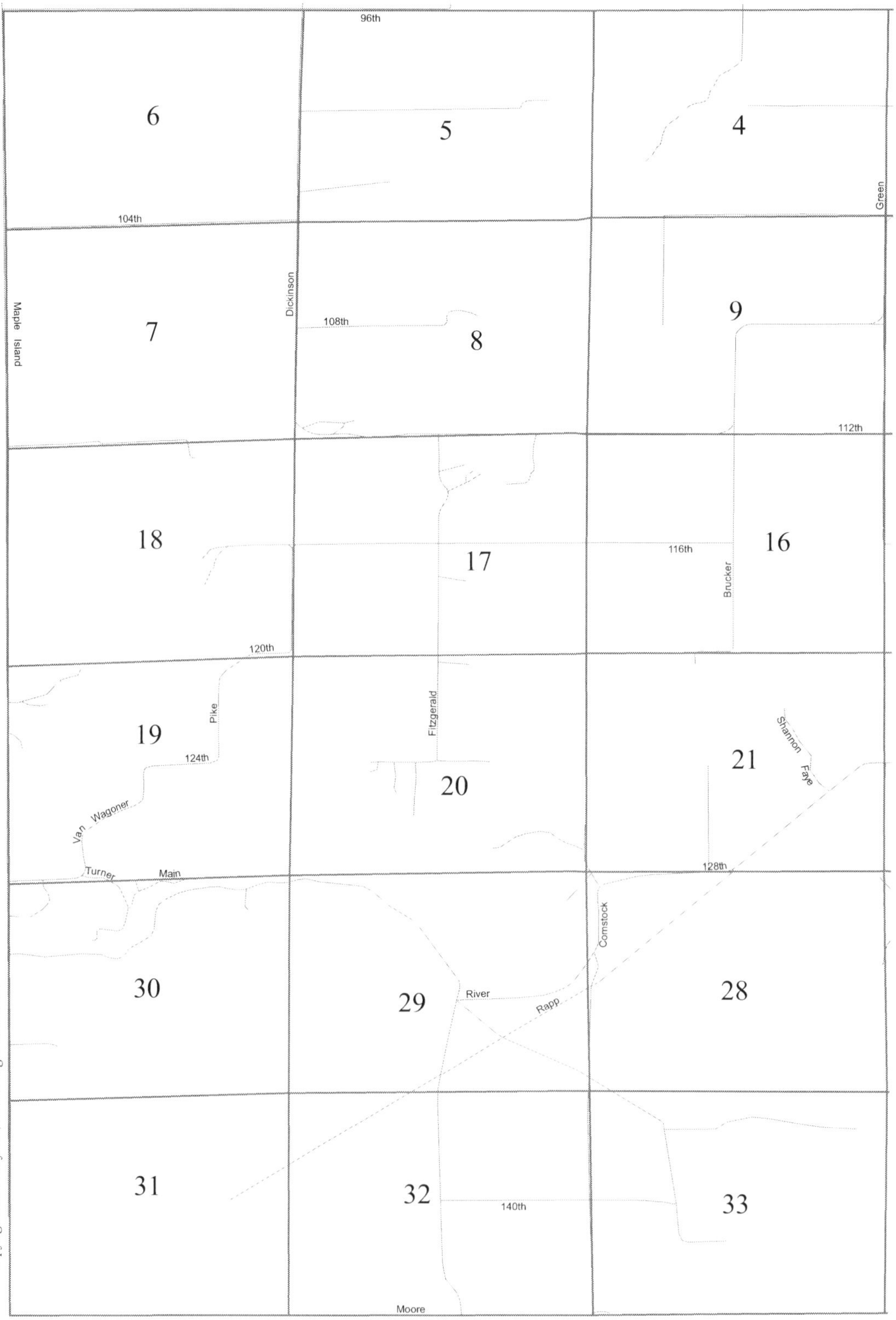

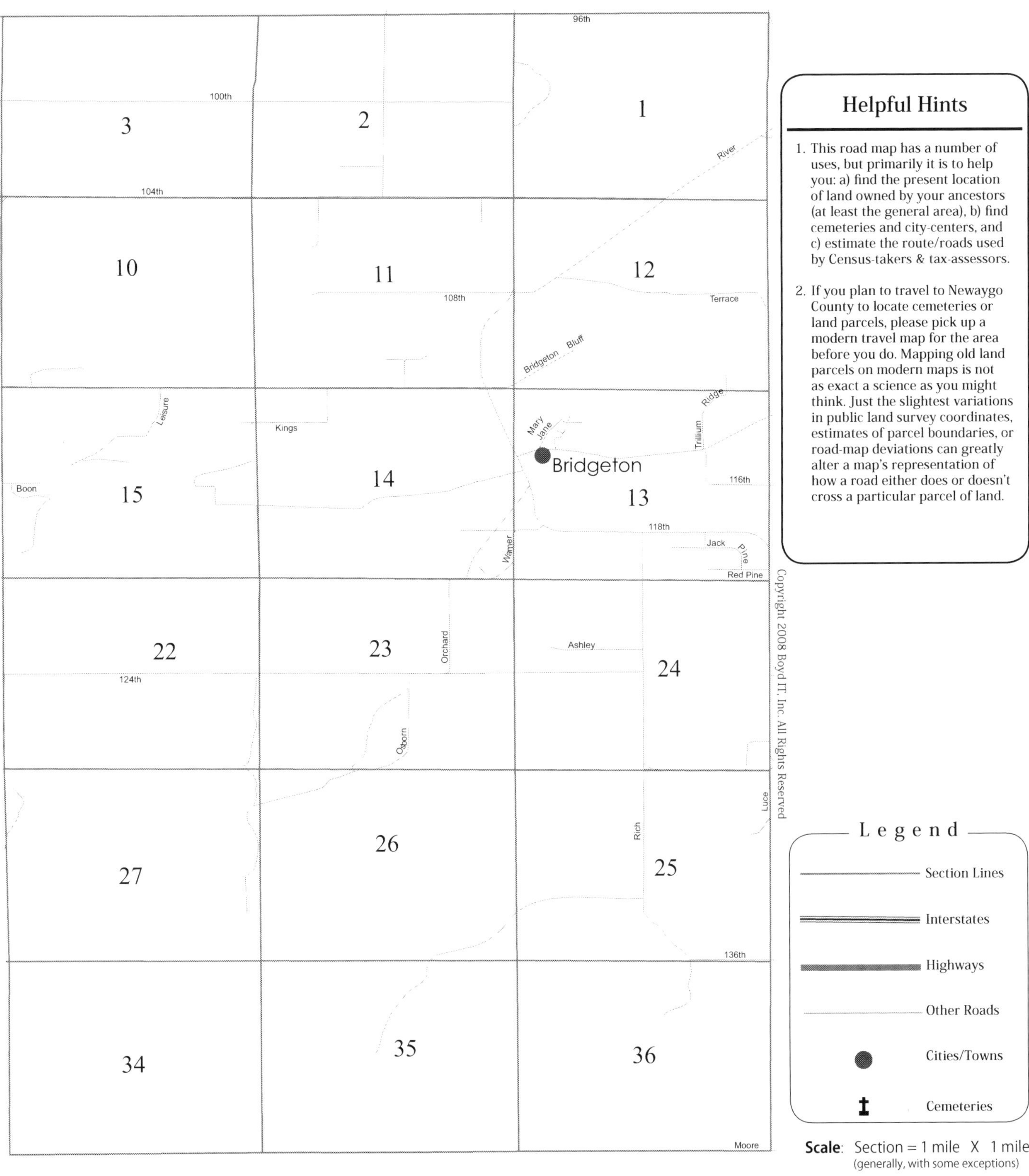

Helpful Hints

1. This road map has a number of uses, but primarily it is to help you: a) find the present location of land owned by your ancestors (at least the general area), b) find cemeteries and city-centers, and c) estimate the route/roads used by Census-takers & tax-assessors.
2. If you plan to travel to Newaygo County to locate cemeteries or land parcels, please pick up a modern travel map for the area before you do. Mapping old land parcels on modern maps is not as exact a science as you might think. Just the slightest variations in public land survey coordinates, estimates of parcel boundaries, or road-map deviations can greatly alter a map's representation of how a road either does or doesn't cross a particular parcel of land.

Scale: Section = 1 mile X 1 mile
(generally, with some exceptions)

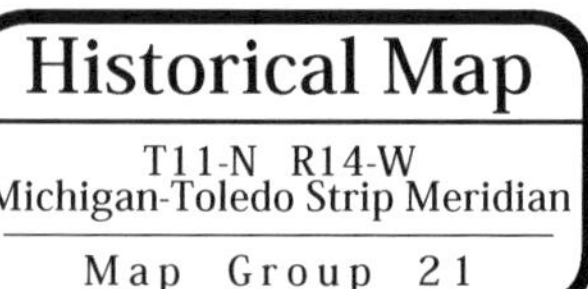

Cities & Towns

Bridgeton

Cemeteries

None

6 5 4

7 8 9

Cow Creek

Brooks Creek

Graham Creek

18 17 16

Mystery Lake

19 20 21

Haverson Lake

30 29 28

Truckey Lake

Maple River

31 32 33

Maple Lake

Chidister Creek

Mosquito Creek

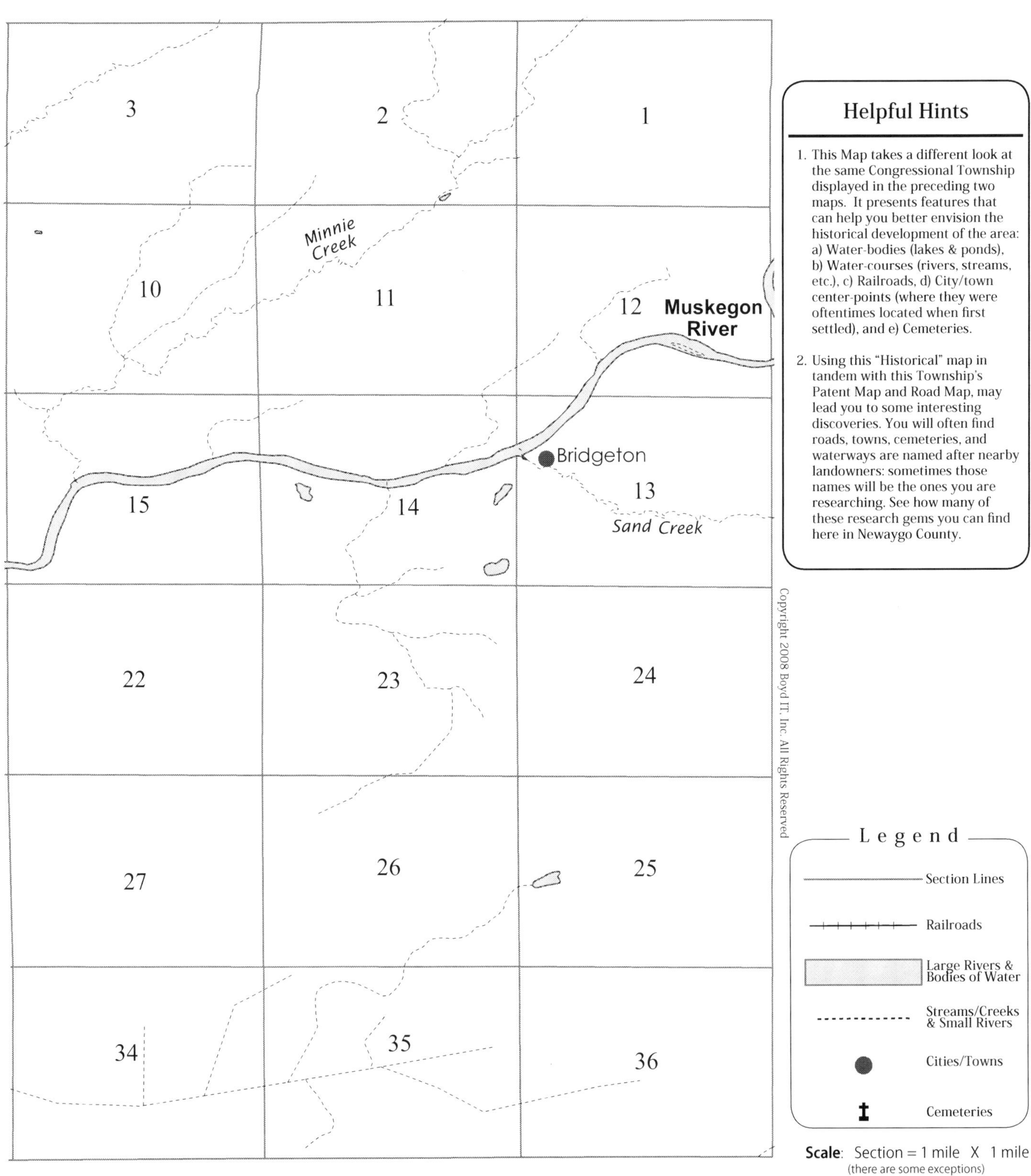
3
2
1
10
Minnie Creek
11
12
Muskegon River
15
14
Bridgeton
13
Sand Creek
22
23
24
27
26
25
34
35
36
Copyright 2008 Boyd IT, Inc. All Rights Reserved
Helpful Hints
1. This Map takes a different look at the same Congressional Township displayed in the preceding two maps. It presents features that can help you better envision the historical development of the area: a) Water-bodies (lakes & ponds), b) Water-courses (rivers, streams, etc.), c) Railroads, d) City/town center-points (where they were oftentimes located when first settled), and e) Cemeteries.
2. Using this "Historical" map in tandem with this Township's Patent Map and Road Map, may lead you to some interesting discoveries. You will often find roads, towns, cemeteries, and waterways are named after nearby landowners: sometimes those names will be the ones you are researching. See how many of these research gems you can find here in Newaygo County.
Legend
Section Lines
Railroads
Large Rivers & Bodies of Water
Streams/Creeks & Small Rivers
Cities/Towns
Cemeteries
Scale: Section = 1 mile X 1 mile
(there are some exceptions)

Map Group 22: Index to Land Patents

Township 11-North Range 13-West (Michigan-Toledo Strip)

After you locate an individual in this Index, take note of the Section and Section Part then proceed to the Land Patent map on the pages immediately following. You should have no difficulty locating the corresponding parcel of land.

The "For More Info" Column will lead you to more information about the underlying Patents. See the *Legend* at right, and the "How to Use this Book" chapter, for more information.

LEGEND

"For More Info . . . " column

A = Authority (Legislative Act, See Appendix "A")
B = Block or Lot (location in Section unknown)
C = Cancelled Patent
F = Fractional Section
G = Group (Multi-Patentee Patent, see Appendix "C")
V = Overlaps another Parcel
R = Re-Issued (Parcel patented more than once)

(A & G items require you to look in the Appendixes referred to above. All other Letter-designations followed by a number require you to locate line-items in this index that possess the ID number found after the letter).

ID	Individual in Patent	Sec.	Sec. Part	Date Issued	Other Counties	For More Info . . .
3335	ARMSTRONG, Alfred F	15	SWSE	1854-06-15		A1
3457	ARMSTRONG, Sullivan	22	NENW	1854-06-15		A1
3395	BALL, John	2	NWNW	1853-04-15		A1 F
3408	" "	7	NENE	1854-09-15		A1
3409	" "	7	SESW	1854-09-15		A1
3399	" "	5	7	1855-11-01		A1
3400	" "	5	8	1855-11-01		A1
3403	" "	6	1	1855-11-01		A1
3404	" "	7	1	1855-11-08		A3
3405	" "	7	2	1855-11-08		A3
3410	" "	7	SWNE	1855-11-08		A3
3406	" "	7	3	1856-03-10		A1 F
3407	" "	7	N½NW	1856-03-10		A1 F
3396	" "	4	NWNW	1858-01-15		A3 F
3397	" "	5	1	1858-01-15		A3
3401	" "	5	NENE	1858-01-15		A3 F
3398	" "	5	6	1861-07-01		A3
3402	" "	5	NWNW	1861-07-01		A3 F
3345	BANKER, Charles A	33	E½SE	1854-10-05		A1
3346	BLOOD, Charles	28	E½SE	1854-09-15		A1
3431	BLOOD, Orin	28	W½SE	1854-09-15		A1
3432	" "	8	NESE	1861-04-01		A1
3394	BROOKS, John A	15	W½SW	1855-12-15		A1
3428	BROWN, Nathaniel H	10	SESE	1854-09-15		A1
3429	" "	11	NWSW	1854-09-15		A1
3419	BUHL, Lewis	34	W½NE	1854-06-15		A1
3368	BURRIL, Ezra N	13	NWNW	1852-03-10		A1
3369	" "	14	NENE	1852-03-10		A1
3393	CARTER, Joel H	1	SENW	1853-11-01		A1
3342	CHAPMAN, Augusta	7		1871-11-15		A1 F
3411	COX, John	20	SESE	1873-05-20		A4
3386	DANA, Josiah P	19	NESW	1854-06-15		A1 G182
3427	ELPHICK, Morgan E	4		1876-05-10		A1 F
3381	FELLOWS, Henry H	24	NWNW	1861-12-10		A1
3382	" "	24	SWNW	1884-12-05		A4
3365	FULLER, Emily	26	S½SW	1855-11-01		A1
3366	" "	27	S½SE	1855-11-01		A1
3341	FURMAN, Ashley B	4	1	1851-05-01		A1
3370	GRIFFIN, George	4	SESW	1877-11-20		A4
3384	HALL, Hiram S	32	E½SE	1854-10-05		A1
3385	" "	32	SWSE	1854-10-05		A1
3383	HARRINGTON, Henry	27	S½NE	1854-06-15		A1
3415	HEADLEY, John	20	NESE	1856-03-10		A1
3433	HEADLEY, Orrin	35	NWSW	1857-03-10		A1
3347	HILL, Charles F	29	E½NW	1854-06-15		A1
3348	" "	29	NWNW	1854-06-15		A1

ID	Individual in Patent	Sec.	Sec. Part	Date Issued	Other Counties	For More Info . . .
3388	HOULDING, Israel	28	NENE	1854-10-05		A1
3389	" "	28	S½NE	1854-10-05		A1
3387	" "	28	E½NW	1857-03-10		A1
3390	" "	28	SWNW	1857-03-10		A1
3391	" "	29	NENE	1866-06-05		A1
3435	HOWLETT, Robert	5	2	1854-09-15		A1
3436	" "	5	4	1854-09-15		A1
3437	" "	5	NESE	1854-09-15		A1
3440	" "	6	NW	1854-09-15		A1 C F
3441	" "	6	NWNE	1854-09-15		A1 C R3442, 3443
3444	" "	6	W½NW	1854-09-15		A1 C F R3445, 3446
3438	" "	6	NENW	1905-06-26		A1 R3439
3438	" "	6	NENW	1905-06-26		A1 C R3439
3439	" "	6	NENW	1905-06-26		A1 R3438
3439	" "	6	NENW	1905-06-26		A1 C R3438
3442	" "	6	NWNE	1905-06-26		A1 R3441, 3443
3442	" "	6	NWNE	1905-06-26		A1 C R3441, 3443
3443	" "	6	NWNE	1905-06-26		A1 R3441, 3442
3443	" "	6	NWNE	1905-06-26		A1 C R3441, 3442
3445	" "	6	W½NW	1905-06-26		A1 F R3444, 3446
3445	" "	6	W½NW	1905-06-26		A1 C F R3444, 3446
3446	" "	6	W½NW	1905-06-26		A1 F R3444, 3445
3446	" "	6	W½NW	1905-06-26		A1 C F R3444, 3445
3424	KEATING, Michael E	27	NW	1844-09-15		A1
3372	KENDALL, George	14	NWNW	1854-09-15		A1
3371	" "	14	E½NW	1854-10-05		A1
3373	" "	26	SENW	1855-03-01		A1
3374	" "	26	W½SE	1855-12-15		A1
3375	" "	35	N½NW	1856-03-10		A1
3376	KENDULL, George	1	E½NE	1854-06-15		A1 F
3377	" "	1	W½NE	1854-06-15		A1 F
3425	KRIGER, Michael	28	E½SW	1854-10-05		A1
3426	" "	34	W½NW	1854-10-05		A1
3336	LOOMIS, Alfred	28	NWNW	1860-06-01		A1
3420	LOVELL, Louis S	22	S½NW	1855-03-01		A1
3447	MALLERY, Samuel	26	E½SE	1856-03-10		A1
3337	MAXIM, Alfred	18	NWNW	1852-11-01		A1 F
3338	" "	4	SWSE	1853-08-01		A1
3332	MAXIM, Alfred A	4	N½SW	1851-05-01		A1
3331	" "	4	2	1861-12-10		A1
3333	" "	4	SWNE	1861-12-10		A1 F
3334	" "	4	SWNW	1868-02-15		A1
3459	MEAD, William J	18	SESW	1869-09-10		A1
3386	MERRILL, Elias W	19	NESW	1854-06-15		A1 G182
3386	MERRILL, Isaac D	19	NESW	1854-06-15		A1 G182
3378	MITCHELL, George	13	SENE	1858-05-01		A1
3422	MORRIS, Robert W	9	E½SE	1851-05-01		A1 G236
3423	" "	9	NWSE	1851-05-01		A1 G236 V3460
3421	" "	2	N½SE	1854-06-15		A1 G236
3351	NORTON, Edwin A	17	W½SW	1854-09-15		A1
3352	" "	19	E½NE	1854-09-15		A1
3353	" "	19	NENW	1854-09-15		A1
3354	" "	19	SE	1854-09-15		A1
3355	" "	20	NENW	1854-09-15		A1
3356	" "	20	NWSE	1854-09-15		A1
3357	" "	20	S½SW	1854-09-15		A1
3358	" "	20	W½NE	1854-09-15		A1
3359	" "	29	W½NE	1854-09-15		A1
3360	" "	32	E½NW	1854-09-15		A1
3361	" "	32	NWNW	1854-09-15		A1
3362	" "	32	NWSE	1854-09-15		A1
3363	" "	32	W½NE	1854-09-15		A1
3460	PATTERSON, William	9	W½SE	1861-12-05		A1 V3423
3379	POLLARD, George	8	SESE	1861-12-05		A1
3380	" "	9	SWSW	1861-12-05		A1
3392	RANDLE, James	34	NWSW	1858-05-01		A1
3422	RYERSON, Martin	9	E½SE	1851-05-01		A1 G236
3423	" "	9	NWSE	1851-05-01		A1 G236 V3460
3421	" "	2	N½SE	1854-06-15		A1 G236
3448	SANFORD, Samuel R	5	3	1868-02-15		A1 C
3449	" "	6	SESE	1868-02-15		A1 C R3450
3450	" "	6	SESE	1885-05-20		A1 R3449
3451	SHELDON, Sarah M	15	NESW	1855-11-01		A1

ID	Individual in Patent	Sec.	Sec. Part	Date Issued	Other Counties	For More Info . . .
3452	SHELDON, Sarah M (Cont'd)	15	SESW	1855-11-01		A1
3339	SHERK, Alfred	2	NWNE	1852-03-10		A1 F
3364	SIMONDS, Elihu A	23	NWNW	1854-09-15		A1
3350	SMITH, David	21	SWSE	1860-10-01		A1
3414	STANDISH, John H	26	SWNW	1856-03-10		A1
3430	STARR, Noble	23	NESW	1853-08-01		A1
3458	STARR, Washington	23	S½SW	1853-11-01		A1
3367	STICKNEY, Eusebeus	22	SW	1854-06-15		A1
3456	STILWELL, Sherman	6	2	1863-09-01		A1
3461	STRONG, William S	18	E½NE	1854-10-05		A1
3463	" "	7	5	1854-10-05		A1
3462	" "	7	4	1855-03-01		A1
3344	SUTLIFF, Calvin	6	4	1864-11-01		A1
3343	SUTLIFF, Calvin A	3	SWNW	1859-10-10		A1 F
3416	THOMAS, John	2	SENW	1854-06-15		A1 F
3412	THOMPSON, John D	6	6	1870-05-02		A4
3413	" "	6	7	1870-05-02		A4
3329	UPTON, Adonijah E	2	NENW	1868-02-15		A1 F
3417	WART, John	8	S½SW	1873-05-20		A4
3418	" "	8	SWSE	1873-05-20		A4
3340	WATSON, Amasa B	8	NENE	1876-07-25		A1
3330	WHEAT, Albert	28	NWNE	1859-10-10		A1
3454	WILCOX, Sextus N	20	NESW	1863-10-20		A3
3455	" "	20	S½NW	1863-10-20		A3
3349	WILSON, Daniel R	3	NWNE	1858-05-01		A1
3434	WOOD, Ransom E	18	SWNW	1854-06-15		A1
3453	WOOD, Sarell	12	W½NE	1855-12-15		A1

Patent Map

T11-N R13-W
Michigan-Toledo Strip Meridian

Map Group 22

Township Statistics

Parcels Mapped	:	135
Number of Patents	:	105
Number of Individuals	:	68
Patentees Identified	:	65
Number of Surnames	:	60
Multi-Patentee Parcels	:	4
Oldest Patent Date	:	9/15/1844
Most Recent Patent	:	6/26/1905
Block/Lot Parcels	:	19
Parcels Re - Issued	:	4
Parcels that Overlap	:	2
Cities and Towns	:	3
Cemeteries	:	1

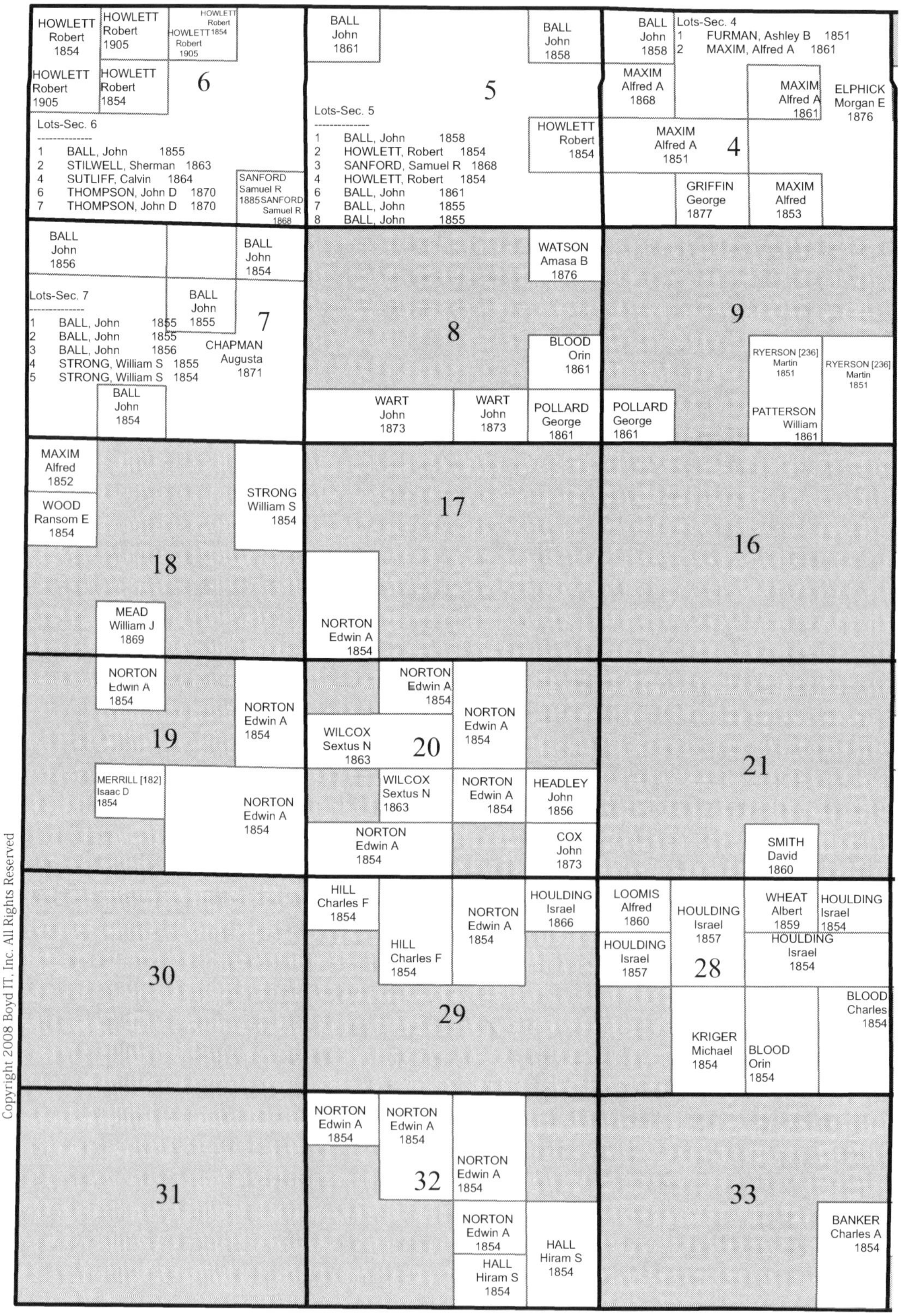

HOWLETT Robert 1854
HOWLETT Robert 1905
HOWLETT Robert HOWLETT 1854 Robert 1905
HOWLETT Robert 1905
HOWLETT Robert 1854
6
Lots-Sec. 6
1 BALL, John 1855
2 STILWELL, Sherman 1863
4 SUTLIFF, Calvin 1864
6 THOMPSON, John D 1870
7 THOMPSON, John D 1870
SANFORD Samuel R 1885 SANFORD Samuel R 1868

BALL John 1861
BALL John 1858
5
Lots-Sec. 5
1 BALL, John 1858
2 HOWLETT, Robert 1854
3 SANFORD, Samuel R 1868
4 HOWLETT, Robert 1854
6 BALL, John 1861
7 BALL, John 1855
8 BALL, John 1855
HOWLETT Robert 1854

BALL John 1858
Lots-Sec. 4
1 FURMAN, Ashley B 1851
2 MAXIM, Alfred A 1861
MAXIM Alfred A 1868
MAXIM Alfred A 1861
ELPHICK Morgan E 1876
MAXIM Alfred A 1851
4
GRIFFIN George 1877
MAXIM Alfred 1853

BALL John 1856
BALL John 1854
Lots-Sec. 7
1 BALL, John 1855
2 BALL, John 1855
3 BALL, John 1856
4 STRONG, William S 1855
5 STRONG, William S 1854
BALL John 1855
7
CHAPMAN Augusta 1871
BALL John 1854

WATSON Amasa B 1876
8
BLOOD Orin 1861
WART John 1873
WART John 1873
POLLARD George 1861

9
RYERSON [236] Martin 1851
RYERSON [236] Martin 1851
POLLARD George 1861
PATTERSON William 1861

MAXIM Alfred 1852
WOOD Ransom E 1854
STRONG William S 1854
18
MEAD William J 1869

17
NORTON Edwin A 1854

16

NORTON Edwin A 1854
NORTON Edwin A 1854
19
MERRILL [182] Isaac D 1854
NORTON Edwin A 1854

NORTON Edwin A 1854
NORTON Edwin A 1854
WILCOX Sextus N 1863
20
WILCOX Sextus N 1863
NORTON Edwin A 1854
HEADLEY John 1856
NORTON Edwin A 1854
COX John 1873

21
SMITH David 1860

30

HILL Charles F 1854
HILL Charles F 1854
NORTON Edwin A 1854
HOULDING Israel 1866
29

LOOMIS Alfred 1860
HOULDING Israel 1857
HOULDING Israel 1857
WHEAT Albert 1859
HOULDING Israel 1854
HOULDING Israel 1854
28
BLOOD Charles 1854
KRIGER Michael 1854
BLOOD Orin 1854

31

NORTON Edwin A 1854
NORTON Edwin A 1854
NORTON Edwin A 1854
32
NORTON Edwin A 1854
HALL Hiram S 1854
HALL Hiram S 1854

33
BANKER Charles A 1854

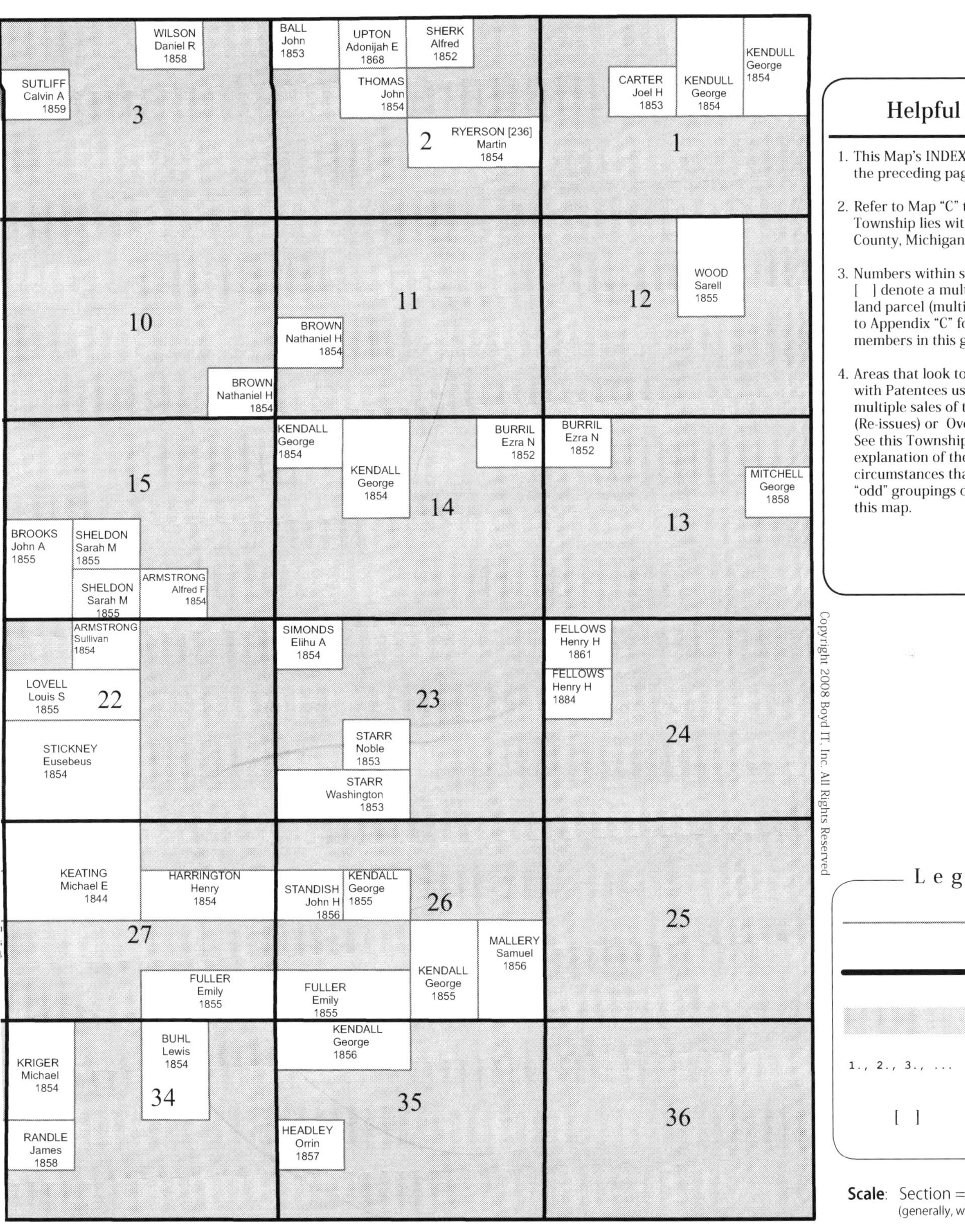

Helpful Hints

1. This Map's INDEX can be found on the preceding pages.
2. Refer to Map "C" to see where this Township lies within Newaygo County, Michigan.
3. Numbers within square brackets [ ] denote a multi-patentee land parcel (multi-owner). Refer to Appendix "C" for a full list of members in this group.
4. Areas that look to be crowded with Patentees usually indicate multiple sales of the same parcel (Re-issues) or Overlapping parcels. See this Township's Index for an explanation of these and other circumstances that might explain "odd" groupings of Patentees on this map.

Legend

———	Patent Boundary
▬▬▬	Section Boundary
(shaded)	No Patents Found (or Outside County)
1., 2., 3., ...	Lot Numbers (when beside a name)
[ ]	Group Number (see Appendix "C")

Scale: Section = 1 mile X 1 mile (generally, with some exceptions)

Road Map

T11-N R13-W
Michigan-Toledo Strip Meridian

Map Group 22

Cities & Towns

Ashland
Ashland Center
Grant

Cemeteries

Shippy Cemetery

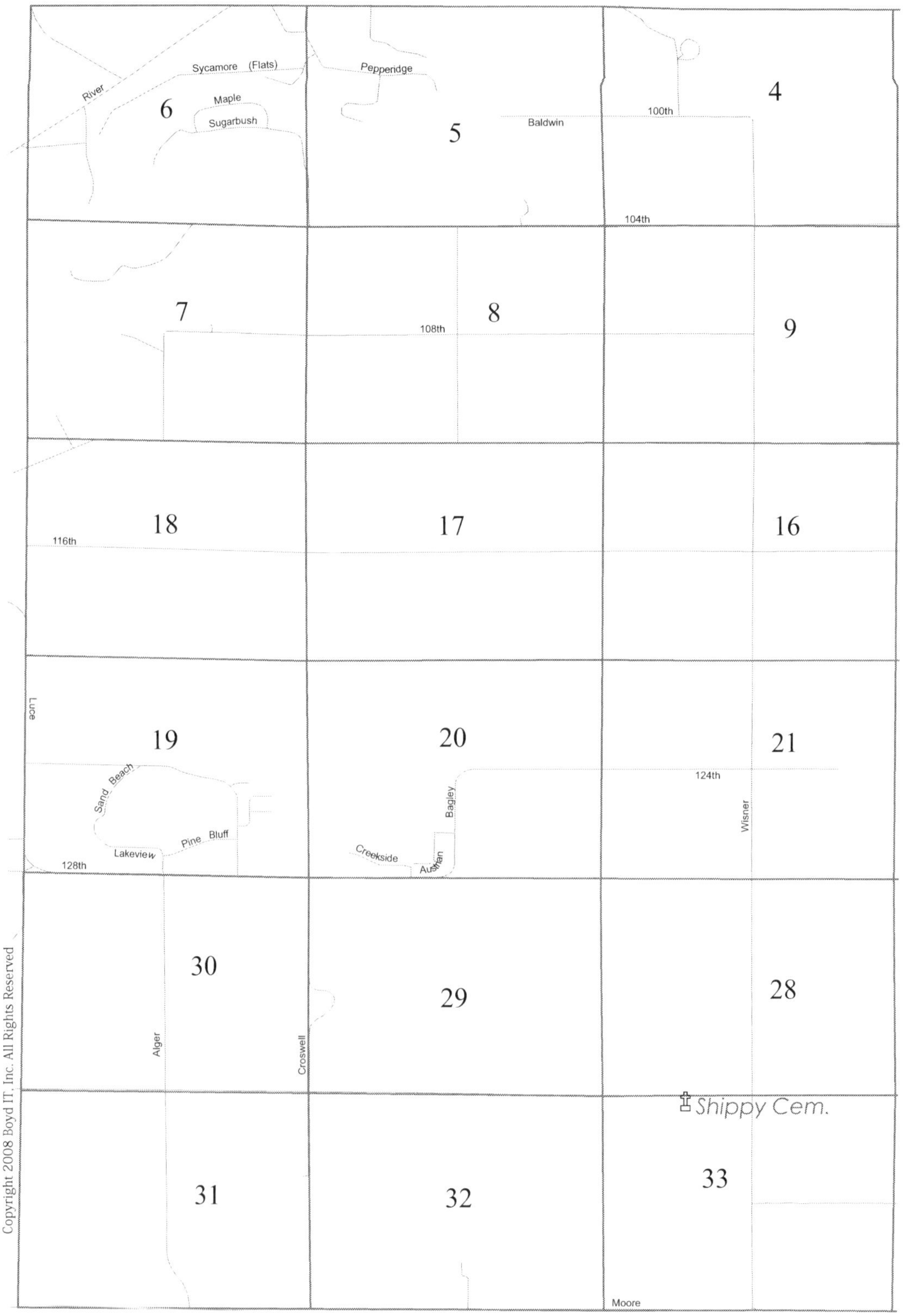

River
Sycamore (Flats)
Maple
Sugarbush
Pepperidge
Baldwin
100th
104th
108th
116th
Luce
Sand Beach
Lakeview
Pine Bluff
128th
Creekside
Austin
Bagley
124th
Wisner
Alger
Croswell
Shippy Cem.
Moore

6 5 4 7 8 9 18 17 16 19 20 21 30 29 28 31 32 33

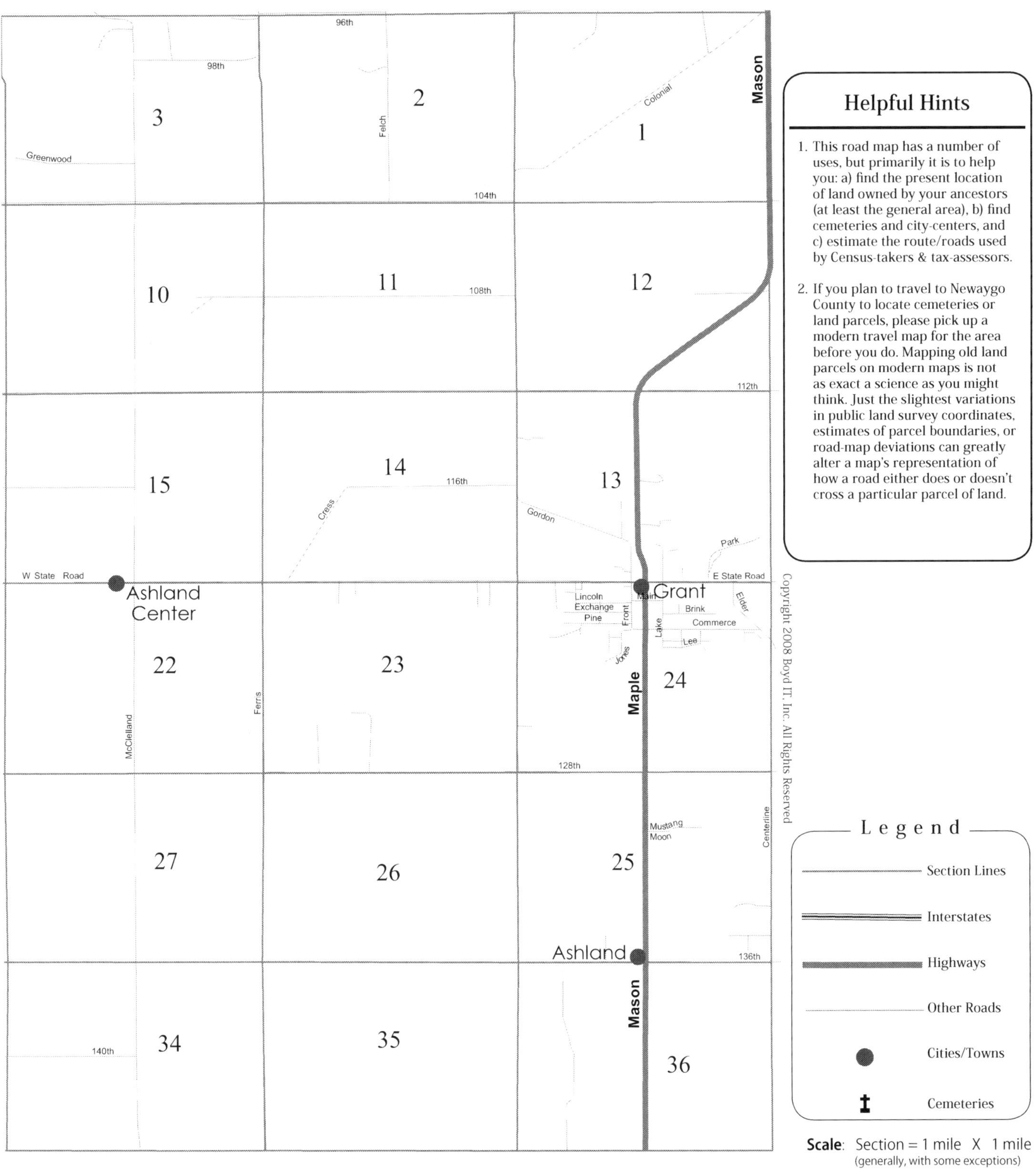
96th
98th
3
2
1
Felch
Colonial
Mason
Greenwood
104th
10
11
108th
12
112th
15
14
116th
13
Cress
Gordon
Park
W State Road
E State Road
Ashland Center
Grant
Lincoln
Exchange
Pine
Front
Main
Lake
Brink
Commerce
Elder
Lee
Jones
22
23
Maple
24
McClelland
Ferris
128th
27
26
25
Mustang Moon
Centerline
Ashland
136th
140th
34
35
Mason
36
Helpful Hints
1. This road map has a number of uses, but primarily it is to help you: a) find the present location of land owned by your ancestors (at least the general area), b) find cemeteries and city-centers, and c) estimate the route/roads used by Census-takers & tax-assessors.
2. If you plan to travel to Newaygo County to locate cemeteries or land parcels, please pick up a modern travel map for the area before you do. Mapping old land parcels on modern maps is not as exact a science as you might think. Just the slightest variations in public land survey coordinates, estimates of parcel boundaries, or road-map deviations can greatly alter a map's representation of how a road either does or doesn't cross a particular parcel of land.
Copyright 2008 Boyd IT, Inc. All Rights Reserved
Legend
Section Lines
Interstates
Highways
Other Roads
Cities/Towns
Cemeteries
Scale: Section = 1 mile X 1 mile
(generally, with some exceptions)

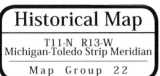

Cities & Towns
Ashland
Ashland Center
Grant

Cemeteries
Shippy Cemetery

6
5
4
Muskegon River
7
8
9
Greenwood Creek
18
17
16
Sand Creek
19
20
21
Sand Lake
30
29
28
Blood Lake
Shippy Cem.
31
32
33

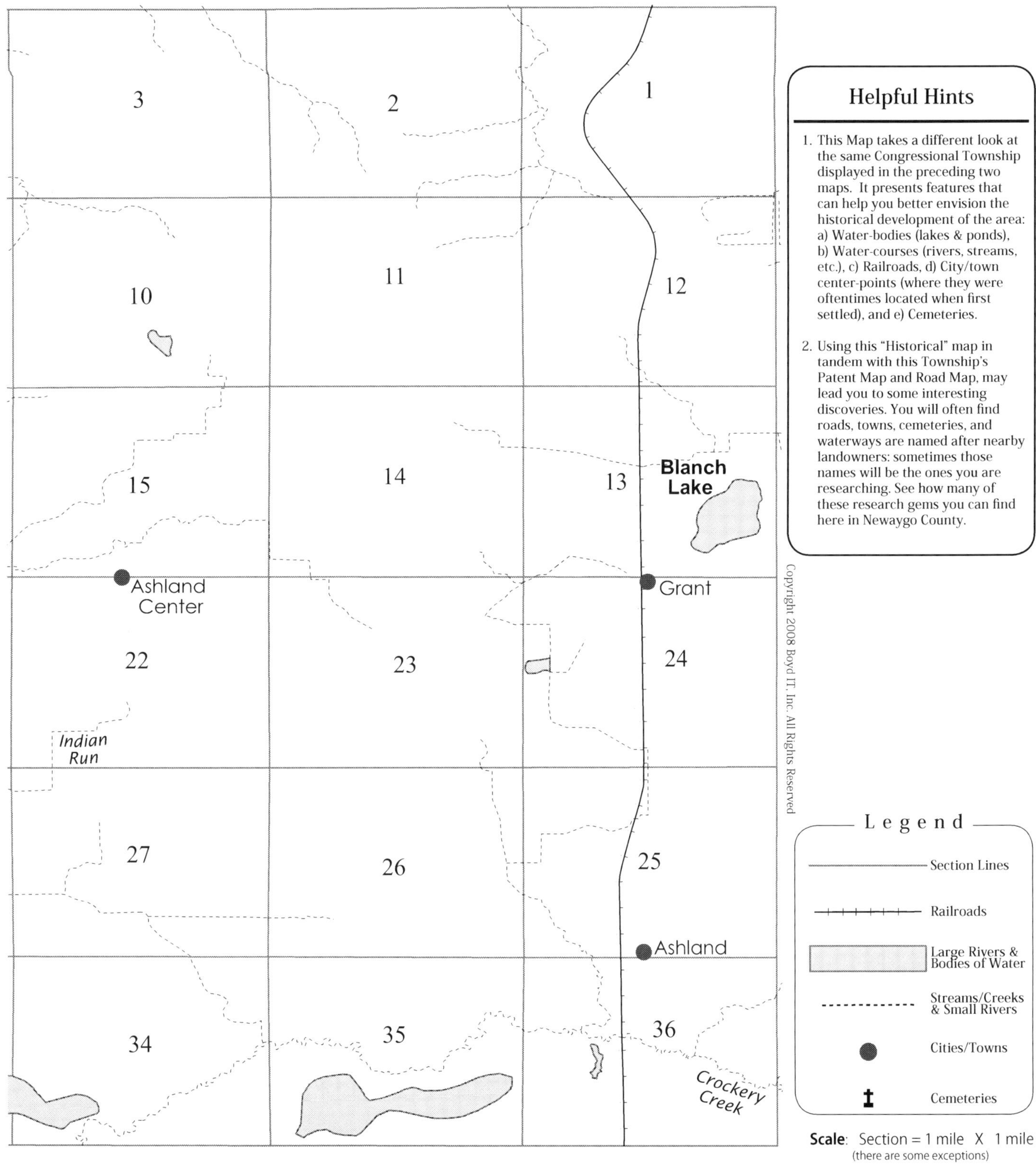

Helpful Hints

1. This Map takes a different look at the same Congressional Township displayed in the preceding two maps. It presents features that can help you better envision the historical development of the area: a) Water-bodies (lakes & ponds), b) Water-courses (rivers, streams, etc.), c) Railroads, d) City/town center-points (where they were oftentimes located when first settled), and e) Cemeteries.
2. Using this "Historical" map in tandem with this Township's Patent Map and Road Map, may lead you to some interesting discoveries. You will often find roads, towns, cemeteries, and waterways are named after nearby landowners: sometimes those names will be the ones you are researching. See how many of these research gems you can find here in Newaygo County.

Map Group 23: Index to Land Patents

Township 11-North Range 12-West (Michigan-Toledo Strip)

After you locate an individual in this Index, take note of the Section and Section Part then proceed to the Land Patent map on the pages immediately following. You should have no difficulty locating the corresponding parcel of land.

The "For More Info" Column will lead you to more information about the underlying Patents. See the *Legend* at right, and the "How to Use this Book" chapter, for more information.

LEGEND

"For More Info . . . " column

A = Authority (Legislative Act, See Appendix "A")
B = Block or Lot (location in Section unknown)
C = Cancelled Patent
F = Fractional Section
G = Group (Multi-Patentee Patent, see Appendix "C")
V = Overlaps another Parcel
R = Re-Issued (Parcel patented more than once)

(A & G items require you to look in the Appendixes referred to above. All other Letter-designations followed by a number require you to locate line-items in this index that possess the ID number found after the letter).

ID	Individual in Patent	Sec.	Sec. Part	Date Issued	Other Counties	For More Info . . .
3503	ALLEN, Lafayette	22	S½NW	1873-02-10		A4
3495	BALL, John	9	E½NW	1855-03-01		A1
3496	" "	9	SENE	1855-03-01		A1
3497	" "	9	W½NE	1855-03-01		A1
3508	BARKER, Neuman	30	NENE	1860-09-03		A3
3509	" "	30	W½NE	1860-09-03		A3
3519	BRACE, Rensselaer	30	E½SW	1861-12-10		A1
3500	BRITTAIN, Thomas	10	NW	1868-02-10		A3 G115
3518	BROWN, Rebecca	28	NW	1869-11-01		A4
3506	COOK, Luke	36	W½SE	1878-06-13		A4
3489	DANIELS, James P	24	NENE	1871-11-01		A4
3490	" "	24	W½NE	1871-11-01		A4
3467	EDMESTON, William	18	S½SE	1865-10-20		A3 G171
3472	EVANS, Daniel W	33	S½SW	1858-01-15		A3 G60
3473	" "	33	SESE	1858-01-15		A3 G60
3474	" "	34	SWSW	1858-01-15		A3 G60
3472	EVANS, George C	33	S½SW	1858-01-15		A3 G60
3473	" "	33	SESE	1858-01-15		A3 G60
3474	" "	34	SWSW	1858-01-15		A3 G60
3502	EWING, Kizzaiah	10	NWNE	1893-10-07		A4
3520	GLOVER, Samuel W	34	E½NE	1870-08-10		A4
3521	" "	34	NWNE	1870-08-10		A4
3468	GOODALE, Austin	24	N½SW	1870-08-10		A4
3469	" "	24	S½NW	1870-08-10		A4
3476	GRAY, Edgar L	32	SWNE	1867-01-10		A1
3493	GREEN, Jeremiah	4	E½SE	1889-11-22		A4
3499	HART, Joseph	2	NW	1874-02-20		A4 F
3475	HEBEL, David	26	SWNW	1875-02-10		A4
3481	HEBEL, Genette	26	S½SW	1870-08-10		A4
3465	HOOD, Andrew	3	SESE	1856-03-10		A1
3464	" "	3	N½SE	1857-02-20		A3
3466	" "	3	SWSE	1857-02-20		A3
3504	HUNSINGER, Levi C	12	SESE	1904-09-08		A1
3467	HUNTER, Nathaniel D	18	S½SE	1865-10-20		A3 G171
3500	JOHNSON, Isaac N	10	NW	1868-02-10		A3 G115
3482	KENDALL, George	6	W½W½	1855-11-01		A1 F
3500	LANCASTER, Joseph	10	NW	1868-02-10		A3 G115
3494	MAPES, Jesse	30	SE	1865-10-20		A3
3529	MARVIN, Stephen L	22	SW	1869-11-01		A4
3467	MEAD, Andrew W	18	S½SE	1865-10-20		A3 G171
3486	MOORE, James H	24	SWSW	1873-05-15		A1
3498	MORGAN, Jonathan R	2	N½SW	1869-11-01		A4
3478	OCONNOR, Eugene	4	SW	1880-11-20		A1
3507	PLATT, Merrit S	3	SW	1857-02-20		A3
3530	POST, William E	4	W½SE	1880-11-20		A1
3470	REED, Carol	31	N½SE	1855-11-08		A3

ID	Individual in Patent	Sec.	Sec. Part	Date Issued	Other Counties	For More Info . . .
3471	REED, Carol (Cont'd)	32	NWSW	1855-11-08		A3
3483	RUSSELL, Isaac	36	E½NW	1878-06-13		A4
3484	" "	36	W½NE	1878-06-13		A4
3491	SANBORN, James W	7	NWSW	1855-12-15		A1 F
3492	" "	7	SWNW	1855-12-15		A1 F
3477	SHAW, Elijah	32	W½NW	1861-11-01		A3
3485	SHAW, Jacob H	28	NE	1869-11-01		A4
3479	TRAIN, Furana	28	E½SE	1873-02-10		A4
3480	" "	28	NWSE	1873-02-10		A4
3501	TREXELL, Joseph	4	E½NE	1879-11-25		A4 F
3505	TREXELL, Lewis	10	NWSW	1875-09-10		A1
3487	WIGGINS, James M	2	SENE	1856-03-10		A1
3488	" "	2	SWNE	1856-03-10		A1
3510	WOOD, Ransom E	20	SESW	1866-04-03		A1
3511	" "	30	SENE	1866-04-03		A1
3514	" "	32	SESE	1866-04-03		A1
3515	" "	32	SWSW	1866-04-03		A1
3516	" "	36	SWNW	1866-04-03		A1
3517	" "	8	SESW	1866-04-03		A1
3512	" "	32	E½NW	1866-05-01		A3
3513	" "	32	N½NE	1866-05-01		A3
3528	WOOD, Sarell	7	SWSW	1854-06-15		A1 F
3522	" "	18	SESW	1855-11-08		A3
3523	" "	19	E½NW	1855-11-08		A3
3524	" "	19	E½SW	1855-11-08		A3
3525	" "	30	E½NW	1855-11-08		A3
3526	" "	31	E½SW	1855-11-08		A3
3527	" "	31	SENW	1855-11-08		A3

Patent Map

T11-N R12-W
Michigan-Toledo Strip Meridian

Map Group 23

Township Statistics

Parcels Mapped	:	67
Number of Patents	:	50
Number of Individuals	:	44
Patentees Identified	:	39
Number of Surnames	:	39
Multi-Patentee Parcels	:	5
Oldest Patent Date	:	6/15/1854
Most Recent Patent	:	9/8/1904
Block/Lot Parcels	:	0
Parcels Re - Issued	:	0
Parcels that Overlap	:	0
Cities and Towns	:	1
Cemeteries	:	1

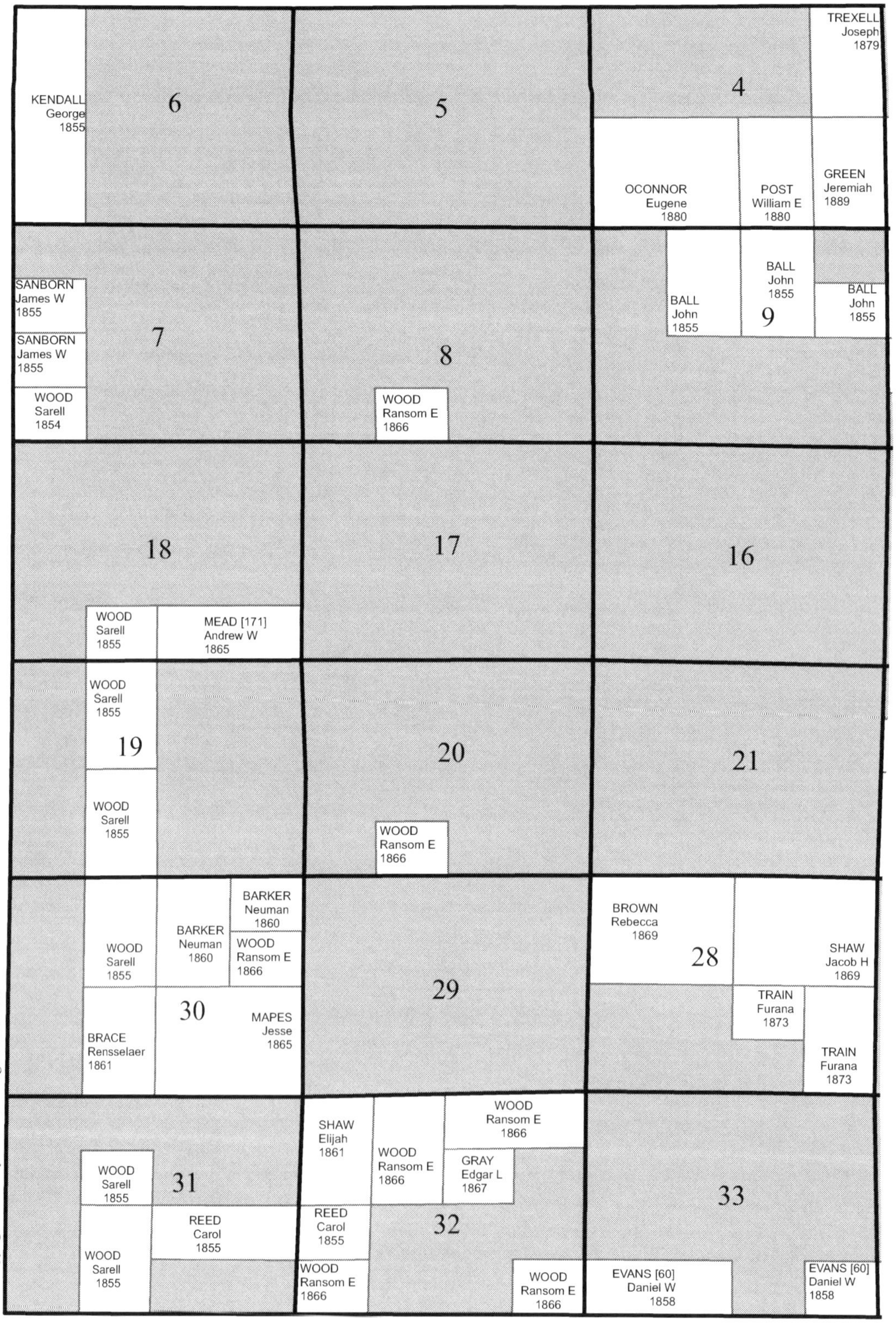

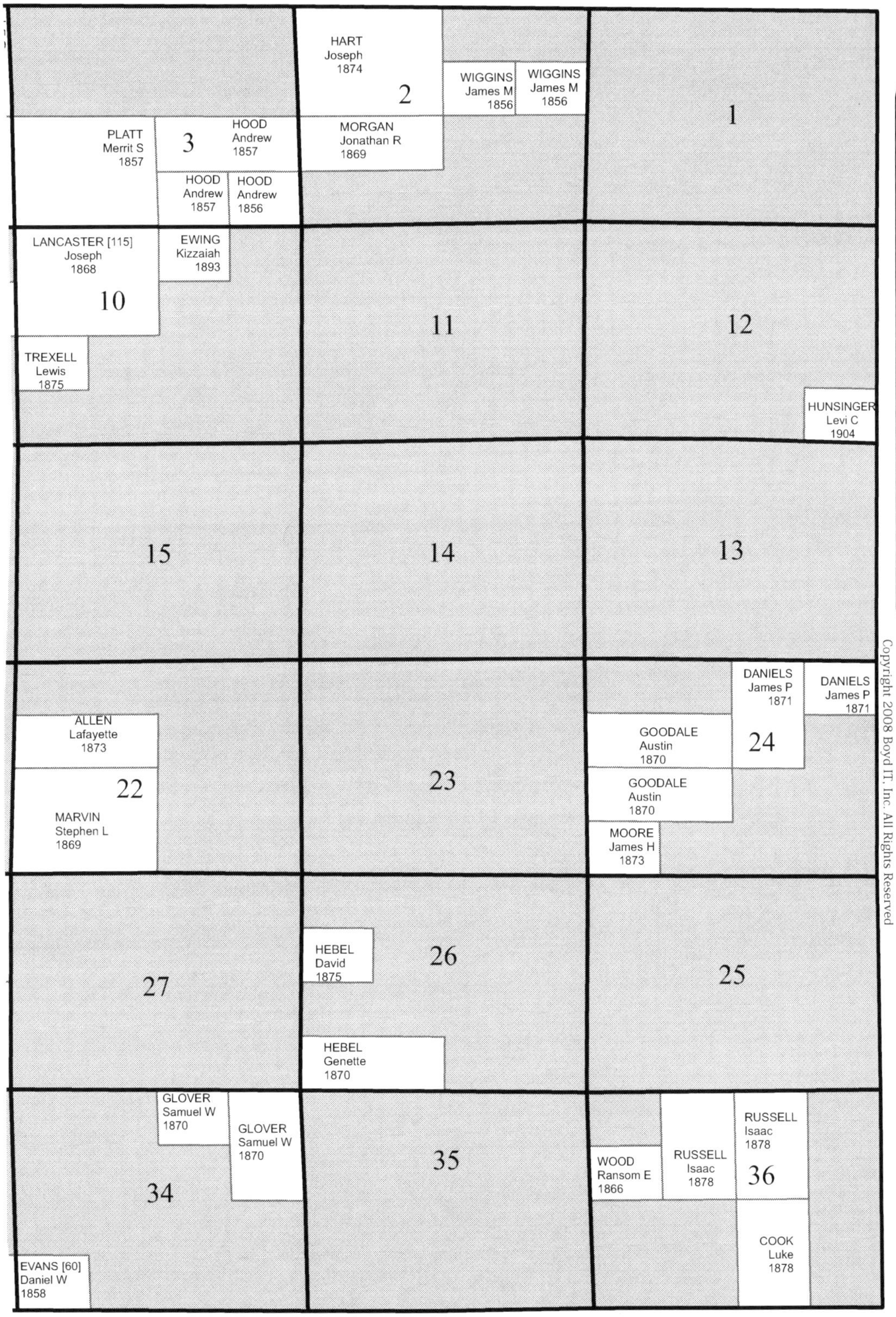

HART Joseph 1874
2
WIGGINS James M 1856
WIGGINS James M 1856
1
PLATT Merrit S 1857
3
HOOD Andrew 1857
MORGAN Jonathan R 1869
HOOD Andrew 1857
HOOD Andrew 1856
LANCASTER [115] Joseph 1868
EWING Kizzaiah 1893
10
11
12
TREXELL Lewis 1875
HUNSINGER Levi C 1904
15
14
13
DANIELS James P 1871
DANIELS James P 1871
ALLEN Lafayette 1873
GOODALE Austin 1870
24
22
23
GOODALE Austin 1870
MARVIN Stephen L 1869
MOORE James H 1873
HEBEL David 1875
26
27
25
HEBEL Genette 1870
GLOVER Samuel W 1870
GLOVER Samuel W 1870
35
RUSSELL Isaac 1878
WOOD Ransom E 1866
RUSSELL Isaac 1878
36
34
COOK Luke 1878
EVANS [60] Daniel W 1858

Helpful Hints

1. This Map's INDEX can be found on the preceding pages.
2. Refer to Map "C" to see where this Township lies within Newaygo County, Michigan.
3. Numbers within square brackets [ ] denote a multi-patentee land parcel (multi-owner). Refer to Appendix "C" for a full list of members in this group.
4. Areas that look to be crowded with Patentees usually indicate multiple sales of the same parcel (Re-issues) or Overlapping parcels. See this Township's Index for an explanation of these and other circumstances that might explain "odd" groupings of Patentees on this map.

Legend

Patent Boundary

Section Boundary

No Patents Found (or Outside County)

1., 2., 3., ... Lot Numbers (when beside a name)

[ ] Group Number (see Appendix "C")

Scale: Section = 1 mile X 1 mile (generally, with some exceptions)

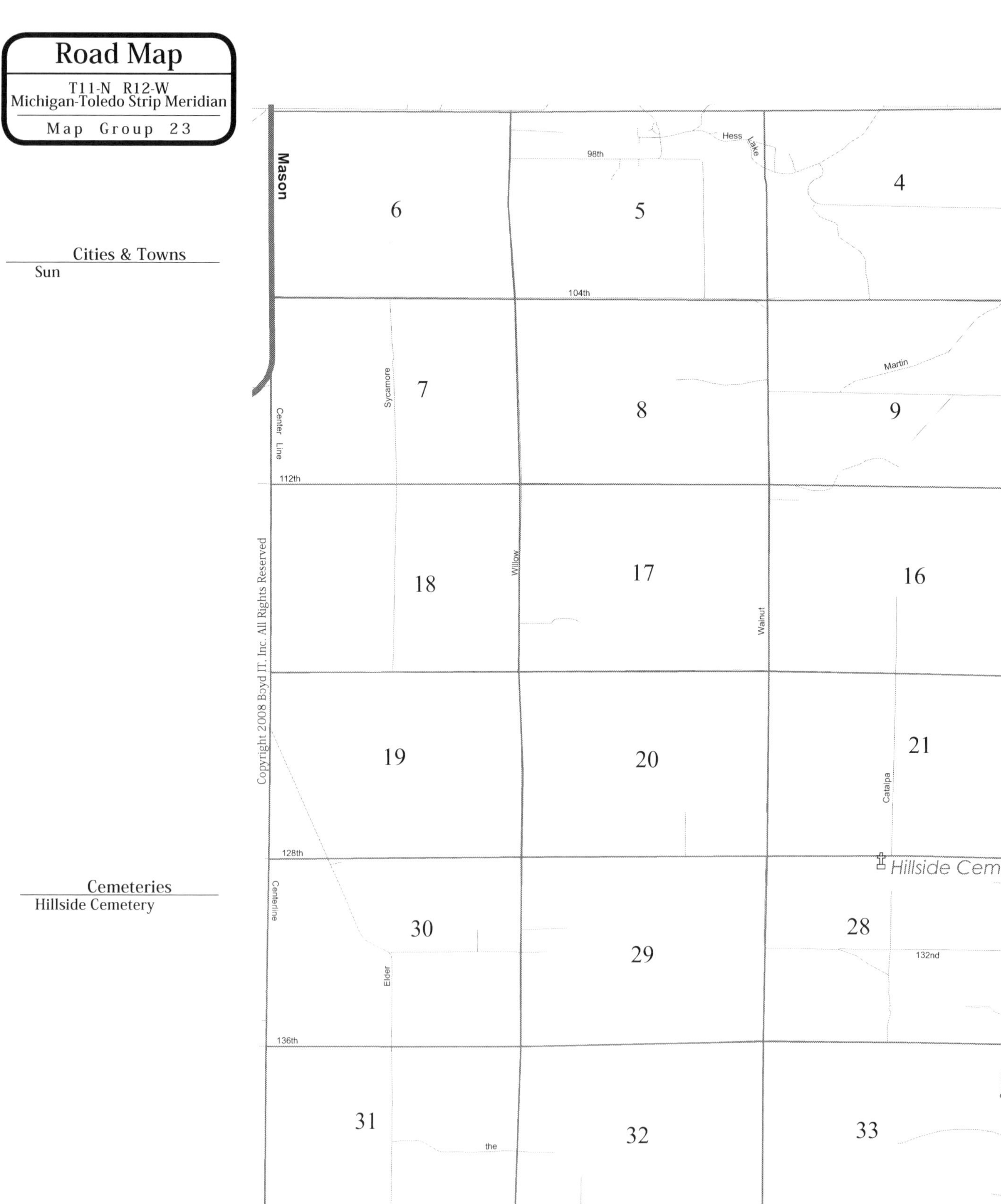
Road Map
T11-N R12-W
Michigan-Toledo Strip Meridian
Map Group 23
Cities & Towns
Sun
Cemeteries
Hillside Cemetery
Mason
Hess
Lake
98th
104th
Spruce
Martin
Sycamore
Center Line
112th
Willow
Walnut
Catalpa
128th
Hillside Cem.
Centerline
132nd
Elder
136th
the
Moore
22 Mile
6
5
4
7
8
9
18
17
16
19
20
21
30
29
28
31
32
33
Copyright 2008 Boyd IT, Inc. All Rights Reserved

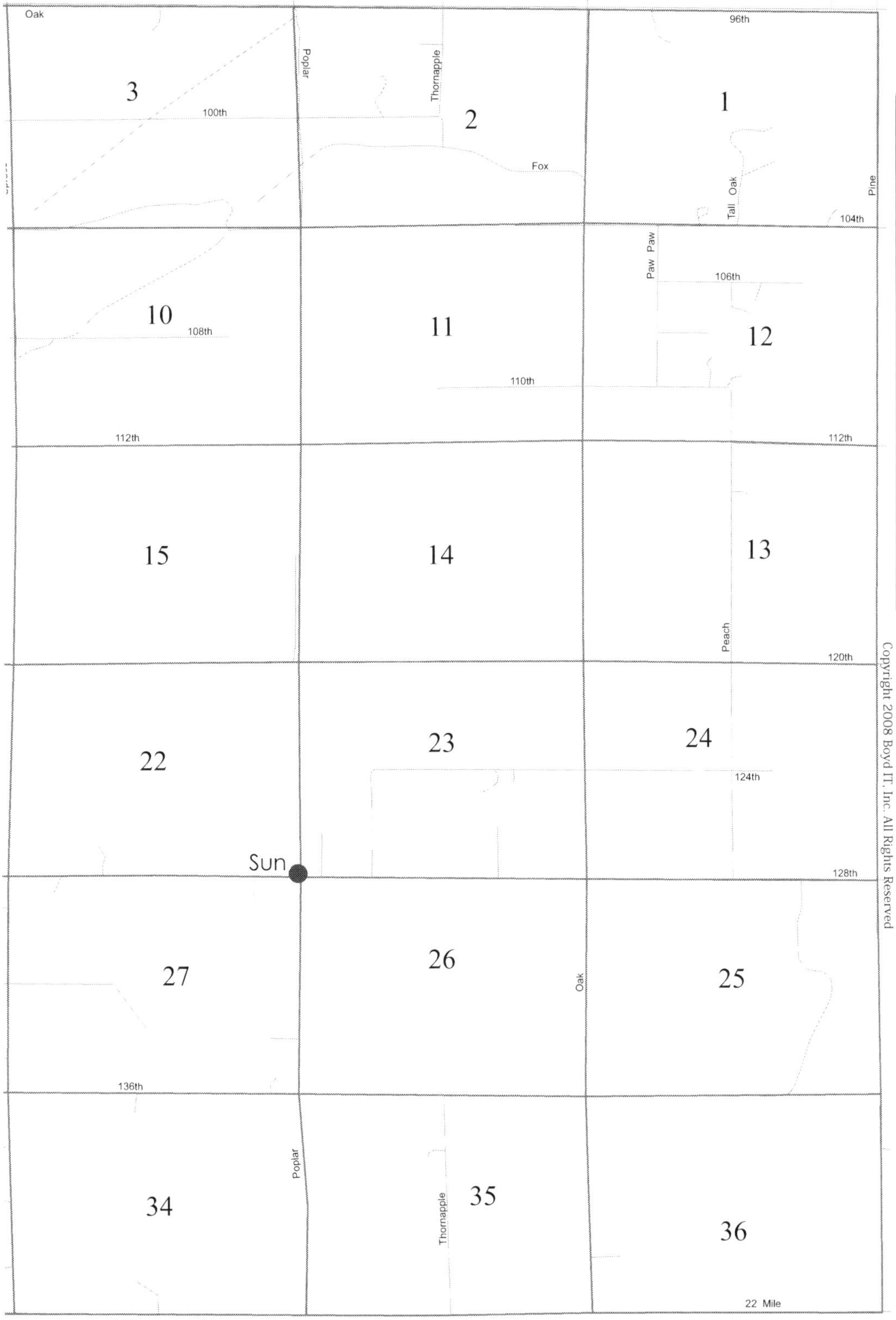

Oak
96th
Poplar
Thornapple
3
100th
2
1
Fox
Tall Oak
Pine
104th
Paw Paw
106th
10
108th
11
12
110th
112th
112th
15
14
13
Peach
120th
22
23
24
124th
Sun
128th
27
26
Oak
25
136th
34
Poplar
35
Thornapple
36
22 Mile

Helpful Hints

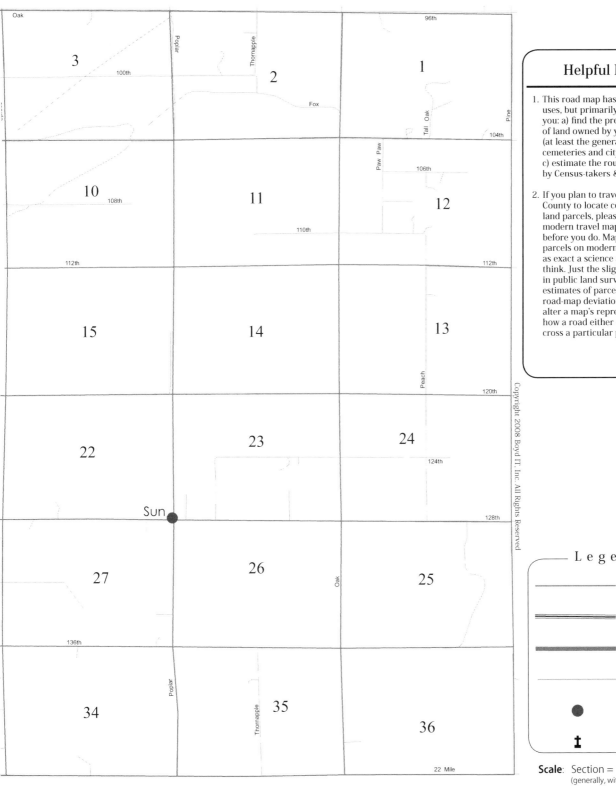

1. This road map has a number of uses, but primarily it is to help you: a) find the present location of land owned by your ancestors (at least the general area), b) find cemeteries and city-centers, and c) estimate the route/roads used by Census-takers & tax-assessors.
2. If you plan to travel to Newaygo County to locate cemeteries or land parcels, please pick up a modern travel map for the area before you do. Mapping old land parcels on modern maps is not as exact a science as you might think. Just the slightest variations in public land survey coordinates, estimates of parcel boundaries, or road-map deviations can greatly alter a map's representation of how a road either does or doesn't cross a particular parcel of land.

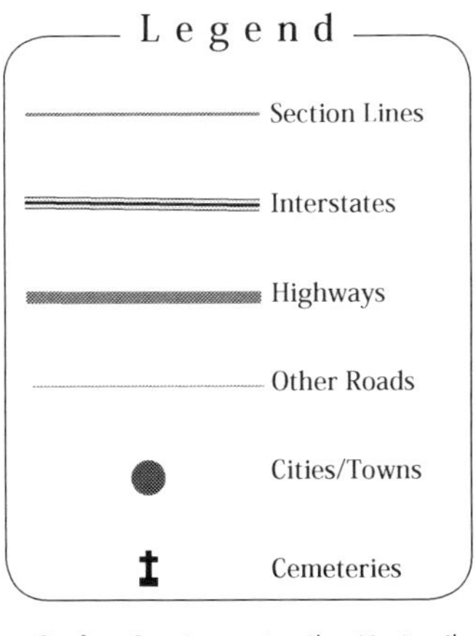

Scale: Section = 1 mile X 1 mile
(generally, with some exceptions)

Cities & Towns

Sun

Cemeteries

Hillside Cemetery

Hess Lake

6
5
4
7
8
9
Wheeler Drain
17
18
16
19
20
21
Hillside Cem.
29
28
30
Skipperville Lake
31
32
Crockery Creek
33

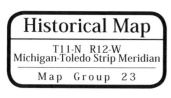

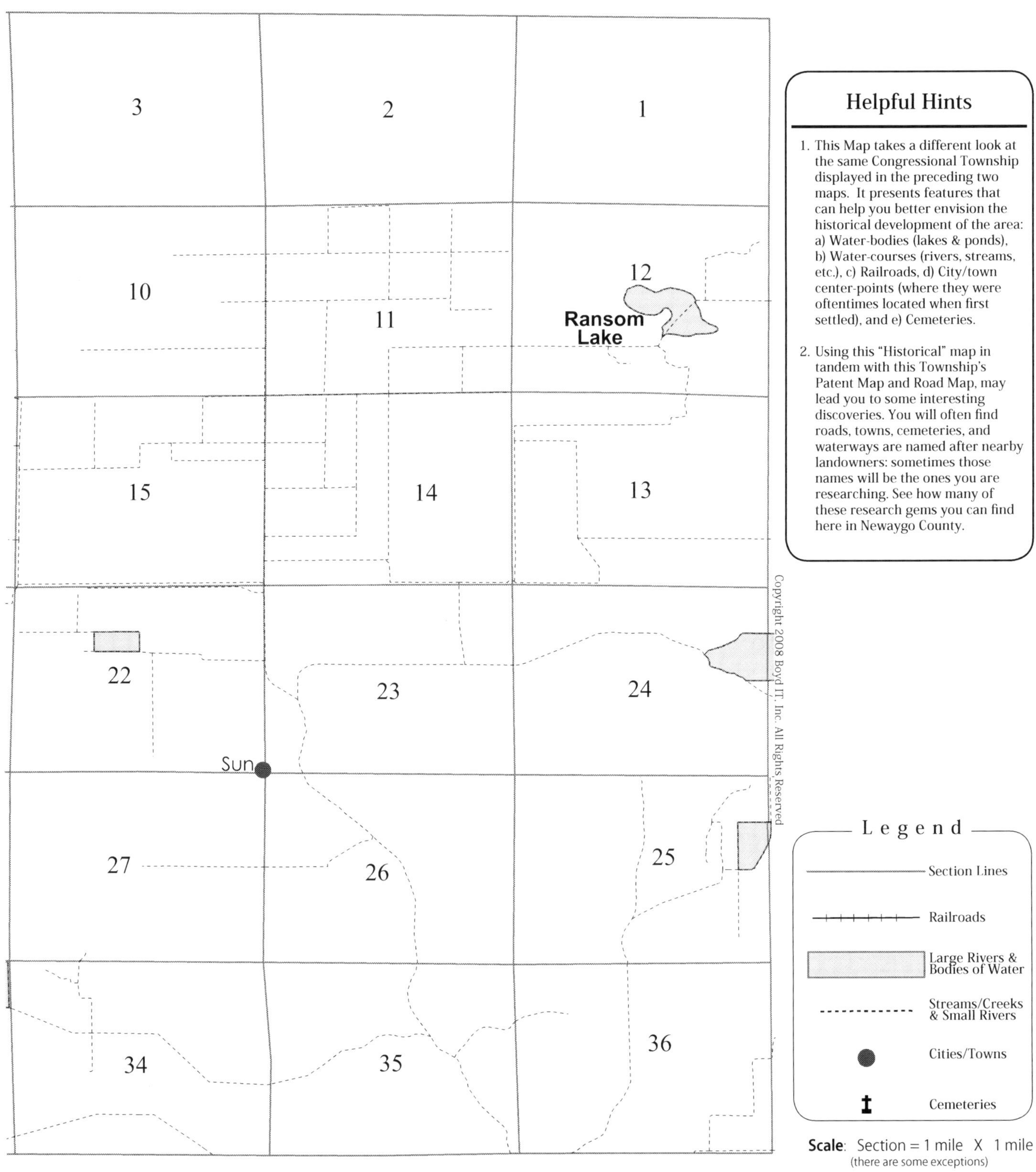

Helpful Hints

1. This Map takes a different look at the same Congressional Township displayed in the preceding two maps. It presents features that can help you better envision the historical development of the area: a) Water-bodies (lakes & ponds), b) Water-courses (rivers, streams, etc.), c) Railroads, d) City/town center-points (where they were oftentimes located when first settled), and e) Cemeteries.
2. Using this "Historical" map in tandem with this Township's Patent Map and Road Map, may lead you to some interesting discoveries. You will often find roads, towns, cemeteries, and waterways are named after nearby landowners: sometimes those names will be the ones you are researching. See how many of these research gems you can find here in Newaygo County.

Legend

- Section Lines
- Railroads
- Large Rivers & Bodies of Water
- Streams/Creeks & Small Rivers
- Cities/Towns
- Cemeteries

Scale: Section = 1 mile X 1 mile
(there are some exceptions)

Map Group 24: Index to Land Patents

Township 11-North Range 11-West (Michigan-Toledo Strip)

After you locate an individual in this Index, take note of the Section and Section Part then proceed to the Land Patent map on the pages immediately following. You should have no difficulty locating the corresponding parcel of land.

The "For More Info" Column will lead you to more information about the underlying Patents. See the *Legend* at right, and the "How to Use this Book" chapter, for more information.

LEGEND

"For More Info . . . " column

A = Authority (Legislative Act, See Appendix "A")
B = Block or Lot (location in Section unknown)
C = Cancelled Patent
F = Fractional Section
G = Group (Multi-Patentee Patent, see Appendix "C")
V = Overlaps another Parcel
R = Re-Issued (Parcel patented more than once)

(A & G items require you to look in the Appendixes referred to above. All other Letter-designations followed by a number require you to locate line-items in this index that possess the ID number found after the letter).

ID	Individual in Patent	Sec.	Sec. Part	Date Issued	Other Counties	For More Info . . .
3609	ADSIT, Eunice	29	S½SE	1859-08-10		A3 G24
3610	" "	32	NENE	1859-08-10		A3 G24
3538	ARMS, Lewis L	6	SESW	1855-12-15		A1 G36
3706	BAKER, Samuel L	4	NWSW	1855-12-15		A1
3619	BALL, John	29	NWSW	1859-08-10		A3 G7
3620	" "	29	SWNW	1859-08-10		A3 G7
3621	" "	30	NESE	1859-08-10		A3 G7
3622	" "	30	SENE	1859-08-10		A3 G7
3543	BANCROFT, Benjamin B	30	N½SW	1859-08-03		A3 F
3544	" "	30	SENW	1859-08-03		A3 F
3582	BARNES, Ezekiel L	4	N½NE	1869-11-01		A4 F
3583	" "	4	N½NW	1869-11-01		A4 F
3747	BEAUCHAMP, Frances	34	E½SE	1857-02-20		A3 G295
3748	" "	34	SWSE	1857-02-20		A3 G295
3651	BEIDLER, Mary Ann	7	N½NE	1857-02-20		A3
3652	" "	7	SENE	1857-02-20		A3
3609	BENTON, James	29	S½SE	1859-08-10		A3 G24
3607	" "	32	N½SE	1859-08-10		A3
3610	" "	32	NENE	1859-08-10		A3 G24
3611	" "	32	SENE	1859-08-10		A3 G25
3608	" "	32	SESE	1859-08-10		A3
3612	" "	32	W½NE	1859-08-10		A3 G25
3581	BIGGS, Elizabeth	6	SESE	1855-12-15		A1
3553	BILLS, Charles	1	W½SE	1854-09-15		A1
3616	BILLS, James K	1	E½SE	1854-09-15		A1
3611	BLINDBERRY, Patty	32	SENE	1859-08-10		A3 G25
3612	" "	32	W½NE	1859-08-10		A3 G25
3623	BORDEN, John D	1	NE	1855-11-01		A1 F
3714	BOYD, Stephen	10	SESE	1876-01-05		A4
3601	BRIGGS, Horace J	35	SW	1857-03-10		A1
3718	BURT, Thomas A	12	S½SE	1871-09-15		A4
3640	CALLAR, Joseph	2	E½SE	1858-05-01		A1
3642	CARPENTER, Joshua C	31	SWNW	1858-05-01		A1 F
3654	CARPENTER, Norman	15	NWNW	1858-05-01		A1
3655	" "	22	SWSW	1858-05-01		A1
3638	CAYWOOD, John W	14	N½NE	1871-09-15		A4
3538	CHENEY, Albert N	6	SESW	1855-12-15		A1 G36
3613	CONOVER, James	24	1	1875-03-22		A4
3552	COOK, Calvin W	34	W½SW	1875-08-20		A4
3711	COOK, Smith	15	W½SW	1857-03-10		A1
3712	" "	22	NWSW	1857-03-10		A1
3713	" "	22	W½NW	1857-03-10		A1
3560	COOPER, Cornelius	33	NW	1858-05-01		A1
3639	COOPER, Jonathan	33	S½NE	1858-05-01		A1
3635	CRANDALL, John V	27	E½NE	1856-03-10		A1
3636	" "	35	NWSE	1857-03-10		A1

ID	Individual in Patent	Sec.	Sec. Part	Date Issued	Other Counties	For More Info . . .
3637	CRANDALL, John V (Cont'd)	35	S½SE	1857-03-10		A1
3641	CROFF, Joseph H	28	N½SE	1871-11-15		A1
3574	DARLING, Elias	24	2	1855-12-15		A1
3575	" "	24	3	1855-12-15		A1
3576	" "	24	4	1855-12-15		A1
3577	" "	24	E½SW	1855-12-15		A1
3578	" "	25	NENW	1855-12-15		A1
3594	DARLING, Henry	23	3	1856-03-10		A1
3595	" "	23	NESE	1857-02-20		A3
3596	" "	23	W½SE	1857-02-20		A3
3722	DARLING, William	25	1	1855-11-08		A3
3723	" "	25	E½SW	1855-11-08		A3
3724	" "	25	SENW	1855-11-08		A3
3725	" "	25	W½SW	1855-11-08		A3
3727	" "	26	NENW	1855-11-08		A3
3728	" "	26	SENW	1855-11-08		A3
3729	" "	26	W½NE	1855-11-08		A3
3730	" "	26	W½NW	1855-11-08		A3
3726	" "	26	1	1856-03-10		A1
3618	DE PUNG, JESSE	12	SWNW	1871-09-15		A4
3562	DENIS, Crist H	2	E½NE	1870-06-20		A4 F
3585	DIXON, George	25	E½	1857-03-10		A1
3715	DOWNING, Susan H	28	W½NE	1869-09-10		A1
3693	DUDLEY, Jane	22	S½NE	1858-01-15		A3 G334
3694	" "	22	SENW	1858-01-15		A3 G334
3624	ECKELS, John	12	N½SW	1871-09-15		A4
3625	ELDRED, John	35	NESE	1855-12-15		A1
3653	ELDRED, Nathan	35	E½NE	1855-12-15		A1
3545	ENSLEY, Benjamin	12	NE	1857-03-10		A1
3646	FRENCH, Leonard	28	N½SW	1859-10-10		A1
3647	" "	28	S½NW	1859-10-10		A1
3662	FRENCH, Ransom E	29	S½SW	1857-03-10		A1
3663	" "	30	SESE	1857-03-10		A1
3664	" "	31	NENE	1857-03-10		A1
3603	FULLER, Jacob	2	NENW	1856-03-10		A1 F
3604	" "	2	NWSE	1856-03-10		A1
3606	" "	2	SWNE	1856-03-10		A1
3605	" "	2	S½NW	1857-03-10		A1
3614	FULLER, James	36	NESW	1871-09-15		A4
3615	" "	36	NWSE	1871-09-15		A4
3627	FULLER, John	36	NWSW	1858-05-01		A1
3628	" "	36	S½SW	1858-05-01		A1
3573	GALLUP, Edwin	12	E½NW	1855-12-15		A1
3709	GARDNER, Hannah	27	NENW	1859-08-10		A3 G66
3710	" "	27	S½NW	1859-08-10		A3 G66
3709	GARDNER, Silas	27	NENW	1859-08-10		A3 G66
3710	" "	27	S½NW	1859-08-10		A3 G66
3732	GRIFFITTS, William	36	NWNW	1858-05-01		A1
3733	" "	36	SENE	1858-05-01		A1
3734	" "	36	SWNE	1858-05-01		A1
3731	" "	36	E½NW	1859-08-03		A3
3735	" "	36	SWNW	1859-08-03		A3
3703	GROVE, Richard A	6	NESW	1872-07-01		A1
3704	" "	6	SENW	1872-07-01		A1
3720	HEATH, Warren	34	W½NW	1869-11-01		A4
3546	HILLMAN, Benjamin	10	E½NW	1857-03-10		A1
3547	" "	3	SESW	1857-03-10		A1
3751	HILLMAN, William	10	W½NE	1857-03-10		A1
3752	" "	3	W½SE	1857-03-10		A1
3754	HILLMAN, William S	3	NESW	1858-05-01		A1
3755	" "	3	SENW	1858-05-01		A1
3554	HOLMES, Charles	13	E½SE	1855-12-15		A1
3556	" "	24	SENE	1855-12-15		A1
3555	" "	24	NENE	1857-02-20		A3
3557	" "	24	W½NE	1857-02-20		A3
3602	HOUGHTON, Ira	34	SENW	1871-11-01		A4
3559	HOUSE, Coonrod	1	N½SW	1857-03-10		A1
3661	HUCKLEBERRY, Phillip	12	N½SE	1870-05-02		A4
3629	HUNTER, John J	36	E½SE	1869-11-01		A4
3597	ISHAM, Henry	30	SWNW	1876-02-10		A4 F
3584	KEENEY, Francis M	18	W½NW	1885-01-07		A1 F
3537	KELLOGG, Agustus	9	NWSE	1858-05-01		A1
3536	KELLOGG, Agustus A	9	NESE	1858-05-01		A1

ID	Individual in Patent	Sec.	Sec. Part	Date Issued	Other Counties	For More Info . . .
3656	KELLOGG, Otis H	28	E½NE	1858-05-01		A1
3657	" "	9	S½SE	1858-05-01		A1
3586	KENDALL, George	6	NWSW	1856-03-10		A1
3630	KENNEY, John	9	SW	1859-10-10		A1
3631	KENNEY, John M	2	NWNE	1888-05-31		A4 F
3659	KINNEY, Patrick	14	N½NW	1875-02-10		A4
3563	LAHR, David	22	S½SE	1869-11-01		A4
3736	LAHR, William H	22	SESW	1870-05-02		A4
3700	LATHROP, Lydia	23	1NW	1859-08-03		A3 G344 C
3701	" "	23	2NW	1859-08-03		A3 G344 C
3702	" "	23	SENW	1859-08-03		A3 G344 C R3699
3697	" "	23	1	1951-11-02		A3 G335
3698	" "	23	2	1951-11-02		A3 G335
3699	" "	23	SENW	1951-11-02		A3 G335 R3702
3695	LAWSON, James	14	SWNE	1861-10-10		A3 G337
3696	" "	14	W½SE	1861-10-10		A3 G337
3695	LAWSON, John	14	SWNE	1861-10-10		A3 G337
3696	" "	14	W½SE	1861-10-10		A3 G337
3695	LAWSON, Lavinia	14	SWNE	1861-10-10		A3 G337
3696	" "	14	W½SE	1861-10-10		A3 G337
3579	LEE, Elias	21	E½NE	1855-12-15		A1
3707	LEONARD, Samuel	28	N½NW	1859-10-10		A1
3708	" "	29	NENE	1859-10-10		A1
3721	LEWIS, William A	26	W½SE	1869-11-01		A4
3717	LINGO, Temperance T	8	SESE	1867-01-10		A1
3591	LUTES, George W	11	N½NE	1857-03-10		A1
3592	" "	12	NWNW	1857-03-10		A1
3593	" "	2	SWSE	1857-03-10		A1
3587	MIDDAUGH, George	18	E½SW	1885-01-07		A1
3588	" "	18	NWSW	1885-01-07		A1 F
3753	MOORE, William	30	NENW	1860-09-01		A1 F
3632	MORLEY, John	28	S½SE	1871-09-15		A4
3580	MURRAY, Elijah R	31	W½NE	1837-04-01		A1
3564	NORTHROP, John O	10	NENE	1857-02-20		A3 G241
3565	" "	10	W½NW	1857-02-20		A3 G241
3571	" "	11	N½NW	1857-02-20		A3 G253
3566	" "	2	SW	1857-02-20		A3 G241
3567	" "	3	E½SE	1857-02-20		A3 G241
3568	" "	3	W½SW	1857-02-20		A3 G241
3569	" "	4	E½SE	1857-02-20		A3 G241
3570	" "	9	E½NE	1857-02-20		A3 G241
3687	ONDERDONK, Anna	21	N½SE	1858-01-15		A3 G336
3688	" "	21	NESW	1858-01-15		A3 G336
3633	OSBURN, John	31	W½SW	1859-10-10		A1 F
3648	PATTESON, Elizabeth	28	S½SW	1864-10-01		A3 G312
3550	PERRIGO, Benjamin T	4	NWSE	1860-09-03		A3
3551	" "	4	S½NE	1860-09-03		A3 F
3634	PHILLIPS, John	1	SWNW	1857-07-01		A1
3540	PROVIN, Andrew	10	SWSE	1858-05-01		A1
3541	" "	15	NWNE	1858-05-01		A1
3626	RAIDER, John F	6	NESE	1858-05-01		A1
3548	RHOADES, Benjamin J	6	NENW	1868-07-20		A3 F
3549	" "	6	W½NW	1868-07-20		A3 F
3705	ROACH, Richard	34	E½SW	1856-03-10		A1
3589	ROBERTSON, George	1	SESW	1857-07-01		A1
3600	RUDES, Henry M	1	SWSW	1857-03-10		A1
3542	RUSSEL, Andrew	10	E½SW	1857-02-20		A3 C
3617	SANBORN, James W	5	NW	1862-04-15		A3 F
3564	SANFORD, Ebenezer	10	NENE	1857-02-20		A3 G241
3565	" "	10	W½NW	1857-02-20		A3 G241
3571	" "	11	N½NW	1857-02-20		A3 G253
3566	" "	2	SW	1857-02-20		A3 G241
3567	" "	3	E½SE	1857-02-20		A3 G241
3568	" "	3	W½SW	1857-02-20		A3 G241
3569	" "	4	E½SE	1857-02-20		A3 G241
3570	" "	9	E½NE	1857-02-20		A3 G241
3749	SANFORD, William H	27	SWNE	1857-02-20		A3 G296
3750	" "	27	W½SE	1857-02-20		A3 G296
3590	SANGER, George	1	SENW	1857-03-10		A1 F
3658	SIMPSON, Parker	24	SE	1857-03-10		A1
3561	SLAIGHT, Cornelius	36	N½NE	1856-03-10		A1
3695	SLAUGHTER, John	14	SWNE	1861-10-10		A3 G337
3696	" "	14	W½SE	1861-10-10		A3 G337

ID	Individual in Patent	Sec.	Sec. Part	Date Issued	Other Counties	For More Info . . .
3598	SMITH, Henry K	33	E½SW	1859-10-10		A1
3599	" "	33	W½SE	1859-10-10		A1
3649	SMITH, Martin	30	SWSW	1858-05-01		A1 F
3650	" "	31	NWNW	1858-05-01		A1 F
3660	SMITH, Peter	18	E½NW	1877-04-25		A4
3644	SPALDING, Kimbol C	32	E½NW	1876-01-20		A1
3645	" "	32	N½SW	1876-01-20		A1
3643	SPAULDING, Kimble C	32	W½NW	1869-11-01		A4
3539	STOCKING, Andrew L	36	SWSE	1871-09-15		A4
3558	SUMNER, Charles	6	SWSW	1885-01-07		A1 F
3571	SUTFIN, Mary	11	N½NW	1857-02-20		A3 G253
3531	TERWILLIGER, Abram	15	E½NW	1857-03-10		A1
3532	" "	15	SWNW	1857-03-10		A1
3533	" "	4	E½SW	1869-11-01		A4
3534	" "	4	SWSE	1869-11-01		A4
3535	" "	4	SWSW	1869-11-01		A4
3572	TERWILLIGER, Edward	2	NWNW	1875-02-10		A4 F
3691	TURNER, Coley B	15	N½SE	1858-01-15		A3 G338
3692	" "	15	NESW	1858-01-15		A3 G338
3756	VAN LIEW, WILLIAM	10	SENE	1874-02-20		A4
3737	WARD, William H	26	E½SW	1857-02-20		A3
3738	" "	26	NWSW	1857-02-20		A3
3739	" "	26	SWSW	1857-02-20		A3
3740	" "	27	E½SE	1857-02-20		A3
3749	" "	27	SWNE	1857-02-20		A3 G296
3750	" "	27	W½SE	1857-02-20		A3 G296
3741	" "	34	E½NE	1857-02-20		A3
3747	" "	34	E½SE	1857-02-20		A3 G295
3742	" "	34	NWSE	1857-02-20		A3
3748	" "	34	SWSE	1857-02-20		A3 G295
3743	" "	34	W½NE	1857-02-20		A3
3744	" "	35	E½NW	1857-02-20		A3
3745	" "	35	NWNW	1857-02-20		A3
3746	" "	35	SWNW	1857-02-20		A3
3716	WARREN, Sylvia S	12	S½SW	1874-06-15		A4
3538	WELLES, William P	6	SESW	1855-12-15		A1 G36
3648	WHITE, Levi	28	S½SW	1864-10-01		A3 G312
3689	WHITEHURST, Daniel	23	NENW	1858-01-15		A3 G340
3690	" "	23	W½NW	1858-01-15		A3 G340
3719	WILKIN, Thomas C	1	N½NW	1859-08-03		A3 F
3666	WOOD, Ransom E	14	E½SW	1858-01-15		A3
3668	" "	14	SENW	1858-01-15		A3
3669	" "	14	SWNW	1858-01-15		A3
3670	" "	14	W½SW	1858-01-15		A3
3691	" "	15	N½SE	1858-01-15		A3 G338
3692	" "	15	NESW	1858-01-15		A3 G338
3671	" "	15	S½SE	1858-01-15		A3
3672	" "	15	SESW	1858-01-15		A3
3687	" "	21	N½SE	1858-01-15		A3 G336
3673	" "	21	NENW	1858-01-15		A3
3688	" "	21	NESW	1858-01-15		A3 G336
3674	" "	21	SENW	1858-01-15		A3
3676	" "	21	W½NE	1858-01-15		A3
3677	" "	21	W½NW	1858-01-15		A3
3679	" "	22	N½NE	1858-01-15		A3
3680	" "	22	N½SE	1858-01-15		A3
3681	" "	22	NENW	1858-01-15		A3
3682	" "	22	NESW	1858-01-15		A3
3693	" "	22	S½NE	1858-01-15		A3 G334
3694	" "	22	SENW	1858-01-15		A3 G334
3689	" "	23	NENW	1858-01-15		A3 G340
3690	" "	23	W½NW	1858-01-15		A3 G340
3686	" "	8	NW	1858-01-15		A3
3675	" "	21	SESW	1859-08-03		A3
3678	" "	21	W½SW	1859-08-03		A3
3683	" "	5	NENE	1859-08-10		A3 F
3684	" "	5	NWNE	1859-08-10		A3 F
3685	" "	5	S½NE	1859-08-10		A3 F
3695	" "	14	SWNE	1861-10-10		A3 G337
3696	" "	14	W½SE	1861-10-10		A3 G337
3665	" "	14	E½SE	1862-11-01		A3
3667	" "	14	SENE	1862-11-01		A3
3697	" "	23	1	1951-11-02		A3 G335

ID	Individual in Patent	Sec.	Sec. Part	Date Issued	Other Counties	For More Info . . .
3698	WOOD, Ransom E (Cont'd)	23	2	1951-11-02		A3 G335
3699	" "	23	SENW	1951-11-02		A3 G335 R3702
3619	WOOD, Susanna	29	NWSW	1859-08-10		A3 G7
3620	" "	29	SWNW	1859-08-10		A3 G7
3621	" "	30	NESE	1859-08-10		A3 G7
3622	" "	30	SENE	1859-08-10		A3 G7
3689	WOODHOUSE, Benjamin	23	NENW	1858-01-15		A3 G340
3690	" "	23	W½NW	1858-01-15		A3 G340
3700	WOODS, Ransom E	23	1NW	1859-08-03		A3 G344 C
3701	" "	23	2NW	1859-08-03		A3 G344 C
3702	" "	23	SENW	1859-08-03		A3 G344 C R3699

Patent Map

T11-N R11-W
Michigan-Toledo Strip Meridian

Map Group 24

Township Statistics

Parcels Mapped	:	226
Number of Patents	:	150
Number of Individuals	:	126
Patentees Identified	:	116
Number of Surnames	:	102
Multi-Patentee Parcels	:	40
Oldest Patent Date	:	4/1/1837
Most Recent Patent	:	11/2/1951
Block/Lot Parcels	:	11
Parcels Re - Issued	:	1
Parcels that Overlap	:	0
Cities and Towns	:	1
Cemeteries	:	3

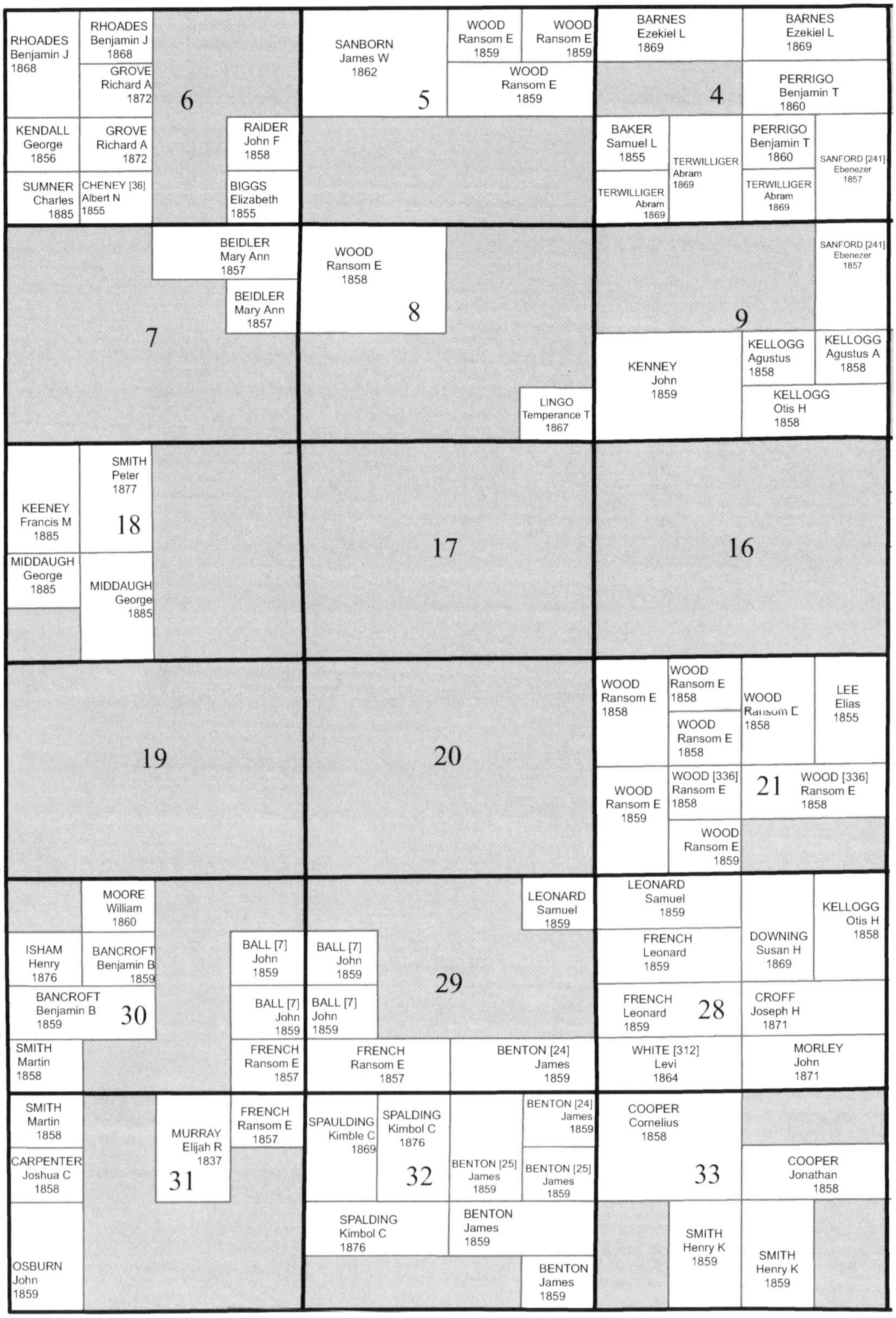

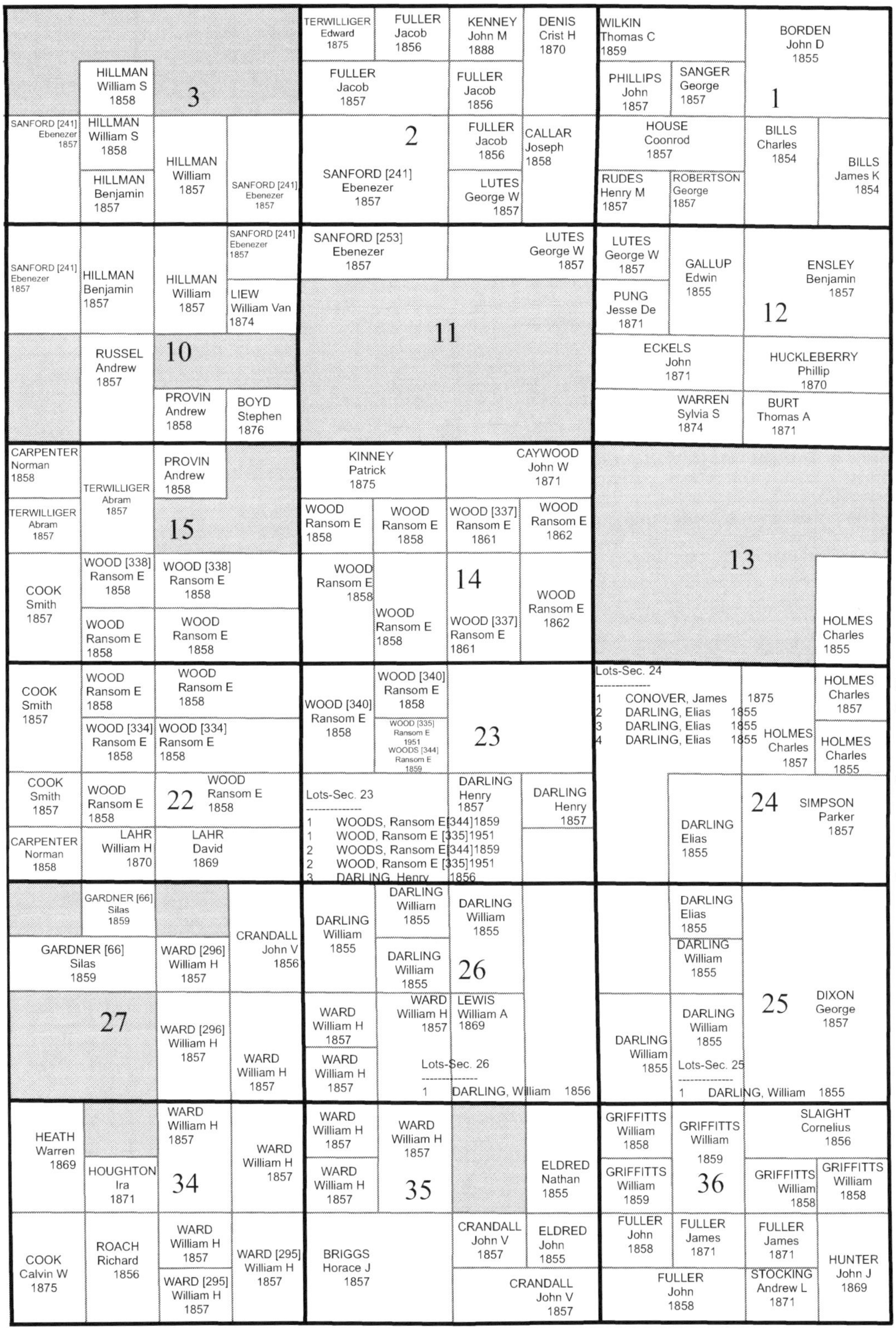

HILLMAN William S 1858
3
SANFORD [241] Ebenezer 1857
HILLMAN William S 1858
HILLMAN Benjamin 1857
HILLMAN William 1857
SANFORD [241] Ebenezer 1857

TERWILLIGER Edward 1875
FULLER Jacob 1856
KENNEY John M 1888
DENIS Crist H 1870
FULLER Jacob 1857
FULLER Jacob 1856
2
FULLER Jacob 1856
CALLAR Joseph 1858
SANFORD [241] Ebenezer 1857
LUTES George W 1857

WILKIN Thomas C 1859
BORDEN John D 1855
PHILLIPS John 1857
SANGER George 1857
1
HOUSE Coonrod 1857
BILLS Charles 1854
BILLS James K 1854
RUDES Henry M 1857
ROBERTSON George 1857

SANFORD [241] Ebenezer 1857
HILLMAN Benjamin 1857
HILLMAN William 1857
SANFORD [241] Ebenezer 1857
LIEW William Van 1874
RUSSEL Andrew 1857
10
PROVIN Andrew 1858
BOYD Stephen 1876

SANFORD [253] Ebenezer 1857
LUTES George W 1857
11

LUTES George W 1857
GALLUP Edwin 1855
ENSLEY Benjamin 1857
PUNG Jesse De 1871
12
ECKELS John 1871
HUCKLEBERRY Phillip 1870
WARREN Sylvia S 1874
BURT Thomas A 1871

CARPENTER Norman 1858
PROVIN Andrew 1858
TERWILLIGER Abram 1857
TERWILLIGER Abram 1857
15
COOK Smith 1857
WOOD [338] Ransom E 1858
WOOD [338] Ransom E 1858
WOOD Ransom E 1858
WOOD Ransom E 1858

KINNEY Patrick 1875
CAYWOOD John W 1871
WOOD Ransom E 1858
WOOD Ransom E 1858
WOOD [337] Ransom E 1861
WOOD Ransom E 1862
WOOD Ransom E 1858
14
WOOD Ransom E 1862
WOOD Ransom E 1858
WOOD [337] Ransom E 1861

13
HOLMES Charles 1855

COOK Smith 1857
WOOD Ransom E 1858
WOOD Ransom E 1858
WOOD [334] Ransom E 1858
WOOD [334] Ransom E 1858
COOK Smith 1857
WOOD Ransom E 1858
22
WOOD Ransom E 1858
CARPENTER Norman 1858
LAHR William H 1870
LAHR David 1869

WOOD [340] Ransom E 1858
WOOD [340] Ransom E 1858
WOOD [335] Ransom E 1951
WOODS [344] Ransom E 1859
23
Lots-Sec. 23
1 WOODS, Ransom E[344]1859
1 WOOD, Ransom E [335]1951
2 WOODS, Ransom E[344]1859
2 WOOD, Ransom E [335]1951
3 DARLING, Henry 1856
DARLING Henry 1857
DARLING Henry 1857

Lots-Sec. 24
1 CONOVER, James 1875
2 DARLING, Elias 1855
3 DARLING, Elias 1855
4 DARLING, Elias 1855
HOLMES Charles 1857
HOLMES Charles 1857
HOLMES Charles 1855
DARLING Elias 1855
24
SIMPSON Parker 1857

GARDNER [66] Silas 1859
GARDNER [66] Silas 1859
WARD [296] William H 1857
CRANDALL John V 1856
27
WARD [296] William H 1857
WARD William H 1857

DARLING William 1855
DARLING William 1855
DARLING William 1855
DARLING William 1855
26
WARD William H 1857
LEWIS William A 1869
WARD William H 1857
WARD William H 1857
Lots-Sec. 26
1 DARLING, William 1856

DARLING Elias 1855
DARLING William 1855
25
DIXON George 1857
DARLING William 1855
DARLING William 1855
Lots-Sec. 25
1 DARLING, William 1855

HEATH Warren 1869
WARD William H 1857
WARD William H 1857
HOUGHTON Ira 1871
34
COOK Calvin W 1875
ROACH Richard 1856
WARD William H 1857
WARD [295] William H 1857
WARD [295] William H 1857

WARD William H 1857
WARD William H 1857
WARD William H 1857
35
ELDRED Nathan 1855
CRANDALL John V 1857
ELDRED John 1855
BRIGGS Horace J 1857
CRANDALL John V 1857

GRIFFITTS William 1858
GRIFFITTS William 1859
SLAIGHT Cornelius 1856
GRIFFITTS William 1859
36
GRIFFITTS William 1858
GRIFFITTS William 1858
FULLER John 1858
FULLER James 1871
FULLER James 1871
HUNTER John J 1869
FULLER John 1858
STOCKING Andrew L 1871

Helpful Hints

1. This Map's INDEX can be found on the preceding pages.
2. Refer to Map "C" to see where this Township lies within Newaygo County, Michigan.
3. Numbers within square brackets [ ] denote a multi-patentee land parcel (multi-owner). Refer to Appendix "C" for a full list of members in this group.
4. Areas that look to be crowded with Patentees usually indicate multiple sales of the same parcel (Re-issues) or Overlapping parcels. See this Township's Index for an explanation of these and other circumstances that might explain "odd" groupings of Patentees on this map.

Legend

Patent Boundary
Section Boundary
No Patents Found (or Outside County)
1., 2., 3., ... Lot Numbers (when beside a name)
[ ] Group Number (see Appendix "C")

Scale: Section = 1 mile X 1 mile (generally, with some exceptions)

Road Map

T11-N R11-W
Michigan-Toledo Strip Meridian

Map Group 24

Cities & Towns
Ensley Center

Cemeteries
Crandall Cemetery
North Ensley Cemetery
Saint John Cemetery

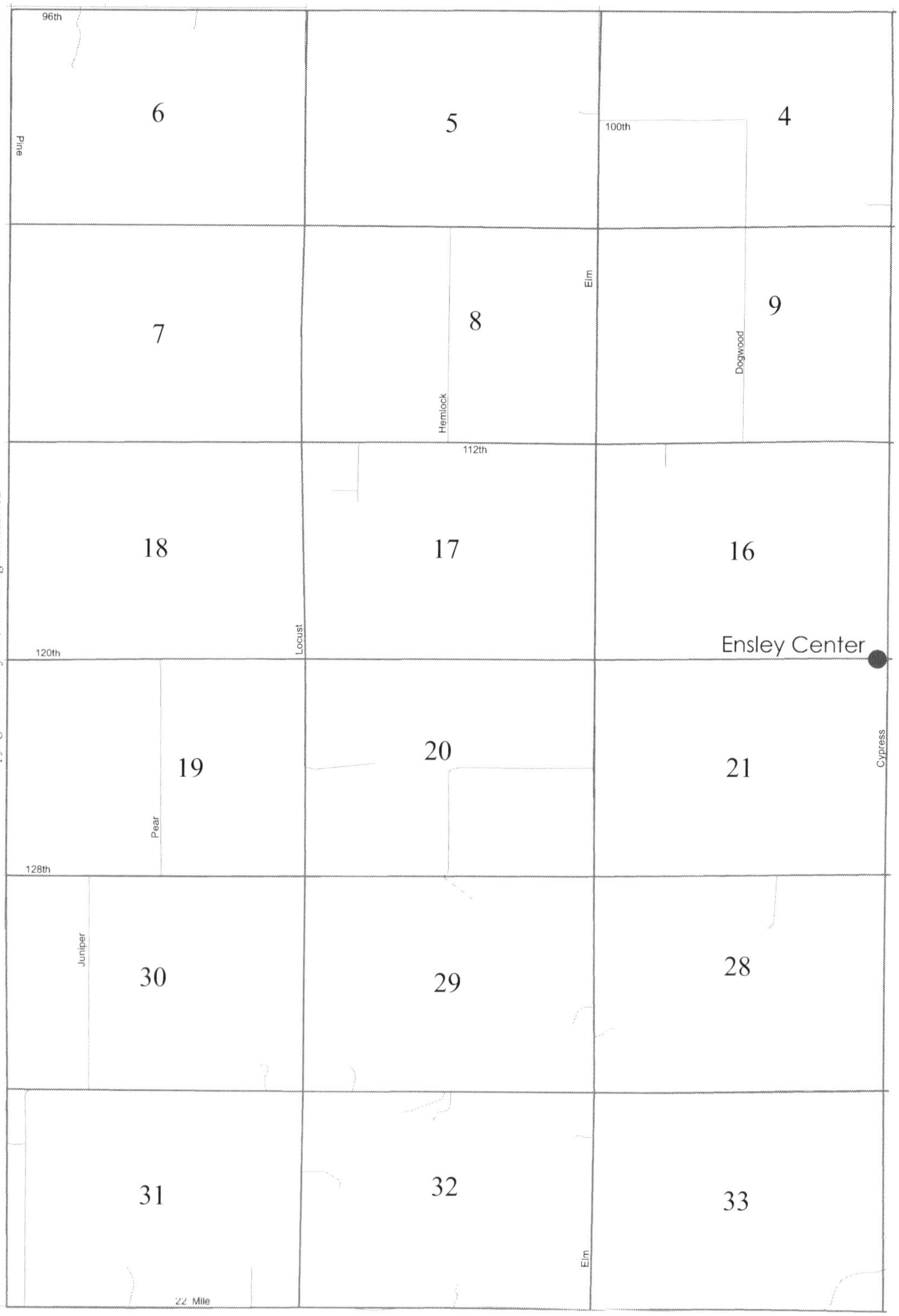

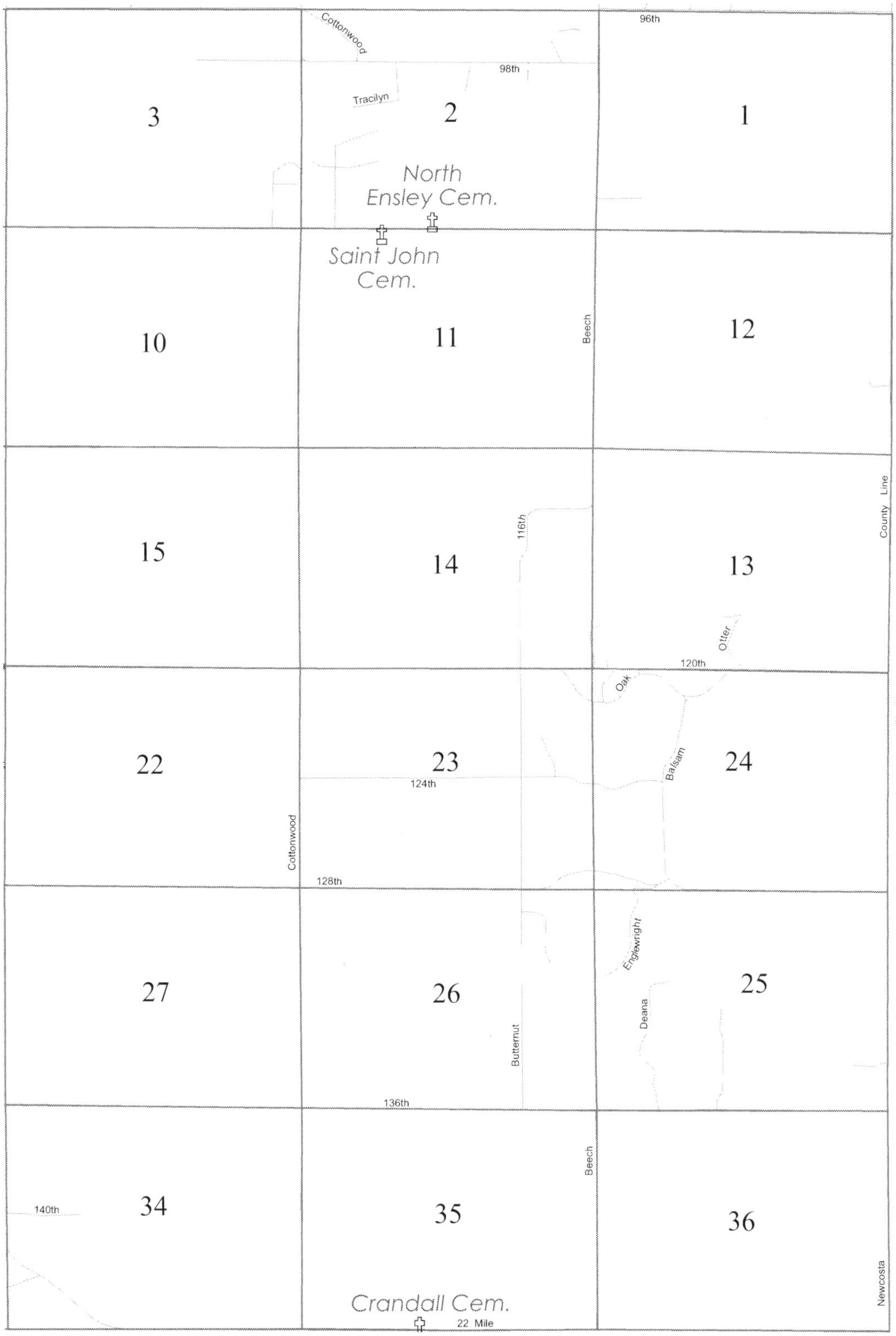

96th
Cottonwood
98th
Tracilyn
3
2
1
North Ensley Cem.
Saint John Cem.
10
11
Beech
12
15
14
116th
13
County Line
Otter
120th
Oak
22
23
124th
Balsam
24
Cottonwood
128th
27
26
Englewright
25
Deana
Butternut
136th
Beech
140th
34
35
36
Newcosta
Crandall Cem.
22 Mile

Helpful Hints

1. This road map has a number of uses, but primarily it is to help you: a) find the present location of land owned by your ancestors (at least the general area), b) find cemeteries and city-centers, and c) estimate the route/roads used by Census-takers & tax-assessors.
2. If you plan to travel to Newaygo County to locate cemeteries or land parcels, please pick up a modern travel map for the area before you do. Mapping old land parcels on modern maps is not as exact a science as you might think. Just the slightest variations in public land survey coordinates, estimates of parcel boundaries, or road-map deviations can greatly alter a map's representation of how a road either does or doesn't cross a particular parcel of land.

Legend
Section Lines
Interstates
Highways
Other Roads
Cities/Towns
Cemeteries

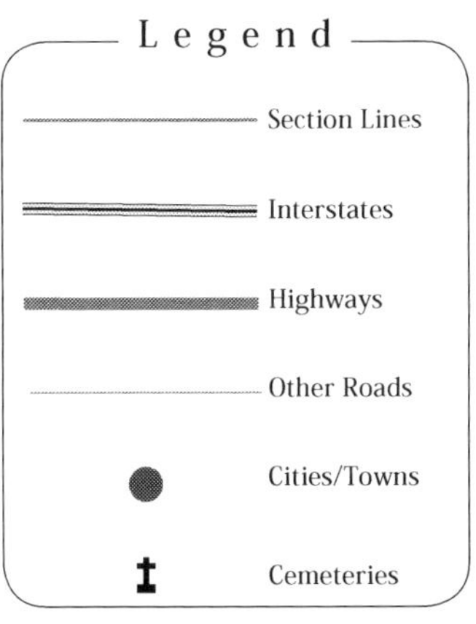

Scale: Section = 1 mile X 1 mile
(generally, with some exceptions)

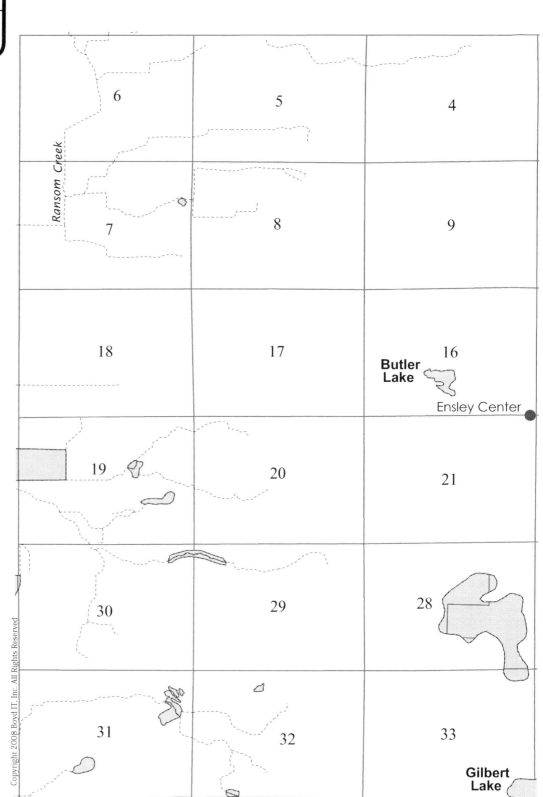

Historical Map

T11-N R11-W
Michigan-Toledo Strip Meridian

Map Group 24

Cities & Towns
Ensley Center

Cemeteries
Crandall Cemetery
North Ensley Cemetery
Saint John Cemetery

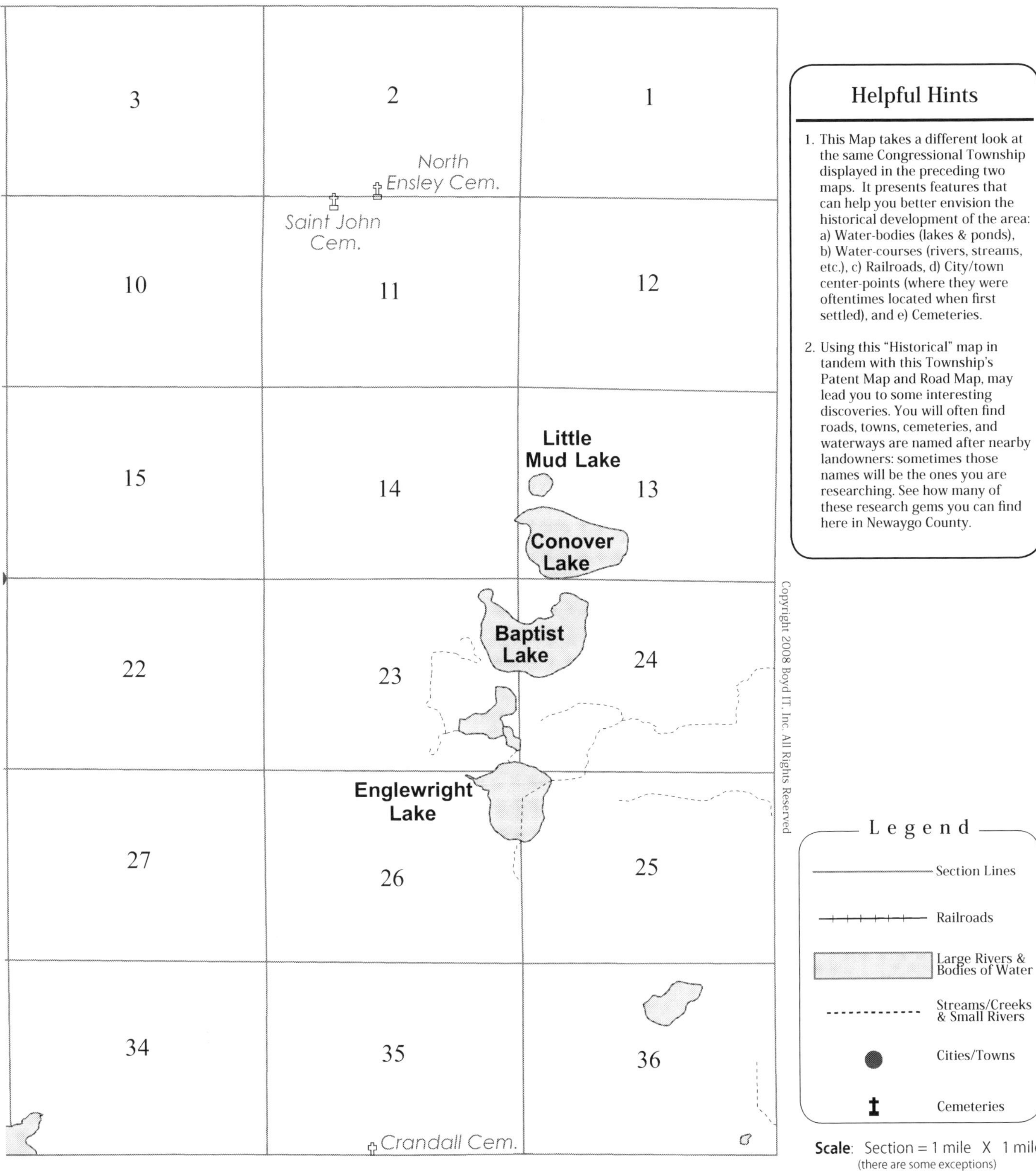

Helpful Hints

1. This Map takes a different look at the same Congressional Township displayed in the preceding two maps. It presents features that can help you better envision the historical development of the area: a) Water-bodies (lakes & ponds), b) Water-courses (rivers, streams, etc.), c) Railroads, d) City/town center-points (where they were oftentimes located when first settled), and e) Cemeteries.

2. Using this "Historical" map in tandem with this Township's Patent Map and Road Map, may lead you to some interesting discoveries. You will often find roads, towns, cemeteries, and waterways are named after nearby landowners: sometimes those names will be the ones you are researching. See how many of these research gems you can find here in Newaygo County.

Appendices

Appendix A - Acts of Congress Authorizing the Patents Contained in this Book

The following Acts of Congress are referred to throughout the Indexes in this book. The text of the Federal Statutes referred to below can usually be found on the web. For more information on such laws, check out the publishers's web-site at *www.arphax.com,* go to the "Research" page, and click on the "Land-Law" link.

Ref. No.	Date and Act of Congress	Number of Parcels of Land
1	April 24, 1820: Sale-Cash Entry (3 Stat. 566)	2112
2	July 2, 1862: State Grant-Agri College (12 Stat. 503)	2
3	March 3, 1855: ScripWarrant Act of 1855 (10 Stat. 701)	1109
4	May 20, 1862: Homestead EntryOriginal (12 Stat. 392)	531
5	September 28, 1850: ScripWarrant Act of 1850 (9 Stat. 520)	1
6	September 28, 1850: Swamp Land Grant-Patent (9 Stat. 519)	1

Appendix B - Section Parts (Aliquot Parts)

The following represent the various abbreviations we have found thus far in describing the parts of a Public Land Section. Some of these are very obscure and rarely used, but we wanted to list them for just that reason. A full section is 1 square mile or 640 acres.

Section Part	Description	Acres
<none>	Full Acre (if no Section Part is listed, presumed a full Section)	640
<1-??>	A number represents a Lot Number and can be of various sizes	?
E½	East Half-Section	320
E½E½	East Half of East Half-Section	160
E½E½SE	East Half of East Half of Southeast Quarter-Section	40
E½N½	East Half of North Half-Section	160
E½NE	East Half of Northeast Quarter-Section	80
E½NENE	East Half of Northeast Quarter of Northeast Quarter-Section	20
E½NENW	East Half of Northeast Quarter of Northwest Quarter-Section	20
E½NESE	East Half of Northeast Quarter of Southeast Quarter-Section	20
E½NESW	East Half of Northeast Quarter of Southwest Quarter-Section	20
E½NW	East Half of Northwest Quarter-Section	80
E½NWNE	East Half of Northwest Quarter of Northeast Quarter-Section	20
E½NWNW	East Half of Northwest Quarter of Northwest Quarter-Section	20
E½NWSE	East Half of Northwest Quarter of Southeast Quarter-Section	20
E½NWSW	East Half of Northwest Quarter of Southwest Quarter-Section	20
E½S½	East Half of South Half-Section	160
E½SE	East Half of Southeast Quarter-Section	80
E½SENE	East Half of Southeast Quarter of Northeast Quarter-Section	20
E½SENW	East Half of Southeast Quarter of Northwest Quarter-Section	20
E½SESE	East Half of Southeast Quarter of Southeast Quarter-Section	20
E½SESW	East Half of Southeast Quarter of Southwest Quarter-Section	20
E½SW	East Half of Southwest Quarter-Section	80
E½SWNE	East Half of Southwest Quarter of Northeast Quarter-Section	20
E½SWNW	East Half of Southwest Quarter of Northwest Quarter-Section	20
E½SWSE	East Half of Southwest Quarter of Southeast Quarter-Section	20
E½SWSW	East Half of Southwest Quarter of Southwest Quarter-Section	20
E½W½	East Half of West Half-Section	160
N½	North Half-Section	320
N½E½NE	North Half of East Half of Northeast Quarter-Section	40
N½E½NW	North Half of East Half of Northwest Quarter-Section	40
N½E½SE	North Half of East Half of Southeast Quarter-Section	40
N½E½SW	North Half of East Half of Southwest Quarter-Section	40
N½N½	North Half of North Half-Section	160
N½NE	North Half of Northeast Quarter-Section	80
N½NENE	North Half of Northeast Quarter of Northeast Quarter-Section	20
N½NENW	North Half of Northeast Quarter of Northwest Quarter-Section	20
N½NESE	North Half of Northeast Quarter of Southeast Quarter-Section	20
N½NESW	North Half of Northeast Quarter of Southwest Quarter-Section	20
N½NW	North Half of Northwest Quarter-Section	80
N½NWNE	North Half of Northwest Quarter of Northeast Quarter-Section	20
N½NWNW	North Half of Northwest Quarter of Northwest Quarter-Section	20
N½NWSE	North Half of Northwest Quarter of Southeast Quarter-Section	20
N½NWSW	North Half of Northwest Quarter of Southwest Quarter-Section	20
N½S½	North Half of South Half-Section	160
N½SE	North Half of Southeast Quarter-Section	80
N½SENE	North Half of Southeast Quarter of Northeast Quarter-Section	20
N½SENW	North Half of Southeast Quarter of Northwest Quarter-Section	20
N½SESE	North Half of Southeast Quarter of Southeast Quarter-Section	20

Section Part	Description	Acres
N½SESW	North Half of Southeast Quarter of Southwest Quarter-Section	20
N½SESW	North Half of Southeast Quarter of Southwest Quarter-Section	20
N½SW	North Half of Southwest Quarter-Section	80
N½SWNE	North Half of Southwest Quarter of Northeast Quarter-Section	20
N½SWNW	North Half of Southwest Quarter of Northwest Quarter-Section	20
N½SWSE	North Half of Southwest Quarter of Southeast Quarter-Section	20
N½SWSE	North Half of Southwest Quarter of Southeast Quarter-Section	20
N½SWSW	North Half of Southwest Quarter of Southwest Quarter-Section	20
N½W½NW	North Half of West Half of Northwest Quarter-Section	40
N½W½SE	North Half of West Half of Southeast Quarter-Section	40
N½W½SW	North Half of West Half of Southwest Quarter-Section	40
NE	Northeast Quarter-Section	160
NEN½	Northeast Quarter of North Half-Section	80
NENE	Northeast Quarter of Northeast Quarter-Section	40
NENENE	Northeast Quarter of Northeast Quarter of Northeast Quarter	10
NENENW	Northeast Quarter of Northeast Quarter of Northwest Quarter	10
NENESE	Northeast Quarter of Northeast Quarter of Southeast Quarter	10
NENESW	Northeast Quarter of Northeast Quarter of Southwest Quarter	10
NENW	Northeast Quarter of Northwest Quarter-Section	40
NENWNE	Northeast Quarter of Northwest Quarter of Northeast Quarter	10
NENWNW	Northeast Quarter of Northwest Quarter of Northwest Quarter	10
NENWSE	Northeast Quarter of Northwest Quarter of Southeast Quarter	10
NENWSW	Northeast Quarter of Northwest Quarter of Southwest Quarter	10
NESE	Northeast Quarter of Southeast Quarter-Section	40
NESENE	Northeast Quarter of Southeast Quarter of Northeast Quarter	10
NESENW	Northeast Quarter of Southeast Quarter of Northwest Quarter	10
NESESE	Northeast Quarter of Southeast Quarter of Southeast Quarter	10
NESESW	Northeast Quarter of Southeast Quarter of Southwest Quarter	10
NESW	Northeast Quarter of Southwest Quarter-Section	40
NESWNE	Northeast Quarter of Southwest Quarter of Northeast Quarter	10
NESWNW	Northeast Quarter of Southwest Quarter of Northwest Quarter	10
NESWSE	Northeast Quarter of Southwest Quarter of Southeast Quarter	10
NESWSW	Northeast Quarter of Southwest Quarter of Southwest Quarter	10
NW	Northwest Quarter-Section	160
NWE½	Northwest Quarter of Eastern Half-Section	80
NWN½	Northwest Quarter of North Half-Section	80
NWNE	Northwest Quarter of Northeast Quarter-Section	40
NWNENE	Northwest Quarter of Northeast Quarter of Northeast Quarter	10
NWNENW	Northwest Quarter of Northeast Quarter of Northwest Quarter	10
NWNESE	Northwest Quarter of Northeast Quarter of Southeast Quarter	10
NWNESW	Northwest Quarter of Northeast Quarter of Southwest Quarter	10
NWNW	Northwest Quarter of Northwest Quarter-Section	40
NWNWNE	Northwest Quarter of Northwest Quarter of Northeast Quarter	10
NWNWNW	Northwest Quarter of Northwest Quarter of Northwest Quarter	10
NWNWSE	Northwest Quarter of Northwest Quarter of Southeast Quarter	10
NWNWSW	Northwest Quarter of Northwest Quarter of Southwest Quarter	10
NWSE	Northwest Quarter of Southeast Quarter-Section	40
NWSENE	Northwest Quarter of Southeast Quarter of Northeast Quarter	10
NWSENW	Northwest Quarter of Southeast Quarter of Northwest Quarter	10
NWSESE	Northwest Quarter of Southeast Quarter of Southeast Quarter	10
NWSESW	Northwest Quarter of Southeast Quarter of Southwest Quarter	10
NWSW	Northwest Quarter of Southwest Quarter-Section	40
NWSWNE	Northwest Quarter of Southwest Quarter of Northeast Quarter	10
NWSWNW	Northwest Quarter of Southwest Quarter of Northwest Quarter	10
NWSWSE	Northwest Quarter of Southwest Quarter of Southeast Quarter	10
NWSWSW	Northwest Quarter of Southwest Quarter of Southwest Quarter	10
S½	South Half-Section	320
S½E½NE	South Half of East Half of Northeast Quarter-Section	40
S½E½NW	South Half of East Half of Northwest Quarter-Section	40
S½E½SE	South Half of East Half of Southeast Quarter-Section	40

Section Part	Description	Acres
S½E½SW	South Half of East Half of Southwest Quarter-Section	40
S½N½	South Half of North Half-Section	160
S½NE	South Half of Northeast Quarter-Section	80
S½NENE	South Half of Northeast Quarter of Northeast Quarter-Section	20
S½NENW	South Half of Northeast Quarter of Northwest Quarter-Section	20
S½NESE	South Half of Northeast Quarter of Southeast Quarter-Section	20
S½NESW	South Half of Northeast Quarter of Southwest Quarter-Section	20
S½NW	South Half of Northwest Quarter-Section	80
S½NWNE	South Half of Northwest Quarter of Northeast Quarter-Section	20
S½NWNW	South Half of Northwest Quarter of Northwest Quarter-Section	20
S½NWSE	South Half of Northwest Quarter of Southeast Quarter-Section	20
S½NWSW	South Half of Northwest Quarter of Southwest Quarter-Section	20
S½S½	South Half of South Half-Section	160
S½SE	South Half of Southeast Quarter-Section	80
S½SENE	South Half of Southeast Quarter of Northeast Quarter-Section	20
S½SENW	South Half of Southeast Quarter of Northwest Quarter-Section	20
S½SESE	South Half of Southeast Quarter of Southeast Quarter-Section	20
S½SESW	South Half of Southeast Quarter of Southwest Quarter-Section	20
S½SESW	South Half of Southeast Quarter of Southwest Quarter-Section	20
S½SW	South Half of Southwest Quarter-Section	80
S½SWNE	South Half of Southwest Quarter of Northeast Quarter-Section	20
S½SWNW	South Half of Southwest Quarter of Northwest Quarter-Section	20
S½SWSE	South Half of Southwest Quarter of Southeast Quarter-Section	20
S½SWSE	South Half of Southwest Quarter of Southeast Quarter-Section	20
S½SWSW	South Half of Southwest Quarter of Southwest Quarter-Section	20
S½W½NE	South Half of West Half of Northeast Quarter-Section	40
S½W½NW	South Half of West Half of Northwest Quarter-Section	40
S½W½SE	South Half of West Half of Southeast Quarter-Section	40
S½W½SW	South Half of West Half of Southwest Quarter-Section	40
SE	Southeast Quarter Section	160
SEN½	Southeast Quarter of North Half-Section	80
SENE	Southeast Quarter of Northeast Quarter-Section	40
SENENE	Southeast Quarter of Northeast Quarter of Northeast Quarter	10
SENENW	Southeast Quarter of Northeast Quarter of Northwest Quarter	10
SENESE	Southeast Quarter of Northeast Quarter of Southeast Quarter	10
SENESW	Southeast Quarter of Northeast Quarter of Southwest Quarter	10
SENW	Southeast Quarter of Northwest Quarter-Section	40
SENWNE	Southeast Quarter of Northwest Quarter of Northeast Quarter	10
SENWNW	Southeast Quarter of Northwest Quarter of Northwest Quarter	10
SENWSE	Souteast Quarter of Northwest Quarter of Southeast Quarter	10
SENWSW	Southeast Quarter of Northwest Quarter of Southwest Quarter	10
SESE	Southeast Quarter of Southeast Quarter-Section	40
SESENE	SoutheastQuarter of Southeast Quarter of Northeast Quarter	10
SESENW	Southeast Quarter of Southeast Quarter of Northwest Quarter	10
SESESE	Southeast Quarter of Southeast Quarter of Southeast Quarter	10
SESESW	Southeast Quarter of Southeast Quarter of Southwest Quarter	10
SESW	Southeast Quarter of Southwest Quarter-Section	40
SESWNE	Southeast Quarter of Southwest Quarter of Northeast Quarter	10
SESWNW	Southeast Quarter of Southwest Quarter of Northwest Quarter	10
SESWSE	Southeast Quarter of Southwest Quarter of Southeast Quarter	10
SESWSW	Southeast Quarter of Southwest Quarter of Southwest Quarter	10
SW	Southwest Quarter-Section	160
SWNE	Southwest Quarter of Northeast Quarter-Section	40
SWNENE	Southwest Quarter of Northeast Quarter of Northeast Quarter	10
SWNENW	Southwest Quarter of Northeast Quarter of Northwest Quarter	10
SWNESE	Southwest Quarter of Northeast Quarter of Southeast Quarter	10
SWNESW	Southwest Quarter of Northeast Quarter of Southwest Quarter	10
SWNW	Southwest Quarter of Northwest Quarter-Section	40
SWNWNE	Southwest Quarter of Northwest Quarter of Northeast Quarter	10
SWNWNW	Southwest Quarter of Northwest Quarter of Northwest Quarter	10

Section Part	Description	Acres
SWNWSE	Southwest Quarter of Northwest Quarter of Southeast Quarter	10
SWNWSW	Southwest Quarter of Northwest Quarter of Southwest Quarter	10
SWSE	Southwest Quarter of Southeast Quarter-Section	40
SWSENE	Southwest Quarter of Southeast Quarter of Northeast Quarter	10
SWSENW	Southwest Quarter of Southeast Quarter of Northwest Quarter	10
SWSESE	Southwest Quarter of Southeast Quarter of Southeast Quarter	10
SWSESW	Southwest Quarter of Southeast Quarter of Southwest Quarter	10
SWSW	Southwest Quarter of Southwest Quarter-Section	40
SWSWNE	Southwest Quarter of Southwest Quarter of Northeast Quarter	10
SWSWNW	Southwest Quarter of Southwest Quarter of Northwest Quarter	10
SWSWSE	Southwest Quarter of Southwest Quarter of Southeast Quarter	10
SWSWSW	Southwest Quarter of Southwest Quarter of Southwest Quarter	10
W½	West Half-Section	320
W½E½	West Half of East Half-Section	160
W½N½	West Half of North Half-Section (same as NW)	160
W½NE	West Half of Northeast Quarter	80
W½NENE	West Half of Northeast Quarter of Northeast Quarter-Section	20
W½NENW	West Half of Northeast Quarter of Northwest Quarter-Section	20
W½NESE	West Half of Northeast Quarter of Southeast Quarter-Section	20
W½NESW	West Half of Northeast Quarter of Southwest Quarter-Section	20
W½NW	West Half of Northwest Quarter-Section	80
W½NWNE	West Half of Northwest Quarter of Northeast Quarter-Section	20
W½NWNW	West Half of Northwest Quarter of Northwest Quarter-Section	20
W½NWSE	West Half of Northwest Quarter of Southeast Quarter-Section	20
W½NWSW	West Half of Northwest Quarter of Southwest Quarter-Section	20
W½S½	West Half of South Half-Section	160
W½SE	West Half of Southeast Quarter-Section	80
W½SENE	West Half of Southeast Quarter of Northeast Quarter-Section	20
W½SENW	West Half of Southeast Quarter of Northwest Quarter-Section	20
W½SESE	West Half of Southeast Quarter of Southeast Quarter-Section	20
W½SESW	West Half of Southeast Quarter of Southwest Quarter-Section	20
W½SW	West Half of Southwest Quarter-Section	80
W½SWNE	West Half of Southwest Quarter of Northeast Quarter-Section	20
W½SWNW	West Half of Southwest Quarter of Northwest Quarter-Section	20
W½SWSE	West Half of Southwest Quarter of Southeast Quarter-Section	20
W½SWSW	West Half of Southwest Quarter of Southwest Quarter-Section	20
W½W½	West Half of West Half-Section	160

Appendix C - Multi-Patentee Groups

The following index presents groups of people who jointly received patents in Newaygo County, Michigan. The Group Numbers are used in the Patent Maps and their Indexes so that you may then turn to this Appendix in order to identify all the members of the each buying group.

Group Number 1
ALLEY, Samuel M; VARNUM, Mercy

Group Number 2
AVERY, Newell; ANDERSON, Patience

Group Number 3
AVERY, Newell; GROVENBERRY, Mary

Group Number 4
AVERY, Newell; MURPHY, Simon J

Group Number 5
AVERY, Newell; MURPHY, Simon J; WELCH, John; HEALD, Joseph

Group Number 6
BALL, John; MCKEE, James H

Group Number 7
BALL, John; WOOD, Susanna

Group Number 8
BENJAMIN, D Marcellus; ARNOLD, Nancy

Group Number 9
BENJAMIN, D Marcellus; CHARLES, James

Group Number 10
BENJAMIN, D Marcellus; CHASE, Tryphena

Group Number 11
BENJAMIN, D Marcellus; DOANE, Clarissa

Group Number 12
BENJAMIN, D Marcellus; HAINES, James

Group Number 13
BENJAMIN, D Marcellus; HALL, Rebecca

Group Number 14
BENJAMIN, D Marcellus; HUNTER, Sarah; HUNTER, Noble W; GASTON, Mary J; GASTON, William S; BALL, Malinda C; MILLER, David M; MILLER, Susanah; MILLER, John W; MILLER, Nancy E; JACOBS, John C

Group Number 15
BENJAMIN, D Marcellus; HUSTON, Tabitha; LENNEN, Peter; WRENN, William B

Group Number 16
BENJAMIN, D Marcellus; JOHNSON, Nehemiah; PRESTON, W E

Group Number 17
BENJAMIN, D Marcellus; MERRICK, Elliott T

Group Number 18
BENJAMIN, D Marcellus; PATEN, William

Group Number 19
BENJAMIN, D Marcellus; RIPLEY, Joseph O; RIPLEY, Mercy J; MERRICK, E T

Group Number 20
BENJAMIN, D Marcellus; SLATER, John M; SMITH, Joseph B

Group Number 21
BENNETT, William; ALLEY, James; ALLEY, George; ALLEY, Samuel M; HASKELL, Nathaniel B

Group Number 22
BENNETT, William; ALLEY, James; ALLEY, George; ALLEY, Samuel M; HASKELL, Nathaniel B; KONKEL, Jacob

Group Number 23
BENNETT, William; ALLEY, James; ALLEY, Samuel M; ALLEY, George; HASKELL, Nathaniel B

Group Number 24
BENTON, James; ADSIT, Eunice

Group Number 25
BENTON, James; BLINDBERRY, Patty

Group Number 26
BRIGHAM, Orlando S; WHEELER, Silas

Group Number 27
BROOKS, John A; LASLEY, William

Group Number 28
BROOKS, John A; MERRILL, Isaac D

Group Number 29
BROWN, Silvester; DOUGLAS, Ann E

Group Number 30
BROWN, Stephen; STUDLEY, Susan

Group Number 31
BRUBAKER, Phares S; MOSS, Elizabeth; MOSS, Charles N; REED, William A

Group Number 32
CARLSON, Charles M; BELL, Darwin G

Group Number 33
CARPENTER, Ebenezer S; CARPENTER, George W; CARPENTER, Anthony W

Group Number 34
CHAFFEE, Joel S; CHAFFEE, Elanor

Group Number 35
CHENEY, Albert N; ARMS, Lewis L

Group Number 36
CHENEY, Albert N; ARMS, Lewis L; WELLES, William P

Group Number 37
CONKLIN, Catharine; CONKLIN, George

Group Number 38
CONKLIN, Frank; CONKLIN, Walter; CONKLIN, Thomas

Group Number 39
COOK, James M; ASHLEY, Samuel M; BENNETT, William

Group Number 40
COOK, John P; EARLY, Sarah

Group Number 41
COOK, John P; HILL, Elizabeth; THOMPSON, J E

Group Number 42
COOK, John P; MABIE, Margaret

Group Number 43
COOK, John P; STEVENSON, James L; WALKER, William L; WATSON, Robert

Group Number 44
COOK, John P; STORMS, Mary

Group Number 45
COOK, Josiah M; JOHNSON, Harley M

Group Number 46
COOK, Josiah M; SMITH, Canton

Group Number 47
CRARY, Stephen; CRARY, Mehitabel

Group Number 48
CUDABACK, Harvey; MCNITT, Catharine H

Group Number 49
DAGAN, John; WHITEHEAD, John

Group Number 50
DANIEL, Elias; DANIEL, Susanna

Group Number 51
DEANE, James M; STILWELL, Sherman

Group Number 52
DICKISON, Frederick; WASHBURN, Deborah

Group Number 53
DOTY, Achsah M; DOTY, Rowena L; DOTY, Edith B; DOTY, Enoch

Group Number 54
DOUGLASS, Everett; BOWEN, Anson

Group Number 55
EASTMAN, George; MCCAB, Owen

Group Number 56
EASTMAN, Mason; EASTMAN, George

Group Number 57
ELDRIDGE, Lorenzo; GARNER, Ranyon; EUT, William; GARNER, Cyrus C; BENDER, John C

Group Number 58
ELDRIDGE, Lorenzo; REASMON, Magdalene

Group Number 59
ELY, John J; RAYNSFORD, Frederick; CLARK, Lafred L

Group Number 60
EVANS, Daniel W; EVANS, George C

Group Number 61
FERRY, Thomas G; FERRY, George F

Group Number 62
FERRY, Thomas W; FERRY, Edward P

Group Number 63
FOSTER, Wilder D; BALL, Daniel

Group Number 64
FOWLER, Thomas; BOWLEY, Polly

Group Number 65
FULLMER, Jeremiah; WHITNEY, Brazill H; GOODRIDGE, Charles

Group Number 66
GARDNER, Silas; GARDNER, Hannah

Group Number 67
GAUWEILER, Frederick; KAUFMAN, Christopher

Group Number 68
GIDDINGS, Jane; WHITE, John; COOPER, Joel M; GIDDINGS, June

Group Number 69
GILBERT, John; GILBERT, Joseph; GILBERT, William

Group Number 70
GODFREY, Solomon; CULP, Christopher

Group Number 71
GOODRICH, Chauncey; ALLEN, John S

Group Number 72
GRAY, Edgar L; ROCHESTER, John W

Group Number 73
GROVESTEEN, John M; NEAL, Aurelia C

Group Number 74
GROVESTEEN, John M; PELTON, Rollin H; HARRIS, Mary

Group Number 75
HALCOMB, Seth; COULTER, John; PRESTON, David

Group Number 76
HALL, Mary E; KITCHEN, James

Group Number 77
HALL, Stephen C; THOMPSON, Samuel C

Group Number 78
HALL, Stephen C; THORP, Lucy

Group Number 79
HALL, Stephen C; TUTHILL, Mehitable

Group Number 80
HAMILTON, Addison R; WEBSTER, Lucretia

Group Number 81
HASCALL, Herbert A; WILLIAMS, Ann

Group Number 82
HASCALL, Lucien A; WEBB, Nancy

Group Number 83
HEALD, Joseph; AVERY, Newell; MURPHY, Simon J

Group Number 84
HEALD, Joseph; MURPHY, Simon J; CREPIN, Ernest E

Group Number 85
HICKS, Julia A; HICKS, George W

Group Number 86
HILDRETH, John P; BUSH, John J

Group Number 87
HILDRETH, John P; BUSH, John J; MANLEY, Franklin Norman; FERRISS, Lucy Maria; MANLEY, Lucy Maria

Group Number 88
HILDRETH, John P; RUSH, John J

Group Number 89
HOWE, William; BARRON, Mary

Group Number 90
HOWE, William; HEATH, Elizabeth

Group Number 91
HUBBARD, Abijah; HALL, Charlotte

Group Number 92
IVES, Chauncey P; BEAZLEY, Martha E; FOGG, Elzer; LEONARD, Frederick B

Group Number 93
IVES, Chauncey P; FARINHOLT, Maria; LEONARD, Frederick B

Group Number 94
IVES, Chauncey P; HOUSTON, Nancy; LEONARD, Frederick B

Group Number 95
IVES, Chauncey P; JONES, William T; LEONARD, Frederick B

Group Number 96
IVES, Chauncey P; LEONARD, Frederick B

Group Number 97
IVES, Chauncey P; LEONARD, Frederick B; FISCHER, Angelles

Group Number 98
IVES, Chauncey P; LEONARD, Frederick B; GATEWOOD, Rhoda

Group Number 99
IVES, Chauncey P; LEONARD, Frederick B; HOLLOWAY, Joanna

Group Number 100
IVES, Chauncey P; LEONARD, Frederick B; PITTS, Nancy

Group Number 101
IVES, Chauncey P; LEONARD, Frederick B; PULLER, Mary A

Group Number 102
IVES, Chauncey P; LEONARD, Frederick B; WARREN, George B; CARTER, Maria

Group Number 103
IVES, Chauncey P; MARTIN, Frederick P

Group Number 104
JEWELL, Joseph B; MULDER, Kornelius

Group Number 105
JOHNSON, Charles; GUSTROUS, John

Group Number 106
JOHNSON, Charles; MCCRACKEN, Otho

Group Number 107
JOHNSON, Charles; PETERSON, Charles

Group Number 108
JOHNSON, Harley M; CRITTENDON, Israel L; CHADWICK, Rachel

Group Number 109
JOHNSON, Harley M; CRITTENDON, Israel L; FRY, Ellen

Group Number 110
JOHNSON, Harley M; CRITTENDON, Israel L; SOEVYN, John; PRESTON, David

Group Number 111
JOHNSON, William A; BALLINGER, John T; BALLINGER, Sarah Ann

Group Number 112
KAUFMAN, Christopher; GAUWEILER, Frederick

Group Number 113
KIDD, William E; SAPP, Dexter T

Group Number 114
LAKE, Samuel; LAKE, Erastus

Group Number 115
LANCASTER, Joseph; BRITTAIN, Thomas; JOHNSON, Isaac N

Group Number 116
LEACH, Paul A; WILLARD, David

Group Number 117
LEONARD, Charles W; TROTT, Levi L

Group Number 118
LEONARD, Charles W; TROTT, Levi L; BISSETT, Bethiah; FOSTER, James

Group Number 119
LEONARD, Charles W; TROTT, Levi L; STEVENS, Jane

Group Number 120
LEONARD, Frederick B; BRUNSON, Rebecca

Group Number 121
LEONARD, Frederick B; IVES, Chauncey P

Group Number 122
LEONARD, Frederick B; IVES, Chauncey P; BARB, Ruth

Group Number 123
LEONARD, Frederick B; IVES, Chauncey P; BENNETT, Mary

Group Number 124
LEONARD, Frederick B; IVES, Chauncey P; BOWMAN, Mary

Group Number 125
LEONARD, Frederick B; IVES, Chauncey P; EANES, Jane T

Group Number 126
LEONARD, Frederick B; IVES, Chauncey P; GATEWOOD, Rhoda

Group Number 127
LEONARD, Frederick B; IVES, Chauncey P; GILLILAND, Elizabeth

Group Number 128
LEONARD, Frederick B; IVES, Chauncey P; GRAHAM, Catharine

Group Number 129
LEONARD, Frederick B; IVES, Chauncey P; HUTCHERSON, Elizabeth

Group Number 130
LEONARD, Frederick B; IVES, Chauncey P; KING, Eunice P

Group Number 131
LEONARD, Frederick B; IVES, Chauncey P; LANNING, Mary

Group Number 132
LEONARD, Frederick B; IVES, Chauncey P; MCCLUNG, Jane

Group Number 133
LEONARD, Frederick B; IVES, Chauncey P; MILLER, Phebe

Group Number 134
LEONARD, Frederick B; IVES, Chauncey P; MILLER, Susannah

Group Number 135
LEONARD, Frederick B; IVES, Chauncey P; RAYBORNE, Sally

Group Number 136
LEONARD, Frederick B; IVES, Chauncey P; SAMMIS, Lydia

Group Number 137
LEONARD, Frederick B; IVES, Chauncey P; SAMUEL, Frances

Group Number 138
LEONARD, Frederick B; IVES, Chauncey P; SELLEARS, Nancy

Group Number 139
LEONARD, Frederick B; IVES, Chauncey P; SHOWARD, Lucy

Group Number 140
LEONARD, Frederick B; IVES, Chauncey P; SIDERS, Ann

Group Number 141
LEONARD, Frederick B; IVES, Chauncey P; SKELTON, Sally

Group Number 142
LEONARD, Frederick B; IVES, Chauncey P; SOUTHWORTH, Lucy

Group Number 143
LEONARD, Frederick B; IVES, Chauncey P; SPARKS, Sarah L

Group Number 144
LEONARD, Frederick B; IVES, Chauncy P

Group Number 145
LEONARD, Frederick B; IVES, Chauncy P; WHITE, Alma

Group Number 146
LOVELL, Louis S; BIRCHARD, W H

Group Number 147
LOVELL, Louis S; HUZZEY, Susannah

Group Number 148
LUDINGTON, James; AGARD, Noah; AGARD, Alexaniller; BALEY, Arma M; TICHENOR, Sarah L A; BAILEY, Gilbert D

Group Number 149
LUDINGTON, James; ATWOOD, Mary

Group Number 150
LUDINGTON, James; BLANCHARD, Irena

Group Number 151
LUDINGTON, James; CADY, Levinia

Group Number 152
LUDINGTON, James; FLAGG, Betsey

Group Number 153
LUDINGTON, James; JOY, Abigail

Group Number 154
LUDINGTON, James; KING, Mary; WILLIAMS, Josephine; KENNEDY, James

Group Number 155
LUDINGTON, James; LAVERGNE, Alexandre; TRAHAN, Onezime; DELAHOUSSAYE, Gustave; ELMS, George O

Group Number 156
LUDINGTON, James; LEMONS, Aley

Group Number 157
LUDINGTON, James; LESUEUR, Napoleon B

Group Number 158
LUDINGTON, James; PLACKARD, Malinda

Group Number 159
LUDINGTON, James; ROUNDS, Mina

Group Number 160
LUDINGTON, James; SAWYER, Polly L

Group Number 161
LUDINGTON, James; TARR, Mary

Group Number 162
LUDINGTON, James; WAKE,

Group Number 163
LUDINGTON, James; WEDD, William; MITCHELL, David T

Group Number 164
LULL, Hiram; EASTMAN, George

Group Number 165
LULL, Hiram; EASTMAN, George; CLAY, Joseph G; CLAY, Nancy; CLAY, William

Group Number 166
LULL, Hiram; EASTMAN, George; DUNN, Hannah

Group Number 167
LULL, Hiram; EASTMAN, George; HEFFERAN, Thomas

Group Number 168
LULL, Walter; EASTMAN, Galen

Group Number 169
MARSH, Carlos; CASE, Lucena

Group Number 170
MATTESON, Freeman; WHEELER, Suphronia

Group Number 171
MEAD, Andrew W; HUNTER, Nathaniel D; EDMESTON, William

Group Number 172
MELENDY, David A; GERRY, Elizabeth

Group Number 173
MELENDY, David A; LEONARD, Mary; LEONARD, Samuel L; ISBELL, Yearby H; LINGLE, John S

Group Number 174
MELENDY, David A; LONG, Priscilla

Group Number 175
MELENDY, David A; MARSHALL, William R

Group Number 176
MELENDY, David A; ROWLAND, James A

Group Number 177
MELENDY, David A; WOODBURY, Joseph B

Group Number 178
MERCHANT, Benjamin P; STEWART, John R; MARTIN, Marion; MARTIN, Hannah; STANLEY, Thomas B

Group Number 179
MERCHANT, Benjamin P; STEWART, John R; MARTIN, Marson; MARTIN, Hannah; STANLEY, Thomas B

Group Number 180
MERRILL, Elias W; MERRILL, Isaac D

Group Number 181
MERRILL, Isaac D; MERRILL, Elias W

Group Number 182
MERRILL, Isaac D; MERRILL, Elias W; DANA, Josiah P

Group Number 183
MERRITT, Titus; BEAN, Emery O

Group Number 184
MILES, James H; MILES, William

Group Number 185
MILES, James H; MILES, William; FERRAN, Jane; BLAZO, Jonathan; BLAZO, William A; CLARK, Susan J; WOODMAN, Horatio

Group Number 186
MILES, James H; MILES, William; MINK, Margaret

Group Number 187
MILES, James H; MILES, William; SAUNDERS, Isaac M

Group Number 188
MILLER, John; HAGERMANN, Charles

Group Number 189
MILLER, Orrin A; MILLER, Samuel

Group Number 190
MITCHELL, Samuel S; LULL, Hiram

Group Number 191
MITCHELL, Samuel; COCHRAN, Fanny

Group Number 192
MITCHELL, Samuel; NICHOLS, James

Group Number 193
MIX, Sylvester; MIX, Sylvenus S; WELLING, Cornelia

Group Number 194
MORGAN, Samuel F; PORTER, Abigail

Group Number 195
MORRISON, Jefferson; DAVIDSON, Miriam

Group Number 196
MORRISON, Jefferson; GARDNER, Anna

Group Number 197
MORRISON, Jefferson; PAGE, Almira Hellen

Group Number 198
MOSES, Henry C; FRENCH, Sarah

Group Number 199
NORTHROP, John O; HINE, John

Group Number 200
NORTHROP, John O; HINE, John; WATERHOUSE, Ruth

Group Number 201
NORTHROP, John O; SANFORD, Ebenezer; MERWIN, Henry

Group Number 202
NORTHROP, Nelson W; SPAIDS, Clarisa

Group Number 203
PADDOCK, Augustus; EDWARDS, Phineas; LYKINE, John; BENDER, John C

Group Number 204
PADDOCK, Augustus; GOLLADAY, David; HOYT, Benjamin

Group Number 205
PADDOCK, Augustus; JUDSON, Zerah; STEVENS, Edward

Group Number 206
PAGE, Stephen F; RESSEGINE, Charles E; CHRISTIAN, Sarah; WINN, William

Group Number 207
PAGE, Stephen F; RESSEGINE, Charles E; DUNGAN, Sarah

Group Number 208
PAGE, Stephen F; RESSEGINE, Charles E; GOODALL, Eliza B

Group Number 209
PAGE, Stephen F; RESSEGINE, Charles E; HARRIS, William S; WITHEROW, John H

Group Number 210
PAGE, Stephen F; RESSEGINE, Charles E; MCCLAIN, Mary

Group Number 211
PAGE, Stephen F; RESSEGINE, Charles E; WITHEROW, John; HARRIS, William S; WITHEROW, John H

Group Number 212
PAGE, Stephen F; RISSEGUIE, Charles E; CLENLEY, Martha

Group Number 213
PALMER, Chandler; GREY, Charles

Group Number 214
PARKER, Samuel E; COLLINS, David

Group Number 215
PELTON, Rollin H; PELTON, Ephraim; PELTON, Abagail

Group Number 216
PETERSON, Charles; BAMBER, Robert

Group Number 217
PILLSBURY, Oliver P; ALEXANDER, Elizabeth; ALEXANDER, Robert C; LANE, Abraham; LANE, William E

Group Number 218
PILLSBURY, Oliver P; BUSHNELL, William

Group Number 219
PILLSBURY, Oliver P; GRANADE, John A; GRANADE, William; HALL, Mary

Group Number 220
PLATT, Nathan H; KNOX, Charles A

Group Number 221
POTTER, Henry C; WEBBER, William L

Group Number 222
PRESTON, David; HARPER, John L

Group Number 223
PRICE, Bartholomew W; PRICE, Parker C; PRICE, John L

Group Number 224
PRUYN, Samuel; HIGGS, Benjamin; HIGGS, Jackson

Group Number 225
RICE, William; RICE, David

Group Number 226
RICHARDSON, Austin; RICHARDSON, James C

Group Number 227
ROBBINS, David; ROBBINS, Hepzibah

Group Number 228
ROCHESTER, John W; DICKERSON, Wallace W

Group Number 229
ROCHESTER, John W; GRAY, Edgar L

Group Number 230
ROSS, James H; SCHURCK, Morris B; BESHER, Cornelia

Group Number 231
RUPRECHT, William; PARK, Sarah A; PARK, Erastus S; KINGSLEY, Thomas G; CHAPMAN, Dwight P; BUMSTED, William H

Group Number 232
RUSHMORE, Silas; CAIRNS, Elizabeth

Group Number 233
RYERSON, Martin; HILLS, Charles T; GETTY, Henry H

Group Number 234
RYERSON, Martin; HILLS, Charles T; GETTY, Henry H; STEVENS, Ezra; KIMBALL, Orson W

Group Number 235
RYERSON, Martin; MORRIS, Robert

Group Number 236
RYERSON, Martin; MORRIS, Robert W

Group Number 237
RYERSON, Tunis; JOHNSON, Peter

Group Number 238
SANFORD, Ebenezer; GAYLORD, Irwin B

Group Number 239
SANFORD, Ebenezer; MERWIN, Henry; NORTHROP, John O; ROBERTS, William

Group Number 240
SANFORD, Ebenezer; MERWIN, Henry; NORTHROP, John O; ROBERTS, William; ELTING, Evelina

Group Number 241
SANFORD, Ebenezer; NORTHROP, John O

Group Number 242
SANFORD, Ebenezer; NORTHROP, John O; BRIGGS, Catherine

Group Number 243
SANFORD, Ebenezer; NORTHROP, John O; EWERS, Sarah

Group Number 244
SANFORD, Ebenezer; NORTHROP, John O; GREGORY, Mary

Group Number 245
SANFORD, Ebenezer; NORTHROP, John O; HAYWARD, Ruth; BLANCHARD, John C

Group Number 246
SANFORD, Ebenezer; NORTHROP, John O; JONES, Elizabeth E

Group Number 247
SANFORD, Ebenezer; NORTHROP, John O; LASHER, Mary

Group Number 248
SANFORD, Ebenezer; NORTHROP, John O; MERWIN, Henry

Group Number 249
SANFORD, Ebenezer; NORTHROP, John O; MERWIN, Henry; CADY, Susannah

Group Number 250
SANFORD, Ebenezer; NORTHROP, John O; MERWIN, Henry; ROBERTS, William

Group Number 251
SANFORD, Ebenezer; NORTHROP, John O; MERWIN, Henry; SHEARMAN, Elizabeth

Group Number 252
SANFORD, Ebenezer; NORTHROP, John O; STAUDT, Anna

Group Number 253
SANFORD, Ebenezer; NORTHROP, John O; SUTFIN, Mary

Group Number 254
SANFORD, Ebenezer; NORTHROP, John O; WOOD, Lydia

Group Number 255
SANFORD, Samuel R; DAVIS, Mary

Group Number 256
SECORD, Sidney; MOODY, Lucy; ROGERS, Abigail

Group Number 257
SIMONS, James V; BROWN, Elsey

Group Number 258
SKEELS, Amos K; WARREN, Persis

Group Number 259
SKINNER, Adolphus L; BROWN, Augustus L; FORSHAY, David F

Group Number 260
SKINNER, Adolphus L; GUDGELL, Van Buren

Group Number 261
SMITH, Arabut F; BOYD, Rufus

Group Number 262
SMITH, Warren; FOWTER, Alvah

Group Number 263
STEBBINS, Joseph D; FRANKLIN, George W; JOHNSON, Charles

Group Number 264
STEVENS, Fitz H; KENNE, Elias G; SHERMAN, Alonzo

Group Number 265
STEVENSON, Thomas G; CRAWFORD, Francis; ROWE, Mary

Group Number 266
STEVENSON, Thomas G; FOLJAMBE, Charles

Group Number 267
STEVENSON, Thomas G; JOHNSON, Davis

Group Number 268
STEVENSON, Thomas G; REWALT, Catharine

Group Number 269
STEVENSON, Thomas G; VAN BUREN, MARIA

Group Number 270
STIMSON, Thomas D; STIMPSON, Thomas D

Group Number 271
STINGEL, Jost; HINDS, Michael

Group Number 272
STOCKING, Erastus P; STOCKING, Adeline M; STOCKING, Jared W

Group Number 273
STROH, Bernhard; KIEFER, Herman; LICHTENBERG, Gustav B

Group Number 274
STROH, Bernhard; KIEFER, Herman; LICHTENBERG, Gustav B; PEAT, James; MATHERS, Nancy; TUTTLE, Elias W

Group Number 275
STROH, Bernhard; KIEFER, Herman; LICHTENBERG, Gustav B; PROBASCO, Mary; PROBASCO, Uzzet H

Group Number 276
STROH, Bernhard; KIEFER, Herman; LICHTENBERG, Gustav B; WRIGHT, Mary

Group Number 277
STROH, Bernhard; KIEFER, Herman; LICHTENBERG, Gustav; SIMMS, Juliet Ann; PRESTON, William E

Group Number 278
STUART, Wilkes L; HOLMES, Susan

Group Number 279
SWAIN, Aaron; MCCALL, Martha R

Group Number 280
SWAIN, Aaron; ORTON, Alonson F; ORTON, Henry F

Group Number 281
SWAIN, Aaron; ORTON, Alonson F; ORTON, Henry J

Group Number 282
SWAIN, Aaron; ORTON, Henry A; ORTON, Alanson F

Group Number 283
SWAIN, Elisha R; ARNOLD, Susan H

Group Number 284
SWAIN, Elisha R; GAMBLE, Sarah

Group Number 285
TAYLOR, James B; CHICK, Charles H

Group Number 286
TENANT, Jonas L; ELY, Phebe

Group Number 287
TENNY, Justus W; SMITH, James M

Group Number 288
TERWILLIGER, Abram; PITTS, Elizabeth

Group Number 289
TINDALL, William A; CILLEY, Susan

Group Number 290
TINKHAM, John F; TAYLOR, Royal; HARPER, John S

Group Number 291
TOWER, Osmond S; HARRISON, Mary A; SEAMAN, Oliver

Group Number 292
TROTT, Levi L; SIBLEY, Anna

Group Number 293
TUCK, Lizzie M; TUCK, George F

Group Number 294
VANO, Peter S; GOULD, John; AYER, Delila; CRITCHLOW, John J

Group Number 295
WARD, William H; BEAUCHAMP, Frances

Group Number 296
WARD, William H; SANFORD, William H

Group Number 297
WARREN, George B; BEDIENT, Eunice; LEONARD, Frederick B; IVES, Chauncy P

Group Number 298
WARREN, George B; LEONARD, Frederick B; IVES, Chauncey P

Group Number 299
WARREN, George B; MILLIMAN, Eunice M; LEONARD, Frederick B; IVES, Chauncey P

Group Number 300
WARREN, George B; REARDON, Betsey; LEONARD, Frederick B; IVES, Chauncey P

Group Number 301
WATSON, Amasa B; WHALEN, Elizabeth

Group Number 302
WELCH, John; HEALD, Joseph; AVERY, Newell

Group Number 303
WESTON, William; COOPER, Sarah

Group Number 304
WESTON, William; HARDEN, Julia; MERRICK, Elliott T

Group Number 305
WESTON, William; JOHNSON, Charles; ADAMS, Abigail

Group Number 306
WESTON, William; JOHNSON, Charles; DAVIS, John G

Group Number 307
WESTON, William; JOHNSON, Charles; LYNN, Mary W

Group Number 308
WESTON, William; JOHNSON, Charles; WILLARD, David

Group Number 309
WESTON, William; JOHNSON, Charles; WOODMAN, Horatio

Group Number 310
WESTON, William; WILLARD, David; JOHNSON, Charles

Group Number 311
WHITE, Cada; WHITE, Jane

Group Number 312
WHITE, Levi; PATTESON, Elizabeth

Group Number 313
WILCOX, Sextus N; LYON, James O; HEALD, Horatio N

Group Number 314
WILCOX, Sextus N; LYONS, James O; HEALD, Horatio N

Group Number 315
WILCOX, Sextus N; PEARSON, Daniel K

Group Number 316
WILSON, Gilbert F D; HAMMOND, Mercy

Group Number 317
WILSON, Gilbert F D; RIGGS, Mary Jane; RIGGS, Clinton D; GAYLORD, Josiah A

Group Number 318
WILSON, Gilbert F D; RYDER, Dinah

Group Number 319
WILSON, Gilbert F D; RYDER, Lurana

Group Number 320
WOOD, Eliphalet; LAWRENCE, John

Group Number 321
WOOD, Eliphalet; LAWRENCE, John; ROGERS, William C; ROGERS, Effy

Group Number 322
WOOD, John L; BARBER, Clara

Group Number 323
WOOD, John L; BELMEAR, Catharine

Group Number 324
WOOD, John L; CLARK, John; WILLIAMS, Simeon

Group Number 325
WOOD, John L; DUNN, Susannah

Group Number 326
WOOD, John L; HANCOCK, William H; HANCOCK, George W

Group Number 327
WOOD, John L; HARNESS, Susan E; HARNESS, James P; DEVER, Rebecca F; DEVER, Joseph M; GLAZE, Sarah S; THOMPSON, Albert C

Group Number 328
WOOD, John L; INGALLS, Mercy

Group Number 329
WOOD, John L; KEINER, Catharine

Group Number 330
WOOD, John L; KILBY, Hannah

Group Number 331
WOOD, John L; PARKER, Jonas

Group Number 332
WOOD, John L; WARREN, James M; MCFARLAN, James

Group Number 333
WOOD, Ransom E; DENSLOW, Polly

Group Number 334
WOOD, Ransom E; DUDLEY, Jane

Group Number 335
WOOD, Ransom E; LATHROP, Lydia

Group Number 336
WOOD, Ransom E; ONDERDONK, Anna

Group Number 337
WOOD, Ransom E; SLAUGHTER, John; LAWSON, Lavinia; LAWSON, John; LAWSON, James

Group Number 338
WOOD, Ransom E; TURNER, Coley B

Group Number 339
WOOD, Ransom E; WALTERHOUSE, Thomas S

Group Number 340
WOOD, Ransom E; WOODHOUSE, Benjamin; WHITEHURST, Daniel

Group Number 341
WOOD, Sarell; CHEENEY, Damon E; WHEELOCK, Addison P

Group Number 342
WOOD, Sarell; GLAZIER, Dexter P

Group Number 343
WOOD, Wesley F; MILLER, John D

Group Number 344
WOODS, Ransom E; LATHROP, Lydia

Group Number 345
WRIGHT, George E; WRIGHT, Susan; WOODMAN, George

Group Number 346
YOUNG, Martin B; SMITH, Mary

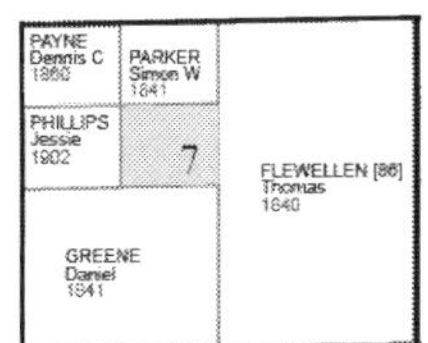

Extra! Extra! (about our Indexes)

We purposefully do not have an all-name index in the back of this volume so that our readers do not miss one of the best uses of this book: finding misspelled names among more specialized indexes.

Without repeating the text of our "How-to" chapter, we have nonetheless tried to assist our more anxious researchers by delivering a short-cut to the two county-wide Surname Indexes, the second of which will lead you to all-name indexes for each Congressional Township mapped in this volume :

Surname Index (whole county, with number of parcels mapped) ....page 18
Surname Index (township by township) ....just following

For your convenience, the "How To Use this Book" Chart on page 2 is repeated on the reverse of this page.

We should be releasing new titles every week for the foreseeable future. We urge you to write, fax, call, or email us any time for a current list of titles. Of course, our web-page will always have the most current information about current and upcoming books.

Arphax Publishing Co.
2210 Research Park Blvd.
Norman, Oklahoma 73069
(800) 681-5298 toll-free
(405) 366-6181 local
(405) 366-8184 fax
info@arphax.com

www.arphax.com

How to Use This Book - A Graphical Summary

Part I

"The Big Picture"

Map A ▸ *Counties in the State*
Map B ▸ *Surrounding Counties*
Map C ▸ *Congressional Townships (Map Groups) in the County*
Map D ▸ *Cities & Towns in the County*
Map E ▸ *Cemeteries in the County*
Surnames in the County ▸ *Number of Land-Parcels for Each Surname*
Surname/Township Index ▸ Directs you to Township Map Groups in Part II

The Surname/Township Index can direct you to any number of **Township Map Groups**

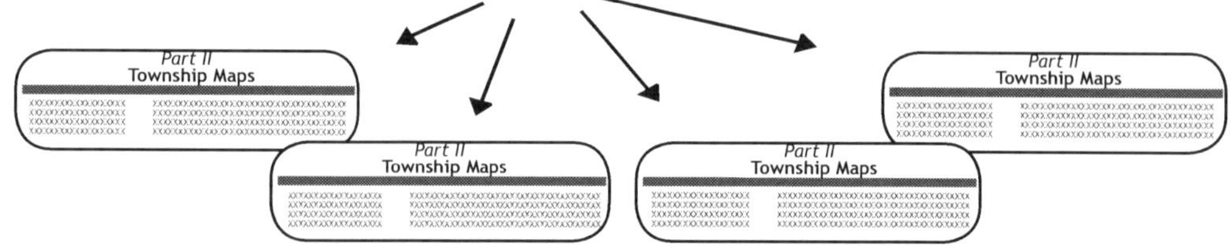

Part II

Township Map Groups

(1 for each Township in the County)

Each Township Map Group contains all four of of the following tools . . .

Land Patent Index ▸ *Every-name Index of Patents Mapped in this Township*
Land Patent Map ▸ *Map of Patents as listed in above Index*
Road Map ▸ *Map of Roads, City-centers, and Cemeteries in the Township*
Historical Map ▸ *Map of Railroads, Lakes, Rivers, Creeks, City-Centers, and Cemeteries*

Appendices

Appendix A ▸ *Congressional Authority enabling Patents within our Maps*
Appendix B ▸ *Section-Parts / Aliquot Parts (a comprehensive list)*
Appendix C ▸ *Multi-patentee Groups (Individuals within Buying Groups)*

(This page is a repeat of page 2 in the text)

Made in United States
Orlando, FL
27 July 2024

49602510R00183